PATRICIA UNTERMAN'S
SAN FRANCISCO
FOOD LOVER'S GUIDE

PATRICIA UNTERMAN'S
SAN FRANCISCO
FOOD LOVER'S GUIDE

PHOTOGRAPHS BY ED ANDERSON

TEN SPEED PRESS

BERKELEY / TORONTO

Dedication

To Tim and Harry

Ten Speed Press
Box 7123
Berkeley, California 94707
www.tenspeed.com

Distributed in Australia by Simon & Schuster Australia, in Canada by Ten Speed Press Canada, in New Zealand by Southern Publishers Group, in South Africa by Real Books, and in the United Kingdom and Europe by Airlift Book Company.

Cover and book design and photography by Ed Anderson, Skout, Cleveland
Maps by Ellen McElhinney, San Francisco

Library of Congress Cataloging-in-Publication Data on file with publisher.

Printed in Canada
First printing, 2003

1 2 3 4 5 6 7 8 9 10 — 08 07 06 05 04 03

ACKNOWLEDGMENTS

This book is the product of over thirty years of reviewing restaurants, shopping, and cooking in the Bay Area with maniacal passion. Many, many, many thanks go to Tim Savinar, who trouped with me everywhere, and to Harry Savinar, who put up with my obsession.

Many thanks go to Sue Moore, eating companion and tennis guru, who made herself available for any kind of eating adventure at any hour of the day or night; Tracy Johnston, who performed emergency research in Oakland's Chinatown with her granddaughter Lauren in tow; Niloufer Ichaporia King, who continues to be my ethnic food advisor and cooking inspiration. Special thanks to Laurie MacKenzie, an expert on the Mission and Latin American culinary arts; Yoko Tahara, my guide to Japantown; Amy Kaneko for her many tips about the best Asian dishes around town; Yanek and Mary Chiu for my Chinese cultural education during hundreds of meals in Chinese restaurants here and abroad; Bruce Cost, Cecilia Chiang, and Sue Yung Li for their expertise on Chinese cuisine and culture; Lin and Kien Nguyen for Vietnamese shopping and eating; Jenn Fox for her knowledge of the Sunset, the environment, and surfer hangs; Stephen Singer and Pam and Jay Heminway for their expertise on wine and wineshops; Tim Savinar for his intimate knowledge of bars; Barbara Mendelsohn for her insight into Pacific Heights, Healdsburg, and everything else in life; John Chalik for his unfailing generosity, grand love of the table, and help with the East Bay.

Special appreciation goes to Alice Waters for her higher vision. Thanks to Paul Johnson, Tom Worthington, and Andy Powning for updating the fish and produce charts; to Laura Shapiro for inspiring journalistic authenticity and help with writing; Wendy Lesser for her unflagging support, editing in a pinch, and inventing the newsletter.

Big thanks to Paula Tevis, the best editor and assistant a writer could have, and to Harry Savinar and Justin Gorski, my tenacious fact checkers. I chose Ed Anderson of Skout to be the designer of this tome and he fashioned a sexy book about food—his first. Endless thanks goes to Ellen McElhinney, my loyal cartographer, who remained nimble until the end. Gratitude goes to Lorena Jones of Ten Speed Press, who has been a model editor, enthusiastic and questioning. Also, thanks to copy editor Sharon Silva, whose depth of knowledge has increased mine.

Special thanks go to my restaurant partner Richard Sander, whose humanity and sense of fun teaches me to keep things in perspective.

—Patricia Unterman

CONTENTS

1   Introduction

8   Seasonal Produce

14 Seasonal Fish and Shellfish

THE NEIGHBORHOODS

21 Chinatown

47 Civic Center & Hayes Valley

67 Embarcadero & Fisherman's Wharf

91 Financial District & Union Square

129 Lower Haight, Upper Haight
    & Cole Valley

147 The Marina & Cow Hollow

171 The Mission District, Bernal Heights
    & the Excelsior

211 Noe Valley, the Castro,
    Diamond Heights & Upper Market

231 North Beach

259 Pacific Heights & Japantown

289 Polk Street, Nob Hill, Russian Hill
    & Van Ness Avenue

313 The Richmond

341 South of Market, Third Street
    & Potrero Hill

367 The Sunset

OUT OF TOWN

391 The East Bay

443 Marin County

463 Wine Country

INDEXES

502 Alphabetical

511 Restaurants

514 Cuisine

518 Price

521 Food Service at Counter or Bar

522 Food Service after 10 P.M.

524 Breakfast or Weekend Brunch

524 Outdoor Seating

524 Child Friendly

525 Banquet Room

526 Of Historic Interest

526 Bakeries/Pastries

526 Bars

528 Cafés

528 Cheese

528 Coffee

528 Cookware and Books

529 Delicatessens/Takeout

530 Ethnic Markets

530 Fish

530 Ice Cream/Chocolates

530 Markets

530 Meat and Poultry

531 Produce

531 Wines and Spirits

531 Recipes

532 Sidebars

INTRODUCTION

The *San Francisco Food Lover's Guide* was written both for visitors and for residents who want to explore the culinary landscape of their own city. Anyone who loves to travel knows the value of a guidebook that dovetails with his or her own passions and sensibilities. An intuitive writer can open up a seemingly impenetrable place and foster a deeper level of understanding and pleasure. Some travelers I know argue that arriving cold in a new place, completely open to any adventure, is provocative, but this argument does not convince me. If we travel to expand our senses and broaden our minds, then setting off unprepared and untutored lessens the scope of our experience. I like to know in advance where to find the qualitative best—especially when it comes to my personal passion, food—and I'm willing to go to the ends of the earth for a taste of the extraordinary.

For three decades I have been developing my sense of taste as a restaurant critic (at the *San Francisco Chronicle*, at the Hearst-owned *San Francisco Examiner*, and currently at the Fang-owned *San Francisco Examiner*), and as a cook both at home and in San Francisco at the Hayes Street Grill, which I own with my partner of twenty-four years, Richard Sander. But what I really am is an eater, someone who loves food of every kind, but with an almost obsessive discrimination. Such openness combined with unrelenting critical consciousness seems like a paradox; being a connoisseur suggests a narrowing of taste. But eating something gorgeous, humble or high as it may be, floods me with pleasure and expands my consciousness. Looking for sensuous food has been an unending quest. I admit it: eating is the center of my intellectual and emotional life. Sounds frivolous, but as far as I can see, the better the food, the happier the person, if even for a moment. My idea of an evolved world pretty much hinges on wanting all people to have access to a good meal when they are hungry.

As I am an enthusiastic user of guidebooks myself, I thought I would contribute to the genre from my own little piece of the earth, San Francisco and environs, and pattern it after a book that has been the source of hundreds of wonderful eating experiences for me, Patricia Wells's *Food Lover's Guide to Paris*. Reading that guidebook and plotting a course from it sends a thrill down my spine, second to actually being in Paris. Wells writes about not only restaurants in every neighborhood, but bakeries, cheese stores, butchers, open markets, and the whole complicated tree of French culinary life, with an intelligent, personal, sensual voice. I can only hope to come close.

Since the last edition of this book five years ago, the restaurant scene exploded in the Bay Area and then contracted a bit as a result of an economic boom followed by a recession. But we haven't drifted backward when it comes to the quality of the Bay Area food supply. If anything, more fresh, organic, and artisan foods are available on a retail and wholesale level than ever before, and I continue to believe that Northern California represents the most exciting and energetic food system in America—indeed, equal to any in the world.

San Francisco has become a culinary crossroads where ethnic cooks and ingredients, especially from Asia and Latin America, enrich our own indigenous products and cooking style. The mild Northern California climate supports an enormous variety of fruits, vegetables, and herbs. Our location on the edge of the Pacific assures a supply of fresh seafood.

The cool fog and protected hills and valleys make for a now world-class wine country. But even more interesting has been the development of artisan producers, some of whom have learned from European techniques, others who use traditional American methods to get a superior product. We have a vital organic farming movement here that not only produces fruits and vegetables, but also meat, poultry, and dairy, plus an efficient distribution system that delivers these foods to consumers, sometimes on the morning they've been harvested, at our many farmers' markets. Furthermore, the Bay Area has become a large enough market to support imports from all over the world. The products we don't make ourselves we ship in. This bounty attracts an ever more sophisticated food community and an influx of people who come here to eat, work, and live within it. San Franciscans never feel culinarily bereft coming home after a trip. They have too many pleasures right here.

ABOUT THE CATEGORIES . . . .

The book is divided into chapters that explore loosely drawn neighborhoods in the city, plus some important centers of good eating outside the city. While not every one of the following categories is represented in every chapter, restaurants always are because they, more than any other culinary institution, excite and entertain us.

RESTAURANTS

Each chapter starts with a very personal selection of restaurants that I have enjoyed over the years for one reason or another. Sometimes a restaurant is included because it makes one dish I adore, or because it provides a useful service to its neighborhood, or because it feels good to be sitting in it. A very few have been included because of the importance of their role in the city's dining-out profile (though not necessarily mine), and I felt I had to say a few words about them. You'll just have to read the entries. Unlike Zagat and newspaper reviews, I am not providing a rating service. The very fact that a restaurant appears in the book means that it is interesting and the writing tells why. After fifteen years of assigning stars and thereby pigeonholing restaurants against my inclinations, these writings come from the heart. Something about these places has grabbed me and demanded inclusion.

There are so many restaurants in the city now that you almost don't need to reserve in advance, especially if you go at a slightly off hour. The weekends can be tougher at the most popular dinner houses, but unlike many European restaurants that will not seat you without a booking, whether they're full or not, San Francisco restaurants want to find you a table. It never hurts to drop by if you can be flexible. Some parties don't show up for their tables, maddening and discourteous behavior though this may be, which allows the maître d' to fit you in. The American appetite tends to be spontaneous (unlike that of Europeans, who all eat at certain hours), and many restaurants cater to this free-spirited dining by serving at the bar, at cocktail tables, and at counters. You can get a good taste of expensive restaurants without spending an arm and a leg by ordering a glass of wine and a few appetizers from a perch at the bar. This impromptu seating also works nicely if you are eating alone. In San Francisco's competitive atmosphere, restaurants want only to accommodate.

Two restaurant trends became evident as I did my research: the popularity of small-plate menus, which allow people to spend less and eat less; and a growing number of high-quality new restaurants in outer neighborhoods like the Lower Haight, outer Noe Valley, and the Mission, where commercial rents are cheaper and residents underserved. The Financial District and SOMA have contracted, while the wine country and the East Bay have exploded with new places. People want to eat in their own backyards these days.

CAFÉS

You can always get something to eat in coffeehouses in San Francisco, but the food service is usually informal, requiring you to order at a counter. Some cafés put out stunning snacks, sandwiches, and light fare, but the draw of cafés is that you can sit, think, talk, write, or read over a beautifully made cup of coffee.

BARS

What are these doing in a food lover's guide? Ask my husband, who considers an ice-cold martini, or a perfectly balanced margarita swirled in ice and served up, as important sustenance. Many bars do serve food, but they are included in this category for their watering-hole identities—their drink making, not their kitchens.

DELICATESSENS/TAKEOUT

With more and more members of the household working, and little time left for shopping and cooking, a good delicatessen can be a godsend. Semiprepared food requiring a minimum of last-minute cooking can greatly improve a meal served at home. The best delicatessens, no matter what their ethnic origins, prepare or import foods that are difficult to make at home, even if you had the time. How many of us have the equipment or patience to air-dry and roast Peking duck, cold-smoke salmon, or make fresh sausages? Delicatessens also sell food to eat on the spot, though usually there are no places in the stores to sit.

BAKERIES/PASTRIES

The Bay Area is now the undisputed American, and arguably the world capital of artisan bread. Of course, San Francisco has a long tradition of bread making, started during the gold rush with our unique sourdough. Few artifacts represent San Francisco to the world as vividly as a crusty, chewy loaf of sourdough bread. Currently one historic sourdough bakery, Parisian, founded in 1856, cranks out ninety thousand fresh loaves every morning to deliver to restaurants and supermarkets. However, with the rise of Acme Bread in 1983, Berkeley became the epicenter for high-quality *levain* and a range of other superb organic breads, albeit on a much smaller scale. Its success set off a renaissance of artisan bakers. These handmade breads are available in many stores throughout the Bay Area and in retail bakery shops that also bake sophisticated sweet and savory pastries—a new development over the last five years. Tartine in the Mission and La Farine on College Avenue in Oakland represent the apotheosis of the artisan bakery, and are well worth a detour.

The ice cream parlor is all but gone, and even simple ice cream scooperies seem to be diminishing. There are no grand ones like Bertillon in Paris or Vivoli in Florence, but a few small independent ice cream makers like Double Rainbow, Gelato Classico, and Swenson's still have retail shops. We do have some wonderful local chocolatiers though, and one of the few artisan chocolate manufacturers in the world, Scharffen Berger. The beloved, ubiquitous See's candy shops represent one end of the spectrum, while Michael Recchiuti's expensive flower- and tea-scented hand-dipped chocolates available online (www.recchiuticonfections.com) and occasionally at the Ferry Plaza Farmers' Market, the other. The economic viability of the one-item shop depends so much on location, and prime location can be very expensive for an artisan operation.

MARKETS

As convenient and tempting as supermarkets may be, I find that I shop in them less and less. I turn to specialty stores, Chinatown stores, and farmers' markets for fresh food, and try to use paper products and disposable goods as little as possible. To meet the challenge, the supermarkets try to be all things to all people. They have large deli counters, cheese sections, and their own bakeries. But too often the quality level is so low that the food is not worth buying even at the cheapest prices. The rock-hard warehoused fruit in towering pyramids in the produce department is tasteless, and overpackaged processed food, often quite expensive, almost is not really food at all. The good general markets included in this book make an effort to carry more and better fresh foods than the gigantic chains. They often have independent butchers and stock some organic produce and meats. They take daily deliveries from local bread bakeries and local dairies, and feature goods from small producers.

ETHNIC MARKETS

Many of the items I buy at ethnic markets are essential for my peripatetic pantry, necessary to the eclectic cooking style so many of us have developed over years of travel and interest in international eating. Visits to these markets are as close as you can get to a trip to another country, and a pastime that I always find stimulating. Seeing the juxtaposition of ingredients and figuring out what to do with them puts me in a mood to cook. Ethnic markets often have a deli component that makes them invaluable if you've decided to cook an exotic meal and you don't quite know how to prepare everything.

PRODUCE

If any kind of shopping has blossomed over the last five years, it has been produce. Invigorated by the influx of Cantonese, then Vietnamese immigrants who buy, grow, and sell a huge array of vegetables and herbs, and by the increasing demand for organic produce, availability and quality of the widest range of produce improves every year. People get turned on to fabulous tomatoes or sautéed pea sprouts in restaurants and want to get their hands on them. Organic produce has moved from natural foods stores (still the major outlet for them) into general produce stores and even onto some supermarket shelves. Farmers' markets have proliferated so that almost every local community has one, several days a week. Our growing season is year-round, so even winter markets have wonderful things. As our diet shifts toward eating more fruits, vegetables, and grains, farmers and retailers are rising to the occasion, bringing greater and greater variety to the market.

MEAT AND POULTRY

The personalized butcher counter is making a comeback. Organic beef and small farm–raised pork and lamb are more and more in demand and growing in availability. Everyone has gone chicken crazy, and the demand for free-range, wholesomely fed birds continues to rise as eaters discover the difference in flavor. Cooks are discovering quail, poussin, squab, pheasant, and other smaller birds, and the best shops are carrying them. Chinatown has always been a source for flavorful chickens and birds of every sort, but specialty poultry is nudging red meat over to the side in Western butcher counters as well.

FISH

How ironic that fish with all its health benefits is finally catching on with home cooks just as the supply of local wild fish is coming under close environmental scrutiny. As I write this, a law has been put into effect that prohibits fishing of sand dabs, petrale, other bottom fish, and all rockfish from coastal waters from the Mexican to the Canadian border. I hope that there will be exemptions for small, certified boats that fish ecologically. San Francisco without sand dabs and petrale would be like the city without sourdough bread or the Golden Gate Bridge. My fingers are crossed that some sustainable fishing of our beloved bottom fish will be allowed.

At any rate, because of higher demand for all kinds of fish, the quality of retail fish has improved over the five years since I wrote the last *Food Lover's Guide*. However, finding pristine fish still remains a challenge. Chinese fish markets are an excellent source for fresh fish, but you have to know what you're doing. The smell emanating from the fish departments in supermarkets is enough to make you walk by quickly, and very few butchers know how to buy and handle fish and shellfish. The fact is that there are only a handful of markets in the whole Bay Area that I fully trust, and whenever you buy fish, you must be proactive. Point to the fish or fillet you want. Ask to see it up close and smell it. You must use good sense, as well as your senses, in buying fish if you want it to be tasty. Also, I feel it is important to know if the species you're eyeing as dinner is endangered by being overfished, like Chilean sea bass; or if it is farmed in an environmentally destructive way, like Puget Sound salmon. The provenance of the food we eat is important, for both health and ecological reasons. You should ask your fishman not only when the fish arrived at the store, but where it comes from and how it's caught or raised. The Monterey Bay Aquarium website, www.montereybayaquarium.com, can help you make the best choices.

CHEESE

Since the last edition of this guide, the cheese scene has exploded in the Bay Area. People are eating cheese as never before, and restaurants and retail stores are responding by offering an ever more sophisticated sampling of artisan cheeses. A good many of them are made locally, like elegant goat and cow milk blends from Soyoung Scalan's Andante Dairy, Bellwether Farms's sheep milk cheeses, and Cowgirl Creamery's tasty washed-rind organic Jersey-milk cheeses, an exciting new development. For the first time, American cheeses equal their European counterparts in quality, mainly because the American artisan cheese makers have learned European techniques. Additionally, cheese departments in high-end supermarkets and delis, and the few shops dedicated completely to cheese, are importing a wider variety and higher quality of cheeses. Many cheese counters offer tastes before you buy, the only way to find out what you like and learn about them. Also, local cheeses, along with artisan yogurt and butter, are available at many farmers' markets. In San Francisco, as in France, many diners now save room for cheese instead of dessert.

WINE AND SPIRITS

The small, personally run wineshop plays an important role in this age of discounters and warehouse stores. If you know what you want, the wine warehouses will save you some money. But if you are interested in exploring or cultivating your palate, the small wineshop makes sense. The best ones comb the international wine market to tease out delicious unknown bottles and good buys. They like to talk to customers about wine and often give tastes. Once a small shop knows what you like, the staff will steer you to bottles or even buy wines for the shop with your preferences in mind. As this book is geared toward the qualitative, I include wineshops where service and knowledge lead patrons to unusual and well-made bottles from all over the world.

COOKWARE AND BOOKS

Cookware chain stores and small cookware shops are everywhere in the Bay Area, but my favorites are Asian, stocked to the rafters with handsome crockery and elegant cooking utensils for a song. Every Asian market street has one or two, and I have stocked my cupboard with a bazaar's worth of unmatched pieces, all of which miraculously seem to go together as needed. As for cookbooks, the best volumes are timeless, making used cookbook sections in bookstores a valuable resource. The Bay Area's best independent bookstores often have a broad selection of both new and used books. Cookware stores also have cookbook sections, but currently there is no bookstore dedicated to cookbooks alone, a hole in the market to my mind.

RECIPES

I never fail to be surprised by the ethnic diversity of the city as I march down the market streets of each neighborhood. The discovery of new ingredients (new at least to me) makes me want to cook with them, and many meals are inspired by finds from my wanderings.

Hence the recipes, a handful of my very favorites, drawn from cookbooks, chefs, and the best home cooks I know, many of whom I've written about for the *San Francisco Chronicle* and the *San Francisco Examiner*. A fabulous product, like Straus organic whole-milk yogurt or prune plums during their short season, also inspires some of the recipes. Sidebars of information that relate to the neighborhoods or to products are scattered throughout the text as well.

INDEXES

By using the indexes you can scan quickly all the recommended bakeries, butchers, coffeehouses, and so forth in the individual subject listings. Restaurants are cross-referenced alphabetically by nationality and by price, among other groupings. But my main impetus was to explore the city neighborhood by neighborhood, so that if you found yourself in a certain part of town you'd immediately know where the good food is.

My friend, food anthropologist Niloufer Ichaporia King, told me that when she used to visit her mother in Bombay, her greatest pleasure was starting a walk in the middle of the city and wending her way outward through layers of neighborhood, observing, tasting, smelling, buying this and that as she went. I have done that with this city on a spontaneous basis over the years, one spot leading to another, but with this book my research became more methodical. People who like to visit parks, monuments, and museums to get a feel for a city have their guides. For those who learn about culture through food, this book is dedicated to you.

KEY . . . .

PRICE

Inexpensive = $15 or less per person without drinks, tax, or tip
Moderate = $16 to $35 per person without drinks, tax, or tip
Expensive = above $35 per person without drinks, tax, or tip

CREDIT CARDS

AE = American Express
CB = Carte Blanche
D = Discovery
DC = Diners' Club
JC = [to fill in]
MC = MasterCard
V = Visa

SEASONAL PRODUCE

A MONTHLY LISTING OF FRUITS AND VEGETABLES

The small family farm is under siege from urban development and big, industrial agriculture, which keeps prices below sustainable levels. When the plastic surgeon from Reno comes along with that big check and a dream of owning a winery in the foothills of the Sierras, how many set-upon farmers with families to support can justify saying no? A half century of pristine apple orchards disappear and one more high-end cabernet hits the market.

The California farmland that produces all the beautiful items listed below should be classified as a national treasure and protected through agricultural trusts. Why should industrial-scale farming get all the subsidies? Small, sustainable and organic farmers need support, too. One way you can help preserve these special farms is to buy locally, directly from farmers at farmers' markets, and at stores that tell customers where and how fruits and vegetables are grown. To my mind a perfect tomato, say, picked ripe and brought gently to market, is worth twice or three times the price of a hard, warehoused supermarket tomato that never tastes like a tomato anyway. The small family farmer deserves to live a sustainable existence.

This list, compiled in collaboration with Andy Powning, a produce specialist at Greenleaf Produce Company in San Francisco, will help you anticipate the pleasures from farm and garden month by month. I have indicated the beginning of the growing season for each item, but keep in mind that most produce is available over a period of months. Everything listed here should be available at farmers' markets or in specialty produce stores. Please note that most of this produce can come from a number of different growing areas through out the state, often moving from south to north as the seasons advance. The towns and areas listed in parenthesis are primary sources for particular crops that are organically and sustainably grown. An asterisk indicates my personal favorites—produce I look forward to eating as it comes into season.

JANUARY

Arugula, mizuna, baby red mustard (Bolinas)
Broccolini (Salinas)
Savoy cabbage (Pescadero)
Baby bok choy, napa cabbage, lemongrass (Fresno)
Baby turnips, White Rose and red Irish potatoes,
    Bloomsdale spinach (Clovis)
Watermelon radish (Watsonville)
Purple cauliflower (Esparto)
Cara Cara navel oranges (Fallbrook)
Seville oranges (Porterville)
Meyer lemons, allspice tangerines, Page and Kinnow
    mandarins, Lavender Gem tangerines (Fallbrook)
Morro blood oranges, kumquats (San Diego)

Carrots, turnips, fennel, leeks, and gold, red, and Chiogga beets (Watsonville)
Lacinato or dino kale (Marin)
Green garlic (Santa Cruz, Bolinas, Guinda)
Choy sum, baby gai choy, *gai lan* (Gilroy)
Yellowfoot mushrooms (north and central California coast)
Chandler strawberries* (Santa Maria)
Rangpur limes (Santa Cruz)
Pomelos, Minneola tangelos* (Fallbrook)
Sour bergamot oranges (Fallbrook)

MARCH

Baby lettuces, *mâche*, Pain du Sucre chicory, lavender and
    chive blossoms (Watsonville, Sonoma)
Treviso radicchio, Catalognia chicory (Guinda)
Young escarole, red and green chard (Pescadero)
Broccoli de ciccio* (Guinda)
Erbette chard* (Aromas)
Flambeau and Easter Egg radishes, salad savoy (Santa Maria)
Dandelion greens (Bolinas, Watsonville)
Mustard greens (Capay)
Sorrel (Escondido, Guinda)
Navel oranges (Livermore)
Star Ruby grapefruit, Fortune and Dancy tangerines (Fallbrook)
Pixie mandarins* (Santa Barbara)
Citron, Buddha's hand *(Fallbrook)
Rhubarb, hothouse grown (Oregon, Washington)

APRIL

Asparagus* (Delta)
English shelling peas,* sugar snap peas (Half Moon Bay)
New-crop Hass avocados* (Southern California)
Spring bulbing onions with tops, snow peas (Fresno)
Kohlrabi, green and purple (Pescadero)
Fiddlehead ferns, morel mushrooms (Pacific Northwest)
Japanese cucumbers, scented and opal basils (Watsonville)
Fava beans (Stockton)
Baby summer squashes, baby corn, baby Japanese eggplants (Selma, Vista)
Chervil, red Russian kale (Pescadero)

Young yellow wax beans, Blue Lake beans, haricots verts (Vista)
Red onions, green almonds, loquats, Thai basil (Fresno)
New-crop creamer,* Bintji, yellow Finn, ruby crescent potatoes (Guinda)
Green and gold zucchini and crookneck, sunburst, and pattypan
    squashes (Fresno, Santa Rosa)
Tartarian, Rainier, and Bing* cherries (Suisun, Santa Clara, Gilroy, Smith Flat)
Royal Blenheim apricots* (Winters, Brentwood)
Cantaloupe (Imperial Valley)
Valencia oranges (Fallbrook)
Field-grown rhubarb (Pescadero)
Red and black currants (Sebastapol)

JUNE

Early Girl tomatoes* (Coachella)
Sweet 100 and Sungold cherry tomatoes (Capay, Winters)
German butterball, French fingerling and red potatoes,
    pickling cucumbers (Bolinas, Fresno)
Baby Blue Lake beans* (Palo Alto)
Romano beans (Fresno)
Summer squash, Costato di Romesco, French grey squash (Bolinas)
Walla Walla onions (Washington)
Sea beans, or *pousse pied*, a seashore succulent (Oregon)
Red and white *fraises des bois*, red and gold raspberries (Watsonville)
Black raspberries (Watsonville)
Ollalieberries (Stockton, Fresno)
Boysenberries, loganberries (Winters, Palo Alto)
Montmorency sour pie cherries (Smith Flat, Placerville)
Santa Rosa plums,* Firebrite* and White Snow Queen nectarines, and
    Red Haven, Babcock, Regina, and Early O'Henry* peaches
    (Brentwood, Fresno)
Green Perlette seedless grapes (Delano)
Yellow and red watermelon (Imperial Valley)

JULY

White, yellow, and bicolored* corn (Brentwood)
Heirloom tomatoes, including Golden Jubilee, Yellow Taxi, Brandywine,
    Green Zebra, Marvel Stripe, Great White, and Purple Calabash, and
    yellow and red plum and pear cherry tomatoes (Capay, Palo Alto,
    Winters, Davenport, Healdsburg)
New-crop red Italian garlic* (Pescadero)

Long beans and Armenian,* Jordanian, and lemon cucumbers (Capay, Stockton)
Persian cucumbers (Madera)
Cannellini shelling beans (Half Moon Bay)
Jacob's Cattle, lima*, speckled butter, fresh cranberry* and
    French horticultural shelling beans, black-eyed and
    Crowder peas, okra (Fresno, Watsonville)
Crimson corn (Yolo County)
Garlic chives, summer savory (Pescadero, Bolinas)
Plums, including Wickson, Elephant Heart, Satsuma,* and
    Mariposa (Placerville, Vacaville, Santa Rosa)
Pluots* (Brentwood)
Red and green Thompson seedless grapes, Champagne grapes (Fresno)
Wild blackberries* (Sonoma)
Green gooseberries (Sebastapol, Pacific Northwest)
Italian butter pears (Walnut Grove)
Asian pears (Brentwood, Sebastopol, Guinda)
Melons, including Charentais, Sharlyn*, Crenshaw, Ambrosia*,
    pink and green honeydew (Guinda, Fallbrook, Brentwood)
Temptation melons (Imperial Valley)
Orange orchid watermelon (Yolo County)
Gravenstein apples* (Sebastopol)
Blueberries* (Oregon)

AUGUST

Chanterelles* (Oregon)
Lobster mushrooms (Pacific Northwest)
Peppers and chiles, including red, green, gold, and yellow bell; jalapeño,
    serrano, long hot sweets, cubanelle, Aconcagua, corno di toro*,
    Gypsy, Cheesecake*, and Lipstick pimientos (Stockton, Winters, Fresno)
Red torpedo onions and Italian flat sweet onions (Capay, Stockton)
Globe, Chinese, and Japanese eggplants (Fresno)
Rosa bianca eggplants (Guinda)
Figs, including black Mission*, Kadota, Adriatic, and brown Turkey
    (Stockton, Maywood, Chico)
Bartlett pears (Lakeport)
Italian and French* prune plums (Vacaville)
French butter pears* (Walnut Grove)
Pink pearl apples (Booneville, Mendocino)
Concord, Italian muscat grapes (Fresno)
McIntosh, Mutsu, and Jonathan apples (Sebastopol, Capay)

Pumpkins, including Sugar Pie, Baby Bear, White Cheesequake, French Red;
　　winter squashes, including delicata, sweet dumpling, red kuri, buttercup,
　　butternut, acorn, blue Hubbard, banana, hokkaido (California)
Red* and white* Belgian endives (Santa Rosa)
Brussels sprouts (Pescadero, Half Moon Bay)
Tomatillos (Capay, Stockton)
Red, gold, and white pearl onions (Central California)
Cippolini onions* (Petaluma)
Chestnuts (Northern and Central California)
Cape gooseberries (Graton)
Pineapple quince (Stockton, Santa Rosa, Reedly)
Granny Smith, Rhode Island Greening, Ozark, Hawaiian Gold,
　　Rome Beauty, Orange Cox pippin, Royal Gala*, and Fuji* apples
　　(Smith Flat, Sebastopol, Capay, Redding)
Huckleberries* (Oregon, Northern California)
Indian red peaches (Smith Flat)
Seckel, Comice, and Bosc pears (Northern and Central California)
Pomegranates (Dinuba, Stockton, Woodland)
Medjool and khadrawi dates (Walnut Grove, Coachella)
Varietal grapes including chardonnay, pinot noir, sauvignon blanc,
　　gamay beaujolais, zinfandel (Napa)

OCTOBER

Small loose artichokes*, fennel (Watsonville)
Many greens, including red and green* chard, rainbow chard,
　　spinach, collard, kale (Central Coast)
Celery roots (Fremont, Watsonville)
Cauliflower and broccoli, including Venetian, purple, and
　　Romanesque varieties, leeks (Central Coast)
Broccoli rabe* (Salinas, King City)
Russet, purple Peruvian, yellow Finn, and Yukon gold* potatoes (Washington, Oregon)
Garnet and Jewel yams, sweet potatoes, Japanese sweet potatoes (Livingston)
Black trumpet, porcini, and matsutake mushrooms (Pacific Northwest)
Gourds, decorative corn (Stockton)
Fuyu and Hachiya persimmons (Aptos, Santa Cruz, Santa Rosa)
New-crop Mission and non-pareil almonds (Guinda)
New-crop walnuts (Hartley)
Cranberries (Michigan, Massachusetts)
Passionfruit* (Carpenteria)
Golden Delicious, Spitzenberg, and Sierra Beauty apples (Philo, Sebastopol)
Crab and Lady apples (Placerville, Hairston)
Sapote, feijoa (Fallbrook)

Cardoons (Salinas)
Curly endive or frisée (Santa Rosa, Watsonville)
Baby turnip greens or rapini (Santa Maria)
Parsnips (Lamont)
Jerusalem artichokes (Watsonville)
Turnips and rutabagas (Fresno)
Uncured Manzanillo olives (Central Coast)
Winesap and Ashmead's Kernel apples (Mendocino, Philo)
Late-harvest Granny Smith apples (Smith Flat)
Winter Nellis pears (Reedly)
Pepino melons (Graton, Santa Maria)
Fairchild tangerines (Coachella)
Orlando tangerines (Orosi, Fallbrook)
Kumquats (Thermal)

DECEMBER

Hedgehog mushrooms (Central Coast)
Green, red, and Dutch Flat cabbage (Central California)
Black Spanish radishes, carrots (Watsonville)
Beets (Oxnard)
Red Russian kale* (Pescadero)
Mixed winter braising greens, including chard, tatsoi, kale,
        and mustard (Central California)
Dried shelling beans, including cannellini, cranberry,
        tongue of fire, flageolet, French horticultural,
        and scarlet runner (Central California)
Wreaths and garlands of cedar, redwood, noble fir, juniper,
        and mistletoe (Pacific Northwest)
Blood oranges (Porterville, San Diego)
Honey tangerines (Fallbrook)
Satsuma mandarins*, oro blanco (a pomelo-grapefruit hybrid),
        pomelo (Orosi, Fallbrook)
Limequats (San Diego)
Barhi dates (Indio)
Kiwifruits (Chico)

SEASONAL FISH AND SHELLFISH

(from Paul Johnson and Tom Worthington of Monterey Fish, see page 436)

	JAN	FEB	MAR
FISH			
Anchovies (local)			
Bluefish (East Coast)			
Black cod (Alaska)			
Cabezon, rockfish, lingcod (Canada or deep water only)	•	•	•
Catfish (aquaculture)	•	•	•
True cod (East Coast hook & line, Alaska)	•	•	•
Flounder, petrale (Canada only)	•	•	•
Grouper (New Zealand)	•	•	•
Northern halibut (Alaska, Canada, East Coast)			•
Pacific halibut (local, hook & line)	•	•	•
Mackerel (local)	•	•	•
Mahi-mahi (both hemispheres)	•	•	•
Opah (local)			•
Salmon (local)	•	•	•
King salmon (Alaskan)	•	•	•
Sand dab, rex sole (Canada only, though perhaps from some local boats certified to fish sustainably)	•	•	•
Sardine (local)	•	•	•
Blue nose sea bass (New Zealand)	•	•	•
White sea bass (Channel Islands)			
Skate (East Coast)	•	•	•

APR	MAY	JUNE	JULY	AUG	SEPT	OCT	NOV	DEC
	•	•	•	•	•	•		
	•	•	•	•				
		•	•	•	•	•		
•	•	•	•	•	•	•	•	•
•	•	•	•	•	•	•	•	•
•	•	•	•	•	•	•	•	•
							•	•
•	•	•			•	•	•	•
•	•	•	•	•	•	•		
•	•							
•	•	•	•	•	•	•	•	•
		•	•	•	•			•
•	•							
•	•	•						
						•		
•	•	•			•	•	•	•
•	•	•	•	•	•	•	•	•
•	•	•				•	•	•
		•	•	•	•			
•	•	•	•	•	•	•	•	•

	JAN	FEB	MAR
Smelt (local)	•	•	•
Tai snapper (New Zealand)	•	•	•
True snappers: opaka, onaga, Gulf snapper (Hawaii, Gulf of Mexico)	•	•	•
Spearfish, ono (Hawaii)	•	•	•
Striped Bass (East Coast)	•	•	•
Swordfish (California)			
Trout (aquaculture)	•	•	•
Tuna (both hemispheres)	•	•	•
Opah (local)			•

SHELLFISH

	JAN	FEB	MAR
Manila clams (Pacific Northwest)	•	•	•
Blue crab (East Coast)	•	•	•
Dungeness crab (local)	•	•	•
Soft shell crabs (East coast)		•	•
Crawfish (Louisiana, Oregon)			
Lobster (East Coast)	•	•	•
Spiny lobster (Pacific)	•		
Mussels (Northeast)	•	•	•
Oysters (local, Pacific Northwest)	•	•	•
Scallops (East Coast)	•	•	•
Spot shrimp (Santa Barbara)			
Spot shrimp (Alaska)			
White shrimp (Florida, North Carolina)	•	•	•
Squid (Monterey)			
Squid (San Pedro)	•	•	•

SEASONAL FISH AND SHELLFISH

APR	MAY	JUNE	JULY	AUG	SEPT	OCT	NOV	DEC
			•	•				
•	•	•			•	•	•	•
•	•	•						
						•	•	•
•	•	•	•	•	•	•	•	•
			•	•	•			
•	•	•	•	•	•	•	•	•
•	•	•	•	•	•	•	•	•
•	•							
•	•				•	•	•	•
•	•	•	•	•	•	•	•	•
•	•					•		
•	•							
•	•	•	•	•	•	•		
•	•	•	•	•	•	•		•
							•	•
•					•	•	•	•
•					•	•	•	•
					•	•	•	•
		•	•	•				
						•		•
•	•			•	•	•	•	•
•	•	•	•	•	•	•		•
•								

THE NEIGHBORHOODS

CHINATOWN

CHINATOWN

RESTAURANTS
1 Bow Hon
2 Dol Ho
3 Great Eastern Restaurant
4 Hing Lung
5 House of Nanking
6 Kay Cheung
7 Lichee Garden
8 Oriental Pearl
9 Pearl City
10 R & G Lounge
11 Y Ben House Restaurant

CAFÉS
12 Imperial Tea Court

BARS
13 Li-Po

DELICATESSENS/TAKEOUT
14 Gourmet Delight
15 Yee's Restaurant

BAKERIES/PASTRIES
16 Eastern Bakery
17 Golden Gate Bakery
18 Mee Mee Bakery

ICE CREAM/CHOCOLATES
19 Sweet World

ETHNIC MARKETS
20 Lien Hing Supermarket

PRODUCE
21 Chung Hing Produce Co.
22 Fruit City
20 Lien Hing Supermarket
23 Lien Hing Supermarket No. 2
24 Wo Chong

MEAT AND POULTRY
25 Guang Zhou King & King Sausage
20 Lien Hing Supermarket
26 Man Sung
27 Ming Kee Game Birds
28 New On Sang

FISH
29 Luen Sing Fish Market
30 New Sang Sang

COOKWARE AND BOOKS
31 Chong Imports
32 Ginn Wall
33 Tai Yick Trading Company

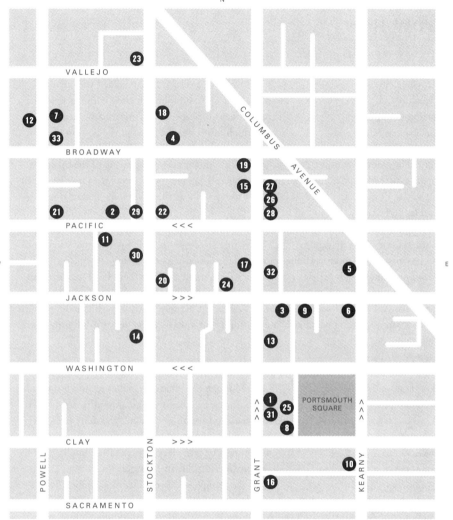

VALLEJO

BROADWAY

PACIFIC <<<

JACKSON >>>

WASHINGTON <<<

CLAY >>>

SACRAMENTO

POWELL

STOCKTON

GRANT

KEARNY

PORTSMOUTH SQUARE

COLUMBUS AVENUE

N

S

W

E

0 SCALE FEET 500

BOW HON . . . .

850 Grant Avenue (between
Clay and Washington)
415-362-0601
Open daily 11 A.M. to midnight
Inexpensive
Credit cards: MC, V

This respected Grant Avenue cafe specializes in what I consider Cantonese soul food: sizzling clay pots. I adore the Bow Hon Special Clay Pot loaded with tender, puffy white-fish dumplings braised with black mushrooms, napa cabbage, and Chinese barbecued pork at superhigh heat until the juices at the bottom of the pot become intense and smoky. I can't stop eating these dumplings sauced with the pot gravy. With this luscious clay pot, or any of the other ten, order a plate of Chinese broccoli in garlic sauce. The long round stems with tiny heads will arrive bright green and lightly sauced, not too garlicky at all. Bow Hon's kitchen does vegetables perfectly.

For casual dining alone or with one other, sit downstairs in the small storefront dining room with its partially exposed kitchen. With a larger group, walk up a narrow stairway to an upstairs dining room with big round tables where the serious eating takes place. Cantonese families always sit upstairs. They concentrate on their food, but I gaze dreamily at the elevated view of Grant Avenue and the roofs of Chinatown and imagine old San Francisco. Whenever I walk down Grant Avenue on the way downtown, I hesitate in front of Bow Hon, debating whether I should drop in for a sizzling clay pot of fish dumplings.

DOL HO . . . .

808 Pacific Avenue (between
Stockton and Powell)
415-392-2828
Open daily 7 A.M. to 5 P.M.
Inexpensive
Cash only

Dol Ho is one of my favorite places to stop for a bite of lunch during a Chinatown shopping trip. Small, very informal, and seemingly chaotic, you don't feel weird having a single plate of sparkling fresh *har gow* (shrimp dumplings) or crisp, lacy-crusted taro dumplings with creamy interiors. Plenty of people do.

The complete lack of amenities combined with the freshness and high quality of the food only make the place more treasured among the cognoscenti. A single dim sum cart barely negotiates a parlor-sized room crammed with ancient black-linoleum tables. Lunchers snatch up the dumplings, the chicken feet, the turnip cakes; the cart returns to the kitchen and everyone waits for the next load of tidbits. Look for any of the shark's fin dumplings, so named because of the crimped edge that runs across the top of the noodle wrapper (not because of a shark's fin filling). Depending on the season, they will be filled with lovely combinations like pea sprouts with shrimp. Saucy tofu skin–wrapped pork and vegetable rolls, three large ones to an order, are a meal by themselves. Flat, chewy rice-flour dumplings filled with garlicky Chinese chives and shrimp are a specialty here. Dol Ho's steamed rice noodle rolls are another. They are meltingly tender and velvety, stuffed with barbecued pork or shrimp aromatic with fresh cilantro. These must be ordered from a waitress and arrive at the table hot and delectable.

I've never been able to figure out the system at this crazy little place. Some items must be ordered from the waitstaff; some come out of the kitchen on the carts; others are distributed from a counter by a front window that's stacked with gigantic bamboo steamers from which to-go orders are dispensed. The selection from all three stations differs depending on the day and hour.

Though the much-worn carpeted floor can look messy and the dining room seems a bit out of control (the women working it barely have time to clear the tables and get the food out), the kitchen keeps sending out mouthwatering little plates. Because the place is so small, the food is cooked to order. Nothing hangs around, which makes this just the kind of place where you want to eat dim sum.

GREAT EASTERN RESTAURANT . . . .

649 Jackson Street (between
Grant and Kearny)
415-986-2500
Open daily 10 A.M. to 12:30 A.M.
Moderate
Credit cards: AE, MC, V

Specializing in high-quality, family-style cooking and seafood, the Great Eastern is one of the more handsome restaurants in Chinatown. Dark wood trim, green carpeting, green-tile wainscoting, and shiny black chairs give it a clubby feel, especially with a similarly decorated old-fashioned basement dining room. Both upstairs and downstairs are brightly lit, well ventilated, and noisy when full. Tanks with clear water and lively fish and shellfish, and a dining room divided into two sections make the upstairs more attractive.

Clear seafood soup, swirled with egg whites, chockful of crabmeat, dried scallops, and other delicacies from the sea, makes an excellent beginning to the meal. Deep-fried shrimp balls in a crisp batter are full of shrimp flavor. A platter of crisp, laboriously trimmed bean sprouts, pale green, julienned Chinese chives, and paper-thin slices of nutty geoduck clam makes for a particularly elegant and tasty dish. And you can't go wrong with a whole fish, such as rockfish strewn with scallions, ginger, and sprigs of cilantro.

As a casual, family-style restaurant, Great Eastern is a find. Service is efficient and the maître d's desk is well-handled during the busiest times. The waiters likely will urge you to order the set seafood dinners, and this is one place where I'd take them up on it.

HING LUNG . . . .

674 Broadway (near Stockton)
415-398-8838
Open daily 8 A.M. to 1 A.M.
Inexpensive
Credit cards: MC, V

Very Cantonese, Hing Lung turns out thousands of bowls of white rice porridge called *congee*, or sometimes *juk*. It is kept hot in a gigantic sunken vat at one side of a wildly active glassed-in kitchen at the entrance to the restaurant. You can watch the porridge being ladled out into saucepans and brought to a rolling boil, at which time it is poured over finely shredded ingredients waiting in deep serving bowls, cooking them instantaneously. Cilantro, ginger, and scallions are a given, along with such things as sliced hard head, a troutlike fish and my favorite, though not always available. (One time, on a take-out order, Hing Lung substituted chicken on me. Oh, the disadvantages of being Caucasian!) First-timers feel confident with sampan porridge seasoned with bits of shrimp, fish, lettuce, and peanuts, but experienced *juk* eaters go for the sweetest, most velvety pork liver, kidney, tripe, and meatballs in Hing Lung's famous pork giblet porridge. I wouldn't try this dish in very many places, but when my surgeon friend and Chinese dining guru was gobbling his up, I snatched a few bites. The pork giblets were impeccable—like silken foie gras. The oblong doughnuts you see on every table, translated as fried bread, are yeasty, airy, crisp, and unsweetened. People tear them up and throw them into the congee or, better still, into bowls of lightly sweetened or salted warm soy milk. The doughnuts also come warm, wrapped in a sheet of rice noodles, cut into sections, sprinkled with sesame seeds and a gingery soy sauce. Wonderful!

The other specialty, pearly rice noodles, is made from a thin batter poured onto an oiled canvas in a rectangular steamer. Bits of that amazingly sweet pork liver, barbecued pork, and shrimp, just to name a few foods, are cooked right into them. The sheets are then folded over, cut with a scissors, and sauced with a mixture of soy, ginger, and peanut oil.

Hing Lung is a madhouse on weekends, but the turnover in the large, cheery, utilitarian dining room is rapid, the wait never too long. People from all segments of San Francisco's Chinese community come here. The owner of my Telegraph Hill cleaners, a city vice-mayor, my most elegant Pacific Heights friends, their Hong Kong nanny, and all the Chinatown chefs getting off the late shift rub elbows at Hing Lung.

I can see why. *Congee* is a restorative. Hot, soothing to the stomach, easy to eat, Hing Lung's superior version is as good for breakfast as it is at midnight, though the place turns out hundreds of bowls for lunch as well. *Congee* is not served after 3 P.M., when Hing Lung switches to its miraculously cheap and generous dinner menu. The *congee* returns to the menu late in the evening, ready to get people home with a full, but not heavy, stomach.

HOUSE OF NANKING. . . . .

919 Kearny Street (between
Jackson and Columbus)
415-421-1429
Open Monday through Friday
11 A.M. to 10 P.M., Saturday noon
to 10 P.M., Sunday 4 P.M. to 10 P.M.
Inexpensive
Credit cards: MC, V

Peter Fang and his wife, Lily, personally have operated this hole-in-the-wall from the day it opened and achieved cult status. They doubled the original tiny restaurant by moving into a storefront next door. Now there are two cramped dining rooms, mirror images of each other, crammed with nine or so tiny tables each and a counter with a dozen stools.

Peter Fang's cooking is nothing if not original. His primary goal is to keep prices about as cheap as they can be, and his next is to please the palates of the mostly young, Caucasian crowd that loves the place. Western broccoli, not Chinese broccoli, white mushrooms, not shiitakes, and enough garlic to satisfy a Sicilian have been incorporated into the style. However, since the restaurant is so amazingly small, with all the cooking, prepping, and dishwashing done right in front of the counters, there is absolutely no place to store anything. So shopping is done sometimes two or three times a day in Chinatown.

Forgo the creative specials for beloved items on the regular menu like Shanghai-style vegetable-filled dumplings made with raw bread dough that's fried, then steamed. I like the tender chicken breast slices with long slices of zucchini and a resonant sauce made with Tsingtao beer. For starters, crisp deep-fried pancakes stuffed with shrimp and vegetables napped in a salsalike mix of diced cucumber, scallions, and peanuts get a meal off to a good start. I also like the clear Nanking fish soup seasoned with lots of coarsely ground black pepper. It wakes up the palate without filling up the stomach. Vegetable dishes like rich Szechwan-style eggplant, simmered in a spicy brown sauce and tossed with broccoli florets and snow peas, are as substantial as a main course. Ice-cold Chinese beer is plunked down on the table without glasses and tastes all the better for it.

I have to admire Peter and Lily for expanding in a way that maintains the spirit of the place, because the House of Nanking magic depends on all its quirks. But what this amazing popular success boils down to is Peter Fang's gentle, generous spirit and sense of fun. He loves the business and schmoozing with his loyal clientele. The walls are lined with doting reviews and accolades. This little place has earned every one of them—as well as those lines out the door.

KAY CHEUNG . . . .

615 Jackson Street (at Kearny)
415-989-6838
Open daily 9 A.M. to 2:30 P.M.
and 5 P.M. to 10 P.M.
Inexpensive
Credit cards: MC, V

This ever-popular dim sum house used to be called J & J, and when I ate there recently still posted J & J reviews in the front windows. The plain dining room is crammed full of tables and seating can be uncomfortably close together. People commandeer tables before they are cleared or grab unoccupied seats at partially full tables, so you may end up lunching with a Chinese grandmother. The moderate size of the restaurant and the volume allows for a wide range of dim sum to be made in small enough batches so they arrive at your table hot and fresh, carried on trays by a cadre of dim sum servers.

But don't grab the first things to come along. Hold out for some of the stars, such as the translucent dumplings with light fillings that feature pea sprouts or Chinese chives. A single tray bearer may carry two or three different dim sum, each in its own steamer, like shark's fin–shaped dumplings filled with cilantro, garlic chives, peanuts, and pork, or fabulous meaty shark's fin dumplings filled only with sweet, gently seasoned pork. Green Chinese chive and shrimp dumplings are round, delicate, and dreamy. The *har gow* (shrimp dumplings) pass the freshness and sweetness tests with flying colors. There are fabulous deep-fried taro dumplings with lovely purple interiors (a must), and tasty chicken feet, stuffed bean-curd rolls, and turnip cake. All and all, this location—despite change of ownership—delivers a consistently delicious tea lunch in a busy and well-serviced dining room. And you can't beat the prices anywhere.

LICHEE GARDEN . . . .

1416 Powell Street (between
Broadway and Vallejo)
415-397-2290
www.licheegarden.citysearch.com
Open daily 8 A.M. to 9:30 P.M.
Inexpensive
Credit cards: MC, V

Lichee Garden earned a reputation as the city's premier home-style Cantonese dinner house when it opened twenty years ago, becoming the forerunner of the new generation of upscale Hong Kong–style restaurants like Flower Lounge. Early on it offered high-quality ingredients in a comfortable, informal environment. As a result, Lichee Garden appeals to middle-class

Chinese families and practically everyone else who lives nearby in North Beach, Telegraph Hill, and Russian Hill. They come in for meals of glistening spareribs, crispy chicken, radiant green vegetables, and creamy tofu cakes in thin gravy. Lichee Garden also has taken on the role of the Chinatown family club, with birthday, anniversary, marriage, and New Year's parties all celebrated here.

Much of the popularity of Lichee Garden can be attributed to the soulful cooking of chef-owner Chak Siu, who has been with Lichee Garden since it first opened. Everything that comes out of his kitchen has the heartiness, the savoriness, of food you could eat every day. He is famous for his crispy-skinned chicken and the house special pork spareribs, thin slices with bones lightly battered, deep-fried, and tossed in a piquant sweet-and-sour sauce. I adore them. From a list of amazingly cheap dishes written in Chinese (you'll have to ask for a translation) comes a huge platter of fried tofu, bone-in chunks of satiny black cod, and wilted iceberg lettuce seasoned with pickled greens, a dish you pile onto rice and slurp up, bowl after bowl. Pan-fried noodles here have the much-prized taste of the wok, which turns chicken-and-black-mushroom chow mein into a crispy pillow slathered with chicken, baby bok choy, and mushrooms. The noodles cook so hot and fast that they caramelize slightly, skirting the edge of burning in the way that barbecue does, taking on a special flavor that only comes from the fire. The wonton soup is also a dream, boasting rich, clean stock and noodles stuffed with sweet-flavored shrimp and pork. If you like egg foo yong (I do)—a soft egg and bean sprout omelet in brown gravy—Lichee Gardens makes the best one in town. Dim sum lunch is excellent and ridiculously cheap. I don't know how these highly competitive Chinatown restaurants can do it, but Lichee Garden's dumplings boast the sweetness of fresh shrimp and other high-quality ingredients. The spacious dining room has the aura of a resonant old Hong Kong café, with wooden chairs and wainscoting, a celadon green carpet, and lots of small square tables interspersed with large round ones— the perfect configuration for a restaurant that accommodates two cultures with single-minded integrity.

ORIENTAL PEARL . . . .

760 Clay Street (between
Grant and Kearny)
415-433-1817
Open daily 11 A.M. to 3 P.M.
and 5 P.M. to 9:30 P.M.
Moderate
Credit cards: AE, DC, D, MC, V

Unlike many Chinatown restaurants where low price is the most important consideration, Oriental Pearl's goal is to offer a civilized dining experience, as well as authentic food, for a still-reasonable tariff. When out-of-town visitors want a top-notch dinner spot in the heart of Chinatown, I always send them here, as do many well-informed concierges. I tell my guests to start with a house special chicken meatball—one for each person at the table—a delicate bundle wrapped in a gossamer pancake made only of egg whites, tied with a Chinese chive. Inside is an ethereal forcemeat of finely chopped chicken, shrimp, black mushrooms, freshwater chestnuts, and Virginia ham. Another must is a dish called *pei pa* tofu, spicy golden-fried dumplings of bean curd in a lush, hot sweet-and-sour sauce. Tofu soup brings a peppery broth spiked with toasted garlic and cilantro leaves, an exciting background for lots of sweet, fresh shrimp. Chiu Chow duck, marinated and then braised with aromatic Chinese spices and served with a dipping sauce of vinegar and red chiles, reminds me of a duck stew, but don't expect the crisp skin of Chinese roasted duck. However, the spectacular spicy braised prawns, first battered and deep-fried, then sauced in a hot, chile-flecked sweet-and-sour syrup on a cloud of crackling fried rice noodles, is all about crunchiness. Even simple vegetables like slightly bitter mustard greens taste different here, set off by tiny slivers of Virginia ham. The crisp-tender stalks refresh the palate at the end of the meal, almost like a sip of strong black tea. If you have room, order a plate of Oriental Pearl's elegant chow mein, made with the thinnest noodles quickly and cleanly tossed with slivers of chicken breast, shiitake, scallion, and bean sprouts—a stellar preparation of an often pedestrian dish. People travel across the city for a glass pie plate of Oriental Pearl's house special noodles *(yee min)*, which are first deep-fried, then braised with Chinese chives and enoki mushrooms so that they achieve a miraculously soft, silky, yet elastic texture. It's hard to stop eating them.

This comparatively small Chinatown restaurant also puts out an accomplished tea lunch, which is ordered from a menu rather than being brought around on carts. This means that each item will emerge fresh and hot from the kitchen, though the tea lunch draw of immediate gratification is lost. The impeccably fresh shrimp and pork dumplings in all their various forms are certainly worth a wait. Be sure to try the scallop and shrimp dumplings, the rustic taro-leaf packets filled with sticky rice and pork, the fantastically crisp taro balls, and the cigar-shaped egg rolls of exceptional crunch. Finish with crisp, thin pancakes filled with red bean paste.

PEARL CITY

641 Jackson Street (between Kearny and Grant)
415-398-8383
Open daily 8 A.M. to 10 P.M.
Inexpensive
Credit cards: AE, D, MC, V

A spot for very inexpensive, rustic dim sum in huge portions, this teahouse is almost unapproachable on the weekends, although unrelenting competition in price and quality from other dim sum houses in Chinatown have somewhat diminished the crowds during the week.

Some of my favorites here are sticky rice–stuffed lotus-leaf packets, more moist and savory than most; vegetarian rolls wrapped in crisp deep-fried tofu skin; and coarsely chopped *siu mai*, which are noodle-wrapped cylinders of pork and shrimp barely bound together. The best dumplings come in translucent wheat-gluten wrappers filled with chopped greens, garlic chives, and a little bit of pork. They have a delightful fresh flavor. Little accommodation is made for non-Chinese speakers here, but the authentic food at fantastic prices allows adventurous eaters to shrug off any unexplained surprises. The women bearing the trays and carts want only to lighten their loads.

R & G LOUNGE

631 Kearny Street (between Clay and Sacramento)
415-982-7877
Open daily 11 A.M. to 9:30 P.M.
Moderate
Credit cards: AE, DC, D, MC, V

Over the years, R & G Lounge has become one of my favorite restaurants anywhere. I celebrate Christmas, my birthday, and Chinese New Year there with glorious banquets of ordered-ahead dishes that never fail to excite and please. I'm always torn between my old favorites and a handful of new ones suggested by Angel Liu, the energetic manager with whom I arrange the dinners. I have learned to take her advice since many of the new dishes immediately gain most-favored status. I used to prefer eating in the more formal upstairs dining room (as opposed to the clamoring basement dining room), but recently R & G expanded into a new area at street level filled with comfortable, large round tables.

The restaurant has made another improvement. If you've ever wondered how to decode the long, often metaphorical descriptions of dishes in our local Chinese restaurants, or more vexing, not been able to figure out how to order the dishes that everyone else seems to know about, R & G has come up with the answer. Just leaf through the glossy, new R & G Lounge menu with color photographs of signature dishes, then choose from the dishes on the House Specialties pages. They represent some of the best food to be had in any restaurant in San Francisco.

Start with No. 1, Minced Seafood in Lettuce Cups. Since everyone loves this dish and finds it unthreatening, it deserves its numero uno status. When I arrange a banquet, I always order No. 2, geoduck sashimi, the siphon of this gigantic Pacific coast clam elegantly sliced and served with wasabi and soy, followed by a soup made with the rest of its body. This two-part geoduck service ranks as one of the most extraordinary food experiences I've ever had. If you've ever dreamed of imbibing the essence of the sea, it would taste like this. Many people come to R & G for No. 6, the incomparable salt-and-pepper crab—an impeccably fresh crab plucked from a tank (they go through so many here), enrobed in a thin batter, dusted with salt and white pepper, and deep-fried. You learn what Dungeness crab should taste like after having it here. No. 11, Beef Brisket and Turnip in a Clay Pot, is a sleeper, a full-flavored, velvety beef brisket so accessible to the Western palate and so delicious, it will win over the most recalcitrant eater at your table. I also must plug No. 12, Dried Scallops with Chinese Melons, a dish that exemplifies the divide between Chinese and Western texture preferences. The featured ingredients are slippery on the tongue and offer no resistance to the tooth. They disappear down your throat leaving only the lingering flavor of scallop and ginger captured in the sauce. On the poultry page resides No. 25, Peking Duck, the crown jewel of all poultry preparations. End your meal with Dried Scallops Egg White Fried Rice listed in the Noodles and Fried Rice section. I know it sounds weird, but just take my word for it.

A favorite dish of mine at R & G is nowhere to be found on the menu: pea sprouts or spinach or amaranth, depending on the season, with three kinds of eggs (fresh, salted, thousand-year-old) that, with the juice of the greens, forms a buttery-tasting sauce. This dish, first recommended to me by a captain no longer at R & G, continues to be made, so ask for it.

What's remarkable about the R & G Lounge, which I first visited in 1988, is the way it has matured and deepened over the years. It gets better and better. Credit goes to owner Kinson Wong who has kept the standards high in both the kitchen and dining room. If you want to explore southern Chinese cooking, you can start here at the R & G with new menu in hand.

835 Pacific Avenue (between
Stockton and Powell)
415-397-3168
Open daily 7 A.M. to 3 P.M.
and 5 P.M. to 9 P.M.
Inexpensive
Credit cards: D, MC, V

I go to this large, roaring dim sum house for turnip cake infused with Chinese bacon and yummy deep-fried eggplant sandwiches, crisp on the outside, creamy within, with a well-seasoned filling of ground shrimp, all napped in an addictive black bean sauce. You see these stuffed, fried eggplant dim sum everywhere. The version at Y Ben is the best. The pork dumplings, *siu mai*, and the shrimp dumplings, *har gow*, are fresh and bright—exemplary. I like them better than a garlicky pork-filled shark's fin–shaped dumpling. You can taste some exotic things here like squares of steamed pig's blood—it tastes a bit liverlike—with strips of fatless, mahogany pig skin that has the gelatinous texture of jellyfish. But there's plenty of less challenging dim sum items like lacy taro balls (the fried potato of Cantonese cuisine) filled with pork. They can be sublime if you get them hot. I like them so much I never let them pass by without asking for a plate.

Y Ben looks as if it had been some kind of meeting hall before it became a dim sum house. The cold terrazzo floors, a raised podium area no doubt for weddings, and pink plastic–covered tables bespeak a utilitarian decor. But the place is full of life, of people coming and going, including quite a few older Chinese from public housing next door. No one can complain about price or quality at Y Ben, and you walk out feeling as if you've made an important urban discovery.

CAFÉS

IMPERIAL TEA COURT . . . .

1411 Powell Street (between
Broadway and Vallejo)
415-788-6080
www.imperialtea.com
Open Wednesday through Monday
11 A.M. to 6:30 P.M.
Credit cards: AE, MC, V

Every time I enter this serene haven in the form of a traditional Chinese teahouse, I wonder why I don't come here more often. I spend a tranquil half hour or so sipping small cups of refreshing and invigorating tea and walk out a new person. Everything about this teahouse works against daily stress and soothes a person back into civilized existence. I don't know why this place has such a strong effect on me because I am not a tea drinker or even someone who likes to linger in coffeehouses, but the minute I sit down at one of the Tea Court's antique square tables and the tea master takes a look at my face and suggests a certain brew, I know that my life will improve. Most recently, he suggested a light herbal tea called silver needle, aptly named for its soft, furry pointed leaves, with two (not three, not one) chrysanthemum flowers in the pot. He set a kettle of water to simmer on a special heater at the table and, when the water reached the right temperature, which he could tell from its sound in the pot, he half-filled the teapot, then poured out the first brewing of tea, then rebrewed and finally served us our first cup. We continued to add water to the pot to drink four more small covered cups of tea. Time flew by, and I felt as if I had just taken a small vacation.

On other occasions I have had strong espressolike tea in thimble-sized cups, and medium-bodied *pu-erh* tea after lunch at Lichee Garden across the street. Each infusion gets a different pot, a different cup, and undergoes a different brewing process. You can learn as much as you want from the eager teachers in the shop, or you can just enjoy your tea. The people who run this charming cafe are friendly and sensitive to their customers' desires.

The room evokes old China. Dark, polished wooden tables and shelving, jade green Chinese-silk insets in the burnished maple walls, marble floor, wooden lanterns, and a beautiful antique tea counter look like they were all airlifted from some pre-Revolution Shanghai teahouse. If you're in the neighborhood, drop by and see what it was like to be a mandarin.

BARS

LI-PO . . . .

916 Grant Avenue (at Washington)
415-982-0072
Open daily 2 P.M. to 2 A.M.
Cash only

Like its sister street-level bars nearby, Bow Bow and Buddha, Li-Po was an historic haunt for seamen visiting the Barbary Coast. With a golden Buddha enshrined in a cave behind the bar, and an entrance that looks like it leads to a temple, Li-Po still provides an atmospheric haven. The women bartenders are welcoming and pleasant, but tough. You pay for each drink as it's served. Although the liquor and beer selection is generally unexceptional, the bar does stock a number of good cognacs, brandy, and Scotch whisky.

DELICATESSENS/TAKEOUT

GOURMET DELIGHT . . . .

1045 Stockton Street (between Washington and Jackson)
415-392-3288
Open daily 7 a.m. to 7 p.m.
Cash only

Many Chinese take-out places line Stockton Street, and three of them vie for customers practically next to one another in the 1000 block. People buy barbecued pork, mahogany-skinned ducks, and chickens. The poultry usually hangs in the front windows on hooks, their skins glistening and darkly burnished. A huge roast pig with crisp, golden rind dangles at the back above a thick slab of wood. The chef hacks off different bits—some ribs, a loin, some leg—cleaves them into bite-sized pieces with the bone, weighs them, and slides them into a carton. Here is the centerpiece of a meal. Kept warm along the counter are scores of Cantonese dishes: Piles of chow mein tossed with bean sprouts and vegetables that can be ordered with or without gravy (bite the bullet, go without for a better texture); crispy deep-fried nuggets of battered chicken coated in a honey-sweet sauce that puts anything at KFC to shame; vegetables of all sorts; sweet-and-sour pork; fried rice; stuffed eggplants in black bean sauce. The variety of both familiar and exotic dishes is endless. New pans keep emerging from the kitchen at the back. Prices are cheap and at the most popular places like this one, the food stays fresh because there's so much turnover. I'm not much of a fan of takeout, but these Chinese delicatessens have it down. They put out dishes that reheat well and can hold in a steam table. I prefer them to Chinese restaurant take-out, because made-to-order restaurant dishes wilt cruelly in those paper cartons. They don't reheat the way the delicatessen dishes do. With Chinese deli take-out, a few tosses in a hot wok and you've got yourself a tasty hot meal.

YEE'S RESTAURANT . . . .

1131 Grant Avenue (between
Broadway and Pacific)
415-576-1818
Open daily 7 A.M. to 9 P.M.
Cash only

I have to credit friend and Asian food expert Bruce Cost (now a honcho at the Big Bowl chain in Chicago) for tipping me off to Yee's, where the roast pig is sublimely velvety, the ducks crackling crisp, and the soy sauce and salt-roasted chickens moist and tender. You can get your barbecued meats to go or you can eat in

the immaculate, light-filled dining room. Either way, be sure to get a plate of that pig, the best in Chinatown.

BAKERIES/PASTRIES

EASTERN BAKERY. . . . .

720 Grant Avenue (between
Clay and Sacramento)
415-392-4497
Open daily 8 A.M. to 9 P.M.
Cash only

A picture of President Clinton with the owners of Eastern Bakery graces the wall behind the counter of this destination for traditional Chinese moon cakes, the varieties of which stand in parade in the front window. These dense pastries, filled with hard-boiled egg yolks and sweetmeats, are eaten at holidays. I am partial to

Eastern's crisp, crumbly almond-egg cookies, and the old Chinatown look of this place in an ancient brick building, with a tiled facade and an ornamental roof over the front door.

GOLDEN GATE BAKERY . . . .

1029 Grant Avenue (between
Pacific and Jackson)
415-781-2627
Open daily 8 A.M. to 8 P.M.
Cash only

I noticed Golden Gate because of the lines of Chinese school kids and adults spilling out the door, eating good-looking turnovers and tarts. I worked my way to the counter of this small bakery and asked for one of each. When I saw that these savory brown pastries were hot from the oven, I understood what was causing the

stir. The curry beef turnover, my favorite, has a supertender, light, flaky crust made up of many tissue-thin layers. Inside is a warm, saucy, curry-scented filling of ground beef, corn, and carrots. They're just delicious. But the superstars here are warm egg custard tarts with a crust that any American grandmother would die to be able to make, filled with barely sweetened egg custard. They're sold as fast as the bakery can make them, so they're either available warm, or sometimes hot, or you've missed them. It's worth waiting for more to come out.

It turns out that Golden Gate Bakery is associated with the historic Eastern Bakery down the street, and that Golden Gate closes three months of the year. Let's just hope that when you read this, Golden Gate will be open because you won't taste a better custard tart or savory turnover anyplace else.

MEE MEE BAKERY. . . . .

1328 Stockton Street (between
Broadway and Vallejo)
415-362-3204
Open daily 8 A.M. to 6 P.M.
Cash only

This is Chinatown's premier fortune cookie bakery. Not only are Mee Mee's fortune cookies fresh and crisp, defining qualities for these simple wafers shaped while hot, but you can order them with your own messages. As you can imagine, the potential for fun cannot be overstated. Even if you settle for precomposed fortunes, the big bags of cookies make for an inexpensive and much-appreciated present for kids. For adults who might enjoy a bag of cookies with risqué messages, Mee Mee always has them on hand. I like both their sandy-textured almond and sesame cookies, too. They're about three inches in diameter, a quarter of an inch thick, barely sweetened, and full of egg and nut or sesame flavor. They finish off a meal with tea.

ICE CREAM/CHOCOLATES

SWEET WORLD. . . . .

601 Broadway (at Grant)
415-989-1228
Open 10 A.M. to 6 P.M. in winter
until 7 P.M. in summer
Cash only

Many Asian sweets are sour, salty, and chewy. At Sweet World, you can taste the whole range from bins of dried kumquats, ginger, mango, tiny plums, and other preserved Asian fruits that seem more like pickles than sweets to Westerners. But some types of vitamin C–enriched chewy fruit jellies are more accessible to Western tastes. I always buy a package of Cocoaland Mango Gummy made in Malaysia and try to make it home with a few of the individually wrapped jellies left. These jellies taste just like fresh mangoes, and I have grown to like their hard, gummy texture that eventually melts in your mouth. They really are addictive. My teenage son loves sour apple jellies from Japan that come in a rectangular package, but I don't like the chemical smell that many of the artificially made jellies exude. The Cocoaland Mango Gummy is made only with natural ingredients.

Sweet World also makes black bubble tea, all the rage now. Different kinds of sweetened milky Thai or black teas are poured over ice and a layer of big, black tapioca balls. You drink this concoction with an extra-wide straw to allow the tapioca balls to be sucked up. All I can say is that bubble tea is an acquired taste and you have to be very careful not to aspirate on the throat-clogging balls. My Chinese friends cannot understand my dislike of their favorite drink.

Also available at Sweet World is twenty-first-century ice cream in the form of pellets of different colors and flavors, called Frosty Bites. This extruded frozen product, which melts quickly in your mouth, tastes less creamy and viscous than regular ice cream. You get the sensation of eating ice cream without the dairiness of it all. Mint-chocolate cookie ice cream, the most popular flavor at Sweet World, incorporates frozen chocolate cookie crumbs that add a little crunch. Sweet World also offers regular ice cream in tropical flavors for the old-fashioned, and prepares fruit juice, and ice cream drinks.

ETHNIC MARKETS

LIEN HING SUPERMARKET . . . .

1112 Stockton Street (between Pacific and Jackson)
415-986-8488
Open daily 6:30 A.M. to 7 P.M.
Cash only

Two chaotic Cantonese supermarkets compete head to head on adjacent blocks in Chinatown. Lien Hing, at this moment, may have a slight edge simply because the operation has two other locations, one on Clement and the other just a couple of blocks away, and has more stuff. This double storefront on the east side of Stockton lures the hordes with tables of good-looking vegetables and fruits spilling out onto the pedestrian-clogged sidewalk. Sexy peas sprouts, huge grapefruitlike pomelos, young ivory-skinned coconuts, durians, pristine Shanghai-style baby bok choy, and Western spinach grabbed my attention the other day, but the availability of exotic and seasonal items and the quality of everything changes by the hour. The butchers at the meat counter will cut and grind the smallest amounts of pork at the fat level you choose. You can buy dry goods—Longevity Brand sweetened condensed milk, soy sauce, the best brand of coconut milk, rice, dried noodles—and refrigerated goods—tofu, fresh noodles, wonton skins, pickled vegetables—at the best prices.

Completely unlike the wide, tidy aisles of Western supermarkets filled with processed foods, all is chaos at Lien Hing and every other Chinatown market. Practically nothing is packaged or labeled; everything is fresh, raw, unprocessed. You can barely push through the crowds—let alone wield a shopping cart or even a basket. And once you've got an armful of stuff, you have to defend your place in line or some Chinese grandmother will elbow her way in front of you. If you can't find what you need at Lien Hing, go next door.

The market streets of Chinatown rival Hong Kong's in their frenzy, smells, and crowds. Chinatown can seem daunting to the uninitiated shopper, but there is no more exciting area in which to buy food in the city. You can find excellent raw materials here in the way of fish, poultry, shellfish, pork, and vegetables for any style of cooking, and of course anything you might need for the Asian pantry. The great shopping blocks are between Broadway and Pacific on Grant Avenue, and Broadway to Washington on Stockton Street, with growing activity on Powell. A scattering of good Chinese markets has jumped over Broadway into North Beach, as have a number of good Cantonese restaurants. Broadway itself, between Stockton and Columbus, offers a number of stores selling produce and groceries. You don't hear much English, although almost everyone does speak it, but the shops and stores want only to move their merchandise, so don't be shy about asking for what you want.

The prices can be very good, but it takes a keen eye to find the best things. One store can have tables of beautiful baby bok choy and moldy water chestnuts. Another will have piles of tiny pea sprouts, yet another mangoes and apricots. One of the fish markets will have rockfish still gasping for breath; another, exquisite live spot prawns swimming in a tank. At first you think the same things are being sold everywhere, but certain places have special things and those things seem to move around from place to place. I approach shopping in Chinatown the same way I do at a farmers' market: I go with empty baskets and cloth bags slung across my shoulder and an open mind instead of a specific shopping list. That way I can walk around and pick up the best things available at six different stores. Once you start shopping this way, you will find it boring to shop in the supermarket where everything is available whether in season or not, and where the emphasis is on packaged, not fresh and often alive, foods.

PRODUCE

CHUNG HING PRODUCE CO. . . . .

1300 Powell Street (at Pacific)
415-693-9634
Open daily 8 A.M. to 6 P.M.
Cash only

You won't find the widest range of produce at this corner store, but you will find some of the prettiest and freshest examples of some of the more precious produce—perfect snow and snap peas, fresh black Mission figs (during the summer and fall), big, perfect bunches of watercress, flawless hairy melons, leafy Chinese celery, fresh, moist, unmoldy water chestnuts, baby bananas. Chung Hing distributes fresh noodles from the local Hong Kong Noodle Company and many restaurants double-park their vans in front of this store to pick up cases of these excellent noodles, along with boxes of produce.

FRUIT CITY. . . . .

1210-1216 Stockton Street (between
Broadway and Pacific)
415-781-8186 or 415-989-2350
Open daily 6:30 A.M. to 7:30 P.M.
Cash only

Fruit City's greens always catch my eye as I move with the crowds down Stockton Street—the *gai lan* (slender-stemmed Chinese broccoli), watercress, tiny heads of bok choy. I have bought hard-to-find fresh bamboo shoots there, and also Western broccoli and cauliflower. In the former location of May Wah (still a major player on Clement Street), Fruit City offers the wide range of produce and meat counter of a typical Chinatown supermarket.

LIEN HING SUPERMARKET. . . . .

1112 Stockton Street (between
Pacific and Jackson)
415-986-8488
Open daily 6:30 A.M. to 7 P.M.
Cash only

The produce spills out onto the congested sidewalks of Chinatown and Lien Hing's buyers know to put the choicest items of the hour in the most prominent location. These might be pristine baby bok choy for a few cents less than the store next door, or extra-large fresh lichees for the same price as smaller ones. Since Lien Hing is the current reigning independent Chinese supermarket in the city, with three branches, they move lots of produce. They sell cheap and, with their turnover, fresh. See page 36 for more information.

POT STICKERS (JIAO ZI)

MAKES ABOUT 3 DOZEN, SERVES 4 (if people restrain themselves)

This recipe draws on Barbara Tropp's *The Modern Art of Chinese Cooking* for proportions, and Cecilia Chiang's advice for technique. (Cecilia founded The Mandarin in Ghirardelli Square, the first elegant northern Chinese restaurant in the United States. She is a superb home cook.) Homemade pot stickers are scrumptious and worth the effort. You can get all the ingredients at a Cantonese supermarket like Lien Hing.

FILLING

½ pound napa cabbage, cut into pea-sized dice

2 teaspoons kosher salt

¾ pound ground pork butt

1 tablespoon fresh ginger, peeled and finely minced

¼ cup chopped scallion

1 tablespoon soy sauce

1 tablespoon Chinese rice wine

1 tablespoon sesame oil

———

1 package pot sticker skins

2 tablespoons peanut oil

1 cup water

Soy sauce, chile oil, and Chinese vinegar for serving

1 Put the chopped cabbage in a colander and toss with 1 teaspoon of the salt. Let this mixture sit for 10 minutes to drain. Then squeeze out all the liquid with your hands and put the cabbage in a large bowl with the rest of the ingredients for the filling. Mix thoroughly.

2 Put a scant tablespoon of the filling in the middle of a pot sticker skin. Fold wrapper in half over filling. Pinch shut at midpoint. Then, beginning to the right of the midpoint, make three tiny pleats on the near side of the wrapper only, folding the pleats toward the midpoint. After each pleat, pinch the dough to join the far, unpleated side of the wrapper. Pinch the extreme right corner of the arc closed. Repeat to the left side of the midpoint, aiming the pleats toward the center. Pinch the left corner closed. Pinch all along the arc to ensure the seal and to thin the ridge dough. There will be pleats on one side of the ridge of the dumpling and smooth dough on the other side. Put each one on a plate as you make it.

3 Heat the peanut oil in a large cast-iron skillet with a lid. When the oil is hot, arrange the pot stickers, flat side down, in concentric circles in the frying pan, starting from the outside and working toward the middle. Snuggle them next to one another. It's okay if they touch. Fry at high heat for 2 minutes once they're all placed in the pan. Then add the water. Cover the pan. Turn down the heat to medium and cook for 7 minutes. All the water will disappear and the dumplings will be crisp and golden on one side.

4 Turn them out onto a plate (in one big cake if you can) crispy side up, and place them in the middle of the table. Let eaters pull off each dumpling with chopsticks. Eaters can make their own dipping sauce from the soy, chile oil, and vinegar placed on the table.

LIEN HING SUPERMARKET NO. 2 . . . .

1401 Stockton Street (at Vallejo)
415-397-2668
Open daily 8 A.M. to 6 P.M.
Cash only

It's easier to shop for produce at Lien Hing No. 2 than the larger Lien Hing, deeper in Chinatown, because it's less crowded, both on the sidewalk in front of this corner store and inside. Though still packed, it feels more spacious and less claustrophobic. (Technically this store is in North Beach, but thematically it belongs in the Chinatown section, so I've included it here.) You can shop here for the likes of big, meaty fresh shiitakes, coconuts, huge green papayas, pineapples, and Shanghai bok choy without getting pushed off the sidewalk into the street.

WO CHONG . . . .

720 Jackson Street (between
Grant and Stockton)
415-982-6137
Open daily 8:30 a.m. to 5:30 p.m.
Cash only

This little shop makes its own fresh tofu and I like to buy it here. A small selection of produce that you may not see anyplace else is often displayed near the cash register or on a few tables on the sidewalk. Most of the vegetables go with tofu or belong in soups with tofu.

MEAT AND POULTRY

GUANG ZHOU KING & KING SAUSAGE . . . .

57 Walter Lum Place (between
Clay and Washington)
415-397-3878
Open daily 9 A.M. to 6 P.M.
Cash only

A charming little shop with a small selection of dry goods and a counter hung with strings of sweet, dry, thin Chinese sausages and mahogany slabs of dry, sweetly cured Chinese bacon, this is the only place that still makes these meats in Chinatown. Steam for 5 minutes, cut up into pieces, and serve the meat and its juices with rice and vegetables.

LIEN HING SUPERMARKET . . . .

1112 Stockton Street (between
Pacific and Jackson)
415 986-8488
Open daily 6:30 A.M. to 7 P.M.
Cash only

This fully manned butcher counter is long and well stocked with pork, though beef and chicken are also represented. Chinatown butchers now carry mostly lean pork, which I find impossible to cook in Western recipes since it dries out so quickly. For Asian recipes, like pot stickers, which call for ground pork, be sure to buy meat with some proportion of fat in the grind for flavor. At a Chinese butcher counter like Lien Hing's, you can select a good-looking piece of pork butt with fat and ask for it to be ground to order. See page 36 for more information on this supermarket.

SERVES 3 TO 4 with rice and other dishes

Adapted from *Hot, Sour, Salty, Sweet* by Jeffrey Alford and Naomi Duguid. A stop at Wo Chong inspires me to make this fast and delicious dish. You can buy hard-to-find Szechwan pepper at Lien Hing Supermarket.

1 tablespoon peanut oil

3 scallions trimmed, cut lengthwise into strips, and then crosswise into 1-inch lengths

¼ cup (2 ounces) ground pork

4 blocks fresh tofu (about 1½ pounds total), cut into ¾-inch cubes

2 to 3 tablespoons chile oil

1 teaspoon kosher salt, plus a pinch

⅛ teaspoon freshly ground Szechwan pepper, or more to taste

1 teaspoon cornstarch, dissolved in 1 tablespoon water

1 Place all the ingredients near your stovetop. Heat a wok over high heat. Add the oil and swirl to coat, then toss in the scallions, reduce the heat to medium-high, and stir-fry briefly. Add the pork and stir-fry, breaking up any clumps with your spatula, until the meat has changed color, about 1 minute. Pour off any water that has drained out of the tofu cubes and add the tofu, chile oil, salt, and pepper to the wok.

2 Raise the heat, turn the ingredients gently to mix well, and cook for 30 seconds to 1 minute. Stir the cornstarch paste, add to the wok, stir to blend, and cook for another 20 to 30 seconds until the sauce thickens. Turn out onto a plate or shallow bowl. Serve hot or at room temperature to accompany rice or noodles.

MAN SUNG . . . .

1116 Grant Avenue (between Broadway and Pacific)
415-982-5918
Open daily 7 A.M. to 6 P.M.
Cash only

Basically a wholesaler with a tiny retail storefront, Man Sung only displays a few of the poultry items it sells. But this is the place to go for fresh chickens and chicken parts. Chinese shoppers insist on free-range chickens, and they bought them long before the rest of us caught on. These hormone-free chickens are raised for flavor and tend to be lean, but oh-so-tasty. Be sure to specify Petaluma chickens at Man Sung; they are specially raised by Petaluma Poultry for the Chinatown market. Take home a whole bird complete with head and feet, appendages that greatly enrich a stock. Birds with head and feet attached are called Buddhist chickens and may be sold because of a religious exemption granted by the U.S. Department of Agriculture, which otherwise requires that these appendages be removed. Since these Buddhist chickens are bled, a method of killing required by Jewish law, they are also sold in kosher butcher shops.

Man Sung also sells Pekin ducks from Reichardt Duck Farm in Petaluma. These ducks do not have huge breasts, so they roast up quickly and stay moist, especially when bathed in an aromatic Asian marinade. The California history of the Pekin duck, first bred in China thousands of years ago, began in 1880 when a Yankee clipper ship, on its way to the East Coast from China by way of South America, docked in San Francisco. Somehow a dozen Pekin ducks in its cargo disappeared and ended up at a small poultry farm in the middle of the city. In 1901, Otto H. Reichardt bought the stock and moved the operation to South City in 1912 and then to Petaluma in 1958, where the duck farm, still in the family, raises over a million ducks a year, supplying most of the West Coast.

MING KEE GAME BIRDS. . . . .

1122 Grant Avenue (between Broadway and Pacific)
415-391-8287
Open Monday through Saturday
8 A.M. to 6 P.M., Sunday until 5 P.M.
Cash only

The word must have gotten out about Ming Kee, because there are signs in the window that ask tourists not to take pictures of the fluffy live hens, quail, squab, and partridges crowded into cages behind the counter. Chinatown women come to the ordering window, point at a handsome brown hen, and watch as the clerk grabs the bird by its feet, pops it into a heavy brown paper bag with holes in it, staples it shut, and puts it into a thin plastic bag for carrying. The shoppers walk off with the live birds, just as if they were carrying bags from the supermarket. Some French cooks I know tell me it's no big deal to kill a chicken, bleed it and pluck it, fry the blood *(sanguette)*, and use every part of the bird in cooking, but I can't imagine doing it myself.

For the faint of heart, freshly butchered birds, vacuum-packed in plastic, fill a small refrigerated case in the store. Expensive black-skinned chickens used for restorative broths (surprisingly their feathers are pure white) and superb quail and squab can be found here. In the spring, game-bird eggs are available, a rare delicacy, especially squab eggs that sell for $50 a dozen.

NEW ON SANG . . . .

1114 Grant Street (between Broadway and Pacific)
415-982-4694
Open daily 8:30 A.M. to 5:30 P.M.
Cash only

New On Sang, with a branch on Clement Street (which takes credit cards), opened right next to Man Sung. You can decide which chickens and squabs look fresher. I have noticed small variations in price for wings or backs for soup—Man Sung is cheaper—and when one has run out of chicken feet (a must for gelatinous chicken broth), the other will have some. Man Sung puts out more product for retail customers than its neighbor. I have seen French chefs shop here for squab and for chicken livers. You simply can't beat Chinatown poultry for quality—or price for the quality. Of course these free-range Buddhist/kosher chickens cost twice as much as mass-produced supermarket chickens, but they're worth it for the superior flavor.

FISH

LUEN SING FISH MARKET . . . .

1207 Stockton Street (between
Broadway and Pacific)
415-399-8788
Open daily 8 A.M. to 6 P.M.
Cash only

Luen Sing holds live crabs in clean tanks with fast-running water. When the counterman pulls one out of the tank, he holds it up to show you how lively it is. You might wonder how you're going to get this wild, gesticulating crustacean with lethal claws home. No problem. The plastic-aproned fishmonger quickly drops the crab into a thick, brown paper bag and then puts it in a pink plastic bag with handles. As you inch your way down Stockton Street with your dinner, you can figure that half the people you squeeze by have live creatures in bags, too—frogs, birds, fish, shellfish. If you're going to eat it, you should be able to kill it. It's only fair.

Luen Sing also displays many clear-eyed whole fish, now dead but recently alive, like large, flat flounders with both eyes on one side of their heads. Usually there will be one bin of fish still flapping. As at every shop in Chinatown, the selection varies from day to day. But when you want fresh, well-stored, live crabs and often live shrimp, check out Luen Sing first.

NEW SANG SANG . . . .

1143 Stockton Street (between
Jackson and Pacific)
415-433-0403
Open daily 8 A.M. to 6 P.M.
Cash only

This large fish store in Chinatown (it used to be called the Dragon Market) gives off a breath of the sea when you walk by it, luring you in by displaying its freshest fish on tables of ice at the front, open to the sidewalk. The other day, huge Monterey spot prawns with bright orange roe caught my eye. They are sublime steamed until just firm, keeping head and roe intact. (The fat in the head and the roe are the best parts of the prawn.) If brilliant blue crabs are in they will be wiggling around in boxes on the street. I always return to this market after a perusal of several others to buy live, whole fish, about 2 pounds each, with clear glassy eyes. You tear off a plastic bag and use it as a glove to pick up your fish by the gills (the slits by the head). A genial counterman weighs it, then scales, guts, and takes out the gills, leaving you with a beautiful whole cleaned fish. Best to cook it simply. Preheat the oven to 450°F, put the whole fish seasoned with salt and pepper in a pan, fill the cavity with sliced fennel, lemon slices, sprigs of rosemary or Chinese aromatics like ginger and green onions, cover it with a piece of aluminum foil, cuts slits in the foil, and bake it for about 20 minutes. The fish comes out of the oven moist and firm, with the glorious chewiness that comes only with the freshest of fish cooked whole this way. These freshest of fish make an easy and very spectacular meal. This fish store carries red-fleshed fish like mackerel, not often seen in Cantonese markets, along with salmon, tiny pomfret, and yellow China cod. Price is keyed to quality. The cleaned and beheaded sand dabs on sale will be flabby. The whole sand dabs with clear eyes at three times the price will be excellent. For selection and quality I head here, expecting to be inspired for many a meal.

SALT-ROASTED WHOLE FISH

SERVES 4

Jean-Pierre Moullé, the former downstairs chef at Chez Panisse, is a hunter, gatherer, and fisher, both on the water and under it. He knows how to cook everything from the sea, including seaweed. One day at his house, he cooked a white sea bass in rock salt and it was the most succulent fish I ever tasted. Here is his recipe. It works for any whole fish with scales, such as a small salmon, sea bass, or local snapper. I used a beautiful green-skinned lingcod, and this method of cooking made it taste extraordinary. The fish is so delicious, moist, and aromatic, it needs no sauce, though you could put extra virgin olive oil infused with lemon zest on the table.

3- to 4-pound whole true snapper, sea bass, or rockfish cleaned and with scales left on

6 to 8 fresh herb sprigs such as parsley, thyme, oregano, and/or rosemary

10 pounds rock salt

1 Preheat the oven to 500°F. Stuff the inside of the fish with the herbs.

Choose a baking pan just large enough to hold the fish. Cover the bottom with a 1-inch layer of rock salt. Lay the fish on top and cover the entire fish with more salt. The fish should be completely mounded with the rock salt. Depending on the size of the fish, bake for 20 to 30 minutes. (My lingcod was 3½ pounds and I cooked it for 25 minutes.)

2 Remove from the oven and let rest for 10 minutes. Break the salt crust. Gently remove the fish from the pan. Lift off the skin. It should peel very easily. Serve the whole fish at the table. Be careful to brush off all the grains of salt.

CHONG IMPORTS . . . .

838 Grant Avenue, Empress of
China building basement (between
Clay and Washington)
415-982-1432
Open Monday through Thursday
10 A.M. to 8 P.M., Friday and
Saturday until 9 P.M.,
Sunday noon to 8 P.M.
Credit cards: MC, V

A huge space filled with all sorts of rare, but mostly very affordable treasures makes the trip downstairs worthwhile. I never fail to find something irresistible: black and red hardbound notebooks for $1.79, handsome celadon dishes for a song, pretty and useful bamboo steamers. Chong also has elegant quince- and melon-shaped antique porcelain bowls at $450 each, and teapots in the shape of pigs with thimble-sized cups for $15. Lotus-shaped teapots with lotus seeds rattling in the tops, packets of Chinese vegetable seeds, and a lot of Chinese tableware make up a small fraction of the stock. Regular Chinatown shoppers drop by just to see what might have come in, like large and very inexpensive glass jars for pickling, and large and small clay pots with covers, one of the finest braising vessels in any culture.

GINN WALL . . . .

1016 Grant Avenue (between
Jackson and Pacific)
415-982-6307
Open Monday, Tuesday,
Wednesday, Friday, and
Saturday 10 A.M. to 6 P.M.,
Sunday until 5 P.M.
Credit cards: MC, V

This Chinese hardware store is filled with Chinese cooking essentials, from woks of all sizes to the utensils necessary to cook in them. Cleavers and knives, huge stockpots and steamers, marble mortars and pestles—the building blocks of an Asian kitchen—are all here at nontourist prices. A section of paperback Chinese cookbooks at the front of the store, including Shirley Fong-Torres's instructive guide to Chinatown, will inspire you to start cooking. But you don't have to be a Chinese cook to use a wok. The wok's versatility as a cooking tool makes it an excellent and inexpensive addition to any kitchen. I steam vegetables, fish (on a glass pie plate), and tamales in mine on top of a beautiful and inexpensive bamboo basket insert. I also use the wok for deep-frying. Its efficient shape makes a small amount of oil go a long way. The oil heats quickly and recovers its temperature after food is dropped in it, which makes deep-frying easy. Try frying fresh corn chips or whole sand dabs in it. Heat a couple of inches of olive oil in the wok until a piece of bread dropped into the oil turns golden. Dip the sand dabs in buttermilk, then in seasoned flour. Carefully slide them into the oil and cook until brown and crispy, about 4 minutes, depending on the thickness of the fish. Cook just a couple at a time so that the oil surrounds each fish and they do not touch. I serve one of these hot, crisp fish with a little green salad as a first course.

TAI YICK TRADING COMPANY . . . .

1400 Powell Street (at Broadway)
415-986-0961
Open daily 9:30 A.M. to 7 P.M.
Credit cards: AE, MC, V

I'm a pushover for celadon, that mysterious gray-green color the bay becomes on certain overcast days. At Tai Yick, a store packed to the rafters with Chinese pottery and porcelain, you can buy a whole set of celadon plates, cups, saucers, and flat bowls at Crate&Barrel prices, though you may have to sort through piles of dishes in a cluttered corner to find them. Celadon china always looks elegant and is particularly beautiful with fish or dark green vegetables served on it—colors you might find in the sea. Fresh fruit on celadon also is stunning. Deep Chinese soup bowls in all sorts of ornate patterns are stacked next to simple blue-and-white china decorated with cheerful brush-painted fish. Dark brown, glazed terra-cotta casseroles for all of $4.50 are suitable both for serving and cooking in the oven or even on top of the stove. You can bake potato gratins in them or heat up stews, and handsomely present them on the table where they will stay hot. Several sizes come with glazed covers. Finally, for fans of cracked-glaze porcelain, Tai Yick has all sorts of vases and planters, some huge, in mustardy yellow and celadon green.

CIVIC CENTER
HAYES VALLEY

CIVIC CENTER &
HAYES VALLEY

RESTAURANTS
1   Absinthe Brasserie and Bar
2   Citizen Cake
3   Destino
4   Hayes Street Grill
5   Jardinière
6   Suppenküche
7   Vicolo Pizzeria
8   Vietnam II
9   Zuni Cafe

CAFÉS
10   Arlequin
11   Caffè Trinity
12   Momi Toby's Revolution Cafe

DELICATESSENS/TAKEOUT
13   DeLessio
14   Saigon Sandwich Cafe

BAKERIES/PASTRIES
15   Citizen Cake

ICE CREAM/CHOCOLATES
10   Arlequin
15   Citizen Cake

ETHNIC MARKETS
16   New Chiu Fong Company

PRODUCE
17   Civic Center Farmers' Market
16   New Chiu Fong Company

WINES AND SPIRITS
18   Amphora Wine Merchant
19   Hayes and Vine Wine Bar

COOKWARE AND BOOKS
20   A Clean Well-Lighted Place for Books

N

W

E

S

GEARY

O'FARRELL >>>

ELLIS   <<<

15 **8**

EDDY   >>>

JEFFERSON
SQUARE

VAN NESS AVENUE

14

TURK   <<<

HAYWARD
PLAYGROUND

19

FEDERAL
BLDG

LARKIN

HYDE

LEAVENWORTH

JONES

GOLDEN GATE   >>>

STATE
BLDG

STATE
BLDG

McALLISTER

FULTON

VETS
WAR
MEM

CITY
HALL

CIVIC
CENTER
PLAZA

UN
PLAZA

16

MAIN
LIBRARY

OPERA
HOUSE

5

7TH

11

GROVE

IVY

2 **7**

SYMPHONY
HALL

1 **10** **17** **4**

CIVIC
AUDI-
TORIUM

STREET

8TH

HAYES

<<<

POLK

9TH

6

18

12

FELL   <<<

LAGUNA

OCTAVIA

GOUGH

FRANKLIN

10TH

OAK   >>>

MARKET

11TH

PAGE

9

12TH

HAIGHT   <<<

WALLER

13

GOUGH

3

VALENCIA

GUERRERO

ABSINTHE BRASSERIE AND BAR . . . .

398 Hayes Street (at Gough)
415-551-1590
www.absinthe.com
Open Tuesday through Thursday
11:30 A.M. to 3 P.M. and
5 P.M. to midnight,
Friday 11:30 A.M. to midnight,
Saturday 10:30 A.M. to midnight,
Sunday 10:30 A.M. to 10:30 P.M.
Moderate
Credit Cards: AE, DC, MC, V

My friend Billy Russell-Shapiro founded Absinthe, Arlequin (see page 60), and Amphora Wine Merchant (see page 65), all on one block of Hayes. He's a former city planner and current philanthropist who believes that establishing labor-intensive businesses, like restaurants, gives people jobs. As a result of his pro-employment philosophy, Absinthe encompasses both high professionalism and a certain degree of winging it. All who work at this romantically lit French bistro with belle epoque flourishes are exceptionally nice and eager to please, but some of the floor staff can be a little befuddled, not fully informed, as if they forgot a few crucial items in a memorized list of duties. The ups and downs of service have not diminished my pleasure in eating here, or having a cocktail with a little bowl of marinated olives in the always busy barroom-café.

Chef Ross Brown always comes up with something unusual and delicious for the menu, like *malfatti*, free-form dumplings of ricotta and spinach, sauced with brown butter and white truffle oil, a delicate treat, or a Greek salad of juicy heirloom tomatoes and thinly sliced peppers. From the raw bar come platters of oysters, marinated white anchovies, or a delicious cold calamari salad with capers and olives. Brown's creamy chicken liver pâté with brioche toasts makes for a substantial treat with a glass of wine. His salads of perfect tiny greens sparkle. A steak from old-fashioned, marbled corn-fed beef tastes guiltily good, especially accompanied with Absinthe's skinny, crisp french fries, stylishly served in a paper-lined metal cup. Chocolate *pots-de-crème* and springtime rhubarb soup with strawberries and crème fraîche ice cream demonstrate the breadth of the pastry kitchen.

I am intrigued by the international wine list and the sommeliers who steer you to treasures like resonant Portuguese reds made with fruit from ancient vines. In the $30 range, you can't find a better bottle. Of course, the list is buoyed by the inventory at Amphora Wine Merchants, and vice versa. The little food empire of operations that start with "A" has done its part to make Hayes Street a destination for culinary pleasure.

CITIZEN CAKE. . . . .

399 Grove Street (at Gough)
415-861-2228
www.citizencake.com
Open Tuesday through Friday 8 A.M.
to 10 P.M., Saturday 10 A.M. to 10
P.M., Sunday 10 A.M. to 9 P.M.
Inexpensive–Moderate
Credit Cards: AE, MC, V

With talented chef Jennifer Cox running the kitchen, this twenty-first-century bakery, *gelateria*, and café has become a viable restaurant where the savory food now matches the polish of Elizabeth Falkner's pastries.

The other day I had the most wonderful little lunch at the bar, waited on by a smart, efficient server who knew the menu and everything about the desserts–bakery–restaurant world. In addition, she intuitively

SPAGHETTINI WITH PECORINO AND BLACK PEPPER

SERVES 4 TO 6

When you eat this kind of simple pasta in Italy, you can't believe how good it tastes. Ross Brown, the chef at Absinthe, first prepared this dish for me at Rosmarino in Pacific Heights, before the restaurant changed identity and moved to the Civic Center. I was hooked forever. The key is to use European-style butter like Plugra or Straus Family Creamery butter, and aged pecorino, such as *locatelli*. Ross Brown uses De Cecco dried pasta.

1 pound dried spaghettini	Bring a large pot of salted water to a boil and add the spaghettini. Bring the pot back to a boil and cook for 8 minutes, or until al dente. Drain the pasta thoroughly and pour it back into the pot. Add the butter and cheese and toss until the pasta is thoroughly coated. Grind in the pepper. Toss again. Check for salt, add if necessary, toss again, and serve.
½ cup unsalted butter	
1½ cups (6 ounces) grated aged pecorino	
30 turns of the pepper grinder set to coarse	
Kosher salt to taste (optional)	

understood the dance of chat and retreat that must be adjusted to each customer. She served me a bowl of luscious, just-cooked baby spinach, a "salad" in whole-grain mustard vinaigrette with big hunks of bacon, creamy Yukon gold potatoes, and a poached egg that enriched all the other juices. Poised between a salad and a sauté, this clever dish, a turn on a classic combination of frisée with lardons, was complete, vegetable-centered, heartily satisfying. It left appetite for the tenderest *panna cotta* made with Redwood Hill goat yogurt, sweetened only by blackberry purée, garnished with a strawberry sorbet and a berry salad, which stood above the hundred versions I've had. With a glass of Joguet Chinon, the perfect lunch wine from Kermit Lynch, and Citizen Cake's own fresh bread, this meal charmed me from beginning to end.

Cox's menu truly draws from the local market—in early summer, Frog Hollow peaches in a salad with soft white Bellwether Farms's *crescenza* cheese, chicken leg confit with apricots, English pea and pea sprout lasagne with *fromage blanc*. I trust her instincts in interweaving fruit with greens, cheese, pork, and birds. She knows how to create whole cloth.

Now with new, more comfortable chairs, the literally edgy, hard-surfaced, loftlike dining room surrounded by windows has become a more welcoming place to dine. The resources of the bakery and *gelateria*, which were the original focus of Citizen Cake, now enrich the food service instead of dominating it, so this multifaceted operation works on many different levels. The best time to come is for nonmatinee lunch and after 7:45 P.M. on symphony, ballet, and opera nights, when the kitchen and staff have time to work their full magic.

DESTINO . . . .

1815 Market Street (between
Valencia and Guerrero)
415-552-4451
Open Monday through Saturday
5 to 11 P.M.
Moderate
Credit cards: AE, MC, V

Tapas—small plates and bites—are everywhere in every flavor. Enough already! But there's one more place you should know about—perhaps the best of all—Destino, a vibrant, sexy, Latin American tapas bar in an easily overlooked location. Had I not met the thirty-year-old owner-chef-designer-manager James Schenk at a dinner party, I would never have set foot in this little joint, though I must have passed it a million times driving down Market Street. Now, whenever I go by, I think about *arepas con queso*, piquant sea bass ceviche, pisco sours. How could I have missed a restaurant that makes me so happy?

Schenk designed, built, and furnished polished little Destino himself, and the energy in the room is palpable. Images bounce off the huge mirrors and noise echoes off all the hard surfaces. There are no tablecloths to dampen the sound—hot Latino music hardly in the background or a live guitarist in the small bar at the front. The bartenders mix pisco sours, a milky, cinnamon-scented, sweet-and-sour drink, as fast as they can. The excitement at Destino is further fueled by an enthusiastic and eclectic crowd who know that they can eat and drink brilliantly for $20 to $25 a person.

Start with a ceviche—either a fruity tuna, avocado, and mango one served in a martini glass, or the scintillating Peruvian-style sea bass ceviche sprinkled with deep-fried corn kernels that ingeniously add nuttiness and crunch. Few pass up the rich, ground beef–filled chile relleno, swathed in guacamole, melted cheddar, smoky chipotle salsa, and fragrant citrus crème fraîche. Pair it with sustainably harvested (I asked) hearts of palm salad in classic orange French dressing, a modernization of a beloved, old-fashioned San Francisco salad. Another must-order is *Pastel de Choclo*, a Chilean casserole layered with Niman Ranch ground beef, shredded chicken, and shards of sharp, dried black olives all blanketed in creamy puréed corn. Schenk knows how to weave flavors and textures together—the sweet, mild, and soft with sharp, pungent, and earthy—so that the components of his dishes, no matter how inventive, taste inevitable. From his Peruvian mother, Schenk inherited a romantic Latin American sensibility, and he stays true to it from beginning to end.

Anticuchos, skewered, marinated, and grilled beef heart, the definitive Peruvian dish, gets authentic treatment here. So delicious. Slices of crispy-skinned duck breast, cooked through but still juicy, lean against a mound of cilantro-green basmati rice cooked like a risotto so the kernels still have a bit of crunch, but have mushed together. *Arepas*, soft, silky, thick white cornmeal-and-cheese pancakes, are slathered with grilled corn and chunky salsa. They are Destino's version of soul food.

If you have any room after an array of little dishes, I highly recommend an amazingly moist fillet of mahi-mahi encrusted with fried plantain crumbs, served with a bacon-infused plantain and yuca mash (denser than potatoes) and soupy black beans drizzled with olive *crema*. This *plato grande* is quite spectacular.

The bar makes the best margarita in town, a piquant lime elixir served in a short tumbler over ice, bright and refreshing. Both margaritas and pisco sours complete the food, but so do the select Spanish, Latin American, and California wines on a succinct list organized according to character. If you can manage dessert, try *Banana con Tres Leches*, a little tower of milk-soaked banana sponge cake and banana cream with warm, caramelized banana slices. Even the espresso is perfect, a sip of dark, rich New World coffee that comes with miniature *alfajores*, butter cookie sandwiches filled with *dulce de leche*. These fresh, exquisite cookies send every customer off with a smile and a vow to return to Destino as soon as possible.

HAYES STREET GRILL . . . .

320 Hayes Street (between
Gough and Franklin)
415-863-5545
Open Monday through Friday
11:30 A.M. to 2 P.M., Monday
through Thursday 5 to 9:30 P.M.,
Friday and Saturday 5 to
10:30 P.M., Sunday until 8:30 P.M.
Moderate
Credit cards: AE, DC, MC, V

I must be completely up front about this twenty-something fish house across the street from the Performing Arts Center. I am an owner and a kitchen presence there. So instead of trying to give my own place a qualitative description, I will tell you what we do each day from the viewpoint of a chef.

The first thing in the morning, the grill chef has a chat with the fish man (Paul Johnson or Tom Worthington of Monterey Fish) to find out what looks good that day, and we base our daily menu on this. The Hayes Street kitchen is divided into three areas: a pantry or salad station, the mesquite grill, and a sauté station. We divide what we order among the three, so that big meaty fish like wild north coast king salmon or buttery swordfish come off the grill, while panfried Hama Hama oysters, petrale sole with chanterelles, or braised California white sea bass with artichokes are under the sauté chef's jurisdiction. The grilled fish comes with a pile of french fries cooked in peanut oil, our trademark, and a choice of at least four sauces and salsas. From the salad station comes our signature fresh crab slaw or an Indian-style scallop, mango, and cucumber salad with *papadum* (crispy lentil wafers). The whole menu benefits from the stunning array of seasonal produce we get directly from the Ferry Plaza Farmers' Market—I shop and haul myself two times a week—as well as Greenleaf Produce, an organic produce broker. Collaboratively the cooks figure out what dishes to make to create a balanced and tempting menu. We use an international mix of recipes with the unifying theme of fish and seafood. Above every other consideration, we want the freshness and pristine quality of the fish, produce, and naturally raised meats to speak for themselves. Though our dishes may be inspired by Southeast Asian, Italian, French, Mediterranean, American, Indian, or Latin American preparations, they are always simple, allowing the ingredients to shine.

We opened the Grill because over two decades ago there simply wasn't a good place to eat before the opera, ballet, or symphony. My partners and I wanted such a place ourselves, so we created a restaurant that cooks unfussy food, casual enough to serve before a performance, but substantial and tasty enough to be a main event. We drew inspiration from old

San Francisco grills like Tadich (see page 115) and Jeanty at Jack's (see page 105), which have always featured local ingredients in straightforward presentations, but we took the grill concept a step further by seeking out more sophisticated ingredients and cooking them in a modern style.

The Hayes Street Grill's walls are covered with autographed photos of the artists who use the restaurant as their club. We used to have bentwood chairs and worn wooden floors, but we remodeled and installed banquettes, chairs with upholstered seats, and carpeting, making the restaurant less noisy. The original brass coat hooks along the walls remain, as does our founding philosophy of cooking only the food we would serve at home to our families—dressed up a little—with a religious dedication to wholesomeness.

CRAB, ENDIVE, AND RADICCHIO SLAW

SERVES 4 as a side dish

At Hayes Street Grill, we use fresh-picked blue crab for this salad, which can be purchased at Monterey Fish Market (see page 436). During local Dungeness crab season, cook a live crab yourself and pick out its meat to use in this recipe, making it extra special.

1 tablespoon sherry vinegar

1 tablespoon minced shallots

½ teaspoon kosher salt

Freshly ground black pepper to taste

3 tablespoons olive oil

2 medium heads Belgian endive

1 small head radicchio

1½ cups (8 ounces) fresh-cooked crabmeat

¼ cup minced fresh chives

1 tablespoon fresh lemon juice

1 In a small bowl, combine the vinegar, shallots, salt, and pepper. Whisk in the olive oil. Set aside.

2 Separate the endive leaves, stack them, and cut them lengthwise into thin strips with a sharp knife. Core the radicchio and cut it into thin strips.

3 In a large bowl, combine the crab, endive, radicchio, and chives. Toss with the lemon juice, then toss with the vinaigrette and serve.

300 Grove (at Franklin)
415-861-5555
www.jardiniere.com
Open Sunday through Wednesday
5 to 10:30 P.M., Thursday through
Saturday until 11:30 P.M.
Expensive
Credit cards: AE, DC, D, V, MC

I consider Traci Des Jardins to be one of the most solid and talented cooks in San Francisco. Her local ingredient-enriched French cooking pleases me on the deepest levels. Her sauces are expressive; her combinations of foods natural; the look of the plates stylish without being fussy. Her training in France in starred kitchens and her experience opening the estimable Rubicon kitchen prepared her for launching her own place. She knows how to deliver a first-class restaurant experience, first making sure the kitchen is turning out food that she likes—and with her New Orleans–Creole background you know that Jardinière food will be richly layered with big flavors. She keeps current all the amenities of luxurious dining: a cheese-aging room; extensive wine inventory administered by knowledgeable staff; a sophisticated bar that pours all the best and the latest in spirits; fresh osetra caviar, but not endangered beluga; platters of tiny cookies and house-made candies that can be packed up for intermission across the street. She believes in informed service at all levels, from the moment you walk in the door to the way your dishes are cleared, and the Jardinière waitstaff in smart steward's jackets have been unfailingly gracious, intelligent, and intuitive.

But above and beyond all this, Des Jardins has become a leader in the local and national restaurant community. She empowered her right-hand man, Larry Bain, to organize a group for restaurateurs concerned about issues of sustainable food production, fair labor practices, and finding ecological solutions. If a community cause needs support, Jardinière is the first name on the letterhead.

So when I spend a sybaritic evening in the soigné, Pat Kuleto–designed supper club, drinking champagne, nibbling on foie gras, relishing my pan-roasted squab with porcini sauce and an elegant red wine, or my Alaskan halibut with asparagus, morels, and a lobster *jus* with a creamy chardonnay, I never feel too guilty because I know how much this restaurant gives back to everyone, customer and community included.

SUPPENKÜCHE . . . .

601 Hayes Street (at Laguna)
415-252-9289
www.suppenkuche.com
Open nightly 5 to 10 p.m.,
Saturday and Sunday brunch
10 A.M. to 2:30 P.M.
Moderate
Credit cards: AE, MC, V

Hayes Valley blossomed after the earthquake-damaged freeway was carted away. What was once a literally shady neighborhood, now basks in the sun of gentrification, full of arty clothing and shoe shops, antiques stores, and some restaurants and cafés.

Oddly enough, the most exciting culinary development in the area has been a German beer house and restaurant called Suppenküche, a lively, inexpensive place that serves superb German beers and simple German food on unfinished pine tables in a vaulted dining hall. From the moment it opened, Suppenküche has attracted a young crowd that appreciates beer and substantial, reasonably priced food. The spare, functional decor fits right into a minimally funded urban lifestyle, and sure enough, it has become the rage among a certain set to tuck into a plate of braised cabbage and bratwurst. The food is so good that people come from all parts of the city to eat here.

Thomas Klausmann, a Bavarian home cook, started the restaurant and runs the kitchen along with an experienced staff. The menu sticks to the traditional, though the cooking seems lighter, fresher, and more seasonal than a lot of German restaurant cooking I have tasted. Fresh pea soup comes out peppery and true flavored; the bread basket boasts moist sprouted-wheat bread and a German rye with a crackling crust; sausages come with sauerkraut resonant with bacon and sweet spices, a far cry from the stuff in cans. The oft-appearing mashed potatoes have a fork-mashed texture and a magical balance of butter, nutmeg, and milk. The mustard is hot, grainy, and delicious.

One of the most wonderful daily specials, from a chalked list that enlarges the small core menu, is an oxtail stew served with the tender noodle-dumplings called spaetzle. Other specials, like huge, soft veal meatballs in a caper-cream sauce, and a dreamy German-style chicken à la king served on noodles with big chunks of amazingly velvety chicken, represent the highest form of comfort food, especially with steins of cold, crisp, sparkly German lager. The small place gets noisy as the large tables fill up, often with several different parties, and the beer bar in the middle of the room gets crowded. The waitresses handle it all with finesse and humor, endlessly describing and recommending dishes for the first-timers. In every way this little soup kitchen knows how to please. It's a marvelous example of grass-roots urban redevelopment.

VICOLO PIZZERIA . . . .

150 Ivy Alley (between Hayes and Grove, off Franklin)
415-863-2382
Open Monday through Friday 11:30 A.M. to 2 P.M.; Monday through Thursday 5 to 9:30 P.M.; Friday 5 to 11 P.M.; Saturday and Sunday 11:30 A.M. to 2 P.M., matinees only; Saturday 5 to 11 P.M.; Sunday 5 to 8:30 P.M.
Inexpensive
Credit cards: MC, V

Once again I have to come clean. Vicolo (which is the Italian word for "alley") is an operation we set up in a corrugated steel shed behind the Hayes Street Grill to serve the overflow pre-performance crowd as well as people who want a fresh, inexpensive lunch or dinner in the Civic Center neighborhood. To that end, Vicolo has expanded its menu to include house-made lasagnas, warm sandwiches on focaccia buns, pizza, oven-roasted chicken, and baked pasta bolognese. Vicolo does not take reservations and the high-ceilinged room can get noisy during the pre-performance crush. Otherwise, the space is a comfortable hideaway. People order at the counter, find their own tables, and eat Italian vegetable salads or house-made soups while they wait for their pizza. The pizzas come by the slice or whole, in black cast-iron pans. The crisp cornmeal crust is sturdy enough to act as a shell for substantial fillings made with high-quality ingredients: whole-milk mozzarella, imported Italian cheeses, fresh and dried wild mushrooms, house-made sausage.

One interesting property of Vicolo pizza is that it can be successfully finished off at home. The half-baked pies cook in 12 to 15 minutes in a preheated hot (425°F) oven. They also freeze well and go right into the oven from the freezer. The crust stays nice and crisp and the rich fillings retain their flavor and texture, whether eaten at home or at the restaurant. Vicolo has been voted best pizzeria in local publications year after year.

VIETNAM II RESTAURANT . . . .

701 Larkin (at Ellis)
415-885-1274
Open daily 8 A.M. to midnight
Inexpensive
Credit Cards: AE, MC, V

Vietnam II has been a fixture in the Civic Center restaurant landscape for years, preparing high-quality Vietnamese and Chinese dishes for residents of the neighborhood. The pleasant, homey dining room with a koi pond and potted bamboo at the entrance, has hosted many a family banquet, but regulars always find a table to order No. 27, Sweet-and-Sour Prawn Soup, which costs around $12 for a small order, which is actually huge. The dreamy look of the soup, with many plump, pink shrimp, pale green spongy Chinese melon, bright yellow chunks of fresh pineapple, reddish green wedges of sour tomato, tissue-thin half-moons of celery, commas of sliced dark green chile, dashes of opalescent bean sprout, all suspended in clear broth aromatic with Vietnamese herbs, excites the appetite. All these flavors dance harmoniously with one another, yet no soup could be brighter, fresher, livelier. The stunning use of vegetables by Vietnam II's kitchen, some contributing aroma, others texture, set this complex version of sweet-and-sour soup far, far apart from others. This is a dish you must eat to understand—especially if you've had too many clunky, Westernized Asian sweet-and-sour preparations. Vietnam II's No. 27 defines the genre. With it order a plate of Salted Fish with Chicken Fried Rice, No. 198. In contrast to the clean, bracing soup, this heap of fried rice is meaty and savory. The background flavor of salted fish, hardly distinguishable, adds richness to the fluffy fried rice, wok-tossed with tender, juicy bits of chicken and egg. Again, the portion is substantial. I reheated No. 198 in a wok at home the next day and it was just as delicious. The combination of Vietnamese soup and Cantonese fried rice at Vietnam II exemplifies the breadth of flavors at this restaurant. The long menu, which offers many vegetables given either Vietnamese or Chinese saucing, a choice section of quail and squab preparations, and tempting clay pot dishes, stands up to deep exploration.

ZUNI CAFE . . . .

1658 Market Street (between
Franklin and Gough)
415-552-2522
Open Tuesday through Saturday
7:30 to 11 A.M., 11:30 A.M. to
3 P.M., and 6 P.M. to midnight;
Sunday 11 A.M. to 11 P.M.
Moderate
Credit cards: AE, MC, V

Zuni Cafe is the most European restaurant-cafe-bar in the city, not just because of the style of the food, but because of its function within the community. The place has grown organically over the years into a social crossroads, a meeting spot, a place that has become indispensable if you want a cocktail, oysters, a late-night hamburger, a wood-oven baked pizza in the afternoon, or a sophisticated full meal. Zuni fulfills your eating and drinking needs no matter what they may be or when they hit. Much better in quality than the grand brasseries in Paris, Zuni plays the same role in San Francisco, always available for the spontaneous passerby or the diner who plans ahead.

The most important development occurred when the restaurant doubled in size by annexing a neighboring triangular space between Market Street and an alley. In this sunny, glass-fronted room, Zuni installed the much-frequented copper-topped bar and indoor and outdoor café tables. Upstairs and deeper into the restaurant, a labyrinth of rooms with built-in banquettes and odd-shaped tables make up the dining areas. In the bar you can get casual food and pizzas from the wood-fired oven, as well as any conceivable drink, be it fresh-lime margaritas or glasses of Condrieu (a hauntingly flowery, but dry white Rhône wine).

Superstar chef Judy Rogers, who put Zuni on the national culinary map, fell into cooking by chance when she lived with the famous Troisgros family in France as an exchange student. She was hooked and returned to cook at Chez Panisse. When she couldn't find the financing to open her own place in Berkeley, she ended up at Zuni as a partner. The match was made in heaven.

Her menus bring together the cooking of southwest France and most of Italy in her own peculiar and winning way. The restaurant's signature dishes come from the brick wood-burning oven in the center of one dining room. Roast chicken for two on a warm bread and currant salad moistened with cooking juices and lightened with arugula has become a San Francisco classic. Her *fritto misto*, a changing array of vegetables, whole little fish, and paper-thin slices of lemon, emerges from the fryer irresistibly crisp. A starter of salt-cured anchovies and thinly sliced celery in olive oil remains my pick if I am not having oysters instead, usually a variety of pristine West Coast mollusks opened to order and presented on a stand holding a tray of crushed ice with brown bread and butter below. Long-braised meats like osso buco or lamb shanks appear regularly and Rogers is never afraid to offer tripe or salt cod. Another innovation started by Rogers pairs a certain cheese with a fresh or dried fruit, the combination of which becomes a revelation. House-made ice creams and ices and biscotti dependably satisfy the sweet tooth. The menus are always so varied that no matter what the state of your appetite you will find something perfect to eat and drink. So people just drop by, knowing that they will run into someone they know and find something very good, and interesting, to eat. She gets big flavor and irresistible texture in the most ingenious ways. She makes a savory stew out of chopped chicken livers and pancetta for crostini or squares of polenta. She uses sweet raw corn kernels in a salad with cherry tomatoes. She lets long-cooked squid make their own sauce with wine and their own dusky ink.

The other part of Rogers's genius is that she instinctively meets the eclectic needs of the widest range of San Franciscans—and tourists—without sacrificing her unique personal style. Actually, she has defined San Francisco style over the years, and now everyone depends on her to show them what they will be eating next.

CAFÉS

ARLEQUIN . . . .

384 Hayes (between Gough
and Franklin)
415-626-1211
Open Monday through Friday
8 A.M. to 8 P.M., Saturday 9 A.M. to
6 P.M., Sunday 9 A.M. to 4 P.M.
Credit cards: AE, D, MC, V

An offshoot of Absinthe (see page 50), Arlequin takes advantage of the bistro's extensive kitchen to offer a full range of house-made treats: lovely buttery pastries (including exemplary croissants), ice creams and fruit ices, soups, salads, and sandwiches. The grilled Crôque Arlequin, ham, Gruyère, and Dijon mustard on thinly sliced *levain,* is a neighborhood favorite, especially on nice days when you can eat the toasted sandwich in the back garden with a glass of wine. As much a deli as a café, Arlequin packages everything they make to go and will tailor orders to specific catering needs.

CAFFÈ TRINITY . . . .

1145 Market Street (between
7th and 8th streets)
415-864-3333
Open Monday through Friday
6 A.M. to 4 P.M.
Cash only

This tiny jewel can be considered a gift to the city from developer Angelo Sangiacomo, whose office building it graces. No expense was spared in adorning this light-filled room with opulent materials—handcrafted mahogany woodwork, marble tables and counters, hand-painted panels of native American animals depicted in the style of seventeenth-century European naturalists, and crystal light fixtures. Sitting in this baroque parlor, pondering the street people across the way at United Nations Plaza, makes you feel like a character in a Charles Dickens novel.

Everything prepared by the young Italian couple who run the cafe is simple and tasty, like a salad of Roma tomatoes, red onions, and capers with tuna, or a cup of minestrone with honest, long-cooked flavor. The prosciutto, mascarpone, and radicchio sandwich on focaccia is moist and delicious. Good coffee made from Mr. Espresso beans is a pleasure to be enjoyed slowly while basking in the richness of the surroundings.

MOMI TOBY'S REVOLUTION CAFE . . . .

528 Laguna Street (between
Hayes and Fell)
415-626-1508
Open weekdays 7:30 A.M. to
10 P.M., Saturday and Sunday
8 A.M. to 10 P.M.
Cash only

Noteworthy for its peaceful ambience, Momi Toby's light-filled corner space has dark-wood-framed windows and window seats, weathered wooden floors, and a handsome marble-topped coffee bar with Victorian slatted-wood shelving behind it. The whispery, soothing tones of gamelan music engulf you when you walk in the door. The coffee is competent and served in handle-less pottery cups. If you are in the neighborhood, this café offers a sanctuary for reading or writing.

DELESSIO . . . .

1695 Market Street (at Valencia)
415-552-5559
Open Monday through Friday
7 A.M. to 7:30 P.M., Saturday 9 A.M.
to 5:30 P.M., Sunday 9 A.M. to 4 P.M.
Credit cards: AE, MC, V

This multifaceted operation has many identities: café, deli, bakery, and caterer. The Parisian red-and-gold-painted facade with sidewalk tables, pulls you into the shop that turns out to be an expansive space mostly filled with kitchen. At the front is a composed-salad bar, not just of naked ingredients, but platters of marinated vegetables, olives, crumbled cheeses, and DeLessio's signature oversized focaccia croutons studded with raisins. The glass deli counter displays more prepared foods, sandwiches, and whole meals ready to be taken home and reheated, plus potential components, like legs of duck confit. Shelves of breads and pastries, pretty wooden cabinets of house-made preserves, caramel and fudge sauces all grab for your attention. I gobbled up a soft but crusty house-baked white roll with a thick filling of gently smoked salmon salad distinctively mixed with currants, chopped celery, and mild aioli. I sat on a woven chair at a metal table outdoors watching the Market Street parade. A cup of Peet's coffee and a buttery wedding cookie later, I was still there. The one drawback of eating at DeLessio is that everything is served on or in paper—maybe okay for a sandwich but terrible for salads, coffee, and hot dishes. At home, you can serve DeLessio's tasty, stylish fare on plates with silverware, and enjoy them even more.

SAIGON SANDWICH CAFE . . . .

560 Larkin Street (at Eddy)
415-474-5698
Open Monday through Saturday
7 A.M. to 5 P.M.,
Sunday 7:30 A.M. to 4:30 P.M.
Cash only

The tiny, overstuffed Saigon Sandwich Cafe, which has been turning out delicious Vietnamese sandwiches for fifteen years, reminds me of snack stalls in the student quarter of Paris, except that the sandwiches are much better. Instead of *saucisson sec*, Saigon fills its soft French baguettes with five-spice chicken, roast pork, or Vietnamese meatballs, then kisses them with a sweet, hot-and-sour dipping sauce, shredded carrots, sprigs of cilantro, and hot green chiles. The juicy, savory, exotic sandwiches soon become addictive. My favorite is the warm meatball sandwich, which tastes like a sparkling sloppy joe. Long, generously filled sandwiches still cost around $2, an amazing buy. I like to eat them with a package of shrimp chips, with the texture of crisp Styrofoam. (They taste much better than the description suggests.) The shop has almost a cult following of Civic Center employees, cab drivers, delivery men, and SOMA types, as well as the Vietnamese community that lives nearby. Many drop in for a glass of powerful Vietnamese iced coffee, creamy with sweetened condensed milk. The pleasant people who work behind the counter are efficient and eager to please. When I call ahead for sandwiches for meetings and the like, they are ready exactly at the assigned time, not before and not after. The Saigon Cafe knows the importance of freshness.

CITIZEN CAKE. . . . .

399 Grove Street (at Gough)
415-861-2228
www.citizencake.com
Open Tuesday through Friday
8 A.M. to 10 P.M.,
Saturday 10 A.M. to 10 P.M.,
Sunday 10 A.M. to 9 P.M.
Credit cards: AE, MC, V

Pastry chef Elizabeth Falkner's true love is designing architecturally whimsical cakes with offbeat fillings and modernist flourishes. If I were getting married, I'd order a snowy white coconut cake filled with passion fruit mousse and iced with vanilla buttercream. You never know what twenty-second-century concoction will emerge from her immaculate, completely open pastry kitchen. With an artist's sensibility and a scientist's precision she bakes a full range of homey American

cookies and brownies, always with her own twist; fresh breads daily; morning rolls like her crumbly strawberry scones; the complex cakes; and a range of other desserts like bread puddings, *panna cotta*, baked custards, and ice creams. You can buy them by the slice, by the cake, by the scoop, or by the pint to eat in the airy, light-filled café or to take home. She's indeed a good citizen in the Civic Center neighborhood, providing uninterrupted service from breakfast through dinner by drawing on the treasures from her pastry kitchen to fill in the cracks, those odd times during the day when only a peanut butter cookie will do.

ICE CREAM/CHOCOLATES

ARLEQUIN . . . .

384 Hayes (between Gough
and Franklin)
415-626-1211
Open Monday through Friday
8 A.M. to 8 P.M., Saturday 9 A.M. to
6 P.M., Sunday 9 A.M. to 4 P.M.
Credit cards: AE, D, MC, V

The woman behind Arlequin's ice cream freezer graciously lets you taste any or all of the sorbets and ice creams. All are house made and change with the seasons. One afternoon I particularly liked a lavender honey–vanilla ice cream with a light, grainy texture that actually tasted like lavender honey and not like soap, as so many lavender-flavored dishes can. Ginger frozen yogurt got a lift from lime. The sorbets—strawberry

and yellow watermelon—reflected the pure fresh fruit from which they were made, while an intense caramel called out for an apple accompaniment. For more information on this multifaceted operation, see page 60.

CITIZEN CAKE. . . . .

399 Grove Street (at Gough)
415-861-2228
Open Tuesday through Friday
8 A.M. to 10 P.M., Saturday 10 A.M.
to 10 P.M., Sunday 10 A.M. to 9 P.M.
Credit cards: AE, MC, V

The ice creams here are as creative and interesting as the pastries. A perennial favorite is a subtle goat-milk honey ice cream that delivers an intriguing tang without being barnyardy at all. You might find burnt orange caramel ice cream, cinnamon ice cream, or Concord grape sorbet. You can order by the cup or cone, but if you're feeling indulgent, you can construct your own ice cream sandwich with Citizen Cake cookies and your choice of ice creams for a filling, a pre-performance snack that will keep you energized through at least the first two intermissions. See page 63 for more information.

ETHNIC MARKETS

NEW CHIU FONG COMPANY . . . .

724 Ellis Street (between
Larkin and Polk)
415-776-7151
Open daily 8:30 A.M. to 6:30 P.M.
Cash only

The most complete Vietnamese market in the city, New Chiu Fong has everything from four-inch-thick chopping blocks made out of slices of tree trunk to imported dried Thai snapper. Fresh rice noodles are by the meat counter, and dried noodles of every conceivable kind, from rice threads to Chinese-style egg noodles, fill up their own aisle. Many are used in the northern Vietnamese soup called *pho*, an amazingly restorative and refreshing concoction that combines handfuls of fresh herbs and hot chiles with noodles, beef, and broth. In the meat counter, strips of fat-marbled beef, precut for *pho* and satays, streamline the preparation of these dishes. Every part of the pig and large fresh stewing chickens are piled high, while shelves of fish sauce, soy sauce, and hot chile pastes await the home cook. The freezer sections of ethnic markets are always worth a look because they hold useful ingredients like banana leaves for wrapping fresh sausage and rice, or *pandan* leaf, which you rarely see fresh.

But the produce section here is the draw, with its boxes of fresh Vietnamese herbs, some with the most delectable perfumes. Of particular interest for creative cooks is the fresh cumin leaf (*ca n au chua rau om*), which smells like the seed but more complex; the minty, pointy-leafed Thai basil, wonderful in seafood stews with coconut milk; and an herb that looks like flat Italian parsley (*bo xao can*), but tastes like a cross between celery and parsnip, used for beef cookery in Vietnamese kitchens. There are big, flat, purple-tinted leaves (*rau kinh gioi*) that have a *shiso*-like, or chrysanthemum, flavor, and aromatic elongated greens with pointy edges (*rau ngo gai*) that are used as salad or accompaniment to *pho* or savory grilled meats. And these are but a few. Many of the herbs are raised in Hawaii and flown in, so prices are not cheap, but at New Chiu Fong they arrive in excellent condition, fresh and aromatic. Since the prices and names of the herbs are not posted in English, the best way to find the flavors that interest you is to taste.

CIVIC CENTER FARMERS' MARKET . . . .

United Nations Plaza
(at Fulton)
Open Wednesday and
Sunday mornings

This heart-of-the-city farmers' market truly serves the local community, especially since parking in the area can be impossible. You can find metered spaces on the other side of Market Street, but that limits your shopping to whatever you can carry for several long blocks. As an expression of a market self-molded to serve a specific community, the Civic Center stalls are heavy on fresh and inexpensive Asian vegetables like long beans, the wonderful purple-leafed Asian spinach called amaranth, Asian mushrooms, bok choys, Vietnamese herbs, lemongrass, and cooking essentials like carrots and onions. As at every vital farmers' market, there will be seasonal surprises, like a stall full of the most fragrant tangerines, thin-skinned Rangpoor limes, or new-crop walnuts. Whenever I want dates to serve with mint tea, I go to the Civic Center date man. He has *barhi* and *medjool*, large and small, sweet and sticky, creamy and juicy.

The beauty of this market is that you can buy fresh food at such cheap prices that a large family can be fed for a week at about half of what it would cost at the supermarket—and the quality will be far superior.

NEW CHIU FONG COMPANY . . . .

724 Ellis Street (between Larkin
and Polk)
415-776-7151
Open daily 8:30 A.M. to 6:30 P.M.
Cash only

The produce section is large and exotic, with an array of fresh Southeast Asian herbs and all the vegetables you'll need to cook Vietnamese food. Though some of it can look tired, it's all there. See the opposite page for more information.

WINES AND SPIRITS

AMPHORA WINE MERCHANT . . . .

384A Hayes (between Franklin
and Gough)
415-863-1104
www.amphorawine.com
Open Monday through Saturday
11 A.M. to 8 P.M.,
Sunday noon to 6 P.M.
Credit cards: AE, MC, V

Let's say you order an exceptionally tasty bottle of wine next door at Absinthe (see page 50), collaboratively teased out of the extensive list with the sommelier. You like it so much that you want to drink more of it at home. Just stroll over to Amphora Wine Merchant where 70 percent of the Absinthe wine list is stocked on the shelves. Like many small shops, Amphora specializes in small lots of artisan wines from all over the world, and its knowledgeable staff is able to supply lots of personal service, including education. The shop sponsors an active schedule of tastings, often in the pleasant back garden that they share with Arlequin (see page 60), or at Absinthe.

HAYES AND VINE WINE BAR . . . .

377 Hayes Street (between
Gough and Franklin)
415-626-5301
www.hayesandvine.com
Open Monday through Thursday
5 P.M. to midnight, Friday and
Saturday to 1 A.M.,
Sunday 3 P.M. to 9 P.M.
Credit cards: MC, V

One of the few bona fide wine bars in San Francisco, Hayes and Vine has become a hit with a young crowd eager to cultivate their palates and have a night out at the same time. Over forty wines are open at a time and over half of these change weekly. Some are available by the half glass, others by the glass. A small menu from the cold pantry—charcuterie, smoked fish, olives, nuts—helps refresh the palate, easing the way from whites to reds. If you don't want to invest in expensive bottles without tasting, or expensive bottles period, here's your chance to taste these wines without maxing out your credit card. Who knows? You may not actually like French Burgundy, or maybe you only like pinot noir from a certain region in Burgundy. Hayes and Vine is the place to find out what tastes like what and which you prefer. The staff knows how to guide you on your journey. There's nothing more informative than tasting wines side by side and no place where it's more fun to do it than this classy little wine bar.

COOKWARE AND BOOKS

A CLEAN WELL-LIGHTED PLACE FOR BOOKS

601 Van Ness Avenue (between
Golden Gate and Turk)
415-441-6670
Open Monday through Thursday
10 A.M. to 11 P.M., Friday and
Saturday until midnight,
Sunday until 9 P.M.
Credit cards: AE, MC, V

The most complete bookstore in San Francisco, A Clean Well-Lighted Place for Books has a well-chosen cookbook section as well as an extensive travel section with much food writing in it. The literature section carries many classic books on food and eating as well. The clerks will help you hunt down anything in the store or out. Authors visit frequently and sign their masterpieces, and if you are a contributor to City Arts and Lectures (a series of talks by authors, the profits of which go to Friends of the Public Library), you get a 15-percent discount at the store. Clean Well-Lighted is community spirited and service oriented but, more important, if you want it, they'll probably have it.

EMBARCADERO
FISHERMAN'S
WHARF

EMBARCADERO & FISHERMAN'S WHARF

RESTAURANTS

1 Boulevard
2 Fog City Diner
3 Gary Danko
4 Harbor Village
5 One Market Restaurant
6 Ozumo
7 Piperade
8 Shanghai 1930
9 Slanted Door
10 Teatro ZinZanni
11 Yank Sing

CAFÉS

12 South Beach Cafe

BARS

13 Cosmopolitan Cafe
14 Pier 23 Cafe

DELICATESSENS/TAKEOUT

15 Arabi
16 In-N-Out Burger

BAKERIES/PASTRIES

17 Boudin Sourdough Bakery and Cafe

ICE CREAM/CHOCOLATES

18 See's Candies

PRODUCE

19 Ferry Plaza Farmers' Market

COOKWARE AND BOOKS

20 Cost Plus World Market
21 Williams-Sonoma

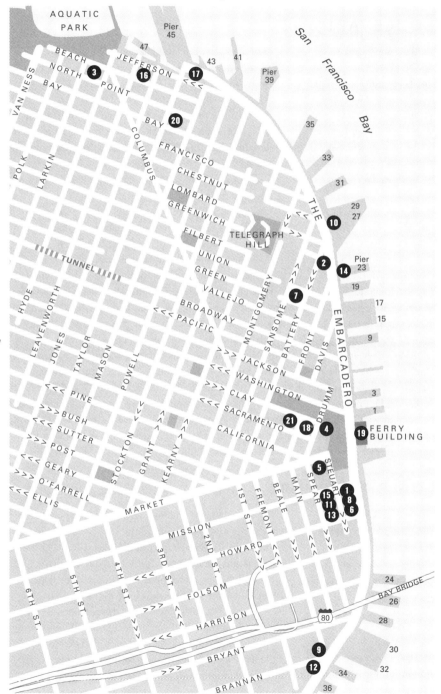

N

AQUATIC
PARK

Pier
45

Pier
39

Pier
23

San
Francisco
Bay

BEACH
NORTH
BAY
POINT
JEFFERSON
3
16
17

47
43
41
35
33
31
29
27

20

BAY
FRANCISCO
CHESTNUT
LOMBARD
GREENWICH
FILBERT
UNION
GREEN
VALLEJO
BROADWAY
PACIFIC

COLUMBUS

VAN NESS
POLK
LARKIN

TUNNEL

TELEGRAPH
HILL

10

2
14
19

17
15
9

THE
EMBARCADERO

7

MONTGOMERY
SANSOME
BATTERY
FRONT
DAVIS

HYDE
LEAVENWORTH
JONES
TAYLOR
MASON
POWELL

PINE
BUSH
SUTTER
POST
GEARY
O'FARRELL
ELLIS

JACKSON
WASHINGTON
CLAY
SACRAMENTO
CALIFORNIA

STOCKTON
GRANT
KEARNY

21
18
4

DRUMM

3
1

19
FERRY
BUILDING

5

MARKET

STEUART
SPEAR
MAIN
BEALE
FREMONT
1ST ST.

15
11
13

1
8
6

MISSION
HOWARD

2ND ST.
3RD ST.
4TH ST.
5TH ST.
6TH ST.

FOLSOM
HARRISON

80

24
26
28

BAY BRIDGE

BRYANT
BRANNAN

9
12
34
36
30
32

S

W

E

0   SCALE MILES   .25

RESTAURANTS

BOULEVARD . . . .

1 Mission Street (at Steuart)
415-543-6084
www.boulevardrestaurant.com
Open Monday through Friday
11:30 A.M. to 2:00 P.M.,
bistro menu 2:30 to 5:15 P.M.;
Sunday through Wednesday
5:30 P.M. to 9:30 P.M.; Thursday
through Saturday until 10:30 P.M.
Expensive
Credit cards: AE, CB, D, DC,
MC, V

Year after year, Boulevard, a collaboration between chef Nancy Oakes and restaurant designer Pat Kuleto, wins the *San Francisco Magazine* readers' poll. Every local knows that Boulevard is the most popular restaurant in the city. Everyone wants one of the 120 seats in this fantasy French bistro in the Audiffred building, built in 1889, across the Embarcadero from the bay.

Oakes's plates are huge, creative, and colorful, with lots of different bells and whistles. She has a special feeling for meat—husband Bruce Aidells is the nationally known sausage maker—and many a plate features a huge chop or steak or roast with interesting, if sometimes incompatible trimmings. I still vividly remember a gargantuan maple-cured pork chop: pink, thick, and juicy, with a divine sauté of chard and bacon, a pile of fried onion rings, and an odd, doughy apple cake seasoned with sage. Even fish dishes, like a moist fillet of salmon with great mashed potatoes and a decadent pool of mustard seed–laced beurre blanc, skinny French beans, and onions, have heft. Desserts are as monumental as main courses, like hot dark gingerbread with melting honey ice cream, a boozy bourbon sauce, raspberry syrup, and bananas. Plain or simple are not part of Oakes's cooking vocabulary. Don't reserve here unless you really want to eat. Boulevard is an upscale, important-night-out kind of dinner house in the vernacular of California-American cuisine. The dishes, both as they read on the menu and arrive at the table, are meant to wow diners not with exquisiteness, but with ebullience, imagination, and the chef's drive to please. Oakes is nothing if not generous, and she uses every conceivable combination of ingredients and cooking technique to extract oohs and ahhs from her adoring public.

FOG CITY DINER . . . .

1300 Battery Street (at the
Embarcadero)
415-982-2000
www.fogcitydiner.com
Open Monday through Thursday
11:30 A.M. to 10:30 P.M.,
Friday 11:30 A.M. to 11 P.M.;
Saturday 10:30 A.M. to 11 P.M.;
Sunday 10:30 A.M. to 10 P.M.
Moderate
Credit cards: DC, D, MC, V

To my mind, the famous Fog City Diner represents the best Pat Kuleto design of all. He took a wood-frame shack on the Embarcadero and turned it into a glamorous and fun dining car with luxurious wooden booths each by a big window, dark wood paneling, a counter with stools, and a long bar that's always crowded. The streamlined metal exterior reminds me of sleek Pullmans with light glowing inside. Whenever you pass it, day or night, you want to stop in because it looks like everyone is having such a good time. When it opened sixteen years ago, it was the first upscale diner in the country.

The menu has changed very little over the years. Daily specials add variety, but to this day I order the same things: grilled pasilla peppers stuffed with goat cheese accompanied with a chunky avocado salsa, and an unintimidating salad of pretty greens tossed with caramelized walnuts, aged goat cheese, and, most recently, peaches. The salads are perfectly dressed, the lettuces of proud California pedigree. At the opposite end of the food chain, Fog City's hamburgers with skinny fries and house-made ketchup are always a temptation. The thick onion rings, though monolithic, are never greasy; you have to like crunchy batter to appreciate them. Tender braised short ribs off the bone are larded with fat, which would be okay if the young broccoli accompaniment weren't drenched in bacon and butter and the gravy pooling around the mashed potatoes unskimmed. The side of sour cream with horseradish is pure overkill. A lot of the food at Fog City is purposely too rich, broad in flavor, and fun but not refined. A towering turtle sundae fits that description, but I always order it because I love the four inches of toothachingly sweet butterscotch pecan sauce at the bottom of the glass, perfect after a big, fat, heavy meal. For the most part, the food is peppy, but don't come here for a serious dining experience.

GARY DANKO . . . .

800 Northpoint (at Hyde)
415-749-2060
www.garydanko.com
Open Sunday through Wednesday
5:30 P.M. to 9:30 P.M., Thursday
through Saturday until 10 P.M.
Expensive
Credit cards: AE, CB, DC, D, MC, V

With its small, sophisticated dining rooms and zinc bar, a highly professional floor staff drawn from the San Francisco culinary community, and the self-assured Gary Danko in the kitchen, restaurant Gary Danko has become the new high-end dining experience that every one talks about.

Exquisite little pre-dinner tastes—warm blini with house-cured salmon, a tiny coin of foie gras terrine speckled with truffles with a bite of *mâche* and endive salad, a corn and lobster custard in a baby-sized cup—are sent out to everyone. This generosity begets self-generosity, immediately putting you in the mood to splurge on beautiful wines, perhaps a glass of champagne. Then the meal starts in earnest.

The menu changes daily. On past visits I've eaten summer corn and mussel chowder distinguished by thin but rich sherried broth; seared foie gras set off by sautéed peaches, fresh raspberries, and caramelized onions, lusciously sweet and sour; superb roast lobster slathered with chanterelles; a thick hunk of tuna as the centerpiece of a Mediterranean composition with olives, anchovies, and Provençal vegetables; quail stuffed with wild mushrooms, leeks, and pine nuts served with a toasty three-grain pilaf, all moistened with a stunning red wine sauce.

I always succumb to the cheese trolley—a cheese service that makes cheese irresistible. They collect them from all over the world so you can, for instance, taste three sheep's milk cheeses from three different continents, or three goat cheeses, or a grand assortment, and every one will be in perfect condition and a perfect representative of its type.

And then, of course, you have to have a little dessert, like a warm chocolate soufflé all puffy and creamy inside and divine with two custard sauces poured right in the middle. Just in case you had the slightest wisp of desire to consume anything else, out comes the shiny silver plate of house-made English toffee, tiny truffles, candied citrus peel, sweet and salty cashews.

Cost is almost irrelevant at this point, but the check won't horrify. At press time, three courses were $48, each additional course an extra $9. You'll ante up more for wine. You can order by the half glass, glass, half bottle, and hundreds of full bottles from around the world at every price range. But this is the place to drink a special wine. Ask for one. Point to a price and say you want to spend that much and see what you get.

At the bar, where you can dine without reservations, you can eat just one course if you want, or two, but who can stop? Seated at a table (as opposed to the bar), you get to be in the middle of the performance and the focus of much attention. The service moves along flawlessly. You feel as if your needs are anticipated. Thus, when the foie gras appears, someone brings over the sweet, raisiny Hungarian Tokay Aszú, anticipating that you might want a little glass. You want it. The combination is delightful. It's best to give yourself over to this staff.

I can't think of a more complete experience, one so right, so true on every level. Everyone working at Gary Danko is so proud and happy to be there that the patrons get a contact high. Owning and working your own top-of-the-line restaurant calls for huge passion, dedication, skill, and a little bit of madness. Danko's got it all. I love the way that everything has fallen into place here. The restaurant gods smiled on this one.

HARBOR VILLAGE . . . .

Four Embarcadero Center
(between Clay and Drumm)
415-781-8833
www.harborvillage.net
Open Monday through Friday
11 A.M. to 2:30 P.M.,
Saturday 10:30 A.M. to 2:30 P.M.,
Sunday 10 A.M. to 2:30 P.M.,
nightly 5:30 to 9:30 P.M.
Moderate
Credit cards: AE, DC, MC, V

This large, bustling branch of a Hong Kong restaurant chain mounts one of the best dim sum services in the city—and there are quite a few now. The variety of dim sum seems never-ending and the quality is invariably high. With a view of the bay from the glassed-in room on Justin Herman Plaza, the tiny, well-appointed dining rooms really do feel like Hong Kong. Women in starched white uniforms push carts silently over the carpeting offering bona fide delicacies. This is one of the few places that makes *xiao long bao,* twisted dumplings filled with shrimp, cabbage, black mushrooms, and an unexpected gush of flavorful stock, which is put into the dumpling as a gelatin, but turns to liquid when the dumpling is steamed. Beautiful shrimp pearl balls, coated in opalescent rice, are filled with chopped shrimp barely bound together with a little egg. Elegant slices of cured pork shank rest on a bed of orange soybeans, waiting for a splash of Chinese vinegar from the server. Tender octopus flecked with hot red chiles and served with a mild green wasabi dipping sauce is one of the most delicious items here. Pork dumplings surprise you with the crunch of peanuts, dried shrimp, and Chinese celery. The measure of every teahouse, *har gow* (shrimp dumplings), meets the highest standards of dim sum cookery. The shrimp are naturally sweet and juicy, and the portion in each dumpling is large.

At night the dim sum carts are garaged and a long dinner menu goes into effect. The dishes, many of them inventive in a cross-cultural, Hong Kong style, are refined and attractively presented. I've had lots of intriguing preparations here, including some excellent lobster and whole fish and a signature chicken salad with fresh fruit that weaves together many different ingredients. Light, flavorful noodle dishes, made here with the thinnest strands of pasta, are a satisfying way to end a meal full of delicacies.

ONE MARKET RESTAURANT. . . . .

1 Market Street (at Steuart)
415-777-5577
www.onemarket.com
Open Monday through Friday
11:30 A.M. to 2 P.M., Monday
through Saturday 5:30 to 9 P.M.
Expensive
Credit cards: AE, DC, MC, V

One Market, now across a plaza from the dramatically refurbished Ferry Building, is celebrity chef Brad Ogden's most urbane venue. It offers a sweeping, sleek glass and granite dining room with power booths, a barroom with separate menu, and private dining rooms that open out onto the soaring atrium of One Market Plaza. The design takes advantage of One Market's location with huge windows that look out to the Embarcadero, the bay, Justin Herman Plaza, the broad tree-lined end of Market Street. One Market suits Financial District business needs brilliantly, priding itself on its professionalism and sophistication in its role as a big, urban restaurant. All the amenities—anything you want to drink, large dishes, small dishes, the bar, and a stunning interior that reminds me of the prototype of all big city restaurants, the Four Seasons in New York—are provided. One Market radiates a sense of place.

But the most important development at One Market has been the hiring of chef-partner Adrian Hoffman. He, more than any of the other name chefs who have passed through this kitchen, has made One Market a destination restaurant. His wide-ranging international experience—Italy, London, France, Japan, Israel, Boston, New York—coupled with innate culinary good sense, result in naturally focused dishes of originality and charm.

A salad of frisée, Bing cherries, and hazelnuts, lavishly blanketed with shaved ribbons of cold foie gras, hides a warm slice of brioche smeared with duck liver at the bottom. The intricate balance of bitter, buttery, fruity, and nutty flavors and the play of textures in essentially a big, hearty salad represents the best of two worlds. Hoffman's ability to combine the rustic and the refined defines his food and makes it unique.

Deep-fried fish fingers on big, creamy-centered french fries on a fresh pea purée with pea sprouts polygamously marries pub food, ingredient-driven California cuisine, and haute French. It works. Succulent braised organic pork shoulder, formed into a glazed roulade, perches atop the most delicious mélange of chewy *farro* (a kind of wheat berry) with grapes, almonds, and cilantro. All the components tasted inevitable—of course pork and cilantro and *farro* belong together. One Hoffman dish after another expands your consciousness and gives deep pleasure at the same time. The desserts, inspired by the farmers' market across the street, sing of the season. Toasted slices of angel food cake slathered with a ripe stone-fruit salad—plums, pluots (a cross between a plum and an apricot), white and orange nectarines, and peaches—moistened with apricot sauce and topped with honey-yogurt ice cream, is motivation enough for a summer visit to One Market.

Service here has always been top-drawer and the extensive California wine list, though pricey, always produces distinctive, exciting bottles. Now under Hoffman's rule, One Market has moved into the highest echelon of San Francisco restaurants.

161 Steuart Street (between
Mission and Howard)
415-882-1333
www.ozumo.com
Open Monday through Friday
11:30 A.M. to 2:30 P.M.,
Monday through Wednesday
5:30 to 10 P.M., Thursday through
Saturday 5:30 to 10:30 P.M.,
Sunday 5 P.M. to 9 P.M.
Expensive
Credit cards: AE, DC, D, MC, V

Ozumo, the resplendent, upscale Japanese restaurant in Harry Denton's old location facing the Embarcadero, combines the Japanese penchant for big city modernity with pristine, elegant cooking. The result is one of the most exciting new restaurants to open in San Francisco lately.

You would never believe that this cavernous, long space with sweeping views of the bay at one end was ever anything but Ozumo. Tokyo designer Noriyoshi Muramatsu transformed it using the mostly natural materials—no plastic, no paint, some steel—of a Japanese tea garden. Through the dark wood front door you enter a similarly dark sake bar that also serves a full range of well-made Western cocktails and wild herb-and fruit-infused tonics. A large mounted video screen silently runs tapes of sumo wrestlers and Kurosawa movies. (The name of the restaurant means sumo championship.) A subtle garden path leads you through the restaurant to the next area, the *robata* room and bar, where the grilling occurs, and finally to a huge square sushi bar with seating on four sides in a radiant dining room filled with natural light. The cohesive design, gradually moving from dark to light, transports you to another world. The decor is a physical and emotional statement about comfort, luxury, simplicity, and peace.

I'll save you the trouble of decoding talented chef Sho Kamio's menu by telling you the best way to order. Since almost everything is served family style, you get to taste a lot of different things, so don't worry about not liking something. Start with a dish or two from the *zensai*, or before meal, page. I recommend *Dohyo*, layers of diced avocado, tuna sashimi, and crumbled tofu molded into a huge round sauced with wasabi cream and sweet soy. A bowl of steamed organic soybeans in their bright green pods provides crisp contrast. And if there are four of you, try the warm Dungeness crab roll wrapped in soft bean curd skin with a juicy micro-green salad in grapefruit vinaigrette. All these dishes go wonderfully with cold sake, served in frosty little tumblers. Ozumo has one of the best lists in the city, by the glass or bottle.

For the next course, send your waiter to the sushi bar to find out what's fresh, local, and interesting. Let the sushi chefs do their job. Then from the *robata* or grill order an assortment of different vegetables, lamb, and Japanese beef, each salted, cooked over char-coal, and sliced or served whole (in the case of the vegetables) on individual plates chosen to complement the color and shape of each item. Finish the meal with steamed rice, crisp house-made cucumber and sweet daikon radish pickles, and handleless mugs of hot, vegetal, soothing green tea. The simplicity and perfection of the meal, so satisfying, so mindfully presented in such lyrical surroundings, will make you giddy with satisfaction.

PIPERADE.........................

1015 Battery Street (between
Union and Green)
415-391-2555
Open Monday through Friday
11:30 A.M. to 3 P.M.; Monday
through Saturday 5:30 to 10:30 P.M.
Moderate
Credit Cards: AE, MC, V

Chef Gerald Hirigoyen, who earned national attention with his SOMA bistro Fringale (see page 350), has returned to his Basque culinary roots with Piperade, located at the site of his former second restaurant, Pastis. He re-opened with a talented twenty-three-year-old Basque cook in the kitchen, a warmer décor, and a menu of small plates *(tipia)*, big plates *(handia)* and a Basque daily special *(euskaldun)*. The wine list from master sommelier Emmanuel Kemiji, enlarges the experience with stellar examples of regional wines and the whole package is bound together by Hirigoyen himself who has taken a more visible role in the dining room, though he shuttles back and forth to the kitchen.

Many of us who have been in San Francisco for a long time remember the Basque restaurants of North Beach, which specialized in multicourse, prix fixe meals much loved by students, the budget minded, and those who liked to eat big and well in a pensionlike environment. There's very little of this homey, fill 'em up, cooking at Piperade. Hirigoyen's version of Basque reminds me more of the refined restaurants in San Sebastian, like Arzak, which turn out subtle dishes using traditional ingredients: fish, shellfish, squid, sheep milk cheese, cured ham, peppers, veal, lamb, and salt cod.

I was transported to my favorite part of the world one night by a tableful of small dishes: raw, marinted sardines with dollops of potato–roasted red pepper purée, acting like a thick sauce; a bowl of creamy-textured gigante beans (gigantic limas), garnished with hard-boiled egg wedges, and marinated sardines in a sparkly vinaigrette; ruby red piquillo peppers stuffed with salt cod in a terra cotta ramekin lined with red pepper sauce and run under the broiler; crisp crab croquettes bound with old-fashioned bechamel; and a plate piled with thinly sliced *serrano* ham.

The delicious big plates can be shared, too, though I would rather eat the signature piperade, a stew of peppers, onions, and tomatoes with sautéed *serrano* ham and a runny poached egg, all by myself. Thick hunks of braised swordfish, tuna, cod, and shrimp in their shells in a roasted pepper and tomato broth are so generous they can easily be shared. And if you come on a Saturday, have the moist, fork-tender veal stew "axoa," infused with peppers. Each night brings a different traditional Basque special.

Of course save room for dessert, like hot, creamy-centered, orange-scented beignets. Remember Hirigoyen started out at a pastry chef.

The modern, low-ceilinged wood and brick room somehow evokes a lodge in a Pyrenees village for me. Each white-linen covered table has a striped sash running down the middle. The thin glassware is French, as is the service, Music plays. The lighting makes the room feel intimate. I love being there.

On the way out one night, I asked Hirigoyen to read aloud the Basque phrase written on the bottom of the check. "Mil esker eta ikus arte," it reads, which translates to "Thank you and see you soon." Spoken, it sounds like no language I've ever heard. Likewise, Hirigoyen's Piperade takes you to a very old and mysterious culinary place while delivering one of the most exciting restaurant experiences to happen in a long time.

131 Steuart Street (at Mission)
415-896-5600
www.shanghai1930.com
Open Monday through Friday 11:30
A.M. to 2 P.M., Monday through
Thursday 5:30 to 10 P.M., Friday
and Saturday 5:30 to 11 P.M.,
Sunday 5 to 9:30 P.M.
Moderate–Expensive
Credit cards: AE, DC, MC, V

After almost a four-year hiatus, I returned to Shanghai 1930, a dark, stylish supper club and bar, expecting to be amused by the ambience, but I fell in love with the food. This cellar restaurant now serves the best Shanghai dishes in town. Owner George Chen has been focusing his attention on the menu—it's longer, broader, more interesting, and seriously executed. The evocative surroundings, full bar and wine list, Monk and Redman on the state-of-the-art sound system, and gracious service have become a bonus, not the main attractions. For those of us old-school types (and there aren't too many of us left) who go to restaurants because of the food, Shanghai 1930 heads the list.

From the Shanghai section of the menu order *Youbao* prawns, small, fresh, sweet-fleshed shrimp with thin, edible shells. Pretty *xiao long bao,* the classic Shanghai pork-filled dumplings with twisted noodle tops, here garnished with red crab roe, explode with juice when you pop them into your mouth. Cold appetizers, always part of a Shanghai meal, are represented by moist, velvet-textured drunken chicken, marinated in Chinese rice wine, and five-spice smoked fish, bony if aromatic pomfret, almost jerkylike in intensity. The highlight for me, also an appetizer, is called Eight Delicacies with Savory Paste. Had I not been introduced to it, I would have missed out on a culinary thrill. Eight Delicacies looks like a little bowl of ratatouille, but instead of Mediterranean vegetables you find pressed tofu, reconstituted dried black mushrooms, raw peanuts, green and red peppers, cubes of shrimp and pork, and fresh soybeans, all bound in a hot, spicy, slightly vinegared dressing. Each bite is a roller coaster of textures and flavors.

Large, lobsterlike scampi are split down the middle, steamed, topped with crab roe, and served next to wide, tender house-made rice noodles. Tiny, tender Mongolian lamb chops rubbed with Chinese five spices are served with whole chestnuts; exquisite-looking Jade and Ebony whole braised black mushrooms with opalescent green, tiny Shanghai bok choy taste like meat, the greens clean and juicy. My favorite fish dish, Princess Fish Delight, turns out to be a small dice of firm rock cod in one of those elegant, clear Cantonese sauces enlivened with pickled cabbage.

The decor and accoutrements of Shanghai 1930 add a dimension of pleasure not found at any other Bay Area Chinese restaurant. Shanghai 1930 has one of the sexiest bars in town, with inventive house cocktails, numerous champagnes and wines by the glass, small bar tables for casual eating with drinks, a piano, and personable bartenders in steward's jackets. Soft white linen, white porcelain, thin glasses, and an oversized free-form flower arrangement give the dining room tony, simple period charm. Shanghai 1930 feels like a Hong Kong restaurant, an international Chinese meeting spot with its world-class surroundings and conscientiously cooked regional Chinese dishes.

SLANTED DOOR . . . .

100 Brannan Street (at the
Embarcadero)
415-861-8032
Open daily 11:30 A.M. to 3 P.M.,
Sunday through Thursday
5:30 to 10 P.M., Friday and
Saturday until 10:30 P.M.
Moderate
Credit cards: MC, V

The Slanted Door has catapulted authentic ethnic cooking into the forefront of the hip restaurant world, incorporating the stylishness of the modern San Francisco bistro with an authentic Vietnamese kitchen. The combination is irresistible, and the Slanted Door dining room is always full, even in its new, roomier, supposedly temporary location on the Embarcadero. While the restaurant's Mission District digs are expanding, chef-owner Charles Phan moved the whole operation into an airy, white-tiled restaurant space with a full bar, a counter, and two dining rooms. Some windows look out onto the bay across the street, others to a leafy plaza in newly developed South Beach. The new location has been such a success that Phan has decided to keep Slanted Door here and put a noodle house in the original location.

At the relocated Slanted Door, Phan continues to execute a changing menu of Vietnamese favorites that not only sparkle with freshness and bright flavor, but also take on new cachet by being served on a stunning mix of Japanese and Western china. Chopsticks, silverware, glassware, plates, tea service, napkins—everything that lands on the table has chic, as does the food itself, which naturally juxtaposes the raw and the cooked, crisp and tender, cold and hot, clean and rich, that characterize Vietnamese cooking. This cuisine is particularly appealing to salad-and-vegetable-loving Californians.

At Slanted Door you will find traditional crisp, fried shrimp and pork rolls, which you wrap in lettuce leaves with sprigs of mint and dunk into sweet, hot dipping sauce, and unusual steamed vegetarian dumplings topped with fried shallots. There is a refreshing green papaya salad, juicy and very finely shredded, and a superb watercress and shrimp soup served in a deep pottery bowl full of clear, elegant chicken broth. Don't miss the velvet-textured five-spice chicken or fresh Maine crabmeat with cellophane noodles and scallions, so delicious with rice. Steamed daikon rice cakes, elegant *pho* (Vietnamese beef noodle soup made here with Niman Ranch London broil), and no less than eight different all-vegetable dishes keep regular customers coming back again and again.

In keeping with the modern decor and presentation, the Slanted Door invented a wine list that groups wines by characteristics—floral and soft, crisp and dry, aromatic and rich. This helps you choose among little-known wines drawn from all over the world chosen especially to go with the food.

The choices offered in fine Western restaurants—house-made desserts (especially tropical ice creams and ices); cocktails, wine, beer; herbal, green, and black teas; espresso; service by course—only seem natural for Vietnamese dining. Indeed, the stylish dishes coming out of Slanted Door's open kitchen have inspired many a Cal-Asian dinner house. How rewarding that the authentic Vietnamese preparations served here delight the most!

When people ask me for suggestions of restaurants with views, I often recommend a meal cruise right on the bay. Two yacht companies currently offer very competent food and drink as they ply the waters between San Francisco and Marin County. Though these cruises are a bit pricey, the beauty outside the expansive picture windows makes a ride on these yachts worthwhile. During the day, and at night as the sun sets, being on the water in these big, comfortable, smooth-riding ships can be very romantic, and you get to see the land from a perspective that makes you appreciate the unique geography of San Francisco.

From a food perspective, I like best the Sunday brunch cruise on the **San Francisco Spirit**, a Pacific Marine yacht that boards near Pier 39 (415-788-0258). The spacious, handsomely appointed boat puts on a generous buffet with miraculously decent poached eggs on English muffins coated in a light, creamy hollandaise, delicious with juicy baked ham sliced to order by a chef on the serving line. The rest of the buffet consists of fruit salad; good, creamy potato salad; warm spinach and other salads, some quite tasty; and the usual bad commercial bread and pastries. A dry Spanish sparkling wine is liberally poured. While sailing during the day may not be as romantic as at night, you see so much more. Sailboats whiz past your table; pelicans slowly drift by in the air. A protected part of the deck lets you view everything from outside. The price ($59 for adults, $25 for children, tax and tip included) and duration (11:30 A.M. to 1:30 P.M.) feel just about right.

The alternative is a Hornblower dinner cruise (415-788-8866, $75 to $89 per person), leaving from Pier 33 at 7 P.M. and returning at 10:30 P.M. The **California Hornblower** is one of the most majestic boats plying the bay. A white wooden structure encircled by rows of large square windows, the Hornblower looks a little like a tiered Victorian wedding cake. Inside, the carpeted salons are dimly lit by art deco wall sconces and candles, letting the windows frame breathtaking views of sparkling city lights. The service is formal and very friendly. Unfortunately, the food is the least satisfying part of the experience. Corners have been cut in the ingredients and the execution is of the nondescript hotel variety. But there is dancing to a three-piece combo and you can get a bottle of Sterling chardonnay, for example, for $28. Even if you don't eat very much, you leave the boat enchanted.

A STRATEGY FOR VISITING FISHERMAN'S WHARF

Who can resist going down to a waterfront, where monstrous sea lions bark and lounge on the piers, where you can hop on a ferry to Sausalito or Tiburon, or visit a wax museum? That's the problem with the wharf: It has turned into a kitschy tourist attraction with a plethora of T-shirt shops and boardwalk-candy emporia. The working part of the wharf, where San Francisco's fishing boats dock with their hauls of crab and salmon, is getting smaller and smaller as fishing is being regulated to protect diminishing supplies and the real estate gets more and more valuable. There are a number of long-established wharf restaurants that charge a pretty penny for indifferent food; you are paying for location when you eat at them. Then there are the sidewalk seafood bars and crab pots that stretch along the wharf, owned by old Italian families. These are your best bets for getting a feel of the old workingman's wharf, when people really bought their live crabs and fresh-caught salmon there. Ideally, you can buy a whole live crab and ask that it be cooked to order in one of the huge, steaming, pressurized crab pots. The cooks will crack it for you, and with a glass or two of icy cold California chardonnay you can have one of the nicest meals in the world. But all too often the crab has been frozen or overcooked, or cooked and then frozen. I've had every kind. You'll never get anything spoiled (the wharf smells only of appetizing fresh seafood), but you never really know what you're getting unless you see the crabs wiggling in crates. Most of the operations sell identical items: crab-salad sandwiches, shrimp cocktails, cold half lobsters, picked Dungeness crab, and tiny bay shrimp cocktails. If I had to choose one stand over another, I like the looks of **Nick's** and the funky old-wharf feeling of the street-level dining rooms of **A. Sabella & La Torre**. I have actually witnessed the guys at Alioto's stand cook the crabs and crack them to order. The **Boudin Cafe**, a freestanding building across the street from these stands, makes the best clam chowder. You can have it in a small hollowed-out loaf of Boudin sourdough, a presentation popular with hungry teenagers.

TEATRO ZINZANNI

Piers 27–29 (Embarcadero at Battery)
415-438-2668
www.teatrozinzanni.org
Show starts at 6:30 P.M.
Wednesday through Saturday,
5:30 P.M. on Sunday
Expensive
Credit cards: AE, MC, V

I include this circus-cabaret-dinner theater in a food lover's guide because I just plain love spending an evening here. The meal service is cleverly interwoven into the show, and each act ends with a parade of athletic servers-actors rushing through the tent dealing out plates. An emotive chef and a moody maître d' with a legendary nose keep the action moving. The five-course meal, prepared by Taste Catering, is imaginative and surprisingly tasty considering how many people must be served at the same time. Everyone sits down at a linen-covered table or velvet-lined booth to a family-style antipasto of all sorts of goodies—hummus, olives, pepperoncini, fennel salami, crudités, cheeses, and breadsticks. Salads, always brightly dressed, and a soup, like corn chowder, usually precede main courses of a Moroccan-spice marinated chicken breast or lamb loin or a vegetarian stuffed pasta with seasonal accompaniments (you get to choose from two each night), all of which land on the tables hot and moist, never overcooked. Desserts, like lemon meringue tarts or summer fruit shortcakes, are always worth eating.

The antique spiegel tent erected right on the Embarcadero provides a romantic belle epoque backdrop for the wacky goings-on. The audience becomes part of the show and even the most skeptical get swept into the fun. Though not cheap—around $100 a person not including tip or drinks—no one leaves disappointed. It's worth saving up your pennies for this extravagant entertainment.

YANK SING

Rincon Center, 101 Spear Street
(at Mission)
415-957-9300
www.yanksing.com
Open weekdays 11 A.M. to 3 P.M.
Saturday, Sunday and holidays
10 A.M. to 4 P.M.
Moderate
Credit cards: AE, DC, MC, V

49 Stevenson (between 1st and 2nd streets)
415-541-4949
Open daily 11 A.M. to 3 P.M.

Henry Chan, a second generation dim sum man, moved Yank Sing from its longtime Battery Street location into the former Rincon Center quarters of Wu Kong a couple of years ago. (I still panic on occasion when I pass the old site and realize I have to travel a bit farther to still my cravings.) The Rincon Center could be in Tokyo or Hong Kong or New York, which probably appealed to the meticulous Chan, who, I happen to know, prefers clean and modern. Yank Sing is installed at the southeast corner of the atrium: it's spacious and softly lit, with a bar anchoring a sea of white linen–covered tables.

Yank Sing is known for innovation—for presenting some traditional Chinese banquet dishes in dim sum portions and for inventing completely new dim sum. Hence, a single airy steamed bun filled at tableside with a slab of crispy Peking duck, a swab of hoisin sauce, and some scallions; a dusky stir-fry of minced chicken, water chestnuts, and shiitakes spooned into an iceberg lettuce cup—a Chinese taco with hoisin for salsa.

Around 11 A.M. the first carts are wheeled from the kitchen, prime time for a dim sum lunch. Do not pass up translucent dumplings filled with tender steamed pea sprouts; Shanghai *bao*, little round dumplings twisted at the top into a spiral, filled with voluptuous, very juicy ground pork; or the crispy, deep-fried rectangular logs of tofu and seafood wrapped in seaweed. They're pure heaven. I also give my heart to vegetarian mushroom dumplings, their meaty filling of black shiitakes peeking through a clear wrapper. Then, there are my beloved deep-fried taro balls filled with creamy mashed taro and saucy pork, the outside lacy, crisp, and golden from the deep-fryer.

I always end a meal at Yank Sing with a deep-fried sesame ball, golden and coated with sesame seeds outside, chewy and white inside, filled with lightly sweetened brown bean paste. They're weird on first encounter and then, irresistible.

CAFÉS

SOUTH BEACH CAFE . . . .

800 The Embarcadero (at Brannan)
415-974-1115
Open Monday through Saturday
5 A.M. to 10 P.M.,
Sunday 8 A.M. to 8 P.M.
Credit cards: AE, DC, D, MC, V

Have a creamy-topped espresso at an outdoor table nestled under plane trees in front of this Embarcadero café with a loyal clientele of soccer fanatics, coffee drinkers, and focaccia aficionados. Latin Americans and Europeans live here during the World Cup, and in the off-season gravitate to South Beach for a peaceful interlude across the street from the water. The weather in this protected section of the Embarcadero tends to be balmy.

BARS

COSMOPOLITAN CAFÉ . . . .

Rincon Center, 121 Spear Street
(between Howard and Mission)
415-543-4001
www.cosmopolitancafe.com
Open Monday through Friday
11 A.M. to 2 P.M., Monday through
Wednesday 5:30 to 9:30 P.M.,
Thursday through Saturday
until 10 P.M.
Credit cards: AE, DC, D, MC, V

This stylish Rincon Center restaurant has two wood-paneled bars manned by cocktail specialists who know how to concoct multihued drinks made with fresh citrus and infused liquors. The barroom at the entrance is packed after work and has several video monitors tuned to the sports event of the moment. The more peaceful bar in the middle of the dining room is more amenable to exploring the layered East-West creations that come out of the kitchen. After one cocktail, you're ready for one of the towering appetizers like a tartare of tuna, salmon, and avocado seasoned with lots of

cilantro, dabbed with spicy *crema*, and garnished with thin Japanese sesame wafers, shredded seaweed, and tissue-thin cucumber pickle slices, an Asian-Latino composition. These multifaceted small plates match the complexity of current mixed drinks just as snuggly as chips do with beer. You drink and nibble upmarket here.

PIER 23 CAFE . . . .

Pier 23 (Embarcadero at Front)
415-362-5125
www.pier23cafe.com
Open Monday and Tuesday
11:30 A.M. to 11 P.M.,
Wednesday through Friday until
2 A.M.; Saturday 10 A.M. to 2 A.M.;
Sunday 10 A.M. to 10 P.M.
Credit cards: AE, DC, D, MC, V

One of the finest locations in town for a bar, this resonant old longshoreman's shack sits just yards from the bay on the water side of the Embarcadero. Patrons warming stools at the copper bar have a direct view of Treasure Island and sailing vessels just beyond a concrete pier. When the weather is warm, tables go out on the pier so you can eat and drink inches from the water. The place revs into high gear at night when live salsa, R & B, and jazz bands perform. Its excellent weekend brunch has become a San Francisco tradition, and whole roasted Dungeness crab has supplanted meat loaf with Cajun gravy as the most popular dish. Owned by local character Flicka McGurrin, who hangs her expressive oil paintings on the walls between the stuffed marlins and sailfish, Pier 23 offers the best neighborhood ambience of any bar on the Embarcadero.

DELICATESSENS/TAKEOUT

ARABI . . . .

Rincon Center, 101 Spear Street
(at Mission)
415-243-8575
Open Monday through Friday
7 A.M. to 2:30 P.M.
Cash only

This Palestinian food stand, the star of the Rincon Center food court, dishes up spicy, garlicky food that tastes home cooked. The meze—bulgur wheat salad, roasted eggplant purée, chickpea puree, dolmas, tomato and cucumber salad, marinated squashes in yogurt— have such depth of flavor, brightness, and balance that you can't stop dipping your pita bread into them. The pita sandwiches filled with falafel sparkle; each bite is gloriously rich, juicy, and spicy. Chicken kabobs made velvety by a lemony marinade seem to melt in your mouth. Also try the *mujadara*, a deeply seasoned stew of rice and lentils topped with caramelized onions. Of course you have to eat all this wonderful food on paper and plastic in the noisy, crowded atrium, where the smells of spicy food waft through the air, but frankly, this environment does evoke Middle Eastern markets, where you probably wouldn't find food as good as this.

IN-N-OUT BURGER . . . .

333 Jefferson Street (between
Jones and Leavenworth)
www.in-n-outburger.com
Open Sunday through Thursday
10:30 A.M. to 1 A.M., Friday and
Saturday until 1:30 A.M.
Cash only

My teenage son turned me on to In-N-Out Burger when the closest branch of this small, privately owned chain was in Marin County. I had my first Double-Double Animal Style standing up at a counter off Highway 101 because no seats were available. The big, juicy double-double—two ground-on-the-premises beef patties, cheese, tomato, pickles, lettuce, special spread, and grilled onions, the addition of which gives the burger animal classification—takes to upright consumption if only to ease digestion. I include only this one fast-food hamburger joint because it fulfills its mission better than any other. Choices are restricted—only simple hamburgers and cheeseburgers, french fries, and milk shakes are offered—but such specialization means that each item is constructed pretty much to order and based on fresh ingredients. You can watch the incredibly enthusiastic workers cut potatoes for the fries and cook the burgers one by one. They take your order with a smile and coach you through the small menu. "Do you want your fries extra crispy? Do you want grilled onions?" The posted menu doesn't mention this option, but the cognoscenti order them. Now the counter people ask. This private outfit pays well, trains assiduously, and turns out a fresh, consistent product quickly, all of which creates happiness and loyalty in both workers and customers. When I get the deep urge for this most American of foods, I head straight to In-N-Out.

BAKERIES/PASTRIES

BOUDIN SOURDOUGH BAKERY AND CAFE

156 Jefferson Street (between
Taylor and Mason)
415-928-1849
www.boudinbakery.com
Open daily 8 A.M. to 9 P.M.
Credit cards: AE, MC, V

When I'm down on the wharf, I always stop at this Boudin outlet to buy one of their 1½-pound sourdough rounds. This particular kind of San Francisco sourdough has a tender crust, a softer but more dense interior, and less sourness than the equally famous Parisian loaf. The breads at this original bakery site are always very fresh because of the volume. You can get six loaves in a travel box, ready to check onto airline baggage. You also can buy a small round, walk up to the wharf to buy crab cocktails and a pound of shrimp in the shell, stroll down to a less crowded spot on a pier by the water, and have the quintessential San Francisco wharf picnic.

ICE CREAM/CHOCOLATES

SEE'S CANDIES . . . .

Three Embarcadero Center
(at Drumm)
415-391-1622
www.sees.com
Open weekdays 10 A.M. to 7 P.M.,
Saturday 10 A.M. to 6 P.M.,
Sunday noon to 5 P.M.
Credit cards: AE, DC, D, MC, V

I find it hard to walk by a See's candy shop and not stop for a small box of peanut brittle or a few toffee-ettes. See page 334 for more information.

FERRY PLAZA FARMERS' MARKET

On the Embarcadero in front of, and on the plaza behind the Ferry Building at Market Street
Open Saturdays around 8:00 A.M. to 2 P.M., Tuesdays 10:30 A.M. to 2 P.M.
Day tables daily.
Cash only

This vibrant farmers' market, with the widest selection of organic and sustainably produced fruits, vegetables, cheeses, breads, pastries, meats, fish, and dairy products, has found its permanent home in and around the gloriously refurbished Ferry Building.

The market has become a culinary Mecca for food lovers all over the Bay Area who have become fiercely loyal to their favorite farmers and eagerly await the seasonal gifts of Early Girl tomatoes, Royal Blenheim apricots, or purple asparagus, local varieties they have come to know and love. They attend the farmers' market religiously, buying for the whole week because the produce is so fresh. The trip to the market with empty baskets and canvas bags has become a Saturday ritual for thousands of urban dwellers, many of whom probably have never set foot on a farm. At first they may have been stunned by the prices, which are high, because most of the produce sold at this market is organic. But once they tasted an organic peach or tomato, picked ripe, carefully packed, and brought to market that morning, they couldn't go back to the flavorless commercial kind. The taste of this ripe organic produce is incomparable, and when you think about the time, effort, and expense of the farmers, paying more for it does not seem out of line. Though supermarket produce may be half the price of the organic produce sold at the market, it's not worth eating if it tastes like cardboard. More and more people, skeptical at first, are being won over. In fact, food shopping directly from farmers has become a movement, a lifestyle decision.

The Ferry Plaza Farmers' Market is more than a produce destination, though one would be hard-pressed to find a better seasonal display of locally grown fruits and vegetables. There is an egg vendor with free-range and organic eggs of every size and color, including exquisite-tasting little pullet eggs; a mushroom stand with domestic brown Italian, oyster, portobello, and shiitake mushrooms, to name just a few; a number of artisan goat cheese producers; an organic cow's milk and butter producer, Straus Family Creamery; a fine producer of sheep's milk cheeses and lamb, Bellwether Farms; Hoffman Ranch with flavorful quail, squab, free-range chickens, rabbit, pheasant, and smoked game birds; Acme Bread from Berkeley; the Downtown Bakery and Creamery from Healdsburg; flower vendors, orchid vendors, rose specialists; and the most dedicated, talented array of farmers anywhere. If you just come down once and take a few tastes, you'll be hooked. Everyone will think that your cooking has improved, and it will when you start using these flavor-packed ingredients. You'll be inspired to cook more often, to try new ingredients, to taste in a way you never have before.

On top of all the beautiful food, there is an ongoing shop-with-the-chef program, in which local chefs walk around the market assembling a basket of ingredients, demonstrate how they would use them, and then raffle off the basket. Every top chef in the city has made the tour, coming up with some extraordinary menus. The Ferry Plaza Farmers'

Market sponsors comparative tastings of many different varietals, and local restaurants set up booths where they cook seasonal bites—like grilled corn with spicy chile butter, grilled salmon sandwiches with tomatoes, or grilled asparagus tossed with Parmesan and olive oil.

The feeling here is different than at any other farmers' market. Although there are few bargains to be found, you can get your hands on the highest-quality produce in the Bay Area for prices under what you would pay at specialty stores, if you could find like quality. That's the big advantage of shopping at a farmers' market: you get the produce in perfect condition, fresh picked, and full of flavor and nutrition.

FRESH EGG PASTA

MAKES 1 POUND DOUGH

2 cups unbleached
all-purpose flour

4 medium eggs, lightly beaten

½ teaspoon salt

1 Process the flour, eggs, and salt in a food processor until the dough forms a ball. Knead in more flour by hand if the dough is too sticky. Wrap in plastic and set aside for 1 hour.

2 Cut the dough into 2 pieces, and flatten each piece. Sprinkle flour on each piece and fold into thirds like a business letter. Set the rollers of the pasta machine to the widest setting and feed the dough through the rollers. Repeat about 8 times, dusting with flour, folding into thirds, and passing the dough through the widest setting, until very smooth.

3 From then on, pass the dough only once (do not fold into thirds, and dust with flour only if the dough feels sticky) through each setting, up to the next to last.

4 The sheet of pasta will measure about 6 inches wide and 60 inches long. Cut it crosswise into 3 pieces.

5 Let the pasta sheets dry for about 45 minutes before cutting them into the desired width.

CHICKEN WITH YOGURT AND MUSTARD

SERVES 8

Adapted from *Chez Nous* by Lydie Marshall, this ingenious chicken dish from French cooking teacher Lydie Marshall practically cooks itself. The trick of blending the pan juices in a food processor when you take the chicken out of the oven produces a voluptuous, silken sauce. If you go the distance and make your own tender egg noodles from her recipe (see opposite page), you'll have an exquisite dish. Otherwise, dried fettuccine will do just fine. Buy a Hoffman chicken or a Rosie organic chicken, both available at the Ferry Plaza Farmers' Market, and a pile of bracing green vegetables—young broccoli called broccoli *di ciccio; cavolo nero,* a kale with long, skinny, nubbly leaves; or young green beans—to accompany. Ask the farmers how to prepare the unfamiliar ones. You can also purchase a quart of Straus whole-milk yogurt at the market, the best cow's milk yogurt I've ever tasted.

1½ cups plain yogurt

⅓ cup strong Dijon mustard

½ teaspoon salt

Freshly ground black pepper

1 teaspoon fresh thyme leaves

2- to 3-pound free-range chicken, trimmed of all fat and cut into 8 parts each, or 4 pounds chicken parts, trimmed of all fat

1 In two 2-quart baking dishes, mix the yogurt and mustard. Season with salt, pepper, and thyme.

2 Dunk the chicken parts in the mixture. If prepared several hours ahead, cover the pans.

3 Preheat the oven to 400°F.

4 Bake the chicken, uncovered, in the middle of the oven for 45 minutes, or until golden brown.

5 Transfer the chicken to a warmed serving platter.

6 Process the curdled yogurt sauce in a food processor or blender to smooth it out, and pour in a sauceboat. Serve immediately.

ROASTED ASPARAGUS WITH SHAVED DRY JACK

When fat purple asparagus from the Sacramento Delta appear at the farmers' market, I prepare them this way. The purple asparagus require no peeling. They are tender and juicy all the way down once you snap off their stem ends. They take particularly well to roasting because they retain so much moisture. Any asparagus, thick, thin, green, or purple, will work beautifully. Simply adjust the roasting time. Even if you cook them too long, they'll still be delicious. This is a very forgiving recipe. Just be sure to sprinkle them with lots of tasty olive oil, kosher salt, pepper, and shaved Parmigiano-Reggiano or Sonoma's Vella Cheese Company's dry Jack.

Standard asparagus, about ½ inch thick at the butt

Extra virgin olive oil

Kosher salt

Freshly ground black pepper

A chunk of Vella dry Jack or Parmigiano-Reggiano

1 Preheat the oven to 425°F.

2 Break off the butt ends of the asparagus and arrange the spears on a cookie sheet in one layer, tips aligned. Sprinkle olive oil on the spears. Roll them about until they are just coated and then liberally sprinkle with salt and pepper.

3 Roast in the oven for 15 minutes, or until just tender.

4 Slide the asparagus off the cookie sheet onto a heated platter, tips aligned. With a potato peeler, shave thin slices of dry Jack or Parmigiano all over the asparagus. Taste a spear for salt and pepper. I like to sprinkle a little more olive oil over the asparagus and shaved dry Jack.

5 Set the platter in the middle of the table and eat communally, using fingers.

COOKWARE AND BOOKS

COST PLUS WORLD MARKET . . . .

2552 Taylor Street (between
Bay and Northpoint)
415-928-6200
www.costplusworldmarket.com
Open Monday through
Saturday 10 A.M. to 9 P.M.,
Sunday until 8 P.M.
Credit cards: AE, D, MC, V

The prices used to be fantastic at this warehouse of imported foodstuffs, glassware, dishes, cotton tablecloths and napkins, and baskets. I once shopped here for platters and serving bowls, but the prices rose and the pieces weren't as attractive as those I could find at Crate&Barrel. But there are always bargains, especially in Asian dishware and handwoven baskets. Cost Plus has one of the largest collections of baskets anywhere, and I have discovered, along with every caterer in town, that flat-woven rimmed baskets in different-sized circles are good for serving foods like cheese, fruit, bread, cookies, and raw vegetables. Baskets are light, unbreakable, and easy to transport. Just by wandering through the aisles at Cost Plus, you'll get some good ideas for presenting food.

WILLIAMS-SONOMA . . . .

Two Embarcadero Center
(between Front and Sacramento)
415-421-2033
www.williams-sonoma.com
Open weekdays 10 A.M. to 7 P.M.,
Saturday 11 A.M. to 6 P.M.,
Sunday noon to 5 P.M.
Credit cards: AE, D, MC, V

This store is full of great-looking high-end kitchenware and tableware. See page 127 for more information.

FINANCIAL DISTRICT
UNION SQUARE

FINANCIAL DISTRICT & UNION SQUARE

RESTAURANTS

1 Alfred's Steak House
2 Anjou
3 Anzu Sushi Bar
4 Aqua
5 B 44
6 Bix
7 Burma's House
8 Elisabeth Daniel
9 Farallon
10 Fifth Floor
11 Fleur de Lys
12 Globe
13 Grand Cafe
14 Jeanty at Jack's
15 Kokkari
16 Le Central
17 Masa's
18 MC^2
19 Millennium
20 Naan 'N' Curry
21 Original Joe's
22 Palio d'Asti
23 Postrio
24 Rubicon
25 Sam's Grill
26 Sanraku Four Seasons
27 Sear's Fine Foods
28 Shalimar
29 Tadich Grill

CAFÉS

30 Armani Cafe
31 Café Claude
32 Café de la Presse
33 Café Niebaum-Coppola
34 Cafe Prague
35 Zero Degrees

BARS

6 Bix
36 Harry Denton's Starlight Room
37 Red Room
38 Redwood Room

DELICATESSENS/TAKEOUT

39 Blondie's Pizza
40 Lee's Sandwiches
41 Palio Paninoteca
42 Specialty's Cafe and Bakery

ICE CREAM/CHOCOLATES

43 Fog City News
44 Morrow's Nut House
45 See's Candies
35 Zero Degrees

WINES AND SPIRITS

46 London Wine Bar

COOKWARE AND BOOKS

47 Crate&Barrel
48 Macy's
49 Sur La Table
50 Williams-Sonoma

N

BROADWAY

COLUMBUS

PACIFIC

34   18 35   12

6

GOLD ST.

JACKSON   <<<

33

15

WASHINGTON   >>>

20

8

PORTS-
MOUTH
SQUARE

MERCHANT

CLAY   <<<

1

SACRAMENTO   <<<

22 14 41   24 46

V
V
V

CALIFORNIA

4 29

ST.
MARY'S
SQUARE

V V V   > > >

PINE   <<<

BATTERY

FRONT

W

TUNNEL

5

BUSH   >>>

17

^
^
^

40 25

42

E

26

32 16

SANSOME

43

MONTGOMERY

31

SUTTER   <<<

45

37   11

36

2

KEARNY

7

9 27

CAMPTON

50

POST   >>>

23

UNION
SQUARE

MAIDEN

LANE

STREET

2ND ST.

19

49

GEARY   <<<

GRANT

28   13 38

44

ST.

O'FARRELL   >>>

48

30

NEW MONTGOMERY

V
V
V

^
^
^

V
V
V

3

47

STOCKTON

MARKET

3RD ST.

SF
MOMA

ELLIS   <<<

39

POWELL

4TH ST.

MISSION

ST.

JONES

EDDY   >>>

TAYLOR

MASON

10

YERBA BUENA
GARDENS

HOWARD

MOSCONE

FOLSOM

21

TURK

S

0   SCALE MILES   .25

ALFRED'S STEAK HOUSE . . . .

659 Merchant Street (alley off
of Kearny, betweeen Clay and
Washington)
415-781-7058
www.alfredssteakhouse.com
Open Tuesday to Friday
11:30 A.M. to 2 P.M.,
nightly 5:30 P.M. to 10 P.M.
Expensive
Credit cards: AE, DC, D, MC, V

Alfred's, one of San Francisco's oldest restaurants, reassures us that the old-fashioned steak house, especially a clubby, traditional one with Italian overtones, will always have a place in San Francisco. At Alfred's the cocktails will be forthcoming, the service professional, and the amenities traditional: heavy white linen, booths, big tables, and large upholstered chairs. If you want comfort and a luscious piece of dry-aged beef, you can count on this restaurant. It is the same today as when I first ate there twenty some years ago and probably when it first opened over sixty years ago.

Although the menu offers a number of Italian dishes, everyone knows to stick to the steaks. The T-bone and the Alfred's Steak, which is a bone-in New York, are exemplary—full of flavor and tender. The porterhouse is magnificent on both sides of the bone. Expert grilling over mesquite means that your meat will be cooked to exact specification without acrid burn marks or a cold center. The grillers at Alfred's know how to control the fire. With these steaks come sweet-fleshed baked Idaho potatoes, properly soft, dry, and light textured, with real, not imitation, fixings.

Everything else on the menu can be hit or miss. The Caesar salad, made at tableside, varies with the mood of the waiter. The house green salad with a ton of blue cheese has a sugary sweet, mayonnaise-based dressing. Believe me, a foray into the Italian section (the antipasto is okay) only underscores that Alfred's remains first and foremost an excellent steak house. In this era of chain operations, Alfred's stands out as an individual—crusty, aging, masculine—and just where you want to go if you're hungry for red meat.

ANJOU . . . .

44 Campton Place (between Sutter
and Post, Stockton and Grant)
415-392-5373
www.anjou-sf.com
Open Tuesday through Saturday
11:30 A.M. to 2:30 P.M. and
6 to 10 P.M.
Moderate
Credit cards: DC, D, MC, V

This cozy, very French bistro around the corner from Campton Place Hotel is a haven for delicious, classic bistro fare, such as calf's liver with bacon and onions, and the sweetest, creamiest chicken liver sauté you'll ever run across. A warm spinach salad with bacon, topped by a juicy grilled quail, and a house-made seafood sausage on warm cabbage salad in a vinegary butter sauce are other signature dishes. One of my favorites is a warm duck-leg confit surrounded by a wreath of endive and watercress in a tart dressing.

Typical of the well-prepared bistro dishes are tender, juicy rib lamb chops on a bed of delicately minted fresh flageolets, and a thin steak topped with a rosette of herb-shallot butter and accompanied with good *pommes frites* and French-cut green beans. Who could ask for anything more? If the hazelnut napoleon is available for dessert, give it a try. When it's fresh, it's a masterpiece. Prices are still amazingly reasonable, and eating at the tiny pushed-together café tables in this brick-walled, bi-level dining room softened by a floral canopy feels very Parisian.

ANZU SUSHI BAR AT THE HOTEL NIKKO . . .

222 Mason Street (at O'Farrell)
415-394-1100
www.anzunikko.com
Open Tuesday through Saturday
6 P.M. to 10 P.M.
Moderate
Credit cards: AE, DC, D, MC, V

Sushi aficionados (or are they affishionados?) followed the classicist sushi chef Kazu Takahashi from Sushi Ran in Sausalito to the Nikko. Takahashi trained for many years in Tokyo and knows his fish. The parade of high-quality seasonal fish that emanates from his bar, first as sashimi with freshly grated wasabi (for mixing with soy sauce) and reprised as sushi, will make you giddy with pleasure. The palette of colors on the sashimi plate may range from opalescent white to rusty red, and the flowing knife work of Mr. Takahashi underscores the differences in flavor and texture of each fish—exemplary buttery *hamachi; chu-toro*, tuna of midlevel fattiness cut from the flesh around the stomach; *tai*, crisp, white Atlantic snapper; red-edged slices of *hokkigai*, the most tender clam I have ever eaten; toothsome *kampachi*, an amberjack; *shimaji*, a flavor-packed white fish with high oil content that Mr. Takahashi calls kingfish. Mr. Takahashi presides at the sushi bar on Tuesdays, and Thursdays through Saturdays. Because most of his fish is flown in from Tokyo, he says Tuesday is the best day to come, unless the weather is stormy in Japan, in which case Thursday might be better. You can call him to inquire, and to reserve a spot at the sushi bar.

AQUA . . . .

252 California Street (between Battery and Front)
415-956-9662
www.aqua-sf.com
Open Monday through Friday
11:30 A.M. to 2:30 P.M., Monday through Saturday 5:30 to 10:30 P.M., Sunday 5:30 to 9:30 P.M.
Expensive
Credit cards: AE, DC, D, MC, V

At this perennially full upscale restaurant that now has a branch in Las Vegas, the kitchen combines French (via New York) formality with the imaginative eclecticism of California. Aqua is an elegant seafood restaurant that has garnered a reputation for sophisticated, first-class service. Once you're known there, your treatment becomes personal, completely tailored to your most minute preferences. Even if you're not known and are throwing a party for business purposes, as many do here, the service is so professional and smooth you never have to worry about making the right impression.

The fact is, Aqua is one of the few dining rooms in the city that offers this degree of comfort and luxury. Conveniently located right next to Tadich Grill (see page 115) in the Financial District, with big plate-glass windows looking out onto California Street and the cable car line, the interior, carpeted and draped in the palest shades of peach and decorated with gargantuan flower arrangements on sculpted pedestals, is a civilized place to dine. While most other rooms in town lean more to the bustling bistro mode, Aqua's heavily linened tables and upholstered armchairs are spaced for comfort. The scale is grander here, yet completely contemporary. People are expected to eat a leisurely full-course meal with wine and indeed, the complicated plates take some time coming out of the kitchen. Some dishes are a revelation, like a pairing of rare tuna with foie gras that is absolutely stunning, as odd as the combination sounds. It must have been inspired by the flavor of *toro*, the belly meat of tuna, which does taste like foie gras. A savory black mussel soufflé has become another constant on the menu, deservedly so. And diners can indulge in full-out culinary luxury—a parfait of Russian osetra caviar molded on top of a crisp potato cake with layers of crème fraîche and chopped egg, or slices of a whole roasted foie gras with fruit garnish and glaze that actually ends up tasting like very delicate calf's liver. One night the kitchen prepared a gorgeous, full-flavored consommé of wild mushrooms with sweet little bay scallops and a roasted Maine lobster with meat juice, a combination that Mina likes. The fish dishes can get elaborate with strong, reduced sauces and fussy presentation, which detracts from their purity, especially when first-rate ingredients are being used. At the best seafood restaurants (European and Japanese), you are awed by the beauty of the ingredient first and then by the art of the preparation. The cooking at Aqua is jazzier than that, and people eat here for the total experience, as opposed to paying homage at a temple of exquisite foods from the sea.

B 44 . . . .

44 Belden Place (between Pine and Bush, Kearny and Montgomery)
415-986-6287
www.beldenplace.com
Open Monday through Friday
11:30 A.M. to 2:30 P.M., Monday through Thursday 5:30 to 10 P.M.,
Friday and Saturday until 10:30 P.M.
Moderate
Credit cards: AE, DC, D, JCB, MC, V

The food at B 44 is stylish, edgy, and real, the flavors true and direct. I could spend hours perched at the long maple bar eating Daniel Olivella's luscious tapas and drinking sherry or wine.

Every visit could start with prosciutto-thin slices of *serrano* ham draped on triangles of soft-crisp garlic toast brushed with olive oil. Olivella presents it perfectly. How good this nutty, salty, moist ham tastes with sherry! This dish gets your mouth ready for Spain. There are other treasures, like *salpiçon negro*, a Spanish-style ceviche delicately scented with orange juice and lime, darkened by a little squid ink. On the opposite end of the richness scale are *canelons*, plump little cannelloni stuffed with fragrantly spiced minced meats, slathered with béchamel and Manchego cheese, and run under the broiler. I lean toward *exqueixada*, house-cured salt cod, delicate in flavor, silken in texture, mounded on top of the classic roasted pepper, eggplant, and onion salad called *escalivada*.

You can make a meal out of tapas (including Olivella's buttery half-dollar-sized fish cheeks sautéed with garlic, parsley, chile flakes, and sherry—one of the best dishes in town), or you can save room for one of B 44's moist paellas. They come in flat cast-iron paella pans paved with rice and different assortments of ingredients—chorizo, chicken, shrimp, squid, mussels, clams in the signature B 44 paella; chicken, rabbit, pancetta, mushrooms, rosemary, and *sofrito* (onions slowly cooked in olive oil with tomatoes) in the *Cazadora*. Each bite is flavorful, whether it is a hunk of boneless chicken or a fresh shrimp—with head still attached.

I like wine with Spanish food (as opposed to beer or sherry, which Spaniards seem to prefer) and the elegant little list of Spanish and California bottles provides some inspired matchups. A smoky red wine made near Barcelona in Villa Franca del Penedes, a Vallformosa Reserva, really completes the food. Olivella grew up next to these vineyards so it's no surprise that wine from this region tastes especially good with his cooking. Even a couple of desserts at B 44 achieve new heights. The best is a small plate of *fromage frais*, fresh, creamy, barely soured white cheese drizzled with honey, sprinkled with walnuts, and served with a *poron* (a glass beaker with a long skinny spout) of cream sherry. You eat a spoonful of the ethereal cheese and wash it down by pouring a thin stream of sherry into your mouth without touching your lips to the beaker. Cleaning bills aside, the interweaving of sweet nutty wine and honeyed cheese is sublime.

Not everything on this ambitious menu will appeal to everyone, but this is your chance to taste some modern Catalan cooking in San Francisco. Belden Alley, with all its little French restaurants spilling out onto the street, does feel like a corner of Europe, and B 44 extends the zone.

BIX . . . .

56 Gold Street (off Montgomery, between Pacific and Jackson)
415-433-6300
www.bixrestaurant.com
Open Monday through Saturday
5:30 to 11 P.M., Friday and
Saturday to midnight,
Sunday 6 to 10 P.M.
Lunch offered on Friday only,
starting at 11:30 A.M.
Moderate
Credit cards: AE, DC, D, MC, V

Doug Biederbeck, the genial host-owner (along with Real Restaurants partners) of Bix, has made this sophisticated, intimate restaurant and bar hidden away in an alley off Jackson Square into one of the most happening venues in San Francisco. Biederbeck is a true boulevardier, a man about town who knows what's going on in every spot in the city because he makes the rounds. He throws a sophisticated affair himself every night in his resplendent art deco quarters with a collagelike mural over the bar, an intimate mezzanine with luxurious booths for diners, and a jazz trio holding forth on the main floor. Everyone stops by Bix for superb cocktails, early and late.

Recently Bix acquired an accomplished new executive chef, Bruce Hill, of Oritalia fame, who has reinvigorated the menu. Beloved Bix favorites—including crisp chicken hash and smoked salmon on a potato pancake—remain and are prepared with new consistency. Hill also has created many new dishes, all fitting into Bix's elegant club ethos.

With a cocktail, perhaps a martini shaken at the table and poured from a silver shaker, I have hot mini ham-and-cheese sandwiches. Each bite-sized sandwich melts in my mouth, reminding me of Harry's Bar in Venice where they were invented. Bix does them as well. Another classic, marrowbones with toasts and a tiny spoon to scoop out the marrow, is another favorite of mine here. Martini drinkers should move on to a tasty steak tartare; wine drinkers to a generous portion of expertly seared foie gras with seasonal accompaniments. A blue crab and avocado salad, neatly molded and sauced in relishy Louie dressing; or the festive tomato cart, wheeled to the table with a rainbow of heirloom tomatoes in late summer and fall, offer a lighter start. The open-faced truffled hamburger on rye toast with skinny french fries is absolutely irresistible, the reason many people eat at Bix, but a crunchy crusted chicken cutlet, buttery like a schnitzel, served with scrumptious mashed potatoes and a big pile of green beans, offers similar straightforward appeal. For dessert, the kitchen makes old-fashioned bananas Foster, bananas heated in butter, brown sugar, and rum, served with vanilla ice cream, a dessert that comes as close to being an after-dinner drink as possible.

With Bruce Hill in the kitchen, Bix has risen in my estimation from being the best bar in town to being a spot where I really want to eat. I'm down for the whole evening here.

BURMA'S HOUSE . . . .

720 Post Street (between Jones
and Leavenworth)
415-775-1156
Open daily 11:30 A.M. to 9:45 P.M.
Inexpensive
Credit cards: AE, MC, V

A Burmese meal can be a roller coaster of hot, sweet, and sour sensations, and Burma's House is a good place to hop on for the ride. Though the large menu looks daunting at first, it can be decoded by referring to small color photographs of selected dishes. The best and most typical plates to order are the Burmese salads, spectacular mélanges of spicy toasted ingredients individually arranged on a plate in little piles and mixed together at the table by the waiter with a squeeze of lime. The ginger salad epitomizes the genre, with tiny threads of fresh young ginger, toasted coconut, lentils and yellow split peas, fried garlic chips, fresh green chiles, and toasted sesame seeds. It's worth a visit to this restaurant just for this or their mango salad, made of finely julienned strips of green and ripe mangoes, cucumber, chiles, and onion topped with deep-fried onion threads. It really is lovely. There are many Chinese-style stir-fries and some strong-flavored stews, my favorite being fork-tender pork, potato, and onions in a classic yellow Burmese curry, served with rice cooked in coconut milk and scattered with fried onion threads. The decor here is nondescript and the service can run hot or cold depending on your waiter, but when you're in the mood for something very spicy, completely exotic, and like nothing you've ever tasted before, head for Burma's House.

ELISABETH DANIEL. . . . .

550 Washington Street (between
Montgomery and Sansome)
415-397-6129
www.elisabethdaniel.com
Open Monday through Friday
11:30 to 1:30 P.M.; Monday through
Friday 6 to 10 P.M., Saturday and
Sunday 5:30 to 10:30 P.M.
Expensive
Credit cards: AE, DC, MC, V

Chef Daniel Patterson is one of those sensitive, artistic, self-taught young chefs who played football and honed a 125-mile-an-hour first serve on the tennis court (I've seen him play) while working every summer in restaurants on Martha's Vineyard. Now you can watch him in his immaculate glassed-in kitchen, athletically dancing his way through service. The five-course $49 prix fixe meals he cooks at Elisabeth Daniel, the understated storefront restaurant he opened with his wife, Elisabeth Ramsey (who is no longer involved with the restaurant), reveal a poetic soul. Inspired, perhaps, by Thomas Keller's witty two-bite dishes at the French Laundry (see page 472), Patterson has developed his own repertoire of small-scale wonders, each exploring a different cooking technique, kaiseki style. Bite-sized ovals of rare tuna suspended in lemon–black pepper *gelée* look like shimmering sushi. A warm foam of sweet butter and black truffles conceals tender sweetbread ravioli beneath. Seared scallops act as nuggets of sugar in a ginger, lemongrass, and cilantro-infused carrot broth. Patterson's crimson venison chop in bitter chocolate–red wine sauce makes you think about the animal. Its extraordinary flavor pays homage to its life. For those who prefer a more abbreviated experience, the restaurant now offers an à la carte menu at both lunch and dinner.

The food, gorgeous and meticulous, still reveals the hand that made it, and the service and decor is a little naive, perhaps a holdover from the couple's first restaurant off the central plaza of laid-back Sonoma. But the modest San Francisco space, hidden across the street from the Transamerica Pyramid, allows an exacting young chef in love with cooking to explore his voice.

FARALLON . . . .

450 Post Street (between
Mason and Powell)
415-956-6969
www.farallonrestaurant.com
Open Tuesday through Saturday
11:30 to 2 P.M; Monday through
Thursday 5:30 to 10:30 P.M.,
Friday and Saturday 5:30 to 11 P.M.,
Sunday 5 to 10 P.M.;
small bistro at the bar open
Tuesday through Saturday
2:30 to 5 P.M.
Expensive
Credit cards: AE, DC, D, MC, V

In the late 1980s, during Stars' highest moment, when Jeremiah Tower and his chef de cuisine Mark Franz were fully engaged, there wasn't a more exciting collaboration anywhere. But some stars burn out, and Franz finally left the restaurant to open Farallon in collaboration with designer-restaurateur Pat Kuleto, who created a phantasmagorical underwater decor with mythic jellyfish suspended from the ceilings. Franz refocused his attention on seafood, and the result is as mind-expanding as the decor, with sophisticated, surprising, multi layered creations that often bring together disparate ingredients.

Franz put on one of the finest displays of cooking for the first Farallon wine dinner, which showcased wines made from Rhône grape varietals grown in

Central California and France. (It was emceed by none other than brilliant British wine writer Jancis Robinson.) He prepared pretty molded crab salad garlanded with jewellike beets and tiny lamb's lettuce to partner viognier; seared fillets of rouget topped with seared foie gras, fava beans, and a briny buttery sea urchin sauce for roussane; wild turbot stuffed with a layer of lobster on a bed of miniscule cubes of aromatic vegetables all moistened with a bacony syrah reduction, to go with Hermitage and California syrah. After an opulent cheese course, pastry chef Emily Luchetti refreshed our palates with strawberries and blackberries splashed with Muscat de Beaumes-de-Venise, pure berry sorbet, and tiny warm gingersnaps. Stars's whimsical American pasty chef now holds court at Farallon with Franz, completing the team.

I love the way Franz uses meat with fish, and red wine with fish, and birds with red wine. He's a true California chef in that all his dishes are inspired by local products. They're often vegetablerich. He, above all other chefs, knows the importance of pristine condition in both fish and produce, and how to fashion a dish that showcases intrinsic quality. And though Franz's cooking is refined, it always has a hearty edge that American eaters can hold onto, a bright New World sensuality that still takes some unexpected turns. I always look forward to a Mark Franz meal, just the way I did a Jeremiah Tower meal.

Like Stars, Farallon is a big operation with a bar and a bar menu, lunch, dinner, and tasting menus, and private rooms for special events. It's managed professionally so you won't get lost in the ocean of tables, but your most rewarding relationship will be with Franz's unique and polished food.

FIFTH FLOOR . . . .

Hotel Palomar, 4th Street at Market
415-348-1555
www.fifthfloor.citysearch.com
Open Monday through Friday
7 A.M. until 10 A.M.,
weekends 8 A.M. until 11 A.M.;
Monday through Thursday,
5:30 until 9:30 P.M., Friday and
Saturday until 10:30 P.M.
Credit cards: AE, DC, D, MC, V

Laurent Gras, a thirty-six-year-old Frenchman who was chef de cuisine at Alain Ducasse's restaurants in Monte Carlo and Paris, and at Guy Savoy in Paris, has taken over the kitchen at Fifth Floor, the small, boîtelike restaurant in the Hotel Palomar. He brings an intellectual approach to the high-end dining experience, dividing the menu into primal categories: Ocean; Field and Forest; Farm; and, in winter, Black Truffle. He designed the menu so that all the dishes go with one another in any combination. Diners can feel free to order any that pique their interest rather than be constrained by a limited number of choices in the typical course progression.

Gras is not the first chef to offer this flexibility. Gary Danko invented the form over a decade ago at the Dining Room at the Ritz-Carlton, when he came up with the idea of charging by the number of courses ordered, not for each item. Then he tailored the size of each dish to make an appetizing meal. This kind of adaptability on the part of the kitchen has become almost expected in high-end San Francisco restaurants, influenced, I think, by the taste for eclectic, small-plate dining that has swept the restaurant scene. At any rate, the current $85 per person chef's tasting menu for the table is roughly equivalent to ordering three dishes of your own choice. As someone who is always tempted by a chef's tasting menu and then regrets it halfway through, I recommend striking out on your own. Gras makes some magnificent dishes of which you will want more than a taste.

Surf & Turf of steamed striped bass and almost raw sautéed foie gras with brussels sprout leaves is pulled together with a bracing sherry vinegar sauce infused with black truffles. It makes a miraculously sparkly composition. His version of Brillat-Savarin's lamb is also mind-expanding. A lamb loin has been baked so slowly that it practically melts in your mouth, but still appears rare and retains the bright flavor of rare meat. Each of three ample rounds are thickly encrusted with black truffles, pistachios, and black olives, respectively, so each magnificent piece responds to a different flavor. Fluffy yellow rutabaga and potato puree and buttery savoy cabbage fill out this edible still life. Every item on the rectangular plate is separate and distinct, but all the flavors meld as you eat the dish, a tour de force of technique, of ever-deepening harmony in taste.

Niman Ranch pork belly presents another texture for Gras to master, and he does so by poaching it ever so slowly, capping it with a thrillingly crispy slab of rind, saucing it with black truffle *jus*, and accompanying it with a winter pastiche of Jerusalem artichoke, apple, salsify, and potato.

If you have worked out all day and not eaten for two, you might be able to eat all three of these winter dishes. A sane person would choose between the lamb and the pork belly. Either way, you can choose a refreshing dessert, such as passion fruit sorbet on tiny-diced tropical fruit salad in juicy vanilla bean–lemon balm syrup. Other desserts are actually composed of several mini-desserts—a Winter Apple Tasting of tart green apple sorbet on a fine mince of apples plus a hot apple fritter, a caramelized apple charlotte, a buttery apple strudel, and a Chinese teacup of mulled apple cider. I'll let you imagine what the Tour de Chocolate brings.

Under Laurent Gras, Fifth Floor has become the most sophisticated and cutting edge of all the high-end restaurants in the Bay Area. When you make the decision to eat here—and the investment—you should approach the experience as you might a poem: the understanding and resulting pleasure will require some thought.

FLEUR DE LYS ·

777 Sutter Street (between
Taylor and Jones)
415-673-7779
www.fleurdelyssf.com
Open Monday through Thursday
6 to 9:30 P.M., Friday and Saturday
5:30 to 10:30 P.M.
Expensive
Credit cards: AE, DC, D, JCB,
MC, V

Chef Hubert Keller put Fleur de Lys back on the map of important San Francisco restaurants when he took over the Michael Taylor–designed dining room in partnership with Maurice Rouas over sixteen years ago. It has been full ever since. This is one of the most romantic-looking restaurants in the city, with the main dining area actually inside a floral print tent that now, after a recent complete renovation, gently suggests North Africa. One side of this draped tent is mirrored so cleverly it provides the illusion that you're in a room twice as large. Sconces protrude from the material, giving this soft structure an intimate glow. In the center of the room, under the peak of the tent, a towering exotic flower arrangement rises up out of the sea of tables to meet a huge chandelier.

Keller's cooking is equally pretty. He starts you out with charming little bites—a morsel of foie gras and chanterelles in a miniature cast-iron skillet; a tiny, savory wedge of Alsatian potato and onion cake; a bite of cauliflower puree topped with caviar and flanked with tiny purple potato chips. And then the meal unfolds with colorful, multifaceted dishes that almost always include a luxury ingredient, sometimes two or three. A thick slice of seared foie gras takes on new dimension with a sauce larded with smoked duck breast. Pink and juicy lamb chops have a crunchy coating that adds both texture and flavor. On his famous four-course vegetarian menu, Keller, one night, came up with two really satisfying creations: a ragout of wild mushrooms with house-made shell pasta that mirrored the texture of the mushrooms, and a braise of celery hearts in a tomatoey Provençal sauce with niçoise olives. As an omnivore, I appreciated eating such a clean but voluptuous meal.

Maurice Rouas works the dining room like the old pro that he is, with beautiful former pastry chef Chantal Keller now schmoozing alongside. Hubert comes out at the end of the evening to pay his regards to his fans. Fleur de Lys is very much a family restaurant like many starred restaurants in France. The owners do the lion's share of the work themselves, setting the tone, giving the restaurant personality. Fleur de Lys, though certainly expensive, fancy, and French, is not stuffy or pretentious. Its owners have kept it a place for a celebratory meal and a good time.

GLOBE . . . .

290 Pacific Avenue (between Battery and Front)
415-391-4132
Open Monday through Friday 11:30 to 3 P.M.; Monday through Saturday 6 P.M. to 1 A.M., Sunday until 11:30 P.M.; light menu at the bar daily 3 to 6 P.M.
Moderate
Credit Cards: AE, MC, V

This insouciant little Cal-Med bistro is always packed for lunch and dinner (until 1 A.M.) with people who like chef-owner Joseph Manzare's witty way with hearty favorites. He serves house-made spaghetti with tomato sauce in a deep ceramic bowl; clay pots of steamed clams, mussels, and calamari in spicy tomato broth; and bowls of frisée salad intertwined with lardons of pancetta and a lusciously runny poached egg. Somehow the rustic pottery makes all these dishes taste better. Many patrons come in especially for a huge grilled T-bone steak for two, slathered with grilled onions, sliced and presented on a pizza pedestal, accompanied with a dangerously hot ramekin of potato gratin. Others go for thin-crusted pizzas topped with mushrooms and truffle oil; or paved with wine-cured salami and a sunny–side up egg. A Wolfgang Puck veteran before he opened Globe, Manzare picked up the clever, stylish, casual Puck vernacular and made it his own.

The red-bricked space with open kitchen, hard surfaces, and tiny service bar at the front can get roaringly noisy, but that only adds to the fun. Globe always feels like a drop-in party. I usually run into someone I know, maybe because off-duty chefs gravitate here for Manzare's hip, easy-to-eat food after a hard night's work.

GRAND CAFE . . . .

Hotel Monaco, 501 Geary Street
(at Taylor)
415-292-0101
www.grandcafe.net
Open Monday through Friday
7 A.M. to 10:30 A.M., Saturday
8 A.M. to 10:30 A.M., Sunday
brunch 9 A.M. to 2:30 P.M.;
Monday through Saturday
11:30 A.M. to 2:30 P.M.; Sunday
through Thursday 5:30 to 10 P.M.,
Friday and Saturday until 11 P.M.
The Petite Café, which offers a light
menu, is open Sunday through
Thursday 11:30 A.M. to 11 P.M.,
Friday and Saturday until midnight.
Moderate
Credit Cards: AE, DC, D, MC, V

One of my favorite chefs, Paul Arenstam, has taken on the gargantuan task of running the kitchen at Grand Café, a La Coupole–scale restaurant in the heart of the theater district. He's doing a stunning job. His soulful French cooking characterized by deep sauces and endless flavors works perfectly in this dramatic belle epoque room.

You can begin with his accomplished cold torchon of foie gras, a generous round encased in walnuts and fig preserves, served with warm brioche toasts. No one does a better presentation. He knows how to elevate the flavor of a chopped salad of romaine, green beans, and chickpeas with big hunks of local Great Hill blue cheese. His lush, savory tarts, like one of rosemary-scented mushrooms, onion, and Gruyère, are made to go with a glass of crisp white wine.

Arenstam loves duck. His confits with crispy skin are only equaled by his pink, juicy duck breast preparations, my favorite being one with Bing cherries and cardamom in a coriander-scented *jus*, accompanied with scallion-studded basmati rice and whole grilled baby bok choy. I dream about this dish. His way with fish charms, too. If you're eating at Grand Cafe in the spring, perhaps you'll encounter his crispy sole with Half Moon Bay peas, pea sprouts, tiny wild *mousseron* mushrooms, all in an earthy mushroom *jus*.

For dessert, order the towering Grand Banana Cream Pie, really an individual tart on a pool of caramel sauce with a generous layer of macadamia nuts on a buttery crust, and inches of banana pastry cream, sliced bananas, and whipped cream.

Arenstam's commitment to this monumental restaurant near Union Square is great news for San Franciscans and tourists alike. Now we have a convenient choice for pretheater dining; a grand room for a moderately priced dinner downtown; a destination for brunch, lunch, or just a bite in the Petite Café; and a dressy bar for both drinks and oysters. Such versatility combined with Arenstam's dedication to high quality is a public service. We can thank the Kimpton Hotel and Restaurant Group for bringing it all together, but our deepest gratitude goes to Arenstam, a chef with enormous and unflagging integrity.

615 Sacramento Street (between
Montgomery and Kearny)
415-693-0941
Open Monday through Thursday
11:30 A.M. to 10:30 P.M.,
Friday and Saturday until 11:30 P.M.
Moderate
Credit Cards: AE, D, MC, V

Philippe Jeanty put together a dream menu for his homey Bistro Jeanty (see page 467) in the wine country. After years of fancy cooking at Domaine Chandon, he came up with the idea of preparing old-fashioned French grandmother dishes, which tend to use the cheapest and most exciting parts of the animal—pig's feet, lamb's tongue, cured pork belly, duck legs, rabbit legs. He grills fat leeks and marinates them in mustardy vinaigrette; he makes frisée and lardon salad with a soft-boiled egg. His coq au vin, served in a ramekin, has a deep, bacony red wine sauce, as does *boeuf aux carottes*, served over puréed potatoes. Prices are reasonable, the food hearty and very French, and Bistro Jeanty has been packed from the minute it opened.

Jeanty has duplicated most of that menu at the historic Jack's restaurant in San Francisco and the formula works. Before the original Jack's closed, it had been a de facto San Francisco men's club for 135 years. Generations of San Franciscans, mostly male, ate their way through Dungeness crab salads, mutton chops with kidneys attached, fillets of beef, wild salmon, and fat asparagus with sauceboats of buttery hollandaise. It took brave new owners to attempt to reinvigorate a fading institution: John Konstin and his father Gus, who worked at Jack's as a waiter for ten years and saved up enough money to buy the historic John's Grill, spared no expense in the restoration, but they couldn't make it fly. So Jeanty took over the restored building from them and turned it into a brasserie.

From the outside Jack's looks much the same, a compact brick building with a small front window shuttered with blinds. A green velvet curtain still hangs in front of the brass-trimmed front door to block out the rush of cold air. Jeanty painted the facade a French shade of red. The interior, now resplendent with gold, polished brass, and wood, does look different. The meticulously restored bas-reliefs of lambs, pheasants, fruit, and jackrabbits glisten in fresh 22-karat gold leaf. (Jackrabbits? There were so many of them in this nine-teenth-century neighborhood that they appeared on the menu as well as inspiring the restaurant's name.) Huge alabaster light fixtures hang from the newly raised ceiling. Sconces alternate with coat hooks along the walls. A stairway with a magnificent wrought-iron and brass railing now fills one side of the small dining room, leading to a cozy mezza-nine, a second floor of private dining rooms, and a third floor under a copper and glass French skylight.

Jeanty's idea to run it like a big city brasserie, open throughout the day and night from early lunch through late dinner, opens the door to all levels of diner. The oversized single page menu looks just like a Parisian brasserie's with sections for *fruits de mer*, charcuterie and pâtés, salads, and so forth. You can eat big or small, light or heavy. As at his wine country place, the food is delicious and reasonable in price. And with every passing month, the memory of the old crusty Jack's disappears and the tradition of the new Jeanty at Jack's takes root, anchored by the resonant building that still echoes of San Francisco's past.

200 Jackson Street (at Front)
415-981-0983
www.kokkari.com
Open Monday through Friday
11:30 A.M. to 2:30 P.M.;
Monday through Thursday
5:30 to 10 P.M., Friday 5:30 to
11 P.M., Saturday 5 to 11 P.M.
Expensive
Credit cards: AE, DC, D, MC, V

You can't help but be seduced by the ambiance at Kokkari. A massive fireplace, big enough to roast whole lambs or goats, dominates a small, high-ceilinged dining room. A rough wooden table placed in front of the fireplace is laid with breads and crocks of olives. Huge, unfinished beams protrude from the ceiling, while antique Oriental carpets are scattered here and there on a polished wooden floor. It's as if you stumbled into a private living room in a Greek country villa—maybe owned by an Onassis.

But wait. People are disappearing into a hallway and if you follow them you discover a spacious second room with even bigger beams, a long, brightly lit open kitchen, and tall wood-framed windows that look out onto Jackson Street. A dramatically long refectory table stretches the length of one wall; other tables fill alcoves suggesting private dining possibilities.

While I could make a meal of those glistening olives, this is one place where restraint is rewarded. Save yourself for additional *mezethes* (appetizers), first and foremost a platter of traditional Greek dips—smoky roasted eggplant and pepper purée; thick yogurt and cucumber subtly seasoned with garlic; creamy *taramosalata* infused with cured pink carp roe—served with scrumptious house-made pita bread served hot from the grill.

In most Greek meals the main courses never seem to be as engaging as the *mezethes*, but Kokkari has some standouts. The moussaka is wonderful, baked and served in its own stunning blue pottery bowl, layered with potatoes, lamb, and eggplant and topped with a tart yogurt béchamel. A lamb shank infused with cinnamon is both tender and flavorful. Especially good is its bed of orzo cooked in rich stock. Quail stuffed with lots of winter greens offers a dish in which vegetables star.

For an aperitif you may choose from eight different ouzos served straight up with water on the side, or mixed with a little ice water. You have to like licorice to appreciate it. Though they resemble nothing I've ever had in Greece, the dreamy desserts do use traditional Greek ingredients: hence, a creamy yogurt sorbet scattered with tangerine granita; or airy, hot apple fritters moistened with apple syrup served with honey ice cream; or a *bastela* of crispy phyllo pastry separated by vanilla custard and spiced nuts drizzled with caramel. And if you're a Greek coffee aficionado, Kokkari mixes stone-ground coffee with water and sugar in special, long-handled metal pots, and puts it to boil in a sandpit, which produces an especially unctuous and aromatic brew.

The accomplished cooking owes as much to California and France as to Greece, for Kokkari's chef, Jean Alberti, is a Frenchman with classical French hotel school training. He knows how to make food taste and look good, no matter what its ethnicity. I suppose one criticism that can be made is that the cooking here is a blend of cuisines, not the pure, rustic Greek food you would find in Greek tavernas, for example. But I think that there's plenty of soulful Greek cooking at Kokkari. If a little local frisée sneaks onto a plate of fried smelt, what's the harm? If a lamb shank is sauced with an elegant meat stock reduction, so what? Like the decor, the food presents a Grecian fantasy.

453 Bush Street (between
Grant and Kearny)
415-391-2233
Open Monday through Saturday
11:30 A.M. to 10:30 P.M.
Moderate
Credit cards: AE, DC, MC, V

What the food lacks in brilliance at Le Central, San Francisco's oldest authentic French bistro, it makes up for in dependability and the exact replication of a beloved French form. The tiny, crowded-together tables covered with butcher paper, the menu written in grease pencil on the mirrors, the celebrity lunchers like Willie Brown and pals strategically seated at tables in the front windows all give Le Central its cachet. When you're at the zinc bar sipping Pernod, you can easily imagine yourself in Paris, and when you're at table, you'll be eating just what you might in the City of Light.

Start with a butterleaf salad with walnuts in a mustardy vinaigrette, tender braised leeks, or celery root *rémoulade*. Continue with roast chicken with watercress, a grilled tomato half, and *pommes frites*. My favorite dish here is the *boudin noir*, blood sausage from master *charcutiers* Marcel and Henri. The fat black aromatic sausages are sautéed to the bursting point, garnished with hunks of sautéed apple. The restaurant often has poached skate wing with capers in a vinegary butter sauce and prepares it perfectly. The house chardonnay and cabernet come from Chalone, the accomplished California winery inspired by the winemakers of Burgundy. So all a diner's needs are met in a thoroughly French way.

MASA'S . . . .

Hotel Vintage Court,
648 Bush Street (between
Powell and Stockton)
415-989-7154
www.masas.citysearch.com
Open Tuesday through Saturday at
5:30 P.M., last seating at 9:30 P.M.
Expensive
Credit cards: AE, DC, D, MC, V

Masa's happens to be one of the few high-end restaurants where I am willing to put my body and pocketbook on the line for four-plus hours of wanton pleasure. Its great chefs, Julian Serrano and now Ron Siegel, are artisans who understand that true culinary elegance grows out of ingredients and technique. I find this conservatism inspiring.

Just before Siegel took over the kitchen, the restaurant closed down for complete redecoration. The burgundy draperies and romantic light sconces of the Serrano era were replaced with chocolate brown walls, black-and-white abstract prints, and overgrown red lamp shades suspended from the ceiling. The dining room's best feature, a luminescent white curtain that separates it from the brightly lit entryway and moderne bar, adds a touch of urbanity.

Oh, but the food and the service! Purposely I chose the smallest menu—a first course, main course, dessert, and coffee—but don't think for a minute that you can get away with just eating three courses. Fabulous bites emerge from the kitchen, single morsels of food on huge white plates. It may be a demitasse of silky textured winter squash soup deepened by rich chicken stock; or a sweet sea scallop perched on top of microscopic florets of cauliflower; or a shrimp paired with a fig.

Yet no dish I've eaten in recent memory has been so drop-dead voluptuous as Siegel's cream of mushroom soup with white truffle *raviolini*—with such pure wild mushroom flavor you could taste a forest in every bite. I spied a squab dish on the six-course tasting menu and asked to have it as my main course. Not a problem. The chef enlarged it from one to two breasts, each red, meaty, and velvety in texture, set off by squab liver mousse and a bed of slivered brussels sprouts with bacon. This still life of fall foods was made even more festive by a 1998 Chassagne-Montrachet from Ramonet. Burgundy and squab at this level make me very happy.

As in the best French restaurants, the Masa's staff choreographs a dance of food and wine with such graciousness and thoughtfulness that everyone feels like a celebrity. Most important of all, the eating, drinking, and service fit together seamlessly. The wine enhances the food; the food makes the wine taste complex. (Let sommelier Michele Morey take care of you. For around $50 a person she can work wonders.) The service supports the refinement of the wine and food.

As you teeteringly stand up to leave, you notice the bowl of handmade caramels on a trolley. You can't help but grab a few to throw in your purse, but the gentlemanly maître d' and intuitive waiter let out a little howl. "We've caught you," they say, as they knowingly hand you a miniature shopping bag of exquisite chocolates, fruit jellies, nougats, candied citrus peel, and those buttery caramels to take home—to augment the ones you've already been served. They've lovingly packed it for you, and it's 1:30 in the morning.

Masa's proudly projects the ethos of the job well done, whether it be at the table, in the wine cellar, or in the kitchen. In these uncertain times when we look for reassurance that traditional values do mean something, a restaurant like Masa's can buoy the spirit.

MC² . . . .

470 Pacific Avenue (between
Montgomery and Sansome)
415-956-0666
www.mc2restaurant.com
Open Monday through Friday
11:30 to 2 P.M., Monday through
Saturday 5:30 to 10 P.M.
Moderate
Credit cards: AE, MC, V

From a choice window table at MC² I watched my Roman friend walk up Pacific Avenue to meet me for lunch. In a tight black T-shirt, Armani sport coat, loose-fitting black slacks, and wire-rimmed sunglasses, he looked like just the kind of patron MC² was designed to attract—chic, understated, timelessly modern.

The room is exhilarating, a striking, light-filled space in an old red brick Jackson Square building. Dramatic steel beams and joists look as if they were part of the plan—not earthquake retrofitting. A mysterious narrow atrium in the back of the dining room appears to be an outdoor alley, except that you notice that people are eating there. You see them through holes cut through the brick wall it shares with the main part of the restaurant. A floating fabric ceiling muffles sound, some of which emanates from a white-tiled open kitchen, where chefs in immaculate white coats work a wood-burning oven.

Stunning furniture—Philippe Starck chairs of beech and chrome, cocktail chairs made of black bungee cords strung over chrome frames, bar stools of brushed metal—enhance the room. Long blond cabinets break up the dining space; tall blue banquettes along one wall soften it. I always like being in MC², especially now that chef Todd Davies, formerly chef for Bradley Ogden at Lark Creek Inn, has taken over.

While some deserving original dishes remain, like Traditional Tarte Flambee, really a thin-crusted rectangular pizza slathered with *fromage blanc*, crème fraîche, onions, and blanched bacon, Davies has reformulated the menu, which now offers flights of small plates of increasing complexity.

The "Covalent" category includes the tarte and other dishes to share, like a huge artichoke, leaves and heart dismantled, dressed with *tapenade* and basil oil, accompanied with a frisée and watercress salad with sheep's milk feta and olives. Though a lot happens on these plates, everything belongs. In "General Theory," I learned about Davies's charming layered potato cake with house-smoked salmon, chopped egg, and horseradish cream. "Continuum" brought two crispy catfish fingers on a slaw with really hot jalapeño vinaigrette, and from "Quantum Mechanics" came juicy pork loin slices on a ragout of corn and favas surrounding a tender corn custard with morels. There's a fabulous Farmers' Market Vegetarian Plate that has all the brightness of freshly harvested produce, and no less than eleven different cheeses, each served with seasonal fruit and walnut bread, to complete a meal. Dessert brings highly original compositions, like a "banana split" of ice cream wrapped in chocolate with a caramel and fudge center, topped with sliced caramelized bananas.

Though the waiters assume that everyone at the table will share, I don't think they should. Each dish is so tightly composed, so well balanced, and frankly, so small, that it should be eaten entirely by one—well maybe by two, so you can taste a few more. Davies, like a skillful miniaturist, offers whole worlds in a few intriguing bites. His cutting edge presentations belong in this lyrical modern space. MC^2, with Davies spinning culinary theories, deserves more and closer attention.

MILLENNIUM . . . .

580 Geary (at Jones)
415-345-3900
www.millenniumrestaurant.com
Open nightly 5 to 9:30 P.M.
Brunch Sunday from
10 A.M. to 2 P.M.
Moderate
Credit cards: AE, D, DC, MC, V

Vegan restaurants are not a rarity in San Francisco now, but none are as sophisticated or as much fun as Millennium. Vegans eat only fruit and vegetables, and even avoid animal products like eggs, butter, and yogurt. Vegetable oils are used sparingly, as is sugar. Protein comes from soy products like tofu and tempeh, seitan (a chewy brown substance made from whole wheat flour), and, of course, combinations of vegetables, nuts, and grains. This restaurant looks and feels like a French bistro until you open the menu and see a dish like Breaded Pan-Sautéed Seitan Medallions. Then you know you're in California.

The kitchen does a pretty good job of turning out appetizing food using such a restricted palette of ingredients. Some dishes work; some don't. But by the end of a meal practically everyone leaves satisfied and feeling good. The food sits lightly on the stomach. Meals begin with warm house-made whole-wheat baguettes and garlicky tofu spread. Starters include some fine salads, such as the Green Gulch butterball, which brings together seasonal fruits with big soft leaves of butter lettuce in a sparkling oil-free, citrus-mint vinaigrette. One would be happy to get a salad like this in any restaurant. Warm spinach salad with mushrooms, red onions, and smoked tofu in a balsamic and extra virgin olive oil vinaigrette falls into this category, too. A grilled portobello mushroom is particularly satisfying in a Moroccan vinaigrette, meaty and bright. Stay away from the phyllo-wrapped dishes. Without butter between the layers, the dough becomes sodden and pasty.

After many years in the Civic Center, Millennium moved to the handsome Brasserie Savoy space, where the staff takes advantage of the commodious three-sided central bar to pour thirty organic wines by the glass. (The restaurant has the first all-organic wine list in the country.) The former shellfish counter in the back has been transformed into a dessert bar. Contemporary décor and dramatic flowers bring new chic to the experience of dining on clean, organic, vegan fare.

NAAN 'N' CURRY . . . .

533 Jackson Street (at Columbus)
415-693-0499
Open daily 11:30 A.M. to midnight
Inexpensive
Cash only

Very much in the Shalimar tradition (see page 115), Naan 'N' Curry specializes in searing-hot, saucy curries and chewy flat breads baked to order on the side of the tandoor oven. The rock-bottom prices and relatively quick counter service classifies this bare-bones joint as an exotic fast-food restaurant. Any of the vegetable curries, such as smoldering *bengan bharta*, smoky eggplant and chopped tomatoes in a turmeric-yellow sauce, eaten with a plate of saffron-speckled basmati rice and a spectacular clay oven–blistered naan stuffed with onions and brushed with ghee (clarified butter), makes for a pretty wonderful $6 meal. I like the food here because it's alive, vibrant with fresh spices, smoldering with really hot peppers, and cooked to order. At these prices don't expect the meats to melt in your mouth, but all the curries generate high energy. If you stick to the advertised naan and curries (as opposed to tandoor-cooked meats), you'll be dropping in again and again. The food is addictive. Naan 'N' Curry does a large to-go business and also delivers.

ORIGINAL JOE'S . . . .

144 Taylor Street (between
Eddy and Turk)
415-775-4877
www.originaljoes.net
Open Sunday through Thursday
10:30 A.M. to midnight, Friday and
Saturday 10 A.M. to 12:30 A.M.
Inexpensive
Credit cards: AE, D, MC, V

Once you've tasted Original Joe's famous ¾-pound hamburger steaks formed from coarsely ground beef, coated in chopped onions, and cooked medium-rare on the griddle, you'll brave the neighborhood to eat here. This restaurant has been cranking out quintessential Joe's-type grill food for over a half century: inexpensive, plentiful, of amazingly high quality. It's a cuisine based on beef (which the kitchen butchers itself from sides); sourdough bread; precooked pasta in meat sauce; fresh, if much-cooked, vegetables; and some daily long-cooked braised dishes. The way the San Francisco sourdough bread is handled, for example—hollowed out, buttered, and grilled for hamburgers; sliced and bakery fresh with lots of pats of cold salted butter for the tables; pressed and griddled for gigantic ham and cheese sandwiches—teaches you something about the practical wisdom of San Francisco's culinary past.

Once you've made it to the front door (there are attended parking lots directly next door and across the street) on one of the funkiest blocks in the Tenderloin, you can sit in one of the commodious ancient booths or grab a seat at the counter in front of the cooking line. Some people like to hide away in the dark, once smoky barroom with booths. Original Joe's feeds a lot of older neighborhood residents every day. They order one of the reasonably priced dishes, eat a third of it, and take the rest home to have for dinner and breakfast the next day. To tell you the truth, that's what I do, too. I'm addicted to that hamburger steak, hot from the griddle and cold in the morning.

PALIO D'ASTI . . . .

640 Sacramento Street (between
Montgomery and Kearny)
415-395-9800
www.paliodasti.com
Open Monday through Friday
11:30 A.M. to 2:30 P.M. and
5:30 to 9 P.M.
Moderate
Credit cards: AE, CB, DC, D,
MC, V

The energy behind this alluring modern Italian restaurant comes from Gianni Fassio, whose family owned the original Blue Fox a block away. In a complete break from family tradition, he insists upon serving the dishes he ate in Italy during his years as an international accountant there. This means house-baked Italian breads and breadsticks; house-made pastas with rustic, long-cooked game sauces in winter; or delicate ravioli filled with fontina and toasted almonds, tossed with spinach and truffle oil. Unfortunately, under the current chef you might also encounter calamari fried in bad-smelling commercial fat, dried-out presliced prosciutto served with tough cheese "crisp," and stuck-together gnocchi. Former chef Craig Stoll left to open his own place, Delfina (see page 179), and the Palio kitchen now lacks consistency. The large restaurant still admirably makes practically everything they serve on the premises, including pasta and focaccia, which they supply to their *paninoteca* (Italian sandwich shop) and café around the corner on Montgomery Street (see page 121).

The theme of the Palio, Siena's fabled bareback horse race that takes place in the central piazza twice a year, is manifested in colorful banners hanging from the ceiling. The expansive modern concrete-and-glass space is broken up by three glassed-in display kitchens, a smart bar, and comfortable upholstered booths and linen-covered tables.

When ridiculously expensive white truffles come to town, or fresh porcini, or very rare, aged balsamic vinegar, you can depend on Palio to have them. Fassio sees his restaurant as an outpost of Italian culture.

POSTRIO . . . .

545 Post Street (between
Taylor and Mason)
415-776-7825
Open Monday through Saturday
11:30 A.M. to 2 P.M., Sunday
11 A.M. to 2 P.M.; Sunday through
Wednesday 5:30 to 10 P.M.,
Thursday through Saturday until
10:30 P.M.; upstairs café open
11 A.M. to midnight
Expensive
Credit cards: AE, DC, D, JCB,
MC, V

The two great originating chefs, Annie and David Gingrass, left to open their own restaurants, Hawthorne Lane (see page 351) and Desiree (see page 163), and the eclectic, flamboyant California food has not been the same, though service continues to be as impeccable and intelligent as always. On two visits I tasted most of the menu. A number of the old dishes remain, but they don't sparkle. Muddled, illogical combinations, over-the-top seasoning, and general lack of restraint characterize the new offerings. This change in the performance of the kitchen has in no way dampened the popularity of this restaurant, however.

The expansive Pat Kuleto–designed dining room with a completely open kitchen practically roars. The restaurant starts at street level with an always-packed bar with its own wood-burning pizza oven and menu, then lowers a level to a mezzanine that is a bit quieter for dining, then cascades down a dramatic staircase into the main dining hall. That staircase has provided an entrance for many a costume, many a celebrity, many an indiscreet pairing. Postrio is fun in that way. It's always full because Prescott Hotel guests get preferential reservations. You have to call way in advance to get a prime-time table, but regulars sneak in. When anyone glamorous comes to town from Los Angeles, they always hit this Wolfgang Puck restaurant. For locals, its location near Union Square makes it a natural for a pretheater dinner or a downtown lunch. The scene has become the draw.

RUBICON . . . .

558 Sacramento Street (between
Sansome and Montgomery)
415-434-4100
www.myriadrestaurantgroup.com
Open Wednesday for lunch
11:30 A.M. to 2:30 P.M.; Monday
through Thursday 5:30 to 10 P.M.,
Friday and Saturday until 10:30 P.M.
Jazz band every Friday 6 to 9 P.M.
Expensive
Credit cards: AE, DC, MC, V

Rubicon, the San Francisco outpost of Manhattan restaurant wizard Drew Nieporent, with backing from local celebs like Francis Ford Coppola (who bottles a blended red wine called Rubicon from his Napa Valley vineyard and winery), is a restaurant built around a wine guru. Professor, lover, and certified master of wine, Larry Stone has put together a deep and personal wine list that he deconstructs for any table that shows an interest. Though not cheap by any means, the list is so broad and interesting that Stone can plumb it for a wine that will titillate the palate and suit the pocketbook, while making your meal taste even better. The other night I saw him presenting bottle after bottle of expensive-looking red to a large table of handsome people headed by Robin Williams, who kept nodding his head. On my other side, wine writer Robert Finnegan went into deep consultation with Stone over the list. Stone keeps up-to-the-minute on every release, practically worldwide, and colleagues pick his brain. An academic-turned-wine-nut, he attacks his field with passion and an infallible nose and palate. He once told me that 40 percent of sales at Rubicon come from wine, an astounding figure considering that the fine dining standard runs about 20 percent. Wine groupies come to Rubicon to pay homage.

He works with a terrific kitchen started by Traci Des Jardins, who now owns Jardinière (see page 55). Under current chef Dennis Leary (formerly sous chef under Des Jardins), the kitchen carries on in the same elegant, local ingredient–driven style, incorporating all the most interesting vegetables. One spring menu was sprinkled with favas, fresh peas, chanterelles, asparagus, spring onions, leeks, bitter greens, rhubarb, fennel, radishes, portobello mushrooms, and Jerusalem artichokes; a recent fall menu offered cardoon, brussels sprouts, parsnips, salsify, porcini, figs, and persimmons. The cooks work them into dishes using traditional European techniques. You never have to suffer piles of undercooked cardoon or greens here.

This is not eclectic, California winging-it cooking, but California-inspired French–New York cooking that boasts depth over style. The food here really goes with wine, and at Rubicon the combination of the two can be a revelation. Just remember to bring an extra credit card.

Drew Nieporent originally made his reputation on two downtown Manhattan warehouse conversions—Montrachet and the Tribeca Grill—and physically Rubicon reminds me of the latter with its location in an earthquakeproofed red-brick firehouse in the heart of the Financial District. While the downstairs with its small bar, cozy tables, and booths draws on the natural charm of the old building, the larger upstairs dining room feels a bit faceless, an open space with earthquake bracing. Try to snag a table on the first floor, though in either location you'll eat and drink superbly.

SAM'S GRILL . . . .

374 Bush Street (at Kearny)
415-421-0594
www.samsgrill.com
Open Monday through Friday
11 A.M. to 9 P.M.
Moderate
Credit cards: AE, DC, D, MC, V

I include historic Sam's because I love the way it looks. The ancient wood-paneled dining room, the private cubicles with buzzers to summon the waiters, the solid-looking facade broken only by a small rectangular window covered with blinds conjure up the old days in San Francisco when Financial District office buildings emptied every day at lunch and people sat down to real noontime meals. Sam's was one of the most popular, masculine, no-nonsense grill rooms and actually, it still is. Order only local fish like sand dabs, petrale, and salmon. Have a seafood salad or cold asparagus with mustard sauce and a few slices of sourdough. Have a cocktail or a bottle of wine and there you are. Don't stray much further than this. The restaurant closes early and the liveliest time is at lunch.

SANRAKU FOUR SEASONS . . . .

704 Sutter Street (at Taylor)
415-771-0803
www.sanraku.com
Open Monday through Saturday
11 A.M. to 10 P.M.,
Sunday 4 to 10 P.M.
Moderate
Credit cards: AE, DC, D, MC, V

An adjunct to an excellent, inexpensive Japanese restaurant that has been open for over twenty years (called Sanraku), the Four Seasons puts on imaginative $30 four-course meals Monday through Saturday nights from 6 to 9 P.M. in a special dining room next door. The meal might begin with a "summer dish" of noodles and various toppings; proceed to a deep-fried dish featuring sea bass and vegetables; then to an outright French presentation of sliced steak in a red wine sauce, with an ending of fruit. Though the order-ahead multi-course *kaiseki* meals are no longer available, Sanraku Four Seasons still offers an opportunity to taste a kind of Japanese cooking gently influenced by the West, presented in traditional Japanese form.

The linen-covered Western-style tables in a peaceful gray and beige dining room are set only with red lacquer place mats and a pair of black wooden chopsticks. A few intriguing brush paintings of geometric shapes and a ceramic pot are the only decorations in the room. The food and its presentation on ceramics appropriate to each dish create the aesthetic.

These meals offer all the lyricism and art of Japanese cooking along with a certain kind of Western exuberance. Though each course is elegant, they add up to generous, almost hearty meals, a bargain for the price. The focus is on freshness and flavor, not garnish, and the presentations seem organic to the food.

SEAR'S FINE FOODS . . . .

439 Powell Street (between
Post and Sutter)
415-986-1160
Open Thursday through Monday
7 A.M. to 2:30 P.M.
Inexpensive
Cash only

This beloved downtown breakfast and lunch spot remains one of the best places in the city for an old-fashioned American breakfast. Always start with a huge fresh fruit cup of high-quality fruit marinated in fresh orange juice, a must order here. If you're a one-fruit person, you can get bowls of berries in season, orange slices, juicy melons, papaya, or a large baked Rome Beauty apple served with cream. Then move on to Sear's famous eighteen Swedish pancakes, six baby stacks of airy pancakes the size and thickness of half-dollars that have real character; or Sear's crisp, dark brown waffles with tender eggy interiors; or French toast made of well-soaked sourdough bread served with a small cup of Sear's own strawberry preserves, really a barely sweetened compote. The Canadian bacon truly is the best obtainable anywhere as the menu boasts, and the smoked country sausage, made especially for Sear's and served in crisp patties, is excellent, too. At lunch, after an egg salad sandwich or a BLT, have fresh strawberry shortcake or a fresh-fruit deep-dish pie that comes in a glass cereal bowl filled to the top. If anyone staying around Union Square asks you to meet them for breakfast, do yourself a favor and suggest Sear's. It's also a big favorite with kids.

SHALIMAR . . . .

532 Jones Street (between
Geary and O'Farrell)
415-928-0333
Open daily noon to 3 P.M.
and 5 to 11:30 P.M.
Inexpensive
Cash only

Grungy Shalimar defines the great, inexpensive neighborhood restaurant, a necessity in San Francisco where housing costs eat up the lion's share of most incomes. With such vibrant food, it's no wonder all sorts of people make their way here—suits and ties at lunch, bike messenger types, international tourists, neighborhood residents getting takeout. The restaurant, located on the better edge of the Tenderloin, is a bare-bones room with fluorescent lighting, vinyl-topped tables, and an open kitchen with seven Pakistani men working in it. A constant stream of people walk through the usually open front door to the front counter to order from a short, descriptive menu of curries, tandoor-cooked meats, and breads. Then, the guests set their own tables and watch for their order to be set on the counter. In very little time their fragrant dishes appear in small rimmed bowls filled to the top. If you don't recognize your order, the counterman will summon you. He remembers every face and every order. For well under $10 you can feast on Pakistani and Indian dishes that are fresh, cooked to order, and alive with aromatic spices.

All five of the vegetable curries are scrumptious. I could make a meal out of any one of them with Shalimar's beautiful basmati rice, the distinct grains dotted with whole spices and dappled with yellow saffron. With generous squirts of chile-heated *raita* (yogurt) in plastic squeeze bottles at the table and naan (tandoor-baked bread), you've got yourself a luscious, bargain vegetarian meal. For diversity add a beef shish kabob, ground meat and spices molded onto a skewer and roasted in the tandoor oven.

Thermoses kept on one side of the kitchen near the silverware keep milky, grass-flavored tea super-hot. You pour it into Styrofoam cups and add your own sugar. Water comes in Styrofoam too, or you can choose a soda or fruit drink from the refrigerator case. Bypass dessert.

When you finish, go back to the counter to settle up. The order-taker will remember everything you've eaten and hand you an adding machine tape with an amazingly modest bill.

Shalimar's food reminds me of Indian food I've eaten in India, full of whole spices, smoldering, alive.

TADICH GRILL . . . .

240 California Street (between
Front and Battery)
415-391-2373
Open Monday through Friday
11 A.M. to 9:30 P.M.,
Saturday 11:30 A.M. to 9:30 P.M.
Moderate
Credit cards: MC, V

A Yugoslavian family has run this historic fish house since the turn of the last century, grilling fresh fish over mesquite charcoal and cranking out a fascinating menu printed daily all these years in offset type. The menus themselves are souvenirs, documents of culinary history, full of dinosaurs such as lobster Newberg, halibut Florentine, and deviled crab. The best way to proceed is to ask your crusty waiter what fish has come in fresh that day and order it simply charcoal grilled or panfried. What a pleasure it is to hang your coat on a brass hook at Tadich's, grab a seat at the long, oval wooden counter, and dig into a fresh seafood salad slathered with an excellent Louie sauce, and a plate of buttery griddled sand dabs or rex sole served with Tadich's gigantic fried potatoes. The rex sole, which are small, flavorful local fish, are also delicious charcoal grilled, eaten with mounds of Tadich's unique and addictive tartar sauce thickened with sieved potato. The waiters will quickly fillet them for you, an old-fashioned luxury. Creamed spinach, sautéed spinach, thick clam chowder, and poached salmon with chopped egg sauce are other Tadich favorites. The wine list is simple and cheap—most people still have cocktails here. For dessert, there are huge baked Rome Beauty apples and rice custard pudding, which work perfectly after the straightforward meals.

The wonderful-looking dining room is paneled in ancient dark wood with compartments that enclose small linen-covered tables and bentwood chairs. The original pressed-plaster ceiling, a white-tiled floor, and a busy wooden counter with wooden chairs that swivel on pedestals set the scene for a timeless experience, especially since most of the uniformed waiters have been here forever. There's always a crowd at the door having a drink at the small bar and waiting for one of the not-so-plentiful tables. However, if you don't want to wait, you can usually get a seat immediately at the counter, where the stools turn over quickly and the regulars are gracious about moving over to accommodate a pair who want to sit together.

CAFÉS

ARMANI CAFE . . . .

1 Grant Avenue (between
O'Farrell and Stockton)
415-677-9010
Open Monday through Saturday
11:30 A.M. to 4:30 P.M., drinks
until 5 P.M., Sunday noon to
4:30 P.M., drinks until 5 P.M.
Moderate
Credit cards: AE, D, DC, MC, V

The Armani Cafe consists of a large oval island of counters and stools in the middle of an imposing former bank building now filled with Armani suits. Sidewalk tables are put out during good weather and are always full. Like the shoes, purses, toiletries, and other accoutrements of the Armani lifestyle, the cafe is an extension of Armani taste. In fact, it was reported during the opening that the king himself designed the menu and cafe. Peculiarly enough, lunch here does have a European graciousness, even if you have to sit on your coat at the counter and drop your bags on the floor. An elegantly suited maître d' seats you, and if you have to wait, he'll track you down among the blouses.

The best dish on the small menu is the pizza Ortolano, a thin, chewy crust paved with fontina, chopped arugula, and radicchio drizzled with truffle oil. The bitter lettuces turn fruity as they melt into the fine imported cheese. A salad of artichokes, shaved Parmigiano, and baby greens with any of the pizzas and a glass of Italian merlot make for one of the best downtown lunches. The pastas are okay, but don't sparkle; the *antipasto misto* is a mishmash. Desserts, however, are worth ordering. I am partial to an espresso granita parfait—icy coffee crystals layered with sweetened whipped cream. The warm chocolate soufflé cake served in a little white dish topped with hazelnut ice cream oozes in a very seductive way. Espresso is top-notch.

CAFÉ CLAUDE . . . .

7 Claude Lane (off Bush
between Grant and Kearny)
415-392-3505
www.cafeclaude.com
Open Monday through Saturday
8 A.M. to 11 A.M. and
11:30 A.M. to 4 P.M.; Tuesday
through Saturday 5:30 to 10 P.M.
Inexpensive
Credit cards: AE, D, MC, V

This is one of my favorite lunch places in the city because it so captures the spirit of the cafés I love in Paris. In fact, all the furnishings come from a small bar and *tabac* in the eleventh arrondissement that was about to be torn down. Café Claude's owner saved most of the interior intact and had it shipped to San Francisco, so the small, hidden-away space is full of vintage fifties French café chairs, banquettes, and tables, a bona fide zinc bar, and old cinema posters. The food and wines are typical: the delicious, crusty grilled-cheese sandwiches called *croque-monsieur*, with a cheesy béchamel broiled on top of the sandwich and smoky Black Forest ham inside; green salad in a simple vinaigrette; *assiettes*, or plates of charcuterie or smoked trout with vegetable salads; an authentic *salade niçoise*; and French-style sandwiches on very fresh buttered baguettes with thin slices of *saucisson sec* or ham inside. To wash all this down, glasses of inexpensive Rhône, Beaujolais, and Mâcon blanc are sold by the glass, just as in France. The coffee is strong and the waiters are French, young, and cute.

CAFÉ DE LA PRESSE . . . .

352 Grant Avenue (at Bush)
415-398-2680
Open weekdays 7 A.M. to 10 P.M.,
weekends 7 A.M. to 11 P.M.
Credit cards: AE, MC, V

Sitting at one of the outdoor tables hugging the building at Grant and Bush, across from the entrance to Chinatown, makes you part of the international tourist circuit that flows by this very corner. I like to dive in, if even for an hour, at Café de la Presse, which is next to the groovily decorated Triton Hotel (check out the lobby). The café not only serves a decent *salade niçoise* and a generous prosciutto and melon plate with a good baguette, but it also houses one of the best international newspaper and magazine stands in the city, so you can buy your *International Herald Tribune* and pretend you're an American in Paris, or your *Le Monde* and pretend you're French. Two drawbacks: the waiters are sweet-natured but incompetent, and the Rhône and Beaujolais taste identical, as if they were bought at a French supermarket, a bit of authenticity I could do without.

CAFÉ NIEBAUM-COPPOLA . . . .

916 Kearny Street (at Columbus)
415-291-1700
www.cafeniebaum-coppola.com
Open Monday through Saturday
11 A.M. to 10 P.M.,
Sunday noon to 9 P.M.
Credit Cards: AE, D, MC, V

Film director Francis Ford Coppola has installed one of his meticulously designed, stage-set cafés in the tiny triangular space on the ground floor of the historic San Francisco building he uses for his Zoetrope offices. If you want to run into locals like Sean Penn, movie directors, actors, a scriptwriter of the moment, or Francis himself, hang out here. Most of the tables are on the sidewalk under awnings, either on Columbus or

Kearny. A few tables and a tiny bar are squeezed inside an exquisite room furnished with marble tables and shelves of Coppola signature products that range from spaghetti and jarred marinara sauce to glassware and Italian pottery. Everything surrounding you, whether it can be purchased or not, looks as if it were airlifted from Italy—including the waiters who have a *molto* casual attitude about service.

Order a thin-crusted pizza with proscuitto and arugula, a tumbler of Coppola rosso, and an espresso, and you'll be playing out a scene in your own movie set in Rome.

CAFE PRAGUE . . . .

584 Pacific Avenue (at Kearny)
415-433-3811
Open weekdays 7:30 A.M. to
midnight, Saturday 11 A.M. to
2 A.M., Sunday 11 A.M. to 11 P.M.
Cash only

If you're lonely for the smoky cafés in the cobblestone alleyways of historic Prague, here's your place. The Czech-speaking staff, the Czech magazines and journals, the notes and cultural announcements in Czech on the walls, the Old World ambience—dark, homey, and old-fashioned with sofas, wooden tables, and a cluttered ordering bar—will make an émigré feel at home. The front opens completely onto the sidewalk where cafe-goers can have a smoke with better coffee than they can find across the St. Charles Bridge. People like to pass the time here at this refuge and hangout on the edge of downtown.

ZERO DEGREES. . . . .

470 Pacific Avenue (at
Montgomery)
415-788-9376
Open Monday through Friday
7 A.M. to 7 P.M.
Credit Cards: AE, DC, MC, V

At Zero Degrees, the airy café next door to MC^2 (see page 108), I had a very pleasant late lunch one day sitting at a high table in the window. I chose from the Zero Degrees specialties section a sandwich evocatively called Devil's Acre that really hit it for me. Layers of smoked prosciutto, black olives, and *peperoncini* came on a thin foccacia roll, served with a simply dressed *mesclun* salad. The salty, smoky sandwich was counterbalanced by the clean, herbal greens. Chef Todd Davies from MC^2 came up with a good one here. I finished with a single scoop of the brightest apricot sorbet I've ever tasted, served in a metal dish with a squared-off European ice cream spoon. The café offers no less than six house-made gelati and *sorbetti*. I tasted until I found the one I liked. I didn't like the thin look of an espresso as it was handed across the counter, so I asked for another. The request was gladly granted by another counterperson, and the second espresso did please me. In fact, the whole little meal buoyed my spirits. I'm coming back to this hip spot, with its magazine rack, tons of light, sidewalk seating, arty clientele, and access to the riches from the MC^2 kitchen. Next time I'm having one of those paper-thin pizzalike Alsatian tarts so I can eat it all myself.

BIX . . . .

54 Gold Street (off Montgomery
between Pacific and Jackson)
415-433-6300
www.bixrestaurant.com
Open Monday through Friday 5 P.M.
to 2 A.M., Saturday 5:30 P.M. to
2 A.M., Sunday 6 P.M. to 2 A.M.

Most sophisticated San Franciscans consider the bar at Bix to be the best in town. Long before owner Doug Biederbeck got the food together at the restaurant (see page 97), the bar shone, stocked with the best and rarest booze, Champagnes, wines, elegant glassware, and classic cocktail shakers, and nimble bartenders in white steward's jackets—all the traditional accoutrements of the urbane American watering hole. A combo plays, the handsome crowd mingles, the drinks flow. When a friend asked me where she should take her twenty-one-year-old grandson for his first public martini, only one place came to mind. I hope to be drinking my last martini there, right along with Doug Biederbeck.

HARRY DENTON'S STARLIGHT ROOM . . . . .

450 Powell Street (atop the
St. Francis Drake Hotel between
Post and Sutter)
415-395-8595
www.harrydenton.com
Open daily 6 P.M. to 2 A.M.
Credit cards: AE, D, MC, V

Bon vivant Harry Denton knows what it takes to throw a party every night. On the twenty-first floor of the Sir Francis Drake, now a Kimpton Hotel, Denton has a venue with wraparound views, a small dance floor, a DJ booth, and yards and yards of red drapery. Small round tables draped in white tablecloths fill every nook and cranny. The room is furnished with couches and chairs, plush, intimate booths, and tall, slender cocktail waitresses in long, clinging black satin. The best booze—Appleton Jamaican rum, Basil Hayden bourbon—is poured in special house drinks. Bar food is inexpensive and ample, like a huge bowl of marinated olives and pickled peppers with breadsticks for a few dollars. Caviar is practically sold at cost. Out-of-towners (i.e., anyone who does not live in San Francisco proper) love this room. It has become a must for a night on the town.

RED ROOM . . . .

827 Sutter Street (between
Jones and Leavenworth)
415-346-7666
Open daily from 5 P.M. to 2 A.M.
Credit Cards: D, MC, V

This is a typical San Francisco bar—intimate, retro, really red. Every surface is red except for the sexy bartendresses who dress in black, have black hair, wear black lipstick, and show plenty of décolletage. You can sit on red stools at the curved red bar or on red banquettes at red vinyl tables. Drinks are well made and generously poured. Located in the Commodore Hotel, which is owned by hip hotel entrepreneur Chip Conley, the successful Red Room still maintains its highly coveted underground status, which, of course, keeps it popular.

REDWOOD ROOM . . . .

Clift Hotel, 495 Geary Street
(at Taylor)
415-929-2300
Open daily 6 P.M. to 2 A.M.
Credit cards: AE, D, MC, V

The best way to experience the multicultural food at Asia de Cuba and the wonders of the new Ian Schrager and Philippe Starck–designed Clift Hotel is to sidle up to the dramatically lit mirrored bar in the still beautiful Redwood Room, redecorated but still, thank goodness, intact. Even Philippe Starck knew that nothing could top the resonant redwood paneled walls, carved redwood columns, and high, high redwood ceiling. He refurnished with groovy squared-off leather sofas and low tables, but the wood-paneled walls remain unscathed, decorated only with projected images of Roberto Clemente works. The grandeur of the historic room lives on.

I like to go for a cocktail early, during cocktail hour before dinner, ahead of the partying hordes. I sit at the bar and have a *mojito* made with lime-flavored light rum, lots of muddled fresh mint, soda, and a floater of dark rum. This drink can make me float, so I order an Asia de Cuba "shooter." Asia de Cuba, a small upscale chain of restaurants started in New York, does the food next door in the old French Room. A shooter is simply a small version of a cold appetizer on the Asia de Cuba menu. For a third of the price you get a very generous serving of a signature dish like Tunapica, a tuna ceviche spiked with chopped Spanish olives, black currants, almonds, and coconut in a soy-lime vinaigrette, and a salad of pickled Japanese cucumbers and daikon, all layered in a cocktail glass and served with wonton crisps. This delicious, juicy appetizer goes particularly well with *mojitos*. To top it off, the cute, professional bartenders tend to be charming and friendly early in the shift, before the crowds arrive.

DELICATESSENS/TAKEOUT

BLONDIE'S . . . .

63 Powell Street (between
Ellis and Market)
415-982-6168
Open Monday through Saturday
10:30 A.M. to 9 P.M.,
Sunday 10:30 A.M. to 8 P.M.
Cash only

Blondie's, the by-the-slice factory on Powell Street near Market, epitomizes the pizza that adolescents love. The huge wedges have pillowy crusts and copious, if well-proportioned toppings of tomato sauce, mozzarella, and spicy, oily pepperoni. The lines never end and the slices are sold as fast as the pies are baked. The original Blondie's, which closed for almost a year during a renovation of its building, reopened in a grander space that looks more like a fast-food restaurant. My resident pizza expert claims that prices are higher and slices smaller. It is true that a slice of pepperoni now costs $2.75, a price hike, but the size of the slice is the same as always. Blondie's confirmed that they still bake 20-inch pies and cut them into sixths. At $2.75, a Blondie's slice is still an enormous bargain, and frankly, I find it difficult to walk by the shop without buying one.

322 Kearny Street (between
Pine and Bush)
415-986-1052
Open Monday through Friday
6:30 A.M. to 5 P.M.
Cash only

Currently there are ten other Lee's Delis scattered throughout the Financial District, all enumerated on their menu of ridiculously inexpensive, quickly made sandwiches. Lee's sandwiches, the Chevrolets of the sandwich world, are simple American workhorse sandwiches, unfrilled, generous, and tasty. The sandwich girls must use the equivalent of a whole can of tuna, properly moistened with decent commercial mayonnaise, on a tuna sandwich on white bread—for $2.75. I like it only with ground pepper, but standard additions include lettuce, tomato, pickles, mayonnaise, and mustard (God forbid on a tuna sandwich) with onions, peppers, and some other condiment options. You only pay a small tariff for the addition of cheese or avocado, and for a roll (Dutch crunch, sweet or sourdough French, and so forth) instead of bread. Lee's serves only freshly roasted turkey breast cut into rather thick slices and piled on the sandwiches. The turkey has earned Lee's many loyal customers.

This particular Lee's branch on Kearny offers seating on two levels in the back overlooking Belden Place, an alley blocked off to traffic and filled with outdoor tables belonging to other restaurants. You may be eating a tuna on white, but the view outside could be Paris.

PALIO PANINOTECA . . . .

505 Montgomery Street (between
Sacramento and Commercial)
415-362-6900
www.paliopaninoteca.com
Open Monday through Friday
6 A.M. to 4 P.M.
Credit cards: AE, DC, MC, V

Just like the sandwich shops you see everywhere in Italy, this *paninoteca* has a case of premade sandwiches ready and waiting, which you can buy by the half or whole and have grilled. Owned and operated by Gianni Fassio of Palio d'Asti around the corner, ingredients and concept are authentically Italian and sophisticated, down to the cleverly designed wrapping. I take the tomatoes out of the prosciutto and mascarpone sandwich on a soft focaccia bun, which I like grilled. Who needs the distraction when such fine proscuitto nestles within? The Nostromo—tuna, capers, red onions, gherkins, diced red pepper, and radicchio all finely chopped and blended together on soft white Italian bread with a crunchy crust gets my vote as the best tuna sandwich in town—even without mayonnaise! It's delicious. So is the espresso. You really feel as if you've stepped into a shop in Milan. For other locations, see pages 111 and 378.

SPECIALTY'S CAFE AND BAKERY . . . .

22 Battery Street
(at Bush and Market)
415-398-4691 (for daily
specials call 415-896-2253)
www.specialtys.com
Open Monday through Friday
6 A.M. to 6 P.M.
Cash only

150 Spear Street
(between Mission and Howard)
415-978-9662

101 New Montgomery Street
(at Mission)
415-512-9550

369 Pine Street (between
Montgomery and Sansome)
415-896-2253

505 Sansome (at Clay)
415-896-2253

1 Post Street
(at Montgomery and Market)
415-896-9550

Americans love sandwiches, but they must be made in our national style. American sandwiches have more filling than bread, unlike the meager slice of prosciutto or cured sausage that gets lost in an Italian or French baguette. We want nothing of the Danish open-faced variety. The English may have invented the sandwich, but their dry, skinny version spread with margarine gives sandwiches a bad name. To Americans, the sandwich is a meal you can hold in your hand. The best ones have to be juicy, rich, texturally varied, a little spicy, and almost impossible to bite through.

Specialty's, a fifteen-year-old sandwich company now with eight Bay Area locations, understands the American sandwich and is a favorite with the office set. The success of its concept revolves around soft, airy, just-baked breads used in forty different sandwich combinations. Each has a multitude of ingredients and the effect in the best matchups is symphonic: the whole is greater than the individually undistinguished parts.

One of my favorites is No. 11, the Italian, a conglomeration of paper-thin slices of salami, bologna, mortadella, Swiss, mild peppers, provolone, *peperoncini*, and the basic setup of lettuce, tomato, pickles, onions, and black pepper, with mayonnaise and spicy brown mustard on potato–poppy seed bread. All these bland American-style cold cuts add up to a savory submarine-style sandwich with a charm of its own.

Another hands-down favorite with everyone is No. 25, the Vegetarian, the classic California combo of avocado, cheese, mushrooms, and ranch dressing—like a salad between two pieces of soft bread. In addition to the sandwiches, a large variety of warm, puffy, gigantic sweet and savory pastries are baked each hour, including huge coiled buns of white bread slathered with great amounts of Cheddar cheese and sliced pickled jalapeño peppers. The outlets are well-staffed counter operations, and the lines that invariably form at 11:30 A.M. move quickly and efficiently. These operations cleverly take the quickly made lunchtime sandwich to a higher level of freshness and appeal.

FOG CITY NEWS . . . .

455 Market Street (at intersection of
Bush, Battery, and 1st Street)
415-543-7400
www.fogcitynews.com
Open Monday through Friday 8
A.M. to 6 P.M.
Credit cards: MC, V

Fog City News is the largest magazine store in the Bay
Area with at least seventy-five different food magazines
and journals on its attractive wooden racks. But what
really qualifies it as a food lover's spot is its comprehensive assortment of high-end chocolate bars from all over
the world. Owner Adam Smith curates a collection of
over 150 stunning chocolates, annotated by an extraordinary "menu" of lively and opinionated descriptions of
each kind. Chocolate, like wine, has complex, evocative aromas and layered flavor and with
Smith's guide in hand, you can cultivate your chocolate palate.

Personally, I cannot walk by Fog City without buying one of Fran's Coconut Gold
Bars, the ultimate Almond Joy, made with pure, whole ingredients, not hydrogenated poly-
unsaturated fats. This scrumptious, dark chocolate coconut bar is actually good for you—if
you're not counting calories. You can lose yourself for hours browsing the imported and
domestic chocolate bars and the magazines.

MORROW'S NUT HOUSE . . . .

111 Geary Street (between
Grant and Stockton)
415-362-7969
Open Tuesday through Saturday
10 A.M. to 5:30 P.M
Credit cards: MC, V
($10 minimum)

I challenge you to walk by this tiny nut shop without
stopping in to buy at least a quarter pound of nuts. The
irresistible aroma of roasting (actually deep-frying) nuts
wafts out the always-open door and practically pulls
you inside. The nuts are of the highest quality: huge,
fresh, and whole. The cashews are the size of a child's
thumb, and the pecans, an adult toe. Almonds, Brazil
nuts, and hazelnuts all look even plumper glistening in
nut oil. Morrow's keeps roasting all day, so the nuts are always warm when you get them,
but never stale or rancid. A box, even a small bag, of these fresh, fragrant mixed nuts makes
just about the best gift I know.

SEE'S CANDIES . . . .

542 Market Street (at Sansome)
415-362-1593
www.sees.com
Open Monday through Friday
9 A.M. to 6:30 P.M.
Credit cards: AE, DC, D, MC, V

Two branches of San Francisco's famous candy store where the buttery chocolates, toffees, and caramels are always fresh. See page 334 for more information.

846 Market Street (between
Powell and Stockton)
415-434-2771
Open Monday through Saturday
9 A.M. to 7 P.M.,
Sunday 10:30 A.M. to 6 P.M.

ZERO DEGREES . . . .

470 Pacific Avenue
(at Montgomery)
415-788-9376
Open Monday through Friday
7 A.M. to 7 P.M.
Credit Cards: AE, DC, MC, V

This airy modern café offers no less than six stylish, house-made gelati and sorbetti. See page 118 for more information.

WINE AND SPIRITS

LONDON WINE BAR . . . .

415 Sansome Street (at Sacramento)
415-788-4811
Open Monday through Friday
11:30 A.M. to 9 P.M.
Credit cards: AE, D, MC, V

Fifteen to twenty California wines and five or so French ones are poured by the glass at this clubby, wood-paneled, British-style wine bar and store, in addition to pours from interesting magnums and jeroboams of older California wines. Half bottles of white Burgundy, glasses of port and sherry, and a veritable wine cellar of bottles await tasting. What a perfect way to decide what to buy! While the English-publike food is serviceable at best, the wine-tasting opportunities are first rate. Owner Gary Lockes picks for the bar, and special sales on wines by the case are worth noting. The dual roles of retail store and tasting room work together to help people find the wines they like.

CRATE&BARREL . . . .

55 Stockton Street (at O'Farrell)
415-982-5200
www.crateandbarrel.com
Open Monday through Wednesday
10 A.M. to 7 P.M., Thursday through
Saturday 10 A.M. to 8 P.M.,
Sunday 11 A.M. to 6 P.M.
Credit cards: AE, D, MC, V

A good place to find simple, handsome dishware and glasses that will wear well and not cost a fortune, Crate&Barrel prides itself on uncovering these bargains from all over the world. About ten years ago I found some delicate, classic U-shaped handblown wineglasses with the thinnest stems and rims, just the right size for white wines and most reds. I bought two dozen and have tried to replace them ever since, but Crate&Barrel discontinued them. So my advice to you is, if you find a plate or a glass that you really like, buy enough of them because you probably won't get a second chance.

MACY'S . . . .

Union Square
(Stockton and O'Farrell)
415-397-3333
www.macys.com
Open Monday through Saturday
10 A.M. to 8 P.M.,
Sunday 11 A.M. to 7 P.M.
Credit cards: AE, MC, V

I always think I can find just the small appliance I need at Macy's, but actually this seemingly large department only stocks one or two brands of items like juicers, toasters, or blenders, often not the one I'm trying to replace. The new model either does more than I want or not quite what I want, but maybe that's the complaint of someone who distrusts gadgets. However, I have found that getting service in this department is no easy matter, so I can't even be persuaded that the model they have in stock is really better.

The extensive pots and pans department at Macy's is another matter. It carries all levels of cooking equipment, from old-fashioned copper-bottomed stainless-steel Revere Ware to the latest generation of space-age, nonstick, nonscratch cooking-surface pans, stopping along the way to pay homage to Le Creuset's heavy enameled cooking pots. To my mind, some pieces from each line serve a cook better than monolithic matching sets. Many people ask my advice on what kind of pans they should buy, but unless I move in with them for a week to see how they cook, an answer is impossible. In my kitchen I couldn't live without a heavy nonstick saucepan with a glass cover for heating milk for coffee, which I bought at Macy's six years ago for $75. Since I use it every single day it was a terrific investment, amortized over the years. I have a nesting set of copper saucepans, a few cast-iron skillets, a few copper sauté pans, a heavy aluminum restaurant-style skillet, a pressure cooker, a large covered stockpot, a big Le Creuset covered casserole, and that's about it—except for a wok from Chinatown that I use all the time.

The casual dishware department harbors some charming painted dishes in five-piece place settings for four. The glassware selection is weak, but you can find treasures among the French white and painted serving dishes that fill one section. Many of them were on sale the last time I dropped by.

SUR LA TABLE . . . .

77 Maiden Lane (between
Grant and Kearny)
415-732-7900
www.surlatable.com
Open Monday through Saturday
10 A.M. to 6 P.M.
Credit cards: AE, D, MC, V

I thought that the Bay Area did not need another cookware store when Sur La Table opened its first store in Berkeley. Then I started sifting through the merchandise. Sure enough I found things that I didn't know I needed that were unique to this chain—a charming square platter hand painted with olive branches at a very attractive price, a huge wooden salad bowl actually big enough to toss a salad for six or eight, and one of the largest collections of cookbooks (over 700 titles I was told). If a recipe calls for a certain cake pan or mold, or you wanted to make cookies in the shape of sheep, or you need any basic kitchen tool or appliance, I would head here first. There are levels of tools at different prices and different styles of the same tool. As a peripatetic cook, I appreciate the depth of the merchandise in these stores. Everyone who has waited on me has been an absolute saint—patient, friendly, and knowledgeable. This really is a store for serious cooks, though the dabbler will find much here, too. Sur La Table also publishes a seasonal catalog and mounts an extensive schedule of cooking classes.

WILLIAMS-SONOMA . . . .

150 Post Street (between
Grant and Kearny)
415-362-6904
www.williams-sonoma.com
Open Monday through Saturday
9:30 a.m. to 7 p.m.,
Sunday 11 a.m. to 6 p.m.
Credit cards: AE, MC, V

865 Market Street (at 5th Street
in the San Francisco Centre)
415-546-0171
Open Monday through Saturday
9:30 a.m. to 8 p.m.,
Sunday 11 a.m. to 6 p.m.

The Post Street location has the biggest selection of merchandise of all the stores, from high-quality pots and pans in copper and high-tech materials to cookbooks, kitchen gadgets, and olive oil. If you're looking for the hard-to-find cooking item, like crème brûlée irons, or paella pans along with the rice, this is the place to look first. The prices are not cheap, but the cookware, small appliances, and utensils carried here have the company's backing, which includes a huge mail-order business and many branches. The buyers do their research; they read *Consumer Reports* and have enough buying power to make a manufacturer improve a product. So the one toaster they carry has been chosen for a reason, winning the competition for quality and price, though quality is the more important factor.

I have always found the clerks to be extremely helpful. If an item is out of stock, they will try to find it for you at another store, and they know their own inventories. They'll tell you exactly why Williams-Sonoma carries a specific item, and they're usually so convincing that you buy one. I've never been let down, and that includes the time I impulsively bought a bread machine for my husband who had yearned for one with every Williams-Sonoma catalog. It really works, if you like soft, airy bread with crisp crusts, and the smell of the warm loaf in the morning is better than an alarm clock. You also can find some handsome dishes and glasses for a moderate sum, and if you are tantalized by catalogs, Williams-Sonoma regularly sends out a thick one full of many items that you didn't know you needed until you saw them there, such as nonstick corn-stick molds in the shape of little ears of corn.

RAISED WAFFLES

MAKES ABOUT 8 WAFFLES

This classic waffle recipe from an early Fanny Farmer cookbook makes the lightest, crispiest, most flavorful waffles I know. I found it in Marion Cunningham's *The Breakfast Book*, which I use constantly. If there was ever a reason to buy a waffle iron, this recipe is it. The waffle irons sold today have Teflon coatings so that the waffles never stick and always come out golden brown.

2 cups milk

½ cup (1 stick) butter,
cut into chunks

1 teaspoon salt

1 teaspoon sugar

1 package active dry yeast

½ cup warm (105° to 115°F) water

2 cups all-purpose flour

2 eggs

¼ teaspoon baking soda

1 Put the milk, butter, salt, and sugar in a small saucepan. Gently warm over low heat until the butter is almost melted. Remove from heat and let cool to lukewarm.

2 In a large bowl, dissolve the yeast in the warm water. Add the milk mixture, then whisk in the flour until the batter is smooth and creamy. Cover with plastic wrap and let stand for 6 to 12 hours at room temperature.

3 The next morning, or just before cooking, whisk in the eggs and baking soda. The batter will be thin.

4 For each waffle, pour ½ to ¾ cup batter into a very hot waffle iron. Bake for about 5 minutes, or until golden and crisp.

LOWER AND UPPER HAIGHT
COLE VALLEY

LOWER HAIGHT, UPPER HAIGHT & COLE VALLEY

RESTAURANTS

1   Burger Joint
2   Burgermeister
3   Cha Cha Cha
4   Eos
5   Hama-ko
6   RNM Restaurant
7   Taqueria el Balazo
8   Thep Phanom

CAFÉS

9   Bean There
10   Boulange de Cole Valley

BARS

11   Club Deluxe
12   Kezar Bar & Restaurant
13   Noc Noc
14   Toronado

DELICATESSENS/TAKEOUT

15   Brother-in-Law's Bar-be-que
16   Estella's Fresh Sandwiches
17   Rosamunde Sausage Grill
18   Twilight Cafe and Deli

BAKERIES

10   Boulange de Cole Valley

ICE CREAM/CHOCOLATES

19   Gelato Classico

COFFEE

20   Coffee, Tea and Spice

PRODUCE

21   Real Food Company

CHEESE

22   Country Cheese
23   Say Cheese

COOKWARE AND BOOKS

24   Cookin'

N

WEBSTER

FILLMORE

STEINER

PIERCE

ALAMO
SQUARE

SCOTT

DIVISADERO

BRODERICK

BAKER

McALLISTER

LYON

W

CENTRAL

MASONIC

USF

PARKER

FULTON
GROVE
HAYES

FELL
PANHANDLE
OAK

PAGE
HAIGHT
WALLER

ASHBURY

CLAYTON

COLE

COLE

SHRADER

STANYAN

GOLDEN   GATE   PARK

CHURCH
MARKET

SANCHEZ

DUBOCE PARK

NOE

CASTRO

DUBOCE

14TH ST.

HENRY

BUENA

VISTA

BUENA
VISTA
PARK

AVE.

CORONA
HEIGHTS

E

BELVEDERE

FREDERICK
CARL
PARNASSUS

16
17 8
14
6 13
9

1

15   22   24

11

20
7

2
23   12   10
5   4

21   19

18

S

0   .25
SCALE MILES

RESTAURANTS

BURGER JOINT. . . . .

700 Haight Street (at Pierce)
415-864-3833
www.burgerjointsf.citysearch.com
Open daily from 11 A.M. to 11 P.M.
Inexpensive
Credit cards: DC, D, MC, V

This diner-style hamburger shop uses naturally raised Niman Ranch ground beef for its burgers and Double Rainbow ice cream for its thick shakes. See page 177 for more information.

BURGERMEISTER . . . .

86 Carl Street (near Cole)
415-566-1274
Open Monday through Saturday
11 A.M. to 10 P.M.,
Sunday until 9 P.M.
Inexpensive
Cash only

This adorable neighborhood place does one thing and does it right—the hamburger. Flavorful Niman Ranch ground beef, shaped into a large, thick, round patty, is beautifully grilled to exact specification and placed on a soft, warm sesame seed–encrusted bun with fresh tomato, generous butterleaf lettuce, red onion, and sliced kosher pickle as garnish. The immaculate tables are set with Dijon mustard, fast-flowing Heinz ketchup, A-1, Worcestershire, and yellow mustard for personal seasoning. No need for mayonnaise-based dressings on this hamburger, or indeed, any of the numerous additional toppings available as extras from the kitchen. You can taste the juicy natural beef licked by the fire in this classic burger, which is the reason to indulge in a really good hamburger in the first place. I like to sit at the sun-warmed metal tables on the sidewalk in front of the little restaurant. The neighborhood still offers up some colorful characters, but it isn't as raffish as Haight Street.

CHA CHA CHA. . . . .

1801 Haight Street (at Schrader)
415-386-5758 or 415-386-7670
www.chachacha.citysearch.com
Open daily 11:30 A.M. to 4 P.M.;
Monday through Thursday
5 to 11 P.M.; Friday, Saturday,
and Sunday until 11:30 P.M.
Inexpensive
Credit cards: MC, V

The vibrancy of this popular Haight Street institution has not diminished over the years, even with Cha Cha Cha's expansion to a larger space on the corner. If anything, this Caribbean tapas spot is hotter than ever. With Cuban rhythm bands blaring on the sound system and fetishy folk art leaping off the black brick walls, the place always buzzes. Next door, but connected to the dining room, people both eat and drink at a very hip bar made of marble and pressed sheet metal in Cha Cha Cha's original tiny space. They come here for tapas, huge plates of tender fried calamari, or deep-fried new potatoes, golden and crisp, dressed with a dollop of dried chile–infused aioli. From the daily specials board might come a large fillet of trout, spicily breaded Cajun-style and panfried, served with grilled asparagus and a capery *rémoulade*—a surprisingly stylish dish for the venue. Platters of excellent black beans, yellow rice with green olives, and seared flank steak or roast leg of pork make for a dreamy meal if you're really hungry. Everything on these Cuban-inspired plates is delicious. More tapas, such as fried plantains with black beans and sour cream; whole mushroom caps sautéed with sherry, garlic, and olive oil; or a good warm spinach salad with bacon and mushrooms, draw on Spain and Latin America with a bit of California thrown in. The mix works, especially when washed down with pitchers of fruity, but not too sweet, sangria. The cooking is eclectic, but not confused or fussy. The unifying theme is spiciness and each buoyant dish stays true to its ethnic origin. A Cuban dish tastes Cuban; a Cajun dish, Cajun.

This restaurant was made for the Haight. It's an extension of the energy on the street. It projects just enough funk to make neighborhood customers feel comfortable, yet the core of the operation is professional and pretty sophisticated. It has become one of the best neighborhood spots around—so good, in fact, that people come to Cha Cha Cha from all over the city. The loud and colorful dining rooms also happen to be a terrific place to take kids: they can eat a little or a lot (everyone gets a small empty plate and helps him- or herself) and drink their own version of sangria—exotic fruit juices in ice-filled glasses.

E O S . . . .

901 Cole Street (at Carl)
415-566-3063
www.eossf.com
Open Sunday through Thursday
5:30 to 10 P.M., Friday and
Saturday to 11 P.M.
Moderate
Credit cards: AE, MC, V

Eos, a restaurant that serves theatrical East-West creations paired with a mind-boggling collection of wines, has become *the* Cole Valley culinary institution. It draws people from all over the city, but has maintained a loyal neighborhood clientele of pedestrians who don't have to worry about parking.

There are two sections to Eos: a wine bar with more than forty wines by the glass, a wine list of tremendous depth and originality, and an ambitious schedule of wine tastings with winemakers; and a loud, happening restaurant where you can order any of the wines from the wine bar along with large and small plates of wild-looking Euro-Asian food. If you can find a seat in the wine bar, you can eat there, too. The combination of dramatic Asian-accented food and limitless wine choice is exciting—even if sometimes the two don't go together.

I like all the starters that bring something meticulously deep-fried, such as crispy rock shrimp cakes with a mayonnaiselike spicy ginger aioli and a radicchio cup full of little dressed lettuces. A clay pot of clams steamed in sake and lemongrass, garnished with whisk brooms of lemongrass and knotted long beans; a signature and aptly named dish called Tuna Tower; and an intensely smoky duck breast served with fruit chutney have all been delicious, if challenging dishes to match with wine. The wine-knowledgeable waitstaff must be used to people throwing up their hands in confusion when they read both the exotic menu and the huge wine list. So the waiters step right in and suggest. You can follow their advice with confidence to get the best out of this restaurant. On the other hand, wine buffs will be ecstatic to see all sorts of rarities available at small markups.

Chef Arnold Wong and wine manager Debbie Zachareas both worked at the Wong family's famous Ashbury Market (now sold to an Indian family) where they became skilled at buying and tasting wines, cheeses, and produce. (Wong also developed fusion skills at Cafe Kati.) Eos offers ten different cheeses to accompany wine. There are no less than twenty dessert wines by the glass to go with fine desserts such as Bananamisu—whole caramelized bananas—or pastry-wrapped pears. And there might be $36 glasses of rare Burgundy, but the question remains, does a green papaya spring roll go with it? If you're a serious wine buff, you might want to stick to cheese and fruit pairings, though plenty of spicy red and white New World wines are available to drink with the likes of a five-pepper, cornmeal-crusted soft-shell crab with savory cabbage slaw and Asian tartar. Eos pushes the envelope of food and wine togetherness.

HAMA-KO

108B Carl Street (at Cole)
415-753-6808
Open Tuesday through Sunday
6 to 10 P.M.
Moderate
Credit cards: MC, V

It's a well-kept secret that you can get some of the best sushi in town at this practically invisible little restaurant, especially if you call ahead and order a special meal from sushi chef–owner Ted Kashiyama. He goes to Pier 33 every day, specifically to Paul Johnson's Monterey Fish stall, to find scallops, live Dungeness crab, and shrimp. He has his sources for *hamachi* (yellowtail), sea urchin roe, and *mirugai* (giant clam), which is practically still moving when he cuts it. For a modest sum, patrons can order a plate of mixed sushi from a small menu, but for a stunning meal let Mr. Kashiyama compose a series of hot and cold courses that are simple, exquisite, and unique. He might begin with a few perfect oysters on the half shell and end with a whole Dungeness crab cooked Japanese style, with delicacies like sushi and sashimi of *toro* (tuna belly) and real, fresh *hamachi* along the way. Call ahead to order these meals and reserve a space; otherwise you can walk in and hope to find a seat at the tiny sushi bar or at one of the few tables.

Mr. Kashiyama's wife handles the floor with unflagging Japanese graciousness, but if more than two or three parties come in at the same time she does not quicken her methodical pace in bringing drinks, meticulously setting places, and taking orders. Service for her is like a stately dance that will not brook syncopation. Yet when she's with you, you bask in her attention.

RNM RESTAURANT

598 Haight Street (at Steiner)
415-551-7900
Open Wednesday and Sunday
5:30 to 10 P.M., Thursday, Friday,
and Saturday until 11:30 P.M.
Moderate
Credit cards: MC, V

This polished bar and restaurant looks like it belongs on the Upper East Side of New York instead of the Lower Haight, a neighborhood that happens to be gentrifying, but still affords plenty of funky sidewalk action. RNM, started by twenty-nine-year-old Justine Miner, a formally trained chef who apprenticed with Julia McClaskey (see Julia, page 266), has put together an eclectic California menu of stylish small dishes that are fun to eat and very fairly priced. She uses only beautiful ingredients, fresh, local—you know the mantra—and molds them into sexy creations that look as wonderful as they taste. Though many, many places make small pizzas these days, I have to say that Miner's are the best. She must have done some heavy research on crusts because hers are miraculously thin but not crackery, soft but not bready, and possess an intriguing chewy edge. They're brilliant, especially when topped with pancetta, shreds of grilled radicchio and thyme, whole-milk mozzarella, and heirloom tomato sauce. This pizza is just about the best piece of food in town. Her grilled prawn salad, starring moist, fire-licked shrimp on a bed of sweet corn and grilled Maui onions, gets a clever little lift from toasted sunflower seeds. They add just the needed degree of crunch and nuttiness. I came here two weeks after opening when tomatoes were full on, and, after eating Miner's cornmeal-crusted fried heirloom tomatoes stacked with layers of buffalo mozzarella and basil leaves, I realized that I like my tomatoes either raw or cooked into a sauce. I am in the minority considering how many people around me raved about this dish.

Miner wanted RNM to be as much a bar in Berkeley's Cesar vein (see page 398) as a restaurant, and the wine and spirits offerings are still under development. Right now I would drive across town to sit in front of Miner's little kitchen at a shiny stainless steel counter and work my way through the small plates. A mezzanine with couches and a video screen playing art loops, a small dining room with polished dark-wood tables, and a dramatically lit bar with eight or so seats give patrons many choices of venues to eat and drink, each with a different feel. Long metal mesh curtains shimmer at the entryway and on the stairway to the mezzanine giving the illusion of solidity and transparency at the same time. They remind me of Miner herself, who seems a little too young, hip, and nice to be running a kitchen, yet knows exactly what she wants. She has a backbone of steel and the delicious dishes coming out of her kitchen show plenty of discipline.

TAQUERIA EL BALAZO. . . . .

1654 Haight Street (between
Clayton and Cole)
415-864-8608
Open daily 10:30 A.M. to 10:30 P.M.
Inexpensive
Credit cards: MC, V

Balazo is a very popular taqueria where people can eat a lot for cheap. A tasty chicken mole fills burritos and tacos with amazing grace. One wouldn't think that chicken in an aromatic sauce deepened by bitter chocolate would work with guacamole, rice, beans, and salsa in a burrito, but it does. The *carnitas* (pork slowly cooked in its own fat) is fresh, moist, and buttery, delicious in soft tacos sprinkled with extra chopped onions and cilantro that are set out on the counter. Grateful Dead references (roses, skulls, and dishes named after certain group members) abound in the colorful, folk art–filled dining room that surrounds the bustling counter. The food here reaches the best Mission District standards: freshness is key, nothing sits around, and good combinations can be put together with a bit of experimentation. The flavors are authentic, although an awful lot of salt is used in practically everything.

400 Waller Street (at Fillmore)
415-431-2526
Open nightly 5:30 to 10:30 P.M.
Inexpensive
Credit cards: AE, DC, D, MC, V

Although Thai restaurants abound in San Francisco, it is not because they are cooking for a Thai community. The ethnic Thai population (as opposed to Vietnamese or Cambodian, for example) is small in the Bay Area. Thai restaurants cook for Westerners, so the trick is to find a restaurant that will prepare dishes authentically. The excitement of Thai cooking lies in the explosiveness of the seasoning (hot being dominant), and in the sweet, sour, fermented, and aromatic flavors in every dish. The best of the Thai restaurants use fresh ingredients, grind their own pastes for curries, and keep their dishes incendiary. That's why many aficionados consider Thep Phanom one of their favorite Thai restaurants. The kitchen doesn't make concessions. When they warn that a dish is hot, be prepared!

The calamari salad is divine, juxtaposing tender squid with hot chiles, cool lettuces, fresh cilantro, and lime juice. A lot of the appetizers and salads balance similar ingredients, and I love them all whether they are made with minced chicken or duck in the *larb* preparations, or with strips of spongy fish cake. The deep-fried dishes here stand out, especially the quail on lettuce with a peanut sauce. Rubbed with dry spices, the plain quail are so flavorful and moist that dipping them is unnecessary. Angel wings—fried chicken wings stuffed with glass noodles—may be the most ordered and delicious dish at the restaurant. If you love chiles, try one of the fiery stir-fries from a special section of the menu. Once you get used to the level of hotness you realize how deep the flavors go in these dishes. They are the most characteristically Thai, but you must be able to tolerate hot, hot seasoning. More delicate coconut-milk curries, red or yellow from the particular spice paste used, are well-represented on the menu. Deep-fried bananas with coconut ice cream end the meal on a cool note.

Besides the good cooking, Thep Phanom impresses with a pleasant, low-lit dining room decorated with elegant Thai artifacts. Lacy gold-trimmed place mats soften the glass-covered tabletops. The waiters and slim, elegant hostesses in Thai dress know how keep the dining room hopping. The place is always full, but somehow the wait is never long.

CAFÉS

BEAN THERE . . . .

201 Steiner Street (at Waller)
415-255-8855
Open Monday through Friday
6:30 A.M. to 7:30 P.M., Saturday and
Sunday 7 A.M. to 7:30 P.M.
Cash only

Good light makes a good café, something that Hemingway knew. Bean There, the Lower Haight's best coffeehouse, not only has wonderful natural light that pours in through tall windows, but a choice location on a residential corner lined with sycamores facing a block of refurbished Victorians. Chairs play an important role in a café and the handsome ones here, made of heavy bamboo with ladder backs, beckon. A painted cement slab floor, wooden benchlike banquettes, and sponged ochre-colored walls give the room airy warmth. Background music has been carefully chosen; local newspapers and the *New York Times* are sold at the counter; and best of all, the espresso is rich and unburnt and the short latte is in perfect proportion. A large selection of teas is also featured. This café merits a trip across town; it transcends its neighborhood while being completely a part of it.

BOULANGE DE COLE VALLEY . . . .

1000 Cole Street (at Parnassus)
415-242-2442
Open Tuesday through Sunday
7 A.M. to 7 P.M.
Cash only

The pleasant-windowed café area in front of the bakery counter has become a popular neighborhood hang. See Bay Bread, page 274, and Boulange de Polk, page 306, for more information.

BARS

CLUB DELUXE . . . .

1511 Haight Street (at Ashbury)
415-552-6949
Open Monday through Friday
4 P.M. to 2 A.M., Saturday and
Sunday 3 P.M. to 2 A.M.
Cash only

When a jazz combo plays on Fridays, Saturdays, and Sundays, it might cost you $4 or $5 to get in the door. At other times, the jazz comes from the sound system and admission to this suave, retro bar is free. The DeLuxe is one of my favorite bars in the city, not only for the mix of people who hang there, some of whom slick back their hair and make vintage clothing look like Armani, but also because the drinks are so good. Bartenders make first-rate fresh-lime margaritas with just the right balance of sweet and sour so that the salt on the rim of the glass becomes part of the thrill. Ron de Barolito rum, so rich in flavor it reminds me of butterscotch, blossoms in a warmed brandy snifter. Dry, ice-cold martinis come in chilled V-shaped glasses, the very embodiment of sophistication. The scene is elevated enough so that people who like to dress feel appreciated. Yet there's nothing snobby about the DeLuxe. Old and young, matronly and hip, casual and dressy—everyone looks good here, and after a perfect drink or two, everyone feels pretty good, too.

KEZAR BAR & RESTAURANT . . . .

900 Cole Street (at Carl)
415-681-7678
Open daily 5 P.M. to midnight
Credit cards: AE, DC, D, MC, V

A cozy neighborhood sports bar that was opened by the people who owned the long-defunct Ironwood across the street, the Kezar offers a comfortable barroom with two video monitors and an adjoining dining room. The food here is terrific, just what you want when you belly up to a bar. There are spicy garlic peanuts and warm, thick corn chips with delicious toma-to salsa. The hamburgers are juicy and full of flavor. More elaborate dishes turn out to be surprisingly good: Greek-style spinach salad, pot roast, and seafood chowder have been standouts. Anchor Wheat beer is on tap and drinks are generously poured. Good spirit per-vades, fellow patrons are friendly, the staff accommodating. Kezar fulfills every requirement of a fine neighborhood pub.

NOC NOC . . . .

557 Haight Street (between
Fillmore and Steiner)
415-861-5811
Open daily 5 p.m. to 2 a.m.
Credit cards: MC, V

Its singular Flintstones-meets-high-tech interior has been lifted by others, but Noc Noc created the original Iron Age–hippie pad look, augmented by a few glowing video screens without vertical hold and collaged sur-faces embedded with bottle openers. Its patronage has gone through stages: supercounterculture, hip, and exclusive; then druggie and nodding out in the crannies; and currently, youngish and bohemian from the neighborhood. Beer is the thing—from microbreweries up and down the West Coast to German lagers and ales, thirty in all on tap.

TORONADO . . . .

547 Haight Street (between
Fillmore and Steiner)
415-863-2276
www.toronado.com
Open daily 11:30 A.M. to 2 A.M.
Cash only

This has become the choice hangout in the Lower Haight—a safe place in a dicey neighborhood. Toronado is mobbed on the weekends by people who arrive in cabs and do not look as if they live anywhere nearby, perhaps because it is a dead ringer for a colle-giate bar with traditional wood wainscoting and green walls. The list of beers goes on and on—from raspberry wheat to Boont Amber from the Anderson Valley to Guinness Stout, all on tap—and there is enough light in this bar to see the differences in brew color. The bartenders know the brews and describe them well.

DELICATESSENS/TAKEOUT

BROTHER-IN-LAW'S BAR-BE-QUE . . . .

705 Divisidero Street (at Grove)
415-931-7427
www.brotherinlaw.citysearch.com
Open Tuesday through Thursday
11 A.M. to 10 P.M., Friday and
Saturday until midnight,
Sunday until 8 P.M.
Credit cards: DC, MC, V

Brother-in-Law's gets crowded late and on the week-ends and sometimes the line can move very slowly. As you wait by the counter, engulfed in the mouthwater-ing aromas of cooking meat, you can barely restrain yourself, especially if you've spent the earlier part of the evening drinking. Too often I have prematurely torn open the sturdy cartons, which really do keep the food hot until you get it home, and coated the car with barbecue sauce. Brother-in-Law's short ends are worth the mess. These are the chopped-off tops or chine bone of the pork rib—thick, stubby, meaty bones laced with fat that melts as the ribs smoke, bathing them in flavor. The regular pork ribs are excellent too, but don't have quite the succulence of those short ends. Think about brisket here, crusty, moist, and full of smoky flavor. Baked beans are sweet and intensely smoky from slow cooking in the barbecue oven. Very sweet corn bread is still preferable to commercial white. Brother-in-Law's medium-hot barbecue sauce does it for me; the hot is incendiary.

ESTELLA'S FRESH SANDWICHES . . . .

250 Fillmore Street (between
Haight and Waller)
415-864-1850
Open daily from 10 A.M. to 5:30 P.M.
Credit cards: MC, V

Estella's, which used to be called Big Sherm's, makes marvelous multilayered sandwiches with fresh ingredients, the sum of which always add up to something more delicious than their many parts. For those of you who have bonded with No. 13, otherwise known as the Big Sherm (real roast turkey, roast beef, smoked Gouda, *peperoncini*, tomato, red onions, avocado, and pea sprouts on an Italian-style soft but crusty roll), it's still the favorite sandwich, although a couple of tuna sandwiches—fresh herbed albacore with Cheddar, avocado, tomato, red onion, and pea sprouts on focaccia; and fresh herbed albacore II with artichoke spread, feta, and *peperoncini*, etc.—have grown in popularity. Estella actually ran Big Sherm's and bought it from the founder. She continues the tradition of making huge, juicy, well-balanced, and lively sandwiches to order so they always taste their best.

ROSAMUNDE SAUSAGE GRILL . . . .

545 Haight Street (between
Fillmore and Steiner)
415-437-6851
Open daily 11:30 A.M. to 10 P.M.
Cash only

Every grilled sausage joint must to be compared to the ultimate: Top Dog in Berkeley. Although Rosamunde isn't quite as wonderful, its griddled sausages on soft sesame rolls taste mighty good after a couple of beers at Noc Noc or Toronado. And you get to condimentize here, a service not offered at Top Dog. You can choose two condiments for each dog: sauerkraut, grilled onions, peppers, or spicy beef chili. Personally, I like the Hungarian, a smoked pork sausage with sauerkraut and grilled onions, especially with a huge kosher-style pickle, a dollar extra and worth every penny. To complete the Eastern European snack, I order a cup of decent, house-made German potato salad. Every sausage—from sweet Italian to *merguez* (spicy lamb and beef) is enhanced by grilling. The skin gets crisp while the interior intensifies in flavor. Unlike Top Dog, Rosamunde doesn't toast the buns on the griddle and they tend to be a tad too bready. The condiments, however, add a whole new dimension.

TWILIGHT CAFÉ AND DELI. . . . .

2600 McAllister Street (at Stanyan)
415-386-6115
Open Monday to Friday
9 A.M. to 8 P.M.
Credit Cards: MC, V

The twenty-year-old Twilight Cafe and Deli is an immaculate, cozy corner spot by the University of San Francisco. The Syrian owners make phyllo pastries, pita sandwiches, stuffed grape leaves, and an absolutely smashing plate of *ful muddamas* with hummus called the Twilight Special. A key to the success of this dish is a superior hummus, creamy chickpea purée enriched with lots of tahini (sesame seed paste), a whisper of garlic, and just the right amount of lemon. Twilight's hummus is nutty, rich, velvety, and a perfect base for the warm stew of plump, tart Egyptian favas topped with cubed tomato, more tahini (thinned with lemon juice), and a healthy splash of olive oil. The dish is prettily dusted with ground cumin and paprika, releasing their flavors when scooped up with pita bread. You have to taste this Middle Eastern meal staple to understand how primally satisfying it is. (I ate Iraqi, Yemeni, and Palestinian versions of this dish every day for three weeks during a trip to Israel and Jordan and never tired of it.)

For dessert have a *barazek*, a thin, hard, crunchy cookie the size of a salad plate, consisting mostly of toasted sesame seeds. If you're a sesame lover (I am), these are the ultimate. Twilight also sells some Middle Eastern groceries, including a mild, nonbitter tahini from Lebanon jarred under the Aiello label. The informative woman behind the counter told me that it was similar to the tahini she used in her stellar hummus.

BAKERIES/PASTRIES

BOULANGE DE COLE VALLEY. . . . .

1000 Cole Street (at Parnassus)
415-242-2442
Open Tuesday through Sunday
7 A.M. to 7 P.M.
Cash only

Pascale Rigo, a baker from around Bordeaux, turns out to have infallible entrepreneurial instincts. He knows just what kind of an operation a neighborhood will embrace and then magically finds the perfect spot for it. In the case of Cole Valley, Rigo took over the former Tassajara bakery-café location on a shady corner and turned it into the most happening café-bakery in the residential Haight. It performs a number of functions. As a bakery, it offers the appealing range of Boulange's very French breads, pastries, and cookies, all made with organic flour, a big plus. As a café with indoor and some outdoor tables, it meets all kinds of social needs. You can get pretty good coffee (cappuccino, latte that is strong, but with a bitter edge) and a buttery croissant; a crispy topped *croque-monsieur* (cheese on top, ham and béchamel inside in this version) or a warmed-up savory quiche; or open-faced sandwiches with salad. And if you want something fast, baskets of premade baguette sandwiches filled with the likes of *cambozola* and pears on a walnut baguette, or salami and cornichons, or just the traditional ham with butter, can be picked up to eat on the run. They are fresh—the secret behind every French baguette sandwich—and replenished often throughout the day.

Most people sit at little tables in the windowed room to have a bite, surrounded by the charming and appetizing counters, bakery cases, and goods-filled baskets of a real French bakery. This congenial atmosphere and the wide range of affordable possibilities make the Boulange a democratic addition to an ever-gentrifying part of the city.

ICE CREAM/CHOCOLATES

GELATO CLASSICO . . . .

201 Parnassus Avenue
(at Stanyan)
415-566-9696
Open Sunday through Thursday
2 P.M. to 10 P.M., Friday and
Saturday 1 P.M. to 10 P.M.,
Sunday 1 P.M. to 9 P.M.
Cash only

A place to get a wide range of flavors from my favorite San Francisco gelato maker. See pages 255 and 332 for more information.

COFFEE

COFFEE, TEA AND SPICE . . . .

1630 Haight Street
(between Clayton and Cole)
415-861-3953
www.coffeeteaspice.com
Open Monday through Friday
7 A.M. to 6 P.M., Saturday 8 A.M. to
6 P.M., Sunday 9:30 A.M. to 5 P.M.
Credit cards: MC, V

A number of funky coffeehouses line Haight Street and environs, but this family-owned shop in a vintage Victorian prides itself on roasting its own coffee beans and carefully selecting teas, both packaged and in bulk. It also provides respite from the wackiness of the Haight in a living-room-like area in the back and up a short flight of stairs, furnished with couches, easy chairs, and a coffee table, of course. A big window looks out to a tree-shaded backyard with a swing set, clearly a family compound. The espresso and coffee drinks made in house are rich and full bodied, thankfully served in ceramic cups, not ubiquitous paper, which ruins any cup of coffee as far as I'm concerned. This shop does a mail-order business and has local patronage from longtime residents.

REAL FOOD COMPANY. . . . .

1023 Stanyon Street
(between Carl and Parnassus)
415-564-2800
www.realfoodco.com
Open daily 9 A.M. to 8:30 P.M.
Credit cards: AE, MC, V

The Real Food group of natural foods stores were the first retailers to make organic produce accessible to San Franciscans, and my hat goes off to the founder for pioneering this important effort. Kimball Allen, the owner of the stores, fell into his successful chain by accident. He owned some property that he wanted to rent and ended up opening a profitable natural foods chain by letting independent managers run the stores. Although a centralized produce department now buys for all the Real Food stores (and the company was recently purchased by Nutraceutical Corporation), produce cognoscenti still consider these health food outlets to be some of the best sources for organic fruits and vegetables in the city. The buyers have established long-term connections with local organic farmers, and all the stores make a point of labeling produce by farm and growing practice. At the Stanyan store, a whole room is devoted to carefully stored and groomed fruits and vegetables. I like the respectful handling here, the informative labeling, and the wide variety. I always find something unusual that can inspire a dinner. For other locations, see pages 227 and 307.

FRESH PEAS WITH SHALLOTS

SERVES 4

2 tablespoons butter

2 large shallots, minced

3 pounds fresh peas in the pod, shelled (about 2½ cups shelled peas)

1 teaspoon kosher salt

Freshly ground black pepper

½ cup water

Melt the butter in a large skillet over medium heat. Add the shallots and cook until soft. Add the peas, salt, pepper, and water. Stir, bring to a boil, then cover and cook over high heat for 3 to 5 minutes, or until the peas are sweet and tender but not mushy. Timing will depend on the size of the peas. If they are still hard after 5 minutes, add a little more water, if necessary, and cook for 2 minutes longer. Most of the liquid should be gone when the peas are ready.

Variation: At the last moment, you may add 2 tablespoons fine-chiffonnade-cut fresh mint leaves or ½ teaspoon minced fresh thyme or chervil. For a wonderful treat, cook peas in this way with chanterelle mushrooms, adding 1 tablespoon olive oil to the butter and continuing on in the same manner with shallots, then chanterelles, then peas, using less water, depending on the moisture in the mushrooms.

FRESH PEAS

Some of the best peas grow in the cooler finger valleys off Half Moon Bay and San Gregorio Beach. When I think about what it takes to bring fresh peas to market, I marvel that it ever happens at all. The peas must be picked at just the right moment before they mature and get starchy, but when they are large enough to make up more than a handful after they're shelled. As so often happens, some peas may be too large and others small and sweet in the same harvest, so picking must be done judiciously with consistency in mind. Always shell and taste a couple before you buy. The picked peas must be cooled immediately and delivered to market quickly so they keep their sugar. (Peas lose up to 40 percent of their sugar in six hours at room temperature.) At the store the same rules apply. The peas must be kept cool and sold fast. Each moment warming on the display shelves and sitting in the coolers in the back detracts from their charm. Too many times I have come away from a market with peas that tasted pretty good when I bought them, but changed overnight in the refrigerator. When you take the time to shell fresh peas at home, you want them to be worth the effort, and the trip from field to the plate is a long one fraught with pitfalls. Careful buying at a farmers' market offers the highest probability for securing sweet peas.

COUNTRY CHEESE . . . .

415 Divisadero Street
(between Oak and Fell)
415-621-8130
Open Monday through Saturday
10 A.M. to 7 P.M., Saturday and
Sunday until 6 P.M.
Credit cards: MC, V

People like to shop here for large hunks of cheese at wholesale prices, like Parmigiano-Reggiano, at least a dollar a pound cheaper than most other stores. Extra sharp cheddars from Vermont and New York, sweet butter in bulk, and huge wedges of Saint-André can make party purchases less expensive. The nuts in bulk could be fresher. The dry goods in bins, like basmati rice, dried beans of all sorts, and popcorn, are the building blocks of dishes that can feed large groups.

BEST MACARONI AND CHEESE

SERVES 6

2 cups milk

¼ cup butter

¼ cup all-purpose flour

1 teaspoon plus 2 generous tablespoons kosher salt

1 bay leaf

———————

4 quarts water

1 pound penne

3 cups coarsely grated sharp Cheddar cheese, such as medium-aged Vermont Grafton

Freshly ground black pepper

Serve this rich, luscious macaroni and cheese with plain, steamed organic broccoli as an antidote.

1 Preheat the oven to 350°F.

2 Heat the milk in a saucepan.

3 Melt the butter in a large casserole on the top of the stove. Whisk in the flour and 1 teaspoon salt. Cook this mixture over low heat for 5 minutes, whisking often. Take off of the heat and add the scalded milk all at once, stirring constantly. Return the pan to the heat and stir until the sauce has come to a boil and thickened. Add the bay leaf. Cover and cook in the oven for 20 minutes or so.

4 Meanwhile, bring the water to a boil. Add the 2 tablespoons salt. Add the pasta and cook for the time specified on the package. Drain.

5 Remove the white sauce from the oven. Remove the bay leaf. Stir in the cheese and ground pepper to taste. Add the hot pasta and toss thoroughly.

SAY CHEESE. . . . .

856 Cole Street (between
Frederick and Carl)
415-665-5020
Open Monday through Saturday
10 A.M. to 7 P.M., Sunday until 5 P.M.
Credit cards: MC, V

One of the better-stocked cheese stores in the city, Say Cheese carries hard-to-find cheeses on a regular basis. Try this store's super-aged Gouda (pronounced HOW-da by the purists), a caramelly, nutty hard cheese that merits a trip across town. Say Cheese will have the seasonal *brin d'amour*, an evocative, mild, but complex Corsican sheep's milk cheese rolled in wild herbs that charms cheese lovers, or a real *abondance* from the Haute Savoie. On a more mundane level, two-year-old Vermont Cheddar is always available, as is English clotted cream (divine on scones if you can get it fresh enough), and a large selection of imported English cheeses. Good imported and local cured meats and sausages are made into sandwiches on the premises or sliced and wrapped to go. Because Say Cheese does carry a large inventory of cheeses, you might want to ask for tastes just to make sure your selection is in good condition.

COOKWARE AND BOOKS

COOKIN' . . . .

339 Divisidero Street (between
Oak and Page)
415-861-1854
Open Tuesday through Saturday
noon to 6:30 P.M., Sunday 1 to 5 P.M.
Credit cards: MC, V

In a town of dueling cookware giants (Sur La Table, Crate&Barrel, Williams-Sonoma), Cookin's unique and ever-changing collection of old cooking utensils, dishes, and glassware stimulates my culinary imagination. Gazing at a collection of butter molds, tartlet pans, and fragile unmatched tea cups, I contemplate serving a tea. Porcelain egg coddlers, small delicate glasses, tin molds, tarnished copper pieces in unusual shapes, Fiestaware, Bundt pans, madeleine tins, cookie cutters, Christmas things, Easter things, the odd, rare, and common have all been sorted through for intrinsic beauty, utility, and good condition. Often you can find the very item you are looking for at Cookin' when it maddeningly has been discontinued or changed in the name of improvement at the other stores, like long, wooden-handled potato mashers, or plain, rectangular spatulas. Like the old-fashioned card catalog they have removed from the new Main Library, I find this store indispensable for finding what I really need.

THE MARINA
COW HOLLOW

THE MARINA &
COW HOLLOW

RESTAURANTS

1 Betelnut
2 Bistro Aix
3 Cafe Marimba
4 Chaz
5 E'Angelo
6 Greens
7 Isa
8 Merenda
9 Pane e Vino
10 PlumpJack Cafe
11 Rose's Cafe
12 Via Vai Trattoria
13 Yukol Palace

CAFÉS

14 Warming Hut

BARS

15 Balboa Cafe
16 Bus Stop
17 Cozmo's Corner Grill
18 Matrix/Fillmore
19 Perry's

DELICATESSENS/TAKEOUT

20 Cafe Merenda
21 Desiree
6 Green's to Go
22 Lucca

BAKERIES/PASTRIES

23 Just Desserts
24 La Nouvelle Pâtisserie

COFFEE

25 Peet's Coffee & Tea

MARKETS

26 Marina Super

WINES AND SPIRITS

27 California Wine Merchant
28 PlumpJack Wines

COOKWARE AND BOOKS

29 Fredericksen's Hardware
30 Williams-Sonoma

N

FORT
MASON
CENTER

GOUGH

⑫
⑳

OCTAVIA

⑧

LAFAY-
ETTE
PARK

⑥

LAGUNA

MOSCONE
REC.
CENTER

⑲ ⑯

BLVD.

BAY

BUCHANAN

㉓

❶

San
Francisco
Bay

MARINA GREEN

WEBSTER

⑱ ㉔

MARINA

CERVANTES

CAPRI

FILLMORE

④ ㉚ ⑰ ㉘ ⑮ ㉙

② ⑦

STEINER

⑩ ⑪

㉒

❾

㉕

LOMBARD

PIERCE

ALTA
PLAZA
PARK

Yacht
Harbor

AVILA

㉗

❺

SCOTT

JEFFERSON

NORTH POINT

BAY

FRANCISCO

CHESTNUT

⑬
㉖

GREENWICH

FILBERT

UNION

DIVISADERO

BEACH

GREEN

VALLEJO

BRODERICK

❸

BROADWAY

BAKER

W   E

LYON

PALACE
OF
FINE ARTS

RICHARDSON

LOMBARD

PRESIDIO

PACIFIC

JACKSON

WASHINGTON

CLAY

HALLECK

LINCOLN BLVD

PRESIDIO

WEST PACIFIC

LOCUST

MASON

MESA

SPRUCE

㉑

MAPLE

GOLDEN GATE
NATIONAL
RECREATION
AREA

MORAGA

ARGUELLO

CHERRY

DOYLE DR.

CRISSY
FIELD

ARGUELLO

COAST
GUARD
PIER

⑭

PRESIDIO

S

0   .5
SCALE MILES

BETELNUT . . . .

2030 Union Street (between
Webster and Buchanan)
415-929-8855
www.betelnutrestaurant.com
Open Sunday through Thursday
11:30 A.M. to 11 P.M., Friday and
Saturday until midnight
Moderate
Credit cards: DC, D, MC, V

I was much taken by this wildly popular *peiju-wu*, or Asian beer house, when it first opened seven years ago. Cecilia Chiang, veteran restaurateur and former owner of the Mandarin in Ghirardelli Square, put together the menu of spicy, pan-Asian dishes and watched over it like a mother hen. She has since left the operation to the management of the Real Restaurants group, who owns the Fog City Diner (see page 70), Bix (see page 97), and other popular restaurants, and the cooking has become more inconsistent. But I am addicted to some of the dishes, like a fiery, intensely salty stir-fry of tiny sun-dried anchovies, *hot* chiles, sliced garlic, scallions, and peanuts that absolutely requires large draughts of cold, house rice beer (and a full commitment to whomever you happen to be eating this with, because no one else would want to be within ten feet after a little plate of it).

The intriguing menu offers dishes from Singapore, Thailand, Japan, Malaysia, Indonesia, Hong Kong, Shanghai, Canton, Taiwan, Vietnam, Korea, each with its own distinctive pantry of flavors. This is not California-style crossover cooking, but true renditions of dishes from many different parts of the Far East. The noodles, dumplings, curries, and soups, the tea duck, pickles, deep-fried squid, seafood, and small plates of vegetables are all served in a stunning collection of hand-thrown bowls and plates. The unifying concept is that they all go with beer, sake, Trader Vic–style cocktails, tea, Chinese sherrylike plum wine, or maybe even Western wine, though the last is a long shot.

Betelnut is as much a bar as it is a restaurant. The look of the bar was inspired by the Long Bar in Singapore's Raffles Hotel. The ever-packed dining areas arranged around an open kitchen are noisy, fun, exciting. True to all Real Restaurants's operations, Betelnut is witty in its details. A whole Asian world of food and drink has been packaged for you to explore. Though I'm a culinary purist, I find the wrapping here to be pretty irresistible.

BISTRO AIX . . . .

3340 Steiner Street (between
Lombard and Chestnut)
415-202-0100
www.bistroaix.com
Open daily 6 to 10 P.M.
Moderate
Credit cards: MC, V

Bistros come and go, but this one has staying power because chef-owner Jonathan Beard stays behind the stove of this small, wonderful place. His exceptional roast chicken with crusty skin and juicy flesh served with superb, buttery mashed potatoes and fantastic, almost caramelized ratatouille for all of $14.95 is one reason people come back here again and again. This is a dish I could eat practically every day. The light flavorful broth in an onion soup lets the sweetness of onions shine through, a single cheesy crouton adding salt and savoriness. A thin paillard of halibut, seared quickly and topped with a ton of delicious mango salsa on a bed of couscous, strikes a surprisingly delicious balance.

Though done all over town in one variation or another, a salad of grilled pears, goat cheese, and walnuts with winter greens has straightforward rustic charm here. You can tell that this cook tastes his food and knows exactly what flavors and textures he wants in each dish. The cooking glows with hominess and good culinary sense.

A small dining area wedged in around an open kitchen with a few counter seats can get noisy and crowded. Luckily, a clean, modern decor does not add clutter, though a cranked-up sound system seems superfluous. Seating is almost doubled by a pleasant out-door patio with heat lamps that toast you on one side. Still, many prefer sitting in the romantically lit, open-air patio because they can hear one another talk. Frankly, when the food is so good and so reasonable—and that describes a small, well-chosen wine list as well—I am happy in any seat I can find.

CAFE MARIMBA . . . .

2317 Chestnut Street (at Divisidero)
415-776-1506
Open daily 11 A.M. to 10 P.M.
Inexpensive
Credit cards: AE, MC, V

Some people confronted by a three-legged stone mortar filled with grilled pork and onions don't know what to do, especially when they are expecting platters of soft, saucy Mexican food finished off under a broiler. At Cafe Marimba, one of the few authentic, full-scale Mexican restaurants in the United States, they learn how to tuck the luscious morsels of pork into small, soft corn tortillas, just off the griddle, and spoon on some hot, smoky chipotle salsa. The taste of such regional, made-from-scratch Mexican food is sublime and unexpected—very earthy but punctuated by explosive flavors.

The kitchen makes everything from scratch, including the most important element of the Mexican meal, tortillas. Prepared *masa* (freshly ground cornmeal treated with lime and made into a dough with water) is delivered from La Palma Mexicatessen (see page 203) every morning. Throughout the day this soft dough is fed through a roller with a round die that turns out perfect tortillas that are then cooked on a griddle.

While it's difficult to stop eating the freshly fried tortilla chips and engaging salsas that welcome you to the table, make the effort. Many other treats are in store, such as sublime Oaxacan mushroom tacos with tiny white beans hauntingly scented with Mexican herbs; spicy calamari tacos with fresh tomatoes, jalapeños, garlic, and cilantro; or the unexpectedly light and savory quesadilla and empanada sampler plate, three little *masa* turnovers filled with wild mushrooms, chorizo, and poblano chiles. Other favorites include a Veracruz-style shrimp ceviche with lots of chopped tomatoes, jalapeños, and lime; and crepelike chicken tamales, steamed in banana leaves and sauced with red and yellow Oaxacan moles. Since Cafe Marimba's menu is divided into small and large dishes, with most plates served family style, diners end up sharing and tasting lots of the new and sometimes exotic dishes without making a major commitment.

Lest one of the pleasures of eating Mexican be ignored, drinks here get special atten-tion. Fresh fruit juice combos like strawberry-lemonade or pineapple-ginger *agua fresca* especially please kids (who love many of the tacos and quesadillas), while fresh lime margar-itas, kept intentionally tart, do fine with the adults. Smooth tequilas from small producers are a revelation—and may cause a few as well.

The restaurant is always full and very noisy. Most people drop by without reservations, actually looking forward to the short wait at the bar so they can have a top-shelf margarita. With so many exciting restaurants continually opening in San Francisco, we tend to overlook the gems that have been around for a while. Cafe Marimba still fills a unique niche in this city, cooking Mexican for us with unflagging integrity and a lot of native style.

CHAZ . . . .

3347 Fillmore Street (near
Chestnut)
415-928-1211
Open Tuesday through Sunday
5:30 to 9:30 P.M.
Moderate
Credit cards: AE, CB, DC, D,
MC, V

Charles Solomon, of the eponymous Chaz in the Marina, has a glittering culinary curriculum vitae—he worked for David Bouley in SoHo and with the late Jean Louis Palladin at the Watergate in Washington, D.C. He did several stints in France, one with Alain Ducasse, and two years with Gerald Pangaud in Washington, D.C.

Solomon came to San Francisco to open Geordy's, a popular Union Square eatery that closed within a year, though Solomon left before its demise when Le Castel in Pacific Heights became available. There, from 1994 to 1997, he operated The Heights, one of my favorite San Francisco restaurants. With only one year left on its lease, The Heights closed over an Americans with Disabilities Act dispute and Solomon disappeared from the cooking scene until he opened Chaz in 2000.

At Chaz, memories of past Charles Solomon dishes flooded back with my first taste of an exquisite saffron and mussel soup, shelled mussels, the tiniest *brunoise* (or dice) of aromatic vegetables, the briny juices of the shellfish, a little wine, and a saffron-scented broth enriched with a little cream. A crab salad with grapefruit, fresh coconut, and slivers of green bean and sweet red pepper danced on the tongue. Opposite in style, crisp nuggets of sweetbreads nestled into a ragout of chanterelles seasoned with paprika. Technique—the crisped sweetbreads—and an unexpected ingredient—the paprika—made this a signature Solomon dish. He also likes to make savory cakes that are wrapped and molded. With lamb chops he serves a chartreuse encased in chard that turns out to hold minced lamb ragout. Baked mushroom risotto, cheesy and firm with mushrooms in the center, is contained in thin, crisp eggplant slices. It's a very unusual dish, a little tangy, a little creamy, a little sharp, but I found it addictive.

Desserts continue to demonstrate the Solomon penchant for unconventional form. The napoleon of chocolate financier, moist, tender-crumbed chocolate cake, looks like a striped cube. Vibrant fresh mint ice cream separates the square layers anchored by chocolate fudge—a smashing invention.

Overall, Solomon is concentrating on keeping things simple. He does not want Chaz to be a special occasion restaurant, but rather a neighborhood place where people can just drop in. Thank goodness he has not abandoned the offbeat foods and preparations that inspire him—sweetbreads, sardines, vegetable tarts, vegetable compotes, vegetable confits, chartreuses, and *galettes*. If you choose the most interesting dishes, the ones that engage him, you can get a high-end meal at a bistro tariff.

The delicious fresh fruit drinks at Cafe Marimba come in many flavors, depending on the season. Once you've made one, you can easily make any of them. The key is a simple syrup of sugar and water, which can be purchased or made at home. Similar *aguas frescas* are ladled from huge glass jars on the counters of taquerias all over the Mission. In the Mission, you find exotic flavors like *jamaica*, or red hibiscus flower, pruney tamarind, and almost always a wonderful cantaloupe. Cafe Marimba adds extra ingredients to theirs, such as vanilla bean and lemon to their strawberry *agua fresca*, or mint to the mango blend. When the fruit drinks are spiked with dark rum, as they often are at Cafe Marimba, they turn into *batidos*.

WATERMELON AQUA FRESCA: MAKES ABOUT 2 QUARTS

About 2 pounds watermelon

1 cup simple syrup (recipe follows)

2¾ cups water

Cut the watermelon flesh away from the rind, remove the seeds, and cut the flesh into small chunks. You should have 4 cups. Blend for 10 seconds in a blender or food processor. The mixture should be chunky. Put in a pitcher and stir in the simple syrup and water. Let stand for 1 to 2 hours. Serve over ice. Best drunk the same day.

PINEAPPLE-GINGER AGUA FRESCA: MAKES ABOUT 2 QUARTS

1 ripe medium pineapple

1 tablespoon grated peeled ginger (a 1½-inch piece)

1¼ cups simple syrup (recipe follows)

3 cups water

Peel the pineapple and remove the eyes. Core and cut into small chunks. You should have 3½ cups. Blend for about 25 seconds in a blender or food processor. The mixture will be pulpy. Put in a pitcher and stir in the ginger and simple syrup. Let stand for 1 to 2 hours, stirring occasionally. Add the water and serve over ice.

SIMPLE SYRUP: MAKES 2 CUPS

2 cups water

2½ cups sugar

Mix the ingredients together in a medium saucepan. Bring to a boil, boil for 1 minute, and remove from heat. Let cool, cover, and chill thoroughly. Refrigerated syrup keeps indefinitely.

E'ANGELO . . . .

2234 Chestnut Street (between
Pierce and Scott)
415-567-6164
Open Tuesday through Sunday
5 to 10:30 P.M.
Moderate
Cash only

Seated at one of E'Angelo's tiny tables, my then nine-year-old and I were horrified to see the host push the table next to us even closer and seat a dad with two young children. This was our grown-up night out, and we did not want two little kids right on top of us. The host thought he was being cute by sticking all the kids and parents together, but that's life at this twenty-something Marina institution. Just be happy you get a seat at all at this popular restaurant, whose dining room is mostly taken up by a partially open kitchen.

In all the years I have been eating here the menu has not changed, but why should it when the traditional house-made pastas are timeless? E'Angelo made them from scratch long before the Italian food frenzy swept the nation. The luscious green lasagne made with the most tender spinach noodles layered with tons of fontina, mozzarella, and a signature dried porcini and chicken liver meat sauce is both refined and rustic. The kitchen is famous for a delicate eggplant parmigiana that melts in your mouth. The small pizzas with crisp, paper-thin crusts and the simplest of toppings, like tomato sauce, mozzarella, and mushrooms, are among the best in town. Ricotta-and-spinach-filled ravioli and soft, tender gnocchi napped in tomato sauce are both classics. A crisp, old-fashioned iceberg lettuce salad, briskly dressed in vinegar and oil and topped with a few anchovies, seems retro in this age of arugula, but it always hits the spot. Although in some respects closer to the old school of Italian-American eateries, E'Angelo continues to satisfy because it executes the basics: a silken noodle dough and a resonant meat sauce.

GREENS . . . .

Fort Mason, Building A
(Buchanan at Marina Boulevard)
415-771-6222
www.greensrestaurant.com
Open Tuesday through Friday
11:30 A.M. to 2 P.M., Saturday
until 2:30 P.M., Sunday 10:30 A.M.
until 2 P.M., Monday through
Saturday 5:30 to 9 P.M.
(Saturday dinner is prix fixe)
Moderate
Credit cards: DC , D, MC, V

When Deborah Madison, the original chef at this groundbreaking vegetarian restaurant started by the Zen Center, put together her first menus, people could not believe how intriguing and satisfying a meatless meal could be. She developed a whole new style of vegetarian cuisine that looked to France and the Mediterranean for flavors, and local farms and producers for pristine ingredients. Her five-course, prix fixe dinners became legendary for their imagination and elegance—a far cry from the hippie health-food genre that had taken hold in California in the 1960s.

Madison moved to Santa Fe and has become a cookbook superstar—no one writes better recipes, vegetarian or otherwise—and Greens has flourished under the guidance of Annie Somerville, an author in her own right (*Field of Greens*), who has kept the standards high and the menus lively. You will find Greens's classics like a Bloomsdale spinach salad tossed with creamy feta, croutons, and threads of red onion in a gorgeous dressing fragrant with mint, sherry

vinegar, and warmed olive oil; or the best tofu sandwich in the world made with smoky charcoal-grilled tofu with horseradish mayonnaise on potato bread. There might be airy vegetable pancakes enriched with ricotta and Gruyère, served with a piquant tomato-sherry sauce and a dab of crème fraîche; or a house-made pasta with chanterelles, leeks, and Parmesan. The range is stunning and the food always tasty. The restaurant uses only the highest-quality ingredients, from olive oil
to nuts.

Greatly improved over the years is the service, which used to be performed, more or less, by Zen students. Now the service is brisk and professional. Another big plus, in addition to the lovely view of the Marina and the airy, art-filled dining room, is a list of eight unusual wine specials, offered by the glass or bottle, that go wonderfully with the food. Just inside the front door of the restaurant there is a handy outlet that sells soups, sandwiches, and pastries made on the premises, an excellent to-go resource (see page 164).

ISA ·

3324 Steiner Street (between
Chestnut and Lombard)
415-567-9588
Open Tuesday though Thursday
5:30 P.M. to 10 P.M., Friday and
Saturday until 10:30 P.M.
Moderate
Credit cards: MC, V

Isa's concept of serving small plates of French food to be shared strikes me as a little odd. Why share a pretty green salad tossed in good sherry vinaigrette or a small, luscious, expertly seared slice of foie gras with sautéed nectarines in a citrus tinged sauce? As far as I'm concerned, that piece of foie gras is just right for me. I also had a hard time being generous with some fresh shrimp sautéed and finished off with a gorgeous lobster and shrimp reduction. I wanted to sop up all the juices myself with a couple of slices of baguette. In fact, very few of those plates are easy to share. A thick, snowy hunk of sea bass wrapped in golden potato slices and moistened with a capery brown butter sauce is awkward to divide. And strands of al dente spaghetti in a creamy basil sauce with slices of grilled eggplant flop all over the table.

I guess the notion is to keep portions small and prices down. Of course, I'm perfectly willing to order two or three of chef Luke Sung's accomplished little creations and eat them all myself. Judging by the crowds that perpetually fill the tiny indoor dining room and the more expansive candlelit tented dining area in the back, most people love the idea of making a meal out of bites. The knowledgeable waiters bring empty plates for everyone and place all dishes in the middle of the table. The interesting, reasonably priced wine list with lots of European imports has been honed to fit this style of dining, with many wines offered by the glass.

The outdoor dining area, securely covered with canvas even when it rains, has the advantage of being less noisy than most crowded restaurants around town. However, strategically placed heaters on stands tend to roast some diners while others stay chilly. The best solution is to wear layers when you eat here. The dance of climate control—adjusting the heaters during the meal—only adds to the fun.

MERENDA . . . .

1809 Union Street (between
Laguna and Octavia)
415-346-7373
Open Wednesday through Saturday
5:30 to 9:30 P.M., Sunday until 9 P.M.
Moderate
Credit cards: AE, DC, MC, V

People like to be nudged into ordering something new. Merenda's menu formula, which charges by number of courses rather than dish, somehow opens up the meal and frees you to order anything you want on the menu. (A minimum of two courses, currently $30, is required; a third course is $38 and a fourth is $42). This means that you can try two first courses that take your fancy and chef Keith Luce will adjust them so that they make a meal. Or you can put together a dinner of a second and a third course, or just a third course and dessert. Since his menu is a mélange of French, Italian, and California creations, you might begin your meal in northern France with a *bouchon*-style dish of sliced *lyonnaise rosette* (a cured sausage) with warm potato salad and cornichons; then head to Provence with cranberry bean and summer squash soup; and end up in California via northern Italy with roasted free-range chicken with organic beets and seventeen-year-old *balsamico*. Not a rustic cook at all, Luce uses lots of rich, reduced sauces on his meats; his house-made pastas are dressed with more complexity than any in Italy; and his desserts are highly composed. You get fancy cooking based on French techniques for a moderate cost.

The small, romantic dining room, with a compact service bar whose stools are always occupied by diners, has become a Pacific Heights and Cow Hollow meeting place. Raney Luce runs the floor and her husband always emerges from the kitchen to talk to his patrons. The personal involvement of this husband and wife team makes their restaurant all the more popular. You must reserve well ahead and it's a good idea to bring an appetite. Luce's food is rich and tempting.

PANE E VINO . . . .

3011 Steiner Street (between
Union and Filbert)
415-346-2111
Open Monday through Thursday
11 A.M. to 2 P.M., Sunday through
Thursday 5 to 10 P.M., Friday and
Saturday 11 A.M. to 9:30 P.M.
Moderate
Credit cards: AE, DC , MC, V

Pane e Vino was one of the first restaurants in San Francisco to cook real northern Italian dishes using first-rate imported ingredients. Simple, authentic preparations like arugula salad; bread and tomato soup; juicy, thick veal chops; a whole striped bass grilled with fennel; lamb stew over soft white polenta; a sparkling warm salad of cuttlefish, mussels, green beans, and black olives rotate on and off of a menu mostly dedicated to pastas. On a recent visit, however, several of the formerly impeccable pastas were ruined by way too much raw-tasting garlic. You can still depend on Pane e Vino's classic bolognese.

Two small rustic dining rooms with terra-cotta floors and beamed ceilings are separated by a tiled open kitchen, cordoned off with counters that display attractive antipasti. The high noise level counterbalances intimately close tables, so you really can't eavesdrop on the local Pacific Heights politicos, doctors, and lawyers who consider Pane e Vino their club. They have come to appreciate the sophisticated Italian wine list and the insouciant but efficient young Italian waiters. You must book well ahead to secure a table at dinner.

3127 Fillmore Street (between
Filbert and Greenwich)
415-563-4755
www.plumpjack.com
Open Monday through Friday
11:30 A.M. to 2 P.M.;
nightly from 5:30 to 10 P.M.
Expensive
Credit cards: AE, DC , MC, V

PlumpJack is a small, sophisticated Pacific Heights hangout named for an opera written by Gordon Getty, the father of one of the owners. (Another is handsome, young politician Gavin Newsom.) With a beige, gray, and silver color scheme, irregularly shaped wood and metal chairs, banquettes upholstered in metallic silver and an abstract crossed-sword motif, the decor somehow suggests things medieval. An internal window looks across a walkway to a large Buddha in an Asian antiques shop, providing a serendipitous bit of decoration, while a completely separate and hidden private dining room in the back stands ready to host society bachelor parties. Service is top-notch.

Over the nine years it has been open, PlumpJack has hired a number of chefs, some okay, some terrific, but the place has remained perennially successful. One reason is that PlumpJack has always been considered a good value by its well-heeled local patrons, who also shop for bargains at the PlumpJack wine store down the street. With the creative and whimsical James Ormsby currently at the helm, PlumpJack has evolved into a destination restaurant with higher prices.

On my last visit, two of us began with the requisite heirloom tomato and fresh mozzarella salad, which needed either better tomatoes or more dressing, and some small, delicious crab cakes made with a big proportion of crabmeat, paired with a juicy grapefruit salad in witty Ormsby style. This chef won me over with his braised oxtails at Bruno's, so I was elated to see them here. The meat of two big sections of tail fell off the bone into a meaty tomato sauce. They were not overcooked and kept plenty of intense flavor. Chewy black Italian rice and sweet corn salad in a tart, bracing vinaigrette made an exciting new dish out of grilled salmon.

Dessert is a high point at PlumpJack. A baked peach coated in hazelnut crumbs with whole toasted hazelnuts inside, next to a Florentine cup of peach sorbet, must have amused Ormsby as much as his appreciative patrons. It's just the kind of playful, seasonal dish that he's famous for. A dense, steaming-hot ricotta-lemon soufflé with blackberry sauce and some pretty, if sour, blackberries, stood tall, cooled by an elegant muscat sorbet. With two glasses of a flaccid rioja and a bottle of still water, the bill came to $145 with a much-deserved twenty-percent tip. Though the food can be complex and inventive, PlumpJack is not cheap anymore.

ROSE'S CAFE . . . .

2298 Union Street (at Steiner)
415-775-2200
Open Monday through Friday
7 A.M. to 4:30 P.M. and
5:30 to 10 P.M.; Saturday and
Sunday 8 A.M. to 4:30 P.M.,
and 5:30 to 10:30 P.M.
Inexpensive
Credit cards: AE, DC, D, MC, V

Rose's Cafe started out as a self-serve bakery-cafe specializing in "bread-centered Italian bar food," but morphed into a warm, casual neighborhood restaurant that serves breakfast, lunch, and dinner as well as Italian-themed baked goods to go. The menu has been somewhat shaped by the inherited cooking equipment in Rose's kitchen—limited stoves and electric grills, but huge baking capacity (the former tenant was Il Fornaio Bakery). The items to order are luscious breakfast pizzas with thin crusts, lots of melted fontina, thin slices of crispy-edged ham, and two runny baked eggs on top. I love this pizza and would order it all day if they offered it. For lunch I like a "cozy," a thin pocket bread filled with juicy salads that often include tomatoes, cucumbers, feta, and olives. If you break the crisp flat bread into it, it becomes a *fattoush* salad, resonant of the Middle East. At dinner Rose's brings out the roasts from the baking ovens—chicken, albacore tuna, pork stew, pork loin, and an array of Rose Pistola–like (see page 240) small plates. (Reed Hearon originally was responsible for the menus of both of these operations.) Because Rose's has a dual identity as cafe and restaurant, prices are moderate, service is quick, and you can eat a little or a lot without worrying about tying up a table. Outdoor lunch under an awning during sunny afternoons is particularly appealing, and the indoor dining area, finished in wood and tile with handsome wooden booths and tables and colorful Venetian glass light fixtures, always welcomes.

VIA VAI TRATTORIA . . . .

1715 Union Street (between
Gough and Octavia)
415-441-2111
www.viavai.com
Open Monday through Saturday
11:30 A.M. to 10 P.M., Sunday
noon to 2 P.M. and 4 to 9 P.M.
Inexpensive
Credit Cards: AE, CB, DC, D,
MC, V

A second venue from the owners of Pane e Vino (see page 156), Via Vai offers a casual and authentically Italian menu of wood-fired thin-crusted pizzas, pasta, vegetable-oriented antipasti, and simple main courses. Though hardly earthshaking, the menu is executed with such honesty and self-assurance that it feels fresh. While I don't recommend a thorough investigation of the entrées, you can't go wrong with the *Insalata di Lattuga Romana*, an absolutely delicious romaine salad with a creamy dressing of mustard, anchovies, and garlic, finished with coarsely grated Parmesan. My favorite pizza is the Tirolese, topped with tissue-thin slices of smoked prosciutto and argula leaves thrown on at the end. The pizzas are big rounds served on wooden boards; they need to be shared, especially if you want to try some of the tasty pasta dishes, such as a classic linguine with clams and mussels in the shells, bathed in olive oil, garlic, and white wine.

At normal dinner hours the dining room roars. Sound bounces off the hard surfaces— the open kitchen with a brick pizza oven, the tiled floors, the tall walls and ceiling. Despite the noise, Via Vai has been a busy neighborhood hangout from the moment it opened. The only successful restaurant in a once-seemingly hexed location, its exceptionally good value and gratifying food has won a steady stream of customers who are happy to drop in and wait for a table.

YUKOL PALACE. . . . .

2380 Lombard Street (near Scott)
415-922-1599
Open Monday through Thursday
5 to 10 P.M., Friday and Saturday
until 10:30 P.M.
Inexpensive
Credit cards: MC, V

This little restaurant has engendered a loyal neighborhood following for its clean, brightly seasoned Thai standards. The restaurant does a lot of take-out business, and in fact that's how I discovered it. My teenage son developed a habit for Yukol's *pad thai,* panfried rice noodles with shrimp, ground peanuts, tofu, egg, and bean sprouts in a well-balanced tamarind sauce. The delicate satays—bamboo-skewered slices of aromatically marinated chicken or beef—are so juicy and sparkly that the mild peanut sauce served with them isn't needed. I do love the juicy cucumber salad accompaniment, however. Shredded green papaya salad is spiked with hot chiles, deepened with dried shrimp, and lifted with lemony dressing. The coconut curries in different hues and degrees of hotness have depth and fragrance. Someone with a refined sensibility heads up the kitchen because all the food here has clarity of flavor, succulence, and a pretty presentation. If you, too, have the urge for sweet and spicy Thai noodles, crispy spring rolls, juicy satay, and perfumed green curry, Yukol Palace will satisfy it.

CAFÉS

THE WARMING HUT CAFE AND BOOKSTORE

1 mile into the walk from Crissy
Field to Fort Point, in the Presidio
415-561-3040
www.ggnpa.org
Open daily 9 A.M. to 5 P.M.
Credit cards: AE, MC, V

The promenade along the beaches and the bay to the towering base of the Golden Gate Bridge at Fort Point is one of the most spectacular walks in the world—out and back. However, the wind whipping through the Golden Gate from the ocean can be cutting; hence the new Warming Hut in a renovated wooden structure in a part of the Presidio now belonging to the Golden Gate National Recreation Area.

Normally you would expect to find hot dogs and potato chips at a snack bar like this, but Alice Waters consulted on the menu. For $3, kids and adults can get a crunchy, warm grilled cheese sandwich on Panorama bakery bread accompanied with a pile of peeled carrot sticks. I opt for the grilled ham-and-cheese sandwich with a layer of tangy spring greens and threads of marinated red onion inside. This sandwich is amazingly light and savory. A welcome clam chowder and other hot soups are brought in from an outfit called Stock Pot. The limited menu works because the two counterpeople can execute it perfectly and still keep the lines moving. Fresh-squeezed orange juice and natural sodas are available, as well as passable espresso and cappuccino.

The light, airy aesthetic of the Warming Hut, whose floor-to-ceiling glass door allows patrons to look directly at the water and the sky, matches the vista, a grand juxtaposition of urban and natural. If the weather permits, patrons can take their lunches outside to solid wood picnic tables on the side of the building protected by the wind. While the Hut itself may not be a destination, the walk certainly is, and having a place to get a respectable bite in this breathtaking setting only enhances the experience.

BARS

BALBOA CAFE . . . .

3199 Fillmore Street (between Greenwich and Filbert)
415-921-3944
Open Monday through Friday
11:30 A.M. to 11 P.M.,
Saturday 11 A.M to 11 P.M. ,
Sunday 11 A.M. to 10 P.M.
Credit cards: AE, MC, V

Balboa anchors one point of the Bermuda triangle, a Cow Hollow intersection with bars at each of three corners, attracting a crowd of aging fraternity and sorority types. The expansive windows let passersby view the party and decide whether they want to join it. During the day, the clubby, light-filled interior makes for a pleasant setting for lunch and that first martini. As a division of the PlumpJack conglomerate, the Balboa continues to be a popular with the Pacific Heights social crowd who go there for hamburgers.

BUS STOP . . . .

1901 Union Street (at Laguna)
415-567-6905
Open Monday through Friday
10 A.M. to 2 A.M., Saturday and
Sunday 9 A.M. to 2 A.M.
Credit cards: AE, MC, V

Though young, single heterosexuals consider the Cow Hollow–Marina area their playground, everyone likes to hang out at Bus Stop, an endearing neighborhood saloon that has been open continuously since 1900. People of all ages watch games on easily visible video screens with impeccable reception, shoot pool at two tables, or gaze at the passing parade on Union Street. Drinks are generously poured and correctly mixed. The good-natured bartenders happily serve both regulars and drop-ins.

COZMO'S CORNER GRILL. . . . .

2001 Chestnut Street (at Fillmore)
415-351-0175
www.cozmoscorner.com
Open Tuesday and Wednesday
4:30 P.M. to 12:30 A.M., Thursday
through Saturday until 2 A.M.,
Sunday and Monday until 11:30 P.M.
Credit cards: AE, MC, V

Formerly Marina Joe's, then a series of other places including a full-scale brewery, Cozmo's Corner now has been transformed into a dark, New York–style bar with wood paneling, shaded light sconces, and TV monitors hanging from the ceiling. The bartenders hand shake classic and creative cocktails made with fresh-squeezed juices and the usual mind-boggling pharmacopoeia of spirits. Fourteen wines by the glass, mostly from the West Coast, are poured and if you get hungry you can eat at the bar or in the red brick dining area at a wooden booth. Personally, I like to indulge in Cozmo's gigantic banana split, easily enough for two or three and distinguished by caramelized bananas. It is a pastry chef's breakthrough on a soda fountain dessert in which the bananas are finally raised to the sugar level of the rest of the dish. The rest of the menu is serviceable.

MATRIX/FILLMORE . . . .

3138 Fillmore Street (between
Greenwich and Filbert)
415-563-4180
Open daily 5:30 P.M. to 2 A.M.
Credit cards: AE, MC, V

When you've met the heartthrob of your dreams in the crowded, pounding front barroom outfitted with cushy ottomans and cocktail tables, you can sequester him in a little velvet booth, draw the curtains, and get naughty. Such seductive cocktails as the "Apple Pie," Stoli Vanilla and Vincent Wild Appel; a thirst quenching *mojito* of sugar-muddled mint, Mt. Gay sugarcane rum, and club soda; or a glass of classy wine from the inventory of the PlumpJack wine store (see page 168) down the street (they share owners) will help things along. Then you can emerge and hit the back room where stylish nibbles conceived by PlumpJack chef James Ormsby emanate from a tiny open service kitchen. The juicy ceviches are particularly bright and tasty, and the trio of ahi tartare cones makes for sensuous eating. Matrix/Fillmore represents the bar of the twenty-first century, with a huge, upscale menu of cocktails, spirits, and wines; exotic bites; a DJ; plasma screens and video monitors; inviting living-room furniture; fireplace; and a sleek, happening bar with polished young, black-clad bartenders. For nighttime imbibing, Matrix/Fillmore is a destination.

PERRY'S . . . .

1944 Union Street (between
Laguna and Buchanan)
415-922-9022
www.perrysunionstreet.citysearch.com
Open Monday through Friday
9 A.M. to 11 P.M., Saturday and
Sunday until midnight
Credit cards: AE, MC, V

Perry Butler practically started the singles' bar movement in the 1960s at his eponymously named watering hole. Now many of his patrons, two or three marriages later, will admit to pushing fifty (well, late fifties), but the spirit of the place remains convivial and fun. As much a spot for a blue cheese salad and a good hamburger with cottage fries as a bar, Perry's continues to serve classic pub food in congenial surroundings.

CAFE MERENDA

2760 Octavia Street (between
Union and Green)
415-885-2712
Open Monday through Friday 9 A.M.
to 7 P.M., Saturday 11 A.M to 7 P.M.
Cash only

This jewellike shop displays its imported artisan pastas,
balsamico vinegars, and dried porcini like treasures in
an antique hutch. You can get grilled Italian sandwiches
to eat at the moment, a few good-looking salads, like a
classic Italian tuna and white bean, and a handful of
Italian cheeses. Some of Keith Luce's handmade ravioli
from his restaurant Merenda (see page 156) around the
corner might also be available. The lucky few sit at the one tiny table inside the shop or at a
few tiny tables outside by the open front window of the café, warmed by the afternoon sun.

DESIREE . . . .

39 Mesa, Suite 108, Building 39
in the Presidio
415-561-2336
Open Monday through Friday
8 A.M. to 4 P.M.
Cash only

When the Presidio's choicest piece of real estate was
liberated from the U.S. Army, a few small private businesses got to move into the nooks and crannies of
abandoned barracks and administrative buildings. One
of them, Desiree, a tiny breakfast and lunch café
conceived and operated by Annie Gingrass, former co-
owner and chef of Hawthorne Lane, is the best kept
secret in town. It's located in the San Francisco Film Centre building, which runs along the
east side of the massive plaza at the center of the Presidio. (Arguello drops you off there if
you take it all the way down from the Presidio Golf Course.)

When you push open the heavy wooden doors to the building, the savory smells of
roasting pork and toasting cheese pull you down the hall to Desiree. You step out of a gray
institutional warren of offices into the warmth and glow of Annie Gingrass's stylish parlor,
not quite believing that a place like this could be there. The little room, mostly occupied
with a handcrafted counter (the real kitchen is located in the building's basement), is filled
with beautiful, simple things: a wooden armoire, a big vase of tall tulips, a smart, floral-
print high banquette with cushions. At the most, fifteen can sit at the peripheries and
throughout the afternoon sixty people do. But Desiree was conceived around the box lunch,
and the cafe doles out many of these corrugated cardboard treasure chests containing made-
to-order sandwich, salad, and freshly baked cookies.

I chose for my picnic a stunning chicken salad sandwich on lightly toasted white
bread. The chicken was so tender, moist, and gently poached that it practically melted into
a mayonnaise scented with orange and lime zest. Shaved purple Persian carrots in a sparkly
Vietnamese dressing performed like a salad and a pickle. Three thin, chewy caramel cookies
came in their own cellophane bag tied with a ribbon. On another day I ate my way through
the rest of the menu, seated at a high table on a soft banquette. A bright green soup of
potato and green garlic served in a thick polka-dotted bowl came to life with several large
pinches of kosher salt. Miniature bay shrimp, asparagus, orange segments, and arugula were

all tossed together into a juicy pile dripping with luscious creamy balsamic dressing, styled out with mustard seed. I was about to forgo dessert until I spotted a lemon tart on the counter. One of the best pastry chefs in town, Rosemary Swan, makes all the desserts and morning breads.

I am a big fan of Annie Gingrass's cool, sophisticated sensibility and her quiet warmth. I see her every Saturday at the farmers' market buying for her café. How often does a big-time chef actually cook lunch for you, as if you were seated in her home kitchen? Gingrass has gone back to the basics here and we box lunchers get all the benefits.

GREENS TO GO . . . .

Fort Mason, Building A
(Buchanan at Marina Boulevard)
415-771-6330
www.greensrestaurant.com
Open Monday through Thursday
8 A.M. to 8 P.M., Friday and
Saturday 8 A.M. to 5 P.M.,
Sunday 9 A.M. to 4 P.M.
Credit cards: D, MC, V

Sometimes the pull of our beautiful bay is too irresistible and all you want to do is sit on a dock and have a bite to eat. Head right over to the Greens to Go counter at Fort Mason for a cup of Greens's famous cumin-scented black bean chili or grilled marinated tofu sandwich with horseradish mayonnaise on soft thick wheat bread. Greens's chef, Annie Somerville, has added other choices: organic egg salad sandwiches; potato salad with green beans, capers, and red onions; vegetable curries and stews. I'm partial to her aromatic southwestern vegetable stews with corn, squashes, and dried chiles. Buttermilk scones, brownies, and cobblers made in Greens's pastry kitchen can also serve as a bayside snack. If you're catering a meeting or a meal, you can call ahead and everything will be packed and ready to go.

LUCCA . . . .

2120 Chestnut Street
(between Steiner and Pierce)
415-921-7873
Open Monday through Friday
9 A.M. to 6:30 P.M.,
Saturday and Sunday until 6 P.M.
Credit cards: MC, V

Food lovers from all over the city migrate to the well-stocked Lucca delicatessen for two house specialties: superb celery-scented bolognese sauce sold by the pint, and tender hand-rolled spinach-and-ricotta ravioli sold by the box. With either of these items in your shopping bag you have the foundation for a gorgeous meal.

Opened in 1929 by Mike Bosco, a man with a great recipe, and two partners, Lucca supplied Nob Hill hotels with ravioli. Now his son Eddie and two grown grandchildren, Linda and Paul, carry on the tradition, thank goodness.

Around lunchtime, a line forms in front of the long counter stocked with always-fresh foods (nothing sits around at Lucca) for made-to-order Italian sandwiches on Italian rolls and wedges of Lucca's famous spinach frittata. Rotisserie chickens; irresistible marinated vegetable salad rife with beans, artichokes, and chunks of avocado; Acme bread; Italian cheeses; an excellent nutty Emmenthal; imported olive oils and pastas; anchovies in salt; and house-made minestrone sold by the pint mean that customers never walk out the door with only one item.

JUST DESSERTS. . . . .

3735 Buchanan Street (at Marina)
415-922-8675
www.justdesserts.com
Open Monday through Friday
7 A.M. to 7 P.M., Saturday 8 a.m.
to 7 P.M., Sunday 10 A.M. to 6 P.M.
Credit cards: AE, MC, V

Elliot Hoffman started this chain of American-style dessert cafés in 1974 on the strength of a cheesecake recipe. This store, across the street from the mammoth Marina Safeway, where relationships blossom among the salad greens, causes particular anguish to those who work on their bodies next door at a popular gym. A hefty wedge of Just Desserts's moist devil's food cake with fudge frosting can obliterate the effects of a good workout. And, despite their healthful ring, the classic carrot cake with cream cheese frosting, homey lemon-buttermilk cake, and banana bread made with sour cream and walnuts cannot be considered diet fare. Just Desserts bakes everything from scratch, using whole butter and wholesome products, and delivers to its cafés every morning. Freshness is key here.

In 1992, when Just Desserts moved its bakery to a large facility in the Bay View–Hunters Point neighborhood, Hoffman was instrumental in securing an adjacent empty lot for the Garden Project, a program started by the San Francisco County Sheriff's Department. Now, inmates and ex-cons grow fresh vegetables for soup kitchens all over the city. The bakery also uses some of the produce nurtured next door in the urban garden.

LA NOUVELLE PÂTISSERIE . . . .

2184 Union Street (between
Webster and Fillmore)
415-931-7655
www.lanouvellepatisserie.com
Open Monday through Thursday
7 A.M. to 10:30 P.M., Friday and
Saturday 7 A.M. to 11 P.M.,
Sunday 8 A.M. to 8 P.M.
Credit cards: MC , V

The croissant, in all its flaky, buttery glory, brings me regularly to this French pastry shop. I take mine home, but many eat the croissants at small café tables in the shop accompanied with decent café au lait. The cases here are full of colorful fruit tarts and handsome French pastries in generally fresh condition. A favorite item, especially among the French customers, is the bamboo, a crisp puff-pastry sandwich filled with raspberry jam. Airy baguettes, just like the ones sold on Paris street corners, are also available.

COFFEE TASTING

Jim Reynolds, the head coffee roaster and buyer for Peet's, invited me to a coffee tasting at the Emeryville headquarters. He set out three flights of short glasses, each with an inch of coarsely ground coffee at the bottom. He poured water that had cooled down a few minutes from the boiling point into each glass and then stirred. We waited to taste until the coffee cooled to warm.

Armed with a brass spittoon and a rounded soup spoon, we began by noisily slurping up, actually drawing in through the teeth, each coffee. We swished each spoonful around our tongues, smelled it in the back of our mouth, chewed it, and spit it into the receptacle. Very distinct characteristics of each coffee became clear.

Coffees from the Americas—Guatemala, Costa Rica, and Panama— define, to my mind, what we dream of in a cup of coffee. They are full-bodied, balanced, unquirky, aromatic, rich. Guatemala is Jim Reynolds's favorite of all the coffees. I preferred the slightly fuller cup from Costa Rican beans. Lightest of the three was Panama coffee, with flowery overtones. Peet's House Blend and Blend 101 are made entirely from Latin American coffee beans.

The African coffees—Kenyan, Ethiopian, and Arabian Mocha Sanani— have a spiciness and pronounced acidity. The rare Arabian Mocha Sanani, because it is harvested and dried so primitively, has a syrupy, fermented quality to it. Coffees from the Pacific—New Guinea, Sumatra, and Sulawesi— have distinctive herbal and earthy qualities. Given the characteristics of the different coffees, you begin to understand the advantages of blends like Peet's Top Blend, which combines coffees from the Pacific and Latin America, or the famous Major Dickason's, whose regional makeup remains a secret. Each bean has something to say.

Peet's generally roasts darker than most other companies. However, two blends, Italian roast and the really dark French roast, get even longer roastings. Very dark roasting produces a cup with less body, but with an intense flavor and smoky overtone that stand up to milk and sugar, good for morning latte or café au lait. After the coffee tasting, I started enjoying coffee in a new way. What was a generic flavor blossomed with complexity and nuance. Here was a food I have every morning and I had never explored its possibilities. An hour at a Peet's tasting could improve the quality of your daily life significantly.

PEET'S COFFEE & TEA. . . . .

2156 Chestnut Street (between
Pierce and Steiner)
415-931-8302
www.peets.com
Open Sunday through Friday 6 A.M.
to 7 P.M., Saturday 7 A.M. to 8 P.M.
Credit cards: AE, MC, V

Widely considered to be the Cadillac of coffee stores, Peet's has set the standard for coffee-bean buying and roasting throughout the country. If you are a true coffee drinker, you will love the intensity and individual character of Peet's carefully roasted beans. Each store, the most famous being the original location at the corner of Walnut and Vine in Berkeley, brews coffee every thirty minutes, throwing out any leftovers. When you buy a pound of beans, you get a free cup—and what a cup it is! You will never taste coffee with as much flavor and depth.

There are many reasons for the heady richness of Peet's brews. Selective buying from known producers all over the world; daily roasting of each type of bean to exact degrees of toastiness; diligent tasting of coffee made with the newly roasted beans; and daily delivery of the beans to the stores all contribute to the coffee's brilliant flavor.

Although the list of different coffees can seem daunting to the uninitiated, the company has published an extremely helpful booklet describing each one, with recommendations from the head roaster and buyer. It sheds light on the difference in flavor among coffees from different regions of the world, lists the components of Peet's blends, and describes the effects of different degrees of roasting. The booklet is free and available at all Peet's stores. Of course, the only way to understand the differences in flavor is to taste the coffees side by side. Peet's personnel are willing to set up coffee tastings for their customers. Take them up on it and come to your own conclusions.

In addition to coffee beans, Peet's offers a variety of teas, coffee- and tea-brewing equipment from all over the world, and a mail-order service. For other locations, see pages 276, 307, 381, 438, and 459.

MARKETS

MARINA SUPER . . . .

2323 Chestnut Street
(between Scott and Divisadero)
415-346-7470
Open Monday through
Saturday 7 A.M. to 9 P.M.,
Sunday 8 A.M. to 9 P.M.
Credit cards: AE, MC, V

With Susan Herrmann Loomis's *Italian Farmhouse Cookbook* in hand, I walked into the Marina Super, next door to Cafe Marimba, one day after lunch. This market, with a butcher and deli counter, has been supplying the Italian community of the Marina with all the ingredients needed to cook dishes just like the ones in any classic Italian cookbook. I picked up a free-range chicken, pancetta, and some very lean ground sirloin.
Rather nice vine-ripened tomatoes, for mid-October, and beautiful red peppers were piled outside on produce tables. Plump heads of garlic, huge bunches of Italian parsley, fresh

thyme, and oregano are regularly available. Though the market does not buy organic produce, they always have the best commercially available representatives of whatever may be
in season. You never see bad green beans here when good ones are available. Organic
canned tomato products earn their own display shelf. Berkeley Farms hormone-free dairy
products are stocked. Baskets of dried beans, ranging from gigantic borlotti to tiny white
beans, call out to be made into a Tuscan soup. A whole rack of fresh breads from artisan
local bakeries completes the family meal. Although very much a neighborhood market, this
can be one of the most useful stops in the city for Italian-American shopping.

WINES AND SPIRITS

CALIFORNIA WINE MERCHANT . . . .

3237 Pierce Street (between
Lombard and Chestnut)
415-567-0646
www.californiawinemerchant.com
Open Monday through Saturday
11 A.M. to 7 P.M.,
Sunday noon to 5 P.M.
Credit cards: MC, V

Hard-to-find California wines line the walls of this tiny
twenty-one-year-old shop guarded by a huge golden
retriever snoring away at the front door. The elegance
of a shop that does one thing well cannot be underestimated. Only high-quality California and a few Oregon
wines tasted and chosen by the owner, Gregory
O'Flynn, get a slot in the floor-to-ceiling wooden racks.
Small production wines like Terrace zinfandel or
impossible-to-find Stony Hill chardonnay or the ele-
gant Shafer merlot can all be found here at fair-market prices. Since the wine selections
have been so carefully edited, shopping here will expand your knowledge of the most exciting California wines. The shop will ship.

PLUMPJACK WINES . . . .

3201 Fillmore Street (at Filbert)
415-346-9870
www.plumpjack.com
Open Monday through Saturday
11 A.M. to 8 P.M., Sunday until 6 P.M.
Credit cards: AE, D, MC, V

The original Cow Hollow PlumpJack specializes in
California wines, allowing the new Noe Valley branch
(see page 229) to deal in interesting and inexpensive
imports. The bottom line is that you can get bottles
and cases from the inventories of either of the stores,
with discounts available on most case purchases, including mixed cases, at either location. The store believes in
personal service—as most small wineshops do—and will steer you to wines that will
enhance the dinner you're cooking or wine that will please the person cooking dinner for
you. They will deliver cases and help you find everyday drinking wines for under $10. The
Cow Hollow branch carries wines that reflect the tastes of its immediate neighborhood,
which tend to be less world beat, more familiar, and a little pricier than the Noe Valley
selection, though many a PJW label merlot and chardonnay gets carried out of the Cow
Hollow store for $9.99.

PASTA WITH FAVA BEANS, POTATOES, AND BASIL

SERVES 6 TO 8

This recipe from the *Italian Farmhouse Cookbook* by Susan Herrmann Loomis, a personal, ultra-accessible cookbook, produces one of the best pesto sauces I've ever tasted. You can use the pesto in other dishes, but it's divine in this pasta, which is just as good with small green beans as harder-to-find favas. You can get all your ingredients at the Marina Super.

VEGETABLES AND PASTA

3 pounds fresh small fava beans in their pods, shelled and skinned, or 12 ounces green beans, trimmed and cut crosswise in half

12 ounces new potatoes, peeled and cut crosswise into ¼-inch-thick slices

1 pound good-quality dried pasta, such as *cavatappi, farfalle*, or *fusilli*

BASIL PESTO

1 clove garlic, cut in half, green germ removed

⅓ cup (generous ½ ounce) grated Parmigiano-Reggiano

1 tablespoon pine nuts

7 cups loosely packed fresh basil leaves

¼ cup extra virgin olive oil

Fine sea salt

———————

1 tablespoon unsalted butter

1 Bring a large pot of salted water to a boil over high heat. Add the fava or green beans, return to a boil, and boil the favas for about 3 minutes or the beans for 5 to 7 minutes, or until they have softened but still have texture. If using favas, remove them at this point with a slotted spoon; the green beans require further cooking. Add the potatoes and cook for 5 minutes or until they are tender. Be sure not to overcook the potatoes so they won't fall apart. Using a slotted spoon, remove the vegetables from the pan and loosely cover them so they retain their heat.

2 Return the pot of cooking water to a boil, add the pasta, stir, and cook for about 7 minutes, or until it is al dente (tender but still firm to the bite).

3 While the pasta is cooking, prepare the pesto. Place the garlic, cheese, and pine nuts in a large mortar or food processor and grind with a pestle or process until they are minced. Add the basil and grind or process until it is minced. Add the oil in a fine stream, mixing or processing all the while so that it combines well with the other ingredients. Season to taste with salt and transfer to a large shallow serving bowl.

4 When the pasta is cooked, drain it, reserving ½ cup of the cooking water. Add the pasta to the pesto along with the vegetables and toss. Add the butter and toss, then add enough of the cooking water so the pasta is pleasantly moist, not watery. Adjust the seasoning and serve.

NOTE: If your fava beans are very fresh, you may not need to peel them. Sample one and see. If the peel is bitter, the favas will be better off without it.

COOKWARE AND BOOKS

FREDERICKSEN'S HARDWARE . . . .

3029 Fillmore Street (between
Union and Filbert)
415-292-2950
Open Monday through Friday
9 A.M. to 7 P.M., Saturday until
6 P.M., Sunday 10 A.M. to 6 P.M.
Credit cards: MC, V

Hardware stores don't get better than this. Not only does Fredericksen's stock every conceivable item you might need for your house and kitchen, but the service is so good that you will be steered to exactly the right thing. One third of this packed store is dedicated to kitchen and housewares and the level of sophistication is high. This is the place to find kitchen timers, food mills, springform pans, juicers, coffee grinders, good basic lines of pots and pans, glass baking dishes, graters—all the building blocks of a practical, old-fashioned kitchen and then some. Fredericksen's will always have the innovation on the traditional item if it is really an improvement, but it does not carry frivolous gadgets. I love the integrity of this store, the dependability, the completeness. I'm willing to pay a bit more here because I know they will have what I need and I won't have to waste time driving around town.

WILLIAMS-SONOMA . . . .

2000 Chestnut Street (at Fillmore)
415-929-2520
www.williams-sonoma.com
Open Monday through Saturday
10 A.M. to 8 P.M.,
Sunday 11 A.M. to 6 P.M.
Credit cards: AE, D, MC, V

Another branch of the tony kitchen and tableware chain started in San Francisco by Chuck Williams. See page 127 for more information.

THE MISSION DISTRICT

BERNAL HEIGHTS

THE EXCELSIOR

RESTAURANTS

1   Alma
2   Andalu
3   Angkor Borei
4   Balompie Cafe
5   Burger Joint
6   butterfly
7   Charanga
8   Delfina
9   El Balazito
10 El Perol
11 Fina Estampa
12 Foreign Cinema
13 La Corneta Taqueria
14 The Last Supper Club
15 La Taqueria
16 Liberty Café
17 Limon
18 Lorca
19 Los Jarritos
20 Luna Park
21 Palatino
22 Pancho Villa Taqueria
23 San Miguel
24 Slanted Door
25 Ti Couz Crêperie
26 Timo's
27 Walzwerk
28 Watergate
29 Woodward's Garden

CAFÉS

30 Dolores Park Cafe
31 Papa Toby's Cafe

BARS

32 Dalva
33 Lazlo
34 Make-Out Room

DELICATESSENS/TAKEOUT

35 Doña Tere's Cart
36 El Tonayense Taco Trucks
37 La Palma Mexicatessen

38 Lucca Ravioli Company
39 Tortas Los Picudos
40 Valencia Whole Foods Market

BAKERIES/PASTRIES

41 Dianda's Italian-American Pastries
42 Panaderia La Mexicana
43 Tartine

ICE CREAM/CHOCOLATES

44 Bombay Ice Creamery
45 Mitchell's Ice Cream

MARKETS

46 Bi-Rite Market

ETHNIC MARKETS

47 Bombay Bazaar
48 Casa Lucas
37 La Palma Mexicatessen
49 Samirami's Imports
50 Val 16 Market

PRODUCE

51 Alemany Farmers' Market
48 Casa Lucas
52 La Loma Produce
53 23rd and Mission Produce
50 Val 16 Market

MEAT AND POULTRY

54 La Gallinita
55 The Lucky Pork Store
56 Mission Market Meat
57 Polarica

FISH

56 Mission Market Fish and Poultry
58 Sun Fat Seafood Company

COOKWARE AND BOOKS

59 Encantada Gallery of Fine Arts

RESTAURANTS

ALMA ·

1101 Valencia Street (at 21st Street)
415-401-8959
www.almacomida.com
Open Monday through Thursday
5:30 to 10:30 P.M., Friday and
Saturday 5:30 to 11 P.M.
Moderate
Credit cards: MC, V

During this moment of the twenty-first century, small personal restaurants with a sense of place feel right. Reasonable, recession-era price points and a world-encompassing diversity also win approval. That's why Alma, which opened in the Mission on September 10, 2001, took hold against all odds. Its creator, Johnny Alamilla, invented his own version of Latin fusion, which in his hands is ingredient inspired and ungimmicky—bright but restrained. This is no glamorous Farallon (see page 100) or monumental Bacar (see page 345), but a sweet neighborhood restaurant so good that it pulls in patrons from way across town.

Each dish boasts Latin flare, but cannot be identified as regional Mexican, Caribbean, or Argentinean. The cooking comes from Alamilla's imagination. Most diners start off with a ceviche—the edible counterpart of a cocktail. I really like Alma's demure presentations—tiny cubes of bluefin tuna dressed with chiles, scallions, and coconut milk; the delicacy of wild striped bass gently teased with tissue-thin torpedo onions and Valencia orange juice; tiny bay scallops in a champagne glass of cucumber-lemon consommé puddled with a few drops of earthy Brazilian *dênde* oil. With palate awakened, move on to Alamilla's signature tortilla soup, a tour de force. The tortillas are not visible, but puréed into this velvety potion of onions, potatoes, and chiles, a drizzle of fragrant cumin and lime *crema* adding the finishing high note. A savory flan always appears on the small menu, such as a tender custard laced with Manchego cheese and puréed spinach. That would be delectable enough, but Alamilla makes it even more maddeningly rich and delicious with a mildly smoky chipotle chile cream sauce. Cream and chiles don't seem like an obvious combination, but Alamilla sure knows how to meld them.

Alamilla's sense of proportion makes his hanger steak plate fun to eat. Instead of a slab, the chewy, flavorful steak, charred on the outside, pink and juicy inside, is cut into thin slices. Alamilla gets his meats from Niman Ranch. You can taste the difference in a spice-rubbed pork chop served with lively garlic- and scallion-infused mashed potatoes and a pile of shockingly orangy cabbage slaw.

One of the thrills of eating at Alma is the one-page wine list, a scintillating tour of wines made all over the Spanish-speaking world (with a little Portuguese thrown in). Pamela Busch, a founder of Hayes and Vine (see page 66) and now a wine consultant, rounds up the most remarkable tasting wines for Alma and keeps prices thankfully affordable. The wines suit the food perfectly and the food makes the wines taste even more delicious. This is the way wine and food should interact.

Alma's decor, even the size of the dining room, resonates with the style of the cooking. Beautiful lanterns held by wrought ironwork descend from the high ceiling. Six stools at a polished wooden bar in the center of the room offer a place to wait for a table or have a bite. Simple white paper- and linen-covered tables and wooden chairs invite you to eat, the way they do in the neighborhood bistros of Paris. Alma brings all the elusive elements of the successful restaurant together. Though it may not have been lucky to open when it did, this small, evocative Mission District restaurant might not have taken hold when everyone wanted $100 bottles of table wine and $35 entrées. Now people seem to be more interested in soul—*alma* in Spanish—and Alamilla has plenty of it.

ANDALU

3198 16th Street (at Guerrero)
415-621-2211
www.andalusf.com
Open Tuesday through Thursday
5:30 P.M. to 11 P.M., Friday and
Saturday until 11:30 P.M.,
Sunday and Monday until 10 P.M.
Inexpensive
Credit cards: AE, DC, MC, V

The small-plate menu at Andalu takes the tapas genre way beyond Spain and even the Mediterranean. The dishes come from all over the globe, but mostly from chef Ben deVries's imagination. DeVries, who formerly headed the kitchen at the now-closed Ristorante Ecco and who also gathered experience at a world-beat collection of groundbreaking San Francisco restaurants, cooks with such self-assurance that almost every dish works. Each of his eclectic preparations possesses internal logic and all have a unifying deVries signature tastiness.

Though the menu changes daily somewhat, look for Ahi Tartar Tacos, three crisp, miniature tacos filled with a ceviche of tuna in a vibrant marinade of chile and lime, topped with finely minced mango salsa and micro-greens. They look as if they were made by an elf. I am also wild about Fritti Misti, an airily layered salad of warm potato and artichoke chips interwoven with tender young leaves of arugula, drizzled with aioli. Ethereal. Duck Confit Spring Rolls are clean and cool, wrapped in rice paper and filled with sprouts. The duck acts as a seasoning, as does the piquant chile dipping sauce. And I have to give Andalu the *brandade* award—their creamy, fluffy version of salt cod beaten with milk and potato, topped with aioli (beware of the searing hot earthenware ramekin it's served in) raises the bar. DeVries knows how to make his bites irresistible. There are twenty-eight small plates ranging in price from $2 to $12. Four shared dishes make a meal for two, so you can eat frugally here—and roughly within one cuisine if you choose carefully. But it's hard because of the tempting wine list with lots of glasses, tasting flights, and many half bottles from all over the world. Andalu's desserts are another siren call to continue eating and spending. You must succumb to Fresh Donut Holes with Castillian Hot Cocoa, one of the greatest desserts in the city. You get a pile of hot, yeasty, sugared doughnut holes with two espresso cups of the sweetest, richest, creamiest hot chocolate you ever dreamed of, each topped with a raft of thick, sweet, stiffly whipped cream. Let me just say that this innovative cook writes with a flourish.

ANGKOR BOREI . . . .

3471 Mission Street (between
Cortland and 30th Street)
415-550-8417
Open daily 11 A.M. to 10 P.M.
Inexpensive
Credit cards: AE, D, MC, V

This neighborhood Cambodian restaurant, decorated
with handsome Khmer artifacts, turns out complex
dishes with surprising finesse. The dishes here are characterized by a ravishing tapestry of flavors, textures,
and colors. Like intricate Khmer carvings, Cambodian
food is composed of many tiny, exquisite, mosaiclike
elements, such as cold white noodles, julienned cucum-
bers, bean sprouts, basil, red chiles, and carrots, all in separate piles that come together with
a fragrant coconut milk dipping sauce; delicate Cambodian spring rolls with moist multi-
vegetable fillings; or crisp Cambodian omeletlike crepes folded over a juicy, crunchy filling
of vegetables, herbs, and nuts. I love the curries at Angkor Borei, particularly a fiery green
one aromatic with Thai basil and lemongrass served on Japanese eggplant and big chunks of
white fish. A milder red curry with many deep layers of flavor enhances tender sautéed
shrimp on a bed of bright green spinach. The charcoal broiling shows equal skill: marinated
chicken or beef skewers come with delicious vinegared vegetables—the perfect accompaniment. Even the rice, served from a covered silver tureen, has a marvelous nutty flavor and
chewy texture. Artfully presented and nuanced, yet immediately delicious, this Cambodian
food enchants everyone—even those trying Cambodian cooking for the first time. This so-
called neighborhood spot would be a find anywhere in the world.

BALOMPIE CAFE . . . .

3349 18th Street (at Capp)
415-648-9199
Open daily 8 A.M. to 9:30 P.M.
Inexpensive
Credit cards: MC, V

This immaculate, friendly, light-filled cafe with a bar on
one side, a couple of televisions, and a decor of soccer
banners makes the best Salvadoran *pupusas*, *pasteles*, and
yuca in the city. It's always busy, especially at lunch
when I like to go. At noon, the dining room is full of
moms and kids, workers on lunch break, and older
people out for a bite.

For $6.95 you can try all three specialties, a plate generous enough to share. The
pupusas—thin, tender, light *masa* pancakes stuffed with fresh cheese and *loroco*, a flowering
herb from El Salvador (my choice of filling, though you can get chicken, pork, or beans
and cheese)—taste like crepes to me. They're toasted on the griddle and the vegetable-
flecked cheese oozes out when you cut into it. A cabbage slaw dressed with assertive
Mexican oregano and fresh lime always comes with *pupusas*. You spoon some on top and
the combination is thrilling. Balompie's elegant pupusas alone with cabbage salad make for
a terrific bite.

I also like Balompie's deep-fried *pasteles*, Salvadoran empanadas of *masa* dough in the
shape of fat little footballs (American footballs with pointy ends) filled with chicken and
egg. Dark golden brown and supremely crunchy, they shatter in your mouth as you bite
into them, but the filling stays moist and juicy. Crispy deep-fried yuca and big, meaty
hunks of fat-laced, deep-fried pork butt (the Salvadoran version of *chicharrón*) fill out this
combo plate. The big chunks of yuca, a starchy vegetable, have creamy interiors and taste

divine with the fried pork. You eat the cabbage slaw with these, too. Have a refreshing glass of *arrayan*, a pale green fruit pulp that tastes like tart guava, or a cold beer.

BURGER JOINT. . . . .

807 Valencia Street (between
18th and 19th streets)
415-824-3494
www.burgerjoint.com
Open daily 11 A.M. to 11 P.M.
Inexpensive
Cash only

The cheerfully decorated, immaculate Burger Joint does what it does perfectly. The organic Niman Ranch hamburgers are cooked exactly to specification over a charcoal grill. They go on delicately crusty buns with decent tomato slices, red onion, and romaine on the side. I go for a pile of grilled onions for 50¢ additional. All condiments are meticulously maintained on each table. The largish fries, with peel still on, stay crisp due to frying in hot, clean-flavored oil. Finally, thick old-fashioned milkshakes made with Double Rainbow ice cream are so big they last as long as the hamburger and finish off this classic American meal. See page 132 for more information.

BUTTERFLY . . . .

1710 Mission Street (between
Duboce and 14th Street)
415-864-8999
www.butterflysf.citysearch.com
Open Tuesday through Sunday
6 P.M. to 1 A.M.
Moderate
Credit cards: AE, MC, V

Four San Francisco chef–restaurant owners (Traci Des Jardins from Jardinière, Mark Franz from Farallon, Rob Lam from butterfly, and yours truly from Hayes Street Grill), who publicly vow not to serve the endangered Chilean sea bass in their restaurants, shivered in a chilly wind blowing hard onto Baker Beach. We had agreed to be photographed for a *Sunset* magazine story on the campaign to boycott the Patagonian toothfish (otherwise known as Chilean sea bass) to stave off its extinction. The photographer decided to shoot at ocean's edge with the Golden Gate Bridge in the background during what turned out to be high tide. Every so often a pushy wave made us scramble up-beach. Then everyone had to be painstakingly repositioned back down on the wet sand. The wind gusted so strongly that chefs' jackets had to be taped closed and hair had to be battened down. At the end of the two-hour session, the four chefs huddled together for a group shot, and that's when I got to snuggle with Rob Lam, the new chef-partner of butterfly, who somehow remained radiantly warm. The next night I was at his restaurant on the edge of the Mission, thawed out and hungry.

When four of us arrived promptly for our 9 P.M. reservation on a Saturday, the warehouselike space was packed. A crowd of young Asians dressed in black, gay couples, and groups of women clustered at the bar, waiting for tables to open in a dining area enclosed within the larger space by tall glass partitions. A deejay held court on a small stage, flooding the restaurant with sound. We waited about forty-five minutes, drinking well-made Herradura margaritas and iced Chopin vodka. Finally, we were seated at a bare wooden table near the stage in front of DJ Label and singer Kayla, a polished soprano with a clear, light voice. Our little table floated in an ocean of noise, but we were able to navigate a conversation within it. (Okay, we had to yell.)

More important, we devoured sparkling pan-Asian food—a fusion of flavors from Korean, Vietnamese, Japanese, Taiwanese, and Chinese pantries—one dish more luscious than the next. We nibbled on toasted sesame seed– and sesame oil–enrobed fresh soybeans, snapping the nutty green beans out of the pod. Each of us got one big piece of crisp, unctuously filled Duck Confit Spring Roll, resonantly rich, spicy, and fruity, the best I've tasted. An Ahi Tempura Roll filled with chewy, sake-marinated Thai black rice and buttery red-fleshed tuna, accompanied by a piquant salad of cucumber noodles, put on a yin-yang balancing act full of contrasting flavors and textures, every one bright, clean, vivid, fully realized. Irresistible hot and spicy fried calamari came piled in a big glass bowl—so tasty that a chile dipping sauce went untouched. Juicy panfried Shanghai noodles interwoven with crunchy julienned vegetables made for a refreshing accompaniment. The crowning glory of any meal here is a superbly crisp, deep-fried tai snapper, standing on end, curled around a fabulous warm rice noodle (*chow fun*) salad on top of a pile of mildly pickled kimchi (fermented Korean cabbage) and a black bean sauce. The fish kept its integrity amidst a sea of flavors.

Dessert is a little hard to face after all this intense, multifaceted food. I would have liked a simple fruit dessert, an Asian tapioca, or something with coconut or fried bananas. The current butterfly dessert list is too rich, sweet, and Western. But all the savory food works wonderfully together. The spectrum of notes and the degree of intensity stay on a consistent, if amped-up, plane. Not one discordant or meaningless flavor made me wonder what I was eating. Every ingredient made culinary sense. You can take in ten different dishes—as we did—and still remember each tune.

I rarely come across inventive food that is so self-assured, complete, and tasty. Next time, however, I'm visiting butterfly on a weeknight, when an acoustic jazz combo plays, conversation will be easy, and I won't have to wait for my duck spring rolls.

CHARANGA . . . .

2351 Mission Street (between
19th and 20th streets)
415-282-1813
Open Tuesday and Wednesday
5:30 to 10 P.M., Thursday through
Saturday 5:30 to 11 P.M.
Inexpensive
Credit cards: DC, D, MC, V

My friend Roger, who lives on Potrero Hill and moves heavy equipment, has an infallible nose for good restaurants. He turned me on to the Universal Cafe (see page 355) and I've been grateful ever since. The last time I ran into him, I asked about a restaurant I'd heard about in his neighborhood.

"Oh, you must mean Charanga," he said.

"What's Charanga?" I asked him.

"Kind of a tapas bar on Mission Street."

"That's not Potrero Hill," I said.

"Yeah, but it's close enough. They have a real tasty hot calamari dish."

"I'll call you," I told him.

I never did. I checked out Charanga alone one Friday night. All the tables were full and the room was noisy, but no one was sitting at the counter, the perfect place for me. I told the waitress that I had to get in and out fast and she told me what to order—ahi tuna. I got a plate arranged with slices of seared, red-fleshed fish still raw in the center, accompanied with little piles of sesame noodles, cucumber salad, and three different sauces. The whole production was delicious. With a glass of Conde de Valdemar Rioja, which went surprisingly well with this multiflavored dish, this turned out to be the ideal quick meal. Once again, Roger was right.

Subsequent visits proved it. That calamari dish Roger mentioned alone is worth a visit. Shrimp and calamari quickly sautéed with hot chiles and ginger come on a wreath of tender, tiny pea sprouts with coconut rice in the center of the plate. This is not a dish I would willingly share, though the restaurant assumes otherwise. I feel the same way about a fabulous seafood stew with coconut rice, spicy mussels, pieces of tuna, shrimp, tender calamari, and velvety new potatoes; and a creamy Latin American risotto that gets its character from the incorporation of nutty Spanish Manchego cheese that melts into the rice. What appealed to me so immediately about Charanga is its persona—substantial, witty, honest, arty. The food has winning, offbeat personality and the scene is fun, affordable, and way cool. It probably would be a good place to take the guy who turned me on to it. Roger, I owe you one.

DELFINA . . . .

3621 18th Street (between
Dolores and Guerrero)
415-552-4055
Open nightly from 5:30 to 10 P.M.,
until 11 P.M. Friday and Saturday
Moderate
Credit Cards: MC, V

Delfina used to be so tiny that there was no place to wait for a table without standing in the middle of the service area and playing dodge 'em with the waitstaff. But now that it's expanded into the storefront next door, Delfina has transformed itself into a grown-up restaurant with just the right level of amenity to maintain its insouciant Mission District ambience without torturing its patrons.

Abandoning the shoestring decor of the old Delfina, the new dining room has acquired a sleek finish. It incorporates some of the original furnishings, such as the small aluminum tables and blue-tiled bar, but the ill-configured wooden benches that used to serve as so-called seating have been restructured into comfortable banquettes. A handsome hardwood floor and pendulous glass lamps dropped from the high ceiling don't do much to muffle sound, but quilted gray baffling installed along the top of the walls somewhat reduces the din of a full dining room. The food is also better than ever.

Chef-owner Craig Stoll has hit upon the perfect cooking voice for this venue—small portions of intensely flavorful Mediterranean-inspired dishes presented in a straightforward Italian manner. A starter of whole grilled squid, lightly charred and aromatic from the fire, perches on top of a salad of tiny white beans, a few leaves of frisée, and lots of good extra virgin olive oil and lemon. It holds the honor, to my mind, of being the best calamari salad in town. Stoll's chicken liver crostini features fresh, sweet chopped livers topped with a mince of pickled onions and a few leaves of wild arugula. Perfect. Main courses come on small plates filled with exactly the right amount of food—not too much, not too little. I love this kitchen's sense of proportion and take pleasure in being able to finish everything—fork-tender, Chianti-braised short ribs with a demure little spoon of polenta and a flourish of piquant chopped lemon peel and parsley; on another night, a Niman Ranch flatiron steak, seared on the outside, juicy and red on the inside with a pile of skinny french fries; a thick slice of Alaskan halibut (the best-eating species of this fish) gently cooked with asparagus, fava beans, and a whisper of tarragon butter; for dessert, an exceptionally rich and delicious *panna cotta*, and chestnut-flour crepes drizzled with honey and topped with vanilla ice cream.

Like everything else about Delfina, the wine list exudes personality. With twelve wines offered by the glass, one is tempted to skip the full bottle list, but it, too, offers reasonably priced and interesting wines, including a number imported by Kermit Lynch.

Since the remodel, one would think that it would be easier to get into this still relatively small place. Not really. The difference now is that a certain number of tables are kept unreserved so waiting is no longer an ordeal. But when a restaurant grows organically the way Delfina has—holding on to its character and ideals while expanding and actually getting better—it deserves to be full.

EL BALAZITO . . . .

2560 Marin Street (at the
junction of Army and Bayshore)
415-824-6684
Open Monday through Saturday
9 A.M. to 5 P.M.
Very inexpensive
Cash only

Fondly called the car wash taqueria, El Balazito dispenses exquisitely simple and authentic tacos from a permanent stand on a self-service car-cleaning lot. Beyond the obvious convenience of being able to shampoo your vehicle and get a sublime taco at the same place, you will get much pleasure from the purity and uniqueness of El Balazito's food. Everyone comes here for tacos filled with a delicious braise of cactus with tomatoes and onions piled into two soft mini-tortillas topped with *salsa fresca* and cilantro. The *huachinango* taco, just grilled rockfish and salsa, and the buttery tongue tacos define what tacos should be. El Balazito's outdoor counter and stools let you watch the progress of amateur shampooers as you lick your fingers and decide if you want another round.

EL PEROL . . . .

2590 Mission Street (at
22nd Street in the Mission Market)
415-550-8582
Open daily 9 A.M. to 6 P.M.
Inexpensive
Cash only

Hidden away in the middle of the Mission Market, El Perol serves delicious, freshly made Peruvian specialties from a cafeteria-style counter. Seating is at meticulously tended tables under a trellis in the center of the market. Dishes change every day, but you can count on a number of Peruvian potato-based mainstays like a *papa rellena*, a big, football-shaped dumpling of seasoned mashed potato stuffed with a piquant mixture of ground beef, raisins, eggs, onion, and olives. It sports a beautiful crisp crust of handmade bread crumbs turned golden brown in the deep fryer. *Causa rellena* is a very substantial cold dish, a layered torta of mashed potatoes mixed with mayonnaise and red chile with a thick central filling of fabulous fresh chicken salad, meaty with moist chicken breast and lightened with finely chopped celery and pickle. The top of this gigantic square is slathered with more tart, chile-spiked mayonnaise. *Causa* is a meal in itself and will pretty much take care of your appetite for the day.

Drink puréed fresh papaya juice or the spectacular *chicha morada*, a purple drink made of dried purple corn boiled with allspice, cinnamon, clove, and dried fruit, puréed and chilled. El Perol's version is delicate and refreshing and goes perfectly with Peruvian food. If *seco de pollo* is available—it's prepared in advance and kept warm on the steam table—order it. A *seco* is a dryish stew that can be made with kid, lamb, or chicken. El Perol's version with moist, not overcooked, chicken has an aromatic dark green cilantro sauce that's luscious. The *seco de pollo* comes with rice and either a salad or a well-seasoned split pea purée. The kitchen also makes many dishes to order, including soups and the delicious *lomo saltado*, sautéed strips of beef with onions and fried potatoes with an egg on top. Save time in your Mission District shopping for a meal at El Perol, or you can buy these excellent Peruvian dishes to go. El Perol also caters.

FINA ESTAMPA . . . .

2374 Mission Street (between
19th and 20th streets)
415-824-4437
Open Monday through Thursday
11:30 A.M. to 3:30 P.M. and
5 to 9 P.M.; Friday through Sunday
11:30 A.M. to 9 P.M.
Inexpensive
Credit cards: MC, V

Although Gus Shinzato might look more like a sushi chef, one taste of his *parihuela de mariscos* makes it clear that he is a masterful Peruvian cook. A third-generation Peruvian now living in the United States, he opened Fina Estampa with his wife, Tamie Takaesu, a Japanese-born Peruvian who runs the dining room. They serve spectacularly delicious food in a comfortable, if modest, Mission Street storefront, the kind of place that puts glass over the tablecloths.

Before I started eating at Fina Estampa, Peruvian food meant boiled potatoes and skewered beef heart (very tasty, actually). But after several visits here, I discovered that the breadth of the cuisine parallels the spectacular geography of the country. From seaside towns come opulent seafood soups like *parihuela*, a deep bowl full of shrimp, squid, mussels, clams, and rockfish in a tomato broth resonant with dried chiles. Another seafood triumph, *jalea de pescado*, brings a gigantic fish fry served with salsa *criolla* (marinated onions and tomatoes) and a fiery dark green salsa called *ají*. The frying is impeccable. A huge, moist seafood paella has remarkable depth of flavor. Since both San Francisco and Peru share the Pacific Coast, the fresh local catch here works particularly well in many of the seafood dishes. From the mountains come potatoes: orange, yellow, purple, white. Fina Estampa includes them in one of the best ceviches in town, a revelatory combination. Chef Shinzato serves them traditionally, *a la huancaina*, in a pungent cheese sauce as an appetizer, or rubs them with red spice paste and deep-fries them as an accompaniment to skewers of marinated beef heart. Wonderful crisp, deep-fried bone-in chunks of chicken called *chicharrón de pollo* come with a bowl of fresh lime juice and chiles and a pile of salsa *criolla*. A luscious dish called *bisteck a la pobre*, a small, tender grilled steak served on a slice of toast that soaks up all the juices, is piled with sautéed onions and tomatoes, a deep-fried banana, and crowned by a fried egg. *Ají panca*, grilled chicken rubbed with a red spice paste, has the texture of velvet. Both Peruvian beer and Chilean and Spanish red wine enhance the food. Don't be put off by the Mission District custom of putting out margarine with soft white bread; the plates to come will be dazzling.

2534 Mission Street (between
21st and 22nd streets)
415-648-7600
www.foreigncinema.com
Open Sunday through Thursday
6 P.M. to 9:30 P.M., Friday and
Saturday until 10:30 P.M.
Moderate
Credit cards: AE, MC, V

Foreign Cinema was *the* iconic restaurant of the dot-com years. Located in a sprawling, hidden warehouse, this hip, arty restaurant brought urbane attitude to an unlikely Mission District location. Large in scale, this operation had two tony, frantically busy bars, an out door courtyard where French films were projected on a concrete wall, and a roaring dining room. Yet, everyone who found the place—probably 500 people a night—felt they had made a discovery. The booze and wine were chosen for quality. The menu was affordable and chic. You could smoke outside in the courtyard, along with the characters in the moody films, while you ate bistro food and drank at long communal tables under electric heaters. The whole scene was very cool.

We all know what happened. Much of the Foreign Cinema crowd lost their jobs and moved out of town, just as tourism dried up. The partners knew they had to do something, so they hired Gayle Pirie and John Clark, two hired-gun chefs who, between them, spent years at Zuni and Chez Panisse. They took over the kitchen, redid the menu in the style of their mentors, and have brought new cachet to the dining room. On the weekends, Foreign Cinema still throws a rollicking party, but on the quieter weeknights it has become a desti-nation restaurant that serves some of the sexiest food in the city.

A lot of the food at Foreign Cinema is meant to go with drinks—warm, marinated olives glistening with olive oil; oysters on the half shell; a gratin of creamy salt cod and whipped potatoes served with thin, crisp toasts; a Zuni-like combo of fresh mozzarella with house-cured sardines on roasted escarole. Thin slices of cold foie gras terrine on toasts come with a superb salad of pickled beets, *mâche*, and sieved egg in the brightest of dressings. I still dream about this salad. A seafood risotto, almost like a fish stew with seared scallops, monkfish, and wild mushrooms, nestles into juicy, flavor-infused rice—a light, bright main course, if not really a risotto. While many restaurants prepare roast chicken, the golden-skinned one here is dusted with a pungent Moroccan spice mixture called *ras el hanout*, as are the crisp roasted potatoes served with it. These join artichoke hearts and barely wilted radicchio—a big, informal, stunningly delicious plate of food. A hunk of impeccably fresh blue nose sea bass gets an Alsatian treatment with braised cabbage, leeks, and sliced potatoes in lots of luxurious, creamy sauce flavored with hard cider. Divine! Pirie and Clark must have learned at Zuni how to choose cheese and pair them with nuts, fruits, aromatic vegetables, and olives that enhance their character. These pairings make you think about the nature of each cheese, and Foreign Cinema offers not less than five of these clever compositions.

Now that Foreign Cinema has turned into a really good restaurant, I'm selfishly hop-ing that at least on weeknights I'll be able to drop in on a whim. I'll concede the bar action, the films, and the scene to the weekenders as long as I can get a place by the fire for my *mâche* salad, a good glass of wine, and maybe a little steak with fries.

2731 Mission Street (between
23rd and 24th streets)
415-643-7001
Open daily 10 A.M. to 10 P.M.
Inexpensive
Credit cards: MC, V

La Corneta is the hottest thing to happen in the Latino Mission for a long time. The taqueria scene has been dominated by Pancho Villa (see page xxx) with its off-shoot El Toro at the north end of the Mission and the meat-oriented La Taqueria (see page xxx) at the other. Both of these are exemplary, wildly busy taquerias, but the radiant La Corneta is pure fun, a taqueria with a huge range of possibilities, including many vegetarian and seafood items, and a big, comfortable, whimsically decorated dining area filled with light and color.

I first tested the water with a tongue taco, my mainstay and indicator of the depth and quality of a taqueria. Two tender, superbly fresh mini–corn tortillas, one on top of the other, were piled with black beans and a huge portion of cubed tongue scooped with a slotted spoon from a thin red chile sauce. These were topped with a big spoon of fresh tomato salsa. I took my heaped taco to one of La Corneta's pretty blond wood tables where I proceeded to devour the whole thing, it was so delicious (and this was after a whole day of eating and tasting in the Mission). The tongue was velvety and full of meaty flavor; the salsa perfectly balanced with lime and salt. The taco had that satisfying, melded depth that comes when the components are all perfect, as they are at La Corneta.

There are many, many directions you can take at this taqueria: mushroom quesadillas, enchiladas, *flautas*, tamales, *chile relleno*, baby burritos, a whole section of vegetarian burritos that includes a *chile relleno* burrito, all sorts of Mexican stews for fillings, plus chorizo and chicken mole. My only advice is to stay away from the shrimp, though one of La Corneta's signature items and very popular. Now, I'm very sensitive, but the shrimp's muddy, almost moldy flavor indicates that they're farmed, and hence a product to avoid. The main seating area in a tall atrium has walls painted to look like an outdoor courtyard complete with real windows and Spanish grills. Sun streams down from on high and you really feel as if you're sitting in a café in Mexico City. See page 184 for more information.

THE LAST SUPPER CLUB . . . .

1199 Valencia Street (at 23rd Street)
415-695-1199
www.lastsupperclubsf.com
Open nightly from 5:30 to
10:30 P.M.; Saturday and Sunday
brunch 11 A.M. to 3 P.M.
Inexpensive
Credit cards: AE, MC, V

The talented young team behind the ever-popular Luna Park (see page 187) has opened a second Mission District hot spot with an active bar and a casual Italian menu. Pasta and salads reign and you can eat very reasonably here if you don't drink too many negronis or Meyer lemon drops. There are plenty of Italian wines in the mid-twenty-dollar range so you don't have to go dry.

Begin with an escarole and radicchio salad with anchovy dressing, shaved egg and Parmesan or The Last Salad, a juicy mix of lettuces with salami, chickpeas, red onions, tomato and provolone. (It's not as heavy as it sounds.) Move on to soft rigatoni in a creamy sauce with cauliflower, capers, and pecorino or the spectacular house-made chestnut ravioli in a stewlike and pecorino; or the spectacular housemade chestnut ravioli in a stewlike roasted guinea fowl sugo, the best dish on the menu. For a few dollars more, the veal saltimbocca is crisp and light, as are the lemony green beans served with it. A side of broccoli rabe braised with garlic and red chile makes a fine accompaniment with the pastas. For dessert, head straight for the towering house-made spumoni, a luscious layered ice cream cake.

While The Last Supper Club does not deliver Incanto (see page 218) or Delfina (see page 179) culinary purity, it certainly throws a good party with tasty, stylish food and drink at inclusive prices.

LA TAQUERIA . . . .

2889 Mission Street (between
24th and 25th Streets)
415-285-7117
Open Monday through Saturday
11 A.M. to 9 P.M.,
Sunday until 8 P.M.
Inexpensive
Cash only

One of the most long-lived (since 1975) and meticulous taquerias in the Mission, La Taqueria earned its reputation through cleanliness, freshness, and efficiency. This family taqueria sports an attractive Mission-style arched facade, adobe walls decorated with a vibrant mural, and a dining room full of rustic wooden tables with leather stools. Jars of excellent green and red salsa sit on each immaculate table. Although a list of typical and well-prepared fillings for burritos and tacos is posted on the wall above the tiled kitchen, La Taqueria's soft, moist, savory, miraculously greaseless *carnitas* (pork slowly cooked in its own fat) deserves special attention. Prepared every day, this rich pork shines brightest in tacos made with two soft, warm corn tortillas and a little salsa. Shredded chicken simmered with tomatoes and chiles, and aromatically spicy chorizo sausage that has been crumbled and fried, also make for exceptional tacos. This friendly taqueria ranks high on my list of favorites because it fulfills its simple menu perfectly, day after day, year after year.

LIBERTY CAFE . . . .

410 Cortland Avenue (between
Bennington and Wool)
415-695-8777
Open Tuesday through Friday
11:30 A.M. to 3 P.M.; Tuesday,
Thursday, and Sunday 5:30 to
9 P.M., Friday and Saturday until
9:30 P.M.; brunch Friday through
Sunday 10 A.M. to 2 P.M.
Moderate
Credit cards: AE, D, MC, V

If I were to invent my dream around-the-corner café, it would be very much like this cozy little place in Bernal Heights, a touchstone for skillful home-style cooking and friendly atmosphere. Moderate prices; organic produce, meats, and poultry from small local producers; warm house-baked breads, rolls, and desserts; a menu that works for omnivores, vegetarians, and children; and the unpretentious good spirit of the place add up to a constant stream of customers. People wait outside on benches with a glass of wine or on a little patio that fronts the bakery at the back; or, weather permitting, stroll the cute neighborhood until their table is ready. Others stand by the small service bar in the middle of the room, trying not to stare at the diners tucking into their warm frisée salads (the best in town) or big bowls of country-style soup.

Since the chef-owner is a baker, the menu always offers a luscious, flaky-crusted chicken potpie as well wonderful dessert pies, but hearty, multifaceted plates of pork chops with creamy white beans, soft polenta, and winter squash, or sliced duck breasts on lentils with baby mustard greens and creamed cabbage travel to more sophisticated culinary territory. What I love about Liberty is that the bright, home-cooked quality of the dishes never diminishes no matter how creative the combination.

LIMON . . . .

3360 17th Street (between
Mission and Valencia)
415 252-0918
Open Tuesday through Friday
11:30 A.M. to 3:30 P.M., 5:30 to
10 P.M.; Saturday and Sunday
noon to 10:30 P.M.
Inexpensive.
Credit cards: V, MC

Charles Phan started the phenomenon of authentic ethnic cooking in hip surroundings at the Slanted Door (see page 78). I thought about this when I visited Limon, a cool little Peruvian cafe, a block away from the old Slanted Door. Passersby are immediately drawn to this interesting space composed of two clean-edged, bright rooms, one painted the color of lemons, the other of oranges. Indeed, many decide to stop by—at night all the tables are full, a line often forms on the sidewalk, and the noise level amped by the hard surfaces makes conversation nearly impossible. In the quieter afternoons, tables of Peruvians (who else would order dozens of Inca Colas?) drop by for customary late lunch. Spanish speakers outnumber English speakers at Limon, making the cafe feel authentically part of the Mission.

At a Limon-style meal, most diners order a bunch of dishes for the table to share, starting with a platter of the signature ceviche. Red chile–spiked lime juice with a whisper of anise "cooks" halibut, small shrimp, octopus, and squid, turning them pearly white and firming their texture. Move on to empanadas Don Walter, two crisp, brown, pastry turnovers plump with chopped beef, olives, raisins, and hard-boiled egg, aromatic with sweet spices. Dip them in a mild, creamy orange sauce like a Spanish *romesco*.

The kitchen drizzles just the right amount of chipotle aioli over a pile of superb deep-fried calamari lightly battered and shatteringly crisp. And tamale lovers will appreciate a *tamal criollo*, a large, flat, rectangular tamale made with mild panca chile–infused *masa* (dried cornmeal), filled with a mixture of pork, salty black olives, and egg. A salsa of thinly sliced onions and chopped tomato marinated in lime transforms the dish, adding sparkle to tamale earthiness.

I like the lively small plates and ceviches better than the main dishes here. Pair them with delicious, reasonably priced glasses of Spanish or South American wines, or the surprisingly sweet and creamy dark Peruvian beer called Cusqueña Malta, a must try.

For dessert try Helado de Lucuma, a burnt orange–colored, caramel-flavored ice cream imported from Peru with haunting tropical overtones.

While Limon may not be the Slanted Door of *nuevo* Peruvian, it delivers the pleasures of pairing food and wine, a clever design, and an exceptionally kind and helpful waitstaff. And best of all, its prices and laid-back Mission style make everyone in the neighborhood and beyond feel right at home.

LORCA . . . .

3200 24th Street (at South Van Ness)
415-550-7510
Open Tuesday through Sunday 6 to
10 P.M.; bar until midnight
Moderate
Credit cards: MC, V, DC

Contemporary Spanish cooking has become the next big thing on the international gourmet circuit. A far cry from rustic paellas and tapas, the new Spanish cooking can be highly conceptualized and wittily self-referential, or it can be regionally rooted, riffing on local ingredients in creative ways. At Lorca, right here in the Mission, we have our own version of this new kind of Spanish cooking in a restaurant conceived by ambitious twenty-seven-year-old Catalan chef, Pepe Desvalls.

Each night Desvalls puts out a different seven-course tasting menu for all of $28. Actually more than seven courses, the meal in unrelentingly original and absolutely delicious. Desvalls calls it a culinary adventure through the various regions of Spain. I call it an exciting trip through Desvall's culinary imagination. We have nothing like it in this town.

Your can start with a drink in the tapas bar with a complimentary tapa and then proceed to the dining room, really a cozy Victorian parlor, painted a deep shade of red, romantically lit with candles and wrought-iron chandeliers. There you will begin with thimble-sized glasses of sherry capped with a tiny. savory-sweet cookie. You're instructed to pop the cookie into you mouths and throw down the *fino*. This opening ritual sets the ground rules for the rest of the meal. Many of the dishes arrive with eating instructions.

A progression of small dishes follows, such as a thick chicken ragout with bits of soft potato and rich broth, and then a flat soup bowl with a dollop or roasted pepper–potato purée, a drizzle of balsamic syrup, and a miniature triangle of toast, over which the waiter pours a rich, almost creamy onion soup from a pitcher. Next dish: two spicy shrimp with heads, jauntily standing on their tails, propped by a mound of baby eel (the width of cappellini) salad, After that, perhaps a cazuela of luscious baked rice, moist with meat stock, smoldering hot piquillo peppers, and little cubes of beef tongue, all followed by a fish course and meat course; and then two light, lively desserts.

The Spanish wine list, small, well annotated, and full of unfamiliar (at least to me) bottles for $20 to $30, plays its part.

The progression of dishes is so ingeniously crafted and proportioned that they add up to one perfectly satisfying, continuously exciting meal. Desvalls makes it work by putting so much passion and energy into each menu. You can order a la carte, but go for the unique prix fixe.

LOS JARRITOS . . . .

901 South Van Ness Avenue
(at 20th Street)
415-648-8383
Open daily 8 A.M. to 10 P.M.
Inexpensive
Credit cards: MC, V

While good taquerias abound in the Mission, the sit-down Mexican restaurants are surprisingly similar and uninspired. One of my favorites, Los Jarritos, distinguishes itself by its colorful, folk art–filled dining room and tasty *chilaquiles*, the current dish of choice in the Mission among those who have partied too hard the night before. *Chilaquiles* are stale tortillas that are fried and then cooked in a sauce, often with other ingredients. At Los Jarritos, the tortillas are fried with eggs, white cheese, and pickled jalapeños, then braised in a lot of piquant *ranchera* sauce. A huge portion comes with mashed red beans seasoned with lard and Spanish rice. Mission families drift in all afternoon for delicious eggs scrambled with cactus and onions and served with beans, rice, and excellent made-to-order tortillas hot from the *comal*. These tortillas are puffy and lighter in texture than any you have tasted from a package. If you are a tortilla fan, you owe it to yourself to try them. They are especially good with *huevos rancheros*, two perfectly poached eggs in *ranchera* sauce topped with melted cheese (ask them to go light on the cheese or the eggs get buried and overcooked).

Jarritos are small clay cups. Strings of them hang all over the immaculate dining room next to shelves of old-fashioned smiling clay piggy banks. A resonant wooden floor and old Formica and aluminum tables with bright blue and red tops add warmth and cheer to this folksy little restaurant.

LUNA PARK . . . .

694 Valencia (near 18th Street)
415-553-8584
www.lunaparksf.com
Open Monday through Friday
11:30 A.M. to 2:30 P.M., Saturday
and Sunday 11 A.M. to 3 P.M.;
Monday through Thursday 5:30 P.M.
to 10:30 P.M., Friday and Saturday
until 11 P.M., Sunday until 10 P.M.
Inexpensive
Credit cards: AE, DC, MC, V

The current dining-out formula for success is to offer great deals on food, lots of drink choices, and a hip atmosphere, and Luna Park does this the best of all. Chef-owner Joe Jack developed his chops from working at Chow (see page 214), but his Luna Park is completely original and very cool.

One afternoon, two of us snagged a wooden booth in the high-ceilinged burnt orange dining room and polished off a huge lunch. We had a pretty chopped salad of romaine, radicchio, radishes, and crumbled blue cheese in a lively vinaigrette; and a pile of pickley, gingery, red onion tuna *poke*—kind of a Hawaiian ceviche—on a tower of deep-fried wonton chips. We drank lovely margaritas with a little glass carafe of overflow served on the side. A crisp, thin, breaded pork cutlet somehow stuffed with oozing mushrooms and Gruyère was just delicious, especially with buttery mashed potatoes and warm shalloty pickled green and yellow beans—a Joe Jack twist. Equally as winning was a flat bowl of sweet corn and dried lima bean succotash with sautéed onion, on which a spice-rubbed, griddled chicken breast perched. It was split to form two pieces that cooked quickly and stayed moist and juicy. Though we were completely full, we couldn't stop nibbling at a spectacular slice of coconut cream pie topped with toasted ribbons of coconut. It was the best version of this American classic I've ever tasted.

I don't imagine that the sexy waitresses in tight black pants with exposed belly buttons eat much of this pie, but they're still nice to those who do. I can see why Luna Park is so crowded every night. People probably are looking forward to the wait at the bar with one of those tasty margaritas in hand.

PALATINO . . . .

803 Cortland Avenue
(near Ellsworth)
415-641-8899
Open Monday through Friday
11:30 A.M. to 2:30 P.M.;
nightly 5:30 to 10 P.M.
Inexpensive
Credit cards: MC, V

Palatino is a neighborhood place with a genuinely distressed wooden floor, a gerrymandered kitchen behind a wall of paned windows that once probably demarcated a back porch, and fifteen or so postage stamp–sized tables pushed very close together in front of hard wooden benchlike banquettes. To discover this gently edgy place in a hidden neighborhood and slip in for a bite would be very hip. To travel across town, wait in the wind, and jockey for a table demands too much, raising expectations to heights that Palatino doesn't deserve or nurture.

The hardworking kitchen should get credit for a couple of luscious dishes. I would make a detour for house-made pappardelle tossed with a meaty sauce of chicken livers, tomatoes, and mushrooms. *Rigatoni alla Vaccinara,* a meat sauce made with gelatinous oxtail, reminds me of classic, long-cooked bolognese, but with a rich braised beef flavor. Delicate ravioli filled with sweet, velvety butternut squash purée, sauced in brown butter, features the gossamer house-made noodle dough—a triumph. Someone in that kitchen loves dessert, if the two fresh fruit desserts I've had are any indication. A warm polenta pound cake slathered with baked prune plums and whipped cream resembles an Italian version of short cake. Scrumptious. And a baked peach topped with buttery amaretti cookie crumbs next to a mound of barely set vanilla ice cream or *semifreddo* also puts summer fruit to highest use.

I have the feeling that the popularity of the restaurant has overwhelmed the kitchen, that the cooks could make these simple Italian dishes better if they just had a moment to catch their collective breath. Though a no-reservation policy works in a neighborhood restaurant where a manageable number of customers casually drop in, for those coming from across town it's a hardship, especially when there's no place to wait. At heart, Palatino could be a trattoria hidden away in the Trastevere, the working-class neighborhood in Rome where the same people eat every night, except that it's in San Francisco and everyone wants to try the latest spot.

PANCHO VILLA TAQUERIA . . . .

3071 16th Street (between
Mission and Valencia)
415-864-8840
panchovillassf.citysearch.com
Open daily 10 A.M. to midnight
Inexpensive
Credit cards: AE, MC, V

When you bite into one of Pancho Villa's monumental burritos, you know why a line always extends past the front door. Though you may have to wait, the endless turnover means that all the components of the various tacos, burritos, and dinner plates have been prepared very recently. This freshness makes the earthy Mexican food sparkle. The Mission District favorite is the *carne asada* special, a huge flour tortilla lined with melted white cheese and filled with about a pound of Spanish rice, red beans, thinly sliced grilled steak, guacamole, and fresh salsa. All these elements work together in some magical way to make a completely satisfying rolled-up meal. If you eat a Pancho Villa burrito for lunch, don't plan on dinner. *Carnitas* (pork slowly cooked in its own fat) also makes stunning burritos or soft tacos with beans and salsa. On the lighter side, try a grilled shrimp burrito with black beans, or a satisfying vegetarian burrito that features firm cubes of tofu in a red *ranchera* sauce. Besides the tortilla dishes, Pancho Villa puts out some gorgeous-looking platters of butterflied garlic prawns, or hot, spicy prawns griddled with whole dried *chiles de árbol*, all cooked to order. Be sure to get a side order of grilled green onions to go with the shrimp. Ladled from huge glass jars afloat with strawberries, cantaloupe, or seeded watermelon and ice, Pancho Villas *aguas frescas* alone merit a visit, especially on a warm afternoon when the kids want something quick to eat and refreshing to drink.

SAN MIGUEL . . . .

3520 20th Street (between
Mission and Valencia)
415-826-0173
Open Thursday through Tuesday
11 A.M. to 8 P.M.
Inexpensive
Cash only

The cozy dining room of this popular Guatemalan restaurant is decorated to look like a trellised garden, and its super-fresh food, garnished with raw vegetables, *crema*, and herbs, reminds me of a garden, too. The plates are as pretty as the cheerful surroundings. Much care is taken with both. I love the *boquitas* here, bitesized appetizers that are often miniatures of larger dishes, like *tostaditas de ceviche* topped with shrimp, or *tostaditas de salpicón*, crisp tortilla chips topped with a spicy sauté of chopped beef seasoned with sour orange, onions, cilantro, and mint. San Miguel makes a Guatemalan-style chicken mole with sesame seeds topped with *crema*, and tamales flavored with Guatemalan herbs. All the food that comes out of the kitchen is composed on the plate and layered in flavor, just as it is in good restaurants in Mexico and Central America. San Miguel happens to be Latin American food anthropologist–chef Laurie Mackenzie's favorite place in the Mission. I can see why she is charmed.

SLANTED DOOR . . . .

584 Valencia Street (at 17th Street)
415-861-8032

Chef Charles Phan bought the building on Valencia Street that houses Slanted Door and is doubling the size of the original restaurant. In the meantime, he has moved Slanted Door to the Embarcadero. See page 78 for more information.

TI COUZ CRÊPERIE . . . .

3108 16th Street (between
Guerrero and Valencia)
415-252-7373
www.ticouz.com
Open Monday through Wednesday
11 A.M. to 11 P.M., Thursday and
Friday until midnight,
Saturday 10 A.M. to midnight,
Sunday 10 A.M. to 11 P.M.
Inexpensive
Credit cards: MC, V

A real *crêperie* like you might find in Brittany, Ti Couz turns out thin, irresistible pancakes filled with everything from ratatouille to ice cream and chocolate sauce. As a cheap, satisfying meal, you can't beat them. In fact, so many people were banging at the doors at Ti Couz's tiny dining room that the *crêperie* has doubled in size. Happily, only the seating has expanded; the menu remains the same.

For me, the simplest crepe is the most sublime, and I can barely walk past Ti Couz without sitting down at the counter for a hot buckwheat crepe spread just with softened butter and sprinkled with sugar. My new favorite, however, has become a crepe spread with almond butter. The Gruyère and ham crepe topped with an egg is completely satisfying as a main course.

The authenticity of this place comes from owner Sylvie Le Mer, who keeps Ti Couz doing just what it does best. A green salad, sometimes a charcuterie plate, and a soup are the only other dishes offered. The crepes come off the griddle tender, but crisp and buttery on the outside. I hate to order them with too much stuff because the pancakes themselves are the treat. Mildly alcoholic French cider on tap comes in whole and half carafes with pottery bowls instead of glasses, a quaint service that only makes the crepes taste that much better. The small wooden tables and chairs, wood floors, French country china cabinets, and blue-and-white color scheme add to the authenticity of this Mission District *crêperie*.

TIMO'S . . . .

842 Valencia Street (between
19th and 20th streets)
415-647-0558
www.timos.com
Open Sunday through Thursday
6 to 10:30 P.M., Friday and
Saturday until 11:30 P.M.
Moderate
Credit cards: AE, MC, V

Carlos and Theresa Corredor took over this funky bar and turned it into a hot spot with their delicious, creative tapas. One fantastic little plate of savory food after another emerges like some kind of miracle from an immaculate kitchen. Crusty roasted new potatoes, the diameter of a quarter, are dabbed with the velvety house-made garlic mayonnaise called *alioli*. Big firm mushrooms, hot off the grill, are tossed in finely chopped garlic and parsley, as delicious as they are simple. Bright green Catalan spinach with pine nuts, raisins, and bits of dried apricot refreshes the palate. Timo's continues to prepare a superior version of a very typical Spanish dish, salt cod and potato cake, creatively pairing it with a lively cilantro-mint salsa. The chef takes a detour to neighboring southwest France with his crispy leg of duck confit surrounded by tender baby turnips. Timo's legendary Potato Decadence, a crisp cake of Yukon Gold potatoes, chanterelles, and lobster mushrooms dusted with fresh marjoram can be sublime.

I love the wine list with plenty of Spanish and California reds by the glass that go so well with the large variety of tapas on the menu, the simplest of which are prepared with conviction. The colorfully painted rooms of this former bar remind me of Beat coffeehouses, complete with a live guitarist who plays Spanish melodies instead of folk songs.

WALZWERK . . . .

381 South Van Ness Avenue
(just south of Division)
415-551-7181
www.walzwerk.com
Open Tuesday through Saturday
5:30 to 10:30 P.M.
Inexpensive
Credit Cards: AE, DC, MC, V

The beauty of small, soulful Walzwerk is that it is unabashedly German. Exuberantly blue collar, it pays homage to the appetite and pocketbook of the hardworking man and woman. The kitchen doles out huge portions of hearty, delicious food in a spare, decidedly low-tech dining room furnished with choice selections from Goodwill. But owners Christiane Schmidt and Isabell Mysyk, who do all the waiting, insist upon friendly, low-key intercourse with customers, which personalizes and softens the experience.

All the appetizers and salads are big enough to serve two or three—even the scrumptious sweet-and-sour *matjes* herring salad in sour cream with apples, onions, and pickles served with thin slices of chewy pumpernickel. Another meal-worthy starter, *soljanka*, a bright, tangy, tomato-based soup mellowed with smoky sausage, onions, and cabbage, is seasoned with fresh lemon and a dab of sour cream, creating a different spectrum of sweet-and-sour flavor. If the starters seem oversized, the main courses are monumental. A plate-sized schnitzel flops over a mound of nutmeg-seasoned mashed potatoes and a buttery sauté of broccoli, brussels sprouts, and onion. A crisp-skinned, juicy Thuringer bratwurst stretches from one edge of the plate to the other, heaped with caraway-scented sauerkraut and mashed potatoes. My favorite Walzwerk dish was a special one night of pork chops split and filled with moist bread, sausage, and apple stuffing, swathed in hot, delicately vinegared green peppercorn sauce ever so lightly scented with cinnamon. Lots of flavor activity and all of it in sync!

Food like this calls for German beer and Walzwerk accommodates with five German drafts, nine German beers in bottle, and two nonalcoholic German beers, Bitburger Drive and Malzbier, a malt beer. Wine drinkers get seven choices by the glass or bottle. Walzwerk is purposely gutsy, rough, and unritualized. The plates and silverware don't match. Neither do the tables and chairs, though they are all made of metal. The painted cement floor and roughly plastered walls contribute to a basement look, though the restaurant is on street level. In contrast, fresh flowers—campanulas, lilies, dahlias—grace every table, and ornately framed old photographs of convoluted machinery and smoking chimneys decorate the walls. Grim social realism, East German style, may be the theme, but the spirit of this place is sunny and generous. Beneath the gritty surface lies pure culinary gold—and a bonanza for anyone looking to eat well, big, and cheaply in San Francisco.

WATERGATE . . . .

1152 Valencia Street
(near 23rd Street)
415-648-6000
www.watergate.citysearch.com
Open Sunday through Thursday
5:30 to 10 P.M., Friday and
Saturday until 11 P.M.
Moderate
Credit cards: AE, DC, MC, V

When I read the menu posted in front of Watergate, I had my doubts. How could any kitchen turn out three courses of ambitious French-Asian food for $25? Corners would have to be cut. Portions would be small. The cooking would be pedestrian. But the restaurant looked so pretty, so well cared for, that I reserved for dinner early one Friday night. By the time I left, the dining room was packed. I had eaten some gorgeous dishes accompanied with excellent wines and spent a fraction of what it would cost to have a meal of similar quality at other venues around town. Chef-owner Walter Liang and his front-of-the-house partner, Rebecca Kwan, are putting so much personal energy into Watergate that they are able to keep their restaurant affordable. I consider a meal at Watergate as their gift.

From a menu of many choices I chose a salad that turned out to be a refined slaw of julienned Bosc pears and endive with crumbled Roquefort and whole pecans in a lively vinaigrette. An odd-sounding combination of buttery sturgeon on top of a roulade of rich short ribs scented with Chinese five-spice powder, surrounded by braised fennel, cippolini onions, and a bright green sauce of baby bok choy turned out to be voluptuous and astoundingly cohesive. The portion was huge, but I cleaned my plate. For dessert, at the friendly waiter's recommendation, I chose Japonaise, a scrumptious, highly composed, layered affair with almond meringue, dense coconut pudding, and trufflelike pecan chocolate caramel. I didn't stop eating that one either. Liang, who worked with one of my favorite French chefs, Fabrice Cannelle, at Brasserie Savoy, uses classic French technique as a foundation for uninhibited culinary self-expression. He's so disciplined that he's able to pull off all sorts of wild ideas. He uses tea, citrus, ginger, Asian spices, and cilantro to flavor sauces based on buttery potato purée. He likes lavish ingredients: venison, lobster, scallops, foie gras, duck breast—cost be damned. He doesn't skimp on any of them. (A few dishes do require a supplement, but most don't.) Eating at Watergate is pure adventure and you can take the chance because the investment is so small. After the fireworks of a meal, sip elegant tea poured into thimble-sized cups from one of Rebecca Kwan's antique Chinese teapots. You'll float out of Watergate having experienced the best of two worlds.

WOODWARD'S GARDEN . . . .

1700 Mission Street (at Duboce)
415-621-7122
Open Tuesday through Saturday
6 to 10 P.M.
Moderate
Credit cards: MC, V

Woodward's Garden, which has been open for over eight years, is as solid and confident as our best San Francisco institutions. One reason is the distinctive and exciting cooking by chef-owner Dana Tommasino, characterized by offbeat combinations, stylish presentations, and deep flavors. Another is that the co-owner, Margie Conard, not only runs the dining room, but also does most of the waiting. You make a safe choice by reserving at Woodward's Garden, but you leave feeling that you've had an adventure.

The space revels in urbanity, inside and out. Edward Hopper could have painted the nocturnal city landscape surrounding it, and if the lace curtains had been pulled from the street-level windows, he would have been drawn to the stark, somehow thrilling interior. The kitchen takes up half of the original dining room and is almost completely exposed. Customers sit around the perimeter of the room at wooden banquettes at narrow, butcher paper–covered tables a few inches away from one another. The lighting is low except for the illuminated kitchen a few feet away; the ventilation hums; cooking smoke gets caught in the light; the air is heavy. Everyone becomes a film noir character. Then, in the midst of these cramped, evocative quarters with the romantic overtones of an E. L. Doctorow novel, comes the most luminous food and drink. The juxtaposition is stunning.

Tommasino's food is polished and luxurious. She prepares arugula salad with toasted hazelnuts, hazelnut vinaigrette and shavings of foie gras, giving each bite a mysterious richness. Her Bibb lettuce salad looks like a green rose scattered with French butter pears, French blue cheese, and sugary walnuts. You can find this salad at many restaurants around town, but none better than this one. A pink package—a wedge of grilled radicchio wrapped in prosciutto—balances atop a salad of tomatoes with fat, slightly underdone white beans. The kitchen and I may disagree on the texture of dried beans, but we don't on an extraordinary penne with chicken livers, bacon, dates, onions, arugula, and parmigiano—a riff on a traditional Venetian calf's liver dish. You could easily make a meal out of two of these smaller dishes because they are rich and the portions large.

Tommasino cooked at Greens (see page 154) so she understands how to make vegetarian dishes that satisfy. Her tender cannelloni stuffed with buttery butternut squash and Swiss chard, slathered with sautéed portobello mushrooms and herbed cream is evidence. At the other end of the food chain, a Niman Ranch rib-eye steak almost tasted like Thanksgiving dinner, the steak perched on a bed of soft, fluffy mushroom bread pudding, showered with scallion-thick baby leeks and a Dijon mustard sauce. The service is as personal as the cooking. How often do you go to a restaurant where the founding owners are behind the stove or performing tableside? The daily involvement of the two women who conceived the restaurant keeps it vital. Woodword's Garden maintains the professionalism of a well-established mainstream restaurant, yet keeps its edgy, arty persona. The diners who find it get the best of both worlds.

CAFÉS

DOLORES PARK CAFE . . . .

501 Dolores Street (at 18th Street)
415-621-2936
Open Saturday through Thursday
7 A.M. to 8 p.m.,
Friday until 9:45 P.M.
Cash only

The location of this popular, sun-filled corner café couldn't be more inviting with its view of the monumental Dolores Street palms and the greenery and tennis courts of Dolores Park across the street. The balmy Mission District climate means that people lounge at sidewalk tables year-round, including summer, but the windowed café area inside and the bar with stools along the immaculate open kitchen are very pleasant places to have a juicy albacore tuna sandwich accompanied with the best potato chips, a salad made of organic vegetables, or a tart, all fruit, yogurtless smoothie. This café makes a point of buying local and organic, and the carefully constructed salads and sandwiches have bright flavor as a result. While the coffee is not exceptional here, the location, efficient service, and clean, tasty food are.

PAPA TOBY'S CAFE . . . .

3248 22nd Street (between
Mission and Valencia)
415-642-0474
Open daily 8:30 A.M. to 10 P.M.
Cash only

Serenity pervades this light-filled space. The pretty interior, designed and executed by the two artist-owners, has golden walls, a polished wooden floor, and table-tops polyurethaned with old maps. The front doors open completely so that tables spill out onto the sidewalk, allowing café-goers to enjoy the balmy Mission District climate. Soft Latin and Caribbean music plays and the coffee is excellent. I like to drop into Papa Toby's for a strong, rich, short espresso served in a real espresso cup just so I can sit for a moment in this island of calmness in the bustling Mission.

BARS

DALVA . . . .

3121 16th Street (at Valencia)
415-252-7740
Open daily 4 P.M. to 2 A.M.
Cash only

Next door to the Roxie Theater, Dalva offers a tonier atmosphere than most Mission District bars, mostly brought about by its sponged, coral-colored walls. Späten and Bass ale, among others on tap, sangria, some women bartenders in tight T-shirts, and nightly deejays who seem to specialize in the 1970s keep the action lively. The bar comfortably fills up early and buzzes throughout the night.

LASZLO . . . .

2534 Mission (between
21st and 22nd streets)
415-648-7600
Open daily 6 P.M. to 2 A.M.
Credit cards: MC, V

Though Foreign Cinema (see page 182) has two working, usually packed bars, the separate Lazlo, right on Mission Street, considers itself a lounge with a late-night deejay, an intriguing cocktail list, and all the advantages of being connected to Foreign Cinema. Lazlo's appealing bar menu comes from Foreign Cinema's kitchens and the world-beat wine list comes from Foreign Cinema's cellars. But at Lazlo, cocktails are the thing. Try a Ruby and Sapphire, Bombay Sapphire gin, muddled lime, and pomegranate syrup imported from Iran, a potent, sophisticated drink just right when you're taking on this bar's Euro-hip, clubby persona.

3225 22nd Street (between
Mission and Valencia)
415-647-2888
Open daily 6 P.M. to 2 A.M.
Cash only

The ancient, dark, Make-Out Room happens to make first-rate drinks. Their margaritas are models of freshness and balance. An oversized bottle of Chopin, my favorite vodka because it's distilled from potatoes, is proudly displayed on the bar. Things heat up when the Latino bands take the stage at 9 P.M., but I'd drop into the Make-Out Room anytime for a cocktail. The old linoleum booths and floor and weathered wooden bar, the colored Christmas lights hanging from Mylar streamers at the back, and the revolving mirrored globe on the ceiling give the Make-Out Room resonance and soul. Plenty of regulars, including the bands, like the eight different beers on tap. For me, the Make-Out Room means margaritas.

DELICATESSENS/TAKEOUT

DOÑA TERE'S CART . . . .

Corner of 21st Street and Alabama
No phone
Open daily 2 to 9 P.M.
Cash only

Diminutive Dona Tere works under the shade of a blue plastic awning attached to her sidewalk cart, dispensing hot ears of corn impaled on wooden sticks, lightly brushed with mayonnaise, coated with grated *queso cotijo* (a dry Mexican cheese), and sprinkled with ground red chile. She also serves her homemade tamales of light, fresh *masa* dough stuffed with savory pork (or chicken or cheese); super crispy *flautas*, deep-fried tubes of *masa* dough filled with chicken and egg; and simple tostadas. She serves these on a paper plate, garnishing them with lots of shredded cabbage in lime juice and grated Mexican cheese. You complete the plate yourself with fresh green or red salsa set out on the cart. The bright green salsa, a purée of cooked tomatillos, chiles, lime, and a whisper of garlic, does it for me. I like to stand on the sidewalk with the hungry kids from the Boys' Club on the corner, enjoying an afternoon snack. Each item costs $1.50. Dona Tere also sells small plastic bags of freshly cut mango, watermelon, and cucumber kept cool on ice, just what you want on a warm Mission afternoon. Later in the evening, *pozole*, a soup with big kernels of dried, rehydrated corn, and *champurado*, a hot chocolate corn drink, may come out. (Her kitchen is in her corner store a block away.) This meticulously clean sidewalk cart seems like a piece of Mexico airlifted and gently set down in the heart of the Mission.

EL TONAYENSE TACO TRUCKS. . . . .

Harrison at 19th Street, and
Harrison at 22nd Street
No Phone
Open 10 A.M. to 8 P.M.
Cash Only

The simplicity of the tacos dispensed from the high side windows of these silver catering trucks pleases me and the nearby warehouse workers who frequent them. Two small, super-fresh tortillas, stacked one on top of the other, get a spoon of meat—tongue, grilled steak,

pork—and a scoop of fresh tomato salsa. The plate is garnished with radishes and a pickled jalapeño. That's all you need when each of the components is honest. Salt, lime, cilantro, chiles—the layers of flavor add up to perfect bites. The small size of taco truck tacos makes them ideal as snacks.

LA PALMA MEXICATESSEN . . . .

2884 24th Street (at Florida)
415-647-1500
Open Monday through Saturday
8 A.M. to 6 P.M., Sunday until 5 P.M.
Credit cards: MC, V

Serious lovers of tortillas make regular pilgrimages to La Palma, a Mexicatessen and small tortilla factory, where thick tortillas are hand-patted Central American style, or thinly pressed Mexican style, or fried into the best thick chips in town. La Palma also sells fresh *masa* dough by the pound for tamales or homemade tortillas. The *masa* has no preservatives in it. Each day a new batch of corn is ground and fresh tortillas are made. A world of difference exists between reheated packaged corn tortillas, even those hot from La Palma's griddle, and ones that are shaped, cooked, and eaten immediately. Just as yeast, flour, and water act a hundred different ways in the hands of bakers, lime-softened ground corn and water can deliver many subtle pleasures depending on how it is handled.

A glimpse into the back of La Palma, where a group of women stand around patting out tortillas from hills of *masa* and slapping them onto a rectangular griddle, will whet your appetite for Mexican food. Hunger can be satisfied on the spot from the counter at the back, which sells tacos and burritos or prepared fillings to go. If you want to cook at home, La Palma is the place to buy your basic ingredients. Bags of freshly ground dried chiles of different varieties (California, New Mexico, pasilla, ancho), fresh epazote and other Mexican herbs and spices, freshly made *chicharrones* (Mexican cracklings), fried-to-order tortillas for tostadas in any size you like, and all sorts of canned and jarred Mexican products fill the immaculate shelves.

La Palma renders its own lard, which is ever so much more flavorful than the preserved bricks on supermarket shelves. The lard is sold by the quart from the refrigerator case. If you happen to see little bags of La Palma's potato chips, which are fried in clean vegetable oil, grab them. You will never taste a more satisfying chip. To wash them down, try a glass of *jamaica*, a refreshing red iced tea made from hibiscus flowers. Every time I go to La Palma, I come away with a new Latin American food, either for eating right there or for cooking.

LUCCA RAVIOLI COMPANY. . . . .

1100 Valencia Street (at 22nd Street)
415-647-5581
www.luccaravioli.com
Open Monday through Saturday
9 A.M. to 6 P.M.
Credit cards: AE, MC, V

At one time, the Mission was home to a large Italian community, and this sixty-eight-year-old Italian delicatessen is one of the last vestiges of it. Lucca maintains its huge neighborhood following because everyone likes its reasonably priced house-made ravioli, tortellini, sauces, and huge squares of pizza for reheating at home. The volume of sales is so large that meat-and-chard-filled ravioli are actually prepared every hour; more perishable cheese-filled ravioli are always frozen, although they cook up well. Chewy house-made spinach tortellini and plain meat-filled tortellini, displayed in beautiful wooden boxes in the refrigerated case along with many different kinds of fresh noodles, offer other mealtime alternatives. A sweet dried mushroom–infused tomato sauce and an excellent pesto—one of the best I have ever come across—complete the package. The freshness of the pesto, especially in regard to the garlic, makes a world of difference. The fast turnover at Lucca ensures a bright-flavored sauce. Certain cheeses, such as the *grana padano* (a less-aged Parmesan-type cheese that Lucca imports itself), aged Jack, and house-imported double-cream Brie, are offered at excellent prices. So are wines. In fact, Lucca Ravioli Company has the best selection of Italian bottles in the $8 range that I have seen in the city. The loquacious ravioli chef, Mike Feno, will steer you to the best bottles, using the huge map of Italy on the ceiling to show you where the wines come from. This store's dedication to good value makes it a shopping destination for olive oils, dried pasta, olives, and all things imported from Italy.

TORTAS LOS PICUDOS . . . .

2969 24th Street (between
Alabama and Florida)
415-824-4199
Open Monday through Friday
8 A.M. to 7:30 P.M., Saturday and
Sunday 7 A.M. to 7:30 P.M.
Cash only

The Mission is full of taquerias, but a whole shop dedicated to Mexican *tortas*, the equivalent of submarine sandwiches, is a new development. At Tortas Los Picudos, soft crusty rolls are layered with thin slices of roasted pork, ham, or breaded chicken cutlets, called Milanese, or all of the above, along with onions, tomato, pickled chiles, avocado, *queso fresco*, and lettuce. Then they're heated in a sandwich press and served hot and toasty. The *tortas*, huge and full of stuff, are wrapped in parchment paper and then cleanly cut in half, which makes for easy sharing. This cheerfully painted and decorated sandwich shop has a fresh-fruit counter at the front with all sorts of cut-up fruits and whole vegetables for juicing. The Vampira, a mix of carrots, beets, orange juice, celery, and pineapple no doubt fortifies the blood—but you have to like the earthy flavor of beets. Whole peeled young coconuts are kept on ice ready to be tapped with a straw for their juice. Or you can just have a big fruit cocktail for dessert. I predict that the matchup of rich tortas and refreshing made-to-order fruit drinks at Tortas Los Picudos will become a big hit.

TAMALES IN THE MISSION WITH A MURAL DETOUR

The differences between tamales from different parts of Latin America will take you by surprise. Although all of them are based on corn *masa* (dried corn softened with a lime solution, then stone ground), what happens to the *masa* next creates the contrasts. You can start at **La Loma** market (see page 205), where three or four kinds of tamales are kept warm in a steamer at the perpetually busy counter. The Mexican tamales wrapped in corn husks have a dense, almost cakey texture with a monochromatic filling of stewed pork or chicken, but the *nacatamales* from Nicaragua are a revelation. Wrapped in foil and thin white paper, they look like fat baked potatoes. Girdled with a banana leaf, which infuses the tamale with a gentle herbal flavor, the *masa* inside has a soft, light texture from being precooked in broth. The ample filling brings together delicious stewed pork, sliced potatoes, green chiles, tomatoes, *chicharrón* (crisped pork rind), huge capers, hard-cooked egg, a prune, and rice. The balance of filling to tasty *masa* is almost one to one, so you feel like you are eating a satisfying casserole.

In Salvadoran tamales, the *masa* has been cooked until it almost turns into custard, and the generous filling is usually one ingredient, such as chicken stewed in a dried-chile sauce with rice. A banana leaf wrapping inside the paper lends this most delicate of tamales its flavor. **La Palma Mexicatessen** (see page 197) also makes an array of tamales to try, and on your walk down Twenty-fourth Street, the Mission's finest market street, you will encounter a living gallery of folk murals in as many styles as tamales. When you get to Balmy Alley on the south side of Twenty-fourth Street between Treat and Harrison, take a right and walk down one side and up the other. The alley must have been named for its microclimate, which is amazingly warm and sunny even within a part of the city that is famous for its tropical temperatures. All the tall wooden fences and garage doors that line the alley have been painted by Latino artists, some depicting Central American solidarity, others the culture of daily life, all sophisticated and original executions. The tradition of Diego Rivera lives on! Along Twenty-fourth Street itself, church walls, apartment buildings, and stores provide more canvases for the street painters. A map to the murals in the Mission can be purchased for $2 at Precita Eyes Mural Arts Center, 2981 Twenty-fourth Street (between Alabama and Florida). While you're mapping out your route, you can restore yourself with a new set of tamales at La Palma.

VALENCIA WHOLE FOODS MARKET. . . . . . .

999 Valencia Street (at 21st Street)
415-285-0231
Open Monday through Friday
8 A.M. to 9 P.M., Saturday and
Sunday 9 A.M. to 9 P.M.
Credit cards: AE, MC, V

Yousef Nazzal, the owner of this well-stocked, lovingly cared for neighborhood health food store, has a palate with perfect pitch. He can throw together an improbable assortment of ingredients and make them taste as if they were meant for one another. His deli counter at Valencia Whole Foods has become a magnet for moms who need the foundations for a wholesome meal, or for anyone who doesn't have time to cook, but wants to eat cleanly and nutritiously. His specialties are vaguely Middle Eastern salads made with chewy grains, diced vegetables, seeds, nuts, and lively dressings. But he also does a wonderful curried tofu salad with toothsome short-grain rice. Each salad tastes completely different and the selections change often. A generous portion in a clear plastic box with a plastic fork makes for an inexpensive to-go meal. You can also buy his substantial rice-stuffed grape leaves, hummus, marinated olives, and fresh pita bread, with the appropriate organic produce to flesh out a meal. If you're undecided about what to order, the countermen generously offer tastes.

BAKERIES/PASTRIES

DIANDA'S ITALIAN-AMERICAN PASTRIES . .

2883 Mission Street (between
24th and 25th streets)
415-647-5469
www.diandas.citysearch.com
Open Monday through Saturday
6:30 A.M. to 6 P.M.,
Sunday until 4 P.M.
Cash only

This old-fashioned Italian bakery specializes in airy whipped cream and custard-filled cakes, most often inscribed to specification and elaborately decorated. Dianda does bake a flat almond cake, moist with almond paste and topped with sliced, toasted almonds, which goes exceptionally well with Italian coffee. Whenever I'm in the neighborhood I pick one up.

PANADERIA LA MEXICANA . . . .

2804 24th Street (at York)
415-648-2633
Open daily 4:30 A.M. to 8 P.M.
Cash only

At Mexican bakeries scattered up and down Twenty-fourth Street, you will encounter shelves of largish, bunlike pastries, all pretty much made out of the same dough, but shaped, glazed, or sugared differently. There are crocodiles, conch shells, rocks, ears, turtles, and shoes, all made of the soft, airy, pleasant pastry called *pan dulce*, or Mexican sweet bread. Among aficionados, Emilio Valle, the former baker at Panaderia La Mexicana, is considered the reigning master of the *pan dulce*. His shapes were the most whimsical, and I can attest to their freshness and lightness. The baker still turns them out. A cinnamon-and-sugar-dusted *concha* with a cup of Mexican chocolate makes for a morning treat. *Pan dulce* delivers the tactile pleasure of a doughnut, but without all the oil because these pastries are baked. At a *panaderia* you do not wait to be served, but grab a tray and tongs from the counter and choose your own pastries, which are then counted and bagged. A dollar will buy you a bagful. Besides the *conchas*, I also pick up sugared sticks of *pan de yema*, which are filled with a layer of sweetened egg yolk; crisp pretzel-shaped cookies sprinkled with rock sugar; and mild spice cookies. Not rich, these cookies boast crumbly texture and gentle flavor.

TARTINE BAKERY . . . .

600 Guerrero Street (at 18th Street)
415-487-2600
www.tartinebakery.com
Open Tuesday through Saturday
7:30 A.M. to 7 P.M.,
Sunday 10 A.M. to 5 P.M.
Credit cards: AE, MC, V

San Franciscans are very lucky to have snagged Tartine from Mill Valley where it first alighted after leaving its home in Point Reyes Station. This bakery started out as Bay Breads, an amazing bread bakery that used a wood-fired oven for baking, a superslow rising dough, and organic ingredients. With its new location and name, the bakery has gone uptown. But bread baker Chad Robertson still creates his glorious, chewy white loaves with thick, crunchy crusts. This magnificent bread is used for sandwiches, hence the name of the bakery (*tartine* is French for sandwich), including a warm open-faced sandwich of tomatoes, Niman Ranch smoked ham, béchamel sauce, and cheese, that makes me crazy with desire whenever I think about it.

Robertson's partner (and wife), Elizabeth Prueitt, specializes in French pastries and they're divine, too. Her croissants, especially her almond croissants, have enormous character just like the bread. They're buttery and flaky and crisp, but also chewy—a miracle. Don't get me started on the sensually moist, bright-flavored lemon-almond pound cake, the cinnamon- and orange-scented morning buns, or the banana-cream tarts.

You can eat and drink coffee here in a light-filled room at wooden tables and chairs, surrounded by the beautiful breads and pastries, or you can try to take your purchases home. I have never succeeded in doing the latter. I always start nibbling away in the car. Tartine is the best bakery in San Francisco, well worth the long pilgrimage if you aren't fortunate enough to live in the neighborhood.

ICE CREAM/CHOCOLATES

BOMBAY ICE CREAMERY . . . .

552 Valencia Street (between
16th and 17th streets)
415 -431-1103
Open Tuesday through Saturday
11:30 A.M. to 9 p.m.,
Sunday noon to 9 P.M.
Cash only

Two kinds of ice cream are sold here: very sweet commercial Western-style ice cream in exotic flavors like caramel-butter cashew, saffron, and ginger, which taste a bit artificial and cloying, and house-made *kulfi*, real Indian ice cream made with boiled-down milk, which I like very much. Bright green pistachio *kulfi* does have an artificial green glow, but possesses real pistachio flavor. Its texture is denser than Western ice cream, though the *kulfi* made here is a little bit icy and somewhat lighter than most. Frozen in cone-shaped metal molds and unmolded under hot water, it's cut into slices, topped with *falooda* (clear vermicelli noodles), a dab of frozen sweetened cream, and a splash of pomegranate syrup. This Indian sundae, not too sweet but with lots of texture and flavor, satisfies my relentless ice cream craving in a new and delightful way.

MITCHELL'S ICE CREAM . . . .

688 San Jose Avenue (at 29th Street)
415-648-2300
www.mitchellsicecream.com
Open daily 11 A.M. to 11 P.M.
Cash only

Although a bulletproof window with sliding panels might seem more appropriate at a bank than an ice cream shop, Mitchell's is a friendly and crowded place—and they do serve ice cream late into the night, which accounts for the safety features. All the ice creams are made on the premises to old-fashioned, light, but creamy specifications, unlike the super-dense ice creams that have become the vogue. This texture allows more delicate, exotic flavors like *buko* (young coconut), avocado, or *ube* (purple yamlike taro) to come through. Personally, I am a big fan of *buko* cones. The tropical Philippine flavors are part of a long and changing list that includes a distinctive Mexican chocolate, a pallid mango, and fresh peach in the summer. The clerks will give you tastes of any flavor before you decide. This ice cream shop also makes ice cream cakes for special occasions, sodas, shakes, sundaes, and fruit-flavored ice slushes.

MARKETS

BI-RITE MARKET . . . .

3639 18th Street (between
Guerrero and Dolores)
415-241-9760
Open Monday through Friday
10 A.M. to 9 P.M., Saturday 9 A.M. to
8 P.M., Sunday 9 A.M. to 7 P.M.
Credit cards: MC, V

Delfina (see page 179) started the culinary hegira to this neighborhood on the edge of the Mission and now this section of Eighteenth Street has become a mecca for the hip, young, discriminating eater. The bountiful shelves of Bi-Rite, and its eye-catching outdoor display of cut flowers, is a good place to wander while waiting for a table at Delfina. As a grocery, Bi-Rite specializes in high-quality goods: Clover organic dairy products from the cooperative in Sonoma, organic fruits and vegetables, local honey, organic jams, the best imported tuna packed in olive oil, big tins of Recca anchovies, their own bottled salad dressing. It's also a destination for an interesting variety of prepared-on-the-premises salads, take-home meals, sandwiches, and party platters. The combination of grocery store and eclectic delicatessen strikes a pleasing balance. You can pick up Bi-Rite's sweet Italian sausages and pints of super-fresh ratatouille for dinner, or put together a party platter of delicious rice-stuffed grape leaves seasoned with plenty of salt and lemon, accompanied with hummus, olives, and feta. The food selection includes the full Mediterranean. I have to curb my impulse buying at Bi-Rite. The two Mogannam brothers who run it know their way around a kitchen and how to make a food store seductive to both eaters and cooks.

BOMBAY BAZAAR . . . .

548 Valencia Street (between
16th and 17th streets)
415-621-1717
Open Tuesday through Sunday
10:30 A.M. to 7:30 P.M.
Credit cards: MC, V

This used to be the most complete Indian dry-goods store in San Francisco, but half of the store has been given over to saris, and the spices, dals, and flours are packaged in cellophane now. A few fresh items like kaffir lime leaves and fresh *kari* leaves occasionally show up. You still can find good buys on basmati rice in sacks ranging from five to forty pounds, and Darjeeling tea. I am drawn to the many shelves of shiny stainless-steel *thali* plates and saucers, covered jars and canisters, both smart and traditional at the same time. They can be adapted to many Western uses. Indian cookware, such as heavy cast-iron woks with sturdy pounded-steel handles (the Chinese wok came from India) and all sorts of stainless-steel skillets and saucepans come at excellent prices. For cooking vessels of similar quality you pay more at Macy's.

CASA LUCAS . . . .

2934 24th Street (between
Alabama and Florida)
415-826-4334
Open daily 7 A.M. to 7:30 P.M.
Credit cards: AE, MC, V

The lines can be long at this popular Latin American market with tables of plantains, jicama, and citrus outside its perpetually open doors. This store carries the most complete selection of Latin American and Caribbean products in San Francisco. There are no carts, so shoppers fill up numerous plastic baskets with young coconuts, tomatillos, fresh and dried chiles in bulk, packets of Latin American herbs, frozen fruit purées for *licuados*, vinegars, capers at good prices, huge purple olives in brine from Peru, cut-up cleaned fresh cactus *(nopal), piloncillo* (cakes of moist, molasses-rich brown sugar), three kinds of chorizo, powder mixes for Mexican drinks, and Mexican cheeses. Customers line up the baskets on the wooden floor by the check-out counters and push the train forward with their feet. If you cannot find what you need at Casa Lucas, it is probably out of season or unavailable anyplace else.

LA PALMA MEXICATESSEN . . . .

2884 24th Street (at Florida)
415-647-1500
Open Monday through Saturday
8 A.M. to 6 P.M., Sunday until 5 P.M.
Credit cards: MC, V

Latino groceries, fresh cheeses, house-rendered lard, dried chiles and spices augment the fresh tortillas at this excellent Mexican and Central American food store. See page 197 for more information.

SAMIRAMI'S IMPORTS . . . .

2990 Mission Street (at 26th Street)
415-824-6555
Open Monday through Saturday
10 A.M. to 6 P.M.
Credit cards: AE, D, MC, V

A long-established store that caters to Middle Eastern ethnic needs, Samirami's shelves are piled with everything from videos in Arabic to North African cooking equipment like *couscoussières.* At least five different kinds of imported couscous are sold in bulk or in packages, along with the Cortas brand of pomegranate molasses, nuts, dried fruits, spices, and olive oils. In the refrigerator section is thick, creamy, deliciously sour Persian-style yogurt, Armenian string cheese, feta from everywhere, and Mexican *queso fresco,* a mild, crumbly whole-milk cheese that also tastes good sprinkled on Mediterranean dishes. The emphasis, though, is not so much on fresh foods, but on the imported Middle Eastern groceries, spices, and grains necessary to stock a pantry.

VAL 16 MARKET . . . .

3100 16th Street (at Valencia)
415-863-8790
Open daily 7 A.M. to 10 P.M.
Credit cards: MC, V

This well-stocked corner market with fruit piled onto sidewalk tables provides a wide range of Latin American produce and grocery items. From the north part of the city, La Hacienda is the closest outpost for warm packaged tortillas made without additives (read the label before you buy) and fresh Mexican cheeses in bulk, kept in a refrigerated case. The excellent *queso fresco* here has a soft, crumbly texture, not gelatinous, and a gentle tang. Stronger *queso cotijo* and smoked and aged Mexican cheeses along with Mexican Jack are sold in large quantities, so they are always fresh. Luscious Mexican and Salvadoran *crema*—Latino crème fraîche—are sold by the pint. Many markets in the Mission dispense *queso fresco* from an unrefrigerated counter, madness when it comes to such a fresh, delicate cheese. At Val 16 and Casa Lucas (see page 203), the bulk cheeses are always refrigerated.

PRODUCE MARKETS

ALEMANY FARMERS' MARKET . . . .

Alemany at Crescent
(parallel to Highway 280)
Saturdays from first light
through the afternoon
Cash only

This is the oldest farmers' market in the Bay Area, started in 1943 by pear farmers who had extra fruit to sell. In 1945 it moved into two long parallel cement structures divided into stalls. So many farmers come today that they spill out on the ends into the rather chaotic parking lot, setting up their own booths. This is the great multiethnic market in the city, with a dazzling array of Asian greens, exotic bird eggs (quail, duck, turkey), unusual citrus, melons, flowers, and tons of local stuff at the peak of the season. If you want the rare find, you have to get there before 8 A.M. If you're looking for great prices on farm-fresh produce, go late when the farmers are trying to unload. Each week brings something new. This market keeps unfolding with every season and every year as farmers experiment with different crops.

2934 24th Street (between
Alabama and Florida)
415-826-4334
Open daily 7 A.M. to 7:30 P.M.
Credit cards: AE, MC, V

Produce spills out onto the sidewalk on tables at this bustling Latin American market. The sexiest stuff—mangoes, avocados, bananas, oranges, seasonal stone fruit—get prominent display. Inside, the nuts-and-bolts ingredients of Latin American cooking—fresh chiles, cilantro, de-spined cactus paddles, cilantro, radishes, jicama, head lettuce, cucumbers, limes—are piled along one side. Casa Lucas carries the widest selection of Central American produce in the Mission, including banana leaves, coconuts, and exotic fruits. You can find all the produce for authentic Diana Kennedy and Rick Bayless recipes, and practically everything else except meat. See page 203 for more information.

LA LOMA PRODUCE . . . .

2840 Mission Street (between
24th and 25th streets)
415-647-4257
Open daily 8 A.M. to 7 P.M.
Cash only

The produce is stacked outside on wooden tables underneath an awning, and the small, dark interior is crammed with Latin American products. There's barely a place to wait in front of the counter, where up to six different kinds of tamales are dispensed along with such delicacies as the best *alfajores* in the Mission. *Alfajores* are elegant sandwich cookies—two thin Mexican butter cookies dusted with powdered sugar and filled with *cajeta*, a rich buttery caramel made with goat's milk—only the best cookies in town. On the produce shelves you are apt to find fresh coconuts and other hard-to-find ingredients in good shape.

23RD AND MISSION PRODUCE . . . .

2700 Mission Street (at 23rd Street)
415-285-7955
Open Monday through Saturday
7:30 A.M. to 6:30 P.M.
Cash only

This neatly stocked Latin American produce store knows how to entice shoppers. During the winter when people are hungry for fruit, the market stacks up huge piles of sweet, juicy yellow mangoes with blushing red cheeks and sells them for a dollar each when they are at least half again as much anyplace else.

Always in perfect condition, the fruit is either ripe or within several days of ripening. Sometimes Haitian flat green organic mangoes with deep orange flesh are available, or fifteen perfect mangoes by the case for $12 to $13. I happen to be crazy about mangoes, and nothing pleases me more than the thought of having my own case at home to eat as they ripen. The other drawing card of this market are Haas avocados, always in good shape and $.25 less per piece than anyplace else, and well-priced limes and lemons. The produce buyer for the store knows what he is doing. Most of the produce here turns over quickly and looks fresh and handsome.

AVOCADO QUESADILLAS

SERVES 4

Val 16 Market has the best selection of Mexican cheeses in bulk at their refrigerated front counter, and you can get all the other ingredients for these quesadillas there, too. Of course, everyone has his or her favorite cheese combo—I like to use half sharp Cheddar and half mozzarella. When we serve these quesadillas at the Hayes Street Grill, we add a small amount of grilled tuna or shrimp and reduce the amount of avocado, or omit it altogether.

½ cup (2 ounces) coarsely grated
queso chataleño

½ cup (2 ounces) coarsely grated
queso cotija

1 cup (4 ounces) coarsely grated
Monterey Jack cheese

1 serrano chile, seeded
and minced

¼ cup minced fresh cilantro

2 scallions, minced

4 teaspoons vegetable oil

4 flour tortillas

2 ripe avocados, peeled, pitted,
and diced

1 large tomato, seeded and diced

Kosher salt to taste

1 In a small bowl, combine the *quesa chataleño, queso cotija*, and Monterey Jack cheese. In another small bowl, combine the chile, cilantro, and scallions.

2 In a 10-inch skillet over medium heat, heat 1 teaspoon of the oil until it spreads over the surface of the pan. Add a flour tortilla. Cook on one side for 30 seconds, then turn over. Reduce the heat to medium-low.

3 Sprinkle over the tortilla one-fourth of each of the cheeses and of the chile mixture, avocados, and tomato, and add a pinch of kosher salt. Cover the skillet and cook until the cheese is melted and begins to bubble, about 5 minutes. Then, with a spatula, fold the tortilla in half to form a semicircle and transfer it from the skillet to a warmed plate or serving platter. Place in a preheated 250°F oven and repeat with the remaining tortillas. Serve immediately.

SERVES 6

This recipe is adapted from Diana Kennedy's *My Mexico*.

2¼ pounds stewing pork with some fat, cut into ¾-inch cubes

1¼ tablespoons dried Mexican oregano

1 tablespoon cumin seeds

2 bay leaves, crumbled

2 whole cloves

5 garlic cloves

1 tablespoon salt or to taste

1 tablespoon mild vinegar

3 ancho chiles, seeded

3 guajillo chiles, seeded

3 cups water, or as needed

3 tablespoons pork lard or vegetable oil

1 tablespoon sugar

½ orange, sliced

1 Put the meat into a bowl. Grind the oregano, cumin seeds, bay leaves, and cloves together to make a powder. Crush the garlic together with the salt and vinegar. Add the powdered herbs, mixing to a thick paste. Rub the paste into the meat with your hands and set aside to season at least 1 hour or overnight in the refrigerator.

2 Cover the chiles with hot water and soak for about 20 minutes or until softened and reconstituted (do not leave too long in the water or they will lose their flavor). Drain, discarding the water. Transfer to a blender with 1½ cups of the water and blend as smoothly as possible.

3 In a heavy flame-proof casserole over medium heat, warm the lard, add the seasoned meat, and fry until the meat is just starting to brown (take care; if the heat is too high, the spices will burn).

4 Add the blended chiles to the pan, pressing them through a fine strainer to remove the tough pieces of guajillo skin that stubbornly remain despite the blending. Fry the sauce for about 5 minutes, stirring and scraping the pan bottom to prevent sticking.

5 Add the remaining 1½ cups of water, cover the pan, and cook over medium heat for about 15 minutes, stirring from time to time. Add the sugar and orange slices and continue cooking for about 45 minutes, or until the meat is tender. Add a little more water if necessary to thin the sauce to medium consistency so it coats the back of a wooden spoon.

MEAT AND POULTRY

LA GALLINITA. . . . .

2989 24th Street (at Harrison)
415-826-8880
Open Monday through Friday
8 A.M. to 6 P.M., Saturday until
5 P.M., Sunday until 2 P.M.
Credit cards: AE, MC, V

You can tell what this tiny, always-packed butcher shop specializes in by the aroma of fried pork wafting out the front door and down the street. On a table at the back of this dark little place are two stainless-steel pans of crisp, warm *chicharrónes* (pork cracklings), which Salvadorans use in their *pupusas* and on salads, but many people buy by the bag for snacks. You pick out your own crispy pieces with tongs and put them in a white bag. I know most people don't eat bags of fatty pork skin these days, but one melting bite is not enough. You have to have another. Besides the *chicharrónes*, people buy butterflied flank steak for *carne asada* and bags of chicken parts for soup. Fresh blood sausage moves quickly from the counter when it is available, and sometimes super-hot plump red chiles are sold individually. Though the principles of modern marketing have passed by this dark hole of a shop, there are many treasures to be mined.

THE LUCKY PORK STORE. . . . .

2659 Mission Street (between
22nd and 23rd streets)
415-285-3611 or 415-550-9016
Open Monday through Saturday
9 A.M. to 7 P.M., Sunday until 6 P.M.
Credit cards: MC, V

This large and very inexpensive butcher counter and market was founded in 1949 by a Chinese-American butcher and is now run by his son. As if you couldn't guess, it specializes in pig. Whole heads, snouts, ears, tongues, feet, shins, fat back, ribs, tripe, liver—almost every conceivable part of the animal—are surrealistically piled in the long glass refrigerated counter. More usual cuts like pork butt and loin, good-looking beef short ribs, oxtails, and other cuts of beef that take to long cooking are all abundant, fresh, and low in price. This butcher shop will find you whole suckling pigs and *cabrito* (young goat) for major Mexican barbecues. When you think of more unusual cuts of animals, think Lucky.

MISSION MARKET MEAT . . . .

2590 Mission Street (at 22nd Street)
415-282-1030
Open Monday through Saturday
9 A.M. to 6 P.M.
Credit cards: MC, V

The long meat counter in the multistalled Mission Market is one of my favorite places to buy meat anywhere in the city. Among the treasures to be found in the immaculate refrigerated case are Harris Ranch beef, thick slices of beef shin for stock or succulent stew, beautiful-looking oxtails, and short ribs. Rocky free-range chickens and the incomparable Rosie organic chickens, freshly ground turkey meat and fresh, not frozen, turkeys (whole and in parts), fresh chicken gizzards and backs, and rabbits are available at the Mission Market Fish and Poultry counter a few steps away.

Strolling by these counters and just seeing what is available makes me want to get cooking. Here are the building blocks you never see for good stocks—poultry and beef—and the cuts you need for the savory stews you crave. Shopping in the Mission Market comes very close to being in the middle of a Latin American *mercado*.

POLARICA . . . .

107 Quint Street (near 3rd Street and Cesar Chavez)

415-647-1300

www.polarica.com

Open Monday through Friday

9 A.M. to 5 P.M.

Credit cards: AE, MC, V

Polarica imports game, meats, and specialty products from all over the world and sells them both wholesale and retail, delivered and on-site, for the same price. Home cooks can visit the attractively facaded storefront warehouse or call ahead to order something specific. This is the place where many cooks go for one of my favorite birds, the rich-flavored, dark-fleshed guinea fowl (roast or grill the breasts, braise the legs, and serve with long-cooked cabbage), as well as fresh pheasant. The fresh California-grown rabbits have no off flavors, and the vacuum-packed fresh lamb from Australia in all cuts is some of the best available. Fresh venison from New Zealand and duck, whole and in parts from the Grimaud duck farm, are always in stock. Both Hudson Valley foie gras and our local Sonoma foie gras, and smoked salmon from Norway and Scotland at half the price you find them in delicatessens (Polarica will sell the salmon in small quantities if you wish) are but a few of the items available and listed on a detailed product list that will be mailed to you if you call. Polarica is also a source for fresh black truffles and all sorts of fresh wild mushrooms. Russian and American caviars are also sold at competitive prices. Finally, if the urge to eat emu or eland overtakes you, Polarica has them. This outfit, which also has an office in Manhattan, prides itself on finding sources for every conceivable kind of domestically raised game, worldwide. In fact if you're looking for any rare or exotic ingredient, you might want to check here first.

FISH

MISSION MARKET FISH AND POULTRY . . . .

2590 Mission Street (at 22nd Street)

415-282-3331

Open Monday through Saturday

8:30 A.M. to 6 P.M.

Credit cards: MC, V

Pristine, wild California salmon, local squid, tuna, swordfish, and a wide assortment of other local fish and shellfish share the case with poultry at this sweet-smelling, neatly arranged counter. The fish is so fresh here you can make ceviche with it. The Mission Market counters provide one-stop shopping for consumers who can take advantage of the specialization provided by separately operated businesses. Both shoppers and goods—the select array of fish, meat, and poultry on sale at Mission Market counters—get lots of personal attention.

SUN FAT SEAFOOD COMPANY . . . .

2687 Mission (between
22nd and 23rd streets)
415-282-9339
Open Monday through Saturday
9:30 A.M. to 6 P.M.,
Sunday 10 A.M. to 5 P.M.
Cash only

Smelt, whitebait, striped bass, live crabs, blue crabs, soft-shell crabs, fresh squid, fresh shrimp, and beautiful rockfish are but some of the selection at this well-stocked if utilitarian fish market. Unusual fish for Filipino dishes are also a specialty. The fish displayed on metal tables of ice disappear by day's end. Nothing sticks around at Sun Fat, which is why you want to shop for fish here.

COOKWARE AND BOOKS

ENCANTADA GALLERY OF FINE ARTS . . . . .

908 Valencia Street (at 20th Street)
415-642-3939
Open Tuesday through Thursday
and Sunday noon to 6 P.M.,
Friday and Saturday until 8 P.M.
Credit cards: MC, V

Owner Mia Gonzales has collected glassware, complete sets of tableware, serving pieces, salsa dishes, wooden utensils, tablecloths, and napkins from all over Mexico. Her artisanal *molcajetes* (flat mortars and oval pestles) look like carved stone frogs. Turn them over and they become grinding tools for dried chiles and guacamole. You can find lead-free blue-and-white Oaxacan bowls and plates, my favorites, or brilliant blue, orange, or earthtone dishes from Puebla. If you come after one of Gonzales's shopping trips, you might find those trendy, colorful plastic shopping bags that are giving Kate Spade a run.

LAURIE MACKENZIE'S WALKING TOURS OF THE MISSION

Encantada is dedicated to promoting Chicano, Mexican, and Latino cultural heritage and memories through exhibitions and popular art. To that end, the gallery sponsors cooking classes and walking tours of the Mission conducted by Laurie Mackenzie, an expert in Latin American studies and a twelve-year resident of the Mission. She also happens to be a professional cook who has worked with Diana Kennedy and Rick Bayless. Her knowledge runs deep and she has fabulous taste. Call Encantada Gallery (415-642-3939) for a schedule of Mission walks and cooking classes. Mackenzie also leads culinary tours to Mexico.

NOE VALLEY
THE CASTRO
DIAMOND HEIGHTS
UPPER MARKET

NOE VALLEY, THE CASTRO, DIAMOND HEIGHTS & UPPER MARKET

RESTAURANTS

1   Chenery Park
2   Chow
3   Fattoush
4   Firefly
5   Home
6   Incanto
7   La Corneta Taqueria
8   Miss Millie's
9   Ristorante Bacco

CAFES

10   Cafe Flore

BARS

11   Bliss Bar
12   Mecca

BAKERIES/PASTRIES

13   Noe Valley Bakery

ICE CREAM/CHOCOLATES

14   Joseph Schmidt

MARKETS

15   Tower Market

PRODUCE

16   Harvest Ranch Market
17   MikeyTom
18   Real Food Company

MEAT AND POULTRY

19   Drewes Brothers Meat
15   Viglizzo's Meat

CHEESE

20   Cooper's
21   24th Avenue Cheese Shop

WINES AND SPIRITS

22   PlumpJack Wines
23   Castro Village Wine Company

COOKWARE AND BOOKS

24   Cliff's Hardware
25   Lehr's German Specialties

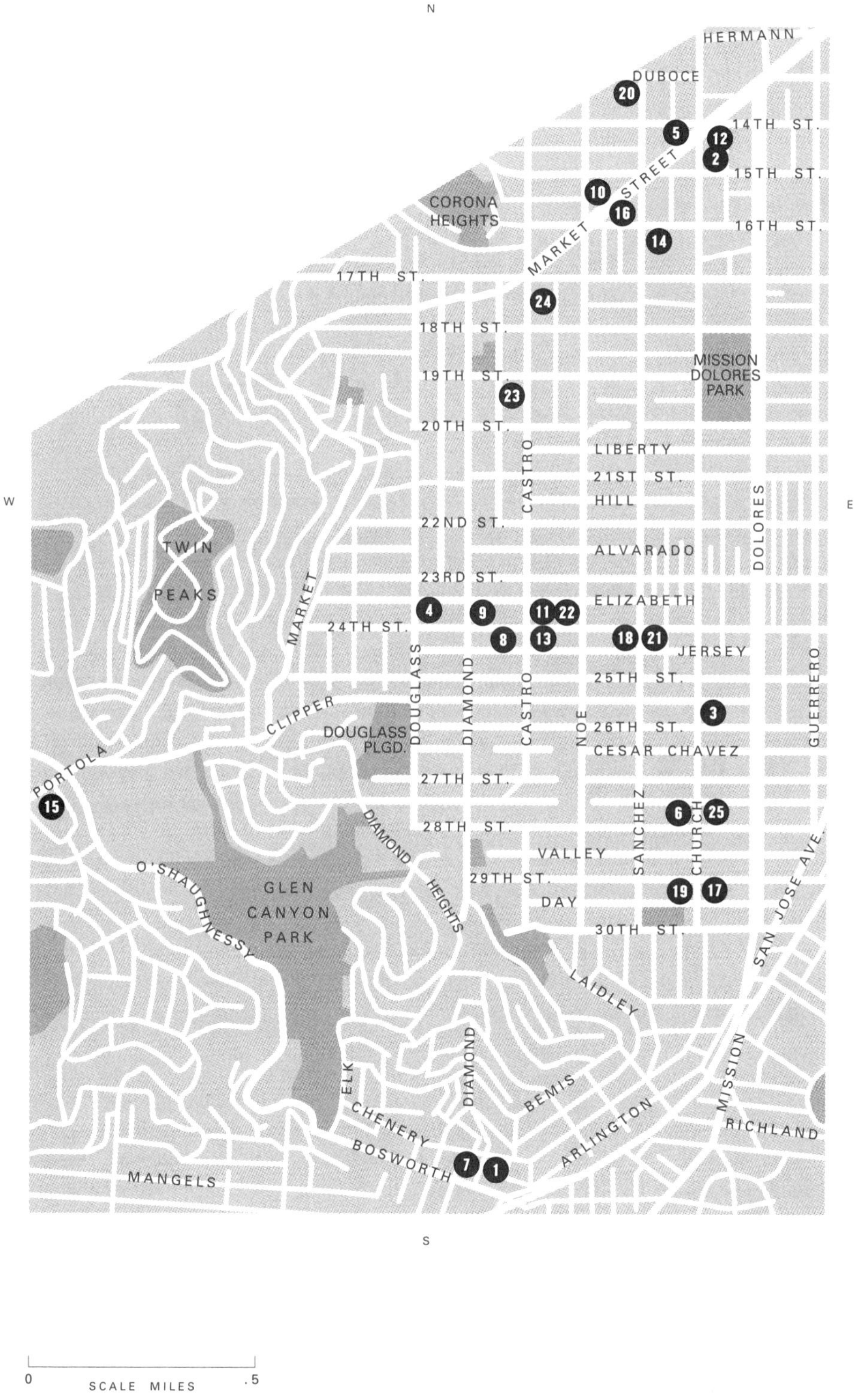
N
S
W
E
HERMANN
DUBOCE
14TH ST.
15TH ST.
16TH ST.
MARKET STREET
CORONA HEIGHTS
17TH ST.
18TH ST.
19TH ST.
20TH ST.
MISSION DOLORES PARK
LIBERTY
21ST ST.
HILL
CASTRO
22ND ST.
ALVARADO
DOLORES
23RD ST.
ELIZABETH
TWIN PEAKS
MARKET
24TH ST.
JERSEY
25TH ST.
DOUGLASS
DIAMOND
CASTRO
NOE
26TH ST.
CESAR CHAVEZ
GUERRERO
CLIPPER
DOUGLASS PLGD.
PORTOLA
27TH ST.
28TH ST.
SANCHEZ
CHURCH
DIAMOND HEIGHTS
VALLEY
29TH ST.
DAY
30TH ST.
O'SHAUGHNESSY
GLEN CANYON PARK
SAN JOSE AVE.
LAIDLEY
MISSION
DIAMOND
ELK
BEMIS
CHENERY
ARLINGTON
RICHLAND
BOSWORTH
MANGELS
1
2
3
4
5
6
7
8
9
10
11
12
13
14
15
16
17
18
19
20
21
22
23
24
25
0
SCALE MILES
.5

RESTAURANTS

CHENERY PARK. . . . .

683 Chenery Street (at Diamond)
415-337-8537
www.chenerypark.com
Open Monday through Thursday
5:30 P.M. to 9:30 P.M.,
Friday and Saturday until 10 P.M.,
Sunday until 9 P.M.
Moderate
Credit cards: AE, MC, V

A treasure in a hidden neighborhood, Chenery Park brings professionalism and smart, tasty food tailored to an upscale microcommunity that previously made do with the offerings on Twenty-fourth Street. What looks like an undistinguished storefront in the tiny village of Glen Park turns out to be a comfortably appointed, multilevel restaurant with small dining areas branching off a central staircase. Because of its vertical layout, the restaurant is actually larger than it appears, and even on weeknights the blond wood tables are full. Plenty of people who live in the hills between Noe Valley and Glen Park are willing to pay downtown prices to eat well close to home.

The menu creates an interesting dialogue between San Francisco and New Orleans—no surprise since one of the chef-owners, Gaines Dobbins, grew up there. The other, Richard Rosen, is from New York, but they hooked up years ago cooking at Nancy Oakes's first restaurant, L'Avenue. Both of them know how to make sexy food and they do it without overfilling the plates or getting too complicated. One of the most gorgeous appetizers in town, the signature Chenery Park Pâté Plate, brings three tiny portions of supermoist, shalloty chicken liver pâté, small slices of smoky country terrine, and a ramekin of unctuous rabbit rillettes. The plate, garnished with a little watercress salad, a few cornichons, a couple of mustards, and some toasts, is generous enough to be shared by two, though so good, one person (me) could easily polish it off. I like to head south for a main course here, like dark, spicy shrimp gumbo with andouille that reminds me of smoky barbecue; or a pounded pan-roasted chicken breast served over dirty rice (a New Orleans–style pilaf with peppers and onions) with andouille gravy. A pasta dish like fusilli tossed with shards of duck confit, sugar snap peas, and a sauce of Madeira cream has the depth of good New Orleans cooking lightened by the sparkle of California produce. These chefs have the touch. They know how to make food with big flavor, yet keep it light.

With full bar and complete wine list, casual if informed service, and a front-of-the-house staff that nurtures ties with many regular customers, Chenery Park has become the local club, but one that welcomes everyone.

CHOW . . . .

215 Church Street (at Market)
415-552-2469
Open Sunday through Thursday
11 A.M. to 11 P.M., Friday and
Saturday until midnight;
Saturday and Sunday brunch
starting at 10 A.M.
Inexpensive
Credit cards: MC, V

Patrons can't believe how lucky they are when they get the check at Chow. How can they eat and drink so well and so much for so little? Tony Gulisano, chef-owner and brain behind the two wildly successful Chows, not only keeps prices low, but also insists on using fresh, local ingredients, including Western Grassland's beef for his delicious hamburgers. This juicy, bright-tasting beef must be ordered rare or medium-rare or it dries out, but it makes for a guilt-free hamburger. No steroids, antibiotics, or bioengineered, fossil fuel–fertilized corn have fed these animals. You're just eating sunlight in the form of grass consumed by the cows, a truly natural food. But I digress.

My favorite dishes come out of the wood-fired oven: stunning pizzas with crisp, yeasty crusts, lots of whole-milk mozzarella, big hunks of warm, peeled Roma tomatoes, and perhaps asparagus and barely wilted arugula leaves thrown on at the last minute; velvety eggplant parmigiana smothered in fresh tomato sauce with whole basil leaves and real Parmigiano; or rich multilayered lasagna. Every day the menu offers a different sandwich special with soup or salad or fries, and they're so hearty and tasty that they feed you for a whole day. The vibrant house salad has a bright lemon and shallot vinaigrette and is full of raw crunchy vegetables. They prepare the palate for a hearty vegetarian dish of grilled portobello mushrooms with soft polenta and roasted peppers; or my husband's beloved homestyle spaghetti and big, soft-textured meatballs, a recipe from Gulisano's mother.

Chow keeps everyone happy with drinkable wines at rock-bottom prices, fresh fruit smoothies, and homey desserts. A warm, crisp crumbly shortcake smothered in fresh strawberries and whipped cream is a perennial favorite, as is the chef's mom's real Sicilian cannoli—crisp shell, creamy ricotta with pistachios—perfect with coffee. So given the high quality of the food and the low prices, the place is packed all the time and only large parties can reserve. But service is so efficient and the kitchen so fast that tables turn and the wait is never long. People don't linger in this madhouse. They eat and talk and drink and move on so the next guy can sit down, participating in the community service ethos that drives this remarkable restaurant.

FATTOUSH . . . .

1361 Church Street (at 26th Street)
415-641-0678
Open Tuesday through Thursday
11:30 A.M. to 9:30 P.M., Friday until
10 P.M., Saturday 9 A.M. to 10 P.M.,
Sunday 9 A.M. to 9 P.M.
Moderate
Credit cards: AE, D, MC, V

Fattoush, a relative newcomer to this neighborhood (it opened in 1998), specializes in dishes from Iraq, Syria, Lebanon, and Palestine, and offers some extraordinary dishes. I recommend going early so you actually can see the colorful food. After nightfall, I could barely read the menu in the candlelit storefront dining room, but did notice the two dark, slim, handsome chefs moving quickly in a brightly lit kitchen window.

Start with the knockout hot appetizer, *hoset sabanech*, spinach sautéed with pickled turnips, green olives, fresh tomato, onions, sour cucumber pickle, and generous clarified butter, creating a tart, complex, perfectly balanced, vibrant cooked salad. It's addictive. Follow it with *mansaf*—a nomadic dish—with a haunting, buttery yogurt sauce. The white sauce fills the plate like a thick soup, with a small mound of nutty basmati rice pilaf tossed with small cubes of braised lamb and toasted almonds in the middle. I still dream about the combination of this luxurious sauce with rice and a little meat. How happy it must make those lucky nomads!

An unexpectedly classy wine list delivers the likes of a lush Testarosa Pinot Noir from Bien Nacido Vineyards in Santa Barbara, which does go with an opening lagniappe of butter-soaked toasted English muffin thickly sprinkled with *za'atar*, the ubiquitous Middle

Eastern herb mix, though the wine's charms get lost when drunk with spicier fare. There are other, less complex wines that complement the food.

FIREFLY . . . .

4288 24th Street (near Douglass)
415-821-7652
Open daily 5:30 to 10 P.M.
Moderate
Credit cards: AE, MC, V

When a restaurant puts out baskets of Acme *levain*, you know it is out to please. Though the cooking of chef Brad Levy falls into the California-eclectic school, his good sense keeps the food appealing. One meal might bring dishes from all over the world, but they are unified by Levy's sensibility. In an affordable neighborhood restaurant, the energy and thought behind his creative menu deservedly causes a stir.

A good way to start is with scallop and shrimp pot stickers, densely filled with a chunky mousse of sweet-flavored shellfish nicely set off with black pepper and served with chopsticks, which adds to the pleasure of eating them. A lemony Caesar salad with huge croutons is also popular and good. Items like Thai salmon cakes apply ethnic forms to Western ingredients. Unlike the spongy fish cakes served in Southeast Asia, these are dense and gingery, presented on a bed of room-temperature wilted spinach. They make for a very substantial starter. Firefly presumes that people will be sharing the first courses, so all the wooden tables are already set with blue-and-white print plates. Main courses are generous as well and span the globe. A moist, perfectly grilled chicken breast crowned a plate of black beans, lemony chayote squash still crisp, and a chunky avocado salsa, sweet and citrusy. The chef likes to season with both sugar and lemon, but not offensively. If any sort of fruit shortcake is on the dessert menu, order it. The crisp, sweet, salty, crumbly shortcakes are so tasty they stand on their own.

The neighborhood atmosphere of Firefly makes it all the more charming. Two small dining rooms, one with a wine bar where people can eat, share the space with a tiny open kitchen. The do-it-yourself decor has homegrown style, yet the service is amazingly professional. This pioneering restaurant in deepest Noe Valley now has achieved institution status.

HOME . . . .

2100 Market Street (at Church)
415-503-0333
www.home.com
Open Sunday through
Wednesday 5:30 to 10 P.M.,
Thursday through Saturday
5:30 to 11 P.M. Backyard Bar
nightly 5 P.M. to late; Sunday
brunch 10:30 A.M. to 2 P.M.
Moderate
Credit cards: AE, D, MC, V

Major restaurants rarely succeed in reinventing themselves: Once business drops off beyond a sustainable level, they have a tough time bouncing back. Owner John Hurley acted decisively when he saw that his sophisticated, upscale JohnFrank was losing ground after the dot-com crash and then the 9/11 disaster. He hired a new chef, the talented Lance Dean Velasquez, but even inspired cooking couldn't restore business. So Hurley closed JohnFrank on December 31, 2001, and reopened eleven days later as Home.

He slashed food prices in half, did away with the white tablecloths, and made the sleek, low-ceilinged dining room feel more casual. To compensate for the loss of revenue from lowered prices, he built a tented, heated patio, called the Backyard Bar, on a section of the restaurant's precious private parking lot. This patio, with its own little bar, counters, and tables, has become the hottest spot in town. Though the roaring restaurant feels like a party anyway when you walk in, the VIP gathering seems to be in the Backyard. Home is now even busier than JohnFrank was during its height, and frankly, this restaurant deserves its success. I've rarely eaten so well for so little. Inspirational credit goes to Tony Gulisano's Chow across Market Street, a restaurant that created the genre of upscale ingredients in downscale dining. But Velasquez does his own version at comparably low prices.

I'm thinking specifically of Lance Dean's braised brisket pot roast with spring onion–potato purée and horseradish crème. It happens to be one of the best plates of food in all of San Francisco, period. He uses Niman Ranch beef, cooking it ever so slowly until the meat becomes meltingly tender while intensifying in flavor. The rich gravy runs into the buttery potatoes, making each mouthful even more moist and velvety. It's worth battling the crowds at Home to order just this one dish.

But there are many others. A bowl of soupy, aromatic *chile verde* made with free-range Niman pork is another treat. Scented with cumin, cilantro, and green chiles, this meaty pork stew becomes almost addictive piled into warm tortillas with a lubrication of guacamole. Another pleasure of eating at Home is the side dish. No domestic god or goddess could put out a more heavenly ramekin of crisp-tender broccoli enrobed in delicious sharp cheddar cheese sauce or a similarly sauced gratin of macaroni with a crunchy topping of rye bread crumbs. Though both are scrumptious, you only want to order one unless you really adore silky Cheddar cheese sauce.

For starters there's a grown-up iceberg lettuce salad with tangy crumbled Point Reyes blue cheese, apple, and spiced pecans, or a piquant asparagus salad smartly dressed in chunky red pepper and caper vinaigrette. Warm dinner sandwiches are distributed all over the menu—a sloppy Joe with creamy slaw and fries is Monday's lunch special; an oyster po'boy, a New Orleans–style fried oyster sandwich, substitutes on Thursday nights; and the always-available pulled-pork sandwich with sweet-and-spicy barbecue sauce and fries. Desserts, made by talented pastry chef Claire Legas, play on the homey, American theme. A classic root beer float in a tall glass comes with crisp ginger cookies. What could go better after a pulled-pork sandwich or a sloppy joe? But I'm partial to her warm, custardy banana bread pudding with toasty edges and bourbon sauce.

Hurley and Velasquez have made the new incarnation of their restaurant as wholesome, as comfortable, as easygoing as dinner at home. Well, the restaurant is noisier—a lot noisier—but at your own home you don't have as many mouthwatering choices, or perky, efficient waiters bringing you your heart's desire. If the post dot-com economy means that we'll have more restaurants like Home, recession can't be all bad.

INCANTO . . . .

1550 Church Street (at 28th Street)
415-641-4500
www.incanto.biz
Open Wednesday through
Monday 5 to 10 P.M.,
wine bar until 11 P.M.
Moderate
Credit cards: MC, V

A space that used to house a German deli and restaurant called Speckmann's has become one of the hottest destinations in town. Incanto, the new Italian wine bar and trattoria, brings together an appealingly simple Delfina-like (see page 179) menu with a Bacar-like (see page 345) wine program that concentrates on Italian wines. The once-dark interior now resembles an airy wine cave with faux stone arches, an open kitchen with counter seating, and a wine library room in the back that has enormous potential for private parties. The food, prepared under the tutelage of longtime California-Italian chef Paul Buscemi, is scrumptious, emphasizing local ingredients in bright, Italian vernacular.

I've never had a warm calamari ragout, peppery, tomatoey, and aromatic of celery, like the one prepared here. Our local squid, barely warmed through, practically melts into the sauce, but it is clearly an Italian dish. The way San Daniele prosciutto works with mango, fresh ricottalike cheese, and peppercress represents a California twist on an Italian classic—prosciutto with melon. Crispy-skinned roast chicken comes with a juicy ragout of cannellini beans, fresh peas in season, and rosemary oil, the whole plate both savory and clean. Pastas may be the most Italian of dishes on the menu in that they are lightly sauced yet full of flavor. A couple of them are offered as main courses, not starters, in the American tradition. And you can find treasures like heaping side orders of broccoli *di ciccio*—nascent, just-sprouted broccoli—sautéed with garlic and red chile flakes. For dessert, crumbly, bright yellow cornmeal cake made with olive oil tastes luxuriantly buttery, a lovely foil for sweet berries and a dab of whipped cream.

The wine list, organized like a chart, tells you everything you need to know about the wines at a glance, including style, grape type, region, and price, often including glass, half liter, and bottle. A master sommelier from Italy, a rare breed according to our waiter, put the innovative list together, along with flights for tasting, and is always on the floor to expound. One advantage of sitting at the bar is that the barmen generously offer tastes of open bottles, a mini–wine education with the informative wine list at hand.

LA CORNETA TAQUERIA . . . .

2834 Diamond Street
(near Chenery)
415-469-8757
Open daily 10 A.M. to 10 P.M.
Inexpensive
Cash only

Fresh and original fillings and an immaculate open kitchen set this neighborhood taqueria apart. See page 183 for more information.

4123 24th Street (between
Castro and Diamond)
415-285-5598
Open Tuesday through Sunday
6 to 10 P.M., Saturday and Sunday
9 a.m. to 2 P.M.
Inexpensive
Credit cards: MC, V

For fresh, home-style American cooking, you can't beat Miss Millie's. Portions are huge and the kitchen makes a point of serving naturally raised meats and seasonal, organic produce. There's even a special wine list with bottles for under $20, a miracle these days. High quality and low prices converge at this charming little restaurant, making Miss Millie's irresistible when you hanker after a buttery-crusted chicken potpie or a heaping plate of real fried chicken in super crisp, golden buttermilk batter with mashed potatoes, chicken gravy, and a pile of sautéed spinach. Begin with a pretty salad that features local greens tossed with tidbits of contrasting flavor like Bing cherries, walnuts, and nuggets of Roquefort.

Desserts are also monumental and homey. I took home half of my banana bread pudding, made with Miss Millie's house-made walnut swirls, and had it for breakfast, the meal that made Miss Millie's reputation. Saturday and Sunday brunch still has the locals lined up for lemon-ricotta pancakes with blueberry sauce.

The interior, with lace-curtained windows, leather banquettes and booths, beautiful painted wooden floors, and tables covered with white linen, is cozy and adorable and service is relaxed but professional. Though it started out as a vegetarian restaurant, the current chef clearly likes to use a wider range of ingredients—Niman Ranch pork, flatiron steaks, and hamburgers and local salmon and lamb. But vegetarians and meat eaters alike can always choose Miss Millie's rich macaroni and cheese with a crispy top.

RISTORANTE BACCO . . . .

737 Diamond Street (at 24th Street)
415-282-4969
www.bacco.citysearch.com
Open Monday through Thursday
5:30 to 10 P.M., Friday and
Saturday until 10:30 P.M.,
Sunday 5 P.M. to 9:30 P.M.
Moderate
Credit cards: MC, V

The brightly lit, cheerful orange dining rooms of this perpetually full restaurant beckon passersby, although a reservation will save you a wait. The small linen- and butcher paper–covered tables turn over at a leisurely pace. The food is similar to that served in a number of small Italian places around town—lively, tasty, just what you want to eat on a casual night out. Start with the terrine of eggplant, peppers, and goat cheese, quite elegantly molded together but rustically flavorful, served with a green salad. Move on to giant ravioli filled with chard and ricotta, drizzled with brown butter and crisp leaves of fried sage. What makes them so lovely is their thin, tender noodle wrappers. For Italian broccoli lovers (those who like the slightly bitter flavor), Bacco makes a wonderful bowl of *orecchiette*, ear-shaped pasta, tossed with anchovies, garlic, red chile flakes, and perfectly cooked broccoli rabe, a classic combination. Simple things like grilled Italian sausages with polenta are dressed up with a tomato and olive purée and accompanied with a favorite Italian vegetable, chard stems. (The green parts, which cook at a different rate, are used in other dishes.) Even desserts, often neglected in small restaurants, get full attention from the kitchen here. One night our meal ended triumphantly with a luscious chocolate pudding cake moistened with hazelnut custard and garnished with strawberries, a culinary event in any neighborhood.

CAFÉS

CAFE FLORE . . . .

2298 Market Street (at Noe)
415-621-8579
Open daily 7 A.M. to 11 P.M.
Cash only

Call me ridiculous, but the stretch of upperish Market Street from Van Ness to Castro reminds me of the Boulevard Montparnasse, Paris's broad, traffic-filled thoroughfare lined with historic cafes (La Coupole, Le Dome, Le Select . . .) and movie houses. Our slanting Market Street has two great triangular cafés, Zuni (see page 57) and Cafe Flore, as well as a row of huge, majestic palm trees on the median in the middle of the street. While Cafe Flore does not come close to having the panache of a French café, it possesses a certain *je ne sais quoi* that makes it a gathering place. Its outdoor tables, on a patio decorated with Cinzano umbrellas and protected from the wind by glass screens, are always full, and the red- and blue-tiled indoor tables turn over constantly. Although the Flore still looks like the gas station it once was, its interior has taken on the patina of age and use. The corrugated-iron roof, the exposed wooden structural bracing, the long Victorian counter where people order their coffees and health-foodish sandwiches and salads (ample and inexpensive), and the wisteria vines all feel organic to the neighborhood. The hundreds of people who come and go at Cafe Flore create the ambience and energy of the place, just as they do at Parisian cafés. The difference is that even cosmopolitan Paris has never seen the likes of a Market Street crowd at practically any time of day or night. By the way, the counterpeople make excellent Graffeo espresso, which they will pour into a small glass with an equal amount of steamed milk (called an Africano). Though coffee stores and cafés abound in San Francisco, very few of them make a decent espresso or cappuccino. Cafe Flore is one of the few.

BARS

BLISS BAR . . . .

4026 24th Street (between
Castro and Noe)
415-826-6200
www.blissbarsf.com
Open nightly 5 P.M. to 2 A.M.
Credit cards: AE, D, MC, V

Any bar that stocks Carpano Antica (a spicy, barrel-aged Italian sweet vermouth) deserves notice, and this sophisticated Noe Valley bar is worth a special detour if you live outside the neighborhood. Co-owner–bartender Pierre Lepheule mixes delicious and original cocktails, cocktails that are so pretty and fun to drink that you just might throw restraint to the winds and try one too many. One afternoon, I found myself with four different-colored cocktails lined up in front of me on the bar. I started off conservatively enough with the Latin

Cosmopolitan—a Herradura silver tequila rose-colored margarita served up, tinted by a splash of cranberry juice—but ended up going wild over the Bliss Apple Martini, which had the fragrance and flavor of fresh, tart green apples. Uncanny how Smirnoff citrus and a schnapps called Sour Apple Pucker can fill your head with the smell of the best apples of summer—and potent too. Lepheule tended bar at the fabulous Bel Air Hotel in Los Angeles for ten years and he also worked in product development. He's come up with a mango martini that captures the nature of mangoes without one drop of the fruit. I think he's motivated to make urbane cocktails that amuse the palate, like tropical drinks, but that don't cloy. He's a real mixologist, and Bliss attracts an ever-broadening attendance of city dwellers who never thought they'd be sipping cocktails in residential Noe Valley.

MECCA

2029 Market (between Dolores and 14th Street)
415-621-7000
www.sfmecca.com
Open Monday through Thursday 5:30 P.M. to 11 P.M., Friday and Saturday until midnight, Sunday 5 P.M. to 10 P.M.
Credit cards: AE, MC, V

Though you can eat at Mecca, everyone goes there for cocktails. It is the meeting place of choice for Upper Market and the Castro, but it draws revelers from all over the city. You can expect lots of come-hither eye contact no matter what your sexual preference. Mecca stocks fine grappas, cognacs, and ports, and an extensive, mostly California wine list organized by varietal. Practically every winemaker is identified, so if you just wanted to drink wines made by women, you could do it and compare them to the same varietals made by men. Fun. The bartenders mix excellent cocktails, even if they do call them by silly names. The campy interior, designed around a huge central bar outlined by a track of fluorescent lights that change color every five seconds, is cavernous, painted black, darkly lit, and filled with the pounding disco beat of the Castro—shades of the seventies. Try to reserve a table in a cordoned-off dining nook somewhat protected from the bar and club activity if you want to eat.

BAKERIES/PASTRIES

NOE VALLEY BAKERY

4073 24th Street (between Castro and Noe)
415-550-1405
Open Monday through Friday 7 A.M. to 7 P.M., weekends 7 A.M. to 6 P.M.
Credit cards: MC, V

This energetic bakery has taken root in the neighborhood, but it thrives because of a citywide demand for its focaccia, morning rolls, and breads. Many cafés and sandwich shops incorporate Noe Valley Bakery's baked goods into their own menus (Palio Paninoteca, page 121 for one). And every Saturday a long line forms in front of the Noe Valley Bakery booth at the Ferry Plaza Farmers' Market. Having met at the ovens of

Il Fornaio, the couple who started the Noe Valley Bakery thought they would make their mark by specializing in dense breads laden with fresh and dried fruits. Now their most popular (and my favorite) items include a soft-centered, crusty Italian-style white bread, buttery croissants, cinnamon twists, and crisp breadsticks. Poppy-seed cakes and pound cakes are sold by the slice or whole cake. Fresh fruit pies are reasonably priced. The bakery turns out old-fashioned treats—chocolate éclairs, large macaroons dipped in chocolate, frosted teacakes, and oversized currant-orange scones of buttery, crumbly texture. A mix of people stream into the attractive shop, piled with a breathtaking variety of freshly baked things, and seem to know exactly what they want. I find it impossible to buy just one item here. Luckily, Noe Valley Bakery's bread stays fresh for several days—and the buttery pastries heat up well.

ICE CREAM/CHOCOLATES

JOSEPH SCHMIDT . . . .

3489 16th Street (at Sanchez)
415-861-8682
www.jschmidtconfections.com
Open Monday through Saturday
10 A.M. to 6:30 P.M.
Credit cards: MC, V

For sixteen years now, Joseph Schmidt has been working his chocolate artistry at this colorful shop filled with seasonal specialties. In the spring, expect lovable Easter bunnies of the richest Belgian chocolate; for Mother's Day, it's long, thin boxes covered with hydrangeas holding a dozen miniature truffles, Joseph Schmidt's signature confection. Truffles may have catapulted him to fame, but his sculptural talent has kept him there. If Schmidt were not working in chocolate, he might have made a career in stone. His large chocolate bowls and vases with ragged, pointed edges, marbled with white and mint chocolate, serve as Baccarat-like containers for more chocolates or even flowers made out of chocolate. San Franciscans order these dramatic bowls for parties and special events. An original confection, slicks, thin round disks of chocolate about two inches in diameter with soft fillings like caramel, coconut cream, or nougat, each disk painted with a colorful and delicate abstract design, now fill one whole case. Rich truffles with flavored fondant interiors fill another. I personally cannot resist the chocolate nut bark and the huge, flat turtles with pecans, buttery caramel, and carapaces of light or dark chocolate, the best of their genre.

While Schmidt chocolates are carried at many upscale food departments around town, a trip to the store can net some unique treasures. Just the other day, I found a bag of round, soft caramel balls encased in milk chocolate, and I haven't stopped eating them since. The dark chocolate bar with biscotti chunks is one of the world's best confections. Schmidt is nothing if not whimsical, and who knows what he will come up with next?

MARKETS

TOWER MARKET . . . .

635 Portola Drive (at Terracita)
415-664-1600
Open Monday through Saturday
8 A.M. to 8:30 P.M.,
Sunday until 8 P.M.
Credit Cards: AE, D, MC, V

In this part of town, Tower Market looms as the best resource for high-quality ingredients under one roof. An independent, medium-sized supermarket, intelligently stocked, it draws a large patronage from St. Francis Wood and West Portal to Glen Park. The produce department always has seasonal treasures such as small, fat stalks of rhubarb in the spring and year-round organic produce. Viglizzo's delicatessen in the Tower Market is a source for prosciutto from Parma as well as German-style cured meats, fresh sauerkraut, and sausages. The butcher counter, also run by the Viglizzo family, has been operating since 1915. They have kept current by offering free-range chickens, freshly ground turkey, and Harris Ranch beef. A large staff of butchers will cut and grind to order, individualized service that is fast disappearing. The dairy department is a source for European Plugra butter, which has a higher butterfat content than American butter and a strong flavor. Sold in half pounds that cost as much as a full pound of other butter, Plugra turns morning toast into the best dish of the day. Also available in this section are glass quarts of Straus Family Creamery organic milk and Straus whole-milk yogurt, a new product from this organic dairy in western Marin. To my mind it's the best yogurt in America, so rich and creamy that you can use it like sour cream. As for the Straus milk, you have to shake the bottles before you pour to dislodge the cream off the top, and the sweet, delicately grassy flavor of this milk will make you take notice of what you're drinking.

PATRICIA WELLS'S CHOUCROUTE GARNI OR CHOUCROUTE L'ALSACO

SERVES 10

You can buy all the ingredients for this marvelous winter dish, including German riesling and salt pork, at Tower Market. With the closing of Speckmann's German deli and restaurant, Tower Market is the only place in San Francisco that carries fresh sauerkraut—not mushy bottled or canned sauerkraut—a requisite for a choucroute. Wells's recipe, adapted from a choucroute restaurant in Paris, is a superior recipe, simple and foolproof as long as you get the fresh sauerkraut.

continued at right...

2 tablespoons pork fat or
goose fat

2 onions, halved lengthwise
and finely sliced

Fine sea salt

1 pound salt pork

10 ounces bone-in smoked
pork butt

3 pounds fresh sauerkraut

SEASONING MIX
(securely wrapped in a
cheesecloth bag)

2 teaspoons coriander seeds

5 whole cloves

2 teaspoons juniper berries

1 tablespoon black peppercorns

1 tablespoon cumin seeds

½ head garlic, unpeeled, crushed

---

1 bottle Alsatian sylvaner or
riesling wine

6 coarse-textured smoked pork
sausages such as small kielbasa

6 fine-textured precooked
sausages such as frankfurters

6 fine-textured precooked grilling
sausages such as knockwurst

1 plump, coarse-textured smoked
pork sausage such as kielbasa, cut
in half lengthwise

Variety of mustards for serving

1 In a large heavy pot, combine the fat, onions, and a pinch of sea salt. Sweat—cook covered over low heat without coloring—for about 5 minutes, or until soft and translucent. Arrange the salt pork and smoked pork butt on top of the onions. Spoon the sauerkraut on top. Add the seasoning mix and the wine. Add just enough water to cover (about 4 cups), cover the pot, and cook at the very gentlest simmer for 1 hour and 20 minutes. Stir the sauerkraut from time to time to distribute the seasoning. Add the smoked pork sausages (kielbasa), cover, and simmer for 10 minutes.

2 Meanwhile, fill a large saucepan with water and bring just to a boil. Add the frankfurters. Immediately turn off the heat and cover the pan. Let the frankfurters sit for 10 to 15 minutes, or until firm to the touch and heated through.

3 In a large, dry, nonstick skillet over medium heat, lightly panfry the grilling sausages (knockwursts) and the halved pork sausages (kielbasa) until browned, shaking the pan from time to time so they cook evenly, 7 to 10 minutes total.

4 Using a large slotted spoon, transfer the sauerkraut to several large warmed serving platters. Cut the meats into serving pieces. Halve or quarter the sausages. Arrange the meats and sausages all around. Serve with a variety of mustards.

HARVEST RANCH MARKET . . . .

2285 Market Street
(between 16th Street and Noe)
415-626-0805
www.harvestranch.com
Open daily 8:30 A.M. to 11 P.M.
Credit cards: AE, MC, V

Really more of a natural foods deli than a market, this flashy store has turned into a Market Street hot spot. Day and night customers come in to cruise the salad bar, filling up clear plastic containers with legume and pasta salads, tofu, and the usual salad bar vegetable assortment with curry dressings. Fast-moving items include giant sushi rolls, about the size of a fist, coated with sesame seeds, pinwheeled with seaweed, and filled with asparagus, cucumber, and *surimi* (imitation crab). Dipped into soy sauce and wasabi, they make for a destination snack or light meal. The sushi, like all the other foods on the salad bar, cost $2.49 per pound and weigh out to about $1 a piece. Two will fill you up. Their best trait is their freshness; they move so fast new trays are constantly prepared. People eat outside on impromptu benches made of wood beams and metal crates. For shoppers, the store carries all sorts of bread, including Acme and Grace Baking Company loaves, and a limited selection of organic produce. The usual natural foods store bulk nuts, cheeses, yogurt, chips, and granola are sexily displayed.

MIKEYTOM . . . .

1747 Church Street (at Day)
415-826-5757
Open Monday through Saturday
7 A.M. to 9 P.M.,
Sunday 8 A.M. to 8 P.M.
Credit cards: AE, MC, V

The residents from Mikeytom's outer Noe Valley neighborhood rejoiced when this modern, brightly lit, organic produce and natural foods store opened. While the selection is small, the fruits and vegetables look inviting, nicely set out in baskets. The small heads of lettuce are particularly beautiful here. Breads from the Metropolis bakery in Emeryville and Clover and Straus Family Creamery products are good to have in any neighborhood market, along with buckets of fresh flowers. Some marble tables have been placed outside for those who want to have a coffee made at the coffee bar inside.

REAL FOOD COMPANY . . . .

3939 24th Street (between
Noe and Sanchez)
415-282-9500
Open daily 9 A.M. to 8:30 P.M.
Credit cards: AE, MC, V

This branch of the Real Food Company, along with the stores on Stanyon, page 142, and Polk, page 307, streets was bought by Nutraceutical Corporation of Park City, Utah, one of the country's largest manufacturers of nutritional supplements sold to health food stores. Peter Gay, CEO of Nutraceutical, promises to maintain the regional character of the stores and is committed to buying from small local farms and producers. It remains to be seen if the Real Food's name and logo will be changed to Fresh Organics, the subsidiary that bought the Real Food Company. At this writing, the Real Food Store on Twenty-fourth Street has a vibrant organic produce department with cut samples of practically all fruit. Second only to shopping at a farmers' market where tastes are the norm, the experience on Twenty-fourth Street makes produce selection a sure thing. You don't want to spend top dollar for organic produce—or any produce for that matter—unless it's sweet and juicy.

MEAT AND POULTRY

DREWES BROTHERS MEATS. . . . .

1706 Church Street (at 29th Street)
415-821-0515
Open Monday through Friday
9:30 A.M. to 7 P.M.,
Saturday 9 A.M. to 6 P.M.,
Sunday 10 A.M. to 5 P.M.
Credit cards: AE, MC, V

The original Drewes was founded in 1889 and the current young proprietors are only the fourth owners. They worked at the market for the second owner and eventually bought it, deciding to specialize in naturally raised meats and poultry. The Meyer natural beef from Montana grazes on grass for nearly two years and finishes on corn. Both rib-eye —which I prefer—and New York have bright flavor and the leanness that comes from ranging over the grasslands. To my mind, this beef does not have the rich, buttery flavor of Niman Ranch beef, which is raised similarly. The Meyer beef I tried was a little leaner and frankly, I think it's easier to digest. Drewes carries Rosie organic chickens from Petaluma Poultry, which also markets Rocky free-range chickens. The Rosie chicken, though expensive, is the tastiest chicken on the market.

Drewes is well worth a stop. Knowing the provenance of your food, how and where it was raised, expands the pleasure of eating it—not to mention health considerations. The young butchers at Drewes take real pride in finding wholesome, flavorful meats to sell to their growing patronage.

VIGLIZZO'S MEAT . . . .

Tower Market
635 Portola Drive (at Terracita)
415-664-1600
Open Monday through Saturday
8 A.M. to 8:30 P.M.,
Sunday until 8 P.M.
Credit cards: AE, D, MC, V

This long, complete butcher counter, which has been operating since 1915, has kept up with the times, or maybe rediscovered old-fashioned, small production, quality. The small army of butchers will cut, grind, bone, and gladly individualize your order. For more information, see Tower Market, page 224.

CHEESE

COOPER'S . . . .

2 Sanchez Street (at Duboce)
415-934-9463
Open Tuesday through Friday
7 A.M. to 9 P.M.,
Saturday 8 A.M. to 9 P.M.,
Sunday 9 A.M. to 8 P.M.,
Monday 7 A.M. to 8 P.M.
Credit card: MC, V

This jewel of a food shop carries a world-class selection of cheeses collected by a former Artisan Cheese (see page 284) store expert, an interesting group of wines from underrepresented wine regions of Europe, and a classy array of prosciutto and *serrano* hams, olives, breads, and imported groceries. Every item is appealingly displayed and packaged. Whoever chose the vinegars, for example, must have been a restaurant cook because the best of them for a moderate price are

offered. But the cheese service is what makes Cooper's so exceptional. The clerks are in love with the cheeses. They handle them carefully, keeping them in pristine condition. They meticulously scrape off the outer layer of plastic-wrapped cheeses before slicing off a tissue-thin taste. They know everything about the cheeses, who made them and how, and they introduce you to new taste sensations. The buyer-owner, Andy Lax, searches out artisan cheeses that he likes and his tastes run to strong, assertive, complicated, layered flavor. But he also offers rich luxuries like *fromage d'affinois*, a soft triple-cream cheese that the staff calls the ice cream of cheeses. Once a clerk knows your taste, he will lead you to an ever-widening circle of cheese and you just may end up broadening your palate. The philosophy behind Cooper's cheese service is education.

24TH AVENUE CHEESE SHOP . . . .

3893 24th Street (at Sanchez)
415-821-6658
Open Monday through Friday
10 A.M. to 7 P.M.,
Saturday until 6 P.M.,
Sunday until 5 P.M.
Credit cards: MC, V

There are only a handful of noteworthy cheese shops in the Bay Area and this is one of them. You can taste anything and the range is extensive. You might find some tangy Pyrenees goat milk cheese set out on the counter, a lusciously runny rice flour–coated Teleme (very fresh in flavor, but it must be eaten quickly), a whole table of Cheddars, or a *pavé d'affinois*, a small cube of soft cheese encased in rind. The staff is meticulous in keep-

ing and cutting the cheeses. All the merchandise looks appealing and fresh, displayed on wooden counters, casks, and shelves. A worn wooden floor only adds atmosphere. A long-time ingredient resource in Noe Valley, this cheese store also carries Molinari salami, lots of olives, crackers, Acme bread, breadsticks, and wine—practically anything you might need for an Italian lunch.

PLUMPJACK WINES . . . .

4011 24th Street (at Noe)
415-282-3841
www.plumpjack.com
Open Monday through Saturday
11 A.M. to 9 P.M.,
Sunday until 6 P.M.
Credit cards: AE, D, MC, V

PlumpJack stepped into the comfortable shoes of the former tenant in this spot, Caruso's, and continues the tradition of scouring the world for surprisingly delicious bottles for under $10, and even more for under $15. Whereas 75 percent of the stock at the PlumpJack wine shop on Fillmore is collected in California, most of the wines at the Twenty-fourth Street store are imported. Noe Valley store manager Drew Spaulding buys independently for his shop and he knows what the 'hood wants. The inventory changes often, so regulars shouldn't become too attached to a specific wine, but Spaulding, once he learns your preferences, will find wines you'll like. I always am looking for reds that will go with spicy foods and the other day I came home with three syrahs—a Pinotage from South Africa, a syrah from Argentina, and a blended red from Healdsburg in Sonoma—all of which pleased. I love getting so much personal service and knowledge of the wines while paying Liquor Barn prices. The store also carries that fantastic Carpano Antica, the complex, aged sweet vermouth from Italy; aged rums from Nicaragua, Haiti, and Martinique; single-malt scotches; and *limoncello*. With the resources of two shops, PlumpJack's staff can hunt down practically anything you fancy.

CASTRO VILLAGE WINE COMPANY

4121 19th Street (between
Castro and Collingwood)
415-864-4411
Open Monday through Thursday
11 A.M. to 7 P.M., Friday and
Saturday 11 A.M. to 8 P.M.,
Sunday noon to 7 P.M.
Credit cards: AE, MC, V

The neatly displayed wines in this twenty-four-year-old pioneering shop all come from California. Though the selection is not as deep or interesting as at the California Wine Merchant (see page 168) in the Marina, the gracious clerks will spend as much time as you like trying to fit you with the best bottle for the occasion. This is a spot to find some of the most elegant California cabernets and French-style blends.

COOKWARE AND BOOKS

CLIFF'S HARDWARE . . . .

479 Castro Street (between
17th and 18th streets)
415-431-5365
Open Monday through Saturday
9:30 A.M. to 8 P.M.,
Sunday 11 A.M. to 5 P.M.
Credit cards: AE, CB, MC, V

Cliff's Hardware has a huge housewares section featuring coffee and espresso makers, Trident knives, pepper mills, water filters, old-fashioned wooden ice cream makers, cast-iron skillets in hard-to-find shapes and sizes, as well as a wide range of the ever-popular Revere Ware pots and pans—the bread and butter of outfitting a kitchen. To meet the entertainment needs of its immediate community, Cliff's stocks coolers from small to gigantic; barbecuing equipment, including Webers, fire starters, charcoal, and wood chips; and many outdoor serving accessories that you never knew you needed until you saw them. Though prices are not cheap, the convenience of shopping in a neighborhood counts for a lot—and Cliff's will have what you're looking for.

LEHR'S GERMAN SPECIALTIES . . . .

1581 Church Street (between
Duncan and 28th streets)
415-282-6803
Open Monday through Friday
10 A.M. to 6 P.M., Saturday and
Sunday 11 A.M. to 6 P.M.
Credit cards: MC, V

A German cultural-necessities store, Lehr's carries everything from German cleaning supplies to liverwurst. The inventory includes some handsome two-toned horsehair brushes with wooden handles for sweeping up crumbs, and tubes of concentrated traveling detergent. (I was tempted to buy one for my husband who does a wash every day on the road, even though he packs a full complement of underwear.) A large assortment of German baking pans ranges from miniature to party size. I was drawn to some patterned springform Bundt pans. You can find old-fashioned potato ricers and handy spaetzle makers, which solves the mystery of how these tiny noodle dumplings are made. The gadget is just a large-holed grater with a slide over it that pushes the dough through. Often seeing the right instrument to make a dish inspires me to cook it. Several long aisles are dedicated to candy and chocolates, including Lindt and liquor-filled Asbach Uralt, a favorite among those who like a shot of brandy with their sweet. Elaborate beer steins fill the front window. The pretty woman with a sexy German accent behind the counter will be happy to show them to you as she hums along to Aretha Franklin on the radio.

NORTH BEACH

NORTH BEACH

RESTAURANTS

1　Café Jacqueline
2　Helmand
3　The House
4　Il Pollaio
5　La Felce
6　L'Osteria del Forno
7　Mo's Grill
8　Moose's
9　Original U.S. Restaurant
10　Rose Pistola
11　San Francisco Art Institute Cafe
12　Tommaso's
13　Washington Square Bar & Grill

CAFÉS

14　Caffè Greco
15　Caffè Roma Coffee Roasting Company
16　Caffe Trieste
17　Mario's Bohemian Cigar Store Cafe

BARS

18　Enrico's Sidewalk Cafe
19　Gino and Carlos
20　Saloon
21　Savoy Tivoli
22　Spec's
23　Tony Nik's
24　Tosca
25　Vesuvio

DELICATESSENS/TAKEOUT

26　Freddie's
27　Golden Boy
28　Juicey Lucy's Organic Juice and Food Bar
29　Molinari Delicatessen
30　North Beach Pizza

BAKERIES/PASTRIES

31　Danilo
32　Liguria Bakery
33　Stella
34　Victoria Pastry Co.

COFFEE

35　Graffeo

ICE CREAM/CHOCOLATES

36　Gelato Classico
37　XOX Truffles

ETHNIC MARKETS

38　La Raccolta

PRODUCE

39　The Nature Stop

MEAT AND POULTRY

40　Little City

WINES AND SPIRITS

41　Coit Liquors

COOKWARE AND BOOKS

42　Biordi Art Imports
43　Columbus Cutlery

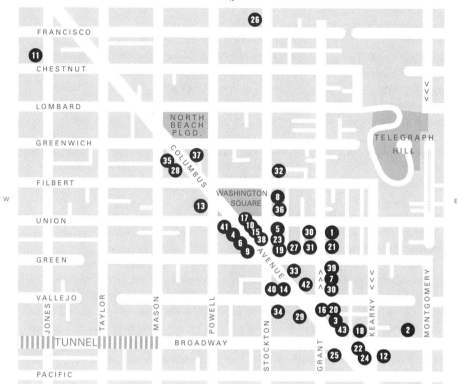

FRANCISCO

11

CHESTNUT

LOMBARD

GREENWICH

NORTH
BEACH
PLGD.

TELEGRAPH
HILL

FILBERT

37

35
28

32

WASHINGTON
SQUARE

8

13

36

UNION

17
41 **10**
4 **15**
6 **38**
9

5
23
19

30
27 **31**

1
21

GREEN

33

39
7
30

40 **14**

42

VALLEJO

JONES

TAYLOR

MASON

POWELL

34

29

16 **20**
3
43 **18**

2

TUNNEL

BROADWAY

STOCKTON

GRANT

KEARNY

MONTGOMERY

25

22
24

12

PACIFIC

S

0   SCALE FEET   1000

CAFÉ JACQUELINE . . . .

1454 Grant Avenue
(between Union and Green)
415-981-5565
Open Wednesday through Sunday
5:30 to 11 P.M.
Moderate
Credit cards: AE, CB, DC, D,
MC, V

Jacqueline Margulis, the sole owner and chef at this very French neighborhood bistro, is the queen of the soufflé. In fact, that's pretty much all she has been serving for the last nineteen years—tall, airy, crusty-topped, aromatic soufflés with sensuous, creamy interiors. The alluring aromas of baking cheese and garlic and the warmth from the ovens enfold you as you walk in the door of this small restaurant, its steamy front windows framed in lace curtains. Each white linen–covered table sports a fresh rose, heavy silverware, thin wineglasses, and huge napkins. High ceilings, worn wooden floors, original wainscoting, and shaded wall sconces bring back visions of pre-earthquake San Francisco. Both the cooking and the surroundings at Jacqueline are timeless.

You start with a salad of butter lettuce or watercress dressed in a traditional mustard vinaigrette. Baskets of warm, crusty baguettes with sweet butter will tie you over until your soufflé finally emerges from the kitchen. In the winter I make a special visit for Jacqueline's magnificent black truffle soufflé made with eggs that have been stored with the truffles (so their aroma permeates the egg shells), Gruyère, and lots of slivered fresh truffles. The expensive soufflé, plenty for two and fine for three, becomes affordable when shared and worth every penny. Her wild mushroom soufflés, textured with roughly chopped morels, boletes, and chanterelles, are also worth a detour. Less lavish, but very savory, are her prosciutto and domestic mushroom, and garlicky broccoli and cheese soufflés. Whatever you order, remember to specify that you want your soufflé runny in the middle. Otherwise, they come baked all the way through and lose their charm. For some reason, Jacqueline thinks that Americans want them cooked airy and dry. If you ever go out for dessert, come here for a spectacular chocolate soufflé. Jacqueline uses tons of dark, rich chocolate, turning the center into a creamy, intense chocolate pudding. One of the best chocolate desserts in the city, it costs $30, but will serve three or four.

HELMAND . . . .

430 Broadway (between
Kearny and Montgomery)
415-362-0641
Open Sunday through Thursday
5:30 to 10 P.M.,
Friday and Saturday until 11 P.M.
Inexpensive
Credit cards: AE, MC, V

Helmand, a graciously appointed Afghan dinner house, rises above exoticism to take its place as one of the most satisfying restaurants in San Francisco of any nationality. Afghan cooking draws on Persian, Indian, and Middle Eastern flavors, but the food at Helmand is immediately appealing to Western palates. Start with *aushak*, large, tender ravioli filled with sautéed leeks and topped with a mild, buttery meat sauce, served on a bed of yogurt speckled with fresh mint; or *kaddo borawni*, pumpkin that has been fried, roasted, and then sauced with garlic-scented yogurt, achieving a melting texture. Another permutation on pasta, a dish called *mantwo*, fills house-made noodles with braised onions and chopped beef, topping them with a delicious sauce of carrots and slightly al dente yellow split peas. All these appetizers are so yummy you want to make a meal out of them alone until you taste the soups at Helmand, served in huge bowls with just a ladleful at the bottom. Try *aush*, a liquid version of addictive ravioli-like *aushak*. Here, thin noodles come in a minted yogurt soup drizzled with the buttery meat sauce. Another warm yogurt soup, *mashawa*, is thick with legumes—mung beans, chickpeas, black-eyed peas, and chunks of beef—a meal in itself.

Several excellent main courses feature different cuts of lamb accompanied with light, airy rice pilaf seasoned with cumin seed and cinnamon. Try *koufta callow*, large soft meatballs in hot cinnamon-scented tomato sauce, or *dwopiaza*, medium-rare lamb kebabs sauced with vinegared onions and yellow split peas on a square of flat bread that soaks up all the juices.

Desserts may seem the most exotic dishes of all, but a cardamom-scented basmati rice pudding or *burfee*, an ice cream made from reduced milk and served in a sundae glass filled with frozen clotted cream, are well worth trying. The long, narrow dining room is decorated with polished antique cabinets with glass doors displaying bowls of colorful ground spices and Afghan artifacts. The brick walls, carpeting, soft light, and tablecloths give the room a dressy look belying the amazingly inexpensive prices. The intelligent and attentive service would be welcome in restaurants that charge three times as much.

THE HOUSE . . . .

1230 Grant Avenue (near Columbus)
415-986-8612
www.thehse.com
Open Monday through Friday
11:30 A.M. to 3 P.M., Monday through
Thursday 5:30 P.M. to 10 P.M.,
Friday and Saturday 5:30 to 11 P.M.
Moderate
Credit cards: AE, MC, V

This is the original restaurant of a young husband-and-wife team, Angela and Larry Tse. With its success, they have opened a larger and more dramatic House in the Sunset (see page 370). The casual North Beach outpost continues to turn out light, colorful, fresh preparations that combine Asian and Western ingredients and techniques with an underlying dedication to freshness. (Someone here shops daily in nearby Chinatown for beautiful fish and good-looking produce, with some stops at nonethnic produce markets as well.) The food is seriously good. Try the house Caesar salad in a creamy, not-too-strong dressing that lends itself to the little bits of warm grilled tuna tossed in it, or a Chinese chicken salad of shredded vegetables and juicy hot chicken breast. The room feels a bit austere in its modernity, especially in contrast to the resonant North Beach spots around it, but this House begins to feel like home when you dig into the clean, tasty food, reasonable enough in price to eat every day.

IL POLLAIO. . . . .

555 Columbus Avenue
(between Union and Green)
415-362-7727
Open Monday through Saturday
11:30 A.M. to 9 P.M.
Inexpensive
Credit cards: MC, V

One of my favorite neighborhood hangs, Il Pollaio does one thing and does it perfectly: chicken. Small chickens with large bones are lightly marinated and grilled over hot rocks, and always come off the fire clean flavored, juicy, and hot. Silver-haired Jose, the Argentinean-Italian owner-griller, never cooks in advance. Served with a mixed salad of crisp shredded cabbage, carrots, shell beans, and chopped lettuce in a tangy Italian dressing, the half-chicken combo always satisfies. The few other items on the menu—tasty Italian sausage made especially for Il Pollaio; a satiny, cold, marinated eggplant antipasto; and fortifying house-made lentil, split pea, and minestrone soups, one offered each day— are also impeccable. The pleasant little dining room, always full, looks onto the passing parade on Columbus Avenue, and smiling Jose knows practically every nontourist who walks in or by the door. Much Italian is spoken here over many bottles of wine. You can call ahead for takeout or be buoyed by the cheerful scene in this popular spot while you eat. Everyone in North Beach considers Il Pollaio an essential resource.

LA FELCE . . . .

1570 Stockton Street (at Union)
415-392-8321
Open weekdays (except Tuesdays)
11:30 A.M. to 2 P.M.; dinner
Wednesday through Monday 5:30
to 10 P.M., Sunday until 9:30 P.M.
Inexpensive
Credit cards: AE, DC, MC, V

At one time, North Beach was considered a mecca for family-style dining in the city, as it was full of restaurants that served copious antipasti of sliced meats and canned beans, tureens of good minestrone, pasta in various forms in tomato sauce, then big platters of sliced meat or roast chicken followed by neon green and pink spumoni. Though their number and quality have diminished, La Felce, which opened in 1974, continues on in fine form, pretty much serving this classic fare with interesting variations. The soup might be a full-bodied chicken stock laced with hundreds of white dots of pasta into which you sprinkle grated Parmesan. A meaty baked lasagna might be the pasta of the night, and chicken cacciatore, in a lively sauce made with tomatoes, mushrooms, green peppers, and onions that have cooked down to a purée, the star main course. An à la carte salad, a platter of sliced tomatoes layered with transparently thin onion slices, anchovies, and fresh parsley in an excellent vinaigrette, is worth sharing. Though the menu will sound familiar, a broader range of entrées to choose from is offered, and the food is alive, prepared with fresh ingredients and a sure hand. I like the white tablecloths and cheery ambience of the dining room, a departure from the utilitarian linoleum decor of many North Beach family-style restaurants.

L'OSTERIA DEL FORNO

519 Columbus Avenue
(between Green and Union)
415-982-1124
www.bstudio.com/l'osteria
Open Wednesday through Monday
11:30 A.M. to 10 P.M.
Inexpensive
Cash only

This little hole-in-the-wall serves authentic and tasty food by keeping its menu tiny and specializing in dishes from the brick-lined oven. The two Italian women who own L'Osteria have attracted a wildly loyal and appreciative following, including my kid Harry, and his parents never complain when he gets his way on this one. We do wrestle over the fingers of crunchy, thin focaccia for which L'Osteria is famous, brought warm from the oven in little baskets during the meal, until Harry moves on to a slice of very thin-crusted pizza, nicely coated with melted mozzarella, good tomato sauce, and tiny balls of Italian sausage. It's also my favorite thin-crust pizza and sometimes the boy has to protect it from being nibbled away by you-know-who. We start with a couple of antipasti: roasted onions sprinkled with breadcrumbs; roasted red peppers in olive oil; tissue-thin *speck* (Italian smoked ham); *bresaola* with arugula salad; or another favorite, canned tuna and white bean salad (see recipe, page 238), a version superior to any I've tasted. I always get a plate of paper-thin sliced roast pork cooked in milk, a traditional method that forms the sublime brown curds that are scattered over the meat. The pork comes with roasted sweet and white potatoes lightly seasoned with herbs—a dish that must be served in heaven. Each day brings one pasta, like house-made green ravioli, tender and light, stuffed with ricotta and sauced in a sprightly marinara; or a ramekin of baked rigatoni in a luscious, slightly creamy beef and tomato sauce.

The women at L'Osteria make one of the best cups of espresso in town—comparable to Caffè Greco's (page 243) I always end with one, then another tiny cup of coffee (very full-flavored, aromatic, almost syrupy, without a hint of bitterness) served with a biscotto. A choice of three or four Italian wines, all inexpensive, by the glass or bottle, completes the experience. (I wish there were a few more interesting bottles.) Only eight tables have been squeezed into the tiny storefront, with several stuck into alcoves by the front windows. Every six months or so the women upgrade a bit—paint the walls, improve the lighting, change the color of the tablecloths under the glass-topped tables—but prices stay amazingly low and everyone understands that any change in scale could ruin the magic.

MO'S GRILL

1322 Grant Avenue
(between Vallejo and Green)
415-788-3779
Open daily 9 A.M. to 10 P.M.
Inexpensive
Credit cards: MC, V

You can see the grill man scooping up big handfuls of bright red, freshly ground beef, gently forming them into patties, and placing them just so on a round revolving grill. All this happens in the front window of this immaculately clean and orderly hamburger joint, strategically located within stumbling distance of Grant Avenue's premier saloons. I like Mo's meticulously prepared hamburgers on their unique soft-crusty buns smeared with mustardy house-made mayonnaise any time of day. The crisp, skinny fries; thick milk shakes made the old-fashioned way in tall silver containers; and the spicy grilled chicken kebabs tucked into pita bread and seasoned with big spoonfuls of coarsely chopped tomato, onion, and cilantro make Mo's a destination even if you're not in North Beach. The one drawback is the chilly decor, an attempt at high-tech design. The white tile, chrome, and black Formica under stark lighting give the small space all the warmth of a locker room. However, the counter seats with a view of the slim, efficient cook and his grill are just fine.

INSALATA RUSTICA L'OSTERIA

SERVES 4 AS AN APPETIZER

This is the best canned tuna salad you'll ever taste. You can get canned cannellini beans at any Italian delicatessen. Fresh shell beans make this preparation superb, and cooked dried cannellini beans are also wonderful, but if you want something fast and really good, use canned. The ratio of beans to tuna is about equal.

One 15-ounce can cannellini beans, or 2 cups cooked cannellini beans

One 6-ounce can tuna, packed in water

½ cup chopped celery

½ teaspoon minced fresh oregano

½ cup thinly sliced red onion

2 tablespoons balsamic vinegar

½ teaspoon kosher salt

Freshly ground black pepper to taste

7 tablespoons olive oil (L'Osteria uses Fortuna extra virgin)

1 Drain the canned cannellini beans, if using. Rinse and drain well again. Drain the tuna. In a serving bowl, combine the beans and tuna. Add the celery, oregano, and onion.

2 In a bowl, mix the balsamic vinegar with the salt and pepper. Whisk in the olive oil. Pour over the beans and tuna and mix gently. Taste for salt. Serve with Italian bread.

MOOSE'S . . . .

1652 Stockton Street
(between Union and Filbert)
415-989-7800
www.mooses.com
Open Thursday through Saturday
11:30 A.M. to 2:30 P.M.,
Monday through Friday 5:30 P.M.
to 10:30 P.M., Saturday and
Sunday until 11:30 p.m.; Sunday
brunch 10 A.M. to 2:30 P.M.
Moderate
Credit cards: AE, DC, MC, V

Publican Ed Moose, a beloved character in this town, has acquired everything any self-respecting North Beach schmoozer-restaurateur could want: a lively bar with two video monitors tuned to timely sporting events; friendly bartenders with impressive memories (once you order a special drink or even ask for something the bar doesn't stock, it will be there the next time you come in); a big, grand café-style dining room with front windows that open on the park; a jazz combo in the evenings; and a menu of stylish California bistro dishes. Moose's has run through a number of chefs, but each has been conscientious about using fresh ingredients and turning out handsome, generous plates of somewhat dressy food.

The last time I was at Moose's, I felt like treating myself so I sat at the bar, with eight other women as it happened, and ate my way through a juicy chopped salad with apples, walnuts, and blue cheese; then plump, potato-filled ravioli slathered with lots of spring vegetables and scented with white truffle oil; and finally a goblet of buttermilk ice cream topped with a paper-thin chocolate cookie star. I washed it down with a big fruity glass of Napa Valley petite syrah. It was a luscious meal. A contingent of old-timers will only order the thick Mooseburger, but you can also get the likes of porcini carpaccio with preserved Meyer lemon vinaigrette, grilled salmon on a bed of sliced celery root in a lobster broth, or Ed's famous gigantic veal chop with seasonal accompaniments.

Everyone who walks through the front door, whether they're part of the regular crowd or not, gets personal treatment. The attitude on the floor and at the door couldn't be more genuine, welcoming, friendly, infecting the entire restaurant with high spirits. People always have hung out at Ed Moose's places, to drink and have a good time.

ORIGINAL U.S. RESTAURANT . . . .

515 Columbus Avenue (at Green)
415-397-5200
www.originalusrestaurant.com
Open Tuesday through Thursday
and Sunday 11 A.M. to 9 P.M., Friday
and Saturday until 10 p.m.
Inexpensive
Credit cards: AE, MC, V

For thirty-three years, the U.S. Restaurant was located on the triangular piece of real estate at the intersection of Stockton and Columbus. This North Beach fixture catered to locals who practically took pension there. They came for the daily special, or a heaping plate of pasta, or a gigantic sandwich on Italian bread. The homey, unadorned food served by Italian grandmothers in pink waitress uniforms was proudly old-fashioned and filling. No embarrassment here about serving soggy vegetables or precooked pasta.

During the latter half of the 1990s, when rents soared and dot-com kids ordered $100 cabs, the U.S. Restaurant lost its cachet—and its lease. In 1998, a restaurant group, which at the time operated the burgeoning Enrico's (see page 245), bought the lease and reopened a remodeled U.S. with an updated, slightly more expensive menu. It was a bomb. The old-timers hated it and a new clientele never took hold. The new U.S. folded and since then several other restaurants have tried to make a go of it in that location. Then, in 2001, the Original U.S. Restaurant resurfaced about a half block away from its triangular origins, unbelievably intact. The menu is almost identical, and miraculously the prices seem unchanged. Although the new space is smaller, the signature open kitchen with counter seating, linoleum floors, and bare wooden tables set with paper napkins are all in place. The major differences I noted are that the waitstaff is younger and wine now comes in wine glasses, not tumblers.

The old menu has been tweaked just the tiniest bit, which hasn't fazed the North Beach denizens who have been crawling out from under rocks to return. The current U.S. is a big hit with everyone—old and young. My adolescent, who started out the evening surly and resentful because he had been forced to leave his room to be taken out for dinner, became talkative and cheerful as he bit into crisp, deep-fried *arancine*, creamy risotto balls filled with mozzarella and a little dab of meat sauce. I have not had them better in southern Italy at shops that specialize in them. The boy and I sparred over the U.S. salad, gently transformed from the old days by small green and black olives with pits and a simple, well-balanced vinaigrette.

I loved my cutlet *milanese*, a thin golden slab of pounded and breaded veal accompanied with a pile of spinach sautéed with massive amounts of garlic and olive oil. (Next time I will order the spinach without the garlic.) The boy worked his way through a huge plate of chewy, meat-filled tortellini in tomato cream sauce. I had one glass of workable Italian sangiovese and we split a pillowy house-made tiramisu blanketed with powdered cocoa. We left as happy companions. Amazing what a plate of pasta will do for a relationship.

ROSE PISTOLA . . . .

532 Columbus Avenue
(between Union and Green)
415-399-0499
Open daily 11:30 A.M. to 4 P.M.,
Sunday through Thursday 5:30 P.M.
to 11 P.M., Friday and
Saturday until midnight
Moderate
Credit cards: AE, CB, DC, D,
MC, V

Reed Hearon, the wunderkind of San Francisco restauranting who invented both LuLu (see page 353) and Cafe Marimba (see page 151), continued his streak with Rose's Cafe (see page 159) and the ebullient Rose Pistola. The restaurant, which stretches from Columbus Avenue to Stockton Street, uses every square inch of space, starting with outdoor tables under amazingly efficient heaters; a white-tiled bar area with tables; an open kitchen with wood-burning ovens, rotisseries, and grills; and two cordoned-off dining areas. The dining room on Stockton Street, tucked away under earthquake bracing, feels the most private.

The place is perpetually packed for lunch and dinner, cocktails, and late-night snacks. Hearon's signature is to provide European style at all levels of service. I personally use Rose Pistola as an Italian tapas bar because I love all the authentic antipasti served in small portions for a small price—things like cured swordfish; shaved artichokes with Parmigiano; plates of fresh green fava beans with percorino cheese; grilled sweet rabbit liver wrapped in pancetta on rosemary skewers; wood oven–baked *farinata* (a pizza made of chickpea flour, topped with olives, sage leaves, and caramelized onions); a tender octopus salad. The bartenders have never failed on my favorite Harry's Bar cocktail, and the wine list offers a wealth of Italian and California bottles. At table, I might move on to a buoyant cioppino made with fresh tomatoes and fish stock, some grilled quail, or a Florentine-style steak on the bone. And who can resist fried cream for dessert? I love the casual family-style presentations, the unadorned plates, the good value. Unfortunately Hearon is no longer working at the restaurant, but if you stick with the antipasti and simple grilled items, you'll be fine. When I walk by Rose Pistola, I almost always find an excuse to drop in.

SAN FRANCISCO ART INSTITUTE CAFE. . . .

800 Chestnut Street (at Jones)
415-749-4567
Open Monday through Friday
9 A.M. to 4 P.M.; call ahead,
as hours vary during the year.
Inexpensive
Cash only

Looking for a great $5 lunch with one of the best views in San Francisco? Check out this funky café in a cement courtyard inhabited by outré art students, and take advantage of the wholesome, first-rate cooking of Peter Stanwood. The café offers two hot-lunch specials each day, homey baked goods still warm from the oven, nicely dressed fresh salads, and thick made-to-order sandwiches. The portions are so large and prices so cheap that no art students starve around this institute.

The setting of the café comes as a spectacular surprise. You enter off Chestnut Street and walk through a tiled courtyard with a fountain. Emotive student art hangs in the arcade surrounding the courtyard and in public galleries to the left. Past these is a large, open plaza with expansive views of the bay and oversized concrete tables and benches. You forget about the utilitarian indoor seating when you gaze through glass walls at the grand vista. I eat at the café often, but I bring my own plate and silverware for perfectly cooked sunny side-up eggs, bacon, crusty hash browns made from real potatoes, good coffee, and toasted bagels with cream cheese. (I can't eat eggs on paper plates with plastic utensils.) For lunch there may be a big blob of soft polenta covered with a southwestern black bean and vegetable stew, or a meatball sandwich on a Bread Workshop baguette, overflowing with sautéed red and green peppers, onions, and tomato sauce. Spicy red beans and rice, based on an old New Orleans recipe from photography teacher Pirkle Jones, or tasty Italian meatballs and spaghetti are perpetual favorites. The café makes hearty minestrone and excellent white bean and escarole soup. The in-house bakers produce crumbly, plate-sized scones, satisfying coffee cakes, chewy oatmeal-butterscotch bars, and large chocolate chip–peanut butter cookies that give Mrs. Fields a run for her money. Though the operation is casual, almost to the point of sloppiness, all the food tastes really good.

TOMMASO'S. . . . .

1042 Kearny Street (between
Broadway and Pacific)
415-398-9696
Open Tuesday through Saturday
5 to 10:45 P.M.,
Sunday 4 to 9:45 P.M.
Inexpensive
Credit cards: MC, V

Time stops when you step down into Tommaso's cave-like dining room with partitioned-off tables along the walls and a long communal table stretching down the middle of the dimly lit room. Nothing has changed in this pizzeria for decades, but that's the way the lines of people waiting to get in like it. They're enticed by the luscious smell of pizza baking in a wood-fired oven. Well before everyone else was cooking in wood-burning ovens, Tommaso's was turning out crisp, sweet, chewy-crusted pizzas scented with smoke and layered with copious amounts of whole-milk mozzarella. The aroma of the vegetarian pizza blanketed with green peppers, onions, fresh mushrooms, and olives really gets to me, though my all-time favorite is the superdeluxe pizza with mushrooms, peppers, ham, and Tommaso's allspice-scented Italian sausage. Ask them to hold the anchovies, which are too strong on this pizza (and I'm an anchovy lover). Tommaso's also makes a massive calzone stuffed with ricotta, mozzarella, prosciutto, and a special spice mixture, which all melt together in a happy way inside a crisp folded-over crust. For starters, order plates of peeled peppers, crisp whole green beans, and trees of broccoli, all lightly dressed in lemon juice and olive oil. Though most people go for pizza, don't overlook an airy lasagna baked in the wood-fired oven. At prime meal hours expect a wait. Reservations are not taken.

WASHINGTON SQUARE BAR & GRILL . . . . .

1707 Powell Street (at Union)
415-982-8123
Open Monday through Friday
11 A.M. to 3 P.M., Sunday through
Wednesday 5:30 to 10:30 P.M.,
Thursday through Saturday
5:30 to 11 P.M.; brunch Saturday
and Sunday 10:30 A.M. to 3 P.M.
Moderate
Credit cards: MC, V

Some restaurants refuse to die, even when new owners take over and try to change them. The rollicking Washington Square Bar & Grill didn't want to be the Frenchified Cobalt Tavern, no matter how hard young owners, Guy and Rose Ferri worked to transform it. So the couple gave in and resuscitated the Washington Square Bar & Grill on what would have been its twenty-ninth anniversary in September 2002.

They reinstalled legendary Washbag mixologist Michael McCourt and a staff of professionals behind the bar. They repainted the blue walls and restored the tarnished brass, red velvet curtains, wooden floors, and plenty of baseball memorabilia. They called up some nimble jazz pianists, putting them to work at the old upright in the back of the barroom. But best of all. Guy Ferri recreated a simple San Francisco-style grill menu, half Italian, half American, that makes everyone happy. The Washbag's food is affordable, satisfying and easy to eat, just what you want from a neighborhood haunt.

As you sit down, the waiter brings over crostini mounded with marinated chickpeas or Tuscan beans enlivened with olives and basil. If you've had a few drinks, they taste like heaven. Even if you haven't, the tone of generosity has been set.

There are Caesars, excellent hamburgers, and Sicilian-style chicken soup with meatballs. But my favorite dish on the whole menu is Ferri's linguine and clams, a bowl of flat spaghetti bathed in olive oil, white wine, toasted garlic and the liquor from small, meaty Manila clams in their shells—perfect balance, perfect ingredients, perfect dish. For serious eating, sage-roasted chicken with a crisp golden skin comes with a big square of potato and butternut squash gratin and buttery spinach. A grilled Black Angus rib-eye gets creamed spinach, those addictive skinny fries, and classic bearnaise. And save room for irresistible freshly made desserts.

As a North Beach dweller, I'm elated that the Washbag is back. The energetic new owners have rekindled the spirit of the old place and improved the food. They figured out how to make a reassuring menu of old favorites fresh and exciting. As Guy Ferri told me, "This space just wants to be a saloon." Why fight the natural order of the universe?

CAFÉS

CAFFÈ GRECO. . . . .

423 Columbus Avenue
(between Vallejo and Green)
415-397-6261
Open daily 6 A.M. to midnight
Cash only

I live on Telegraph Hill because I like the European amenities of North Beach, and the place I walk down to the most is Caffè Greco, owned by Hanna Suleiman. His coffee, made from Illy espresso beans on a machine kept as finely tuned as a concert grand, has the depth, aroma, and body of the best coffee in Italy. Yes, Caffè Greco does offer the option of low-fat milk for its cappuccinos and lattes, and the portion of espresso does exceed the thimbleful of ambrosia you get in Italy, but Greco's coffee is always delicious. I particularly like a mixture of espresso and hot milk served in a little glass, which has been called at various times the Algerian or the Africano, stronger than a latte and without the bland foam of a cappuccino.

The original café has large sliding windows facing Columbus and a few tables on the street. The floor is so tightly packed with chairs and tables that you have to plot out a path before you make a move—especially with several cups of coffee in hand. But now Greco lovers can spread out to a second room opened in a storefront next door. For those who like to read or work in cafés, the new room is a blessing. You don't feel guilty lingering at a table now that there are more of them. Happily, the new room with its big windows on Columbus feels as much like Greco as the original room. I actually prefer it.
Everyone still orders at one end of a counter that holds baskets of fresh croissants and raisin rolls. A refrigerated glass section displays truffle cakes from the great Emporio Rulli (see page 453) and an exceptional house-made tiramisu from a special family recipe. Excellent Italian ice creams from Gelato Classico are offered.

At prime coffee hours—in the morning, after lunch, and late evening after dinner—Greco is a melting pot. The crowd is completely mixed—young, old, local, tourist, Asian, European—attracting anyone who appreciates a great cup of coffee in a clean, well-lighted place.

CAFFÈ ROMA COFFEE ROASTING COMPANY

526 Columbus Avenue (between
Green and Union)
415-296-7942
www.cafferoma.com
Open Monday through Thursday
6 A.M. to 7 P.M., Friday until 8 P.M.,
Saturday 6:30 A.M. to 11 P.M.,
Sunday 6:30 A.M. to 8 P.M.
Credit cards: MC, V

One of my favorite spots to sip a strong, creamy espresso is on the sunny bench in front of Caffè Roma Coffee Roasting Company, a coffee roastery and café much frequented by the filmmakers whose offices are upstairs. Both the beans to take home and the espresso made in the café have extraordinary character and richness. Only coffee and a few biscotti are served here, but the coffee is so good that many folks regularly stop by for a quick shot. For other location, see page 357.

CAFFE TRIESTE. . . . .

601 Vallejo Street (at Grant)
415-392-6739
www.caffetrieste.citysearch.com
Open daily 6:30 A.M. to midnight
Cash only

I had a delicious, strong, creamy, not-bitter espresso here the other day and it took me by surprise. Consistency has not been a strong point at Trieste, though its scruffy regulars would wrestle me to the ground over this one. There may be new attention to coffee quality—certainly Trieste has stepped up its marketing of house-roasted coffee beans to restaurants and consumers. On the weekend afternoons when live opera singers hold forth, you can't get near the place. During the week, Trieste is the home of vestigial and nouveau beatniks who eye everyone who orders a cup of coffee as a potential soul mate. If you're in the mood, you can talk all afternoon.

MARIO'S BOHEMIAN CIGAR STORE CAFE . .

566 Columbus Avenue (at Union)
415-362-0536
Open Monday through Saturday
10 A.M. to midnight,
Sunday until 11 P.M.
Credit cards: MC, V

People gravitate from all over town to little Mario's to eat delicious warm focaccia sandwiches straight from the miniature Baker's Pride pizza oven. They also come to drink coffee expertly made from Graffeo beans, or to drink a cold imported beer or a glass of wine. Seating is so close at this sardine-can of a café that you cannot help but exchange a few words with the person next to you. I always find Mario's to be an exceptionally friendly, low-key spot. The people who frequent it tend to like eating, which means that attitude does not take precedence over humanity. Mario's actually was a cigar store at one time, though Mario, Liliana, and son Paul Crismani have been running it for the last eighteen of its seventy-plus years as a coffeehouse with a counter and six or so tables. Windows that look across the street to Washington Square slide open on warm days, letting a breeze into the almost claustrophobic interior, lined with photographs of beloved patrons. Mario's luscious sandwiches are made on soft, olive oil–rich focaccia from nearby Danilo and Liguria (see page 253) bakeries, with rich, savory fillings like tender house-made meatballs in a buttery tomato sauce spiked with thinly sliced onions. Both the chicken and eggplant sandwiches use crisp, breaded cutlets, which are slipped into the focaccia with just the right amount of tomato sauce and melted mozzarella. On the lighter side, try a warm open-faced tuna salad sandwich with melted cheese and onions, the best tuna melt in the world. A tumbler of Chianti with any of them does a world of good for the digestion. These are the kind of sandwiches that stay with you all day.

BARS

ENRICO'S SIDEWALK CAFE . . . .

504 Broadway (at Kearny)
415-982-6223
www.enricossidewalkcafe.com
Open Monday through Friday
11:30 A.M. to 10:30 P.M., Saturday
and Sunday until 11:30 P.M.
Credit cards: AE, MC, V

Everyone in the city eventually gravitates to Enrico's, the raffish, historic café on Broadway with prime outdoor seating. It took an inspired chef, Rich Hackett, and a group of investors to bring Enrico's back to life after it went belly-up and its former owner, colorful North Beach character Enrico Banducci, sold the building. Hackett and group leased the space when Broadway was at an ebb, poured tons of money into refurbishing it, and turned it into one of the tastiest and most exciting cafés in town. Then the group made some fatal attempts to bring back two other withering North Beach spots and ended up having to sell Enrico's. It remains more popular than ever, a prime meeting ground in North Beach at all hours of the night and day. But the once-vibrant cooking has become pedestrian, if serviceable. Some of the best modern music ensembles on the West Coast play here nightly without a cover charge. The bar stays open until 2 A.M., and many's the time I've dropped in for an espresso or a glass of cognac on the way home from a night out.

GINO AND CARLO'S . . . .

548 Green Street (between
Columbus and Grant)
415-421-0896
www.ginoandcarlo.com
Open daily 6 A.M. to 2 A.M.
Cash only

Just a bar with a couple of television sets, Gino and Carlo's belongs to the North Beach old-timers who have staked out a stool and like cheap booze, friendly talk, and no constraints on their habits, like smoking.

SALOON . . . .

1232 Grant Avenue
(at Fresno near Vallejo)
415-989-7666
Open daily noon to 2 A.M.
Cash only

Junkies and ex-cons prefer the Saloon during the day; at night when local R & B bands play, passersby and everyone in the neighborhood stop in for a drink and a dance, pulled in by the music and the nostalgic beery, smoky Saloon breath that pours out the front door. Started in 1861, the Saloon's ancient bar and funky walls have seen it all.

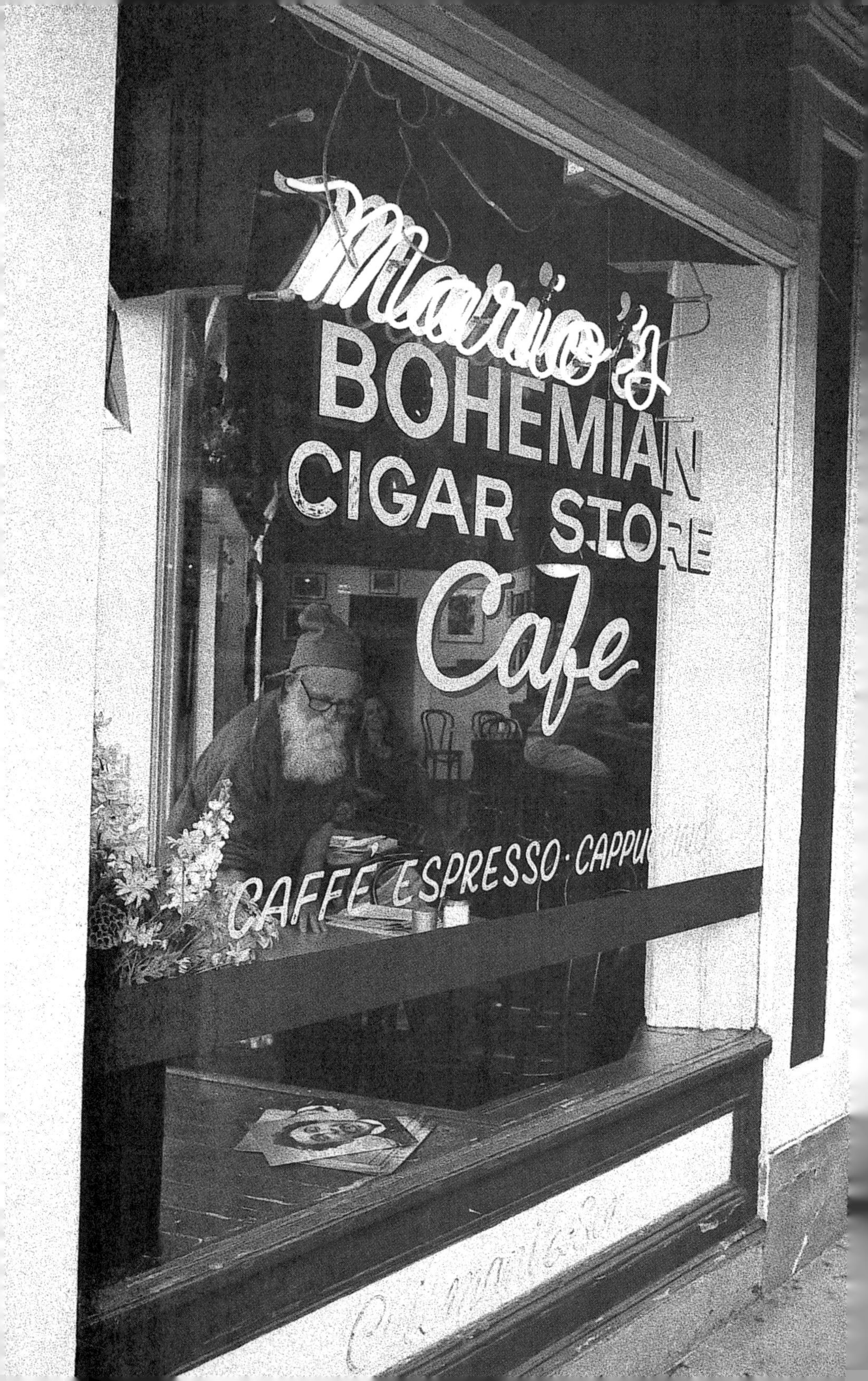

Mario's
BOHEMIAN
CIGAR STORE
Cafe
CAFFÉ ESPRESSO · CAPPU

SAVOY TIVOLI . . . .

1434 Grant Avenue
(between Green and Union)
415-362-7023
Open Tuesday through Thursday
5 P.M. to 2 A.M., Friday through
Sunday 3 P.M. to 2 A.M.
Credit cards: AE, MC, V

A great outdoor venue in North Beach, along with Enrico's (see page 245), Savoy Tivoli's patio attracts a young, cruising crowd that congregates on Grant Avenue every evening, leaving the Savoy's spacious indoor bar and café empty even on the coldest nights. The roar from the patio rivals the noise coming out of the biker bars down the street. People who hang here check out one another, plus everyone else who walks by on the narrow street.

SPEC'S . . . .

12 Saroyan Alley (on Columbus
between Broadway and Pacific)
415-421-4112
Open daily 5 P.M. to 2 A.M.
Cash only

Artists, photographers, and merchant marines hang out at this historic seamen's bar with a worn wooden interior that looks like the hold of a ship. On any drinking tour of North Beach, Spec's is a required stop.

TONY NIK'S . . . .

1534 Stockton Street (between
Columbus and Union)
415-693-0990
Open daily noon to 2 A.M.
Credit cards: D, MC, V

This happens to be my favorite bar in North Beach. It's small, moderne, and neighborhoody, but cosmopolitan enough to attract a city-wide crowd. North Beach bar aficionados (of which there are many) remember Tony Nik's from the old days when it opened at 9 A.M. for its regulars. The nephew of either Tony or Nik—I have never gotten the story straight—recently cleaned up the place, restoring its swanky 1940s blond wood bar and wood-paneled walls. It's just a narrow room that barely holds a bar and a few tables and a banquette at the back, but when I'm sipping my Harry's Bar cocktail (equal parts Punt e Mes and gin with a splash of bitters, shaken vigorously with ice and strained into a martini glass with a twist of lemon), I feel immersed in Sinatra-style North Beach.

TOSCA . . . .

242 Columbus Avenue (between
Pacific and Broadway)
415-391-1244
Open nightly 5 P.M. to 2 A.M.
Cash only

Jeannette Etheredge, proprietor of this beloved, seventy-eight-year-old North Beach bar, knows every ballet dancer, movie star, and filmmaker in this town and many others all over the world, and when any of them are in her neighborhood they drop by Tosca. The long bar, vaulted front windows, and antique espresso machine are just half the picture: Beyond lies a large room filled with booths and tables, plus another back room with a pool table where luminaries tend to hang out with their entourages. It's been the setting for hundreds of arty, impromptu parties. Even if you're a nobody, you might enjoy a special house cappuccino served in a glass and composed of hot espresso, steamed milk, sugar, and brandy, guaranteed to warm you up on a cold summer night. A jukebox filled with arias competes with the pounding bass from a dance club in the same building.

VESUVIO . . . .

255 Columbus Avenue (between
Pacific and Broadway)
415-362-3370
www.vesuvio.com
Open daily 6 A.M. to 2 A.M.
Cash only

This original beatnik bar next to City Lights bookstore has remained true to its founding spirit year after year. The walls are like a work in progress, full of scribblings, ever-changing photographs, and pieces of art. The upstairs mezzanine overlooking the historic conjunction of Columbus Avenue and Jack Kerouac Alley affords a choice view of North Beach shenanigans, and if you insist, the bartender will flick on a slide show that pays homage to James Joyce.

DELICATESSENS/TAKEOUT

FREDDIE'S . . . .

300 Francisco Street (at Stockton)
415-433-2882
Open Monday through Friday
7:30 A.M. to 4 P.M.,
Saturday 8:30 A.M. to 3 P.M.
Cash only

Italian-sub aficionados rank Freddie's multilayered marvels as some of the best in the city. Italian sandwich loyalties run deep because many of the best spots for them have been in business for decades. Freddie's has been making sandwiches since 1926 in an old grocery store across the street from the Francisco Middle School. The aged wooden shelves hold giant cans of tuna, olive oil, and vinegar used to make the sandwiches, and potato chips and candy bars to round out your lunch. You order at the counter at the back from a long list of fillings and trimmings and breads. Everyone seems to know exactly what they want. I go for the small prosciutto sandwich on sour hard without mustard, but with oil and vinegar and *peperoncini*. Thin slices of cheese, tissue-thin slices of tomato and red onion, shredded lettuce, mayonnaise, mustard, and pickles are a given. One member of my family unfailingly orders the popular Italian combo (salami, *salame cotto*, pressed ham, and cheese) on sour soft because he says the sour hard brutalizes the roof of his mouth. The soft Dutch crunch roll with a crumble crust represents the middle ground. The other day, the guy in line behind me ordered a salami and egg salad combo sandwich that made me rethink my usual. The permutations are unending. You have to be decisive. All the meats are sliced to order just a few minutes before your sandwich is assembled, and the tuna, egg, and chicken salads are dewy fresh. A visit to Freddie's resonant shop is well worth a walk off the beaten North Beach track.

542 Green Street (between
Columbus and Grant)
415-982-9738
Open Sunday through Thursday
11:30 A.M. to 11:30 P.M.,
Friday and Saturday until 2 A.M.
Cash only

They put big sheet pans of hot, fragrant pizza right at nose level in the open front window, so when you walk by the smell practically grabs you. How can anyone resist eating a slice of pizza that has just come out of the oven? Golden Boy makes its pizzas on soft, olive oil–rich focaccia dough and slathers them with lots of stuff, so that one piled-up square slice makes a satisfying meal. I am partial to the vegetarian, heavily layered with the thinnest slices of zucchini, fresh tomato, olives, onions, and mushrooms, then drizzled with pesto, but if I don't want to wait for a reheat (and Golden Boy slices do reheat well in the countertop oven), I go for the pizza still warm from its first cooking, whatever it may be. I usually walk down the street eating the slice, trying not to dribble on my shirt, but for the more civilized, there is a high counter and stools plus a few boothlike tables in the back. Only pizza and beer, wine and espresso are sold here, and that's why the pizza stays so delicious, slice by slice, year after year.

JUICEY LUCY'S ORGANIC JUICE
AND FOOD BAR . . . .

703 Columbus Avenue (at
Greenwich)
415-786-1285
Open daily, seasonal hours
Cash only

Many chain juice bars have opened up throughout the city, but Juicey Lucy is the real thing. I see Lucy at the Ferry Plaza Farmers' Market every Tuesday and Saturday buying organic fruits and vegetables for her drinks and salads. She uses only whole fruits for her imaginative drinks, pulverizing them in her Champion juicer. She serves them in thick, colorful pottery bowls at cool room temperature. An apple-orange-lemon-lime combo, made with unpeeled apples and peeled whole citrus, is delicately sweet and aromatic, lighter in texture than squeezed juice. Maybe it's my imagination, but it feels alive on your tongue. Salads, served in Japanese pottery bowls with pointed wooden chopsticks, draw on a farmers' market worth of vegetables, fruits, nuts, and seeds juicily dressed in balsamic vinegar, olive oil, and tamari, an unlikely but tasty combination.

The little shop looks like a hippie pad from the sixties, with purple walls, blue ceiling, green floors, painted furniture, yoga wall murals, and a shelf of health food books with such titles as the *Encyclopedia of Healing Juices*. Juicey Lucy's loyal customers actually read these as they sip their invigorating juice. The absolute freshness of all ingredients, the colorful presentations—and surroundings—and Lucy's good palate give her version of pristine health food genuine style.

SAVORY MEATBALLS WITH SPAGHETTI

(adapted from *Chez Panisse Café Cookbook*)
SERVES 6

¼ cup soft breadcrumbs

½ cup milk

1 small yellow onion,
very finely diced

Extra virgin olive oil

Salt

1 pound freshly ground
beef sirloin

1 egg, beaten

3 tablespoons freshly grated
Parmigiano-Reggiano cheese,
plus more for serving

4 tablespoons chopped fresh
Italian parsley

1 teaspoon finely chopped
fresh thyme

⅛ teaspoon cayenne pepper

Black pepper

1 red onion, thinly sliced

Olive oil

2 to 3 cloves garlic,
very finely chopped

2 cups Simple Tomato Sauce
(see recipe at right)

¼ teaspoon hot-pepper flakes

½ teaspoon finely chopped
fresh oregano

Salt

1 pound spaghetti

Everyone loves spaghetti and meatballs and you can certainly find this dish in many a North Beach trattoria like the Original U.S. Restaurant. But the best version I have ever tasted comes from the *Chez Panisse Café Cookbook*. The meatballs in this recipe, fragrant with fresh herbs and poached in tomato sauce, melt in your mouth. They have a divine texture. The outcome of this recipe is worth the effort. You can get all the ingredients for it in North Beach.

1 Put the milk and breadcrumbs in a small bowl and mix with a fork. When the bread has softened, squeeze out most of the milk with your hands. Discard the milk.

2 Sauté the yellow onion in a little olive oil without letting it color. Season with a light pinch of salt and set aside to cool.

3 Combine in a medium-sized bowl the beef, bread crumbs, onion, egg, 3 tablespoons cheese, 2 table-spoons of the parsley, thyme, cayenne, black pepper, and 1 teaspoon salt. Work the mixture gently and thoroughly with your hands until it has an even consistency. With wet hands, shape the mixture into walnut-sized balls. This can be done a few hours ahead. Store the meatballs in the refrigerator in one layer, tightly wrapped, until you are ready to cook them. The meatballs can be cooked in the time it takes to boil the spaghetti.

4 Heat a skillet large enough to hold all the meatballs in one uncrowded layer. Add the red onion with enough olive oil to coat it lightly and cook over medium heat. When the onion begins to sizzle, add the meatballs, shaking the pan to keep them from sticking. Using tongs or a wooden spoon, gently turn and toss the onions and meatballs so they brown lightly. Add the garlic and cook for a few seconds, taking care that it doesn't color. Add the tomato sauce, hot -pepper flakes, oregano, and the remaining 2 tablespoons parsley. Season with salt to taste. Simmer gently, uncovered, stirring the meatballs to coat them with sauce. Test for doneness by cutting 1 meatball in half with a paring knife. Keep warm.

5 A rule of thumb for gauging how much pasta to cook—one that actually uses the thumb—is to make a ring about the size of a dime with your thumb and forefinger. A dime-size bundle of pasta is one portion. Dry spaghetti will take 7 to 10 minutes to cook. Boil the pasta in a large quantity of salted water. Drain the spaghetti and turn into a deep warmed platter or pasta bowl. Pour the meatballs and sauce over the pasta. Serve with more Parmesan cheese.

SIMPLE TOMATO SAUCE

MAKES ABOUT 2 CUPS

2 tablespoons extra-virgin olive oil

1 yellow onion, finely diced

3 cloves garlic, finely chopped

2 pounds sweet, ripe tomatoes, peeled, seeded, and chopped

1 teaspoon salt

Bouquet garni of fresh parsley, thyme, and basil sprigs

1 Warm the olive oil in a heavy-bottomed nonreactive saucepan over medium heat. Cook the onion, stirring occasionally, until softened and slightly browned, about 5 minutes. Add the garlic and let it sizzle for 30 seconds. Stir in the tomatoes and salt, and add the herb sprigs, bundled together with kitchen twine.

2 Bring the sauce to a boil, then reduce the heat to low. Simmer the sauce, uncovered, for 30 to 45 minutes; it will thicken as it cooks. Remove and discard the herb bundle. Taste for salt and adjust. The sauce will keep for 5 to 6 days refrigerated.

3 Note: for a more refined sauce, pass through a food mill or purée in a blender.

MOLINARI DELICATESSEN . . . .

373 Columbus Avenue (at Vallejo)
415-421-2337
www.molinarideli.com
Open Monday through Friday
8 A.M. to 6 P.M.,
Saturday 7:30 A.M. to 5:30 P.M.
Credit cards: MC, V

The front window of this popular Italian deli is a mosaic made of tightly fitted-together imported tins, jars, and boxes of olive oil, biscotti, anchovies, olives, artichokes, peppers, pasta, polenta, and tomatoes. Just walking by makes my mouth water. Inside, the small, narrow store is similarly packed to the rafters with foodstuffs. Many a great sandwich has been composed around Molinari's spectacular hot red pepper–flecked salami. Behind the counter, Italian pickled peppers, marinated artichokes, mushrooms, red peppers, olives of every sort—all the stuff you need to construct a dream sandwich—await selection. Fresh mozzarella from Ferrante in Benicia and imported buffalo milk mozzarella sit next to each other not far from handy two-ounce tins of Columbus anchovies. I like the frittata here, a cold cheese, spinach, and breadcrumb cake held together with eggs. The fresh sausages are excellent. The sweet Italian with fennel, which cooks up slightly pink in color, is out of this world, and so are the tiny pure pork breakfast links. Any pantry ingredients called for in any Italian recipe, including imported Italian cheeses in good condition, can be found here.

NORTH BEACH PIZZA . . . .

1499 Grant Avenue (at Union) and
1310 Grant Avenue (at Vallejo)
415-433-2444 (both stores)
www.northbeachpizza.com
Open Monday through Thursday
11 A.M. to 1 A.M., Friday and
Saturday until 3 A.M.,
Sunday until 1 A.M.
Credit cards: AE, DC, D, MC, V

I mention the two North Beach Pizza parlors not so much for their sometimes soggy, extremely cheesy, often indifferently put together pizzas, but for the fact that they have an amazingly efficient call-in and delivery system that gets your pizza to your door hot and within forty-five minutes. North Beach pizza is a hundred times better than the chain-style pizzas, and this independent operation has figured out how to beat the chains at their own game. A lot of people do love this thick, rich pizza and often line up outside the Union and Grant corner door to wait for a booth. (The branch down the block near Green stays full, but isn't as wildly popular.) When made well, the vegetarian pizza has a pleasant balance of savory and fresh vegetables that melt in the oven into pillows of cheese. So much cheese is piled on the pepperoni that it gets lost underneath. However, it takes only a few slices to fill you up, which is just what prompts all those young, hungry, budget-minded kids to cool their heels on the sidewalk.

DANILO . . . .

516 Green Street (at Bannam)
415-989-1806
Open daily 6:30 A.M. to 6 P.M.
Cash only

Bakeries that look just like Danilo are found all over
Italy with shelves full of hard Italian biscotti, hard toast
for seafood soups, and crumbly Italian cookies. In back
of the cookie counter are wooden shelves of baked
breads, the most notable being the yeasted Italian corn
bread, so popular that Danilo has started to bake it every day. (It's excellent toasted, buttered, and slathered with caviar.) Rounds of focaccia scattered with coarse salt and rosemary,
scallions, or tomato sauce have a soft, olive oily texture that appeals to kids. The grand-
motherly Italian women behind the counter have a soft spot for children and often hand
them a crisp, yard-long breadstick. I have never walked into Danilo without seeing an elderly man or woman peacefully sitting in the chair by the open door, carrying on a running
conversation with the counter ladies and anyone else who walks in.

LIGURIA BAKERY . . . .

1700 Stockton Street (at Filbert)
415-421-3786
Open Monday through Friday
8 A.M. to 4 P.M. (earlier if sold out),
Saturday 7 A.M. to 4 P.M.,
Sunday 7 A.M. to noon
Cash only

A focaccia store catercorner from Washington Square,
Liguria sells plain, tomato, or scallion-topped focaccia
in big flat sheets, which they cut in half, wrap in waxed
paper, and tie with string. If you don't get there before
11 a.m., there's a good chance that your focaccia of
choice will be sold out. Not only does everyone in the
neighborhood stop by for a square, but Liguria whole-
sales to lots of cafés that use the focaccia for warm
sandwiches. PlumpJack (see page 157), the restaurant off Union Street, came up with the
idea of using the tomato focaccia as a bun for hamburgers, thereby internalizing the
ketchup. Try it. It really works. Early in the morning you can smell the baking dough and
see the golden sheets coming out of the huge brick ovens in the back. The singleness of
purpose and the perfect consistency of their product make Liguria part of many people's
regular North Beach ritual.

STELLA . . . .

446 Columbus Avenue
(between Green and Vallejo)
415-986-2914
Open Monday 7:30 A.M. to 6 P.M.,
Tuesday through Thursday
until 10 P.M., Friday and Saturday
until midnight,
Sunday 8:30 A.M. to 6 P.M.
Credit cards: AE, D, MC, V

This tiny bakery specializes in *sacripantina*, an Italian
cake made with soft yellow layers soaked with Marsala,
then filled and frosted with airy zabaglione enriched
with whipped cream. Twenty years ago these molded
cakes—juicy, boozy, and light, with a pleasant sherrylike flavor—were served in every Italian restaurant
in town. Now, of course, restaurants have their own
pastry departments, but they would do well to create a

cake as good. I much prefer the original Stella *sacripantina* to some of the flavored ones that have slipped into the repertory since the bakery has taken to preparing single servings in clear plastic cups. Recently, one of these was soaked in orange liqueur, an unexpected and not welcome surprise. Be sure to ask for the original Marsala cake and buy a whole one rather than an individual serving if you want the proportions to be right. The whole cakes, which must be refrigerated, come in several sizes, the smallest quite workable for an intimate dinner party.

VICTORIA PASTRY CO. . . . .

1362 Stockton Street (at Vallejo)
415-781-2015
www.victoriapastry.com
Open Monday through Saturday
7 A.M. to 6 P.M.,
Sunday 8 A.M. to 5 P.M.
Credit cards: MC, V

Each bakery in North Beach has made its reputation on a certain cake. At Victoria, it's the St. Honoré, a festive white-frosted cake rimmed with miniature custard-filled cream puffs. Inside, layers of crunchy Italian leaf pastry, custard, and rum-soaked cake make each sweet bite an adventure. Generations of families have celebrated special occasions with the St. Honoré, which can be ordered ahead in many different sizes. The other specialties at Victoria are their molded refrigerator cakes: the *zuccotto*, a bright-red mound soaked in cherry liqueur with custard; my favorite, the Fantasia, a tasty conglomeration of soft cake, mocha cream, and shaved chocolate; and a cheesy tiramisu. All the cakes now come in single-serving sizes so you can try them before you commit to a larger cake. I also like the powdered sugar–dusted cornmeal pound cake, much lighter than a regular pound cake, with a hint of grit. Sliced and toasted, buttered and spread with jam, or as a vehicle for macerated berries and whipped cream, this simple cornmeal pound cake is nothing if not versatile. I can see it as a base for your own Italian cake of custard, fruit, and liqueur. Victoria now has a second location in the Bon Air shopping center in Greenbrae.

COFFEE

GRAFFEO . . . .

735 Columbus Avenue (between
Greenwich and Filbert)
415-986-2420
www.graffeo.com
Open Monday through Friday
9 A.M. to 6 P.M.,
Saturday until 5 P.M.
Credit cards: MC, V

The smell of roasting coffee makes passersby stop dead in their tracks and ponder the conceptual window displays of this old San Francisco coffee bean roaster and seller. A slanted mock tabletop with oversized biscotti, coffee cups, wineglasses, and wineglass stains on the tablecloth suggests that Paul Bunyan might have stopped by for coffee. But the only item that Graffeo sells is coffee beans, either dark roast or light roast, or a combination of your choice. Water-processed decaf beans are also available. For over seventy years, Graffeo has supplied the best restaurants in town and a coterie of loyal retail customers who request their own private blends—one quarter light, half and half, one-third light—as evidenced by the row of stamps on the counter with a mind-boggling range of fractions.

GELATO CLASSICO . . . .

576 Union Street
(between Stockton and Grant)
415-391-6667
Open daily noon to 9 P.M.
Cash only

Lots of Italian ice cream shops have opened and closed, but Gelato Classico (with two other locations, see pages 141 and 332) thrives because it's the best. The ice creams taste natural, and the tricky creamy-thick texture has always been consistently maintained through proper storage and handling. This ice cream is so soft it gets shoveled into little cups. I cannot pass the shop without stopping in for a *coppa mista*, a lovely mixture of chocolate, pistachio, vanilla, and rum-flavored ice creams all swirled together. The true tropical fruit flavors—coconut, banana, mango—have been the base for a tropical fruit sundae I make at home layered with fresh pineapple, kiwifruit, papaya, toasted nuts, coconut, and whipped cream. The guys behind the counter at the North Beach store deserve a medal for patience and generosity; they proffer endless tastes and have a particular affection for children.

XOX TRUFFLES . . . .

754 Columbus Avenue
(near Filbert)
415-421-4814
www.xoxtruffles.com
Open Monday through Saturday
9 A.M. to 6 P.M.
Credit cards: AE, MC, V

Casimira and Jean-Marc Gorce hand-make miniature truffles in their tiny shop. Their small size means that each truffle constitutes one, or maybe two, heavenly bites of rich, buttery chocolate scented with rum or orange or cognac or coffee. My favorites happen to be the chocolate-caramel truffle, essentially creamy chocolate sweetened by burnt sugar, and any truffle coated with finely chopped nuts. The outside coating of these truffles is almost as soft as the inside, so the flavors and textures merge. A box of twenty mini-truffles as of this writing costs around $7, a bargain for such true-flavored artisan chocolate. I much prefer these tiny truffles to the gigantic domes and spheres that most other chocolate makers offer. One of these with an espresso makes the perfect ending to a meal, or an afternoon pick-me-up. I walk down Columbus to the XOX shop, pick up a few truffles, and then walk up to Caffè Roma (see page 244) or Greco (see page 243) to eat them in the heart of North Beach.

LA RACCOLTA. . . . .

521 Columbus Avenue (between
Green and Union)
415-693-0199
www.laraccolta.com
Open Thursday through Sunday
11 A.M. to 8 P.M., Friday and
Saturday 11 A.M. to 9 P.M.
Credit cards: MC, V

La Raccolta means "harvest" in Italian and the two
partners who import artisan Italian foods and ceramics
to sell at their two tiny stores and over the Internet
indeed have harvested a soulful market basket from
their travels. Black olive spread from Liguria; strong,
hot, organic red peppers stuffed with capers and
anchovies from Calabria; dried organic borlotti beans
from Umbria; peaches in Muscat wine from Piedmont;
panforte from a wood-oven bakery in Tuscany; fennel
seed *taralli* (a pretzel) from Apulia; extra virgin olive oils from different regions; pastas from
very old factories whose techniques and equipment have remained unchanged for centuries;
luscious canned Italian tuna in olive oil—well, you get the picture. The shop on Columbus
is packed with treasures. The former tenant sold candies and people still wander into La
Raccolta looking for a sweet. They will not be disappointed because baskets of bite-sized,
individually wrapped Italian fondants, soft, white candies with intense fruit flavor, have
been set out by the front door.

PRODUCE

THE NATURE STOP . . . .

1336 Grant Avenue
(between Vallejo and Green)
415-398-3810
Open Monday through Friday
9 A.M. to 10 P.M., Saturday and
Sunday 10 A.M. to 9 P.M.
Credit cards: AE, D, MC, V

I have watched this roomy Grant Street natural foods
store upgrade its inventory over the years, so that now
it carries a growing variety of organic fruits in season,
such as white peaches and nectarines, berries, and
melons, along with commercial fruits and vegetables.
Metropolis and Semifreddi breads are delivered daily,
and the full complement of bulk nuts, seeds, and grains
from Sun Ridge Farms fills up a portion of the store. A
smoothie bar at the entrance takes advantage of the plentiful tropical fruit by offering such
delights as fresh mango or papaya yogurt drinks, thinned by fresh orange juice, swirled in
the blender to order.

LITTLE CITY . . . .

1400 Stockton Street (at Vallejo)
415-986-2601
Open Monday through Friday
8 A.M. to 6 P.M.,
Saturday until 5:30 P.M.
Credit cards: MC, V

This Italian butcher shop specializes in veal shanks, baby beef liver, veal breast, and other favored Italian cuts. The friendly butchers will order anything they don't have, as well as cut and grind on the spot. They also make their own Italian sausages, hot and sweet. Carlo Togni, my Roman friend who lives near Precita Park, travels all the way across town to buy his meat here (and to have an espresso at Caffè Greco) because the butchers understand what he needs for his meat sauces and roasts. Excellent fat-marbled boneless chuck roasts are always available, along with fresh pork tenderloin and meaty country-style pork ribs for American cooks. Little City carries Petaluma Poultry chickens, which have excellent flavor and texture. If you're not a regular, be specific about which piece of meat in the counter you fancy. If the meat on display does not look fresh enough to you, ask for something from the back. Every old-time Italian shop in North Beach is under siege in these days of sky-rocketing rents and an Italian population that has moved out of the city. Maybe the meat doesn't move as fast it used to, which means that both customers and butchers need to be more vigilant.

WINE AND SPIRITS

COIT LIQUORS . . . .

585 Columbus Avenue (at Union)
415-986-4036
www.coitliquor.com
Open Monday through Saturday
9 A.M. to midnight,
Sunday 11 A.M. to 7 P.M.
Credit cards: MC, V

This vital neighborhood liquor store carries a far-ranging selection of wine carefully chosen for value and quality. When the new Beaujolais arrives in the fall, Coit always has the one from the best producer. If a California wine from a small grower gets some media attention, Coit will get it and mark it up the least. The spirits inventory is complete and sophisticated while still catering to mass tastes. Many locals buy their cigarettes and lottery tickets at Coit, but this independent store aims to please a wider audience with excellent prices on some classy wines, knowledgeable service, and enlightened buying.

COOKWARE AND BOOKS

BIORDI ART IMPORTS . . . .

412 Columbus Avenue (at Vallejo)
415-392-8096
www.biordi.com
Open Tuesday 11 A.M. to 5 P.M.,
Wednesday through Saturday
9:30 A.M. to 6 P.M.
Credit cards: AE, CB, DC, MC, V

I used to think the hand-painted Italian pottery in the window of Biordi was pretty hokey until I looked deeper into the store. At first I was shocked by the high prices; then I saw a hand-painted pasta bowl in the most elaborate and imaginative geometric design, every inch covered with brilliant color. I could imagine pears in it, spaghetti, or a green salad. I bit the bullet and bought it, as expensive as it was, and haven't regretted the purchase since. I use that flat bowl all the time, and when food isn't in it, I set it in the middle of the dining-room table just to gaze on its peculiar rustic opulence. That piece of ceramic radiates humanity. You can feel the sensibility of the person who painted it. I must say that year after year, washing after washing, it has neither chipped nor faded. Since that time I have bought wedding presents and presents for myself at Biordi in the form of plates, cups, saucers, pitchers, and platters, all with different patterns, but all wonderful together. In this Italian food–crazed time, a few Biordi pieces will make your Italian favorites look and taste better, I promise.

COLUMBUS CUTLERY . . . .

358 Columbus Avenue
(between Vallejo and Grant)
415-362-1342
Open Monday, Tuesday, and
Thursday through Saturday
9:30 A.M. to 5 P.M.
Credit cards: AE, D, MC, V

Every cook in town goes to Columbus Cutlery for knife sharpening and purchasing. Packed into a tiny space are scissors, pocketknives, hunting knives, and an abundance of cooking knives of every size and shape from the foremost makers in the world and at the fairest prices. The sweet elderly woman behind the counter moves very deliberately, bringing out the samples and carefully looking up the prices. She does one thing at a time, but the shop has such an old-world ethos about it, you hesitate to break into the ritual. I did that the other day when I was parked in a red zone at the corner, and just wanted to drop off some knives for sharpening. I stuck my card into my gray canvas knife case and rushed out. I think it was okay, but I felt that I had breached custom. The head sharpener is the counterwoman's husband, red of cheek and always with an army-style hat made out of a folded brown paper bag on his head. Over the years, this couple has hired extra sharpeners, so you can get your knives back quickly, crucial if you're a working chef. The sharpeners have been trained to take off as little of the metal as possible while still giving the blades a clean, razor-sharp edge; they never butcher your knives. The sharpening charge is reasonable, but one drawback is that the store is closed on Wednesdays. Plan accordingly.

PACIFIC
HEIGHTS
JAPANTOWN

PACIFIC HEIGHTS & JAPANTOWN

RESTAURANTS

1 Cafe Kati
2 Chez Nous
3 Ella's
4 Florio
5 Jackson Fillmore
6 Juban Yakiniku House
7 Julia
8 Kiss
9 Maki
10 Meetinghouse
11 Mifune
12 New Korea House
13 Vivande Porte Via

CAFÉS

14 Tan Tan

BARS

15 G Bar

DELICATESSENS/TAKEOUT

16 Bryan's Quality Meats
17 Maruya Sushi
13 Vivande Porta Via

BAKERIES/PASTRIES

18 Bay Bread
19 Patisserie Delanghe
20 Sweet Stop

ICE CREAM/CHOCOLATES

21 Tango Gelateria

COFFEE

22 Peet's Coffee & Tea

MARKETS

23 Cal-Mart

ETHNIC MARKETS

24 Maruwa Foods Company
25 Oliviers & Co.
20 Super Mira
26 Uoki Market

MEAT AND POULTRY

23 Antonelli's Meat, Fish, and Poultry
16 Bryan's Quality Meats

FISH

23 Antonelli's Meat, Fish, and Poultry
16 Bryan's Quality Meats
26 Uoki Market

CHEESE

27 Artisan Cheese

WINES AND SPIRITS

28 Wine Impression

COOKWARE AND BOOKS

29 Book's, Inc.
30 Forrest Jones
31 Kinokuniya Bookstore
32 Mashiko Folkcraft
33 Sanko Cooking Supply
34 Soko Hardware Co.
35 Sue Fisher-King
36 Viking Homechef

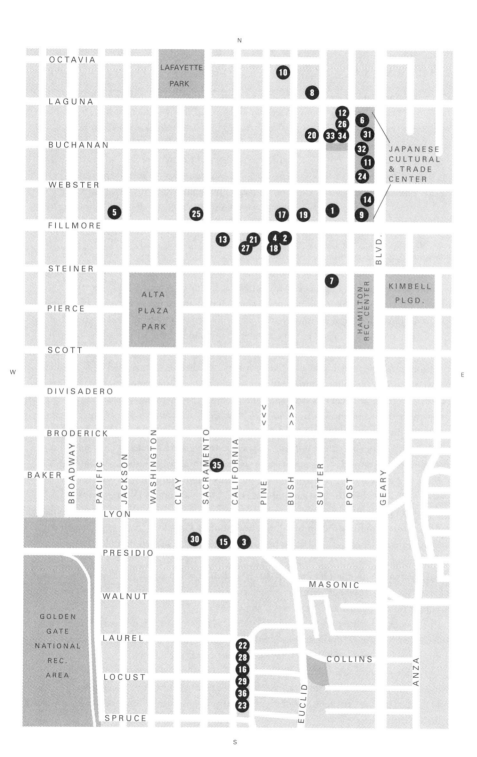

N

OCTAVIA

LAFAYETTE
PARK

🔟

8️⃣

LAGUNA

12
6
26
20 33 34 31
BUCHANAN
32
11
24

WEBSTER

14
5️⃣   25   17 19 1️⃣   9
FILLMORE

13   21   4 2
27   18

STEINER

ALTA
PLAZA
PARK   7️⃣
PIERCE

BLVD.

JAPANESE
CULTURAL
& TRADE
CENTER

KIMBELL
PLGD.

HAMILTON
REC. CENTER

SCOTT

W   E

DIVISADERO

BRODERICK

V V V   > >
V V   >

BAKER

BROADWAY
PACIFIC
JACKSON
WASHINGTON
CLAY
SACRAMENTO
CALIFORNIA
PINE
BUSH
SUTTER
POST
GEARY

35

LYON

30   15   3
PRESIDIO

MASONIC

WALNUT

GOLDEN
GATE
NATIONAL
REC.
AREA

LAUREL

22
28
16
29
36
23

COLLINS

ANZA

LOCUST

EUCLID

SPRUCE

S

0   .25
SCALE MILES

CAFE KATI . . . .

1963 Sutter Street (at Fillmore)
415-775-7313
www.cafekati.com
Open Tuesday through Sunday
5:30 to 10 P.M.
Moderate
Credit cards: AE, D, MC, V

I resisted going to Cafe Kati for the longest time because I was afraid that I would not like chef Kirk Webber's highly stylized blend of East and West cuisines. But when I finally got there, I had one of the nicest evenings I can remember. The plates did attain new heights of visual whimsy and the menu did combine French and Southeast Asian flavors with the crossover aplomb of Wolfgang Puck's Chinois on Main, in Venice, California.

Cafe Kati is, above all, a personal statement. This long, narrow storefront with one charming tiny dining room in the front, an incredibly small kitchen, considering the elaborateness of the food, in the middle, and a somewhat larger back dining room could only support the efforts of a single chef with perhaps a couple of assistants. Webber runs it with his wife Tina and a small, dedicated professional staff who seems as enamored of the restaurant as its fanatically loyal customers are. I can see why it would be a pleasure to work here. Every time a new set of plates reaches a table, diners cannot help gasping with delight.

The first dish that came my way won me over forever, a flat bowl of elegantly clear vegetable consommé tasting exactly like tomatoes. A delicious Caesar salad of richly dressed whole romaine leaves bundled together and standing on end had to be toppled in order to be eaten. A fabulous salad of whole spot prawns deep-fried with heads and dramatic tendrils attached were bound in crispy noodles, filled with a spicy Thai mousse, and accompanied with little lettuces; nests of beet, carrot, and daikon radish threads; and a lemongrass vinaigrette. Divine. Succulent nonfish sushi made with grilled shiitake mushrooms and sheets of toasty seaweed; and mango spring rolls flamboyantly garnished with vegetable threads and carved vegetables bring joy to the hearts of vegetarians. Cafe Kati must be a godsend for them because a wonderful meal could be made out of meatless starters.

For a main course, a clay pot of spot prawns in the most delectable, creamy, aromatic red Thai curry could be the center of my meal, though I would be hard put to pass up a velvety seared fillet of rock cod in a crisp mustard seed crust bathed in pink crawfish hollandaise.

The fantasy does not let up with desserts, such as butterscotch pudding under a hive of spun sugar or a plate of warm, gooey chocolate cake splashed with three fruit purées and arranged on the plate like a Sam Francis canvas.

Of course, by the time you read this, the whole menu may be different. Webber likes to change his dishes with the seasons. However, the spirit will be the same, and I would be surprised if his patrons will let him take certain items off the menu.

Webber mounts a series of quick-to-sell-out wine dinners throughout the year in which a winemaker from a small, choice local estate brings his or her best bottles. The food and wine matchups are often provocative and expand your idea of how food and wine can enhance each other.

CHEZ NOUS . . . .

1911 Fillmore Street
(between Bush and Pine)
415-441-8044
Open Tuesday through Sunday
11:30 A.M. to 3 P.M., Tuesday
through Thursday 5:30 to 10 P.M.,
Friday and Saturday 5:30 to 11 P.M.,
Sunday until 10 P.M.
Moderate
Credit cards: MC, V

Despite its French name, Chez Nous is a tapas bar that serves a wide range of Mediterranean dishes in small portions. It took off the moment it opened, and snagging one of the postage stamp–sized tables is like winning the lottery. My advice is to be flexible. Come to Chez Nous alone or with just one other person so you can eat wherever you find a spot. Anyone who has jockeyed for a few inches of counter at a busy tapas bar in Spain knows what I mean.

Standing or sitting, the food at Chez Nous satisfies. The small portions of bright, full-flavored California-Mediterranean food are easy to eat. I particularly love the excellent *tsatziki* (thick creamy yogurt, mixed with shredded cucumber, mint, and dill) paired with warm, marinated green and black olives; juicy, aromatic, tiny lamb chops provocatively scented with herbes de Provence; and a plate of spinach sautéed with toasted pine nuts and golden raisins. What a lovely meal these dishes make together, the perfect combination of flavors.

Dessert is not even a consideration at most tapas bars, but Chez Nous offers a number of delightful possibilities. To finish off a glass of wine, you might want a mini–cheese plate composed of treasures from the nearby Artisan Cheese shop (see page 284). But I would never leave Chez Nous without ordering a little bowl of thick, creamy Lebanese yogurt with poached dried fruits, almonds, Greek honey, and a few wisps of shredded mint. Heaven!

Though Chez Nous is not an authentic tapas bar, it has adapted the form to its own needs and the concept works on many levels. The narrow, echoing space, once a Leon's Barbecue, now with a smart paint job, Italian lighting, and wooden tables, really can accommodate only casual dining. So the tapas bar format works perfectly given the physical limitations, as does the no-reservation policy. Standing up at the counter or sitting at pushed-together tables, you appreciate how well the small, varied dishes suit this necessary informality. Essential to its success is the honesty of the food—while the menu may be a blend of ingredients and cooking styles, everything is tasty, fresh, and fully realized.

ELLA'S . . . .

Presidio Avenue (at California)
415-441-5669
www.ellassanfrancisco.com
Open Monday through Friday
7 to 11 A.M. and 11:30 to 4 P.M.,
Saturday and Sunday brunch
8:30 A.M. to 2 P.M.
Inexpensive
Credit cards: AE, MC, V

A sunny, charming corner café that puts out a delicious breakfast is a gift to a neighborhood. I know many people who live in the neighborhood who could not start their day without stopping at Ella's. The delicious breakfasts are bolstered by excellent home-style baking and first-rate coffee, both American and Italian. Even the white bread is baked from scratch, and what a difference that makes when your poached eggs come on thick slices of yeasty, buttered, gently crisp white toast. Ella's moist banana-nut-cinnamon coffee cake; sticky buns thick with pecans and orange zest; and light, buttery, sweet potato–raisin muffins capture the spirit of inventive American home cooking. The orange juice is freshly squeezed; the buttermilk pancakes are airy and flavorful, especially when drizzled with real maple syrup.

Ella's small lunch menu is also enlivened by home baking. The hamburgers come on buns still warm from the oven; a classic chicken potpie has a meltingly flaky top crust. Salads are prepared with proper conviction and lovely greens and sparkly dressings. The delicious warm spinach salad makes for a fine lunch, leaving room for a tall, judiciously sweetened slice of fresh apple pie.

FLORIO . . . .

1915 Fillmore Street
(between Bush and Pine)
415 -775-4300
Open Sunday through Thursday
from 5:30 to 10 P.M., Friday and
Saturday until 11 P.M.
Moderate
Credit cards: AE, MC, V

Patrons feel as if they've just stepped off a Left Bank *rue* when they enter cozy Florio. While the ambience, service, bar, (Florio is owned by bar man extraordinaire Doug Biederbeck, see page 97), and wine list have always been just right, the food was faceless and disappointing until chef Rick Hackett came along. He has infused life into a menu of bistro classics and, for my money, made Florio one of the best reasonably priced restaurants in town. I'm not the only one who thinks so, because on Wednesday night, September 12, 2001, at 8:45 P.M., the bar was packed and every table was full. Thankful for small blessings, I was glad I had a reservation.

I like to begin with a slab of sweet, buttery chicken liver pâté with pickled onions and slices of toasted currant-studded baguette, and a big bowl of assorted radishes to dunk into *fleur de sel* (a moist, coarse-grained sea salt) and sweet butter. Hackett also makes a stellar Lyonnaise-style salad of frisée with lardons of sugar-cured bacon topped with a poached egg that melts into the salad and moistens it like a dressing.

As for main courses, you can't do better than Florio's bone-in New York steak, licked by the fire, cooked exactly to specified doneness, juicy and flavorful. You can dip the thin, crisp fries that come with it into a ramekin of classic béarnaise. For dessert, Florio makes a charming, molded summer pudding of berries and berry-soaked bread with whipped mascarpone. It's barely sweetened and delightful. If you have room, order one of the clever cheese combos, like an aged Redwood Hill goat cheese with *medjool* dates or the lovely Matos Farm St. George from Santa Rosa with quince paste.

Florio strikes me as the French version of Delfina (see page 179), the standard for many new restaurants in the city. Both are small, stylish places where the food is simple, seasonal, and perfectly executed, and the prices seem extremely fair.

JACKSON FILLMORE . . . .

2506 Fillmore Street (at Jackson)
415-346-5288
Open Monday through Thursday
5:30 to 10 P.M., Friday and
Saturday 5:30 to 10:30 P.M.,
Sunday 5 to 10 P.M.
Moderate
Credit cards: AE, MC, V

The seating policy at Jackson Fillmore can be aggravating. Reservations are taken only for parties of three or more, and twosomes and singles often have to wait while they are accommodated. Also, the wait is always longer than the hostess says it will be, and feels even longer when it's chilly outside. You have to stand on the sidewalk because there's no room inside this tiny restaurant. But at least the tenor has changed at this everpopular Pacific Heights trattoria over the years. The people at the door now are cordial and understanding. The counter seats do turn fairly quickly, and eating at the counter suits the tasty, short-order Italian cooking well. This is just the place to drop in for a plate of pasta and a glass of wine, and many, many people do.

The daily menu tempts with first courses like a salad of baby arugula and juicy chilled shrimp in a luscious shallotty *rémoulade*-style dressing; and a tasty, warm asparagus salad with prosciutto, radicchio, and toasted breadcrumbs. From the regular menu comes the classic Jackson Fillmore dish, *radicchio al forno*, small wedges of radicchio wrapped in pancetta roasted crisp in the oven. Al dente pastas served in flat bowls, such as *spaghetti all'amatriciana*, in a copious, spicy tomato sauce with pancetta and onions, hit the spot. Spaghetti in lots of red chile–spiked marinara with those excellent shrimp and some scallops (I ask them to hold the scallops) makes for a satisfying bowl too. House-made ravioli amply filled with a mixture of ricotta, spinach, and Parmesan are smothered in tomato sauce, topped with cheese, and stuck under the broiler. They arrive very hot.

Veal, chicken, and fish dishes make up the rest of the long menu. For dessert have cold zabaglione layered with amaretti crumbs and fresh strawberries, a luscious Italian version of a sundae.

For those of you who remember the great counter restaurant, Vanessi's on Broadway, Jackson Fillmore's menu almost seems like an updated version. The inspiration for much of the cooking at Jackson Fillmore comes from Italy, but the North Beach–Italian influence has flowed right up Broadway to Pacific Heights. Jackson Fillmore has taken on the aura of an old-time San Francisco spot.

JUBAN YAKINIKU HOUSE . . . .

1581 Webster Street
(in the Japan Center)
415-776-5822
www.jubanrestaurant.com
Open daily 11:30 A.M. to 9:30 P.M.
Moderate
Credit cards: AE, MC, V

This modern Japanese grillroom strikes me as an Asian version of a California brew pub, at least in spirit. Drinking cold beer or sake is essential to the Yakiniku experience, which entails barbecuing thin, often frozen slices of animal innards, among other cuts, over a small gas grill sunken into the middle of a black table. At first, the idea of grilling beef tongue—one of my favorite foods—sawed into rectangles depressed me. But it cooks amazingly fast over the down-ventilated grill and ends up amazingly tender and tasty, especially dipped into a bowl of sweetened soy sauce. We drank and grilled, working our way through little plates of chewy, lusciously suety beef tripe; soy-marinated beef liver; rib-eye steak; and slices of bone-in short rib. Each slice comprised one nice bite. If we wanted to go upscale, we could have ordered *wagyu* beef, a tender, extensively fat-marbled beef flown in from Japan.

A big bowl of rice and an ample spread of Japanese salads that include cooked spinach, shredded daikon, nutty soy sprouts, and tender bean sprouts round out the meal. For a finale, you can drink a soothing bowl of hot chicken broth with seaweed. The soup works much better than dessert.

JULIA . . . .

2101 Sutter Street (at Steiner)
415-441-2101
Open Monday through Saturday
5:30 to 10 P.M.
Moderate
Credit Cards: AE, MC, V

When Julia McClaskey opened her much-anticipated restaurant on the seemingly doomed corner of Steiner and Sutter, prognosticators pooh-poohed this hidden location in the middle of a transitional neighborhood. But Julia brings obscure glamour to this intersection, making it the perfect offbeat spot for a chef who has always been her own woman. McClaskey and her front-of-the-house manager Robert Hill finally have their own place, and their followers from all over the city are clamoring for a table.

Count me in as one of the faithful. I'd follow McClaskey anywhere. I first tasted her cooking four years ago at the Universal Cafe where owner Gail Deferrari hired her after eating one trial meal. Deferrari signed McClaskey, a self-taught cook who worked with Donia Bijan at L'Ami Donia in Palo Alto, even though she had never run a professional kitchen. After two years at Universal, she and Hill launched Dine on Mission at Third Street, moving into the quarters of a failed restaurant and inheriting its many investors. Designer Michael Brennan redid the space and McClaskey cooked to ecstatic reviews. Dine, however, carried heavy baggage from the former operation and McClaskey and Hill left to open their own place with Brennan as the sole investor.

Indispensable in more ways than one, Brennan created a space for the current restaurant that is replete with light and air, taking advantage of two full sides of windows and a high ceiling. The dramatic interior, with distressed painted wood, drapes, and painted sky, is both rustic and romantic. Half the restaurant is given over to a square, three-sided bar surrounded by tables for walk-ins. The dining room tables radiate out from the open kitchen where a wood-fired rotisserie sends out mouthwatering smells.

The cooking, like the interior, is nothing you've seen before, yet feels familiar. It's playful yet reassuring. No matter how far out she gets, McClaskey's governing principle is to produce luscious, voluptuous food. A number of McClaskey classics appear on the menu: the chicken liver salad; the soul-satisfying pot roast; her extraordinary, multilayered green curry sauce on king salmon with asparagus and jasmine rice. But there are new dishes as well, like velvety braised pork belly, brioche stuffing, asparagus, and a soft-cooked egg, a turn on brunch that works perfectly at dinner. Pickled sole, in the style of a sweet and sour Venetian *agrodolce*, is smothered with pickled Maui onions and dried cherries and accompanied with an earthy potato and watercress salad as a foil. Though you might want to forgo pot roast if you order braised beef cheeks with parsnip purée and freshly grated horseradish as a first course, it's worth it to experience the melting, foie-gras-like texture of these morsels. They're unearthly.

McClaskey takes advantage of her sexy, custom-made, live-fire cooking equipment for main courses like rotisserie young chicken with a spring vegetable potpie and her signature pea sprout and radish salad; or spit-roasted pork loin with creamy polenta, port-mustard sauce, and a salad of radicchio, arugula and pancetta. I love the way she pairs rich meats with bright salads even if we don't think of them as salads, as is the case with the cabbage slaw and pickled corn and cucumber relish that come with chipotle-glazed braised short ribs and mashed potatoes. She knows how to balance a plate, how to incorporate some of every food group in her creations. She boldly weaves the elements together, the warp and the woof in contrasting colors and textures, creating strong, stunning, complete material.

McClaskey has such a sure culinary sensibility that anything she comes up with tastes as if it were a natural—an obvious combination waiting to be discovered. Only other cooks know how elusive such clarity can be.

KISS . . . .

1700 Laguna Street (at Sutter)
415-474-2866
Open Tuesday through Sunday
5:30 to 9:30 P.M.
Moderate
Credit Cards: AE, MC, V

You would never find tiny Kiss if you didn't know about it. Tucked under a new Japantown condo development, it has only five seats at a handsome blond wood sushi bar and three white linen–covered tables. But this treasure is well worth seeking out. Chef-owner Nakagawa Takao creates a menu of sparkly small dishes, sushi and raw fish, which can be ordered à la carte or as an eight course *omikase*, the chef's selection, for $35. I put myself in his hands.

One night we began with a few bites of black seaweed salad in a tiny celadon saucer and joyfully ate our way through vegetables napped in whipped tofu; a five-fish sashimi course highlighted by exquisite giant clam, halibut flavored with *kombo* (kelp) and marinated *kohada*, a kind of shad; Japanese custard in broth (*chawan mushi*) scented with enoki mushrooms and snow peas, with pieces of crab and creamy gingko nuts hidden in the delicate custard; then the highlight of the prepared dishes—four shatteringly crispy, deep-fried spring rolls the size of my little finger, stuffed with amberjack and a *shiso* leaf, served with gently pickled *myoga*, a fragrant, ginger-scented bulb like an onion—then a sushi course with a reprise of some of the fish from the sashimi course, then a steaming miso soup aromatic of the four different kinds of mushrooms floating on the top, and finally a perfect slice of sweet green Crenshaw melon with five plump blueberries.

Each course came on ceramic or glass serving pieces that made the foods more enticing. Naka-san (as he is affectionately called by his loyal patrons) has a lyrical eye and skillful hand. His selection of dishware and his simple presentations turn food into art. His dishes are almost unadorned so when he adds a wisp of opalescent *myoga* to a mound of tofu-napped cold vegetables, it not only gives the mass form but also emits a delicate scent. The aroma of a single snow pea, slant-cut and mounted in the custard of the *chawan mushi*, informs the whole dish. Every detail of every dish has been considered and contributes to both the appearance and flavor. There was not one extraneous element. Nakagawa Takao's cooking is liltingly elegant.

High-quality sake served cold by the stunning narrow glass completes the meal. The single waiter helped me choose. Her recommendation of Shimeharizura from Nigata province had a fruity nose balanced by a dry finish.

The small but airy modern room with pure white walls, wooden floor, sushi bar, and chairs serves as a canvas for the chef. I can't think of a room where I'd rather be.

MAKI . . . .

Japan Center, 1825 Post Street
(between Webster and Laguna on 2nd
floor of the Kinokuniya Building)
415-921-5215
Open Tuesday through Sunday
11:30 A.M. to 1:45 P.M. and
6 to 8:30 P.M.
Moderate
Credit cards: MC, V

A tiny (four small blond wood tables, five counter seats), very charming Japanese restaurant hides behind a cotton banner in a Japan Center hallway. Maki specializes in *wappa meshi*, rice cooked in a covered bamboo steamer topped with meats or fish. These delicious rice-based dishes are clean, filling, and savory all at the same time. My favorite, of course, is topped with sweetly glazed fillets of freshwater eel, a luxury. I like to order it as a dinner to get a lacquered tray full of pretty containers, each with its special food. Maki also features

high-quality sakes, served cold in special decanters that allow an ice cube to cool the rice wine without actually touching it. With sake you can have appetizers like a pristine mixed sushi plate; mosaic-centered vegetarian sushi rolls; or an unctuous braise of yam, fresh bacon, and daikon that melts your mouth. Elegant Mrs. Makaguchi, in refined kimono, presides over the dining room. Her sense of style gives this little gem its sparkle.

MEETINGHOUSE . . . .

1701 Octavia Street (at Bush)
415-922-6733
www.themeetinghouse.com
Open daily 5:30 P.M. to 9:30 P.M.,
Sunday brunch 9:30 a.m. to 2 P.M.
Moderate
Credit cards: AE, MC, V

The Meetinghouse is a small, stylish neighborhood restaurant that serves exceptional American food, much in the tradition of my other favorites, Woodward's Garden and Liberty Cafe. The cooking goes well beyond typical neighborhood fare, yet it has a heartiness and hominess about it that makes you want to drop in anytime. Chef-owner Joanna Karlinsky set up her dream restaurant in a former Victorian apothecary.

Hundreds of little drawers with green wooden knobs line the walls, and vases of seasonal flowers now fill the shelves. Large tables are spaciously placed in a square dining room with huge plate-glass windows on two sides. It's a very welcoming place to eat house-pickled salmon with colorful beet, fennel, and cucumber salads and house-baked rye bread, or airy rock shrimp and scallion johnnycakes served with watercress salad.

Fork-tender braised pork butt with crispy skin, celery root mashed potatoes, and warm cabbage salad is my idea of heaven on a cold night. Pan-roasted chicken on a warm frisée and bacon salad flanked by thick fried potato batons is another. Karlinsky is a baker and her warm, moist, flavorful whole-grain breads are reason enough to come to the Meetinghouse. For dessert she serves warm, fragrant gingerbread with lemon sauce, and rich chocolate layer cake with house-made coffee ice cream. A charming, efficient waitstaff all know the well-composed American wine list (with a number of half bottles) and can steer you to some interesting choices. Karlinsky herself likes being in the dining room, making you feel at home at this most personal of restaurants. I love the intimacy of the Meetinghouse and the fact that it is so professionally run, well above the standards of most neighborhood restaurants.

MIFUNE . . . .

1737 Post Street (between Webster and Buchanan in the Japan Center)
415-922-0337
Open daily 11 A.M. to 9:30 P.M.
Inexpensive
Credit cards: AE, MC, V

One of the most beloved small restaurants in Japantown, Mifune has been satisfying San Franciscan's yen for noodles for eighteen years, its thirty-one or so noodle offerings cast in realistic plastic gracing a glamorously lit front window. First-timers would do well to take a look, because service brooks few explanations. Noodle houses serve quickly; in fact, they really represent a superior version of fast-food outlets.

For well under $6, you can get either house-made *udon*, which are thick white-flour noodles, or *soba*, thin buckwheat noodles, in big bowls of hot, tasty soup topped with the likes of grilled beef and green onions or shrimp and vegetable tempura. True noodle lovers prefer them cold, as in the Mifune Special, a wooden boat with a cargo of white and brown noodles on deck, sprinkled with seaweed, hot shrimp, and vegetable tempura on the prow, and a bowl of cold, gingery dipping sauce with green onions, wasabi, and grated daikon on the stern. You dip the noodles and tempura into your custom-made sauce.

Many of the noodle and rice dishes (several *donburis* are available) are designed to give you protein in the form of seaweed, egg, or miso without meat, making this a good restaurant for vegetarians. Even if you're carnivorous, try No. 3, *wakame udon*, thick white noodles with toasty seaweed, or No. 17, *udon* with mountain fern. Mifune also appeals to kids who always like noodles and don't want to wait for their food. You can be in and out in half an hour, but are never rushed. You can sit and sip tea all afternoon if you'd rather. I have long treasured Mifune as my haven of noodley comfort in the middle of the city.

NEW KOREA HOUSE . . . .

1620 Post Street (at Laguna)
415-931-7834
Open daily 7 A.M. to 11 P.M.
Inexpensive
Credit cards: MC, V

I go to this rather luxurious street level branch of New Korea House specifically for two dishes, both fantastic. (There's an upstairs Korea House down the block at 1640 Post with the same menu and owners.) *Tofu chi gae*, a powerful hot-and-sour, chile-laced red broth with big squares of soothing soft tofu and bits of pork, oysters, and pickled vegetables tastes particularly good during a summer cold spell. One bite leads to another and after a couple you'll find that your internal organs start radiating heat.

My other favorite, delectable little oyster pancakes or mini-omelets, each containing one plump, juicy oyster, deliver a tamer experience. I like them any time. They're delicate and fresh and you need to dunk them in a soy-chile-scallion dipping sauce to complete the flavors. Midway through your oyster pancakes, the waitress brings additional hot, crisp potatolike mung bean pancakes and I could make a meal out of them. Both dishes are preceded by a tableful of starters—pungent Korean pickles, soft tofu, marinated cucumbers, bean sprout salad, daikon and carrot slaw, pressed tofu—each in a tiny pottery plate or bowl. With a tall, cold Korean beer, these two dishes with the introductory pickles come to $26, more than enough for two people and a bargain by any standard, New Korea House has a serene and cozy wood-paneled dining room and gracious service. Just make sure that you eat this garlicky meal with the person you share a bed with or you may get kicked out.

VIVANDE PORTA VIA . . . .

2125 Fillmore Street (between
California and Sacramento)
415-346-4430
www.vivande.com
Open daily 10 A.M. to 10 P.M.
Moderate
Credit cards: AE, DC, D, MC, V

Carlo Middione's celebration of all culinary things Italian is headquartered at this bustling delicatessen-trattoria on Fillmore. His Pacific Heights patrons eat both lunch and dinner at tiny pushed-together tables in the narrow, brick-walled dining area, really an extension of the kitchen. They come in for Carlo's silken house-made pastas; antipasti that put to use all the gorgeous Italian imports he stocks, and main courses that feature his famous flattened chicken. Vivande's Italian desserts are the best of their kind in the city, none more so than a whole juicy peach stuffed with almond paste and encased in chilled zabaglione, a summer dream come true.

People also can take home a tempting selection of Italian salads, baked savories, and great desserts. You can buy such prepared foods as roasted chickens from the open-flame rotisserie, whole onions slowly baked in balsamic vinegar, crusty walnut breads, and Italian tortas to incorporate into your own meals.

If you want to cook an Italian meal at home, Vivande presents a high-level resource. The purest, richest extra virgin olive oils, rare aged balsamic vinegars, Arborio rice for risotto, dried and house-made fresh pasta, Parmigiano-Reggiano, a selection of other hard and soft Italian cheeses, prosciutto from Parma, and Middione's *biscotti di Prato* are but a few of the treasures here. With exquisite Italian ingredients and cookbooks (including Middione's growing opus), you're well on your way. Vivande also does catering of any size. Everything that Middione turns out reflects his sense of integrity and the ebullience with which he cooks and creates in his shiny open kitchen.

Sapporo-Ya (415-563-7400) is catercorner from Tan Tan, the dessert café (page 272). Sapporo-Ya stays open until midnight. People regularly drop by for a late-night bowl of Chinese-style *ramen* in broth or wok-fried noodles with meat and vegetables. Two-story Iroha (in the Japan Center mall, on Buchanan between Sutter and Post, 415-922-0321), owned by the Mifune people, is a good spot for inexpensive Japanese *ramen* noodles (as opposed to soba and udon) in soup. They also do a nice bowl of *soba* noodles in broth with a generous pouf of *tororo*, grated mountain potato, which adds a slimy okralike texture to the noodles that I find addictive.

In the Miyako Mall of the Japan Center on the second floor, closest to the Miyako Hotel, **Takara** (415-921-2000) offers a $5.95 lunch *bento* box filled with tasty tempura, white tuna sashimi, an iceberg salad in a fabulous gingery salad dressing cum relish, and four little pieces of a California roll plus a bowl of miso soup. Also good are *panko*-encrusted fried oysters; a bowl of *soba* noodles, and *dashi* with *tororo*.

Everyone loves **Isobune** (across the walkway from Mifune, page 269), for its amusement-park delivery of sushi on wooden boats, which circulate in a waterway around a long oval sushi bar. The sushi makers stand in the middle of the counter, cutting fish and slapping together rice. Diners pluck little plates off the boats as they sail by. At the end of the meal, the number and sizes of saucers at your place determine the check. You can always ask for specially made pieces from the sushi makers, something I like to do because you never know how long some sushi have been traveling.

For dessert stop by **May's Coffee Shop**, a booth in the Kintetsu Mall behind Mifune, for hot *tai-yaki*, pancakes filled with red bean paste cooked in a carp-shaped mold. The pancake is salty, savory, and crisp, a nice contrast to the delicately sweet, thick red bean filling. *Tai-yaki* really satisfies the sweet tooth after a bowl of noodles. Or you can get a bun filled with red bean paste at **Amrie Antoinette** next door. The combination may seem odd, but the salty, highly flavored soft white bread really tastes great with the sweet bean filling. It works as dessert after a clean Japanese meal. Then you can buy a loaf of soft but chewy white sandwich bread or swirled cinnamon bread, sliced to order, to take home.

TAN TAN . . . .

Japan Center, 1825 Post Street
(between Webster and Laguna on 2nd
floor of the Kinokuniya Building)
415-346-6260
Open daily 10:30 A.M. to 7 P.M.
Cash only

Many people stop in at this tiny Japanese dessert café off the skylit second-floor atrium of the Japan Center, right next to the gigantic Kinokuniya bookstore. A tall window looks out to Geary Boulevard below. Now furnished to look like an Austrian coffeehouse, the once very Japanese Tan Tan has taken a turn toward the West. Western-style tarts and cakes are displayed in a refrigerated glass case, but the real treats are the Japanese desserts served on their own square lacquer trays with decorative and culinary accompaniments. A glass bowl of red beans in sugar syrup topped with tiny white rice dumplings, called *shiratoma*, are served with a ceramic mug of green tea. I also like *tokoroten*, cubes of shimmering agar-agar, crystal-like cubes of gelatin with bits of strawberry, canned peach, and fruit juice for flavor and dots of red bean for color. It's very refreshing. Yoko Tahara, a resident of the neighborhood long before the Japan Center was built and a patron of Tan Tan, loves a hot red bean dessert called *zenzai*, with superglutinous *mochi*, sticky-rice-flour balls, all presented in a lacquer bowl. I found all the red bean desserts wonderfully satisfying after meals at nearby Japanese restaurants. The pleasure of Japanese sweets is subtle for the Westerner: you are not assaulted by sugar or butterfat, but really feel as if you have had dessert. For those who insist on something a little more sybaritic, green-tea ice cream topped with a dab of red beans and decorated with sliced strawberries offers a compromise between Eastern and Western tastes.

Many people use Tan Tan as a tea- and coffeehouse for iced coffee, green tea, hot cappuccino, and green tea floats. If the indoor space gets too crowded, you can sit outside in the atrium at café tables and thumb through a Japanese or English magazine that you have just purchased at the bookstore next door.

BARS

G BAR . . . .

488 Presidio Avenue
(at California)
415-409-4227
Open Monday through Saturday 5:30
P.M. to 1:30 A.M.
Credit cards: MC, V

The black-clad bartender at G Bar mixed me the most delicious Cosmopolitan the other night—Grey Goose vodka, Cointreau, freshly squeezed limes, which happened to be in season when I ordered it, and a splash of cranberry. It was not a large drink—it came three-quarters of the way up a medium-sized martini glass—but it had intensity of flavor and perfect balance so that one was sufficient. This drink cost $9 but was worth every penny. (I love perfection of any kind for under $10.) Two of us started at the somewhat sticky stainless steel bar inset with an ice trough holding bottles of gin and vodka and then moved to the conversation area furnished with modern sectionals. Flames emerged from a sand-filled fireplace, looking disembodied in the purple dimness of the lounge. Connected to the redone, Chip Conley–managed Laurel Inn, formerly just a midtown motel, G Bar has the hipness of SOMA bars in staid Pacific Heights. It has become a big hit with a young Inner Richmond crowd and the discriminating who prefer elegant, top-shelf cocktails.

DELICATESSENS/TAKEOUT

BRYAN'S QUALITY MEATS. . . . .

3473 California Street
(between Spruce and Laurel)
415-752-3430
Open Monday through Friday
8 A.M. to 7 P.M.,
Saturday until 6 P.M.
Credit cards: MC, V

An appealing prepared-food case at the back of this butcher shop offers a wide array of reheatable prepared-meal components. See page 281 for more information.

MARUYA SUSHI . . . .

1904 Fillmore Street (at Bush)
415-921-2929
Open Tuesday through Sunday
11:00 A.M. to 6:30 P.M.
Cash only

On the face of it, sushi seems to be the perfect food to go. After all, it's supposed to be served at room temperature (though the fish is kept chilled before it is cut), and unlike salad, it doesn't wilt. But the fact is, held or refrigerated sushi loses its charm. The rice dries out and starts to separate and the delicate flavors of raw fish disappear. I always hesitate to buy prepackaged sushi in groceries because you don't know how long ago it was made. That's why tiny Maruya is such a find. All the delicate sushi is made to order, and only the delicious vegetarian selection, No. 9, which includes two kinds of nonfish sushi, is prepackaged, though usually the woman behind the counter only has one order available at any time. When that one is sold she prepares another. The four large pieces of pickle-and-vegetable-filled *maki* (a fat, seaweed-wrapped roll that is sliced into rounds), and three large balls of sushi rice sweetened just a bit and tossed with threads of seaweed, then wrapped in deep-fried tofu skin, add up to a light, delicious, and satisfying meal. You can almost feel each slightly chewy grain on your tongue, yet each finger of rice holds together as if by magic. A pyramid of wasabi, a packet of soy sauce, and a mound of pickled ginger threads nestle into one corner of the package along with green plastic grass and wooden chopsticks. Other types of sushi can be ordered by the piece or off a small menu of combinations. If the order is large or even small, calling ahead is a good idea since everything is made to order. The tiny shop holds a kitchen so miniature that you know that everything is made from scratch each day. Since Maruya is dedicated to takeout, the full attention of the sushi chef can be lavished on your order, with no demanding customers eating at the sushi bar to distract her. When a shop can sustain itself at this level of specialization, you know it makes something people really want.

VIVANDE PORTA VIA . . . .

2125 Fillmore Street (between
California and Sacramento)
415-346-4430
www.vivande.com
Open daily 10 A.M. to 10 P.M.
Credit Cards: AE, DC, D, MC,V

A wealth of Italian prepared dishes and ingredients
are temptingly offered at Carlo Middione's upscale
delicatessen and trattoria. See page 270 for more
information.

BAKERIES/PASTRIES

BAY BREAD . . . .

2325 Pine Street
(just below Fillmore)
415-440-0356
Open Tuesday through
Saturday 8 A.M. to 6 P.M.,
Sunday until 4 P.M.
Cash only

This very French bakery was the first in the Pascal Rigo
empire. (See Boulange de Polk, page 306) It is a
straight bakery without café amenities. However, Rigo
does own Chez Nous and the crêperie Galette around
the corner on Fillmore Street if you want to sit down.

DELANGHE PATISSERIE . . . .

1890 Fillmore Street (at Bush)
415-923-0711
Open Tuesday through Friday
7 A.M. to 6 P.M.,
Saturday 8 A.M. to 6 P.M.,
Sunday 8 A.M. to 2 P.M.
Cash only

What wonderful, buttery French sweet rolls come out
of the open kitchen of this one-man bakery run by
Dominique Delanghe! They are filled with fresh strawberries, plums, or apricots and a bit of custard. His
croissants taste like the real thing, flaky, buttery, handmade. Large *palmiers*, palm-leaf-shaped cookies made
of crisp, sugar-glazed puff pastry, dissolve on your
tongue. Miniature éclairs, chocolate-covered

madeleines, and meringue mushrooms make for charming after-dinner desserts with demi-
tasses of coffee. M. Delanghe makes a small version of the classic French wedding pastry
called *croquembouche*, a tower of little cream puffs filled with custard and held together with
caramel. These towering constructions serve twelve or more, and each serving of the dismantled puffs can be made more festive by drizzling a homemade chocolate sauce over or
under them. I can't walk by the shop, especially in the morning when the pastries are still
warm from the oven, without stopping in for at least one cheese-filled roll with a cup of
good coffee.

CHOCOLATE SAUCE

MAKES ABOUT 1 CUP

This is my recipe for the easiest and most luxurious dark chocolate sauce ever to moisten a cream puff.

¼ cup unsalted butter

3 ounces unsweetened baking chocolate

1 cup sugar

1 cup heavy whipping cream

In a saucepan over medium heat, melt the butter. Add the chocolate and melt, stirring constantly. Stir in the sugar until completely dissolved. Add the cream. Stir until incorporated and bring to a simmer for 1 minute. Serve hot or warm. This will keep in the refrigerator for at least a month if tightly covered, and may be rewarmed or eaten cold like fudge.

SWEET STOP . . . .

1790 Sutter Street (at Buchanan)
415-931-8165
Open Monday through Friday
9:30 A.M. to 5:30 P.M., Saturday
9:30 A.M. to 5:00 P.M.
Cash only

A little bakery counter in the Super Mira market, Yasukochi's Sweet Stop's claim to fame is the old Blum's Coffee Crunch Cake, so beloved by generations of San Franciscans. Somehow, Yasukochi became the repository for the secret recipe for this angel food cake layered with whipped cream, coffee cream, and paved with the famous crunch. The super-crisp coffee-flavored candy melts instantaneously on your tongue after delivering a thrilling initial crunch. It is a lovely cake with textural fireworks. The sliced white breads and coffee cakes are light and airy and beloved by children and people who like soft bakery products. Many people order whole coffee crunch cakes for special occasions, but if you shop early enough, before they have run out, you might be able to buy a slice.

ICE CREAM/CHOCOLATE

TANGO GELATO . . . .

2015 Fillmore Street (between Pine and California)
415-346-3692
www.tangogelato.com
Open Sunday through Thursday
noon to 10 P.M., Friday and
Saturday until 11 P.M.
Cash only

This Italian/Argentinean ice cream shop serves bright-flavored gelato and *sorbetto* in a pretty, cafélike environment. In summer when raspberries are plentiful, the *sorbetto* is thick with puréed berries including seeds. You really feel as if you're eating pure fruit. The lemon *sorbetto* has incredibly fresh, natural flavor, as if it were just squeezed. Unusual gelato flavors like coconut mix nicely with the fruit ices so you can construct your own spectacular *coppa mista*.

I'm a fan of smooth, semifrozen Italian ice cream because it is made with milk instead of cream. Hence it has low butterfat content (4 to 6 percent), which allows flavors to be more assertive. If the flavoring ingredients—chocolate, coffee, hazelnuts, fruits, and so forth—are fresh and natural as they are here, you get an exciting, voluptuous ice cream for half the calories.

The Argentina-Italy connection happened after World War II when many Italians immigrated to Argentina during the forties and fifties, creating a large community in Buenos Aires. The gelato maker at Tango Gelato, Eduardo Speco, has been making ice cream for twenty years in Buenos Aires and was persuaded to come here by the young Argentinean founder of Tango Gelato. There are currently two shops—the one on Fillmore Street and one in Oakland.

Those of you interested in tango dancing as well as gelato can come to free tango sessions (with demonstrations) put on by the Bay Area Argentine Tango Association at the *gelaterie* on the first and third Sundays of each month.

COFFEE

PEET'S COFFEE & TEA. . . . .

3419 California Street
(between Spruce and Laurel)
415-221-8506
Open Monday through Friday
6:30 A.M. to 7 P.M., Saturday and
Sunday 7 A.M. to 6 P.M.
Credit cards: AE, MC, V

A branch of the Bay Area's most impeccable coffee seller. See page 167 for more information.

MARKETS

CAL-MART . . . .

3585 California Street (at Spruce)
415-751-3516
Open Monday through Saturday
7 A.M. to 8:00 P.M.,
Sunday 8:30 A.M. to 6:30 P.M.
Credit cards: MC, V

A fine, versatile neighborhood grocery with a comprehensive produce section, Cal-Mart is further strengthened by Antonelli's Meat, Fish and Poultry counter (see page 281), one of the best in the city. While most of the produce is commercial, the Cal-Mart produce buyers do seek out local and organic farms for specialty items like little Yukon Gold potatoes, small red creamer potatoes, beautiful Flambeau radishes (pink and white oval shaped), organic cherry tomatoes from del Cabo farms in Baja California, out of season and local heirlooms tomatoes in season. Piles of stone fruits and myriad different berries look luscious, but are of varying quality. Ask one of the produce people always grooming the displays what has come in that's particularly delicious.

An active deli counter cranks out made-to-order sandwiches, rotisserie chickens, and pre-pared salads and entrées, while a bakery counter run by Sweet Things from Marin offers time-saving items like pints of fresh lemon curd and raspberry purée along with rich bar cookies and gooey cakes. All the major local bread bakeries deliver here daily, and all the upscale grocery standbys, like a full range of Häagen-Dazs ice cream products (a find at this level of completeness), make Cal-Mart a very useful independent grocery store. I consider it a destination supermarket worth a drive across town.

WARM BERRY COMPOTE

SERVES 4

The Cal-Mart produce section features berries, usually commercial ones, but a number of different kinds. This fast, simple recipe, adapted from Jeremiah Tower's *New American Classics*, turns any kind of berry into an opulent warm compote that tastes heavenly with vanilla ice cream.

½ cup sugar

¼ cup water

2 teaspoons fresh lemon juice

1 cup hulled fresh strawberries, halved

1 cup fresh blueberries, halved

1 cup fresh blackberries

¼ cup unsalted butter, cut into pieces

1 pint vanilla ice cream

In a large skillet, dissolve the sugar in the water by stir-ring over medium heat. Bring to a boil. Add the lemon juice and berries and cook over medium heat for 2 to 3 minutes. Swirl in the butter until it melts. Remove from the heat. Spoon into 4 shallow soup bowls and place scoops of vanilla ice cream in the center.

CHERRY CLAFOUTIS

SERVES 6

During the relatively short season in early summer for local Bing cherries, I make this unusual version of *clafoutis* from *Chez Panisse Fruit*. Because the fruit and the custard stay relatively separate, the flavor of the cherries dominates, gently set off by the barely sweetened spongelike custard. A subtle dessert, this cherry *clafoutis* with pits grows on you. I like it best cold or room temperature for breakfast. I made three of them during the season.

2 tablespoons unsalted butter

1 pound sweet or sour cherries, washed and stemmed

⅓ cup plus 3 tablespoons granulated sugar (⅓ cup for sweet cherries, ½ cup for sour cherries)

⅛ teaspoon ground cinnamon

¼ teaspoon grated lemon zest

2 eggs, separated

3 tablespoons flour

1 teaspoon vanilla extract

¼ teaspoon almond extract

⅓ cup heavy cream

Pinch of salt

Powdered sugar for dusting

1 Melt the butter in a sauté pan over medium heat. When the butter is foaming but hasn't begun to brown, add the cherries, ⅓ cup sugar, cinnamon, and lemon zest. Cook for 7 to 10 minutes, stirring occasionally, or until the cherries are tender when pierced with point of a small knife and the juices have begun to thicken. Arrange the cherries in the bottom of a 9-inch baking dish.

2 Preheat the oven to 375° F.

3 Beat the egg yolks and 3 tablespoons sugar together for several minutes, until light and creamy. Beat in the flour, vanilla and almond extracts, and cream.

4 In a separate bowl, beat the egg whites with the salt until they form soft peaks. Fold the whites into the batter just until blended, and pour the batter over the fruit.

5 Bake in the upper third of the oven for about 20 minutes, or until the batter is puffed and well browned. Let the *clafoutis* cool slightly, dust with powdered sugar, and serve.

MARUWA FOODS COMPANY . . . .

1737 Post Street (at Webster)
415-563-1901
Open daily 10 A.M. to 7 P.M.
Credit cards: MC, V

Owned by Koreans, Maruwa epitomizes the modern Asian supermarket, which features lots of precooked convenience foods to take out. A quick look at the pickle section confirms the Korean influence. Kimchis of chile-spiked daikon and cabbage share refrigerator space with salted Japanese pickles. Farther along the refrigerated case, simple steamed daikon mixed with other Asian vegetables, wrapped in plastic on Styrofoam boards, stands ready for immediate eating. Lots of fresh pristine-looking fish have been cut and packaged for sashimi, or marinated whole (but gutted and scaled, of course) in sake lees (*kasu*) or miso paste. Fish cakes in all shapes can be bought in bulk. The grocery aisles are stocked with Japanese ready-to-eat products: cereal, soft drinks (cold cans of Calpis Water), snacks, candy, as well as soup bases, rice, noodles, and other ingredients for cooking at home. For dessert, cartons of green tea or litchi ice cream beckon.

OLIVIERS & CO. . . . .

2208 Fillmore Street
(at Sacramento)
415-474-1408
www.oliviers-co.com
Open Monday through Saturday
11 A.M. to 7 P.M.,
Sunday until 6 P.M.
Credit cards: AE, MC, V

Olive oil is finally taking hold in the United States as more people begin to appreciate both its flavor and health benefits. Oliviers is a company from Haute Provence that has set up shops in France, Britain, and the United States to sell olive oil from different growing regions around the Mediterranean and Uruguay. While prices at these olive oil boutiques are hardly bargains, you do have the advantage of tasting before you buy, and that can really save you money. Nothing is worse than dropping $25 on a bottle of extra virgin oil that you don't like, especially since the ones you do can transform your cooking. You can use Oliviers as a learning tool, discovering that you really love the buttery Greek oil from the Peloponnese peninsula and don't actually like grassy French oils. Artisan oils from the best growing regions are all represented so you really can cultivate your palate.

Oliviers sells many other products as well—olive pastes, biscuits, kitchenware, books, olive oil soap, salts, herbs, and spices—which are available at the shops and on-line. But the value of visiting the stores to taste the different oils cannot be underestimated. If you want to explore olive oil—and you should because it's so delicious and versatile—drop in at Oliviers.

SUPER MIRA. . . . .

1790 Sutter Street (at Buchanan)
415-921-6529
Open Monday through Saturday
9:30 A.M. to 7 P.M.,
Sunday 11 A.M. to 6 P.M.
Credit cards: MC, V

The cognoscenti in Japantown shop at the immaculate Super Mira grocery, where the fish cut for sashimi, tightly wrapped in clear plastic, look opalescent. A trip to this market inspires you to serve your own Japanese meal at home since you can buy most of the components already prepared: seaweed salad in sesame oil with red chiles; octopus and cucumber salad; jellyfish salad; ready-made sushi; sliced fresh *hamachi* (yellowtail) and *toro* (the rare belly cut of tuna) for sashimi; all sorts of other ready-to-eat sliced raw fish. With Japanese beer of every kind and sake, you have the components of an impressive Japanese spread.

For dessert you can go Western with a Blum's-style Coffee Crunch cake from the Sweet Stop bakery counter inside the store (page 275), or Japanese with the packages of four homemade mochi balls filled with red bean paste at the cash register. These *mochi* balls made by a local Japanese woman will make you rethink the Asian dessert. The homemade red bean paste has richness and depth of flavor that almost makes it taste chocolatey. The *mochi*, usually made of straight rice flour, has amazing texture, with whole grains of sticky rice barely holding together. One ball is dusted with toasted sesame seeds; another with ground peanuts; another with black sesame seeds and ground black tea; and one is encased in red bean paste with the luscious sticky rice in the center. These rice balls will finally make you understand the appeal of Japanese sweets.

For slightly more ambitious cooks, paper-thin slices of beef for sukiyaki, *capellini*-thin baby eels, fish cakes, fresh tofu, and fresh roe of all kinds inspire you to get out a Japanese cookbook. All the makings for miso broth and bonito stock are here, along with a healthy-looking produce section, the nicest in Japantown, with fresh burdock root, baby turnips, *shiso* leaves, firm Japanese cucumbers, plump unblemished lotus root, mountain potatoes, and even tiny green plums for pickling. Whole fish, staring out at you with clear, glassy eyes from behind the immaculate sashimi counter, and fillets marinating in sake *kasu* (the lees of sake) or white miso paste stand ready to be broiled. Everything at Super Mira looks so neat and pristine, from the vegetables to the fish, that you trust that even the marinated fish will be fresh.

UOKI MARKET . . . .

1656 Post Street (between
Buchanan and Laguna)
415-921-0515
Open Monday through Saturday
9 A.M. to 6 P.M.,
Sunday 10 A.M. to 5:30 P.M.
Credit cards: V, MC

The fish at the ever-busy Uoki Market fish counter is not prepackaged or precut, and often not precleaned. You have to wait for service at this counter, as you do in the Chinatown bustle, to get your allotment of small clams, fresh squid, fat tentacles of octopus, hunks of tuna, and whole salmon. The busy fish clerks will cut small pieces to order and the quality is generally high.

The produce section is not as carefully weeded of old vegetables as at Super Mira, but there is a larger section of vacuum-packed cured and pick-led vegetables. Of course Uoki Market has whole aisles of jarred pickles in neon colors to put on rice, tea, soup mix, candy, big sacks of organic California short-grain rice for the larder, plus up-to-the-minute imports of Japanese breakfast cereal and snacks.

MEAT AND POULTRY

ANTONELLI'S MEAT, FISH, AND POULTRY . .

3585 California Street (between
Laurel and Spruce, in the Cal-Mart)
415-752-7413
Open Monday through Saturday
8 A.M. to 7 P.M.,
Sunday 8:30 A.M. to 6:30 P.M.
Credit cards: MC, V

Antonelli's is the only source in the city for some of my favorite lamb, Bruce and Nancy Campbell's C. K. Lamb from Healdsburg. Their lambs may be a bit larger than the Superior lambs from Dixon sold at many butcher shops in the city, but they have real character without ever being muttony. One evening I roasted C. K. and Superior racks of lamb next to each other; the C. K. lamb had a deeper flavor and more personality while being just as tender. The C. K. racks turned out to be a couple of dollars more expensive because the bones were larger, but this lamb earns its higher price.

The chicken counter features hormone-free Fulton Valley chickens, which to my mind are some of the best commercial chickens on the market. They have character without any off flavors and they roast up like a dream. The small, fresh Fulton Valley turkey parts carried here are also delicious and an underused meat alternative. What could be better, or easier to cook, than golden-skinned roast turkey breast for dinner, with leftovers for sandwiches the next day?

Since Antonelli's started out as a fish and poultry vendor, you can expect to find seafood treasures, like jars of tiny Pacific oysters from Johnson's Oyster Company in Point Reyes or fresh whole sand dabs with clear eyes. Antonelli's still cuts halibut and salmon steaks, which actually grill up more evenly than fillets (which are also sold), though you have to contend with a few bones and skin. The meat and fish counter is as complete as Bryan's down the block, with a stronger everyday poultry section and special lamb that make it an invaluable resource.

BRYAN'S QUALITY MEATS . . . .

3473 California Street (between
Spruce and Laurel)
415-752-3430
Open Monday through Friday
8 A.M. to 7 P.M.,
Saturday until 6 P.M.
Credit cards: MC, V

Bryan's operated the meat counter at the Cal-Mart for thirty years, but nine years ago opened its own store a few doors away. Now Bryan's has become one of the best all-around butchers in the city. In addition to meat, the shop has separate counters for fish, poultry, and an ever-growing selection of attractive prepared foods. Although the fresh corn salad, old-fashioned potato salads, platters of roasted vegetables, and rotisserie-roasted organic chickens entice as you walk in the back door from the Laurel Village parking area, the beauty of the raw ingredients here inspires home cooking.

Bryan's dry ages its own prime beef for four weeks. You can taste the pedigree in an expensive Prime market steak (call for availability)—fat-marbled, tender, with tons of flavor. The Choice beef comes from Harris Ranch, which I have come to admire for its consistency and lively western flavor. Bryan's dry ages its California lamb for two weeks as well, and the racks, completely trimmed of fat and with a plump loin, are marvelously juicy and refined in flavor. Fresh country-style pork ribs and pork roasts and chops make for another dinner alternative. Anyone who has run out of cooking ideas only needs to step into this shop.

Of course chicken and fish have become staples in a health-conscious diet and Bryan's has taken up the banner. Terry Flannery, the son of the founder, has put together the prettiest fish counter in town. He knows how to buy and who to buy from. I have seen salmon, tuna, striped bass, fresh day-boat scallops, fresh shrimp, delicious northern halibut, swordfish, and seasonal items like soft-shell crabs and shad roe in pristine condition. He is not afraid to stock unusual fish like bright red true snappers from the Gulf of Mexico, whose eyes were so bright one day they looked as if they had just been pulled in from the water. The seafood chowder, sold refrigerated by the pint, is one of the best I have tasted anywhere, and the notion of offering fresh mango salsa at the fish counter is inspired. Moving over to poultry, Bryan's carries poussin, or baby chicken. Pale-skinned and without fat, they cook up moist, tender, and full of flavor. Ducks from Grimaud Farms, local quail, and excellent, tender squab figuratively fly out the door. The freshest little rabbits I have seen in a market are displayed next to the game birds.

On top of all the choice raw materials, Terry Flannery knows where to get the best restaurant-quality cured and smoked items, like Hobbs's bacon and hams. He's got artisan breads; a few crucial produce items like shallots, garlic, onions, lemons, and potatoes and a few seasonal vegetables like asparagus and slender green beans.

When you buy something of the highest quality, hand cut and perfectly fresh, you do not need a lot of it. Bryan's charges for the quality, but the pleasure of eating fine meat, fish, and poultry goes a long way.

FISH

ANTONELLI'S MEAT, FISH AND POULTRY . .

3585 California Street (between
Laurel and Spruce in the Cal-Mart)
415-752-7413
Open Monday through Saturday
8 A.M. to 7 P.M.,
Sunday 8:30 A.M. to 6:30 P.M.
Credit cards: MC, V

Antonelli's started out as a fish and poultry vendor before it branched out to meat, so the counter is an excellent source for fish and shellfish. See page 281 for more information.

LAMB'S TONGUE SALAD

SERVES 6 TO 8

I made this salad for a "spare parts" dinner celebrating Alice Waters's birthday. My cooking guru, Niloufer Ichaporia King, came up with the theme and she made *kharia*, a spicy Parsi stew of pig's feet and black-eyed peas. The salad was a big hit with the fourteen women who attended the party. The tender, velvety tongues, cut into little slices, were not identifiable, and the combination of sparkly, tart dressing, greens, and turnips was stunning. Antonelli's Meat, Fish and Poultry (see page 281) in the Cal-Mart will get the tongues for you with two days' notice.

TONGUES

6 lamb's tongues

3 quarts water

1 tablespoon kosher salt

1 celery stalk

1 carrot

1 onion stuck with 4 cloves

6 sprigs thyme

SALAD

6 young turnips
(about 2 inches in diameter)

2 bunches watercress

2 heads frisée

DRESSING

½ cup chopped shallots

1 teaspoon kosher salt

Juice of 2 limes

1 jalapeño chile, finely chopped

1 bunch cilantro, finely chopped

1 cup light olive oil or peanut oil

1 Combine the tongues with the water, salt, celery, carrot, onion, and thyme. Bring to a boil and simmer for 2 hours, or until very tender. The tongues should offer no resistance when pricked with a knife. Let cool in the cooking liquid, then peel them and trim off any fat and little bones. Set each tongue on its side and slice crosswise.

2 Peel the turnips and into ¼-inch julienne. Bring a small pan of salted water to a boil and add the turnip sticks. When the water returns to a boil, set your timer for 1 minute. They should be crisp-tender. Drain the turnips and place under running cold water. Let drain again.

3 Remove most of the stems from the watercress. Cut off green parts of the frisée. Wash and dry the greens.

4 Prepare the dressing. Put the shallots in a bowl and add the salt and lime. Let sit for 10 minutes. Add the chile to taste and the cilantro. Whisk in the oil. (The dressing should be more like a bright, tart relish than a vinaigrette.) Taste for salt. The intensity of the salt and lime should be equal. You should be able to taste both immediately in a balanced dressing.

5 Toss the watercress and frisée with some of the dressing and line a platter or large, flat bowl with the greens. Toss the tongue and turnips together with some of the dressing and scatter on top of the greens.

BRYAN'S QUALITY MEATS . . . .

3473 California Street (between
Spruce and Laurel)
415-752-3430
Open Monday through Friday
8 A.M. to 7 P.M.,
Saturday until 6 P.M.
Credit cards: MC, V

Though Bryan's made its reputation on meat, I consider its retail fish counter to be the best in the city. See page 281 for more information.

UOKI MARKET . . . .

1656 Post Street (between
Buchanan and Laguna)
415-921-0515
Open Monday through Saturday
9 A.M. to 6 P.M.,
Sunday 10 A.M. to 5:30 P.M.
Credit cards: V, MC

A small selection of seafood tailored for the Japanese kitchen is freshly cut and portioned here. See page 280 for more information.

CHEESE

ARTISAN CHEESE . . . .

2413 California Street (at Fillmore)
415-929-8610
www.cowgirlcreamery.com
Open Monday through Friday
11 A.M. to 6 P.M., Saturday and
Sunday 10 A.M to 6 P.M.
Credit cards: V, MC

As its name implies, this sliver of a shop is dedicated to selling only handcrafted and farmstead cheeses. It barely looks stocked, but the plain wooden counter holds a wealth of unique cheese. Its co-owner, Peggy Smith, and her French assistant work the counter like a piano, rhythmically unwrapping, shaving, cutting, and rewrapping cheese until their customers find what they want.

Each cheese has a story that you can taste. It's quite phenomenal. An aged Gouda—crumbly, buttery, nutty, amazingly complex, like none other I've tasted—turns out to come from Winchester, California (seventy miles north of San Diego), made by the daughter of a Dutch-American dairyman with five hundred Holsteins. They sold their first cheese in 1996. It won the highest honors at the cheese judging in Holland. Another rarity is a stunning buttery but sharp Cheddar from Bravo farms in Visalia (in the heart of the Central Valley)—the only farmstead raw milk Cheddar made in California.

While Smith combs America for artisan cheese, she and partner Sue Conley, of the Cowgirl Creamery in Inverness, also bring in artisan cheeses from Europe and Britain, such as the farmstead cheeses from Neal's Yard Dairy, and cheeses from Jean d'Alos, Bordeaux's great cheese gatherer and *affineur*.

Now I can hear you muttering, "I don't really like strong cheese or smelly cheese, and I'm not fond of goat cheese and isn't sheep cheese like that?" Stop. It's time to cultivate your cheese palate. The rewards are enormous. You will actually be able to experience something that is the best in the world for a few affordable dollars—depending, of course, on how much you buy. Here's how to start: visit Artisan Cheese. Tasting is encouraged.

WINES AND SPIRITS

WINE IMPRESSION . . . .

3461 California Street
(at Locust in Laurel Village)
415-221-9463
Open Monday through Saturday
10 A.M. to 8 P.M.,
Sunday 10 A.M. to 6 P.M.
Credit cards: AE, D, MC, V

My spirits expert (who happens to be my husband) says that Wine Impression carries the best and hardest to find booze no matter what the type: Chinaco Tequila, Bookers and Basil Hayden bourbons, organic Juniper Green gin, high-quality French and Italian vermouths, rye whiskey like Old Overholt, cognacs, Armagnacs, and single-malt scotches, to name just a few of the bottles that attract the connoisseur of spirits. If you're a cocktail lover or like your liquor straight up, stock your cabinet here.

COOKWARE AND BOOKS

BOOKS, INC. . . . .

3515 California Street
(at Locust in Laurel Village)
415-221-3666
Open daily 9 A.M. to 7 P.M.
Credit cards: AE, D, MC, V

This smallish, but amazingly well-stocked bookstore has a cookbook remainder table, with interesting titles at 50 to 90 percent off retail price. Next to the remainders, a whole table of new books at full price titillates the seemingly insatiable cookbook buyer. (The repetition of subject matter in books stylishly devoted to one ingredient makes me wonder how many recipes anyone needs for potatoes, green salad, or chicken.) Books, Inc.'s many shelves of cookbooks do contain an intelligently chosen inventory of classics. For those who associate food with travel, the excellent travel section is stocked with an unusual number of food guides to different countries.

FORREST JONES. . . . .

3274 Sacramento Street
(between Presidio and Lyon)
415-567-2483
www.forrestjones.com
Open Monday through Saturday
10 A.M. to 6 P.M.,
Sunday 11 A.M. to 5 P.M.
Credit cards: AE, MC, V

This cleverly stocked housewares shop often has the very thing you've been looking for all over town, like a plain, heavy glass cake dome (without the plate) or large, white rectangular platters at half off the original price, which I found there between Thanksgiving and Christmas one year. Tons of baskets, including the current rage, Via Motif–covered storage baskets from Indonesia, tote bags, dish towels, Roger and Gallet soaps by the bar, sturdy glassware, and an ever-changing array of goods that households really need make Forrest Jones an invaluable resource, well worth checking out before or after you've shopped elsewhere.

KINOKUNIYA BOOKSTORE . . . .

Japan Center, 1581 Webster
(between Post and Geary)
415-567-7625
Open daily 10:30 A.M. to 8 P.M.
Credit cards: AE, D, MC, V

This spacious book emporium has racks full of Japanese food and housekeeping magazines written in Japanese, but also a large, interesting collection of Asian cookbooks in English. This is the place to find Chinese, Indian, Thai, Burmese, or Indonesian cookbooks in paper- and hardback, not to mention a superior collection of Japanese cookbooks, including Shizuo Tsuji's *Japanese Cooking: A Simple Art*, the definitive Japanese cookbook in English with a foreword by M. F. K. Fisher. Books on Japanese country cooking, on culinary artifacts of Japan illustrated with lively black-and-white photos, and an international survey of rice cookery are but a few of the gems to be mined. Kinokuniya has the best vegetarian and macrobiotic cookbook section in the city; the titles fill many shelves. The variety of meatless dishes in Asian cuisines stretches the imagination, and even the most exotic ingredients for many of the recipes can be found nearby. The cookbook aisle segues right into the Asian massage and sexual instruction section, a juxtaposition I find salubrious.

MASHIKO FOLKCRAFT. . . . .

Japan Center, 1581 Webster
(between Post and Geary)
415-346-0748
Open Wednesday through Monday
11 A.M. to 6 P.M.,
Sunday 11 A.M. to 5 P.M.
Credit cards: AE, MC, V

The uncased displays in this intimate shop of antique Japanese tableware tempt you to pick up things for close examination, but the eagle-eyed store owner will scold you if he catches you. Nineteenth-century wooden buckets for $7,500 and small antique chests sit next to contemporary bamboo noodle trays. There are lyrical, handmade rice containers carved of cedar; hand-thrown tea mugs at $22; wooden water ladles for the garden fountain; and ladles made of bamboo for the Japanese tea ceremony. The shapes and sizes of the singularly glazed ceramics expand your idea of dinnerware. Many of the prices here have caught up to those at Gump's, but there are still bargains to be found. A visit to this small shop of exotic and beautiful things would certainly solve the problem of finding an exquisite house gift or wedding present for people with worldly taste.

SANKO COOKING SUPPLY . . . .

1758 Buchanan Street (at Sutter)
415-922-8331
Open Monday through Saturday
9:30 A.M. to 6 P.M.,
Sunday 11:30 A.M. to 5 P.M.
Credit cards: AE, MC, V

Looking for an electric rice maker, a rectangular cast-iron skillet for making sweet Japanese omelets, a ginger grater, Japanese knives, ridged Japanese mortars, cast-iron sukiyaki pots, or any shape and size of ceramic dish and lacquered bowl? These and every other utensil or vessel you might need for Asian cooking and serving can be found here at reasonable prices.

SOKO HARDWARE CO. . . . .

1698 Post Street (at Buchanan)
415-931-5510
Open Monday through Saturday
9 A.M. to 5:30 P.M.
Credit cards: MC, V

My husband spotted a most attractive cracked-glaze Japanese vase in the window here nine years ago. It looked like something rare, but it cost $70. Now, anytime either of us walks by Soko Hardware, we dash in for a quick look at the ceramics on the main floor. You never know what treasure you might find. Downstairs, everything from child-sized chopsticks with Eggplant Club, Potato Club, and Turnip Club inscribed on them to gorgeous, heavy $295 cast-iron *miso shiro* kettles with thick wooden tops are filed away someplace in the vast housewares department. I'm a sucker for this store. I love the tiny dishes the size of a half dollar, and the earthy, glazed rectangles of pottery that look as if their edges were torn and bent. I imagine putting together an elegant Japanese table with this pottery, and salads, sushi, and sashimi bought at Super Mira (see page 280), but laying Super Hero chopsticks at each place. Upstairs, along with the Japanese carpentry tools and larger ceramics, a rack of Japanese seeds for burdock, cucumber, and *shiso* snags you on the way out.

SUE FISHER-KING . . . .

3067 Sacramento Street
(between Broderick and Baker)
415-922-7276
www.suefisherking.com
Open Monday to Saturday
10 A.M. to 6 P.M.
Credit cards: AE, MC, V

If you're looking for top-of-the-line imports like Italian tablecloths and napkins, or wonderful, oversized French silverware with bone or wooden handles at top-of-the-line prices, Sue Fisher-King has an exclusive, personal selection. Her table of cookbooks is also worth a look for the quirkiness of what's there. I usually find something I didn't know I was looking for.

VIKING HOMECHEF . . . .

3525 California Street (at Locust)
415-668-3191
www.homechef.com
Open Monday through Thursday
10 A.M. to 6:30 P.M., Friday and
Saturday 10 A.M. to 6 P.M., Sunday
11 A.M. to 5 P.M.
Credit cards: AE, MC, V

A complete collection of cooking utensils and some serving and tableware fill the shelves of this densely packed store. It seems to me that the most important tool in any kitchen is a decent knife that is heavy enough to keep an edge, yet many home kitchens overflow with doodads without a decent cutting tool to be found. Viking Homechef does everyone a favor by putting first-class imported knives from Solingen, Germany, plus their own brand of chef's knives, front and center in the shop. Before people move on to the miniature tart pans and the food processors, they ought to buy themselves one good knife. Having gotten that off my chest, I was happy to see Krups ice cream makers, an ingenious invention that only requires the freezer section of your refrigerator and a minimum of arm power to quickly turn out fresh fruit ices and ice cream (so wonderful during the summer fruit season). If you're a pots-and-pans fan, the store carries the latest in nonstick technologies. And if you want cooking inspiration, the store puts on cooking classes in its glassed-in demonstration kitchen, the aromas from which make you want to sign up on the spot.

A SMALL JAPANTOWN DETOUR

A whole row of original Victorian cottages still stands along one side of a miniature park on Cottage Row, a block-long street that runs between Sutter and Bush just west of Webster Street. These dwellings are the only remnants of the original Japanese neighborhood that was destroyed during the redevelopment of Japantown, according to Yoko Tahara, a personal friend and longtime resident of the neighborhood both before and after her family's deportation to relocation camps during World War II. Take a stroll down the brick pathway to get a closer look at the lovingly maintained cottages and gardens. This is one of the most charming secret streets in San Francisco.

POLK STREET
NOB HILL
RUSSIAN HILL
VAN NESS AVENUE

POLK STREET, NOB HILL, RUSSIAN HILL & VAN NESS AVENUE

RESTAURANTS

1 Acquerello
2 Antica Trattoria
3 Cordon Bleu
4 East Coast West Delicatessen
5 Golden Turtle
6 Harris' Restaurant
7 House of Prime Rib
8 La Folie
9 Le Petit Robert
10 Nob Hill Grille
11 Pesce
12 Ritz-Carlton Dining Room
13 Spoon
14 Swan Oyster Depot
15 Tai Chi
16 Venticello
17 Zarzuela

BARS

18 Cinch Saloon
6 Harris' Restaurant
19 Laurel Court Bar at the Fairmont
20 Pasha
21 Top of the Mark

DELICATESSENS/TAKEOUT

4 East Coast West Delicatessen
22 Piccadilly Fish and Chips

BAKERIES/PASTRIES

23 The Bagelry
24 Bob's Donuts
25 Boulange de Polk

ICE CREAM/CHOCOLATES

26 See's Candies
27 Swenson's

COFFEE

28 Peet's Coffee & Tea

MARKETS

29 Real Food Company
30 Whole Foods Market

PRODUCE

29 Real Food Company

MEAT AND POULTRY

30 Whole Foods Market

FISH

13 Swan Oyster Depot

CHEESE

31 Leonard's 2001
30 Whole Foods Market

WINES AND SPIRITS

32 The Jug Shop
33 William Cross Wine Merchants

COOKWARE AND BOOKS

34 City Discount

N

COLUMBUS

FILBERT

34
2
17

UNION
8
25
9
27

GREEN

33
11
13

VALLEJO

28 29
5
20 23

BROADWAY | | | | | | | | | | | | TUNNEL | | | | | | | |

15
6
31

PACIFIC

32

W

JACKSON <<<

AVENUE

NESS

POLK

7

WASHINGTON >>>

4
18

16

VAN

CLAY >>>

1 24

SACRAMENTO <<<

26
14 3

> >
> >

GRACE
CATHEDRAL

19

E

CALIFORNIA

30

^
^ ^
^ ^

v
v v
v v

v v v
v v v

^ ^ ^
^ ^ ^

v
v 21
v

12

PINE

22

10

<<<

FRANKLIN

LARKIN

HYDE

LEAVENWORTH

JONES

TAYLOR

MASON

POWELL

STOCKTON

BUSH

>>>

SUTTER <<<

POST >>>

S

0 SCALE MILES .25

RESTAURANTS

ACQUERELLO . . . .

1722 Sacramento Street
(between Polk and Van Ness)
415-567-5432
www.acquerello.com
Open Tuesday through Saturday
5:30 to 10:30 P.M.
Expensive
Credit cards: AE, DC, D, MC, V

Chef Suzette Gresham and maître d'–Italian wine expert Giancarlo Paterlini have formed an inspired partnership at their jewel of a restaurant. They both believe in refinement and civility, and insist on the highest quality in performance and ingredients. A meal at Acquerello affords its patrons a moment of pure luxury, not necessarily of the elaborate or showy sort, but of the quiet, deeply satisfying sort—perhaps because the wrapping on the package is Italian rather than French.

The food is a little bit fancy, but held down to earth because of the Italian idiom. Gresham's house-made pastas have the texture of silk, yet her rustic sauces deliver the vitality of the countryside even though they're really quite refined. She uses fresh herbs like a fine oil painter, each small stroke adding dimension. Her antipasti are particularly inventive, as evidenced by a warm squab salad with chard sprinkled with extra-virgin olive oil and toasted pine nuts; or tomato slices spread with a paste of anchovies, capers, and cooked egg yolk. The main courses bring roasted quail stuffed with pancetta; a classic Florentine preparation of sole rolled around spinach; or beef fillet stuffed with prosciutto, Parmesan, and rosemary. Her cooking imagination is fertile and she is not timid about trying new dishes, though always with the control of a dedicated professional chef. An ambitious program of special dinners, based around the wines of a certain region or celebrating a single ingredient, such as tomatoes, pasta, or seafood, is worth following because they represent excellent all-inclusive buys.

Equal to the pleasure of eating such lovely food is the experience of being in Paterlini's watercolor-filled dining room. To my mind he has always been the best captain in the city. He knows how to make everyone feel like a million bucks—special, cared for, intelligent, sophisticated—by gently offering guidance, helping people get to the best his restaurant has to offer in just the way that will please them. His expertise on Italian wines, and his generosity in cracking open wonderful bottles to pour glasses that fit each course, expands the whole sensual landscape of the meal. The quiet, anticipatory service, the sparkle of the silver and glasses on the table, the unflagging attention to every detail, all speak to Paterlini's highly trained European sensibility, one that understands and appreciates the tradition of service. This unique restaurant maintains a loyal following of people who like to be treated well.

ANTICA TRATTORIA . . . .

2400 Polk Street (at Union)
415-928-5797
Open Sunday, Tuesday through
Thursday 5:30 to 9:30 P.M.,
Friday and Saturday until 10:30 P.M.
Moderate
Credit cards: DC, D, MC, V

I was first attracted to Antica by its spare, timeless, essentially Italian look. Everyone loves Antica's resonant dark wood walls and floors. A distressed cream-colored paint job covers the ceiling from which hang stunning bowl-shaped light fixtures. Dark wood banquettes run along two walls with brown wooden chairs pushed up to them. The rest of the decor consists of white linen–covered tables with white butcher paper. A partially open kitchen at the back and a maître d' stand at the front with flowers are the only other visual details. Being in this stark and rustic room makes you want to drink Italian wine and eat pasta.

The food matches the decor. A bare-bones menu offers a handful of antipasti, pasta dishes, and main courses served in European-sized portions. For once, they aren't gigantic. If it's winter, start with a ramekin of braised leeks napped in *fonduta* (a white sauce of melted fontina) infused with white truffle oil, or a plate of brussels sprouts in brown butter and capers. Have a flat bowl of whole wheat spaghetti tossed in a lot of deep-flavored bolognese sauce. A rosemary-scented seared chicken breast comes on a bed of saucy white beans and black cabbage presented on a small oval plate. Drink soft, fruity sangiovese or dolcetto. Prices for wine and food are wonderfully affordable. I like everything about Antica's authenticity, restraint, simple presentation, no-nonsense Italian waiters, muted lighting, international clientele. Somehow the folks behind it have come up with a concept that's so old, it feels new.

CORDON BLEU . . . .

1574 California Street (near Polk)
415-673-5637
Open Tuesday through Saturday
11:30 A.M. to 2:30 P.M. and
5 to 10 P.M., Sunday 4 to 10 P.M.
Inexpensive
Cash only

The tiny Cordon Bleu, one of the city's first Vietnamese eateries, reminds me of food stalls in tropical Asia where cooks set up their steamers and grills right on the street. I have eaten the best chicken of my life at a card table and folding chair on a Bangkok sidewalk; the Cordon Bleu uncannily replicates this experience. Though there are a front door and ceiling, the painted brick walls suggest food operations set up in a crevice between two buildings with a canopy overhead. Very little light filters into Cordon Bleu during the day; at night a few dim bulbs barely do the job. People squeeze onto stools at a counter in the front of a small stove and grill or sit at two tiny tables at the back. Every time the door opens a blast of cold air sweeps into the room.

This authentic atmosphere only makes the five-spice roast chicken, the house specialty, taste better. For an extremely small tariff you get a half chicken, aromatically marinated, and a pile of crunchy cabbage and carrot salad with a large dollop of rice moistened with a Vietnamese version of bolognese sauce. Only two other dishes are available: crisply deep-fried imperial rolls stuffed with ground shrimp, pork, and vegetables, and beef on skewers, both of which come with the sauced rice and salad. Whatever the combination, all these foods are wonderfully satisfying eaten together. While not as refined or authentic as the top Vietnamese places, Cordon Bleu has maintained a strong neighborhood following by turning out hearty plates of good chicken year after year.

EAST COAST WEST DELICATESSEN . . . . . .

1725 Polk Street (near Washington)
415-563-3542
Open daily 8 A.M. to 9 P.M.
Inexpensive
Credit cards: AE, D, MC, V

I'm happy to report that this scrappy little deli does it all: matzoh ball soup, chopped chicken liver, gefilte fish, pickled herring, herring salad, smoked whitefish salad, stuffed cabbage, braised brisket, chicken in a pot, potato pancakes, and blintzes. All of it tastes home-made—good homemade, not bad homemade. This is a big event for our westward-looking Pacific Rim city with a Jewish population so assimilated they only eat chicken liver on crostini and smoked salmon with capers. (I know because I'm one of them.) The two professionally trained San Francisco chef-owners apply the principles of good cooking to all these traditional East Coast Ashkenazi dishes, but understand their homey nature. East Coast West chicken broth, for example, is clear and full flavored. It captures the essence of real chicken—not powdered chicken soup base—and you can feel each spoonful restoratively coursing through your system. And the matzoh balls have delightful springiness and actually make something out of the elusive qualities of matzoh meal and egg, gilded with a soupçon of chicken fat. I could go on and on about the prepared foods here, but most people immediately think of corned beef and pastrami sandwiches with the mention of deli. East Coast West puts out a properly spicy, peppery, fat-laced hot pastrami sandwich accompanied with an ample portion of clean, sprightly coleslaw as well as a small new pickle. The corned beef, locally cured, is too lean and boring for my taste.

East Coast West feels like a real deli with a long counter at the front for takeout and a small dining room at the back for sit down at sturdy Formica deli tables and wooden chairs. But the service is way too nice for a deli. No crusty, short-tempered waiters here; just fresh, young faces eager to please.

GOLDEN TURTLE. . . . .

2211 Van Ness Avenue (between Broadway and Vallejo)
415-441-4419
www.goldenturtle.net
Open Tuesday through Sunday
5 to 11 P.M.
Inexpensive
Credit cards: AE, MC, V

A visit to the comfortable dining room of this first-class Vietnamese restaurant will net you one of the nicest meals in town for the most reasonable price. The small multilevel restaurant is decorated with wall murals hand-carved in wood, and light sconces made of gnarled tree branches. The tables are set with wine-glasses and tablecloths. At first, you think you've walked into a French restaurant—until the piles of exotic fresh herbs, cold noodles, and lettuces start coming. Many dishes at the Golden Turtle deliver the classic Vietnamese juxtaposition of hot and savory with cold and crisp, such as hot, crisp crab-filled spring rolls, which you eat in lettuce leaves with sprigs of fresh mint, cilantro, cold white rice noodles, and a dip into a piquant sauce.

Another brilliant combination brings five-spice roast chicken with golden skin and velvety, aromatic flesh, served on a bed of juicy Vietnamese vegetable slaw in a sparkly dressing—a dish I could eat every day. The menu offers one delight after another: a whole fresh sea bass gently steamed, cleanly sauced, and topped with fresh herbs and ginger threads, or thinly sliced grilled beef marinated in lemongrass and served on a watercress salad. Quail, for which Vietnamese cooks have a special affection, is prepared in several different ways and all are worth ordering. The consistently meticulous preparation and high-quality ingredients insisted on in this kitchen make almost every dish a revelation. The graceful waitstaff in long skirts or tunics and pants is well-informed and efficient, and they know how to serve the wines on the small but choice wine list, which includes some French whites that go superbly with the food. Golden Turtle meals work as either satisfying, everyday fare or as special-occasion food. The beauty is that you can eat so well and so elegantly for a song.

HARRIS' RESTAURANT . . . .

2100 Van Ness Avenue (at Pacific)
415-673-1888
www.harrisrestaurant.com
Open Monday through Thursday
5:30 P.M. to 9:30 P.M.,
Friday 5:30 P.M. to 10 P.M.,
Saturday 5 P.M. to 10 P.M.,
Sunday 5 P.M. to 9:30 P.M.
Expensive
Credit cards: AE, DC, D, MC, V

Anne Harris, the founding spirit behind Harris', moved to Phoenix and opened a second restaurant, and her longtime San Francisco chef took over the helm here and became a partner. He maintains the standards in this luxurious restaurant with king-sized upholstered booths, tall potted palms, a huge wall mural by Barnaby Conrad, and a clubby bar (see page 303). The menu is steak-house simple and well executed: juicy grilled Harris Ranch steaks (my favorite is the Harris Steak, a New York with the featherbone left on), baked potatoes with butter, sour cream, and real bacon bits;

excellent creamed spinach; and for starters, oysters on the half shell; a tasty Caesar with freshly made croutons; spinach salad with sieved eggs. Wine drinkers can find a big California red with some age on it on the multipaged wine list, but many stick to cocktails. The Harris combination of luxury and steak works.

HOUSE OF PRIME RIB . . . .

1906 Van Ness Avenue (between Jackson and Washington)
415-885-4605
www.houseofprimerib.citysearch.com
Open Monday through Thursday
5:30 to 10 P.M., Friday 5 to 10 P.M.,
Saturday 4:30 to 10 P.M.,
Sunday 4 to 10 P.M.
Moderate
Credit cards: AE, DC , MC, V

A restaurant that serves slabs of roast beef (with a bone if you want, and I do) carved tableside from huge silver carts should be protected like a national treasure. In this town, the House of Prime Rib practically has that designation since it's the last outpost for this kind of eating nearly anywhere. For one all-inclusive, astonishingly moderate price you get a heap of chopped salad dressed tableside in the famous spinning salad bowl. The waitress spins the bowl on a bed of ice as she pours pink dressing from on high and then madly tosses. She dishes it up on chilled plates and hands out frosted forks right from the freezer. This ritual is follow by the slicing of the roast beef, which is served with a baked potato with real sour cream, bacon bits, chives and butter, and Yorkshire pudding. You can decide if you're up to dessert—a sweet but well-made pecan pie. The chef, Chuck Phifer, is an old friend of *Fannie Farmer* cooking doyenne Marion Cunningham and has a like-minded affection for American desserts. The old-fashioned windowless restaurant has many rooms and a large bar that is particularly active preprandially. Thick carpeting, booths, and heavy linen set a steak-house tone, while the exterior of the building is decorated with an arresting trompe l'oeil mural. Service is professional if scripted, the wine list barely serviceable, and the experience of dining there totally and wonderfully predictable. People who love prime rib don't want any surprises.

LA FOLIE . . . .

2316 Polk Street (between
Green and Union)
415-776-5577
www.lafolie.com
Open: Monday through Saturday
5:30 P.M. to 10:30 P.M.
Expensive
Credit cards: MC, V

Though La Folie is ranked as a top San Francisco restaurant year after year, I had no occasion to eat there in over a decade. Chef-owner Roland Passot reminded me of this when I ran into him at the Ferry Plaza Farmers' Market one Saturday where he was giving a cooking demonstration. He told me that his cooking had changed, and he looked so radiantly happy and self-confident that I had to believe him.

Passot was a wunderkind, one of those precociously talented French chefs who starts cooking at fifteen. Through the network of French chefs here and abroad, he eventually ended up heading the kitchen at the meteoric Le Castel on Sacramento Street, after which he spent five years as chef at the superexpensive French Room at the Adolphus Hotel in Dallas. Finally, he returned to San Francisco, and opened La Folie in 1988. His huge technical skill allowed him to cook anything, no matter how arcane, and his artistic, whimsical sensibility led him actually to do it. He fell in love with presentation, and I remember thinking at the time that his style favored decoration over flavor. But standing in the middle of the farmers' market with newly gray hair, his two young children pulling on his trousers, Passot came off like a different person, less the hyperactive cherub and more the energetic adult.

Not long afterward, I sat down at La Folie one Friday night and Passot came out of the kitchen to say hello. His brother Georges, the sommelier, remembered me so I can't pretend that the attentive service and friendliness of the staff took me by surprise. But looking around, I observed a well-run dining room full of casually dressed patrons eating and drinking freely and having a good time. Georges Passot, a sweet and knowledgeable presence, sets the tone. La Folie has always exuded the warmth of a family-run place, and that's why it has so many loyal patrons.

But the food has changed. Now the cooking revealed Passot's roots in Lyon, where good value, French classics, and rich and luxurious ingredients reign in the starred restaurants. Take for example Passot's asparagus soup, a soup whose flavor eludes many a chef. Passot captures the pure essence of asparagus with unabashed use of cream and practically nothing else. It is divine, made more so by the natural sweetness of a small sea scallop flan.

I knew from my first taste that this meal would soar. I followed the soup with a whole roasted lobster tail perched on a shalloty salad of haricots verts next to a fennel tart; an exceptionally tasty, tiny roast rabbit rack and braised, herb-stuffed legs on a plate scattered with fresh peas, tiny favas, and carrots; and a voluptuous special of tournedos Rossini, a gigantic hunk of fillet topped with a huge slice of seared foie gras next to a crisp, buttery fried potato cake and asparagus drizzled with truffle oil. My instincts were correct.

Complex and rich and sometimes excessive, a meal at La Folie is a culinary—and financial—commitment, but you don't have to wear suit and tie or endure stuffy, ritualized service. Rather, Passot's restaurant performs a unique function by offering high level, luxurious French food in a low-key, neighborhood setting. I feel as if I've discovered a new restaurant.

LE PETIT ROBERT . . . .

2300 Polk Street (at Green)
415-922-8100
Open Thursday through Sunday
11:30 A.M. to 3 P.M., Wednesday
through Monday 5:30 to 10:30 P.M.
Moderate
Credit cards: MC, V

Chef Robert Cubberly, formerly of Fog City Diner, and owner Pascal Rigo, a Frenchman who has colonized San Francisco with authentic French bakeries and casual restaurants, have created in Le Petit Robert an endearing neighborhood haven so good, it's worth the proverbial Michelin detour. (Part of the journey will probably be on foot since it's impossible to park anywhere near the restaurant.)

The chewy walnut rolls delivered in a canvas-lined basket hooked me immediately. What flavor! With sweet butter, a tiny bowl of kosher salt, a bowl of marinated olives, and a few tissue-thin slices of dry sausage, the stage was set for French immersion. When a thick-bottomed glass bottle of Rhône was set on the table, just as in Lyon, the scenario was complete. Among the appetizers, fat, fork-tender leeks served cold, marinated in mustardy vinaigrette, and draped with *serrano* ham are a dream come true. Le Petit Robert's onion soup, winey and naturally sweet, is enriched by a small raft of melting toast and Gruyère—the proportions are just right. For main courses, the kitchen prepares a fantastic roast chicken, juicy, savory, deep in flavor, served on a bed of wilted escarole. My mouth waters when I think of it. Braised Niman Ranch beef short ribs fall off the bone into a high-pitched, highly reduced wine sauce mellowed by the bass notes of parsnip purée. Traditional French desserts come from Rigo's bakery next door and they're top-notch, particularly a warm *tart Tatin* with many-layered puff pastry crust and darkly caramelized apples bathed with melting vanilla ice cream. Simple wines from the Rhône and lesser known wine-growing regions of southwest France are priced to be freely imbibed—$12 gets you more than half but less than a whole bottle of many of them. They suit the country-style French cooking like a *campagnard's* beret. And so does the staff, who must have been chosen to make customers feel at home.

The relatively small restaurant inhabits a cavernous, high-ceilinged space. A handsome zinc bar runs along one side of the room. Jazz plays in the background. Lights hang on long wires from on high. However, the coziness built in by all the French bistro details gets dispersed in the expanse of the towering ceiling. The room becomes noisy as sound bounces off all the hard surfaces and it can feel a bit cold. But personally, I am so content at Le Petit Robert that I don't care if the ceiling is too high. One bite of roast chicken and I'm floating on a cloud anyway.

NOB HILL GRILLE . . . .

969 Hyde Street (at Pine)
415-474-5985
Open Monday through Friday
7 A.M. to 3:30 P.M.,
Saturday 8 A.M. to 3 P.M.,
Sunday 8:30 A.M. to 3 P.M.
Inexpensive
Cash only

In a town blissfully short on franchise restaurants and fast-food chains, an independently owned coffee shop like the Nob Hill Grille fills a real need. It offers the inexpensive everyday food beloved by Americans, prepared with integrity and flair. Located across the street from St. Francis Hospital, the Grille is busy all day with a steady stream of orders for platters of eggs, top-notch home-fried potatoes (baked potatoes broken up and crushed against the griddle until they get brown and crusty), sausages, and crisp bacon. The No. 1 club sandwich is thick with real, moist roast turkey, and it comes with a tasty cucumber salad in cumin-scented dressing. Devotees of bacon, lettuce, and tomato sandwiches should make a pilgrimage here—the sandwich comes with a pile of carrot sticks, instead of french fries, and freshly cut coleslaw, a nice touch. Milk shakes, malts, and fresh lemonade highlight the drink card. The Nob Hill Grille understands what makes all these seemingly simple things taste so good and unfailingly executes them with high standards.

PESCE . . . .

2227 Polk Street (between Green and Vallejo)
415-928-8025
Open Sunday through Thursday 5 to 10 P.M., Friday and Saturday until 11 P.M.
Moderate
Credit cards: MC, V, D

Ruggero Gadaldi, the chef-owner of Antica Trattoria down the street (see page 293), has transformed a narrow Polk Street storefront into a handsome Venetian-style *cichetti* bar that specializes in small plates of seafood. A long bar stretches down the center of the room with tiny butcher-paper covered tables scattered at the front and back. Wood-paneled walls and a white tile floor evoke similar operations in Venice.

Galdaldi is a European so he knows that the most important quality of seafood is freshness. The bottom line on all his little plates, hot and cold, is that the fish and shellfish are rigorously fresh. His exciting, northern Italian preparations become a lovely bonus. You can trust Pesce with the handling of fish, which I consider no small accolade.

Some of my favorite Pesce dishes include a properly chewy squid ink risotto topped with fire-licked whole grilled calamari; satiny, not salty, salt cod in a casserole with big, creamy borlotti beans and a spicy tomato sauce; and any pasta with Pesce's perfectly balanced sauce of olive oil, white wine, garlic and parsley. If it's Dungeness crab season you can have linguine studded with luxuriously big hunks of shelled crabmeat in their shells. Start with a bowl of arugula with shaved fennel and Parmesan simply dressed in olive oil and vinegar; or a platter of moist smoked fish. For dessert, the *sgroppino*, a slush of fresh lemon ice with vodka and sparkling prosecco will send you out of the restaurant tipsy, especially after glasses of superb northern Italian white and red wines at attractive prices. This thoroughly professional little place is a gem, well worth the aggravation of figuring out where to park anywhere near this popular restaurant district in a crowded residential neighborhood.

RITZ-CARLTON DINING ROOM . . . .

600 Stockton Street (at California)
415-296-7465
www.ritzcarlton.com
Open Tuesday through Saturday
6 to 9:30 P.M.
Expensive
Credit cards: AE, DC, D, MC, V

Hotel dining rooms have traditionally earned a bad rap for overpriced luxury and fancy, but soulless institutional cooking, but the Dining Room at the Ritz-Carlton is actually one of the best high-end restaurants in the city. Run almost like an independent restaurant (except for the fact that it is subsidized by the hotel), the Dining Room came up with an appealing format: various set-price meals that allow diners to order as many dishes as they want from any section of the menu. If you feel like having two appetizers and a fish course, or a fish course as an appetizer and an appetizer as a main course, or two fish courses and a cheese course and dessert, the kitchen will adjust the portions to make the meal work. The courses can be mixed and matched because they are stylistically related.

Chef Sylvain Portay's style, while very French, is ingredient driven and inventive. He draws on his classic technique to create dishes with layers of flavor and sublime textures, but sometimes adds an unexpected twist, as in a voluptuous Crayfish Velouté Cappuccino, a shellfish soup deep in flavor enriched with a little cream, lightened by a froth of steamed milk. I love every dish here that involves lobster, such as an exquisite salad or a huge three-tail main course serving of roasted Maine lobster bathed in a velvety coral sauce, showered with artichokes and chanterelles. I also come here for Portay's impeccable sweetbreads meunière, the best in town, and a warm shellfish salad with white beans accompanied with a pile of piquantly dressed arugula.

Whatever you order, save room for cheese. The former maître d'-manager Nick Peyton pioneered a groundbreaking world-beat cheese cart, and the current staff has maintained the service. Now it's much easier to find interesting local and American cheeses as well as artisan imports, and the cart offers many a treasure. Even after cheese you may want dessert. The pastry department comes up with lovely seasonal ones. In the fall, you may find two small Seckel pears baked in crisp pastry. Chocolate soufflés are offered here (I think they should be oozier), and house-made ice creams and sorbets. Or you can opt for a plate of tiny chocolates and cookies that arrive with coffee. During both white and black truffle season, Portay puts on astonishing all-truffle dinners with truffles in every course, including dessert. Some of these truffle dishes make it to the regular menu during the season. Though they're expensive, they actually constitute a great buy. Portay's principle is to be always generous with the fragrant shavings.

The Dining Room is traditionally luxurious, appointed with soft heavy linens, thin china, weighty silver, and even thinner glassware, heavily draped tall French windows, and lots of polished wood and thick carpeting. You settle into large upholstered chairs at tables placed far enough apart for intimate conversation above the glissandi of a harpist. The bartenders make perfect martinis; the waiters know what goes into every dish; the brilliant young sommelier administers a huge wine list of bottles and glasses in every price range, and loves to come up with just the right wines to suit your pocketbook and the dishes you're eating. This town's great food reputation does not come from our high-end restaurants. In fact, we have only a handful of interest. But Sylvain Portay's Dining Room at the Ritz-Carlton happens to be one of them.

SPOON. . . . .

2209 Polk Street (at Vallejo)
415-268-0140
Open Tuesday through Sunday
5:30 to 11 P.M., Sunday brunch
10 A.M. to 3 P.M.
Moderate
Credit cards: AE, D, MC, V

The small plate craze has taken San Francisco by storm, and Spoon's playful chef-owner Erik Hopfinger gives the genre an American twist (as opposed to pan-Asian, pan-Latin American, Mediterranean, or Spanish). He's a master of deep-frying as proved by his fried calamari and rock shrimp, perked up with fried parsley leaves and capers and served in a tall beer glass, a ramekin of creamy lemony aioli on the side. Though plump juicy shrimp wrapped in crispy pancetta on a bed of creamy lima beans may seem Mediterranean, the mild roasted new garlic cloves and the size of the portion make it a California creation. The macaroni and cheese has a crunchy rye breadcrumb topping; a plate of spinach is demurely seasoned with garlic and shallots. Fried chicken—actually a little disappointing because the chicken is poached first and then breaded and fried so its crust falls off the skin—comes with creamy, piquant coleslaw, mashed potatoes, and flavorful brown chicken gravy, an American dream come true.

In the spirit of California eclecticism, Hopfinger offers Thai chicken pizza, Waldorf pizza (apple, blue cheese, pear, and arugula), ravioli of the day, and Greek salad, but he's such a good, clever cook that he can pull it off. His smart presentations—he uses an equally eclectic mix of elegant and rustic dishes—and iconoclastic style somehow make sense.

The narrow, cramped room, with a long bar and tiny tables pushed up against a banquette along the wall, is always full and noisy. The young crowd can choose from many beers and a less interesting selection of wine to go with their food, but many come for a drink and a nibble. Like all small plate places, Spoon is as much a bar as a restaurant. You eat a little or a lot depending on your pocketbook and mood. Given the post-dot-com economy, the wine bar–small plate places make perfect sense.

SWAN OYSTER DEPOT. . . . .

1517 Polk Street (between
Sacramento and California)
415-673-1101
Open Monday through Saturday
8 A.M. to 5:30 P.M.
Moderate
Cash only

I always have considered Swan's, founded in 1912, more of a fish market than an oyster bar, but I'm in the minority. People line up on the sidewalk to wait for one of the eighteen stools at the handsomely worn marble counter. Both the ambience and the simple menu of cold seafood (except for clam chowder) posted on the wall resonate of old San Francisco. See page 310 for more information.

TAI CHI . . . .

2031 Polk Street (between
Broadway and Pacific)
415-441-6758
Open Monday through Thursday
11:30 A.M. to 10 P.M., Friday and
Saturday 11:30 A.M. to 10:30 P.M.,
Sunday 4 to 10 P.M.
Inexpensive
Credit cards: AE, MC, V

Over the years, this modest neighborhood spot, which prepares hot, spicy Hunan and Szechwan dishes, has grown in popularity so that during prime dinner hours you might face a wait. The draw, besides very cheap prices and a Western orientation (which means that the dining room and kitchen are set up to accommodate parties of two instead of large round tables of ten), is the saucy, incendiary food. When I get a yen for pot stickers I come here. I could eat a whole plate of these well-seasoned pork dumplings with thick but tender wrappers, dipped into vinegar and red chile oil. Any of the chile-marked hot dishes will be pretty good, like dry-fried long beans with pork, or the indulgent Hunan-style preparations in which chunks of boneless chicken or pork are thickly battered, crisply deep-fried, and tossed in a copious amount of garlicky hot sweet-and-sour sauce, divine over rice. Hot-and-sour soup is also okay, but this is not the place to order seafood or even plates of simple vegetables. Bowls of spicy noodles are the focus, not to mention congenial waiters who are used to dealing with a mostly Western clientele.

VENTICELLO . . . .

1257 Taylor Street (at Washington)
415-922-2545
Open daily 5:30 to 10 P.M.
Moderate
Credit cards: AE, D, DC, MC, V

At Venticello, a chic trattoria hidden away in a valley between Nob Hill and Russian Hill, diners feel as if they are seated in a Tuscan country kitchen complete with enticing aromas emanating from the tiled oven in the middle of the room. Antique china cabinets, polished wooden floors, heavy wooden chairs, and rosy, mottled walls make the room look as if it had been airlifted from some ancient inn in Chianti. The tables, covered with linen and butcher paper, are decorated with little pots of fresh herbs. The windows from the lower dining room afford a glimpse of the Bay Bridge through the apartments across the street. Venticello is the kind of neighborhood secret that savvy tourists consider a trophy.

The meals start with freshly baked loaves of whole-wheat bread and a saucer of black olives. Soft red and crisp white Italian wines are poured by the glass for reasonable prices. A lush antipasto brings grilled endive, zucchini, and Japanese eggplant, ripe tomatoes in season, fresh mozzarella, melon wrapped in prosciutto, and fabulous marinated shrimp on a bed of radicchio and Italian parsley. Every item on the plate shines. Grilled shrimp wrapped in pancetta make for another fine starter, as do country vegetable soups. Thin-crusted pizzas from the wood-fired oven are delicious, especially the classic pizza Margherita, sublime with only tomato sauce, mozzarella, and basil. House-made ravioli stuffed with spinach and ricotta and wide noodles sauced in duck or rabbit ragout are but some of the satisfying, often rustic pastas. The menu changes daily, but if you find roasted poussin (baby chicken) with wild mushrooms, peppers, and garlic, served with mashed potatoes and arugula, order it. For dessert, both tiramisu and *panna cotta*, cooked cream slathered with fresh berries, are lovely.

ZARZUELA . . . .

2000 Hyde Street (at Union)
415-346-0800
Open Tuesday through Saturday
5:30 P.M. to 11 P.M.
Moderate
Credit cards: D, MC, V

The highly visible corner location at Hyde and Union that used to be the Marcel and Henri charcuterie and butcher shop, then La Ferme Beaujolais, found the perfect identity in a Spanish restaurant that specializes in tapas and paella. The wine-cellarish back room, used as a cheese-ripening room in its former incarnation, lends itself to a Spanish *cava* motif, while the glass deli counters showcase a tempting display of tapas. The small front room, with a terra-cotta tile and stone interior and big windows that look out to the cable car line, evokes the Mediterranean. I can't imagine a more suitable match of place and purpose.

The delicious food is as traditional as it can get—if you're eating on Spain's Costa del Sol. Start with, or make a meal of, tapas, little servings of hot and cold dishes that draw on the entire Spanish pantry. Try a plate of the paper-thin, cold, marinated grilled vegetables called *escalivada*, or a ramekin of hot, miniature, spicy chorizo sausages served in a gravy that you'll want to sop up with pieces of good rosemary bread or baguette, brought to the table with a saucer of olives. Or have a typical Spanish tapas plate of bread slathered with a purée of fresh tomatoes and garlic, thin slices of nutty *serrano* ham, and slices of Manchego cheese (a great all-around cooking and eating cheese). If you don't make a meal of these excellent small plates, by all means have the paella, an absolutely stunning Spanish rice preparation that comes in an authentic flat cast-iron pan. The pearly, short-grained rice soaks up all the juices from impeccable shrimp, clams, mussels, bits of chicken, and a colorful scattering of fresh peas and red peppers, yet the dish is voluptuously moist and flavorful. Zarzuela makes one of the best versions I have tasted in this country. You can have glasses of cold *fino* sherry with tapas or a bottle of light, fruity Spanish red wine, a number of which are on the wine list. It's amazing how wonderful these wines are with the food, made more so by their reasonable prices.

BARS

CINCH SALOON . . . .

1723 Polk Street (between
Clay and Washington)
415-776-4162
www.thecinch.com
Open daily 6 A.M. to 2 A.M.
Cash only

Outside are a wooden Indian and three signs: 17 Draught Beers, Patio, and 30 Fine Tequilas. Every time the front door opens, bar heat pours out. Inside is raucous activity, sometimes bordering on rowdy, but good natured and fun, befitting the Texas cowboy and cactus motif of the place. Video games, TVs, pool tables, pinball, cases and cases of beer, peanut and candy vending machines, an outdoor patio, a bar like a ranch front porch, Navajo blankets, 1980s music, neighborhood guys with gray mustaches in flannel shirts and jeans—all are welcome, all are cared for in this local bar, between Bob's Donuts (where the hot doughnuts are born late at night and early morning; see page 305), and the Jewish deli, East Coast West (see page 294).

HARRIS' RESTAURANT

2100 Van Ness Avenue (at Pacific)
415-673-1888
www.harrisrestaurant.com
Open Monday through Thursday
5:30 P.M. to 9:30 P.M.,
Friday 5:30 P.M. to 10 P.M.,
Saturday from 5 to 10 P.M.,
Sunday 5 to 9:30 P.M.
Credit cards: AE, DC, D, MC, V

As you enter this posh steak house, you can go left into the dining room or straight ahead into the bar. I suggest you start any evening in this bar, even if you are dining elsewhere. The walnut wood and black-and-teal upholstered lounge has the feeling of the 1950s. Bartenders in starched white shirts with black ties and burgundy vests serve martinis from a small carafe nestled in a tiny wine barrel of ice, pouring your first cold splash into a chilled glass. Smooth saxxy jazz mixes with the smell of beef cooking next door, and you can swivel your bar chair around to eavesdrop on diners eating and chatting at the four tables in the room, somehow both intimate and sporty. A portrait of Jack A. Harris, with his beloved cattle in the background, watches over the bar from the library.

LAUREL COURT BAR . . . .

Fairmont Hotel, California and
Mason streets
415-772-5259
www.fairmont.com
Open daily 6:30 A.M. to 10:30 A.M.,
11:30 A.M. to 2:30 P.M.,
afternoon tea 2:30 P.M. to 4:30 P.M.,
Tuesday through Saturday
6 P.M. to 10 P.M.
Credit cards: AE, CB, DC, D,
MC, V

Comfortable padded and upholstered chairs and well-spaced tables are found under a pleasant marble colonnade in this lounge just through the Fairmont lobby. A clubby, soft ambiance pervades. If a pianist is not playing, chamber music or French dances are the soundscape. A full menu of food is served until 10:30 each night.

PASHA . . . .

1516 Broadway (between
Van Ness and Polk)
415-885-4477
www.pasharestaurant.com
Open Tuesday through Sunday
6 P.M. to 2 A.M.
Credit Cards: AE, DC, MC, V

An arcade protects the entrance to what looks like a walled city. Golden doors engraved with scenes from a garden of paradise part and you enter a dark, carpeted and pillowed tent. You are an honored guest in a culture where hospitality is a revered art, even a duty. From the dining room, through an archway, comes the sensual rhythms of Turkish, Persian, and Armenian music, mixed with the aromas of spicy cooking and the heat of belly dancing. But here in the bar, either at low tables or standing at the copper bar, you revive your spirits and cleanse your palate for the night to come with an Ali Pasha cocktail of vodka, pomegranate juice, and lime. Ornate Turkish lamps just illuminate the oil portrait of a happy sultan, owner Jalal Takesh, playing the *kanon*, a traditional stringed instrument. And at the side of the bar is a television that receives any of seventy stations by satellite dish, direct from the Middle East.

TOP OF THE MARK . . . .

Mark Hopkins
Inter-Continental Hotel
999 California Street (One Nob Hill)
415-616-6916
www.topofthemark.citysearch.com
Open Sunday through Thursday
5 P.M. to 11 P.M., Friday and
Saturday until midnight
Credit cards: AE, DC, D, MC, V

The Crown Room at the top of the Fairmont has closed, leaving the Top of the Mark in the Mark Hopkins to glow it alone as the bar at the highest point in the city. You must sit at the tables that ring the almost 360-degree space, because even more than view, this bar is about light. It is too bright when the sun gets low; conveniently, billed baseball caps can be bought at the bar for $20 to shade your eyes. But as the setting orange sun colors the foggy haze and the crystalline city lights come up into the dark night, you relax into an only-in-San Francisco mood. Boogie-woogie piano gives the night a bit of Barbary Coast atmosphere that Herb Caen (to whom the Top of the Mark is dedicated) would have loved. Appetizers are cooked on the premises, and a drink list has nearly one hundred martinis named and described.

DELICATESSENS/TAKEOUT

EAST COAST WEST DELICATESSEN . . . . . .

1725 Polk Street (near Washington)
415-563-3542
Open daily 8 A.M. to 9 P.M.
Credit cards: AE, D, MC, V

All the standards of real East Coast Jewish delicatessens can be purchased to go, of course, and the prepared ones like gefilte fish, chicken soup, and stuffed cabbage actually taste homemade. See page 294 for more information.

PICCADILLY FISH AND CHIPS . . . .

1348 Polk Street (at Pine)
415-771-6477
Open daily 11 A.M. to 11 P.M.
Cash only

When the urge to eat a big pile of fish and chips sprinkled with malt vinegar overtakes you, come to this immaculate little shop that does nothing but fry up fish and potatoes. The cod fillets come from Ireland; they're battered and deep-fried to order, staying moist inside a crunchy golden batter. The thick-cut potatoes are precooked to a creamy consistency, then barely browned in oil a second time. They stay limp and potatoey—just the way true fish-and-chips lovers like them. Though the oil in the gigantic fryer is kept very clean—you can see this—it does have its own special smell, which we neutral-oil fanatics have to get used to. My longtime dining-out companion (otherwise known as Chicken Bucket for his love of fried chicken) says that the oil is fine, and that Piccadilly is the best fish and chips place this side of the Atlantic.

THE BAGELRY. . . . .

2139 Polk Street (between
Vallejo and Broadway)
415-441-3003
Open Monday, Tuesday, and
Thursday 6:30 A.M. to 5 P.M.,
Wednesday until noon, Friday,
Saturday, and Sunday until 4 P.M.
Cash only

To my mind, the Bagelry makes the best bagels in the
Bay Area. They are chewy and carry some weight. They
have a good, deep flavor and toast up fragrantly. Unlike
the lite bagels being sold everywhere—in supermarkets,
natural foods stores, and bagel chains that use bagels for
ham sandwiches—the one main purpose of a Bagelry
bagel is as a landing for cream cheese and, on flush
days, smoked salmon, both of which are sold prepackaged in a small refrigerator at the front of the bakery.
The singleness of purpose at this store underscores how important the quality of their product is to them and their customers. In fact, if you don't get there early, the egg bagels will be
gone (they run out first) and several others, like sesame seed or onion, will be in short supply. The seedy bagel sticks attract a following and will do if the bagels have run out. If you
are a true bagel aficionado, The Bagelry merits a trip across town.

BOB'S DONUTS . . . .

1621 Polk Street (between
Clay and Sacramento)
415-776-3141
Open daily 24 hours
Cash only

There are doughnuts and there are doughnuts, and
90 percent of them are inedible. Bob's, a small doughnut shop that has been open for years, not only makes
edible doughnuts, but delicious doughnuts. First of all,
they are fresh. They're made in batches and turn over
quickly because everyone in the north end of the city
makes doughnut pilgrimages there. Secondly, they are perfectly fried in clean, neutral oil.
Thirdly, they're made from scratch, just an old-fashioned conjunction of flour, yeast, eggs,
and sugar, so they're free of artificial preservatives and off flavors. These doughnuts, crumbly or airy, iced, glazed, or sugared, sprinkled with cinnamon or plain, are never cloying,
rancid, sticky, stale, or greasy. Since I am the only one who feels that doughnuts don't taste
good with coffee (which makes them taste greasy, except for the milky chicory coffee at
Café du Monde in New Orleans, which goes perfectly with their hot beignets), the serve-
yourself Colombian coffee station at Bob's gets lots of action. The women behind the
counter—efficient, intelligent, not overly friendly—know their regulars and have their
doughnuts ready as the familiar faces walk through the door. Once you compare Bob's to
other doughnuts, you'll buy them here.

BOULANGE DE POLK . . . .

2310 Polk Street (at Green)
415-345-1107
Open Tuesday through Sunday from
7 a.m. to 7 p.m.
Cash only

It took me a while to be won over by Pascal Rigo's operations because of my Acme bread prejudice. When it comes to *levain* or baguettes, no bakery surpasses Berkeley's Acme. But Rigo's *boulangeries*, which also use organic flour, fill a different niche by baking unique, very French items, unavailable regularly any place else, like *pain de mie* (light white sandwich bread with the thinnest and shiniest of crusts); loaves of airy brioche; and fabulous chewy walnut rolls in which the earthiness of whole wheat plays off against the butteriness of pristinely fresh nuts. Their texture fights back against the teeth but eventually gives in—just what you dream of in a rustic roll. This bakery also has café seating indoors and out where you can have coffee in bowls, crisp *croque-monsieurs* (toasted ham and cheese sandwiches, but with the cheese on top of the sandwich instead of inside), and pastries. On sunny days, the adorable sidewalk tables are much coveted.

ICE CREAM/CHOCOLATES

SEE'S CANDIES . . . .

1519 Polk Street (between
Sacramento and California)
415-775-7049
Open Monday through Saturday
9 A.M. to 6 P.M.
Credit cards: AE, MC, V

Another indispensable branch of San Francisco's favorite chocolate and candy store. See page 334 for more information.

SWENSON'S . . . .

1999 Hyde Street (at Union)
415-775-6818
Open Tuesday through Friday
noon to 10 P.M., Friday and
Saturday until 11 P.M.
Cash only

On the cable car corner of Hyde and Union, Swenson's has been making its own ice creams and scooping its generous cones for generations. The ice cream is old-fashioned, middle-of-the-road, all-American quality, not as rich as Double Rainbow or Häagen-Dazs, but creamier and of much higher quality than Baskin-Robbins. I like Swenson's light ice creams (lower in fat), which still have a voluptuous texture and bright flavor, particularly the toasted almond, a personal favorite. In fact, I can barely taste the difference between the two. If I did, I certainly would opt for the creamier. Why waste calories by eating something that doesn't satisfy?

PEET'S COFFEE & TEA. . . . .

2139C Polk Street (between
Vallejo and Broadway)
415-474-1871
www.peets.com
Open Monday through Friday
6:30 A.M. to 7 P.M.,
weekends 7 A.M. to 7 P.M.
Credit cards: D, MC, V

A much-visited branch of the Bay Area's impeccable
coffee roaster. See page 167 for more information.

MARKETS

REAL FOOD COMPANY. . . . .

2140 Polk Street (between
Vallejo and Broadway)
415-673-7420
www.realfoodco.com
Open daily 9 A.M. to 9 P.M.
Credit cards: MC, V

The Polk Street location is the most active branch of
the Real Food Company and has become a full-service
market over the years by installing a meat, fish, and
poultry counter in the back of the store. As in the produce section, the emphasis is on natural and organic
(grass-fed beef, Fulton Valley Farms chickens) and
locally made sausages, many made of chicken, many
from Bruce Aidells. A small fish section is not inspiring. The major draw of Real Food is
the wide range of pristine, organic produce at expectedly dear prices. When it's good, it's
very good and worth every penny. When fruits or vegetables come from small local farms,
the produce managers say so on signage. They'll give you tastes of anything, a real advantage when you're spending $3 a pound. This kind of personal attention and the long-nur-
tured relationships with small local farmers makes me want to support Real Food.

Early on this Real Food carried Acme bread, which now arrives fresh, and excellent
Italian-style breads from Metropolis Bakery in Emeryville. The store stocks much of what I
like—extra-rich Clover Guernsey milk for caffè latte, Plugra butter, organic flours, organic
nuts and dried fruits in bulk, fruit juices, vitamin C in every form, and hormone-free
brown eggs—for which I am willing to pay the premium charged here. For other locations,
see pages 142 and 227.

BUTTERMILK BREAD

MAKES TWO 9 BY 5-INCH LOAVES

The Real Food stores sell organic unbleached flour, stone-ground whole-wheat flour, yeast, wheat germ, oat bran, and every other conceivable flour in bulk for bread baking. This buttermilk bread has a light, firm texture and an amazingly full flavor; it's an old-fashioned white bread, great for toast. I found it in *The Margaret Rudkin Pepperidge Farm Cookbook*, which has a number of excellent American bread recipes, including a yeasted corn bread and a full-flavored wheat-germ bread. The volume is worth seeking out for these three recipes alone.

1 cup buttermilk

3 tablespoons sugar

2½ teaspoons kosher salt

⅓ cup butter, cut into chunks

1 cup warm (105° to 115°F) water

1 package active dry yeast

5¾ cups unbleached all-purpose flour

¼ teaspoon baking soda

1 In a small saucepan over low heat, combine the buttermilk, sugar, salt, and butter and warm until the butter is almost melted. Remove from the heat and let cool to warm (105° to 115°F).

2 Pour the warm water into a large bowl. Sprinkle in the yeast and stir until it dissolves. Add the warm milk mixture to the yeast mixture. Stir in 3 cups of the flour and the baking soda. Beat with a wooden spoon until smooth. Alternatively, use an electric mixer with the paddle attachment and beat until smooth.

3 Mix in the remaining 2¾ cups flour to make a dough that has a rough, dull appearance and is a bit sticky. Turn the dough out onto a lightly floured board and knead for 8 to 10 minutes, oruntil smooth and elastic. Or use the dough hook of the electric mixer and knead for 7 minutes.

4 Grease a large bowl with butter. Form the dough into a ball and put into the prepared bowl, turning the dough to coat all sides lightly with butter. Cover with a clean, damp cloth and let rise in a warm place free from drafts until doubled in bulk, about 1 hour. Punch the dough down, turn it out onto a lightly floured board, and let rest for 15 minutes.

5 Divide the dough in half. Shape into loaves and place in 2 buttered 9 by 5-inch bread pans. Cover and let rise in a warm place free from drafts for about 1 hour, or until doubled in bulk.

6 Preheat the oven to 375°F. Bake the loaves for about 35 minutes, or until golden brown. When you turn out the loaves onto a rack, knock the bottom with your knuckle. The breads should make a hollow sound.

ORECCHIETTE WITH CAULIFLOWER AND PECORINO

SERVES 4

Peggy Knickebocker came up with this cunning little recipe in her ode, *Olive Oil: From Tree to Table*. It's ridiculously simple to make and beautiful to eat if you use a fresh, white, tight head of cauliflower and good extra virgin olive oil. I, of course, use the greater amount of oil.

¾ pound orecchiette

1 head cauliflower, cut into small florets

¼ to ⅓ cup extra virgin olive oil

⅓ cup grated pecorino cheese

Chopped fresh Italian parsley

Salt and freshly ground black pepper to taste

Put a large pot of salted water on a stove and bring to a boil. Taste the water to make sure there's enough salt in it. You should be able to taste the salt. Add the pasta and cauliflower to the boiling water at the same time and cook until the pasta is al dente, 8 to 10 minutes. Drain and transfer to a warmed serving bowl. Add the olive oil and toss well. Sprinkle with the pecorino and parsley, season with salt and pepper, and serve at once.

WHOLE FOODS MARKET . . . .

2140 Polk Street (between Vallejo and Broadway)
415-673-7420
www.realfoodco.com
Open daily 9 A.M. to 9 P.M.
Credit cards: MC, V

The arrival of a branch of the Whole Foods chain to San Francisco was regarded by many as the second coming. Indeed, its prime location in the north end of the city, its large size, and its parking lot made it seem like a miracle. I have mixed feelings about it. As part of a publicly traded national chain, Whole Foods buys bulk produce. Though a lot of it is organic, it tastes like the same kind of produce I find at Safeway, picked underripe for transport and warehousing and lacking in character. (I prefer to buy organic and locally, something I do at the Ferry Plaza Farmers' Market, see page 85, and at the smaller, local operation, Real Food, see page 307). I do frequent the meat counter, which carries a delicious, naturally raised New York steak, ground white and dark turkey meat, and free-range chickens. The pork at Whole Foods is too lean. Also, I like dealing with an actual butcher who will cut to order. And the Whole Foods store in San Francisco is the only West Coast outlet for Major Farms sheep's milk cheese from Vermont, one of the best cheeses produced in America. The cheese department carries a wide international range of products at top prices. Tastes are freely offered, and some of the clerks really know their stuff. I've been led to some tasty surprises. Come armed with a healthy pocketbook when you shop here. There are many temptations and none of them comes cheap.

PRODUCE

REAL FOOD COMPANY. . . . .

2140 Polk Street (between
Vallejo and Broadway)
415-673-7420
www.realfoodco.com
Open daily 9 A.M. to 9 P.M.
Credit cards: MC, V

The pretty, mostly organic produce often spills out
onto the sidewalk at this branch of the pioneering Real
Food Company, a destination for locally grown fruits
and vegetables. See page 307 for more information.

MEAT AND POULTRY

WHOLE FOODS MARKET . . . .

1765 California Street (at Franklin)
415-674-0500
www.wholefoods.com
Open daily 8 A.M. to 10 P.M.
Credit cards: AE, MC, V

This long, manned butcher counter features hormone-
and antibiotic-free meat and poultry. I particularly like
the flavorful beef. See page 309 for more information.

FISH

SWAN OYSTER DEPOT. . . . .

1517 Polk Street (between
Sacramento and California)
415-673-1101
Open Monday through Sunday
8 A.M. to 5:30 P.M.
Cash only

This little store, half oyster bar with counter and stools,
half fish market, has been the premier source for high-
quality local fish for decades. I have had the most beautiful wild salmon, elegantly filleted, pristine, full of wild
flavor, as well as good specimens of local halibut; the
biggest, sweetest Dungeness crabs cooked, cleaned, and
cracked per request; as well as some Eastern items like
scallops and Swan's standby, Blue Point oysters. These mollusks are sweeter and milder than
Pacific oysters. You can eat them with an old-fashioned ketchup-horseradish cocktail sauce
at the counter, or take them home—but ask that they not to be rinsed in water after they
are opened. Regulars sit down at the counter for slabs of velvety smoked salmon on buttered bread and Swan's good, not overly thickened clam chowder. The white tile walls, resonantly worn counter, and pleasant, oceany smell draw people who like their seafood chilled,
unadorned, and in large quantity.

LEONARD'S 2001 . . . .

2001 Polk Street (at Pacific)
415-921-2001
Open Monday through Saturday
9:30 A.M. to 7:30 P.M.,
Sunday 10 A.M. to 6 P.M.
Credit cards: D, MC, V

Leonard Born, the proprietor of this store, is serious about cheese. He likes to turn his customers on to his favorites from all over the world, and he buys a wide and interesting selection. He seduces you with tastes so you often end up buying two or three more cheeses than you planned. (Even if you know what you want, always ask for a taste first to insure freshness.) The one problem is that all cheeses are cut and prewrapped so you can't get the size you want, especially under a half pound, a big mistake if Leonard wants his customers to expand their cheese repertoires. You really have to think twice about buying a huge hunk when you know you will only eat a small part of it. However, prices are excellent on popular cheeses like imported Italian fontina, Parmesan, delicious Manchego from Spain, and high-quality French cooking cheeses. To go with the cheese, Leonard's carries a variety of fresh baguettes and crackers. The large, light-filled corner store also stocks grains, dried fruits, spices, and pastas in bulk and in packages, but the cheese is the draw, along with the enthusiastic service.

WHOLE FOODS MARKET . . . .

1765 California Street (at Franklin)
415-674-0500
www.wholefoods.com
Open daily 8 A.M. to 10 P.M.
Credit cards: AE, MC, V

The clerks at this serious cheese counter have personal favorites because they taste the cheese right along with the customers. The cheese manager at this branch of Whole Foods makes a point of carrying American artisan cheeses, which attain new heights of complexity with each succeeding year. See page 309 for more information.

WINES AND SPIRITS

THE JUG SHOP . . . .

1567 Pacific Street (at Polk)
415-885-2922
www.jugshop.com
Open Monday through Saturday
9 A.M. to 9 P.M.,
Sunday 9:30 A.M. to 6:30 P.M.
Credit cards: AE, MC, V

This well-stocked liquor store is noteworthy for an extensive wine selection at good prices as well as a huge inventory of beers and spirits. Open since 1959, The Jug Shop has kept up with the times by installing a wine bar and offering personal service. If I'm buying cheese at Leonard's across the street, I always like to drop in to see what they have on special.

WILLIAM CROSS WINE MERCHANTS . . . . . .

2253 Polk Street (at Vallejo)
415-346-1314
Open Sunday and Monday
11 A.M. to 7 P.M., Tuesday and
Thursday until 8 P.M.,
Wednesday until 9 P.M.,
Friday and Saturday until 10 P.M.
Credit cards: MC, V

This neighborhood wine shop specializes in wines from small California and international producers. The owner–wine buyer has a keen palate—he bought for the Real Food chain and others before he opened his own store—and I've been led to some luscious and little-known wines, such as Wild Horse pinot noir from Philo in the Anderson Valley, for amazingly reasonable prices. The clerks know the inventory. Or you can taste for yourself at a friendly wine bar at the back of the store.

COOKWARE AND BOOKS

CITY DISCOUNT . . . .

2436 Polk Street (at Union)
415-771-4649
Open Monday through Saturday
10 A.M. to 6 P.M.,
Sunday 12 P.M. to 6 P.M.
Credit cards: AE, D, MC, V

You never know what you might find at this funny little cookware shop, which stocks more and more stuff each month. You can depend on kitchen gadgets and utensils, pots and pans, but dishware and ramekins shift with the tides of restaurant-supply surplus. Large platters with Chinese motifs, heavy white china in all sizes, thick glasses, thin silverware—really everything you need to set up mismatched housekeeping—can be found here at reasonable prices, especially if you grab something on special.

THE RICHMOND

HOT OR COLD

house coffee 1.00/1.50
tea 1.00
iced coffee 1.50
cafe au lait 1.00/1.75

latte 1.75/2.50
chai 1.75/2.25
hot chocolate 1.50/2.00
mocha 2.00/2.75
italian soda 1.50
fresh squeezed orange juice 1.75/2.50
smoothie 3.50

torani or soy milk 50¢

RESTAURANTS

1 Al Masri
2 Chapeau!
3 Clementine
4 Dragon House
5 Kabuto
6 Katia, A Russian Tea Room
7 King of Thai Noodles
8 Mayflower
9 Parc Hong Kong
10 Pizzetta 211
11 Q
12 Straits Cafe
13 Taiwan
14 Tekka
15 Ton Kiang

CAFÉS

16 Sam and Henry's Cool Beans

BARS

17 Pat O'Shea's Mad Hatter

DELICATESSENS/TAKEOUT

18 European Food
19 Gastronom
20 Haig's Delicacies
21 New World Foods
22 Seakor Polish Delicatessen

BAKERIES/PASTRIES

23 Allstar Donuts
24 House of Bagels
25 Moscow and Tbilisi Bakery
26 Schubert's

ICE CREAM/CHOCOLATES

27 Gelato Classico
28 Joe's Ice Cream
29 See's Candies

ETHNIC MARKETS

30 Lien Hing Supermarket #3
31 New May Wah Supermarket
32 Super Tokio Japanese Market

PRODUCE

33 Clement Produce
34 4th Avenue and Geary
   Farmers Market
35 Fruit Basket
36 Village Market

MEAT AND POULTRY

37 New On Sang
38 Wycen Foods

FISH

39 Seafood Center

COOKWARE AND BOOKS

40 Green Apple Books
41 Kamei Household Wares
42 Kamei Restaurant Supply

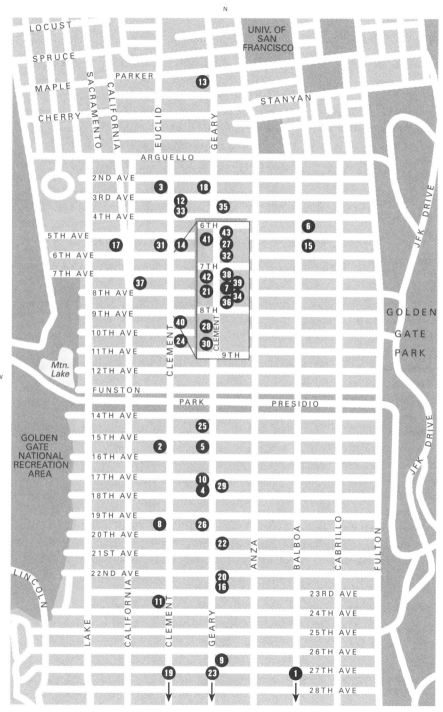

AL-MASRI ....

4031 Balboa Street
(at 42nd Avenue)
415-876-2300
www.almasrirestaurant.com
Open Thursday through Monday
6:30 P.M. to 11 P.M.
Moderate
Credit cards: AE, D, MC, V

More of an intimate nightclub than a restaurant, Al-Masri nonetheless serves tasty Egyptian food for those who have the patience to wait for it. My husband, besotted by a voluptuous belly dancer in a red spangled bra, had absolutely no problem with the practically nonexistent service on our first visit, but four other people at the table were hungry, thirsty prisoners of the entertainment. We couldn't talk over the amplified playing and singing of the one industrious musician, and until the show was over we could not establish communication with anyone on the dining room floor.

But eventually, miraculously delicious food did trickle out from the kitchen, dish by dish. And wine, perfectly matched to the spicy food, appeared on the table for us to pour. Though it took three and a half hours, we ate our way through appetizers, main courses, and dessert and enjoyed another swirl of scarves and breasts.

Egyptian dishes will not be totally unfamiliar to anyone who has eaten Middle Eastern or Moroccan food, but the Egyptian versions are different. The *maza*, or appetizer plate, brings a smooth purée of roasted eggplant and garlic (*babaghanuug*); a smooth purée of chickpeas with sesame paste (hummus); a very fresh feta cheese drizzled with olive oil; salt-cured black olives; a fluffy parsley salad (*taboula*); and deep-fried Egyptian-style falafel (*ta'miya*) made of ground, dried fava beans instead of chickpeas.

Given the inexperience on the dining room floor, I didn't expect the kitchen to handle the extensive main-course menu, but I was pleasantly surprised. We ate succulent, crispy-skinned rabbit and savory spice-rubbed lamb kebabs made with leg of lamb. Even better were ground lamb kebabs, *kufta mashwiya*, seasoned with garlic and mint. Two sensitively cooked fish dishes impressed me with their freshness: an expertly sautéed fillet of petrale sole, *samak mashwi*; and Cairo-style halibut, *taggen samak*, a thick fillet baked with onions, raisins, and tomato sauce, sprinkled with almonds. All the main courses come with an airy pilaf of rice and vermicelli and your choice of saucy Egyptian vegetables served in a little glass bowl. These traditional vegetable dishes are a highlight of the menu, especially *ul as*, creamy cubes of taro root in a haunting green gravy.

Al-Masri is managed by belly dancers (which explains a lot), and the overall experience strikes me as a bit surreal. The small dining room, brightly painted with whimsical murals, scarabs, and hieroglyphics, is made to feel even more intimate with an internal tiled roof. The music is loud and the scene intense. The Moroccan chef, Bouchra Belouzi, is a professed Egyptophile, and her earthy cooking keeps Al-Masri from spinning out into the ozone over the nearby ocean.

1408 Clement Street
(at 15th Avenue)
415-750-9787
Open Tuesday through Thursday
and Sunday 5 to 10 P.M.,
Friday and Saturday until 10:30 P.M.
Moderate
Credit cards: AE, D, MC, V

Philippe Gardelle, owner of little Chapeau!, always seems to find the most talented French chefs to head his kitchen. They may be chefs in-between jobs; or chefs who have burned out running big operations but still want to cook; or chefs waiting to open their own restaurants. The same thing seems to happen with wait-staff. So diners at Chapeau! often get four-star food and extremely knowledgeable service for neighborhood bistro prices. In addition, Gardelle, a brilliant sommelier, has put together one of the most impressive French wine lists in town and prices it as if he were selling the wines retail.

There is a $35 four-course prix fixe menu offered in addition to the regular à la carte menu. You can begin with foie gras, either cold in a *ballotine* or seared. A vichyssoise enlivened with fresh pea purée or a green salad could follow. Butter-tender braised beef cheeks with potato purée, or rack of lamb chops call for a major red wine. For dessert, try crème brûlée, profiteroles, or a cheese plate.

In fact, the reasonably priced food allows you to spend more on wine, and Philippe Gardelle's multipage wine list will tempt you. The bubbly Gardelle cheerfully guides you to wines in the price range you're comfortable with. But if you want to splurge, this is a good place to do it. The markups on the more expensive bottles are reasonable, so once again you get good value. Gardelle will guide you to some complex, currently drinkable bottles. He always pours a tiny sip for himself first—to check the bottle—and consequently he keeps up with every wine on his list. It's a pleasure to order wine from the person who constantly tastes it all. Gardelle wants nothing more than to make his customers happy.

The one drawback is that diners are packed in like sardines at tiny linen-covered tables reminiscent of New York restaurants, but sometimes the service goes beyond professional to inspired. Pros from Masa's and Farallon put in shifts here while they decide what to do next. They know food and wine and how to put them together during a meal. If they suspect you're a player, someone who is interested in doing some top-flight eating and drinking, they spring into action. The little glass of Monbazillac appears with the foie gras terrine. A taste of white Bordeaux may come out before the big red Bordeaux is poured. You get this kind of treatment from the big boys when you're dropping $150 a person. At Chapeau!, you can have a like experience for $150 for two—and you can wear your jeans. Order the most elegant foods on the menu, pair them with some top-flight wines, and consider the savings over a trip to Paris.

CLEMENTINE . . . .

126 Clement Street (between
2nd and 3rd avenues)
415-387-0408
Open Tuesday through Thursday
and Sunday 5:30 to 10 P.M.,
Friday and Saturday until 10:30 P.M.
Moderate
Credit cards: MC, V

Clementine reminds me of Parisian bistros in the well-heeled 14th arrondissement. Here and there customers get good food and good value; the difference is that at Clementine, they also get good service. The staff here really wants to please. They run a tight ship with waiters and support staff bringing everything you need before you start looking around for it. I am always buoyed by professional French service, even in a casual dining room. Such attention to detail in the dining room makes the food taste better.

The chef at Clementine actually cooked in a rather fancy Paris restaurant, Arpège, and his dishes have French complexity and polish. Cured raw salmon molded over creamy boiled potato slices slathered in shalloty vinaigrette has Left Bank chic, as does a buttery blue cheese tart paved with pears and garnished with a pouf of frisée salad and a surrounding drizzle of balsamic reduction. Seared foie gras smothered with sweet onion marmalade on a brioche crouton brings appreciative smiles from Francophiles. *Steak frites* boasts divine, crispy thin fries. A salad lover like me appreciated a duck dish in which buttery rare slices of duck breast were draped over greens with a pile of garlicky lentils and duck leg confit on the side. For dessert, don't pass up the exquisite *pain perdu*, buttery, custardy French toast drizzled with caramel and topped with a little *boule* of hazelnut ice cream. It's crisp on top and cream inside.

The predominantly French wines, with a number of good ones from Bordeaux, are moderate in price and enhance the food. The cozy dining room is packed with banquettes, small linen-covered tables pushed close together, and mirrors and heavily framed French impressionist oils on the salmon-colored walls. You know you're in a French dining room. The overall package at Clementine satisfies and that's why it's perpetually full, mostly with regulars. The casually dressed maître d' seems to recognize everyone, and if you're a first-timer, he'll remember your face by the second visit. I don't think you can find a dining experience as complete as this one for the price in Paris today. Indeed, it feels as if Clementine was airlifted from France and gently set down on Clement Street.

DRAGON HOUSE . . . .

5344 Geary Boulevard (between
17th and 18th avenues)
415-751-6545
Open daily 11 A.M. to 3 P.M.
and 4 to 9:30 P.M.
Inexpensive
Cash Only

With only ten or twelve small tables, Dragon House still offers a huge menu, but everyone comes here for the Shanghai specialties. Unfortunately, many of these are listed only on the Chinese menu. Luckily, you have me to steer you to some of the best, like tofu skin with preserved mustard greens and beans—salty, chewy, vegetarian, and delicious with rice. Lion's head, large meatballs glistening with brown gravy served with bright green spinach, melt in your mouth. Begin with superb Shanghai dumplings called *xiao long bao*, juicy, pork filled, and served with Chinese vinegar with threads of fresh ginger. Jellyfish salad makes for a refreshing starter. It tastes like chewy, sesame-scented pasta. Also try the soup with tofu, preserved mustard greens, and pork. It's both clean and fortifying. On the English menu, you can't go wrong with mu shu vegetables or pork with pancakes and hoisin sauce, or a clay pot of Chinese cabbage with vermicelli and pork. During crab season don't pass up a pristinely fresh Hunan-style crab coated in spicy black bean sauce. I love the red-cooked carp, pulled live from a freshwater tank, braised in thick, sweet, salty gravy with tons of scallions that melt into the sauce. Every dish uses fresh ingredients yet prices are astoundingly cheap. The waitresses who have been there forever are cheerful and friendly. They want you to get to the dishes you like. Just ask for the Shanghai specialties.

KABUTO . . . .

5121 Geary Boulevard (between 15th and 16th avenues)
415-752-5652
www.kabutosushi.com
Open Tuesday through Saturday
5:30 to 11 P.M.,
Sunday until 10 P.M., closed the last Sunday of every month.
Inexpensive-Moderate
Credit Cards: MC, V

For twenty-three years, sushi chef–owner Sachio Kojima has presided over the fish counter here, wielding his knife like a Kabuki samurai executing a jerky sushi-making dance at top speed. For five and now sometimes six nights a week, Sachio has personally overseen every ceramic bowl, lacquer tray, and wooden pedestal of food that has come out of his sushi bar and small adjacent kitchen. That is why the food at Kabuto remains so delectable, so innovative, so honest. The authenticity of this place emanates from Sachio's personal involvement in its operation. In Japan, personal accountability is a way of life. In the United States, you're lucky to find it at all.

On a recent visit I asked Sachio, as everyone does, what he liked for sushi and he quickly rattled off what turned out to be three thrilling fish: white-fleshed albacore tuna that was astoundingly buttery; meaty but mild king mackerel topped with a microscopic mince of scallion and ginger; and sweet, pearly amberjack with a dreamy, velvety texture. Sachio put one piece of each sushi on our wooden serving pedestals, just the way we would have arranged it. He intuits what his customers want.

Kabuto also specializes in small plates of great originality that are listed on their own menu board and on small standup menus at the sushi bar. There are delicious salads of shredded mushroom-flavored burdock root and carrot; and *hijiki*, seaweed threads simmered in soy and mirin (sweet rice wine); sake-marinated slices of grilled black cod; skate wing poached in soy- and mirin-seasoned broth accompanied with a large, split shiitake mushroom, stunning on an aqua ceramic plate. On a cold night, start with a rustic bowl of orange Japanese squash, stewed until tender with bits of tuna in a salty, sweet sauce.

One fairly recent development at Kabuto is the sake list, with each sake rated for level of dryness. The higher the plus (+4, +8, +12) the drier it is. The location of origin is also indicated. These pure rice wines are poured chilled from giant bottles into fat, cut-glass tumblers. I love sake, but I must admit that I am a beginner at knowing it. Its gentle fruitiness really enhances raw fish.

I started tasting here with sakes recommended by Sachio, Karatamba (+3) and Yamada-Nishiki (+4), both considered slightly dry from the Hyogo district near Kyoto. They turned out to be my favorites. I also liked the crisp Onigoroshi (+8), also from Hyogo, because it had a full finish, unlike Hakushika (+5), also from Hyogo, which did not. The extra dry Onino Shitaburui (+12) from Tottori was too austere for me, though I know dryness in sake is prized, the ideal being dry combined with long finish, or high acidity. No matter what sake you choose, you'll find it immediately appealing, more immediately accessible than wine. I much prefer drinking chilled sake to warmed sake, perhaps a holdover from wine drinking, but the flavors of fine sake emerge more distinctly at cool temperatures.

That Kabuto offers this sophisticated, informative sake list points to its continuing vitality. This restaurant reinvents itself with each new generation of customers. It has remained gratifyingly unchanged by maintaining high standards, but it has adjusted to the times by adding more vegetarian dishes, fine sakes, and a greater variety of prepared side dishes. I am deeply moved by any restaurant that has stayed so good for so long.

KATIA, A RUSSIAN TEA ROOM . . . .

600 5th Avenue (at Balboa)
415-668-9292
Open Wednesday through Friday
11:30 A.M. to 2:30 P.M.,
Wednesday, Thursday, and
Sunday 5 P.M. to 9 P.M., Friday and
Saturday 5 P.M. to 10 P.M.
Inexpensive
Credit cards: AE, D, DC, MC, V

Katia Troosh prepares home-style Russian food with a light hand at her charming little restaurant, really the best Russian restaurant in the city. Start, of course, with *zakuski*, small plates of cold appetizers that always begin a formal Russian meal. Katia's include house-pickled cucumbers, marinated mushrooms, the most delicious chopped Russian salad called Vinaigrette, and garlicky eggplant caviar. Frankly, I could make a whole meal out of the chopped salad with the thick slices of moist rye–whole wheat bread set out on the table.

Katia's blini are thin, crêpelike, and slightly sour. The best. They come with sweet-and-sour pickled herring and smoked salmon. The beet borscht made me think of my grandmother. Main courses change often, but small meat-filled dumplings called *pelmeni* served in rich chicken broth with a dollop of sour cream are a mainstay. They should be. I adore the crisp chicken pancakes made of ground chicken breast. For dessert, look for crisp meringues topped with whipped cream and fresh fruit. They are lovely.

Service can be slow, but the food is so marvelous, the atmosphere so warm and friendly, that you don't care. This little family-run place has true Russian soul.

KING OF THAI NOODLES . . . .

639 Clement Street
(between 7th and 8th Avenue)
415-752-5198
Open daily 11 A.M. to 1:30 A.M.
Inexpensive
Cash only

I know of three branches of King of Thai Noodles, but personally, I always go to the original hole-in-the-wall with an open kitchen, a few stools, and a couple of tables at the back for my green papaya salad and Thai beef noodle soup.

At King of Thai, the salad cook tosses shredded

green papaya and sliced long beans with an incendiary dressing he pounds to order in a Thai mortar and pestle of dried shrimp, lime, lots of tiny, potent red chiles, and toasted peanuts. If you're wondering what that thick slice of undressed cabbage is doing on the plate, you'll know once you start eating the papaya salad. A bite of the cool, naked cabbage helps mitigate the heat. The signature beef noodle soup, No. 1 on the menu, has a dark brown, slightly sweet broth, fragrant with cinnamon, star anise, and handfuls of Chinese celery. Rice noodles conveniently cut with a scissors to edible lengths and bean sprouts intertwine for texture, and slices of raw beef cook to chewy juiciness in the hot broth. Plenty of red chiles contribute smoldering heat.

The other favorite at King of Thai is a daily special that seems to be offered every day—Thai green curry with coconut milk and tender, juicy sliced chicken breast served with a big plate of jasmine rice. The green curry, seductively perfumed with minty Thai basil, throws off medium heat that even the chile-challenged can handle, especially with rice.

When the cooks get a break they sit on stools at the counter stripping the leaves off big piles of fresh herbs and the scents follow you out the front door—one more reason to eat here.

MAYFLOWER . . . .

6255 Geary Blvd (at 27th Avenue)
415-387-8338
Open Monday through Friday
11 A.M. to 2:30 P.M., Saturday
and Sunday 10 A.M. to 2:30 P.M.,
nightly 5 to 10:30 P.M.
Moderate
Credit cards: MC, V

This smallish Hong Kong-style seafood house has had its ups and downs, most notably a reputed gang-related fire that destroyed it completely not long ago. It has since been rebuilt and looks quite fresh and clean. Live-seafood tanks hold a menagerie of sea beasts—geoduck clams, shrimp, Pacific lobsters, bony fish—and the kitchen works wonders with them.

My strategy, learned from my Chinese eating partners, is to call the general manager, currently Eric Lau, and tell him how many will be at the table and how much I want to spend, usually around $35 a person. That way the dishes appear one after the other banquet style; you don't have to decode the menu; you can bring your own wine; and the service is always more attentive. At my last meal there, Mayflower put out a feast for six of us for $45 a person, and worth every penny.

The table is always set here with plates of sweet pickled daikon and cucumbers; honey-roasted walnuts sprinkled with sesame seeds; and spice-dusted roasted peanuts. A savory small appetizer plate arranged with crispy-skinned, spice-dusted deep-fried tofu; chile-spiked jellyfish salad; a couple of tender slices of roast pork; and a little pile of roasted soy-beans got the meal off to a promising start. A surf clam, tender-chewy body meat and round slices of adductor muscle (which looks like a scallop), wok-fried with ginger, scallion, cilantro, and soy sauce was piled back into its six-inch-wide shell, a spectacular presentation. We each got our own, as we did a huge conch shell, this time stuffed with a fabulous Thanksgiving-like forcemeat of the chopped shellfish, chicken, water chestnuts, and black mushrooms. It reminded me of New Orleans. It couldn't have been more fun to eat.

The star of the meal was a gigantic five-pound lobster served in two courses. A lobster bisque tinged with tomato made out of the head would have impressed any connoisseur of haute French cuisine. The lobster tail and enormous claws, cut up in the shell and wok-cooked with ginger and scallion, delivered huge chunks of sweet, tender meat. We gorged ourselves. Crabmeat in a clear sauce served in a casserole with bright green broccoli stems refreshed our palates for a whole crispy chicken with deep golden skin stuffed with sticky rice flavored with Smithfield ham and dried shrimp, and served with a brown gravy studded with minced black mushrooms.

For dessert came warm, sweet red bean soup scented with dried orange peel and studded with creamy lotus seeds, and cubes of shimmering coconut pudding (pudding in a Cantonese restaurant means a chilled gelatin). My long-suffering husband was about to pass on the black turtle gelatin—pleasantly herbal and gingery with a slight bitter edge—in favor of his beloved mango pudding pooled with evaporated milk when one of my female guests told him, "You'd better eat your turtle Jell-O. It will give you virility."

"Give me two," he said. But I could tell that he felt fortified anyway by the luscious, unusual seafood dinner.

PARC HONG KONG . . . .

5322 Geary Boulevard
(at 17th Avenue)
415-668-8998
Open Monday through Friday
11 A.M. to 2:30 P.M.,
Saturday and Sunday 10 A.M. to
2:30 P.M., nightly 5 to 9:30 P.M.
Moderate
Credit cards: AE, D, MC, V

Although operating under new ownership, I am relieved to report that very little else, besides the name, has changed at Parc Hong Kong (formerly the Hong Kong Flower Lounge). Manager Jorge Wong still presides over the dining room, Chef Lern Lau still commands the kitchen at dinner, and the original dim sum chef, Tim Ho, keeps tea lunch fresh and light.

I always begin a banquet with Parc Hong Kong's signature roast suckling pig service, served cold, with rectangles of crackling crisp skin; a pile of sparkling, red chile–flecked seaweed salad; and thick, chewy ribbons of sesame-scented jellyfish. Tiny warm white pancakes, scallions, and hoisin sauce are served separately to go with the cracklings. All these seemingly disparate foods create a pleasing yin-yang tension of textures and flavors. Velvety-chewy pork and clean-chewy jellyfish; crisp-juicy seaweed and crisp-rich pork cracklings make for playful juxtapositions. Whoever invented this cutting edge dish—it shows the flair of Hong Kong—has come up with a new classic, and the kitchen at Parc Hong Kong executes it superbly.

More traditional cooking makes its appearance with small Shanghai-style steamed dumplings, plump with pork and broth. You gently remove them from the bamboo steamer with chopsticks, dip them lightly in a little saucer of ginger threads and Chinese vinegar and place the dumpling on your soup spoon. Holding the flat spoon with dumpling in your left hand (presuming you are right-handed), you eat the Shanghai dumpling off the spoon close to your mouth with chopsticks, thereby catching and consuming all the juices. (You'll thank me for this advice.)

I also love a Cantonese double broth called soup of the day, Chinese watercress (*ong choy*) and pork simmered in stock to make a fortifying broth, the soft meat and vegetables strained out and served on the side. The simplicity of this soup refreshes and cleans the palate after the busy appetizers and prepares the mouth for the savory courses ahead: silken Soy Marinated Chicken; Honey Glazed Barbecue Pork, sweetly glazed and toothsome; and cloudlike *pei pa* tofu, dumplings of soft bean curd and crab in a clear sauce, served with miniature heads of steamed baby bok choy—a must-order dish here. A huge pile of snow pea leaves, not tiny pea sprouts, but spinach-sized leaves and stems of pea vine, couldn't be fresher or tastier, dotted with whole browned cloves of garlic. The dim sum, ordered from a form and delivered piping hot from the kitchen, sparkles. Especially tasty are crispy, deep-fried fillets of black cod sprinkled with hot chiles and scallions; slices of cold marinated tofu with brown, chewy exteriors and super-soft, creamy interiors; shimmering seaweed salad; all the very clean steamed dumplings; and sesame-marinated duck tongues (weird for the uninitiated but delectable). There are many more from which to choose.

In every respect, the new Parc Hong Kong lives up to the standards and performance of the former occupant here, the Hong Kong Flower Lounge. (You have to drive to Millbrae now to eat at the mother ship.) Parc Hong Kong remains one of the premier Cantonese dinner houses in the city, which means that patrons can expect pristine ingredients and a light, skilled hand in the kitchen.

PIZZETTA 211 . . . .

211 23rd Avenue (between
California and Clement)
415-379-9880
www.pizzetta211.com
Open Wednesday through Friday
noon to 2:30 P.M. and
5 P.M. to 9 P.M., Saturday and
Sunday noon to 9 P.M.
Inexpensive
Cash only

The tiny Pizzetta 211 defines the adult pizza. The individual, thin-crusted pizzas are artfully constructed to order, sparingly topped with such arcane ingredients as mustard greens, yams, Gruyère, and fried bread crumbs, or an organic Petaluma Poultry egg, Neal's Yard (an artisanal cheese shop in London) Lancashire, and wild arugula. More conventional pizzas with tomato, mozzarella, and basil with variations like pepperoni are also available. But the hallmark of all Pizzetta 211 pizzas is a thin, crisp crust with yeasty chewiness (it's not a cracker), topped with ingredients that have distinctive flavor.

While you're waiting for your pizza, you can nibble on a lightly dressed organic green salad with spiced walnuts that comes with a sampler of farmhouse cheeses purchased from the Artisan Cheese shop (see page 284). In fact, an owner of Pizzetta 211 worked there with founder Peggy Smith and learned about the possibilities of nontraditional cheeses on pizzas. Really more of a take-out place than a restaurant since it has such limited seating, Pizzetta's popularity with the tony Lake Street and Seacliff crowd in the neighborhood keeps it afloat. Neighbors call in and then swing by to pick up their elegant pizzas and salads to eat at home.

Q . . . .

225 Clement Street (between
3rd and 4th avenues)
415-752-2298
Open Monday through Friday
11 A.M. to 3 P.M. and 5 to 11 P.M.,
Saturday 10 A.M. to 11 P.M.,
Sunday 10 A.M. to 10 P.M.
Inexpensive
Credit cards: MC, V

Q is the ultimate neighborhood restaurant, where loyal customers drop in everyday for brunch, lunch, or dinner because it's so affordable. They can be vegetarians or meat lovers. They can drink beer or wine or lemonade. They can read a newspaper or chat up a date. Q is one of the generalists, fulfilling the role of the small town café with a hip, big-city demeanor. This exuberant, loud, trashy Inner Richmond hang beckons those who appreciate good value, amusing decor (if it can be called decor), and hearty and delicious eats.

Craggy, golden boulders of southern fried chicken crunch with each bite. They rest against a volcano of mashed potatoes with sweet brown country gravy pooled in its crater, surrounded by foliage—a buttery braise of peppers, spinach, and zucchini. A thick hunk of buttery-textured swordfish crisscrossed with golden grill marks comes with a mountain of compatible sides—crisp fennel salad, braised kale, and spicy, moist jambalaya rice. Thick slices of dense, spicy meat loaf, reheated on the grill—the best—are infused with smoky barbecue sauce, the overtones of which are intensified by the fire. For dessert, have roasted bananas, split and grilled in their skin, scattered with toasted walnuts, softly whipped cream, and caramel-fudge sauce: the whole thing is an ingenious turn on both bananas Foster and a banana split.

Q's ambience is as original and soulful as the cooking. The space is one big collage of collected materials—lots of sheet metal of one sort or another—including many invented objects. Banquettes and booths of gold-and-silver flecked polyurethane sparkle gaily in light bouncing off the corrugated tin ceiling. Tables are actually wooden boxes on pedestals with one glass side. A panorama inside might be a papier-mâché snake in a purple desert; or crinkled silvery Mylar with a photo of sky and clouds positioned in the middle. The distressed cement floor, industrial sheet metal bar, and proudly open kitchen are softened somehow by layers of wacky abstract objets d'art. Q is deafening with hard surfaces, loud talk, clanking kitchen, and the sound system always cranked up to full volume.

What about that name? Q does stand for barbeque, and it's true that Smilin' Andy's BBQ Pork Spare-Ribs with Mom's Baked Beans, Spicy Slaw, and Garlic Fries transcend any plate of ribs anywhere, and I've never tasted better baked beans. Andy Gillen was lucky when it came to moms. And so are we to have him and his edgy, soulful cooking.

STRAITS CAFE . . . .

3300 Geary Boulevard (at Parker)
415-668-1783
Open Monday through Thursday
11:30 A.M. to 3 P.M. and
5 to 10 P.M., Friday and Saturday
11:30 A.M. until 11 P.M.
Moderate
Credit cards: AE, MC, V

If you find explosive Asian flavors and exotic tropical ingredients seductive, you must eat at Straits Cafe, a charming Singaporean restaurant operated by chef Chris Yeo. His potent Malaysian cooking will sweep you off your feet. Yeo keeps the hot, sweet, sour, gingery, garlicky, perfumey, fermented riot of flavors in each preparation under strict control. Working with an intense palette in which balance is everything, he creates a quintessen-tial tropical-cross-roads cuisine: a unique mix of Malaysian, Chinese, Indian, and Burmese influences.

You may think you recognize some of the dishes on the menu, but even the most familiar will surprise you. Satays, skewers of juicy beef, are fragrant with layers of flavor from wet and dry *masalas* of spices and herbs. The unique peanut sauce served with them has its own spicing that somehow fits into the larger picture like a jigsaw puzzle. The presentation with chunks of cooling cucumber is simple and beautiful. An appetizer called *murtabak*, an Indian-style flat bread filled with minced beef, comes with a luscious coconut milk curry dipping sauce and a pile of pickled red onions, a must-order dish. Spring rolls turn out to be a room-temperature crepe stuffed with slivered vegetables and pungent dried shrimp, each section topped with its own dab of plum sauce and a perfect cilantro leaf. Angel hair noodles get an exquisite, if pungent, treatment in a hot-and-sour tamarind broth, topped with hard-cooked eggs and tender pink shrimp. Dark green long beans stay crisp, stir-fried with hot chiles, dried shrimp, and minced pork. How good this dish tastes with aromatic jasmine rice! A mild, creamy coconut milk–based chicken curry, in which the chicken retains its character, will please everyone. Although the desserts sound completely odd, they, too, are surprisingly delicious. One of my favorites, sago pudding, is a custard of large pearl tapioca in a heavenly palm sugar syrup.

Even the look of the restaurant conjures up tropical romance. The interior resembles a Singaporean street with columns transformed into palms, faux windows with wooden shutters, and balconies high up on one wall, an internal sheet-metal roof, and wainscoting, ceiling fans, slatted doors, and vents. Straits Cafe does remind you of the all-night street food stalls of Singapore, but it also offers such Raffles Hotel fillips as Singapore slings and gin and tonics, along with vanilla bean sodas, sweetened iced tea, and coffee, wines, and beer. In every respect, Straits Cafe promises exotic fun and adventure at the foot of San Francisco's avenues.

TAIWAN . . . .

445 Clement Street
(near 6th Avenue)
415-387-1789
Open Monday through Friday
11 A.M. to 10 P.M.,
Saturday 10 A.M. to 11 P.M.,
Sunday 10 A.M. to 10 P.M.
Inexpensive
Credit cards: MC, V

This small café specializes in superb dumplings and noodles and a wide range of spicy northern Chinese and Shanghai dishes. It's one of my favorite restaurants of any nationality. Once I started eating here I couldn't stop. I had to return every day to taste a few more things. The compact noodle and dumpling kitchen situated right in the front window lets you know how fresh these items are. Behind, a rosy little dining room with a skylight gets constant turnover. People come here for a bite or a full meal all day.

Start with hot-and-sour soup—bright, clean, and bracing. Then choose a mu shu dish, a stir-fry of julienned vegetables, egg, and sparkling shrimp that you pile onto thin white pancakes. Smear them with bean sauce. I can't eat at Taiwan without having at least one plate of gingery, pork-filled boiled dumplings (you get ten to an order); shrimp, leek, and pork boiled dumplings, which have a lovely wild onion edge; or steamed vegetarian dumplings with that slightly grassy herbal flavor lovers of greens adore.

The noodles are also superb. Try the thick, chewy Shanghai noodles tossed with vegetables and slivers of pork or the stunning mustard green and pork noodles bathed in a smoky broth. In braised beef 'ligament' noodles, gelatinous cuts of brisket add texture and buttery flavor to a beef broth.

Lest you think that you have to stick to noodles, try the luscious crispy chicken, a burnished bird with velvety meat in a rich brown sauce—great with a plate of perfectly cooked young bok choy. Unctuous red-cooked eggplant is sublime over rice, as are the addictively tasty dry-fried Chinese long beans.

In 1973 the island of Taiwan inherited uprooted northern chefs from Shanghai, Beijing, Hunan, Sichuan, and Shandong provinces, while many of the Cantonese master chefs emigrated to Hong Kong. Reflecting the northern influence on Taiwanese cooking, a special menu offers soulful cold-weather dishes with lots of tripe, pickled greens, and fish paste for the adventurous.

On top of all the exciting cooking, the obliging waiters will pace your meal so you don't get all your dishes at once. What's hard to believe is that these sensuous, spicy, well-served meals cost under $10 a person.

TEKKA . . . .

537 Balboa (at 5th Avenue)
415-221-8455
Open Monday through Saturday
7 P.M. to midnight
Moderate
Credit cards: MC, V

I shouldn't even be telling you about this tiny neighborhood spot because outsiders really don't belong here. There are only eight seats at a low counter, plus one minuscule table with two chairs wedged into the front window. There's no sign, no menu, no sake list, no fish display—just an older man working behind the counter and a younger woman who shuttles between the kitchen, where she cooks behind a curtain, and the dining area.

The scene is so intimate and personal that I felt like an intruder on my initial visit. I must have been regarded as one, because I wasn't given a hot towel and was treated as if I had wandered into the place by mistake. (The only other Caucasian there, a woman, spoke fluent Japanese.) I asked for some cold sake, which was poured into a wooden box, and then forged ahead, ordering a combination plate of sashimi and a good-looking dish that the other Caucasian had been eating. The sashimi was brilliant—tender cooked octopus, raw *hamachi*, tuna, mackerel, and salmon—but the *agedashi-tofu* that came from the kitchen was one of the most delicious Japanese dishes I've ever tasted, the crispy-skinned cubes of creamy tofu in a sweet, sticky, salty sauce, a masterpiece of textural and flavor contrast. I ordered what other people were eating, like a sushi roll filled with asparagus and avocado, the rice pressed onto the outside of the seaweed wrapper sprinkled with sesame seeds. After polishing off a round of sushi, generously cut fish on perfect rice, I asked the woman to bring me one last little something from the kitchen.

"Do you want something grilled?" she asked.

I told her I wanted something she had cooked. She knew exactly what I was after and returned with a luscious, melting braise of beef, daikon, and yam in a sweet, aromatic gravy—Japanese home cooking at its best. And then the sushi chef, who had just returned from a trip to Japan with blowfish and was feting the Japanese couple next to me with a whole meal based around it, gave me a blowfish sushi as I was paying my bill. Its crisp-tender texture sent a little shiver down my spine. I knew then he wanted me back.

TON KIANG . . . .

5821 Geary Boulevard
(at 22nd Avenue)
415-387-8273
www.tonkiang.com
Open Monday through Thursday
10:30 A.M. to 10 P.M.,
Friday 10:30 A.M. to 10:30 P.M.,
Saturday, Sunday, and holidays
9:30 A.M. to 10:30 P.M.
Inexpensive
Credit cards: AE, CB, DC, D,
MC, V

The relatively small two-story Ton Kiang excels at dim sum. It's the freshest in town. At the bigger houses you never know how many rounds the dumplings have made before the carts pull up to your table. At Ton Kiang, the dim sum arrive hot from the kitchen and the variety is astounding. You cannot eat fast enough to keep up with the stream of new temptations.

What surprises me is the quality of it all. Clean, lean, bright, fresh, Ton Kiang's dim sum taste homemade. Different delicate noodle-wrapped dumplings are filled with a stunning combination of scallops and shrimp or shrimp and pork or just very fresh, sweet shrimp, a sign of well-made dim sum. Look for deep-fried taro croquettes, the outside coated with crackling shredded taro threads, the inside filled with soft, creamy mashed taro. The Shanghai-style dumplings, filled with pork and Chinese chives, are wrapped in thinly rolled raw bread dough. They are fried on one side and then steamed to create a taste sensation. The miniature egg custards have shimmering fillings and warm, flaky crusts. For a change, try a plate of miniature doughnuts, soft and chewy with a rich egg-custard filling.

The first-floor dining room has more amenities than the incredibly low prices of its food would warrant. Painted pale rose with Chinese landscapes on the walls and patterned carpeting, the room comfortably seats parties of four at blond wood booths and larger groups in the center of the room at round tables. The big family parties sit upstairs.

CAFÉS

SAM AND HENRY'S COOL BEANS . . . .

4342A California Street
(at 6th Avenue)
415-750-1955
Open daily 7 A.M. to 5 P.M.
Credit cards: D, MC, V

Painted blue like the summer sky, this miniscule coffeehouse has but four or five stools and a counter, with a few indoor tables newly added and a tiny table and a bench outside next to a metal newspaper rack with the local sheets and the daily *New York Times*. The two owners, Sam and Henry, make absolutely exquisite coffee: intense, rich, and aromatic without any bitterness, on a par with what you get in Italy. At last they don't have to serve it in paper cups. With a mini-expansion into a space next door, they now can wash dishes. They also offer first-rate House of Bagels bagels (see page 331) with cream cheese and a few nice sandwiches.

The Cool Beans guys never forget a face. They know practically everyone who hangs out in their shop and most of the patrons seem to know one another. Laid-back reggae seems to be the sound of choice, a background for talk and reading. People also buy their coffee beans here and pluck cookies from jars to munch. A funny assortment of photographs and containers of wrapped candy constitutes the decor, along with the whimsical paint job. Everyone who steps into Sam and Henry's knows that something special is happening here. If you love coffee, get over there and see for yourself.

BARS

PAT O'SHEA'S MAD HATTER. . . . .

3848 Geary Boulevard
(at 3rd Avenue)
415-752-3148
Open Monday through Friday
11 A.M. to 2 A.M., Saturday and
Sunday 10 A.M. to 2 A.M.
Credit cards: AE, D, MC, V

This rollicking neighborhood sports bar was catapulted to culinary fame when Nancy Oakes started cooking lunch here. No self-respecting, beer-guzzling football fan could believe he was eating and loving the likes of stuffed quail, grilled veal sweetbreads, and roasted monkfish with mussels, but Oakes put it out for the price of barroom hamburgers. She went on to open the multimillion-dollar Boulevard with superdesigner Pat Kuleto, and Pat O'Shea's food service floundered. But now, barman Johnny Love owns Pat O'Shea's and he hired a culinary school grad to run the kitchen, who puts out the best fish and chips and fried onion rings in town. Both fresh fish fingers and big onion rings have a thick if light batter that shatters as you bite into it. The flat-cut fries are crisp, golden, and creamy inside. The kitchen uses clean-tasting vegetable oil, one secret behind successful deep-fried food. A pink, house-made tartar sauce tastes spectacular as an accompaniment.

And Pat O'Shea's maintains its sports bar identity with many easily visible televisions mounted high on the walls, new pool tables, and fourteen different beers on tap.

DELICATESSENS/TAKEOUT

EUROPEAN FOOD . . . .

3038 Clement Street
(between 31st and 32nd avenues)
415-750-0504
Open daily 10 A.M. to 9 P.M.
Credit cards: AE, MC, V

The familiar smells of smoked fish and garlic of the Jewish delis I grew up with in Chicago engulf me when I walk into European Food. But the familiarity ends there. A dizzying range of Eastern European products in Cryovac fills the glass-doored refrigerators. You need to speak Russian if you want any guidance on the myriad fresh and cured sausages; the case of whole cold- and hot-smoked fish; the prepared foods counter laden with Eastern European specialties I've never seen before. European Food sells wholesale and cheap, but if you're not familiar with its products you might end up with a lot of something you don't really like. There are lots of things here I do like:

chubby, mild veal hot dogs; garlicky Ukranian sausages called *kabanosy*; gigantic hunks of creamy Havarti cheese at terrific prices; superfresh white farmers' cheese for blintzes; pint cartons of fresh salmon roe caviar; smoked pork loins for sandwiches; bags of frozen home-made meat filled *pelmeni* (meaty Russian tortellini that I poach in boiling salted water and serve with a spoonful of Straus whole milk yogurt, or Russian sour cream and fresh snipped dill on top).

I like the Russian salads and pickled things at the prepared foods counter at the front. The Russian potato salad doesn't skimp on mayonnaise. The finely cubed soft-cooked pota-toes melt into it along with pickles and celery to make a potato salad cum tartar sauce. It's yummy. So is the generously oily Russian-style eggplant and pepper salad with pickles, scented with a hint of cumin; the supergarlickly, mayonnaise-bound chopped mushroom salad; and the colorful layered salted herring salad in which minced beets, cabbage, and hard-boiled eggs are seasoned by the stratum of strong fish. You could make a fabulous *zakuski* table of these salads and other items from European Food to serve with iced vodka. Or you could bring your treasures to nearby Land's End and have a fabulous Russian picnic overlooking the ocean.

GASTRONOM . . . .

5801 Geary Boulevard
(at 22nd Avenue)
415-387-4211
Open daily 9 A.M. to 9 P.M.
Credit cards: MC, V

If you want to put on a Russian meal, call Gastronom. They'll put together a buffet of *zakuski* (Russian salads), smoked fish, stuffed fish, stuffed cabbage, piroshki, *pelmeni*—the works. Or you can drop in to buy excellent Russian-style dairy products like quarts of pourable yogurt, a wonderful drink; farmer's cheese for blintzes; and whipped farmer's cheese for drizzling with perfumey Australian honey or pre-served apricots. One advantage of shopping at Gastronom is that the counterwomen speak English. Another is the selection of smoked fish, house-made cucumber and tomato pickles, and dairy.

HAIG'S DELICACIES . . . .

642 Clement Street
(between 7th and 8th avenues)
415-752-6283
Open Monday through Friday
9:30 A.M. to 6:30 P.M.,
Saturday 9 A.M. to 6 P.M.
Credit cards: MC, V

One of the oldest international food shops in the city, Haig's shelves are packed with jars and cans of exotic products from all over the globe: Indian curry pastes and Anglo-Indian curry powders; Indonesian *kecap manis* (the ancestor of ketchup); Middle Eastern sumac; hard-to-find Aleppo pepper (medium-hot, sweet, moist red pepper flakes that are my favorite of all the dried chiles); bulgur in fine, medium, and coarse grains; Armenian-prepared foods; coffees; teas; Louisiana hot sauces; halvah; Turkish delight; six different fetas in bulk; olives—any sort of packaged food necessary to prepare a mind-bog-gling variety of ethnic dishes. If you can't find it here, you might have to hop on a plane.

5641 Geary Boulevard
(at 21st Avenue)
415-751-8810
Open Monday through Saturday
9 A.M. to 9 P.M.,
Sunday until 8 P.M.
Credit cards: MC, V

This spacious, modern, well-stocked Russian deli has a self-serve hot table near the front door, and one of the dishes on it, a baked mushroom and sour cream pudding mysteriously called *julien* is worth a drive across town. You pay by the pound. That doesn't stop the Russian women who shop at New World from filling large Styrofoam cartons right to the top. I can't blame them. I'm addicted, too. I love the densely packed thinly sliced mushrooms and the voluptuous sour cream and egg custard that binds them together and the way the top gets golden and crusty. I love the way sweet buttery braised onions melt into the casserole. You can make a meal around this dish, and a vegetarian one at that.

I also like New World's *plov*, a saffron-tinted pilaf studded with big hunks of fatty beef and lots of julienned carrots because the fluffy yellow rice has so much character. A big pile of hot *plov* adds up to a very yummy and inexpensive lunch.

PICKLED SALMON

SERVES 10 TO 12

Multitalented cookbook writer Joyce Goldstein used to make this marvelous pickled salmon at Square One in the spring, around Passover. Actually I first tasted it at a seder of restaurant people. We each brought a dish, but this is the one that knocked me out. If someone ever gives you a whole salmon that they just caught, don't freeze it. Pickle it.

2 cups white vinegar

1½ cups water

6 tablespoons sugar

2 tablespoons kosher salt

2 pounds salmon fillet, skin removed

2 tablespoons mixed pickling spices

6 bay leaves

2 white or yellow onions, sliced ¼ inch thick

1 Bring the vinegar, water, sugar, and salt to a boil. Let this mixture cool completely.

2 Cut the salmon into pieces that are approximately 1 inch by 2 inches.

3 In a ceramic crock, glass bowl, or plastic container, place a layer of salmon pieces, then a sprinkling of pickling spices and bay leaves, a layer of onions, then salmon, spices and bay leaves, onion, continuing until you have used all. Pour the cooled marinade over the fish. Cover the container and refrigerate for 3 to 4 days.

4 Serve the salmon, along with its marinated onions, with matzoh and butter and sliced cucumbers with a sour-cream dressing.

SEAKOR POLISH DELICATESSEN

5957 Geary Boulevard (between
23rd and 24th avenues)
415-387-8660
Open daily 10 A.M. to 8 P.M.
Credit cards: MC, V

This is a small polish sausage factory and deli that
makes gorgeous smoked and fresh kielbasa. Smoky,
dark-hued hunters' sausage is a specialty as is a delicious
hunters' stew of sauerkraut and smoked meats that you
buy by the pound. Sides of smoked pork ribs hang
from a metal rack behind the counter; cured and
smoked pork loins and slabs of bacon fill one side of the immaculate glass case. A constant
stream of Polish-speaking customers buy sausages and smoked meats at this cozy little shop.
Waiting your turn, it's hard to imagine that you're in San Francisco.

A display rack of Polish magazines sits by the front door along with a shelf of florid-
looking Polish greeting cards. Shelves of imported Polish fruit jams, hot-pepper purée, preserved cherries, and other delicacies fill the wall opposite the sausage counter. Someone
always seems to be sitting at the single table in the window with two chairs, reading a
Polish newspaper while munching on a sausage or some stuffed cabbage topped with a big
dollop of ketchup. Of all the Eastern European delis in the immediate area, Seakor is the
best place for fresh and smoked sausages.

BAKERIES/PASTRIES

ALLSTAR DONUTS

901 Clement Street
(at 10th Avenue)
415-221-9838
Open daily 24 hours
Cash only

There are a number of Allstar Donut shops around
town, but this particular branch turns out exceptionally
light, airy doughnuts cooked in clean oil. A classic
maple bar filled with custard may be just the dessert
you're looking for after a bowl of Thai noodles. The
glazed doughnuts have character without tasting artifi-
cial, and chopped coconut and cinnamon are used as a topping for crumb doughnuts here.
The immaculate shop is much frequented by neighborhood mothers with small children,
and the young women behind the counter are models of patience.

HOUSE OF BAGELS

5030 Geary Boulevard (between
14th and 15th avenues)
415-752-6000
Open daily 6 A.M. to 6 P.M.
Cash only

Bagel lovers from all over the city converge on this
Jewish bakery for authentic, chewy, substantial bagels.
The onion bagels are not coated with burned bits but
rather a scattering of sweetly caramelized onion. The
sesame bagel is judiciously sprinkled with the perfume
of the Middle East. When you buy the bagels at the
bakery they are always fresh, which means chewy, the correct texture for a bagel. The difference between a House of Bagels bagel and Noah's bagels is one of style. Noah's bagels are
soft and bready: the Wonder Bread of bagels. The House of Bagels product has soul.
This bakery also makes an old-fashioned rye bread, a bit soft but full of flavor. The rye with

seeds is laced with too many assertive caraway seeds; the plain rye is better. Other Jewish baked goods are available, such as corn rye and sweet rolls, but the bagel reigns supreme at this house.

MOSCOW AND TBLISI BAKERY. . . . .

5540 Geary Boulevard (between
19th and 20th avenues)
415-668-6959
Open daily 7 A.M. to 9 P.M.
Cash and checks only

The line never stops at this neighborhood crossroads for the Russian community. Very few words of English are uttered by the counterwomen, who grab your delicious, amazingly light-textured black bread or tall, crusty-but-soft white (the rye is okay, but not as wonderful as these two loaves), and slap them into plastic bags. Both loaves miraculously demonstrate that bread can have character, flavor, and a real crust while still having a soft texture. These are breads even children will like. The one thing the women do ask is if you want them sliced.

I happen to like this bakery's heavy cherry and almond strudel, but the sweet rolls are too light and airy. The richly filled poppy seed rolls are a poppy-seed lovers dream come true. A big hunk of spicy honey cake studded with walnuts is a must with tea. Also delicious are the meat, cheese, or mushroom-filled pierogi, deep-fried turnovers of yeasty, light dough crisped in the deep fryer. I think they're the best in town.

The bakery really looks like preglasnost Russia: just a counter with bread, a man counting money, the actual ovens and bread tables visible through an open door. A community bulletin board outside the bakery will no doubt be helpful to you if you read Russian.

SCHUBERT'S . . . .

521 Clement Street (between
6th and 7th avenues)
415-752-1580
Open Monday through Friday
7 A.M. to 6:30 P.M.,
Saturday 7 A.M. to 6 P.M.,
Sunday 9 A.M. to 5 P.M.
Credit cards: MC, V

Among the whipped cream-cake set, Schubert's has been a hangout since 1911, but I like the old-fashioned coffee cakes, particularly an almond ring filled with almond paste and paved with toasted sliced walnuts on top. The walnut sour cream ring tastes gloriously of sour cream. The coffee cakes are lighter and less sweet than most others of their ilk, but full of honest flavor. Simple sugar cookies are similarly excellent.

ICE CREAM/CHOCOLATES

GELATO CLASSICO . . . .

750 Clement Street (at 9th Avenue)
415-751-1522
Open Monday through Saturday
11:30 A.M. to 8 P.M,
Sunday 11:30 A.M. to 7 P.M.
Cash only

Bubble teas and bubble smoothies are also served at this cheerful little ice cream shop along with Gelato Classico's bright-flavored ice creams and ices. Since Italian gelato has less butterfat than American ice cream, it works better after a clean Asian meal. See pages 141 and 255 for more information.

JOE'S ICE CREAM . . . .

5351 Geary Boulevard
(at 18th Avenue)
415-751-1950
www.joesicecream.citysearch.com
Open Sunday through Thursday
11 A.M. to 10 P.M.,
Friday and Saturday until 11 P.M.
Cash only

The home of the It's-It, a chocolate-encased ice cream sandwich made with two oatmeal cookies, Joe's charms by remaining so old-fashioned. All the ice cream is made on the premises and scooped to order. The wonderful milk shakes are constructed with a lot of ice cream, and blended with enough milk to make them drinkable. The young counterpeople couldn't be sweeter or more meticulous, and the place looks timeless and well used. There is a small sit-down counter with stools where you can get grilled sandwiches and fountain items, and a ledge with short stools in the window provides just the place to sip a shake and watch the activity at the Alexandria Theater across the street. Joe's also sells chocolate-covered frozen bananas, another old-fashioned classic. The only concession to modern trends comes in the form of frozen yogurt.

SEE'S CANDIES . . . .

754 Clement Street (at 9th Avenue)
415-752-0953
www.sees.com
Open Monday through Saturday
10 A.M. to 6 P.M.,
Sunday 11 A.M. to 4 P.M.
Credit cards: AE, MC, V

Everyone in San Francisco knows about See's peerless peanut brittle: crunchy, buttery, and liberally studded with fresh peanuts. You find yourself nibbling one piece after another until you're a quarter pound into a box. The brittle is as beloved and symbolic of San Francisco as Dungeness crab and sourdough bread, and it travels a lot better. Hence the convenient stands at the San Francisco airport. The company was started by the See family in Los Angeles in 1921 and expanded to San Francisco in 1934.

Many treats present themselves in long glass cases in See's immaculate, white-tiled candy shops. The thrill of putting together a box of your favorites piece by piece—dark and light chocolate–covered nuts; turtles; the fabulous milk chocolate–covered English toffee rolled in chopped almonds called toffee-ettes (you can tell I'm a nuts and chews gal)—ranks with a walk across the Golden Gate Bridge on a sunny day. See's makes solid, middle-of-the-road, moderately priced, American-style chocolates of the highest order. Their candy is always fresh, and with every purchase, large or small, the buxom ladies behind the counter in their white uniforms hand you a free chocolate. For other locations, see pages 124, 306 and 380.

LIEN HING SUPERMARKET #3 . . . .

400 Clement Street (at 5th Avenue)
415-386-6333
Open daily 8 A.M. to 7 P.M.
Credit cards: MC, V

Many bargain-conscious Chinese shoppers claim that Lien Hing is even cheaper than New May Wah across the street. It does have two other branches in Chinatown (see pages 36 and 40), so this small chain buys in volume. Very attractive specials like packages of six fresh jumbo quail for amazingly cheap, or a good price on usually expensive fresh litchis (one of the most aromatic and sensual of all fruits) bring shoppers in. I always make a pass at both Lien Hing and New May Wah to see what's around. If one features gorgeous huge bunches of watercress, the other may have cellophane bags of tiny, sweet prune plums. Both markets are definitely working hard for your patronage.

NEW MAY WAH SUPERMARKET . . . .

525–547 Clement Street
(between 6th and 7th avenues)
415-668-2583
Open daily 7:30 A.M. to 7:30 P.M.
Credit cards: MC, V

May Wah, which used to have branches in Chinatown and on Irving Street, has consolidated its operations on Clement by taking over two large storefronts, one for groceries, pork, and produce; the other for fish, poultry, and other meat items. Between the two stores, New May Wah covers all Asian, and most Western, cooking needs. A huge variety of bottled Asian sauces, condiments, and spice pastes fills the aisles. Rice wines and Chinese spirits, citron honey tea, noodles, tofu, pickled vegetables, spices, the mundane and the unusual are all there. Sidewalk produce tables stretch down the block, piled high with seasonal fruits. What better way to get passersby to stop? Next door in a utilitarian cement-floored room, bright red live shrimp swim in tanks and clear-eyed whole fish rest on ice. Between the two stores, New May Wah is as large and complete as any Asian grocery.

SUPER TOKIO JAPANESE MARKET . . . .

251 Clement Street
(between 3rd and 4th avenues)
415-668-1118
Open daily 10 A.M. to 7 P.M.
Credit cards: AE, MC, V

Super Tokio is as orderly and packaged as the Chinese supermarkets down the block are free form and bulk. Everything is about packaging at Tokio, a food store much frequented by teenagers who gravitate to the extensive candy and snack section and the expansive cold drink case where cold cans of Japanese milk tea share the shelves with small, elegant bottles of Coke. The look and shape of the container becomes part of the fun of drinking it. This is the place to pick up amazingly bright-flavored Morinaga grapefruit or green apple candies, packaged Japanese curries, *panko* crumbs, Hawaiian Sun tropical fruit drinks, and a fairly wide selection of sakes.

PRODUCE

CLEMENT PRODUCE . . . .

645 Clement Street
(between 7th and 8th avenues)
415-221-4101
Open daily 7 A.M. to 8 P.M.
Credit cards: MC, V

This long, narrow, bustling produce store does not carry unusual produce, but the prices are cheap. Sometimes there are piles of desirable things like blood oranges or Fuji apples that are especially inexpensive. Clement Produce is but one of many serviceable produce stores within five blocks or so on lower Clement. Each one might display one or two special items—mangoes, some good-looking pea sprouts—at an excellent price to tempt people into the store, so on a serious shopping trip you might want to give them all a quick visit to grab the best things.

4TH AVENUE AND GEARY
FARMERS MARKET . . . .

3931 Geary Street (at 4th Avenue)
415-831-1067
Open daily 8 A.M. to 9 P.M.
Cash only

A new development in San Francisco, the 4th Avenue and Geary Farmers Market approximates the great produce stores in Berkeley—Monterey Foods and the Berkeley Bowl—in its scope, size, and prices. It even has a parking lot behind it so you can pick up watermelons or a selection of casabas, crenshaws, and honeydews. Fruit is currently the draw at this expansive, freestanding market dedicated solely to produce. It's piled into huge containers outside and big wooden tables inside. You even might run into a farmer standing by his plums offering everyone tastes. In this price-conscious neighborhood, a produce store has to offer specials. The other day you could buy five small, ripe, but not too ripe, avocados for $1, a pair of smooth-skinned mangoes for $1, and a pint of sweet, plump Oregon blueberries for $1.50. Whoever buys for this market knows what he or she is doing. They're getting ripe fruit from the best growing areas just at the moment when it's the most plentiful. They're buying lots of it and selling it for cheap. I'm very excited about the opening of this store. Though this is not the place to shop for organic produce, the balance of quality and price definitely works in the shopper's favor. You're inspired to try new varieties of fruit, buy lots of old favorites, and even pick up some vegetables, too. As far as I'm concerned, you can never buy too much produce, and the 4th Avenue and Geary Farmers Market is one place to indulge.

661 Clement Street (at 8th Avenue)
415-221-0656
Open daily 8:30 A.M. to 7:30 P.M.
Cash only

From the outside, this small, disorganized corner market may not look like a destination for produce, but the store carries a small selection of high-quality greens, like baby Shanghai bok choy and pristine, thick-stemmed *yu choy* that are trucked up from Los Angeles. These special greens are in perfect condition, leaves aglow with health and freshness. You might find some plump beige lotus root or bright green fuzzy melon. In the summer, fresh litchis sit in a box on the counter where the cashier can count them out. For prime Asian vegetables and some fruits, stop in here.

VILLAGE MARKET . . . .

4555 California Street
(at 8th Avenue)
415-221-0445
Open weekdays 8 A.M. to 8 P.M.,
weekends 9 A.M. to 7 P.M.
Credit cards: MC, V

This market has one of the prettiest organic produce sections in the city and it begins outside on the sidewalk under an awning. Wooden shelves of fruit and buckets of the most luscious flowers—in spring, daffodils, tulips, and ranunculus at excellent prices—make you want to fill your arms with them. Indoors, the old wooden floors are stacked with casually arranged displays of organic strawberries, white asparagus, organic bananas, spring greens, and del Cabo tomatoes (organically grown tomatoes from Baja California to get you through most of the winter).

The Village Market combines a commitment to healthful and organic foods with an aesthetic that makes you want to join up. Two wooden benches with cast-iron legs have been placed outside the store between large wooden flower boxes, and you are tempted to plop down and admire the beauty and color of nature's gifts, so appealingly offered.

MEAT AND POULTRY

NEW ON SANG . . . .

617 Clement Street (at 7th Avenue)
415-750-8250
Market open daily
8:30 A.M. to 7:30 P.M.; rotisserie
open daily 11 A.M. to 9 P.M.
Cash only

At New On Sang you can get Chinese-style butchered chickens with head and feet, partridges, pheasants, and ducks with all appendages attached. Nothing enriches a chicken stock more than gelatinous chicken feet. Duck wings and feet by the pound are also available. You find this impeccable poultry past the Chinese deli counter with hanging roast ducks and premade dishes kept warm on steam tables. A branch of the bustling On Sang Poultry Company on Stockton Street in Chinatown (see page 42), New On Sang's raw birds can induce real culinary excitement if you're a cook.

WYCEN FOODS . . . .

625 Clement Street
(between 7th and 8th avenues)
415-751-3981
Open Wednesday through Monday
10 A.M. to 6 P.M.
Cash only

From the outside you're not exactly sure what this shop sells, but once inside you notice two types of food: Chinese sausage and mango gummies in small, medium, and large bags. These happen to be two of my favorites. The small, skinny, dry-cured Chinese sausages hang in pairs in back of the counter. There are many different kinds, but I can attest for the "regular" pork sausages (not the "lean," an oxymoron when linked to sausages), which are delicious sliced and placed on top of rice as it cooks. Chinese sausages are sweet rather than salty and their juices bring out the sweetness in rice. Wycen's sausages, sweetly cured Chinese bacon, and cured duck legs, all made in San Leandro and sold at this store and one at 903 Washington Street in Chinatown, have a pleasant, meaty, not too aged, middle-of-the-road appeal, accessible to all palates.

As for the large, medium, and small packages of individually wrapped Cocoaland mango gummies from Malaysia, the truest flavored and the best of all gummies in my humble opinion, I couldn't find them at any other store in this busy Richmond District Chinatown. Wycen has clearly cornered the market. Happy to find them, I bought several large bags at a very good price.

FISH

SEAFOOD CENTER . . . .

831 Clement Street
(between 9th and 10th avenues)
415-752-3496
Open Monday through Saturday
9:30 A.M. to 6 P.M.,
Sunday until 5:30 P.M.
Cash only

This fresh-smelling Chinese fish store features fresh local fish and pomfret, a small silvery fish that bakes and barbecues well. I have spotted skate wing, live sea bass, carp, catfish, crab, and lobsters. The water in the tanks of live fish and crustaceans is always clean and bubbly and the fish on ice always look dewy. This is my favorite fish store in the Richmond and the one that I go to for flatfish. The beauty of whole flatfish, like sand dabs or rex sole, is that they cook quickly in the oven. Here's how: Preheat the oven to 400°F. Sprinkle the whole fish with chopped shallots, salt, pepper, a little white wine, and some olive oil or butter. Cook for about 5 minutes, depending on the thickness of the fish. You can test for doneness by sticking a knife into the bone. If the fish is ready, the delicate meat will easily lift off, and you will have a delicious main course in no time at all.

COOKWARE AND BOOKS

GREEN APPLE BOOKS . . . .

506 Clement Street (at 6th Avenue)
415-387-2272
www.greenapplebooks.com
Open Sunday through Thursday
10 A.M. to 10:30 P.M.,
Friday and Saturday until 11:30 P.M.
Credit cards: MC, V

In the heart of the best food-shopping section of
Clement Street, Green Apple Books holds down the
food literature front with one of the largest collections
of new and used cookbooks in the city. Shelves and
shelves of practically new volumes marked down to half
price, plus many rarities (like Doris Muscatine's guide
to San Francisco restaurants with recipes, published
thirty years ago, a book many of us cut our culinary

teeth on), make it difficult to leave the store without an armful of books. By thumbing
through some of the treasures, such as a yellowing volume called *Southern Cooking* by Mrs.
S.R. Dull, a 1928 edition for $10, you might find a recipe for orange juice (cut oranges in
half…) or Foolish Pie. More current works by the best food writers are well represented in
the used section, which indicates that the store's cookbook buyers know what they're doing.

KAMEI HOUSEHOLD WARES . . . .

606 Clement Street (at 7th Avenue)
415-666-3688
Open daily 9 A.M. to 7 P.M.
Credit cards: MC, V

Some stunning china for both serving and setting the
table can be purchased for a song at the many Asian
cookware stores in the city. At the two Kamei stores
practically across the street from each other, one finds
Japanese bowls with intricate, speckled glazes, Chinese

bowls in gorgeous shades of jade green, and a selection of small, elegant, weighty iron tea
pots in strong colors. Heavy stone mortars and pestles at a fraction of the cost at tony
houseware stores, and hard-to-find coconut graters in both stool and portable configura-
tions, can be gleaned from the piled-high shelves. There might be seven-gallon calibrated
plastic food containers with covers for home pickling, woks large and small, bamboo steamers, and a whole section of hanging car deodorizers, which lends Kamei the authentic aroma
of Hong Kong.

KAMEI RESTAURANT SUPPLY . . . .

507 Clement Street (at 6th Avenue)
415-666-3699
Open daily 9 A.M. to 7 P.M.
Credit cards: MC, V

Though the division of merchandise between Kamei
Household and Kamei Restaurant Supply is not clear to
me—lots of the same stuff—I somehow find more
treasures at the restaurant supply store, where you can
find sturdier items that cost a little more. There's a

wider range of Asian ceramics here, and some of them are stunning, a blend of traditional
shapes and bold, modern colors and patterns. For serving pieces, like platters, I prefer this
Kamei. Since the two loaded shops are so close to each other, I always check out both.

RED-BRAISED WHOLE PORK SHOULDER

SERVES 10 TO 12

This opulent braised pork has been a favorite dish of mine since Bruce Cost once cooked it for my birthday, surrounded with baby bok choys. The recipe, from Bruce Cost's *Asian Ingredients*, is not difficult to make, and the cooking pork fills the kitchen with the most seductive aromas. You can buy all the dry ingredients you need at any of the Chinese markets listed in the book, and the pork at any of the Chinese meat counters.

3 to 4 quarts water to cover

5- to 7-pound pork shoulder, with bone and rind

¾ cup Shaoxing wine (Chinese rice wine)

6 star anise pods

One 3-inch cinnamon stick

8 cloves garlic, smashed

Fresh ginger cut into 10 thin slices

2 or 3 pieces dried tangerine peel

2 dried red chiles

1 whole scallion

1½ cups soy sauce

6 Chinese rock sugar crystals, each about 1 inch square

1 tablespoon kosher salt

1 In a large pot, bring the water to a boil and add the pork. When it comes to a boil again, skim off any foam and reduce the heat to medium. Add the wine and cook, partially covered, for 20 minutes.

2 Add the star anise, cinnamon stick, garlic, ginger, tangerine peel, chiles, and scallion and cook for another 20 minutes.

3 Add the soy sauce, sugar crystals, and salt, and continue to cook, turning the meat occasionally, for another 2 to 3 hours. The rind and fat should be very soft when the pork is done.

4 Remove the pork from the liquid and keep warm. Strain the sauce into a large skillet and, over high heat, reduce to a syrup. This may take 15 minutes or longer.

5 When the sauce is the consistency of thin syrup, put the pork in the center of a large platter and pour the sauce over the meat. Eat with lots of rice and a green vegetable.

SOUTH OF
MARKET
THIRD STREET
POTRERO HILL

SOUTH OF MARKET, THIRD STREET & POTRERO HILL

RESTAURANTS

1 Acme Chophouse
2 Bacar
3 Bizou
4 Chez Maman
5 Chez Papa
6 chez spencer
7 Fly Trap Restaurant
8 Fringale
9 Hawthorne Lane
10 Kyo-ya at the Sheraton Palace Hotel
11 LuLu
12 South Park Cafe
13 21st Amendment
14 Umbria
15 Universal Cafe

CAFÉS

16 Brain Wash
17 The Butler & The Chef Café
18 Caffè Centro
19 Caffè Roma Coffee Roasting Company
20 Farley's
21 Soma Caffè

BARS

22 Asia SF
2 Bacar
23 42 Degrees
9 Hawthorne Lane
24 Kelly's Mission Rock
25 The Ramp
26 XYZ

MARKETS

27 Rainbow Grocery
28 Trader Joe's

PRODUCE

27 Rainbow Grocery

FISH

29 California Sunshine

WINES AND SPIRITS

30 K & L Wines
31 Wine House Limited

COOKWARE AND BOOKS

32 Economy Restaurant Supply
17 The Butler & The Chef

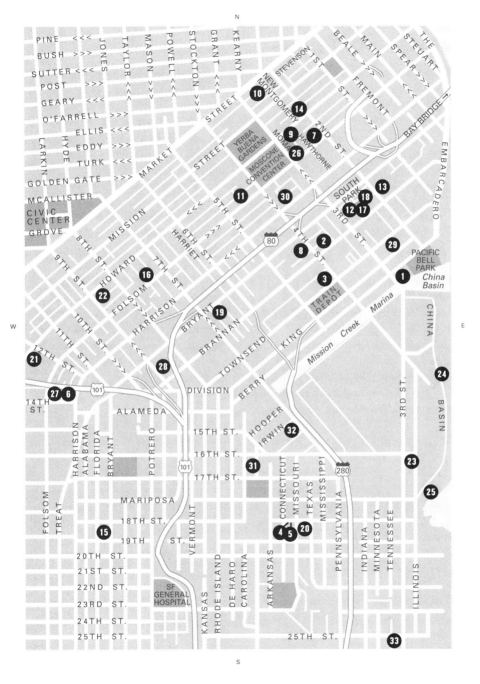

ACME CHOPHOUSE . . . .

24 Willie Mays Plaza (at 3rd Street)
415-644-0240
www.acmechophouse.com
Open nightly 5:30 to 10 P.M.;
open on day-game days
10:30 A.M. to 2:30 P.M.
Moderate-Expensive
Credit cards: AE, DC, MC, V

The steak dinner reigns iconic—not only for poor souls pondering their last meal, but for many of us on celebratory occasions. Every year when I ask my son what he wants for his birthday dinner, he tells me in great detail: a lean but juicy, thick New York steak cooked medium; Caesar salad; crisp roasted new potatoes; green beans; and a poppy seed cake with strawberry–whipped cream frosting, à la mode. Every year I make this meal for him, and every year he complains that I undercook the steak (which I do unconsciously, because I can't stand to cook steak beyond medium-rare. He honestly enjoys the rest of the meal).

This year, the Acme Chophouse opened right before his birthday and I suggested that we go there only because I thought that this steak house could do as good a job of the birthday dinner as I. I also assumed that they could cook a steak medium without having a nervous breakdown. My confidence in the performance of this new restaurant stemmed from the fact that I know all the players—Traci Des Jardins from Jardinière, veteran chef Thom Fox, and enlightened twenty-first-century director of operations Larry Bain—all of whom know how food should taste. If they decided to launch a steak house, it would have to be right in every detail. And so with much fear, debate, and conflicted feeling, three of us went to Acme for my son Harry's eighteenth birthday.

Just off the majestic plaza planted with twenty-four full-grown palms trees on the east side of Pacific Bell Park, the space is a sweepingly dramatic room, a man's room, a natural spot for a steak house. Judging from the menu, the Des Jardins group is well steeped in the American steak-house tradition. I know that at least one of them has eaten at the temple of steak, Peter Luger in Brooklyn, where the beef tastes like foie gras, but the sides are pedestrian. The Des Jardins group have culled a handful of classic side dishes and salads and fleshed out the menu with the most appealing set of bar items anywhere. (The bar items are always available no matter where you sit.) So the three of us hunched over the menu and the birthday boy exclaimed that there were so many dishes he wanted with his steak that he didn't know what to order.

"Get them all," I said. "We'll share." Which is exactly what Acme intends because everything is served family style.

We ate wedges of iceberg lettuce slathered in really good blue cheese dressing—a sharp vinaigrette made creamy with blue cheese puréed into it, plus little hunks of blue cheese folded in at the end. A Caesar of whole leaves of crisp, pale romaine had a dressing redolent of anchovies. And the dreamy wilted spinach salad was clean and light (not soggy), and dressed with smoky bacon and balsamic vinegar.

Acme's steaks come from either grass-fed cattle that graze progressively higher in the Sierras as the weather gets warmer in Northern California, or grain-finished Niman Ranch cattle raised to a natural protocol. The provenance of each cut of meat is indicated on the menu and the steak aficionado is in for two distinctly different experiences—both first-rate. A huge 32-ounce Niman rib-eye for two arrived partially sliced à la Peter Luger, cooked to a perfect medium-rare. Each buttery bite bespoke of meat naturally larded with fat. My son's 16-ounce Niman New York, cooked exactly medium, trimmed of fat and full of flavor, won highest marks from the severest critic at the table. But the steak that took me by surprise was the grass-fed butcher steak, which turned out to be a thick tri-tip, cooked medium-rare and sliced. Part of the sirloin, tri-tip is usually chewy to say the least, but this steak was astonishingly tender, juicy, and, best of all, full of bright, rich, beefy flavor. I loved it. Now I want to try every cut from a grass-fed animal.

And the sides? Thin, crisp onions rings with real onion flavor; unctuous, but not heavy scalloped potatoes in a gratin dish with an enticing crusty top; mild macaroni and cheese, just cheddary enough to act as an accompaniment to beef; tender, skin-on french fries that taste like potatoes; and the best creamed spinach I have ever tasted—just loads of tender spinach and barely thickened sweet cream. We wrapped things up with a demure, shared banana split, of which I got only one bite of chocolate ice cream with an Italian *amarone* cherry. The rest disappeared.

When the great feast was over, the birthday boy said, "This is like a dream restaurant. It has all dishes I love and they make them just right!"

I didn't know whether to be happy that the boy was so pleased, or sad that I hadn't cooked it myself. But I certainly am glad that we now have a steakhouse in San Francisco that lives up to the standards of our best restaurants.

BACAR . . . .

448 Brannan (between
3rd and 4th streets)
415-904-4100
Open Monday through Thursday
5:30 P.M. to midnight,
Friday and Saturday until 1 A.M.,
Sunday until 11 P.M.
Moderate-Expensive
Credit cards: MC, V

Prior to my first visit, I had imagined Bacar (Latin for "wine goblet") to be a grand brasserie with a dramatic entrance—like La Coupole in Paris or Balthazar in New York. But the sleek, airy glass-and-brick restaurant has an unsigned front door hidden in the middle of the block. (I was sure the restaurant would be in the flamboyant building of lofts across the street.) Arriving without reservations, the hostess gave us a table at a banquette in the main dining room when we promised we'd leave by 7:30 P.M. I set to speed-reading the clipboard of wines by the glass and the multipage menu, passing up the book of wines by the bottle.

Ordering food was a snap because the menu offers but a handful of dishes, some of which jumped out at me as tempting—house-cured salt cod cake with horseradish cream; crispy wok-fried sardines and lemon slices; a cracker-thin-crusted pizza with serrano ham, asparagus, and Manchego cheese; a wok-cooked Maine lobster, and a side order of scalloped potatoes. Deciding on wines took a bit longer, but with the waiter breathing down my neck I managed to find a crisp Spanish white, Godeval Valdeorras from Galicia, and a velvety, smoky Rhône, a St. Joseph from Chave.

The lobster arrived in a mouthwatering pile, cut up into chunks with the shell still on, smothered in smoky onions, thyme branches, and garlic cloves. The scalloped potatoes, just creamy and cheesy enough, got along nicely with it. The oven-toasted Spanish manchego cheese made the pizza buttery and nutty, and the asparagus, intensified in flavor from roasting, tasted wild. We ate and drank happily and at about 7:20 P.M. I started looking for our waiter. The dining room was full, but jazz in the background seemed to smooth out the din. A roving manager caught my eye and immediately came over to clear the table. He asked about dessert.

"We have a performance at Yerba Buena and we're walking. Is there time for bananas Foster?" The open kitchen behind me looked awfully busy.

"Sure," he said and rushed off to put in the order. It arrived twenty minutes later, warm bananas in caramel sauce with banana ice cream and a crispy meringue. We wolfed it down, paid the check as we licked the spoons, and dashed out, getting to our seats with two minutes to spare.

Intrigued by that vast wine-by-the-glass list, I returned early one Sunday evening and sat at the bar. Oddly enough, it was the one facet of the operation that really didn't hold up on a second visit. If you are lucky enough to order a glass from a just-opened bottle, you are fine. But if your pour comes from a bottle that has been opened the night before and has sat above the steamy bar (from the constantly running glass washer), the wine can taste pretty dead. It happened with a glass of 1994 Château Musar, a Lebanese wine I like. The bartender graciously poured a new glass from a freshly opened bottle, but if I had been sitting at a table with friends, would I have gone through the process? The condition of the wines by the glass poses a problem, but I may be the only one who thinks so because the place is full of bona fide wine geeks. Major wine talk circulated around me in the bar. Maybe the geeks know to order their wine by the bottle.

BIZOU . . . .

598 4th Street (at Brannan)
415-543-2222
Open Monday through Friday
11:30 A.M. to 2:30 P.M.,
Monday through Thursday
5:30 to 10 P.M., Friday and
Saturday 5:30 to 10:30 P.M.
Moderate
Credit cards: AE, CB, DC, D,
MC, V

This small, terrific bistro boasts an unusually creative menu of Mediterranean-inspired dishes and a smart, resonant decor. The chef, Loretta Keller, a Star's veteran, and her husband, Joseph Graham, have put together a model restaurant and bar: small, manageable, visually uncluttered, culinarily sophisticated, yet moderate in price. Bizou works because it is a unified statement, a completely realized vision anchored in a European tradition, but free enough to draw on the New World eclecticism of California.

The menu derives its energy from a wood-burning oven in which all sorts of surprising things are cooked, such as sand dabs, our wonderful local flatfish served on the bone, or a ramekin of rich rigatoni baked with pancetta, ricotta, and tomato. Addictive thin-crusted pizzas emerge from the oven, topped perhaps with bitter broccoli rabe, smoky wood-roasted onions, and thin slices of pancetta. My favorite dishes here mine the French country repertoire, but imbue them with current style. *Chou farci* comes as a wedge of a round cake made of layers of savoy cabbage, thinly sliced ham, and sliced apples in a sauce of crème fraîche enriched with the cooking juices. Keller's ethereal *brandade* of salt cod is one of the best versions to be found anywhere. The pastas tend to be nontraditional, like chewy fresh *pappardelle* moistened with a hot, spicy tomato broth, onions cooked in the wood-fired oven, eggplant, and assertive feta. They work because the kitchen understands how to balance a dish of disparate ingredients, making a reason for them to come together.

True to form, the concise one-page wine list is culled from many small importers and introduces interesting bottles from lesser-known wine-growing regions of France and Italy. Cocktails are also available, and it is fun to have them at a small, handsome bar at the front of the restaurant with a signature Bizou flat bread, crisp and paper-thin, studded with olives, onions, and cheese.

Small white linen–covered tables are pushed very close together and the noise level can be high despite carpeting. The walls of the restaurant are painted a particularly delicious color of mustard yellow. Lots of light pours in through oversized square windows during the day, and soft light from hanging glass lamps adds a glow to the dining room at night. A lyrical flower arrangement on a buffet represents the only nonfunctional object in the room. I find the economy of space, scale, and decor as refreshing as the food.

CHEZ MAMAN. . . . .

1453 18th Street (between
Connecticut and Missouri)
415-824-7166
Open daily 11:30 A.M. to 11 P.M.
Inexpensive
Cash only

A tiny offshoot of Chez Papa (see below), Chez Maman offers both savory and sweet crepes. The savory crepes made with buckwheat flour have a pleasant heft and chewiness, though they are still very thin and delicate. They stand up to fillings of melted ham and cheese. The sweet crepes, filled with fresh sugared berries and crème fraîche, are made with white flour and are about as thin as a pancake can be.

Really more of a café than a restaurant, the tiny Chez Maman is painted a resplendent shade of coral. Seating is at a counter in front of the kitchen or at a few aluminum tables inside and, on nice days, outside on the sidewalk. Many of the amenities of Chez Papa are here—tasty, affordable French wines, simple food in small portions, adorable young French waiters, and sophisticated design. The Chez family has colonized this part of Potrero Hill and the natives are celebrating by keeping them both full.

CHEZ PAPA. . . . .

1401 18th Street (at Missouri)
415-824-8210
Open Monday through Saturday
11:30 A.M. to 3 P.M.,
nightly 5:30 to 11 P.M.
Inexpensive
Credit cards: AE, MC, V

The minute this sleek little French-Mediterranean bistro opened on restaurant-starved Potrero Hill it was packed, and deservedly so. Professionally run by the group of Frenchmen who colonized Belden Place in the Financial District (Plouf, Cafe Bastille, B 44), Chez Papa exudes panache on all fronts—food, service, and ambience. The trademark low price for all this value is no small consideration in the current economic climate.

People like to order meals of small plates these days, and Ola Fendert, the former chef at Plouf and now chef at Chez Papa, fills the menu with them. First of all, a crusty baguette with a delicious, olive oil–rich tapenade is set on the aluminum table, which immediately warms everything up. This puts you in the mood for a glass of red wine, like a reasonably priced Chapoutier Crozes Hermitage, a pretty Rhône, for under $30 a bottle. Then you can tuck into little plates of potato, artichoke, and asparagus salad with bacon in a grain mustard vinaigrette; signature mussels served in a metal bucket bathed in sparkling wine and tomato sauce ; two tiny, tender thin-boned lamb chops on bright-flavored ratatouille; or black Mission figs stuffed with Roquefort with prosciutto and *Mâche* salad. Well, you get the idea. One of my favorite dishes is actually a main course, marinated tombo tuna, cooked delectably rare so that this white-fleshed tuna stays juicy, on a bed of the excellent ratatouille and fat, creamy white beans. The simpler, more rustic dishes are the best, like crisp, deep-fried whitebait with fried lemon slices. The fancier dishes, like seared scallops on favas with butter sauce and too much basil, aren't prepared with the same sureness.

The red walls, dark wood floor, bright red chairs, Italian light fixtures of metal and frosted glass use modern materials to achieve old-fashioned bistro warmth. The corner location, which affords lots of light through huge plate-glass windows, adds to the physical appeal of Chez Papa. The hard surfaces and tight seating make for a high noise level and no room to spread out. Potrero Hill locals have already made the place their clubhouse, so it's always crowded, part of the fun of going to a good bistro.

CHEZ SPENCER . . . .

82 14th Street (between
Folsom and Harrison)
415-864-2191
Open Thursday through Saturday
11:30 A.M. to 2:30 P.M.,
Tuesday through Saturday
5:30 to 10:30 P.M.
Expensive
Credit cards: V, MC, D, AE

One reason that insider cachet surrounds stylish chez spencer is that it's hard to find on a narrow street in back of Rainbow Grocery (itself hidden under the freeway along Division). Look for a high fence between apartment buildings with "chez spencer" in a black graffitolike srawl. You enter through a door in the fence, walk through a concrete yard with tables, a can vas awning, and heat lamps, and finally arrive at a small indoor space in a warehouse.

The ceiling of the space soars and is vaulted with arched wooden beams. Your eye is drawn to the wood-burning oven in the middle of the room, then a slate bar with an emphatic flower arrangement to your left, and finally a handful of white-clothed tables to your right. An adept player scrunches over the keyboard of an upright piano wedged between the front wall and the bar. The compact, exposed kitchen nestles in the back of the room next to another tiny dining area on the blind side of the wood-burning oven. All of this inhabits maybe a thousand square feet, but the ceiling makes chez spencer feel airy and spacious.

The surfaces set the tone—the flagstone wainscoting, the polished cement floor, the sculpted wooden chairs with spindly stainless-steel legs, the unfinished walls hung with line drawings in black ink slashed across coarse canvas. The drawings echo the chez spencer graffito on the entry fence, a script replicated on small hand-thrown ceramic plates set at each place. Artists reign here and chez spencer projects so much interesting character that the look may have been the motivation for the restaurant.

The cooking dispels that notion. The food turns out to be as modern and delectable as the visual surroundings. Chef-owner Laurent Katgely, who has headed a number of kitchens around the city, including Foreign Cinema, and Alfy's in San Anselmo, fashioned an elegant bistro menu that is meticulously executed by chef de cuisine Yasu Ueno. A meal of a first course, a main course, and either cheese or dessert with wine costs $75 a person and exactly satisfies your appetite.

Of all the starters, I'd come back for a warm mackerel salad with yellow wax beans, dressed in an herby, shalloty vinaigrette, and a smoked duck breast salad "lyonnaise"—tissue-thin slices of smoky duck breast swimming in a sauce of red wine vinegar and bacon, scattered with lardons of bacon. The prosciuttolike duck is garnished with a little pouf of frisée topped with a runny if tepid poached egg, which makes the whole composition fly.

The theme of thinly sliced and fanned birds and meat carries into the main courses as well. Thin, rare slices of antelope, with a delicate, gamey edge identical to farm-raised venison, stay warm in a superb natural *jus* scented with juniper berries and peppercorns. Thick slices of potato baked in mountain cheese and cream run into the juices on this voluptuous plate. I still think about it.

I'd be hard pressed to choose between antelope and a tender, juicy, suggestively gamey wood-oven-roasted squab, also in copious and delicious *jus*, with big hunks of smoky butternut squash and an uplifting drizzle of orange *gastrique*, a savory though naturally sweet orange reduction.

After two refined courses at chez spencer you still have appetite for cheese. You get to try three out of six, the portions of which allow you to finish every morsel. A warm, individual apple tart with buttery multilayered crust makes for an alternative ending, along with excellent espresso.

Chez spencer attracts a slim, hip, edgy Eurocentric crowd that appreciates the personal aesthetic of both the food and decor. Though I'm older and fatter than most of the other patrons, I appreciate the way the kitchen plays off restraint and refinement with true, intense flavor. I like the portion size because I can indulge in a full meal and not feel stuffed. (In fact the nine-course $75 prix fixe actually strikes me as doable here, and it's a terrific buy.) But I'd hate to be on a budget at chez spencer, and I certainly wouldn't want to share as a way to save money. Personally, I wouldn't get enough to eat, but maybe that's how chez spencer's clientele stay so skinny.

FLY TRAP RESTAURANT. . . . .

606 Folsom Street (at 2nd Street)
415-243-0580
Open Monday through Wednesday
11:30 A.M. to 9 P.M., Thursday and
Friday 11:30 A.M. to 10 P.M.,
Saturday 5:30 to 10 P.M.
Moderate
Credit cards: AE, DC , MC, V

The Fly Trap re-creates a famous San Francisco restaurant that operated from the turn of the century until 1963 in various locations. Indeed, a glance at the Fly Trap's daily printed menu conjures up meals taken at Jack's, Sam's, Tadich, and the Old Poodle Dog; the bentwood chairs, wooden floors, butcher paper–covered tables, shaded wall sconces, and a tailored wooden bar all seem familiar and appealing.

The decor suits the menu, which offers lots of old-fashioned salads, chops, steaks, pastas, and grilled fish with à la carte accompaniments, a number of them very good. A spectacular celery Victor brings a gigantic half head of gently braised chilled celery, generously garnished with niçoise olives, anchovies, and slices of hard-boiled egg, all moistened with a mild French dressing. Perfection. The classic Caesar is enhanced with high-quality anchovies and big house-made croutons. One of my favorites, white salad, brings together hearts of palm, endive, and mushrooms in a sour-cream dressing topped with a round of goat cheese.

For a main course, two chicken dishes stand out: a wonderful old creation called chicken Raphael Weill, napped in sour cream with lots of mushrooms and big pieces of braised celery (ask for it if it's not on the menu); and coq au vin, chicken in a rich red wine sauce full of bacon and mushrooms. This is one of the few restaurants where you can get grilled calf's liver with bacon and onions, a personal favorite. The kitchen can come up with some lovely hand-formed tortellini stuffed with minced ham and sauced in cream and wild mushrooms; and perfect plates of steamed asparagus and broccoli in hollandaise. For dessert, have a chocolate sundae.

True to old San Francisco grill form, not all the dishes on the long menu are worth ordering, but the Fly Trap does evoke a beloved native restaurant style that is as much fun today as it was eighty years ago. Given the choice between a trendy SOMA statement and the updated Fly Trap, I'd buzz into the Trap any day.

FRINGALE . . . .

570 4th Street (between
Brannan and Bryant)
415-543-0573
www.fringale.citysearch.com
Open Monday through Friday
11:30 A.M. to 2 P.M., Monday
through Saturday 5:30 to 10:30 P.M.
Moderate
Credit cards: AE, MC, V

J'ai la fringale means "I'm starving" in colloquial French; it's what you utter when you're overtaken by a sudden hunger. If this condition should hit you, Gerald Hirigoyen's smart, casual little bistro, Fringale, provides the antidote. This French-Basque chef turns out an inventive repertoire of dishes that will satisfy deep hunger without taxing a shallow pocketbook.

Start right in with a frisée salad with bacon, croutons, and a poached egg tossed in a warm vinaigrette; or if you're really hungry, have the Fringale classic mashed-potato cake studded with shredded duck confit and walnuts, and sauced with a mild, savory vinaigrette. Tricky presentations that draw on classic French technique, such as a chilled terrine of lentils with a rosette of pink lamb tenderloin in the center, sauced in a shalloty mustardy *rémoulade*, are as delicious as they are stunning.

Hirigoyen has a fine touch with fish. His poached halibut drizzled with nutty brown butter served with a psychedelic purée of beets, a mound of buttery spinach, and a pile of green beans is dreamy. If monkfish swathed in a lively bordelaise sauce of shallots and red wine is on the menu, don't pass it up. Of course a tasty *steak frites*, with a shalloty red-wine butter and thin fries, is always a welcome sight at a good price, but so is a tender roast rack of lamb with the most luscious potato gratin and green beans tossed with fresh herbs, a plate made in heaven, for only a few dollars more.

Since Hirigoyen started his cooking career as a pastry chef, better save room for a crisp, warm apple tart with a puff pastry crust, a Biarritz *rocher* of chocolate mousse on a crisp meringue surrounded with crème anglaise, or a palate-cleansing iced Armagnac and coffee parfait.

The cheerful interior has been done in beiges and shades of white with blond wood trim and an elegantly curved bar. Very small tables covered with linen and white paper are pushed close together in front of banquettes. The ambience is 100 percent French bistro. The waiters are mostly French and completely professional; the wine list reasonably priced and full of good little imported wines; the noise level high. From the moment Hirigoyen opened his bistro, it has been packed with discriminating diners who recognize a great bargain trying to edge out the customers who are there for a great time. Be sure to call ahead, particularly for dinner.

HAWTHORNE LANE . . . .

22 Hawthorne Lane (between
Howard and Folsom where
New Montgomery ends)
415-777-9779
www.hawthornelane.com
Open Monday through Friday
11:30 A.M. to 1:30 P.M., Monday
through Thursday 5:30 to 9 P.M.,
Friday and Saturday 5:30 to 10 P.M.;
Café menu Monday through Friday
2:30 to closing
Expensive
Credit cards: D, MC, V

My husband, a civilized, meticulous person, likes Hawthorne Lane better than any other San Francisco restaurant (except mine, of course, Hayes Street Grill). He naturally gravitates to the long oval cherrywood bar where several of the bartenders know him. They churn his Boodles martini until it turns cloudy with ice crystals. They set a bowl of marinated olives and tiny, thin ovals of house-made salami in front of him along with thick crunchy breadsticks. An artist himself, he appreciates the prints on the walls, a changing collection from Crown Point Press that he says is brilliantly curated.

He feels particularly comfortable at the perfectly proportioned upholstered booths in the handsome dining room. It's quieter there than the hard-surfaced barroom and easy to hold a conversation. He admires the look and feel of the elegant glassware and substantial silverware. He can't suppress a smile when the bread basket is brought—a bouquet of breads, rolls, biscuits, and flat breads, that he rifles through, plucking out his favorites. He slathers them with sweet butter and sprinkles on kosher salt from a miniature bowl.

Most of all, he adores the service. He says no other restaurant treats him with such dignity, such intelligence. He claims that the sommelier, Nabil Abi-Ghanem, reads his mind and always finds him the bottles that he craves at that moment. The waiters not only serve, but also listen. They seem to want to accommodate, to personalize the experience for every customer. When the hefty check comes, and it can be breathtaking, my husband says he is happy to pay it because he believes that Hawthorne Lane is a generous restaurant. Its owner, David Gingrass, creates an elevated experience for his patrons—not kid entertainment, not attitude—that makes my husband feel like an adult at a very good party.

Dishes such as artichoke gratinée particularly delight my husband, a fan of both artichokes and dip. And one night, the kitchen came up with an exhilarating grilled peach salad epitomizing the restaurant's American sensibility. Some really good early peaches, sweet, tart, and juicy, were grilled and fanned out on a plate around a little pile of arugula topped with pickled red onion. Two wafer-thin toasts, one with a thin slice of Old Chatham sheep's milk Brie and toasted pistachios, the other spread with peach chutney, completed the composition, a balancing act of sweet, sour, and buttery. I love the rib-eye steak, a thin one with tons of flavor served with a ramekin of soufléd crème fraîche potatoes and watercress. An old standby, Chinese-style roast duck with steamed scallion buns and mango chutney, continues to boast succulent flesh and crispy skin.

Be prepared to spend on wine. The pricey list has few bottles under $30 and lots that cost over $100. So use that spot-on sommelier to get something really interesting.

I have always been a food-first critic. For me good cooking makes up for any number of flaws in service and ambience, but if the food isn't good, the best service and smartest decor will never get me back. At Hawthorne Lane, the whole experience is so integrated that the food, service, and surroundings produce something greater than the sum of its parts.

KYO-YA AT THE SHERATON PALACE HOTEL

2 New Montgomery Street
(between Mission and Market)
415-512-1111
www.kyo-ya-restaurant.com
Open Tuesday through Friday
11:30 A.M. to 2 P.M., Tuesday
through Saturday 6 to 10 P.M.
Prices: Sushi bar, expensive;
restaurant, moderate
Credit cards: AE, DC , D, MC, V

A branch of a Japanese restaurant chain, Kyo-ya brings a higher level of ingredients to San Francisco, so if you hit it on the right day, it can be the best sushi bar in town. To eat here, have about $75 in your pocket, then don't worry about the cost of each pair. You'll get some of the most exquisite sushi you have ever tasted, along with a couple of martinis or a glass carafe of elegant cold sake. The most fabulous sushi at Kyo-ya are made with raw scallops flown in live from Boston in the shell, scooped out and sliced to order, and fresh *hamachi*, or yellowtail, which tastes completely different from the frozen served everywhere else. Also spectacular are the *toro*, tuna-belly meat not even available most places, which reminds me of a slab of butter; sea urchin roe that has a creaminess and nuttiness I've only experienced when I've pried them off the rocks myself; and delicacies like clean-flavored and refreshing Japanese red snapper. There are no fireworks, no inventions, nothing to distract the diner from the perfection of nature. The fish is framed by fingers of rice, each grain huge, fragrant, and chewy, barely adhering to the mass, seasoned with the most judicious application of hot wasabi. If you want to experience sushi at its best, a meal here is worth every penny.

The food is much less expensive in a series of small, luxurious, simply appointed dining rooms in the restaurant. In fact, many of the authentic dishes served here are tasty, unusual, and a terrific buy. A selection of sushi served at table will be much less expensive than at the sushi bar, but of a more mundane quality. Instead, try a whole crab, stir-fried with *matsutake*, enoki, and shiitake mushrooms enriched with egg, which all melts together into a fantastic sauce that you spoon over a bowl of chewy Japanese rice; or a butter-tender steak, sliced into thick pieces and brought sizzling to the table in a covered ceramic dish with two dipping sauces. In addition to these hearty dishes, a whole range of vibrant

Japanese salads and small dishes, soups, and rice porridges are artfully presented and carefully made. Service by waitresses in kimonos brings traditional graciousness to the dining room floor, where you hear as much Japanese spoken as English. This Tokyo-based restaurant, set up to accommodate Japanese visitors to San Francisco, is an emissary of the best of Japanese culture for those of us who live here.

LULU . . . .

816 Folsom Street (near 4th Street)
415-495-5775
www.lulu.citysearch.com
Open Sunday through Wednesday
11:30 A.M. to 10 P.M.,
Thursday through Saturday
until 11 P.M.
Moderate
Credit cards: AE, DC, MC, V

When LuLu opened in the early 1990s, I thought it was the most exciting restaurant in the Bay Area. Reed Hearon had come up with a concept that enshrined a cooking method—the open fire—and both the physical space and the menu paid homage to it. The hearth became the focal point of the experience. Like an altar, it blazed in the middle of the gigantic, barnlike room, chickens and hunks of meat turning over it sending out primal, hunger-inducing smells.

But as much as I was attracted to LuLu, I stopped going. The huge restaurant became so crowded, it collapsed under its own weight. The service turned ragged, patched together with untrained, young waiters, and the food could be inconsistent. You might get something very delicious, or cold food cooked too far in advance, or dishes sloppily thrown together at the last minute. You never knew.

Recently I floated in late on a Wednesday evening after an inspirational Paul Taylor dance performance at Yerba Buena Center. I didn't expect much and ordered conservatively—a chilled half Maine lobster from the oyster bar, English pea and fennel soup, pork loin with fennel and olive oil–mashed potatoes from the rotisserie, and a side order of peas, carrots, and pearl onions. The lobster was fresh and sweet, served with three ramekins of sauce, none of which was needed as far as I was concerned. The puréed pea soup was thick and comforting. The vegetables, so-so. But the pork was fantastic—two, inch-thick moist slabs with two crusty detached rib bones and a mound of hot, creamy mashed potatoes enlivened with just the right amount of olive oil. Practically every dish is served family style on colorful, hand-painted oval platters, and this portion of succulent pork easily satisfied two of us. For dessert, we had lovely warm apple crepes with Calvados ice cream.

I liked the meal so much that I came back two nights later, again after a performance. At 10:15 P.M. on a Friday night, every seat in the gigantic restaurant was taken and we were told to wait at the bar. At 11 P.M. we were seated in the side dining room, which was completely full, where we were presented with a smashing dinner. Still, I thought I should go back just to make sure that I wasn't dreaming. This time I reserved a table early, at 6 P.M., before an 8 P.M. performance. Again, the meal was terrific—every choice stellar.

LuLu's physical size and volume of business enables it to offer a wide selection of both wine and food. With so much to choose from and so much of it good, LuLu has renewed my faith in the big restaurant experience. The huge roaring room, the big, exciting menu, the endless wine cellar, and the packed bar define urban vitality. My hat goes off to founder Reed Hearon who had the vision, and the subsequent management who have the good sense to carry on in the original spirit.

SOUTH PARK CAFE . . . .

108 South Park (between 2nd and
3rd streets, Bryant and Brannan)
415-495-7275
Open Monday through Saturday
5:30 P.M. to 10 P.M.
Moderate
Credit cards: AE, MC, V

From the moment this charming, very French café and restaurant opened fifteen years ago, I wanted to be there. The design of the narrow room, with front windows that open completely onto the sidewalk, a copper bar, and painted wooden banquettes that stretch the length of the restaurant, is so simple, yet so perfectly done, that I felt I was sitting in a Left Bank bistro in Paris. The food here has had its ups and downs with partnership and chef changes, but you can always find something tasty.

I have sat at the bar in the evening and eaten crispy *brandade* and potato cakes, savory quail salad, and juicy slices of roast pork loin with luxurious potato purée. You can have a perfect roast chicken with skinny pommes frites, or aromatic *boudin noir* sautéed with apples and surrounded by watercress, served by a French-speaking waitperson. The wine list, augmented by many interesting, inexpensive glasses listed on a blackboard, only waits to be mined. The prices are gratifyingly moderate, and the casual bistro atmosphere allows you to order as much or as little as you like.

21ST AMENDMENT . . . .

563 2nd Street (between
Brannan and Bryant)
415-369-0900
www.21st-amendment.com
Open daily 11:30 A.M. to 11 P.M.
Moderate
Credit cards: AE, D, MC, V

Brew pubs are not my cup of tea, because I don't like big, chewy house-made ales and the food at these operations usually gets short shrift. But 21st Amendment is the exception in that the food is absolutely terrific, conceived and executed by Eddie Blyden, a talented chef who has roots in the Caribbean and experience in Europe. He put together the casual, reasonably priced menu you'd expect to see in a SOMA warehouse-brewery, but the seasonality, simplicity, and excellence of preparation set it apart.

Start with a plate of deliciously charred fresh calamari from Monterey in a toasted coriander seed vinaigrette. An organic beet and goat cheese salad boasts sweet beets, lively vinaigrette, and a drizzle of balsamic reduction, a play of sweet and sour. A fabulous, juicy Niman Ranch pork chop, again grilled beautifully so the fat just blackens around the edges, is enhanced by a spice rub, but not overpowered by it. Glazed plantains, green and yellow beans, and a peppery *jus*, made from classic stock, makes this a dish to remember. A roasted, crisp-skinned half chicken on a pile of buttery mashed potatoes is showered with fresh favas and a chiffonade of Smithfield ham, which also flavors the natural gravy on this dish. 21st Amendment also makes its own root beer and ginger ale, and the strong, aromatic versions of these soft drinks make distinctive ice cream floats for dessert. But you may not want to pass up a warm fresh-fruit crisp.

I like everything about 21st Amendment except the beer. The service is friendly but professional, and the high-ceilinged warehouse space furnished with wooden tables and booths, a large U-shaped bar at the front, and a sparkling open kitchen at the back unites form and function. If you actually like the kind of beer made here, 21st Amendment will put you over the top, I'm bringing my own wine next time (and shall gladly pay corkage). Eddie Blyden's cooking deserves its own audience.

UMBRIA . . . .

198 2nd Street (at Howard)
415-546-6985
www.umbria.citysearch.com
Open Monday through Friday
11:30 A.M. to 2:30 P.M., Monday
through Saturday 5:30 to 10:30 P.M.
Inexpensive-Moderate
Credit cards: AE, MC, V

Umbria, with its tile floors, white linen– and butcher paper–covered tables, rustic wood slat benches and chairs, and moss green walls, looks like tourist restaurants in hill towns like Orvieto. The pizzas here are fabulous—much better than Umbrian tourist pizzas—with thin, crisp crusts, bright tomato sauce, just the right amount of mozzarella. Not to be eclipsed by the pizza, authentic Italian pastas shine as brightly. Umbria's pasta dishes sparkle because they are cooked perfectly. You can bite through the noodles, yet they offer provocative resistance (not rawness or starchiness), and the sauce tastes like fresh tomatoes, not garlic or oil. All the pastas I've tried here have been prepared in that same noble, traditional way. When it comes to pasta pleasure and those thin-crusted pizzas, the cooks here have the touch. Umbria makes for a convenient and comforting place to have a light bite before edgy performances at Yerba Buena.

UNIVERSAL CAFE . . . .

2814 19th Street (between
Florida and Bryant)
415-821-4608
Open Tuesday through Friday
5:30 to 10 P.M., Saturday and
Sunday 5:30 to 11 P.M.,
Saturday and Sunday brunch
9 a.m. to 2:30 p.m.
Moderate
Credit cards: AE, MC, V

Universal Cafe was the first of the superhip SOMA restaurants to win an ecstatic following and it has deservedly kept it, even with the dot-com bust that has put so many SOMA operations out of business. Owner-manager Gail Defferari discovered Julia McClaskey, the brilliant chef who put Universal on the culinary map, and when McClaskey left to open another restaurant and then her own restaurant, Julia (see page 266), Defferari promoted the sous-chef, Peter Erickson, who has been cooking sparkling food ever since.

Erickson understands how to cook seasonally with lots of flavor. In early July, for example, when the first sweet peaches come in, he makes a salad with them, arugula, dabs of goat cheese, and toasted hazelnuts in a perfect sharp dressing that ties everything together. Crisp, thin flat breads that emerge from the oven topped with smoky cheese and bright tomato purée get a last-minute garnish of wild arugula. A rich, lamby moussaka, crusty and bubbling in its own ramekin, comes with a refreshing side salad of pea sprouts, tomato, cucumber, and olives, a raw-cooked matchup made in culinary heaven. An interesting risotto of chewy *farro* studded with favas, squashes, and morels, has deep melded flavor, but you can taste each vegetable. Erickson uses ripe fruit for crisps, but my favorite dessert here is the classic *affogato*—vanilla gelato, espresso, and sweetened whipped cream.

It's a downright pleasure to eat here. The craftsmanship that has gone into converting a small wooden warehouse into a very hip café, on an unexpectedly charming, semi-industrial South-of-Market block, still resonates ten years later. Half the room is taken up by a long benchlike banquette with tables, the other by an open kitchen and counter. Cement, cast aluminum, and maple veneer plywood have been used in witty ways. A bank of floor-to-ceiling windows with hefty-looking aluminum hardware opens entirely onto a quiet block dotted with trees. Smart aluminum and wood chairs and marble-topped tables from the workshop of South Park Fabricators, Jeff and Larissa Sand, somehow combine modernity with cafe tradition.

CAFÉS

BRAIN WASH . . . .

1122 Folsom Street (between 7th and 8th streets)
415-861-3663
www.brainwash.com
Open Monday through Thursday 7 A.M. to 11 P.M., Friday and Saturday 7 A.M. to 1 A.M., Sunday 8 A.M. to 1 A.M.
Credit cards: MC, V

This café-laundromat kills two birds with one stone. One part of this eye-catching two-story glass building contains thirty-two state-of-the-art, heavy-duty computer-operated washers, twenty-four dryers, a wash-and-fold service, and a dry cleaners. Separated from the machinery by a diagonal glass wall is a self-service café with cement floors, clever metal chairs covered with epoxied collages, and a loud jukebox, giving it a Cafe Flore (see page 220) feel. Though most of the food is mediocre, with the exception of a tasty Chinese chicken salad in a light soy and walnut-oil dressing, you can fill yourself up with the likes of thick focaccia pizzas or baked apples. The scene is so weird and happening that it makes washing your dirty clothes an important social experience.

THE BUTLER & THE CHEF CAFE . . . .

155 South Park (between 2nd and 3rd streets)
415-896-2075
www.thebutlerandthechef.com
Open Monday through Friday 7:30 A.M. to 6 P.M., Saturday 9 A.M. to 4 P.M.
Credit cards: MC, V

I include this café because it looks as if it were airlifted from a Parisian arrondissement and set down on charming, tree-lined South Park. That's because it's furnished by The Butler & The Chef store (see page 366), so many of the classic chairs and tables you're sitting at and bowls you're drinking from are for sale. Surrounded by all the authentic trappings, you're apt to think more kindly about the food and coffee, which actually replicates what you get most of the time in Paris these days. Stay simple—baguette with butter and jam, a bowl of café au lait, a salami sandwich on a buttered baguette—and you'll be transported.

CAFFE CENTRO . . . .

102 South Park (between 2nd and
3rd streets, Bryant and Brannan)
415-882-1500
www.caffecentro.com
Open Monday through Friday
7:30 A.M. to 5 P.M.,
Saturday 8:30 A.M. to 4 P.M.
Credit cards: AE, MC, V

Caffe Centro's South Park location gives it its cachet. Outdoor tables on the sidewalk around the perimeter of the café bask in the ample sun in this protected good-weather belt in the middle of the city. Light floods in through usually open windows and seems to make the creamy-colored walls glow. Details in the design of the café, like a poured and painted floor that looks like a mosaic, bottle-glass light fixtures, tiny round metal tables that tend to wobble, and metal chairs, set the backdrop for lots of arty, expressively dressed young patrons.

Delicious open-faced sandwiches of roasted red peppers with melted Gruyère on toasted bread star on the menu. Frittatas layered with all sorts of vegetables held together with garlic-scented custard are also good, as are the house-made soups. Unfortunate in a café, the coffee consistently has a bitter edge.

CAFFÈ ROMA COFFEE ROASTING COMPANY

885 Bryant Street (at Gilbert
between 6th and 7th streets)
415-296-7662
www.cafferoma.com
Open Monday through Thursday
6 A.M. to 5 P.M.,
Friday 6 A.M. 4:30 P.M.
Credit cards: AE, MC, V

Another outpost for good coffee made with signature house-roasted beans. See page 244 for more information.

FARLEY'S . . . .

1315 18th street (at Texas)
415-648-1545
Open Monday through Friday
6:30 A.M. to 10 P.M., Saturday and
Sunday 8 A.M. to 10 P.M.
Cash only

There are many reasons to seek out Farley's if you're a café aficionado. The Mr. Espresso coffee is strong, deep, and always well made. An unusually spacious Victorian cottage with a genuinely distressed wooden floor, beat-up wooden tables and chairs, and wood-slat walls painted white, hung with revolving shows from local painters and photographers, makes for a comfy and peaceful environment. On top of all this, Farley's offers a juicy selection of hip and special interest magazines for sale—or browsing—including the likes of *Wallpaper*, surfer magazines, and all the food magazines. Ceiling fans keep it airy; boxes of Trivial Pursuit cards and chess sets provide entertainment; groovy music, mostly Seattle rock, plays not too loud; and the people behind the counter are genuinely gracious. Locals spend hours here, working, reading, hanging out, but newcomers are welcome, too. Farley's defines the ethos of the best neighborhood cafés.

SOMA CAFFE . . . .

1601 Howard (at 12th Street)
415-861-5012
Open daily 6 A.M. to 7 P.M.
Cash only

At 7:30 one morning, after dropping off my car the second time in one week for a repair, my nasty mood was transformed by the performance of two SOMA businesses: City Rent-A-Car and Soma Caffe. It took no longer than five minutes to complete the paperwork for a rental car, allowing me time to have the morning coffee I'd missed at home. The City Rental man sent me two blocks away to the Soma Caffe. There I asked for a double shot of espresso in a caffe latte. The *barrista* assured me that every latte at Soma Caffe gets two shots and he handed me the perfect tall glass of coffee and steamed milk—strong, hot, aromatic. As I ate a fresh Italian almond roll from Dianda's bakery (see page 200) with the coffee, I felt as if I were in Rome—except that the newspapers were in English. The *New York Times* and the local rags were generously scattered on the tables. Jazz played. Light poured in from big plate-glass windows on two sides of the café. Life was good. I went up to the counter when I was finished to tell the man who made the coffee how good it had been and how much I liked the café. He said, "And look at how handsome and intelligent the people are behind the counter." He was absolutely right.

BARS

ASIA SF . . . .

201 9th Street (at Howard)
415-255-2724
www.asiasf.com
Open daily 5 to 10 P.M.
Credit cards: AE, CB, DC, D,
MC, V

The highly designed Asian-fusion appetizers served here are almost as much fun as the multitalented transvestite staff who wait on tables one minute and then hop on the bar to lip-synch to throbbing tunes the next. Everyone has a great time because every aspect of the operation is done with conviction. The whimsical food is tasty, drinks well made, and the service professional. But nothing beats the thrill of having your very own waiter-waitress turn into a star on the bar.

BACAR . . . .

448 Brannan (between
3rd and 4th streets)
415-904-4100
Open Monday through Thursday
5:30 P.M. until midnight,
Friday and Saturday until to 1 A.M.,
Sunday until 11 P.M.
Credit cards: MC, V

Many meet in the upstairs or downstairs barroom before or after a Giant's game for a celebratory glass of wine, an elegant cocktail, or a just a straight shot of top-of-the-line spirits. See page 345 for more information.

42 DEGREES

235 16th Street
(just east of 3rd Street)
415-777-5558
Open Wednesday through
Saturday 6 to 11:30 P.M.
Credit cards: MC, V

Northern Spain, the Basque country, Provence, and Tuscany all happen to be on 42 degrees latitude. What a happy coincidence! Geography thus becomes the unifying theme at this striking warehouse district bar and restaurant whose menu of small and large dishes sometimes reads better than it tastes. No matter. The space, originally developed as a café for the clothing manufacturer Esprit, whose wholesale outlet is next door, has enough cachet to carry a visit. At night, the restaurant becomes a hip, dimly lit clubhouse for graphic artists, multimedia types, and book publishers, who drink at the long bar, take in the live music, and nibble at small plates of food. Serious eaters should try to get a seat upstairs in the mezzanine, which has a view of the shipyards and bay, and stick to the main course dishes like Niman Ranch rib-eye steak, sand dabs with lentils, braised chicken, and chocolate *pots-de-crème* for dessert.

HAWTHORNE LANE

22 Hawthorne Lane (between
Howard and Folsom where
New Montgomery ends)
415-777-9779
www.hawthornelane.com
Open Monday through Thursday
5:30 to 9 P.M., Friday and Saturday
5:30 to 10 P.M.
Credit cards: D, MC, V

This restaurant has a separate barroom and is a destination for cocktails and delicious small bites, like crispy breadsticks and thin slices of house-made salami that appear when you order a drink. A bar menu is always available to go with perfect drinks served in smart, elegant glassware. This is one of my favorite bars in town. See page 351 for more information.

KELLY'S MISSION ROCK

817 China Basin Road
(off 3rd Street)
415-626-5355
www.kellysmissionrock.com
Open Monday through Saturday
11:30 A.M. to 3 P.M. and 4 to 8 P.M.;
Sunday brunch 10:30 A.M. to 4 P.M.
Credit cards: AE, DC, D, MC, V

This multilevel bar and restaurant sits right on the water in a section of the working bay where monumental cargo ships dock for repairs. Nothing is more fun than lounging on a deck at Kelly's Mission Rock with drink in hand, gazing at looming hulls in the shipyards, small pleasure boats in an adjoining marina, water birds, the city skyline, and the water itself, all washed in bright, clear light.

The two-story sheet-metal building protects the restaurant's many waterside decks from the wind, so diners and drinkers sitting outside bask in warmth—a unique San Francisco experience. Owner Jim Kelly is a barman from way back. He ran the infamous Pat O'Shea's Mad Hatter in the Richmond (see page 328) and gave now-famous Boulevard chef Nancy Oakes her first cooking job. He knows how to stock a bar, pour generous beers, mix every kind of drink, and supply the food you need to keep the party going. This Taj Mahal of a bar with glorious outdoor patios and decks on the water is worth a special trip—especially with out-of-town guests who want to get a feeling for San Francisco's unique geographical setting.

THE RAMP . . . .

855 China Basin
(off 3rd Street at Mariposa)
415-621-2378
Open Monday through Friday
11 A.M. to 9 P.M., Saturday and
Sunday 8:30 A.M. to 9 P.M.
Credit cards: AE, MC, V

The Ramp's location, right next to a working shipyard with towering cranes and dry docks, tests your perspective after a few bloody Marys or margaritas. The outdoor bar looks straight at the water where massive ships are repaired in front of a small boat marina. Though the food is acceptable, eating it outdoors under an umbrella by all the intriguing activity on the water makes it taste all the better, especially a breakfast of sunny-side up eggs and spicy Italian sausage. The Ramp is a must-stop for breakfast on the way to Giants day games if you're coming from the south bay.

XYZ . . . .

181 3rd Street (at Howard
in the W Hotel)
415-817-7836
www.xyz-sf.com
Open Monday through Friday
6:30 A.M. to 10:30 A.M. and
11:30 A.M. to 2:30 P.M.,
Saturday and Sunday 8 A.M. to
2:30 P.M.; Sunday through
Thursday 5:30 to 10:30 P.M.,
Friday and Saturday until 11 P.M.
Credit cards: AE, MC, V

One would expect that a restaurant and bar as hip as XYZ would be dripping with attitude. But my very first encounter with the restaurant, which happened to be over the telephone, was surprisingly pleasant and civil. When I pulled up to the W Hotel, in which XYZ is located, and saw the male-model valets in black turtlenecks and earphones, I thought I was in for some real disdain, but the car jockeys were sweet and welcoming. And when I approached the host's desk at the restaurant and the gorgeous, young black-clad maître d' greeted me with a big, beautiful smile, I was ready to faint. Something unusual is happening at this up-to-the-minute hotel restaurant and bar.

That something may be Gail DeFerrari, who was lured over from the Universal Cafe, which she also manages. She has created a haven of graciousness and friendliness in a haute SOMA setting. The juxtaposition of cool appearance and warm attitude makes this hot spot immediately appealing and ultimately very useful.

XYZ is located directly across the street from the Yerba Buena Center, a block from the Moscone Convention Center. At the hub of much activity, it serves as a convenient meeting place, a chic spot for cocktails, and a venue for stylish if casual dining. In other words, it fulfills all the traditional requirements of a major hotel, but in a fresh, exciting way. XYZ is top drawer but not stuffy; pricey, as most hotel restaurants are, but accessible and fun.

A good way to experience this happening scene is to station yourself at Cafe W, a bar with some small tables in the compact lobby at the entrance to the restaurant. Cafe W's bar menu is served continuously from 11 A.M. to 11 P.M., so you can survey the action while eating, say, a grilled tuna club sandwich.

RAINBOW GROCERY . . . .

1745 Folsom Street
(at 13th Street and Division)
415-863-0621
www.rainbowgrocery.org
Open daily 9 A.M. to 9 P.M.
Credit cards: D, MC, V

The Rainbow Grocery cooperative, which preceded the Whole Foods chain by a number of years, has become a San Francisco institution in the best sense. The check out people are still tattooed and pierced. You still have to bag your own groceries, but the array of foods is mind-boggling. Things you only see in small cellophane packages at other places come in bulk here, ready to be scooped out—seaweed of every color and shape, preserved lemons, organic jasmine rice, Thai jasmine rice, basmati rice, beautiful dried beans in all hues and patterns, maple sugar, chestnut flour, spelt, *masa harina*, organic vegetable-flavored penne, organic linguine, and organic dried anchos. This eclectic list only skims the surface.

The large produce department looks terrific. Everything is meticulously labeled as to origin, down to the bunches of herbs. Of particular note is all the produce bought directly from farmers, like romaine and red butter lettuce from Dale Coke. You come pretty close to shopping in a farmers' market here, though prices are higher.

To compete with stores like Andronico's and Whole Foods, Rainbow has its own olive bar and a fine little cheese section with interesting selections that include lots of fresh goat cheeses, sheep's milk ricotta, and rice flour Teleme. Top-of-the-line imported groceries like Capezzano extra virgin olive oil and Rustichella hard-durum-wheat pastas made on ancient machines in Italy fill out your market basket and empty your pocketbook. If you want a Juicerator, you can buy it here, as well as natural fragrant oils, soaps, candles, cosmetics, organic pet food, and recycled paper products. Rainbow has taken itself into the next millennium, much to the surprise of everyone who frequented the grungy old store, and has reinvented itself as a whole-foods superstore on the cutting edge. It's worth traveling across town to shop here.

TRADER JOE'S . . . .

555 9th Street (at Brannan)
415-863-1292
www.traderjoes.com
Open daily 9 A.M. to 9 P.M.
Credit cards: D, MC, V

I've never really found shopping at Trader Joe's to be totally satisfying. Who wants giant tubs of frozen lasagne or mediocre snack chips? But this particular branch now carries fresh Empire Kosher chickens, some of the best chickens available anywhere. The last time I was at Trader Joe's I noticed ten-pound bars of Ghirardelli chocolate for $19.99, a $60 savings over purchase of the same bar at a Ghirardelli outlet. Amazing. I also bought a pound of fresh, new-crop pecans, whole and perfect for half price. I needed these things to make milk chocolate–pecan clusters, this year's Christmas gift. Then I noticed huge bottles of Stolichnaya vodka for a song. Try the natural-tasting grapefruit soda in cans and the thinly sliced almond and raisin biscotti. For certain odd items, some of which seem to shift on and off the shelves, you can't beat Trader Joe's. You just have to discover what they might be.

MILK CHOCOLATE–PECAN CLUSTERS

MAKES 2 DOZEN

This recipe is adapted from a session with my friend Sydney Goldstein, who learned how to make them from Emma Jones, a longtime family employee. I promise you that they will be the best chocolate-covered nuts you've ever tasted.

1 pound Ghirardelli milk
chocolate, chopped

½ pound pecan halves

4 tablespoons salted butter

Pinch of kosher salt

1 Preheat oven to 375°F.

2 Put the chocolate in the top of a double boiler placed over hot water, or in a large metal bowl placed over a pot of hot water, to melt.

3 Put the pecans in another bowl. Melt the butter in a saucepan. Pour the melted butter over the pecans. Add the salt. Toss. The pecans should taste buttery and a little salty. Spread the buttered pecans on a cookie sheet and roast them in the oven for 10 minutes, or until they become fragrant.

4 Stir the chocolate, making sure it is completely melted. Pour the hot, buttery pecans into the melted chocolate. Mix them together.

5 Spread waxed paper on a counter. Scoop out a teaspoon of the mixture containing three or four chocolate-covered pecans and drop onto the paper. Each candy will look different, the beauty of hand-dipped chocolates. Let set for 2 hours, after which the clusters will be ready to box or bag. Eat within a week or so. Their sparkle comes from their freshness.

RAINBOW GROCERY . . . .

1745 Folsom Street
(at 13th Street and Division)
415-863-0621
www.rainbowgrocery.org
Open daily 9 A.M. to 9 P.M.
Credit cards: D, MC, V

Rainbow's large and expensive produce section specializes in organic fruits and vegetables from local farms.
See page 361 for more information.

FISH

CALIFORNIA SUNSHINE . . . .

144 King Street (between
2nd and 3rd streets)
415-543-3007
www.tsarnicoulai.com
Open Monday through Friday
8 A.M. to 5 P.M.
Credit cards: AE, MC, V

Mats and Dafne Engstrom have ascended the throne as
the king and queen of American, Iranian, and Chinese
caviars, having been in business now for twenty-six
years. Their seven-ounce tins of Tsar Nicoulai (their
trademark) osetra, the medium-sized caviar with a
nutty flavor that I like the most, offers the best price
for the quality I have encountered. California
Sunshine's American osetra is astoundingly good. They
have pioneered sturgeon farming in the Sacramento River and have begun harvesting and
curing some truly top-rate local roe. Buying caviar, of course, is a crapshoot because every
fish produces eggs of different quality. The ideal is to get it as fresh as possible, which is
why buying new-crop caviar in the spring will net you the best flavor. Of course, most
Americans want caviar around the winter holiday season, but once you've tasted the fresher
eggs, you'll be tempted to have it earlier in the year. When I was in Soviet Georgia, we ate,
with a spoon, small plates thickly paved with the most delectable, nutty, barely salted sturgeon eggs and washed it down with icy vodka. Now I serve caviar this way here, in
California. You can do it for a special occasion. On a smaller budget, you can make a rather
pretty and not too expensive presentation of caviar toasts using California Sunshine's
crunchy, bright golden whitefish caviar, orange salmon roe, and black Russian sevruga.
Though the wholesale outlet does not have a retail sales room per se, people are welcome to
drop in if they are planning to buy.

RED LENTIL SOUP WITH LIME

SERVES 4 TO 6

Deborah Madison, the groundbreaking vegetarian chef who opened Greens, is the best recipe writer I know. She's a born teacher and knows how to explain procedures and techniques. She always adds an interesting little twist that makes her dishes unique and surprisingly delicious. This red lentil soup, inspired by Indian dal, can be a meal. The layering of flavors and textures gives it complexity that belies how easy it is to make. You can get all the ingredients, including the red lentils and fresh bulk spices, at the Rainbow Grocery.

2 cups red lentils, picked over and rinsed several times

2½ quarts water

1 tablespoon ground tumeric

4 tablespoons unsalted butter

1 tablespoon kosher salt, plus a sprinkling for the spinach

1 large onion, finely diced (about 2 cups)

1 tablespoon ground cumin

1 teaspoon ground coriander

1½ teaspoons mustard seeds

1 teaspoon cayenne pepper

1 bunch cilantro, chopped (about 1 cup)

Juice of 3 large limes

1 large bunch spinach leaves, chopped into small pieces

4 to 6 tablespoons plain yogurt

1 Put the lentils in a soup pot with the water, tumeric, 1 tablespoon of the butter, and the 1 tablespoon salt. Bring to a boil, then lower the heat and simmer, covered, for about 20 minutes, or until the lentils are soft and falling apart. Purée. (An immersion blender is especially helpful here.)

2 While the soup is cooking, sauté the onion in 2 tablespoons of the butter. Add the cumin, coriander, mustard seeds, and cayenne. When soft, about the time the lentils are cooked or after 15 minutes, add the cilantro and cook for 1 more minute. Add the onion mixture to the soup, then add the juice of the limes. Don't be timid about adding lime. The soup should be sour.

3 Just before serving, add the last tablespoon of butter to a wide skillet. When foamy, add the spinach, sprinkle with salt, and cook just long enough to wilt. To serve the soup, divide the spinach among the bowls, ladle in the soup, and swirl in a spoonful of yogurt.

K & L WINES . . . .

766 Harrison Street
(between 3rd and 4th streets)
415-896-1734
www.klwines.com
Open Monday through Friday
9 A.M. to 7 P.M.,
Saturday 9 A.M. to 6 P.M.,
Sunday 10 A.M. to 5 P.M.
Credit cards: AE, MC, V

A parking lot makes it easy to shop at this small, but fully stocked wineshop, where most bottles are displayed in wooden racks. An excellent Bordeaux selection at some surprising prices draws collectors here. In fact, on a recent visit I saw several elegant Bordeaux on sale below cost. An eclectic selection of imported wines from Chile, Spain, and Australia entices adventurous and cost-conscious buyers. K & L also sells fine spirits like grappa and double-malt scotch. Nestled onto its shelves you will find at least one of the Gourmel cognacs, a cognac whose smoothness, delicacy, and finesse make the inevitable headache you get the next morning, when one taste has led to another, worth the pain.

WINE HOUSE LIMITED . . . .

129 Carolina (between
16th and 17th streets)
415-355-9463
www.winesf.com
Open Monday through Friday
10 A.M. to 6 P.M.,
Saturday until 5 P.M.
Credit cards: AE, MC, V

The Wine House has moved into new industrial digs at the bottom of Potrero Hill, which affords them much more space and better browsing for wine buffs. The yeasty smell of wooden wine crates still greets you when you walk into this concrete block warehouse with a cool cement floor. Stacks of these boxes full of Cru Bordeaux at decent prices—a 15 percent discount on two cases—call out to be examined. Many Bordeaux are available in hard-to-find half bottles. The Wine House also brings in the Robert Kacher selection of Burgundies, a favorite label of wine guru Robert Parker. The Wine House sells no liquor, and 90 percent of the twenty-two-year-old wine store's bottles are imported, making the Wine House a real bottle shop, not just a room filled with very good wines. The people who work here care about wine and want to help you find great bottles. This is one of the few places of its kind left in the city, and is well worth a trip if only to visit a wine operation with old-style values. Parking in this industrial neighborhood is a snap.

ECONOMY RESTAURANT SUPPLY . . . .

1200 7th Street (at Irwin)
415-626-5611
www.bigtray.com
Open Monday through Friday
8 A.M. to 5:30 P.M.,
Saturday 10 A.M. to 5 P.M.
Credit cards: AE, MC, V

All the restaurant people come here to buy supplies. There are rows and rows of restaurant-style aluminum skillets and pots, all sorts of large cooking utensils, cutting boards, knives, metal bowls—all the essentials for a production kitchen. I have outfitted many a home kitchen here as well, with basic, useful equipment. All the marked prices are 10 to 15 percent higher than the actual price, so remember to ask for a discount. Just tell them you're opening a restaurant, and thank your lucky stars that you really aren't.

THE BUTLER & THE CHEF . . . .

1011 25th Street (at 3rd Street)
415-642-6440
www.thebutlerandthechef.com
Open Monday through Friday
10 A.M. to 6 P.M.,
Saturday 11 A.M. to 5 P.M.
Credit cards: MC, V

If you're planning to set up a French bistro, a tabac, or a little café, this is the place for you. Most of the droolingly desirable antique French café and rustic household furnishings, like refectory tables, country-kitchen tables, armoires, brass-trimmed bars, zinc bars, café bowls, oversized silverplate, and old posters, would be beautiful in any San Francisco apartment. Look here first before you buy that new dining room table. If you want to see the furnishings and appointments in use, have a bite at The Butler & The Chef Café (see page 356).

THE SUNSET

RESTAURANTS

1   Hana
2   House
3   Just Won Ton
4   Lam Hoa Thuan
5   New Hai Ky
6   Old Krakow
7   Park Chow
8   Pho Hoa Hiep II
9   Ristorante Marcello
10   Riverside Seafood Restaurant
11   San Tung
12   Shanghai Restaurant
13   Win's
14   Yummy Yummy

CAFÉS

15   Canvas Cafe/Gallery
16   Java Beach Cafe

BARS

17   Beach Chalet

DELICATESSENS/TAKEOUT

18   Palio Paninoteca
19   Sunrise Deli & Cafe
20   Yumma's

BAKERIES/PASTRIES

21   Arizmendi Bakery

ICE CREAM/CHOCOLATES

22   Double Rainbow
23   Polly Ann Ice Cream
24   See's Candies

COFFEE

25   The Beanery
26   Peet's Coffee & Tea

MARKETS

27   Andronico's
28   Sunset Super
29   22nd and Irving Market

PRODUCE

29   22nd and Irving Market

MEAT AND POULTRY

30   Guerra's

FISH

28   Sunset Super
31   Yum Yum

WINES AND SPIRITS

32   Mr. Liquor

COOKWARE AND BOOKS

33   Irving Housewares & Gifts
34   Williams-Sonoma

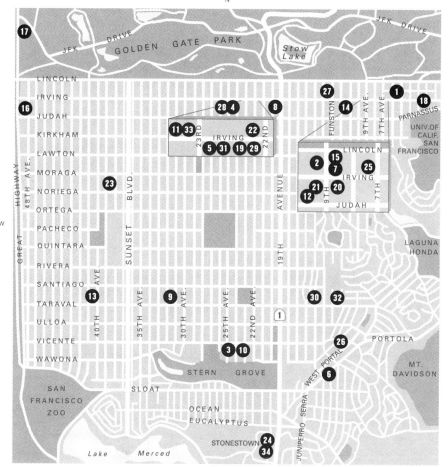

HANA . . . .

408 Irving Street (between
5th and 6th avenues)
415-665-3952
www.hanarestaurant.citysearch.com
Open Monday through Friday
11:30 A.M. to 2 P.M., Monday
through Saturday 5 to 9:45 P.M.
Inexpensive
Credit cards: MC, V

The dining room at Hana looks like an old Japanese inn, with weathered wooden booths, thick wooden tables, and a beautiful deep blue and red paint job. The prices are reasonable and the Japanese mainstays on the menu delicious. Although sushi is available at both a sushi bar and in the dining room, I prefer the cooked dishes. The kitchen has a way with chicken, like a breast with wing attached, basted in the lightest of teriyaki sauces and sprinkled with sesame seeds. The meat stays miraculously tender and juicy. The same extraordinary texture makes chicken *tonkatsu*, a battered and fried chicken cutlet, a standout. Frying is always nicely done at Hana. The fried oysters are barely coated in a crumbly batter and cooked in very hot oil until they are just firm. They melt in your mouth. *Gyoza*, Japanese pot stickers with a spicy pork filling in a crimped noodle wrapper, have an intense gingery flavor and a light texture. Hana is also famous for its *yosenabe*, a perfectly cooked stew of clams, shrimp, oysters, and vegetables in a ginger-scented broth. Portions are geared to Western appetites and dinners include little plates of pickled cabbage, miso soup, and a lettuce salad, albeit with cellophane noodles and a delicate sweet-and-sour dressing. Service by a group of Japanese women in kimonos could not be friendlier, though sometimes it is slow. The waitresses know most of their customers and will quickly get to know you.

HOUSE . . . .

1269 9th Avenue (between
Irving and Lincoln)
415-682-3898
www.thehse.com
Open Monday through Thursday
5:30 to 10 P.M.,
Friday 5:30 to 11 P.M.,
Saturday 5 to 11 P.M.,
Sunday 5 to 10 P.M.
Moderate
Credit cards: AE, MC, V

House, a stylish, minimally decorated Euro-Asian bistro, makes a strong, sophisticated statement with a tempting menu of pan-Asian appetizers, unusual main courses that feature underused varieties of fish, and a cutting-edge wine list keyed to the difficult-to-match flavors in the cooking. Prices are moderate for a high level of dining. As a result, House draws patrons from all over the city. This is remarkable considering how difficult it is to park around Golden Gate Park, but a meal here rewards the hassle.

I will circle the block for this restaurant's impeccably deep-fried green bean tempura and five-spice calamari, both with vibrant dipping sauces. Grilled lamb tongue with Szechwan pepper sauce challenges the adventurous, while steamed chicken and shiitake dumplings reassure the timorous. Saucy satay chicken wings also have their following. But what I really love here are the thick hunks of butterfish, loaded with natural oil and silken of texture. It's marinated and served with flavorful jasmine rice and bright green long beans, making for well-balanced, satisfying plates. The smart, high-concept decor and handsome modern table appointments, ennobled by thin, elegant wineglasses, add cachet to the simple presentations of the food. House has both style and substance. For those who like Euro-Asian food that is not complicated and overwrought, House feels like home.

JUST WON TON . . . .

1241 Vicente Street (between
23rd and 24th avenues)
415-681-2999
Open Tuesday through Sunday
11 A.M. to 10 P.M.
Very inexpensive
Credit cards: MC, V

This tiny place in a converted house in the Sunset devotes itself entirely to making wontons. The skins are gossamer thin, tender, and flavorful, the filling simple and sublime: roughly chopped sweet, impeccably fresh shrimp bound with just a little ground pork. The wontons come in soup with noodles, soup without noodles, with fish balls, roast duck, barbecued pork, spicy chicken, different cuts of beef, innards, and pig's feet.

For a pittance you can get wonton soup with any of the above and extra wontons. Also good is beef *chow fun*, wide, white rice noodles tossed with bright green bok choy and bits of velvetized beef. Although this is primarily a noodle house, it is also known for two appetizers: vegetarian duck, made with ribbons of tofu skin wrapped around a filling of savory mushrooms, and something called a Chinese tamale, a gigantic mound of sticky rice with a center of braised Chinese sausage and taro paste. The beauty of a visit here is that you can take the wontons to go and serve them in your own rich chicken broth, a meal that pleases a lot of kids I know.

LAM HOA THUAN . . . .

2337 Irving Street (at 25th Avenue)
415-661-1688
Open daily 9 A.M. to 9 P.M.
Inexpensive
Cash only

Though no Vietnamese beef noodle soup will ever live up to Pacific No. 2's homemade-style *pho*, (alas, this Jones Street *pho* house closed in 2001), the *pho* at Lam Hoa Thuan has its own charms. The broth is similarly clean, fatless, and beefy, just about perfect except for the missing hint of star anise I loved at Pacific No. 2.

Generously beefy—with the thinnest slices of raw sirloin that cook in the broth, long-cooked beef brisket, beef tendons, and tripe—each bite of noodle and soup is meaty at Lam Hoa Thuan. You add the finishing touches yourself from a side plate of bean sprouts, branches of Thai basil, fresh mint, sliced jalapeño chiles, and lemon, tearing the aromatics to release their fragrance. This juxtaposition of raw and cooked gives Vietnamese cooking its unique character. And Lam Hoa Thuan also specializes in roast pig, the delicious smell of which draws passersby into the cheerful, muraled dining room. A plate of cleaver-cut roast pig with crackling skin and white, salty flesh makes for a hearty snack. Crispy squares of deep-fried tofu, dusted with aromatic five-spice powder with a dipping sauce on the side, delight with their delicate creamy interiors. You can eat a huge meal here for well under $7 a person.

NEW HAI KY. . . . .

2191 Irving Street (at 23rd Avenue)
415-731-9948
Open daily 9 A.M. to 9 P.M.
Inexpensive
Cash only

Burnished ducks, chickens, and slabs of barbecued pig hang in the front window of New Hay Ky, and a crowd always mills around the front door waiting for takeout or for a table in the relatively small but fast-paced dining room. New Hai Ky sells a lot of Chinese barbecue to go. But the reason I come here is for No. 6 on the eighty-some item menu, Preserved Orange Skin Duck with Egg Noodle Soup (thick or thin noodles), an elegant dish that costs a pittance. What arrives at your Formica table is a large bowl of noodles and clear broth topped with a glistening barbecued duck leg and garnished with a big pouf of perfect, bright green cilantro leaves that could grace the centerfold of a glossy food magazine. The duck leg has the texture of a firm confit, its skin crisp and salty and its flesh delicately scented with dried orange peel. The velvety meat adds depth to the light broth and clean noodles and the fresh cilantro provides sharp counterpoint. This clean, exquisitely balanced duck leg–noodle soup refreshes and satisfies at the same time, the perfect dish. If I'm not careful, I can also pack away a platter of addictive, wok-smoked beef *chow fun* with thin gravy, chewy-sticky wide rice noodles, pristine baby bok choy split in half lengthwise, and tender slices of beef—along with the soup.

Although many people eat noodles and plates of Chinese roast duck over rice here, another draw of this place is Chinese barbecue to go. New Hai Ky makes several different kinds of roast and barbecue duck and pork that stay moist and fresh from generally quick turnover. For a change, try the Roast Duck Chinese Guitar, in which the bird is splayed out (in a vaguely guitarlike shape) to take on extra-strong curing and deeper roasting. The guitar duck's skin and flesh is saltier, sweeter, and more aromatic of Chinese five spices than the regular roast duck, and the meat still keeps its velvety texture.

OLD KRAKOW. . . . .

385 West Portal Avenue
(near 15th Avenue)
415-564-4848
Open Monday through Thursday
5 to 10 P.M., Friday through
Sunday noon to 10 P.M.
Inexpensive
Credit cards: AE, MC, V

This cozy Polish art café in the mist and fog belt of the Sunset has soul. It's warm and comfy inside, even though dramatic Polish expressionist oil paintings stare down from the walls. As is true in all Eastern European kitchens, the delicious soups are a mainstay. Try the intense, creamy mushroom soup full of chopped mushrooms, the thin, sweet beet borscht with meat-filled dumplings, or the fortifying garlic soup with garlic croutons. Or start with strong-cured herring with marinated onions, pickles, and peppers; the tasty chopped potato and vegetable salad napped in mayonnaise; or sliced cucumbers with fresh dill and sour cream.

My favorite main course is a thickly breaded but crisp pork cutlet served with crispy fried potatoes, a double whammy. The *bigos,* hunter's stew of beef, pork, and sausage, comes with smoky sauerkraut and mashed potatoes, a real comfort plate. Stuffed cabbage is a little bland here, smothered in tomato sauce, but still satisfying, while house-made Polish sausages (kielbasa) are very garlicky, moderated by the smoky sauerkraut and mashed potatoes. Glasses of Polish beer (the stronger, more hoppy Zywiec, or the light, crisp Okocim) add much to the meal. Don't miss the house-baked desserts, a tall, multilayered apple cake with a crisp brioche crust, or a five-inch-tall farmer's cheese cake with raisins that is barely sweetened, both fine with tea or well-made coffee.

PARK CHOW . . . .

1240 9th Avenue (between
Irving and Lincoln)
415-665-9912
Open Monday through Thursday
11 A.M. to 10 P.M.,
Friday 11 A.M. to 11 P.M.,
Saturday 10 A.M. to 11 P.M.,
Sunday 10 A.M. to 10 P.M.
Inexpensive
Credit cards: MC, V

The menu at this second branch of Tony Gulisano's Chow is exactly the same as at the Church Street restaurant (see page 214), but the physical surroundings are smarter, airier, cleaner, and more comfy, with polished hardwood floors, a long bar with stools, brick walls, and outdoor eating areas at the front and back of the restaurant. Neither Chow takes reservations, but you can call ahead to put your name on the waiting list, an easy compromise that allows for spontaneity without too long of a wait.

PHO HOA HIEP II. . . . .

1833 Irving (between
19th and 20th streets)
415-664-0469
Open daily 10 AM. to 10 P.M.
Inexpensive
Cash only

This branch of a small local chain of *pho* (Vietnamese noodle soup) houses actually is known for its sparkling shrimp cakes, golden deep-fried pillows of coarse shrimp paste studded with moist pieces of fresh shrimp. A generous platter of them comes with sliced raw carrots, cucumber, daikon, crisp red leaf lettuce, and a bowl of classic Vietnamese dipping sauce. You wrap a shrimp cake with a slice or two of vegetable in a piece of lettuce, liberally dunk the package into the dipping sauce, and eat. The hot, savory, gently garlicky shrimp cake, crisp on the outside, firm, juicy, and pink in the middle, is completed by the cold, crunchy vegetables and the tart-sweet clear dipping sauce imperceptibly deepened with Vietnamese fish sauce. They are amazingly delicious.

RISTORANTE MARCELLO . . . .

2100 Taraval (at 31st Avenue)
415-665-1430
www.marcello.citysearch.com
Open Tuesday through Saturday
5 to 10:30 P.M.,
Sunday 4 to 10 P.M.
Moderate
Credit cards: MC, V

The food, the customers, the look and feel of Ristorante Marcello take you back to another era when arugula, grilled radicchio, and balsamic vinegar hadn't entered the common culinary vocabulary and spaghetti with meat sauce held sway. To tell you the truth, this was not a bad time, and at Ristorante Marcello its best qualities have been preserved. This restaurant reminds me of the old Vanessi's on Broadway: it has the same raffish spirit and the same broad cooking style—and it's still appreciated by a loyal following who have been coming now for twenty-four years. Furnished with red vinyl banquettes, padded wooden chairs, linen-covered tables pushed close together, and a long, active bar where people also eat, the room has that classic Italian dinner-house style. The waiters, in tuxes, know the menu and have a sense of humor. They don't coddle their customers, but they serve efficiently. This is the place to get a classic Caesar salad or hearts of romaine in a fabulous shalloty, mustardy, relishy, *rémoulade*-like vinaigrette. The spaghettini comes bathed in a celery-scented bolognese sauce with an authentically gravelly texture from finely chopped beef, chicken livers, and prosciutto. The house-made ravioli, moistened with a little bit of this sauce, are plump with well-seasoned ricotta. The tender green *panzotti*, large ravioli also filled with ricotta and spinach, are sauced with a clean-flavored tomato purée. Don't pass up the old-fashioned *cannelloni della casa*, made with hand-rolled dough and stuffed with finely chopped veal, spinach, and prosciutto, covered with a creamy tomato sauce. The spicy *spaghetti all' matriciana* juggles bacon, tomatoes, and onions masterfully. People come to this restaurant for two main courses: *pollo ai ferri*, a flattened-on-the-grill half chicken with a superb satiny texture, and a gigantic veal chop, very tender but pink enough to have flavor. Try the rest of the menu at your own risk. The wine list is woefully short on good Italian or California red wines, but most people who eat here prefer their martinis and Manhattans anyway. When the place is packed on the weekends, you can almost feel the specter of crusty old San Francisco North Beach hovering overhead.

RIVERSIDE SEAFOOD RESTAURANT . . . . . .

1201 Vicente Street
(at 23rd Avenue)
415-759-8828
Open daily 11 A.M. to 3 P.M.
and 5 to 10 P.M.
Inexpensive
Credit cards: MC, V

A chef and a manager from the well-regarded Fook Yuen on the Peninsula opened this neighborhood restaurant several years ago and it maintains its popularity and quality. The room is clean, comfortably appointed, and miraculously quiet due, perhaps, to low-acoustic ceilings; large groups of eight or ten can eat well here for a very reasonable sum. Value is much prized in the Sunset and Riverside aims to please.

Saucers of barely pickled cucumbers tide you over while you order your dinner off the handwritten list of specials clipped to the cover of an otherwise long menu. The list simplifies the entire process. Start with soup of the day, a magnificently rich and restorative chicken broth. Have Peking duck: Tuck the crackling skin into tender white buns smeared with plum sauce and green onions. Then eat the meat of the duck as a separate course, minced with crisp white rice noodles, which you eat rolled in lettuce leaves. The spicy pork ribs are hot, sweet, vinegary, and chewy, just the way they should be. The oxtails in wine sauce with carrots could have come out of a French kitchen. They are delicious over rice. The sake-marinated black cod, a large, thick hunk, defines the sensation of velvety and rich. The service is pleasant, the experience civilized. You pay more here than at some bargain-driven places in the Sunset, but the price is less than at many Richmond District restaurants for equally high quality.

1031 Irving Street (between
11th and 12th avenues)
415-242-0828
Open Thursday through Sunday
11 A.M. to 9:30 P.M.
Inexpensive
Credit cards: D, MC, V

The first San Tung, a hole-in-the-wall at 24th Avenue and Irving, closed, but now everyone goes to the bright new San Tung, which is larger, more comfortable, and has somewhat easier parking. Most important of all, the northern-style noodles, dumplings, and soups have remained spectacularly good. People make a pilgrimage here for San Tung's famous shrimp and leek dumplings—juicy, garlicky from garlic chives (which the menu calls leeks), and addictive. Many people polish off a plate of twelve themselves. I have. But then I don't have room for San Tung's luscious little round pork dumplings vibrant with ginger. Steamed or fried potstickers are also much ordered here. I also love the seaweed soup, jellyfish and cucumber salad, dry sautéed green beans flecked with bits of pickled mustard and crisp garlic, and, of course, hand-pulled noodles. These are noodles so tender they practically melt in your mouth. They shine in a dish called Three Deluxe Spicy Sauce Noodles, a chile-flecked soup with seafood and vegetables. Kids like them slathered in a mild peanut sauce. Shantung (the restaurant's alternative transliteration of the province name Shandong, to which it refers) is a coastal province between Shanghai and Beijing that has its own distinctive cooking style, and the delicious handmade dumplings, noodles, and seafood soups prepared here are fine examples of it.

SHANGHAI RESTAURANT . . . .

420 Judah Street (at 9th Avenue)
415-661-7755
Open daily 11 A.M. to 10 P.M.
Inexpensive
Credit cards: MC, V

My Asian restaurant expert–filmmaker friend Paul Kwan turned me on to the cold rice wine–marinated Drunken Chicken at Shanghai Restaurant. "Good wine chicken," he wrote. "The meat is very flavorful." Indeed it is. It's the best drunken chicken I've tasted.

This comfortable, pleasant neighborhood restaurant with two separate dining rooms has many treasures on its menu, not the least of which is the drunken chicken. A warm, crisp-skinned vegetarian goose, layers of soybean skin filled with black mushrooms and quickly fried, is also a stellar version of a much-prepared dish. A big portion of pale pink rock shrimp, velvetized with egg white and a dusting of cornstarch, gets a quick sauté. You season this typical Shanghai dish yourself with a spoonful of dipping sauce, mild Chinese black vinegar. It's a taste sensation.

Vegetarians can eat well here, especially if they order famous Shanghai bean curd skin (or leaf as they call it), cut into noodle lengths, wok fried with bits of pickled cabbage, and topped with bright green soybeans. You get the mouth feel of buttery pasta from this dish. The other day we finished off the meal with a gigantic pile of nascent pea sprouts, the delicate green that captures the flavor of fresh peas, lightly sautéed with a whisper of garlic. Newcomers can order off a page of special dishes written in English—salt and pepper pig's knuckle, tea-smoked duck, crispy eel—my mouth waters just thinking about it. In a town dominated by Cantonese restaurants, Shanghai offers a genuine taste of a different culinary region that's becoming all the rage as more and more San Franciscans travel to this exciting mainland city. The homey Shanghai restaurant will give you a little taste without leaving town.

WIN'S . . . .

3040 Taraval Street (between
40th and 41st avenues)
415-759-1818
Open Tuesday through Sunday
11 A.M. to 10 P.M.
Inexpensive
Credit cards: MC, V

People come here to eat Chinese-style roast duck, especially at lunch when it is still hot and juicy from the ovens. The burnished skin crackles; the velvety brown flesh is infused with the perfume of the Chinese spices that have been rubbed into the meat before roasting. You can get these ducks and other good barbecued items such as hunks of pork belly and Chinese spareribs to go, or you can eat them there over rice accompanied with steamed iceberg lettuce leaves, a luscious combination. Although many of the dishes on the amazingly long menu are not worth trying, there are some standouts: excellent rustic pot stickers, crisp-skinned soy sauce chicken, stir-fried Chinese broccoli, and crisp, pan-fried Hong Kong–style chow mein noodles topped with lots of bok choy or Chinese broccoli and chicken.

YUMMY YUMMY . . . .

1015 Irving Street (between
11th and 12th avenues)
415-566-4722
Open Monday, Wednesday through
Saturday 10 A.M. to 9:30 P.M.,
Sunday 10 A.M. to 9 P.M.
Inexpensive
Credit cards: MC, V

I was sent to Yummy Yummy, the relatively new Vietnamese *pho* house and restaurant, by an excook pal who is a climber and likes to stay lean and strong. No surprise that he likes *pho*, the clean rice noodle and beef soup that fills your stomach without weighing you down. Yummy Yummy's No. 2 special combo beef noodle soup is particularly satisfying because it has such a high proportion of beef—thin raw slices that cook in the hot broth, braised brisket, garlicky beef balls, chewy shreds of tendon, spongy beef tripe—and tons of noodles. When you garnish the soup with the bean sprouts, minty Thai basil, a lemon wedge, and sliced green chiles served on the side, and attack with saucerlike flat-bottomed spoon and chopsticks, each bite becomes symphonic, a melding of many flavors and textures. But it's the beef in every bite that sets Yummy Yummy *pho* apart. This is a very hearty version.

But there's another preparation that catapults Yummy Yummy to the hallowed best Asian dish hall of fame—squid salad. It's magnificent. A huge slaw of ever-so-finely julienned cabbage, onion, celery, carrots, and Vietnamese mint is scattered with tidbits of sweetly fresh, white scored squid, all dressed in a balanced Vietnamese dressing of fish sauce, sugar, lemon, and red chiles. Crisp, golden fried shallots and toasted chopped peanuts blanket the top, and large, white shrimp chips—the Vietnamese version of potato chips—surround it. There isn't a more stunning salad in town. Each juicy, crunchy bite is interwoven with aromatics, a vivid tapestry of flavors.

CANVAS CAFE/GALLERY . . . .

1200 9th Avenue (at Lincoln)
415-504-0060
www.thecanvasgallery.com
Open Sunday through Wednesday
8 A.M. to 11 P.M., Thursday
through Saturday until midnight
Credit cards: AE, MC, V

The coffee making is competent here, and the Canvas Cafe's location across the street from the 9th Avenue entrance to Golden Gate Park, where the park's magnificent botanical gardens and arboretum are located, make it a good place for a coffee after a walk. Half of the expansive, sky-lit space is a gallery with revolving exhibits; the other half, which looks across to the park, has Plexiglas café tables and distressed concrete floors. Soothing new-age music plays in the background to match the twenty-first-century decor. Service is efficient.

JAVA BEACH CAFE . . . .

1396 La Playa Boulevard (at Judah)
415-665-5282
Open Monday through Friday
6 A.M. to 8 P.M., Saturday and
Sunday 7 A.M. to 11 P.M.
Cash only

A civilized little café at the end of the N-Judah streetcar line, Java Beach is a hangout for surfers, cyclists, and the kind of person who would live no place other than the edge of the ocean. The smell of the sea, the moist soft air, and the beach stretching for miles just over an embankment make a good cup of coffee taste even better. The juxtaposition of a café that turns out full-flavored, not bitter, espresso and offers ten or so blends of brewed coffee (kept warm in Thermoses on the counter) with laid-back beach life gives Java Beach its cachet. A brisk walk could be planned with a payoff at this welcoming café.

BARS

BEACH CHALET . . . .

1000 Great Highway (between
Lincoln and Fulton)
415-386-8439
www.beachchalet.com
Open Sunday through Thursday
9 A.M. to 10 P.M., Friday and
Saturday until 11 P.M.
Credit cards: MC, V

What a location! The historic Willis Polk building on the edge of the Pacific, at one end of Golden Gate Park, lay empty for years until a young Sunset couple finally won the lease from the city and reopened it as a rollicking brew pub. Everyone watches the sunset and drinks handcrafted beer at this fabulous two-story colonnaded building. The owner wrote a business plan for the property when he was a business student at San Francisco State. Then years later, he and his wife ended up developing the ground floor as a museum of Golden Gate Park memorabilia with restored wraparound murals of San Francisco life in the 1930s, and the upper floor as a vast restaurant and bar with expansive views of the crashing Pacific.

Most of the food on the menu goes well with beer, though the Beach Chalet offers a full bar and wine list. Delicate fried calamari with tartar sauce, an orzo chicken salad, and barbecued pork ribs are good bets. The real draw is the magnificent natural setting and a San Francisco crowd that gives the place resonance, especially later in the evenings. Live jazz makes the bar area, furnished with raised stools and tables so you can look out at the ocean, an even better place to have a drink on the edge of the continent.

DELICATESSENS/TAKEOUT

PALIO PANINOTECA . . . .

500 Parnassus Avenue
(UCSF Milberry Union)
415-681-9925
www.paninoteca1.citysearch.com
Open Monday through Friday
7 A.M. to 5 P.M.
Credit cards: AE, MC, V

Delicious, authentic Italian *panini*, grilled to order or ready to go, plus good espresso in the middle of the UCSF complex. See page 121 for more information.

SUNRISE DELI & CAFE . . . .

2115 Irving Street (at 22nd Avenue)
415-664-8210
Open daily 10 A.M. to 6 P.M.
Credit cards: MC, V

A small, homey Middle Eastern deli, Sunrise makes light, crisp falafel (fried chickpea balls) aromatic with spices, that go into juicy pita bread sandwiches moistened with Sunrise's special salty, creamy tahini (sesame sauce) with cucumber. The store also stocks a variety of Middle Eastern cooking supplies, like fruity Lebanese extra virgin olive oil, flat breads in several sizes, and huge sheets of whole wheat flat bread. Rich whole-milk Persian yogurt takes up a section of the deli case along with tabbouleh (parsley and bulgur wheat salad), hummus (chickpea purée), baba ghanoush (eggplant purée), grape leaves—all the usual. The crisp falafel are better eaten hot on the premises. People sit at a few round tables in the store to eat their pita bread sandwiches and dab their chins with paper napkins.

YUMMA'S . . . .

721 Irving (between
8th and 9th avenues)
415-682-0762
Open daily 11 A.M. to 10 P.M.
Credit cards: MC, V

Of all the places to have a *shawarma*—a Middle Eastern wrap—I would choose Yumma's, which means "mother's" in Arabic. The Palestinian couple that runs this immaculate little shop indeed make you feel right at home. They also know how to construct a gigantic meal inside of fresh *lavash* (a thin flat bread) that will fill you up for a whole day. My favorite creation at Yumma's is the Jerusalem wrap. It begins with crusty bits of Niman Ranch beef and lamb sliced off a revolving vertical spit strung with many packed-down slices of meat—kind of a layered roast. Hot french fries, roasted eggplant, roasted tomatoes (they are in a tray at the bottom of the spit so they get basted in the meat juices), tahini, garlicky yogurt, pickles, and onions seasoned with sumac are piled on top of the meat and the whole thing is rolled up. Each spicy, salty bite tastes like a tour of the Middle East. It's a marvelous experience. Yumma's makes hummus; beautiful, light falafel, delicately scented with cumin, fennel seed, and coriander; tabbouleh; and smoky baba ghanoush. My one admonition is that everyone in the same household eat at Yumma's together, because your whole body seems to broadcast that you have committed to these juicy, pungent Middle Eastern burritos.

BAKERIES/PASTRIES

ARIZMENDI BAKERY . . . .

1331 9th Avenue (between
Irving and Judah)
415-566-3117
www.arizmendibakery.org
Open Tuesday through Friday
7 A.M. to 7 P.M.,
Saturday 8 A.M. to 7 P.M.,
Sunday 9 A.M. to 4 P.M.
Cash only

This cooperatively owned bakery is a spin-off of the mother of all bay area co-ops, The Cheese Board in Berkeley (see page 437). Only the bakery portion of The Cheese Board operation has been somewhat replicated here. Many of the same recipes are used, though some baked goods are locally generated. If I had not eaten the original Cheese Board versions of City and Suburban Bread and baguettes and daily pizzas, I would be ecstatic about the baked goods at Arizmendi. But I have, and the spin-off bakery is not as good yet.

Arizmendi is still a boon to the neighborhood. If you happen to stop by on a Wednesday, try the moist, cheesy corn-cheddar loaf, almost a meal in itself, or pick up a chewy, slowly risen City bread. Each day brings three different bread specials and two different pizzas, which are sold hot by the slice, half or whole, or lite-baked to finish off at home. If you're fond of assertive cheese breads, you will be very happy to find Arizmendi.

ICE CREAM/CHOCOLATES

DOUBLE RAINBOW . . . .

2116 Irving (between
21st. and 22nd avenues)
415-564-9412
www.doublerainbow.com
Open Sunday through Thursday
noon to 10 P.M., Friday and
Saturday until 11 P.M.
Cash only

For the ultimate Outer Sunset dessert, order a Fresh Strawberry Bubble Shake at this Double Rainbow, a sweet shop that exemplifies the diverse cultural currents flowing together on this great market street. This location not only sells rich Double Rainbow ice creams and ices by the cup and the cone, but many different fruit juice and bubble tea drinks with purple tapioca pearls at the bottom. The crowning achievement is the Fresh Strawberry Bubble Shake that brings together the tastes of the Far East and West. Fresh strawberries, a scoop of strawberry ice cream, shaved ice (it goes through an ice crushing machine to order), and simple syrup are liquefied in a blender and the bright pink result is poured into a large, clear plastic cup with a few ice cubes and an inch of big purple tapioca balls. An extra-wide straw, to allow for the free passage of the tapioca bubbles, is pushed through the lid. The strawberry bubble shake has intense strawberry flavor and luxurious creaminess, but is lighter and more refreshing than a Western milk shake. The tapioca bubbles add heft, chewiness, and somehow taste like caramel. They belong in this shake. This twenty-first-century drink would be incomplete without them, just as San Francisco would be incomplete without this international stretch of Irving.

POLLY ANN ICE CREAM. . . . .

3142 Noriega Street (between
38th and 39th avenues)
415-664-2472
www.pollyann.com
Open Sunday through Thursday
11 A.M. to 10 P.M., Friday and
Saturday until 11 P.M.
Cash only

There are so many exotic flavors at this Sunset ice cream institution that a huge ice cream wheel has been mounted on the wall behind the counter for those customers who cannot decide what to order. If you commit to the wheel you must order the flavor it stops on or the one before or the one after. This leeway means that if the wheel stops at durian ice cream, strongly suggestive of fermented garlic, you have a reprieve. I myself almost always order Polly Ann's sharp, herbal green tea ice cream, which is served in many Asian restaurants. The vegetal quality of green tea with its edge of bitterness makes for a lively and refreshing ice cream, an authentic yin-yang bonding of creamy and clean. My other favorites are ginger and litchi, but the gigantic ice cream menu changes often. The young, very hip counterpeople, their hair streaked in primary colors, have the patience of saints, even when they wait on the most indecisive of customers who waffle back and forth between flavors they know and love and risky new ones. Going for ice cream at Polly Ann is always an adventure.

SEE'S CANDIES . . . .

Stonestown Galleria,
20th Avenue (at Winston)
415-731-1784
www.sees.com
Open Monday through Saturday
10 A.M. to 9 P.M.,
Sunday 11 A.M. to 6 P.M.
Credit cards: AE, MC, V

Another indispensable branch of San Francisco's favorite chocolate and candy store. See page 334 for more information.

THE BEANERY. . . . .

602 Irving Street (at 7th Avenue)
and 1307 9th Avenue (at Irving)
415-661-1090
Open Monday through Saturday
6 A.M. to 7 P.M.,
Sunday 7 A.M. to 7 P.M.
Cash only

This beloved neighborhood coffee roastery dispenses both bags of beans and well-made cups of espresso and caffe latte. For those who disavow chains (and many people in San Francisco do, which is why we don't really have very many of them in the city), The Beanery is the local hang in the Sunset. They carry organic coffee beans and make a strong, rich, but non-bitter espresso. The counterpeople know most of their customers and hand-tailor coffees to suit them. Newcomers are treated with equal graciousness. I like supporting small shops like these.

PEET'S COFFEE & TEA. . . . .

54 West Portal Avenue
(between Ulloa and Vicente)
415-731-0375
www.peets.com
Open Monday through Friday
6:30 A.M. to 7 P.M., Saturday 7 A.M.
to 7 P.M., Sunday 7 A.M. to 6 P.M.
Credit cards: D, MC, V

I'm always glad to see a Peet's coffee shop. See page 167 for more information.

MARKETS

ANDRONICO'S . . . .

1200 Irving Street (at Funston)
415-661-3220
Open daily 7 A.M. to 11 P.M.
Credit cards: AE, D, MC, V

The only San Francisco branch of Androncio's, an independently owned chain of grocery stores with four branches in Berkeley, is getting better and more focused since it opened eight years ago. This huge, clean supermarket shows particular strength in luxury cheeses in ready-to-eat condition. I've picked up some obscure, prewrapped treasures based on well-written descriptions and been delighted. I also have found fresh, not moldy coconuts and organic bananas. Tempting aromas always waft from a large prepared-food counter with café seating. Some of the best features of the market are an olive bar with eight different kinds that customers scoop into containers and bring to the checkout line. In the long deli case, salads and prepared foods (like four different kinds of lasagna to take home and warm up) cater to the family that does not have time to cook. You'll also find delicacies such as smoked salmon sliced to order and real Italian prosciutto. In front of the deli case are breads from the best local bakers: Acme, Metropolis, and Semifreddi, to name but a few. The meat department will cut to suit and has hard-to-find items like freshly ground turkey and chicken and a variety of naturally raised meats like Niman Ranch pork and beef. Andronico's has brought Western grocery shopping to new heights in this part of town.

NILOUFER'S TURKEY KABOBS

MAKES ABOUT 8 KEBOBS, SERVES 4

My Parsi friend Niloufer Ichaporia King makes these turkey kabobs all the time, and now I do, too. I serve them with basmati rice, Persian yogurt purchased at the 22nd and Irving produce market (see opposite page), cucumbers, and mango sliced and marinated in lime, salt, and red chile flakes. You can serve these kabobs with almost any accompaniment and they will disappear.

½ cup fresh bread crumbs

¼ cup half-and-half or milk

1 pound ground turkey, preferably dark meat

1½-inch piece fresh ginger, peeled and minced

1 teaspoon kosher salt

3 cloves garlic, minced

3 serrano chiles, seeded and minced

½ bunch cilantro, finely chopped

1 egg

Vegetable oil for frying

1 Soak the bread crumbs in the half-and-half. In a large bowl, combine all the rest of the ingredients, except the oil, with the soaked bread crumbs. Heat a little oil in a large skillet and cook 1 teaspoon of the turkey mixture. Taste for salt and correct the seasoning if necessary. Form the turkey mixture into patties about 2 inches in diameter and 1 inch thick.

2 Heat 1 to 2 tablespoons vegetable oil in the skillet. Sauté the kabobs until they are crisp and brown on one side. Then turn and cook for about 5 minutes longer, or until firm to the touch. These kabobs are almost as good cold as they are hot.

SUNSET SUPER . . . .

2425 Irving (between
25th and 26th avenues)
415-682-3738
Open daily 8:30 A.M. to 7:30 P.M.
Credit cards: MC, V

Moving west on Irving, but east culturally, the great Sunset Super takes you on a trip exclusively through Asia, covering a lot of geography. Specials are hand-written on butcher paper taped to the front windows—fresh oxtails at $2.69, Honey Citron Tea, $3.99. A pallet of the latter greets you at the door. Honey Citron Tea is actually a stunning marmalade, lightly sweet, hauntingly aromatic of citron, and divine on toast. It transforms a cup of hot water into a restorative, grapefruity tea, but it's too good just for that. Put a dish of it on your breakfast table and bask in praise. These big jars of Honey Citron Tea make brilliant hostess gifts, much cleverer than bottles of wine or flowers. (I know because my Parsi friend gave me a jar, which is how I discovered it.)

The scope and depth of food groups at Sunset Super is unsurpassed at any other market in the city. I base this assessment on the fresh noodle section that offers every shape (fine through thick, flat through round), every grain (wheat, rice, buckwheat), and every national style (Indonesian, Chinese, Vietnamese, Japanese); the pickled vegetable department with every conceivable pickled vegetable neatly set out in plastic bins in the refrigerated case; the fresh and dried seaweed selection; or the tofu and tofu products array; or the bottled sauces from every country in Asia. The produce department is mostly Asian with particularly fresh Asian greens, vegetable melons, and fruits, such as bunches of sweet, tiny bananas, each banana no more than three inches long. The fish department is one of the best in the city. Geoduck clams wave their long syphons in tanks like a Busby Berkeley chorus. The other day I spotted such fresh delicacies as tiny cuttlefish, squid, spot shrimp, and clear-eyed fresh flounder. Clean, bubbling tanks hold small, live farmed sturgeon, catfish, and black bass. The fish department smells like the sea. The countermen will clean and fillet. Next to it stretches the long pork counter with every imaginable cut of the animal taking in muscle, bone, and innards, all dewy fresh. A modest selection of beef, oxtails, and some poultry round out animal protein, but pork and fish rule at Sunset Super. This store is a cook's paradise.

22ND AND IRVING MARKET . . . .

22nd Avenue (at Irving)
415-681-5212
Open Monday through Saturday
7 A.M. to 6:30 P.M.,
Sunday 7:30 A.M. to 6 P.M.
Cash only

Only in the Sunset can a market with so many eddying cross-cultural currents thrive. The Outer Sunset (19th Avenue toward the ocean) has become the place where immigrants from Russia, the Middle East, Eastern Europe, and Asia converge, and this store caters to everyone. In one small area of the refrigerator case, for example, I sighted tofu, *queso fresco*, Armenian string cheese, Persian yogurt, Greek feta, and Danish cream cheese in glass jars. On the grocery shelves, bottles of Cortas pomegranate syrup, Bulgarian jam, Kalamata olives, Polish

MUSSELS WITH BLACK BEANS AND FLOWERING GARLIC CHIVES

SERVES 4

I couldn't believe how addictively delicious this mussel recipe is from local food writer Sara Deseran. I was drawn to it because I'm crazy about the flavor of Chinese fermented black beans. (I consider them the anchovies of Chinese cooking.) Carry her book, *Asian Vegetables*, when you shop in Asian markets, and I guarantee that a new world of ingredients will open up for you. The Sunset Super will have everything you need— and then some.

2 tablespoons of peanut oil

1 teaspoon finely chopped garlic

1 tablespoon peeled and finely chopped fresh ginger

2 shallots, thinly sliced

2 tablespoons fermented black beans, chopped

1 cup chicken broth

2 tablespoons Shaoxing wine (Chinese rice wine)

1 tablespoon soy sauce

½ teaspoon sugar

2 pounds mussels, washed and debearded (pull off the hairy bits of seaweed caught between their shells)

1 cup cut-up flowering garlic chives (1-inch lengths)

4 lemon wedges

1 In a large wok or frying pan with a lid over medium-high heat, warm the oil. Add the garlic, ginger, shallots, and black beans. Cook, stirring, for 1 minute, or until the shallots are translucent. Add the chicken broth, wine, soy sauce, and sugar and bring to a boil. Add the mussels, cover, and cook for 3 to 4 minutes, or until the mussels have opened. Add the chives, toss to incorporate, cover, and cook for 30 seconds more to cook the chives.

2 With a slotted spoon, transfer the mussels to bowls, discarding any that have not opened. Ladle the broth into each bowl. Accompany each serving with a wedge of lemon.

cookies, and pitted sour cherries sit next to one another in mind-boggling proximity. You
think that you're in the Adriatic or Mediterranean section until you notice the boxes of
Japanese soup base. Such variety, such turnover. No dust gathers on the jars.

The other great draw of this market is the produce section, full of fresh nut meats and
seeds along with hard-to-find seasonal items such as olives to cure at home, green almonds,
pickling cucumbers, and other products most often found at farmers' markets. Maybe
because rents are cheaper out in the Sunset, the markets can be large and variously stocked
and prices can be low, which encourages a large volume of shoppers. Fuji apples, a loss
leader at practically every other store, cost 39¢ a pound here ($1.29 for extra-large ones at
Andronico's, 29¢ for blemished ones in the Richmond). The 22nd and Irving Market is one
more reason to grant the three or so blocks on Irving between 21st and 24th the best-food-
shopping award.

PRODUCE MARKETS

22ND AND IRVING MARKET . . . .

22nd Avenue (at Irving)
415-681-5212
Open Monday through Saturday
7 A.M. to 6:30 P.M.,
Sunday 7:30 A.M. to 6 P.M.
Cash only

A full and ever-changing array of produce starts on the
sidewalk and takes up more of the store. See page 283
for more information.

MEAT AND POULTRY

GUERRA'S . . . .

490 Taraval Street (at 15th Avenue)
415-564-0585
Open Monday through Friday
9 A.M. to 7 P.M.,
Saturday until 6 P.M.
Credit cards: D, MC, V

Guerra's, a family-owned-and-operated butcher and
delicatessen, has been selling house-cured corned beef
briskets, delectable house-made Italian sausages (hot,
sweet, and fennel), and lush made-to-order deli sandwiches featuring some of the creamiest sliced Havarti
around for over fifty years. I would happily travel across
town to shop at this vibrant meat counter with all sorts
of underused cuts. I love the personal treatment and the pristine freshness of everything.
Guerra's carries a small, if crucial array of produce, imported Italian dry goods and olive
oils, cheeses—basically anything a cook might need to prepare dinner. Having served its
neighborhood for so many years, Guerra's knows what to stock. All inventory turns over
quickly. The codependence of this shop and its neighborhood is not only healthy, but an
exemplary urban model of the benefits of small and local.

EGG
SALAD
$8.99 LB

PAU..
STUF..
EGG..
$..

CRAB
SALAD
$19.99 LB

FRITTA
$5.

GUERRA'S
MEATBALLS
$7.99 LB

..ERRAS
..SAGNA
$..99 LB

SUNSET SUPER . . . .

2425 Irving (between
25th and 26th avenues)
415-682-3738
Open daily 8:30 A.M. to 7:30 P.M.
Credit cards: MC, V

Sunset Super has one of the best fish counters in the
city. See page 283 for more information.

YUM YUM . . . .

2181 Irving Street (at 23rd Avenue)
415-566-6433
Open Tuesday through Sunday
9:30 A.M. to 6:30 P.M.
Credit cards: D, MC, V

Western shoppers like Yum Yum, a branch of Nikko
Fish on 3rd Street, for its neat refrigerated counter full
of easy-to-handle filleted fish. However, the selection at
nearby Sunset Super surpasses the one here. If you need
a salmon steak or two, Yum Yum has them. A sushi-
to-go bar prepares sushi to order, a nice amenity at a
fish store.

WINE AND LIQUOR SHOPS

MR. LIQUOR . . . .

250 Taraval Street (at Funston)
415-731-6222
www.sfwtc.com
Open Monday through Saturday
10 A.M. to 6:30 P.M.
Credit cards: AE, MC, V

A friendly, sophisticated wineshop in the outer reaches
of Parkside? That's correct. Though Mr. Liquor also
carries beer and liquor, this twenty-one-year-old operation knows how to put together a tasty selection of
California, French, and a few Italian wines from the
best importers (Kermit Lynch, Chambers and
Chambers). Beautiful Champagnes and elegant
Burgundies share the limited shelf space with handpicked wines in the $6 to $15 range,
some of which you can taste at a serve-yourself wine bar for 50¢ a pour. I recommend that
you do so. Some of the least-expensive wines may not be worth the savings. The knowledgeable clerks are eager to guide you. They hold special vertical tastings every Saturday as
part of their education program, and Mr. Liquor's monthly newsletter is both informative
and literate. If you are a serious collector or just a drinker, Mr. Liquor is well worth a trip.
The store also stocks hard-to-find single-malt scotches and specialty bourbons, grappas, and
imported stouts and ales.

COOKWARE AND BOOKS

IRVING HOUSEWARES & GIFTS . . . .

2200 Irving Street (at 23rd Avenue)
415-759-1559
Open daily 9 A.M. to 7 P.M.
Credit cards: MC, V

Visit Irving Housewares & Gifts for sturdy, well-made kitchen equipment at decidedly non–Williams-Sonoma prices. Cooking pots with glass covers—my latest fixation—in both medium-weight stainless steel and new-age nonstick materials in all sizes feed into my current cookware phase. (I like to see what's happening in a pot even when it's covered.) A long shelf of cleavers and knives hovers over a similar shelf of cutting boards made of many different materials. Woks and rice cookers, juicers and blenders, cutting and grating tools, long-handled wok utensils—fabulous for the Western kitchen as well—heavy, lidded casseroles that can go on top of the stove and in the oven, and all sorts of dishes and glassware only scratch the surface of this store's inventory.

WILLIAMS-SONOMA . . . .

3251 20th Avenue
(Stonestown mall)
415-242-1473
Open Monday through Friday
10 A.M. to 9 P.M., Saturday and
Sunday 11 A.M. to 6 P.M.
Credit cards: MC, V

Another branch of the upscale kitchenware store. See page 127 for more information.

OUT OF TOWN

N

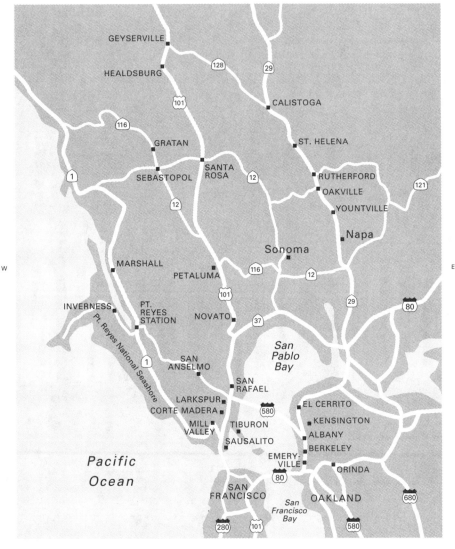

GEYSERVILLE

HEALDSBURG

128

29

101

CALISTOGA

116

GRATAN

ST. HELENA

1

SANTA
ROSA

SEBASTOPOL

12

RUTHERFORD

OAKVILLE

121

YOUNTVILLE

12

Napa

W

MARSHALL

Sonoma

E

PETALUMA

116

12

INVERNESS

PT.
REYES
STATION

NOVATO

101

29

80

37

San
Pablo
Bay

Pt. Reyes National Seashore

1

SAN
ANSELMO

SAN
RAFAEL

EL CERRITO

LARKSPUR

580

KENSINGTON

CORTE MADERA

MILL
VALLEY

TIBURON

ALBANY

BERKELEY

SAUSALITO

EMERY-
VILLE

ORINDA

Pacific
Ocean

80

SAN
FRANCISCO

OAKLAND

680

San
Francisco
Bay

280

101

580

S

0   SCALE MILES   10

THE EAST BAY

RESTAURANTS

Ajanta
BayWolf
Breads of India
Brennan's Restaurant
Café at Chez Panisse
Café Rouge
Casa Orinda
Cesar
Chez Panisse
Citron
Daimo
Doña Tomás
Downtown
Fonda Solana
Grasshopper
Jojo
Mezze
Nizza La Bella
O Chamé
Oliveto
Picante Cocina Mexicana
Rivoli
Siam Cuisine
Sushi Zone
Uzen
Zax Tavern

CAFÉS

Caffe 817
Café Fanny
Cafe at Oliveto
Caffe Strada

BARS

Brennan's
Cesar

DELICATESSENS/TAKEOUT

Blondie's Pizza
Cheese Board Pizzeria
Doug's Bar-B-Q
Market Hall Pasta Shop
Phoenix Pastaficio
Vik's Chaat Corner
Yung Kee

BAKERIES/PASTRIES

Acme Bread Company
Bread Workshop
The Cheese Board
La Farine
Katrina Rozelle
Semifreddi's

ICE CREAM/CHOCOLATES

Scharffen Berger Chocolate Maker
Yogurt Park

ETHNIC MARKETS

G. B. Ratto and Company
Milan International
New Saigon Supermarket
Oakland Market
Sam Yick
The Spanish Table

PRODUCE

Berkeley Bowl
Berkeley Farmers' Market
Market Hall Produce
Monterey Foods
Old Oakland Farmers' Market

MEAT AND POULTRY
Alan's Meats
Enzo
Magnani's Poultry
T & S Market
Taylor's Sausages
Ver Brugge Meats

FISH
Abraham's Seafood
Berkeley Bowl Fish Market
Monterey Fish
New Basement Seafood Market
Rockridge Fish Market

CHEESE
The Cheese Board
The Pasta Shop

COFFEE
Peet's Coffee & Tea

WINES AND SPIRITS
Kermit Lynch Wines
Odd Lots
Paul Marcus Wines
Vino

COOKWARE AND BOOKS
Black Oak Books
Cody's
The Gardener
The Spanish Table
Sur La Table

RESTAURANTS

AJANTA . . . .

1888 Solano Avenue
(near The Alameda), Berkeley
510-526-4373
www.ajantarestaurant.com
Open daily 11:30 A.M. to 2:30 P.M.
and 5:30 to 9:30 P.M.
Inexpensive
Credit cards: AE, DC, D, MC, V

Laxman Moorjani, the owner of Ajanta, presides over his restaurant like a mother hen. He wants everyone to be pleased with his monthly changing menu of specials drawn from all the states in India. He sends out chatty, informative newsletters announcing the dishes and developments in the restaurant—who's gone back to India, who has returned. Once you've visited a couple of times, he knows what dishes you love and can usually conjure them out of the kitchen, even though they are not on the menu. Some of my favorites are chicken *makhanwala*, a boneless breast in a velvety cream sauce, and the stunning chicken *tikka*, an appetizer of boneless tandoori chicken kebabs that are so juicy and tender I always order them along with *aloo tiki*, crisp potato and onion patties served with chutney. I like many of the fresh okra dishes and the spectacular *badal jam*, thick creamy slices of eggplant topped with a garlicky tomato sauce and yogurt, a must order. Mr. Moorjani and his staff gently remind you that Ajanta makes its own Indian desserts and that it would be a shame to miss them. He's right. The house-made *kulfi* (dense Indian ice cream), studded with pistachios, and *ras malai* (*paneer*-cheese patties in yogurt sauce) are exceptional, and both the mango mousse and mango ice cream boast fresh fruit flavor.

BAYWOLF . . . .

3853 Piedmont Avenue
(at Rio Vista Avenue), Oakland
510-655-6004
www.baywolf.com
Open Monday through Friday
11:30 A.M. to 2 P.M.,
6 to 9 P.M., Saturday and
Sunday 5:30 to 9:30 P.M.
Moderate
Credit Cards: AE, MC, V

Michael Wild, the intellectual, twinkly-eyed chef-partner of BayWolf, has been putting out a different seasonal menu every two weeks for over twenty-five years now. This East Bay institution is ensconced in a graciously converted house with two wood-paneled dining rooms with good modern art on the walls and a pleasant little bar. The food has gotten better and better over the years, simpler rather than fussier, as it draws on a marketplace offering ever more naturally delicious ingredients and focuses more directly on Provençal- and Italian-inspired preparations. BayWolf has always had a style of its own: generous, homey, good on meats and duck, great on wines, with a few mannerisms. Over the years, the kitchen has been influenced by a number of its different chefs, but French-born Wild has been a steadying constant, insisting on luscious Provençal dishes like roast chicken with chickpea flour crepes and grilled leeks, juicy leg of lamb with garlic custard, grilled northern halibut with roasted rosemary potatoes, and, of course, a duck dish with a fruit sauce, a BayWolf specialty. You might find wild salmon on a bed of french lentils, braised lamb with creamy polenta, a luscious sliced steak with white beans.

For a starter look for an authentic Tuscan minestrone, chilled shrimp salad in mustard vinaigrette with greens, or a yellow pepper stuffed with goat cheese. An apple *galette* with lavender honey, or a chocolate-ginger *pot-de-crème* might be dessert.

I actually don't think that this East Bay institution has changed much over the quarter century it has been open, but as it matured, the restaurant has achieved a sureness, an appealing self-confidence, a glowing patina of graciousness that makes customers feel great the minute they walk in. Wild and partner Larry Goldman keep working on the physical space, making the odd-shaped dining rooms more accommodating and pleasing. They've enclosed the redwood front porch and installed electric patio heaters to create a spacious dining area, cozy even in cold weather. Their longtime staff, both in the front of the house and the kitchen, work along with them to improve the restaurant continually. You get the feeling that the line between owners and employees has blurred, that the restaurant has become a family, a dedicated community, proud of its home.

This high-minded spirit informs the essentials and the details of this restaurant: the congenial, honest service; the art-driven decor; and especially, the delicious, assured food. Longtime patrons, many of whom live nearby, take obvious pleasure in having such a superb neighborhood spot. That's what BayWolf reminds me of—a charming little chef-run place that happens to seat over a hundred. Diners get all the advantages of the local bistro along with the professionalism and broader range of a larger operation. BayWolf has evolved into this divine state like a great wine. There are no more rough edges, just depth, complexity, and sensual completeness.

BREADS OF INDIA & GOURMET CURRIES . .

2448 Sacramento Street
(at Dwight), Berkeley
510-848-7684
Open daily 11:30 A.M. to 2:30 P.M.
and 5:30 P.M. to 9:30 P.M.
Inexpensive
Cash only

This informal little place specializes in naan—yeasted flat bread baked on the side of a tandoor oven—with different fillings, like cauliflower and *paneer* and seasonings like dill and herbs, plus a daily array of two vegetable and four nonvegetable curries that taste bright and individual. Because the menu is small and changes every day, the dishes are freshly made. Such simplicity pays off in flavor. The problem, of course, is that you have to wait for a table outside on the sidewalk and when seats open up, they might be at a table where other people are eating. I suppose you could wait for your own table, but I have never known anyone who could resist the aroma of spices and the fragrance of the breads one minute longer than needed. The rather bare-bones dining room with some cheerfully hand-painted decoration and Indian artifacts is not a place for quiet conversation anyway. Like Shalimar (see page 115) and Naan 'N' Curry (see page 110) in the city, Breads of India is a place for Indian food that is alive and kicking, not an ordinary restaurant at all.

BRENNAN'S . . . .

720 University Avenue
(at 4th Street), Berkeley
510-841-0960
Open daily 11 A.M. to 9:30 P.M.;
bar open Sunday through Tuesday
11 A.M. to midnight, Wednesday and
Thursday 11 A.M. to 1 A.M., Friday
and Saturday 11 A.M. to 2 A.M.
Inexpensive
Credit cards: MC, V

This beloved Berkeley hofbrau and bar has undergone a couple of gentle face-lifts during its forty years, but the pensioners and students who depend on its first-rate cafeteria food for basic sustenance don't have to worry that the place is going upscale. A coat of bright Egyptian-green paint has been rolled over the old, amazingly drab institutional shade, and customers are dazzled by such modern turns as clear glass windows, perimeter lighting, wooden partitions with coat hooks, and two large new televisions for sporting events.

Though Brennan's has taken on a publike cachet—well, kind of—prices have stayed the same. The blown-up photos of Mr. Brennan posing in front of prize steers at 4-H auctions still gaze down at customers tucking into their chewy roast beef sandwiches, French dipped, of course. And the same cast of characters—artists, sailors from the nearby marina, metalworkers, people off the dinner shift from restaurants around Berkeley—still stops by for late-night drinks.

The food on the cafeteria line includes gigantic roast turkeys, whole briskets of corned beef, and massive top rounds of roast beef, thickly sliced to order and generously stacked onto French rolls, rye bread, or white. Excellent coleslaw in a creamy dressing and incendiary horseradish on the tables enhance all the sandwiches. Turkey plates with nicely seasoned bread stuffing, mashed potatoes, canned or frozen vegetable of choice, and gravy mean that hundreds can celebrate Thanksgiving every day. Some people make a point of going to Brennan's on Wednesdays for the smoked tongue plate with boiled potatoes and cabbage; others always get there early enough to grab the almost giraffe-sized turkey necks while they last. One truly new development is the chicken rotisserie, the source for a juicy half-chicken plate, which has become the most popular to-go item. For cheap, substantial eats and a friendly bar, Brennan's is still the best.

CAFÉ AT CHEZ PANISSE . . . .

1517 Shattuck Avenue (between
Cedar and Vine), Berkeley
510-548-5525
www.chezpanisse.com
Open Monday through Thursday
11:30 A.M. to 3 P.M., Friday and
Saturday until 3:30 P.M.; Monday
through Thursday 5 to 10:30 P.M.,
Friday and Saturday until 11 P.M.
Moderate
Credit cards: AE, DC, D, MC, V

Not enough can be said about the influence of Alice Waters's vision and the enormous impact she has had on cooking and eating in America. Thank goodness her culinary Mecca now takes reservations, though booking lunch affords the quickest turn-around time from phone call to sitting down at a Chez Panisse table, always a rare experience when you consider the unsurpassed quality of everything that is served at this temple of beautiful ingredients. Still anchoring the menu are crusty pizzas, aromatic from the wood-fired brick oven, and the definitive green salad of the tastiest, tiniest lettuces with garlic croutons and a perfect vinaigrette. The rest of the menu changes with the seasons, but you can always count on something sublime and ingenuous, like toasts covered with wild mushrooms drizzled in fragrant olive oil and baked in the wood-fired oven; or LuLu Peyraud's Provençal-style grilled steak served in thin, juicy, rare slices topped with anchovy butter, a few bitter greens, and some roasted potatoes that taste better than any others. That's the thing about Chez Panisse. You get food here that you think you have tasted before—roasted peppers, tomatoes, melon, lamb chops, scallops—that take you by surprise: you never realized that they could taste like this. The key to serving such naturally delicious food goes way, way back to the growing, the picking, the collecting. In fact, the restaurant employs full-time foragers, who discover and commission superb ingredients. They encourage farmers to raise certain species, and teach everyone, through the lusciousness of the stuff they find, about the importance of ecologically sound growing practices. Of course, the cooking itself certainly plays a large part, but letting the ingredients—when they're at their peak—dictate the menu has been the Chez Panisse breakthrough. I marvel at the presentations, so simple, yet so beautiful. Nothing is crowded onto the plates or fussy; the arrangements are naturally full of color and life. Eating here is always a pleasure. You feel nourished, refreshed, delighted, meal after meal, year after year. So if you're a believer, you might as well be nourished at the source.

CAFÉ ROUGE . . . .

1782 Fourth Street (between
Hearst and Virginia), Berkeley
510-525-1440
www.caferouge.net
Open Monday 11:30 A.M. to 3 P.M.,
Tuesday through Thursday
11:30 A.M. to 9 P.M., Friday and
Saturday 11:30 A.M. to 10 P.M.
Moderate
Credit cards: MC, V

Chef-owner Marsha McBride runs this buoyant bar, restaurant, and butcher counter with conviction. She's a meat expert—she knows how the animals she serves are raised, how to break them down, the best ways to cook them. The restaurant specializes in naturally raised meats and often prepares them with grillroom simplicity. Eating anything here—pork chops with rutabaga-potato purée, braised leeks, and spiced prunes in natural juice; crisp-skinned rotisserie chicken; jewel-like salads of endive, persimmon, and pomegranate; house-made charcuteries—is pure pleasure. This is market-inspired cooking and quite appropriate to Café Rouge's market-hall location.

Café Rouge also fills a niche by bringing a Zuni-style (see page 57) zinc bar complete with oysters, a sophisticated wine list, and lots of well-made cocktails to this busy East Bay shopping nexus. The front of the restaurant opens completely onto a patio of tables and umbrellas, a fine spot for lunch. At night, the lighting softens the warehouselike interior so that it feels more intimate than it does during the day. The noise level can be high. People drop by for drinks and food throughout the day and into the evening, making Café Rouge a significant addition to the Bay Area dining scene—especially for a juicy steak and authentic french fries.

CASA ORINDA . . . .

20 Bryant Way (at Moraga Way),
Orinda
925-254-2981
Open Sunday through Thursday
4 to 10 P.M., Friday and
Saturday until 11 P.M.
Moderate
Credit cards: AE, MC, V

I have a soft spot in my heart for this old-fashioned steak, prime rib, and fried chicken house in Orinda with its long western bar, wonderfully warm service, and practically everything made from scratch. John Goyak is the second generation of his family to run this seventy-something-year-old roadhouse with a racy past. Though he has called on some chef friends from no less than Chez Panisse to help him update the menu, he could only change it a little without disappointing his regulars, thank goodness. No customer would tolerate giving up the hot cream biscuits with honey that go with Casa Orinda's southern-fried chicken. Casa Orinda actually uses the original Kentucky Fried Chicken cooking equipment and formulas, which they bought when the Colonel was selling his process door to door. The way the chicken comes out at Casa Orinda makes the greasy fast-food version seem flaccid. People buy tons of prime rib and steak and a delicious chicken cutlet breaded in fresh Acme bread crumbs and fried in clarified butter. The pastry department makes all sorts of fresh fruit pies and cobblers, and even old customers love a sparkling fresh lemon tart taught to the kitchen by Patricia Curtan from Chez Panisse. There aren't many old-fashioned American restaurants left, and very few that are owned by individuals with integrity. Casa Orinda is one of them and you can tell the moment you walk in the door: people are happy to work here, the dining rooms are immaculate, and the food is comforting and tasty.

CESAR . . . .

1515 Shattuck Avenue (between
Cedar and Vine), Berkeley
510-883-0222
Bar open daily noon to midnight;
kitchen open Sunday through
Thursday noon to 3 P.M. and
4 to 11 P.M., Friday and
Saturday until 11:30 P.M.
Inexpensive
Credit cards: MC, V

Cesar gets better and better every time I go there. First I considered it a bar, but a bar extraordinaire with the widest range and highest quality selection of spirits anywhere; a Kermit Lynch–inspired wine list that celebrates the eccentricity of the wine maker and sense of place; artisan ciders and beers; imaginative cocktails made with top-shelf bottles; tasting flights of every kind of booze; and a small menu of stunning bites with a Spanish motif. Right next door to Chez Panisse, and started by veterans of the mother ship, Cesar has become an eating place in its own right. People can make affordable light meals of the tapas; they like the versatility of ordering a little, like a ramekin of olives or toasted almonds and a plate of velvety *jamón serrano*; or something more substantial such as a huge pile of signature flat shoestring potatoes fried crisp with whole leaves of herbs that scent every bite. Another beloved Cesar dish, bite-sized thin-skinned green peppers deep-fried whole, provides the Vegas-like excitement of never knowing which little pepper will blow your mouth out. There's always one or two per plate. The tiny open kitchen turns out resonant miniature fish stews; toasts with anchovies or grilled sardines; and traditional Spanish tortillas, wedges of potato and onion cake molded by egg.

You can reserve the big central table and have a paella party. Otherwise it's first come, first serve, but with supervision. A floor man monitors the door during busy times and keeps turnover orderly. Personally, I like to have a drink standing at the wide, modern blond-wood bar until a stool opens up and eat there because it reminds me of actually being at a tapas bar.

CHEZ PANISSE . . . .

1517 Shattuck Avenue (between Cedar and Vine), Berkeley
510-548-5525
www.chezpanisse.com
Open Monday through Saturday; seatings from 6 to 9:15 P.M.
Expensive
Credit cards: AE, DC, D, MC, V

The famous prix fixe dinner that has been served for over three decades continues to be a reflection of Alice Waters's uncompromising standards about the purity of ingredients and her sensibility that requires elegant simplicity in preparation. As the week proceeds, prices for dinner increase. Three-course Monday meals, such as an interesting pot-au-feu with duck confit, cabbage *crepinette*, and beef short ribs simmered in savory broth served with caper sauce and coarse-grain mustard, are the cheapest and the most rustic. Courses and complexity are added as the week goes on. A winter offering menu might include a green garlic and potato *galette* with garden salad, turnip soup with turnip-green flan, grilled black sea bass with Barolo sauce, leeks, spinach, roasted fennel, and celery root, and end with a caramelized banana gratin. Weekend menus begin with an aperitif, an elixir of white wine infused with fruit or herbs, and continue with salads of Chino Ranch vegetables, shrimp beignets with fried leeks, succulent tiny lamb chops and loin in a fresh shell bean and chanterelle ragout, and for dessert a fresh berry soup with vanilla ice cream. Currently, longtime Chez Panisse veterans Christopher Lee and Kelsie Kerr share cooking responsibilities downstairs. Kerr leans a little more to Italy; Lee to the Mediterranean and France.

Once you eat at Chez Panisse you'll know how magically everything fits together; how superb the individual dishes are; how every detail from flowers to lighting to bread to wine service flows out of a single vision. I've praised this restaurant to the skies so many times that now all I want to say is that it continues on at the highest level; that no other restaurant in the world possesses its purity and charm; that a meal here is worth every penny—even though they can really mount up what with tax and 15 percent service added right onto the bottom of the check—and that I'd rather eat here than anywhere else in the world.

CITRON . . . .

5484 College Avenue
(at Taft), Oakland
510-653-5484
www.citron-acote.com
Open nightly 5:30 to 9:30 P.M.
Moderate
Credit cards: AE, DC , D, MC, V

Chef Craig Thomas's neighborhood bistro continues to charm the picky East Bay crowd, even in competition with his own wildly popular wine bar and small plate venue, À Côté, next door. Romantic yet low key, Citron's small dining room glows with warmth. Someone got all the details down just right: the wicker chairs and banquettes, the little bar, the soft lighting, the tile floors, the casual large arrangements of flowers. The menu is small, interesting, nicely executed, and always delivers a couple of clever new twists on classic dishes. Generous portions and simple presentation complete the picture.

The first courses sound heavier than they are—they're really green salads accompanied with a tiny puff pastry filled with goat cheese or a few shreds of duck confit. These light starters work well with the substantial main courses: a smoky coq au vin served with polenta, flanked by sweet little turnips; a seafood couscous with harissa on the side. Real bistro fare featuring pork loin, duck breast, or thick fillets of fish on lentils is the order of the day. Desserts follow suit with a more American bent, like fresh fruit crisp with ice cream or crème brûlée.

An elegant but reasonably priced international wine list plays a large role in the pleasure of meals taken here. Each bottle on the list has won its place for versatility and character. Citron reminds me of one of my favorite restaurants in San Francisco, Woodward's Garden (see page 192), in that it is very small, personal yet professional, and delivers outsized satisfaction for its size.

DAIMO . . . .

Pacific East Shopping Mall
(off I-80 at the Central Avenue
Exit), El Cerrito
510-527-3888
Open daily 9 A.M. to midnight
Inexpensive
Credit cards: MC, V

Bruce Cost, the Asian-food expert whose classic book, *Asian Ingredients,* opened up a whole new culinary world for Western cooks, feels that Daimo, a casual eatery in the Pacific East Shopping Mall, is the best Cantonese restaurant in the Bay Area. The cooking is personal there, he believes. The chef takes food preparation a step further than any other Asian restaurant: the threads of ginger are finer in the dipping sauces, the chiles more finely sliced, aromatics added with more finesse. The cooking of stomach and tripe and all those parts of the animal that Americans don't eat is superb. Daimo cooks for a discriminating Asian audience. So, of course, I stopped by for lunch one day before a shopping spree at the Ranch 99 Asian supermarket.

I might as well have been in Asia for all the English spoken. Luckily, the daily specials were printed in English. A brisket-noodle soup full of tender if gelatinous tendon had tremendous depth in its aromatic, star anise–scented broth. Soft rice noodles layered with shrimp had a meltingly soft texture punctuated with a whisper of chewiness. The shrimp were sparkling and sweet; the texture of the noodles poetic. Then, for textural contrast, we had a big plate of crispy, garlicky, salt-and-pepper-fried spareribs, actually thin slices of pork with bone in, that made for addictive nibbling. Though it's a schlep to visit Daimo from San Francisco (one mitigating factor is that it's right off a freeway exit), I'm going to take my Cantonese-speaking food experts there to help me order a big adventurous meal. There is treasure to be mined at this nondescript outpost of south China in an East Bay Asian shopping center.

5004 Telegraph Avenue
(near 51st Street), Oakland
510-450-0522
Open Tuesday through Thursday
5:30 to 9:30 P.M., Friday and
Saturday 5:30 to 10 P.M.
Inexpensive–Moderate
Credit Cards: AE, MC, V

The pretty Doña Tomás space, in a renovated commercial building across the street from a new shopping center, has high ceilings, wooden floors, and tall front windows. The white-washed walls display Mexican textiles; the long room is furnished with heavy wooden Mission-style tables and chairs. Interior windows look onto a Mexican-style lobby with a pretty ceramic fountain. Chef–co-owner Donna Savitsky left her head chef's job at Cafe Marimba (see page 151) to open this place with Thomas Schnetz, who actually does most of the cooking. But Doña Tomás is not a Marimba knockoff. It has plenty of its own charming character, reflected in both ambience and food.

The food is as clean and uncluttered as the surroundings. Start with a house margarita made with fresh lime juice, served in a tall glass over ice, accompanied by a blue-and-white bowl of hot, roasted pumpkin seeds tossed with garlic cloves and tiny hot red chiles. You won't be able to stop eating them. For *antojitos* "little bites" try the juicy lime-cooked scallop ceviche or the *empanada de calabaza y queso*, two freshly made rounds of masa with a filling of puréed butternut squash slathered in a tart tomatillo salsa enlivened by roasted *guajillo* chiles. One of my favorite main courses is enchiladas stuffed with wild mushrooms and goat cheese in a piquant tomatillo salsa that sets off the rich filling. Another great tortilla dish comes in the form of shrimp tacos—three soft mini–corn tortillas piled with onions sautéed on a superhot griddle with shrimp, garlic, and hot chiles. They're the best shrimp tacos around.

Doña Tomás offers the amenities of a sophisticated restaurant—pure, often organic ingredients, one-of-a-kind preparations, high-quality tequilas and wines, artful décor—mixed with youthful energy, quirkiness, and a few rough edges. That's okay, because eating and drinking at Doña Tomás is refreshingly affordable. Everyone has fun—customers and workers alike—free from the pressures that creep in from high-rent locations and high prices.

DOWNTOWN. . . . .

2102 Shattuck Avenue
(at Addison), Berkeley
510-649-3810
www.downtownrestaurant.com
Open Tuesday through Friday
11:30 A.M. to 2 P.M.; Tuesday,
Wednesday, and Thursday 5:30 to
9:30 P.M., Friday and Saturday until
11 P.M.; late-night menu until
midnight; Sunday 5 to 9 P.M.,
late-night menu until 10:30 P.M.
Moderate
Credit cards: AE, MC, V

Downtown's large central room reverberates with the confident buzz of big-city restaurants. High-quality materials and stylish details enliven the spare open space, while wooden floors with some carpeting and a floating translucent square of material near the ceiling help to dampen noise. Comfortable, modern chairs fashioned from one heavy slice of bentwood deserve design awards. All the artifacts that diners touch—tabletops, chairs, substantial silverware, thin, graceful wineglasses, white linen napkins—provide tactile pleasure. The changing lineup of jazz musicians who play the baby grand prominently placed in the dining room really know how to warm up the room, without drowning conversation.

Of the many facets of Downtown, the food gleams the brightest. The daily menu written on a long page offers a mix of large and small dishes. From the cold and raw bar come Marin Myagi and East Coast Malpeque oysters on the half shell and some inspired chilled and marinated seafood dishes like a savory and piquant Hawaiian *ono*. Everyone loves deep-fried tidbits and Downtown satisfies with a *fritto misto*, every bite a surprise. You might find an oyster, a scallion, a finger of zucchini or halibut, a thin slice of lemon, a fillet of sardine beneath a crunchy crust. For those who crave soft, saucy food, the juices of steamed mussels mingle with tomato, basil, and a square of focaccia to make a thick, savory bread soup.

You certainly can make a sparkling meal of small plates here, especially with glasses of wine from Downtown's extensive drinks list. Stephen Singer, who put the list together, knows his way around a European wine cellar. Downtown's bar concocts inventive cocktails, always made with fresh citrus juices, and stocks a dizzying selection of spirits and liqueurs—no problem if you're walking or taking BART home.

If you can resist all the little dishes, you'll have room for one of Downtown's main courses like sliced, dry-aged White Mountain Organic New York steak drizzled with twelve-year-old balsamic vinegar and accompanied with thin fries and a bacon and radish salad. Another night I ate a lovely, creamy piece of wild salmon with a seasonal mix of small potatoes, green beans, and a galvanizing tomato relish. In both these dishes, the parts made for a cohesive whole, a rarity in main courses these days.

With one thousand theater and concert seats across the street, twenty-five movie screens within two blocks, the Berkeley Community Theater and UC's Zellerbach Hall a ten-minute walk away, and the Berkeley BART station next door, Downtown's founders, the owners of Cesar (see page 398), recognized an opportunity. Throw in an active bar, a kitchen that serves late, live music, and a staff that can handle the crush of pre-performance crowds, and it's apparent why Downtown has been a hit from the moment its doors opened.

FONDA SOLANA . . . .

1501 Solano Avenue
(at Curtis), Albany
510-559-9006
www.fondasolana.com
Open nightly 5:30 P.M. to 12:30 A.M.;
brunch Friday 11:00 A.M. to 3:00 P.M,
Saturday and Sunday 10:00 A.M. to
3:00 P.M.; siesta (light menu with
full bar) Friday through Sunday
3 to 5:30 P.M.
Inexpensive
Credit Cards: AE, DC , MC, V

This Latin American newcomer strikes out on its own exotic path and takes adventurous diners to new territory. Chefs Steve Jaramillo and David Rosales have come up with some stunning small plates, all reasonably priced and shareable, that add up to a satisfying meal. *Molotes*, Oaxacan-style "cigars" of cornmeal with lots of tasty chorizo and potato filling and a drizzle of crema, become a little meal in themselves with the accompanying pile of pickled cabbage slaw, a great combination. Plump tamales with more chicken filling than cornmeal wrapping get a frisky-hot mole sauce layered with flavor. Quesadillas here turn out to be empanadalike turnovers, a little chewy but nicely filled with Oaxacan white cheese and hot green chiles and onions. They're delicious with bright, uncooked tomatillo salsa. To cool the palate have a goblet of cucumber and jicama sticks bathed in lime juice—just avoid the tops that are gaily sprinkled with cayenne. If you like heat, then this is the perfect refreshing salad. Finish with mango slices with lime and a plate of assorted cookies that includes one of my favorites, buttery Mexican wedding cookies made with pecans.

Latin-themed cocktails, like *mojitos* and *caipirinha*, and a cleverly selected list of wines by glass and bottle that stand up to the chile-spiked food make Fonda all the more fun. The high-ceilinged room, a converted garage, handsomely restructured with rough wood and metal bracing can be deafeningly noisy. Sit in the mezzanine for slightly less sound, though you won't be able to enjoy the excitement of the ground floor open kitchen and bar.

GRASSHOPPER . . . .

6317 College Avenue
(near Claremont), Oakland
510-595-3557
www.grasshoppersaki.com
Open Tuesday through Saturday
11:30 A.M. to 3 P.M., Tuesday
through Thursday 5 to 10:30 P.M.,
Friday and Saturday 5 to 11:30 P.M.,
Sunday 5 to 10 P.M.
Inexpensive
Credit cards: AE, MC, V

Everyone has jumped on the small-plate bandwagon, but you can have no better experience of small-dish eating than at Grasshopper, the pan-Asian *sakana* (little dishes that go with sake) spot on the Oakland-Berkeley border. At Grasshopper, the concept feels natural, not gimmicky.

A meal of small Asian dishes makes the most sense anyway. Additionally, small dishes from the pan-Asian pantry are unified by a universal accompaniment: rice. I left satisfied after dinner at Grasshopper and excited about returning. From nuts and pickles to East-West dessert, the food delighted and nourished.

Large, crisp cashews delicately coated with sugar and cumin; and tidbits of turmeric-tinted cauliflower, red onion, and baby turnip pickle prepare your palate for the flavor contrasts of the rest of meal, especially with an initial tiny cup of cold sake chosen from a helpfully annotated list. Then move along to bracing, superfresh tuna *poke*—a kind of ceviche with fruity, citrusy overtones that work against the earthiness of sesame oil. A baby *tatsoi* and *mizuna* salad, two characteristically cabbagelike Asian greens, is lightened by a fine, clean mince of avocado, cherry tomatoes, and a soy-ginger dressing.

In the fertile small-plates category are irresistible crunchy fried calamari with lime *sambal*, a fruity, chile-flecked dipping sauce; soft, garlicky, juicy pork *gyoza*; and satisfying roasted Gypsy peppers stuffed with curried sticky rice. Soy-braised pork and kabocha squash come straight from the Japanese lexicon, a stew in which orange squash and meat become equally velvety and tender, the sweet and smoky cooking liquid enriched by the melding of flavors. Ask for a bowl of jasmine rice to eat with this one.

Many people just order from the amazingly affordable grill section of the menu where you will find a generous portion of miso-marinated rib-eye steak with grilled broccoli rabe, a spectacular combination in which the slightly bitter bite of the broccoli underscores the richness of the beef. Meaty twelve-spice pork ribs stacked on a small ceramic plate alone would make a sufficient main course. And I am much taken by grilled miso-marinated *ono*, three generous scallops on a piquant warm slaw of napa cabbage, carrots, and radish.

You can eat all these dishes with several different sakes. Like wine, the flavor of fine sake is complex and the more you cultivate your palate, the more you will enjoy it.

Grasshopper is the place to start. The list is long and carefully categorized; each sake gets a rather poetic description of its own special combination of floral, fruity, and spicy notes that proves spot on. For $10 you can get a tasting flight of three, one from each category, *junmai* (superior), *ginjo* (premium), and *daiginjo* (ultrapremium). The servers are eager to explain the differences.

There's no other place like Grasshopper in the Bay Area or, I imagine, anywhere in the world. This restaurant brings together Berkeley's obsession with pure ingredients with wittily presented Japanese and Southeast Asian dishes, a vibrant, polished decor, and a whole new world (for most of us) of drink. Grasshopper is so fully realized and so much fun, a visit is well worth a drive across the bridge.

JOJO . . . .

3859 Piedmont Avenue
(near Rio Vista), Oakland
510-985-3003
www.jojorestaurant.com
Open Tuesday through Thursday
5:30 to 9:30 P.M., Friday and
Saturday 5:30 to 10:30 P.M.
Moderate
Credit cards: AE, DC, D, MC, V

I am transported by Jojo, the tiny country French restaurant next door to BayWolf in Oakland. Jojo looks backward, not forward. When I walked into this modest storefront restaurant, I was reminded of the first time I ate at Chez Panisse thirty years ago. There is something pure and ingenuous about the place.

The chef-owners, Mary Jo Thoresen and Curt Clingman, obviously thought about all the physical factors that make sitting in a restaurant pleasurable. They understand the importance of the sensual landscape—what each patron sees, hears, and touches. As a diner, you feel that your needs have been anticipated, your comfort considered. I got the impression, for once, that the customers were the focus of the restaurant, not profitability, concept, or the ego of the chef.

The small menu of just seven starters, five main courses, and five desserts, printed on a single page, follows suit with its simplicity. We're so used to big menus that this one almost seems meager, but it's wonderfully complete, especially if you factor in dessert—a must here. Because every dish goes with every other dish, you can construct a number of different and satisfying meals.

You might start with an herby, flavorful, roughly textured *pâté de campagne*, garnished with radishes, cornichons, and hot mustard; and a big, poufy green salad of small lettuces dressed in a tart, tasty vinaigrette. A trio of little salads may include seasonal sweet beets, celery root, and Gruyère cut into matchsticks. (The trio changes daily.) With the country pâté, they make for a traditional charcuterie service. If a salad of dandelion, endive, and warm slices of cured rabbit loin in spicy-hot mustard vinaigrette happens to be on the menu, order it. I also love the hearty main courses like a winter vegetable and bean gratin served like a cassoulet with a crunchy breadcrumb topping. Braised lamb is also unusually tasty in that the tender pieces of leg slowly absorb the cooking liquid while also infusing it with flavor.

The wine list is small and select, a combination of French and California bottles, each with a one-line editorial comment. This soupçon of friendly guidance not only helps you choose, but lets you know how carefully each wine was chosen. Many of the most desirable wines can be ordered by the glass.

Desserts share the same page as the appetizers and main courses, because Jojo wants you to look forward to having one or two, right from the start. Mary Jo Thoresen made desserts at Chez Panisse with the late Lindsey Shere for twelve years and her creations at Jojo hit the spot. The measured portions and balanced composition of all that has come before allow you to appreciate every lovely dessert. The whole meal sits just right.

Jojo is such an intimate statement by such dedicated, highly skilled restaurant people that you feel lucky to be included. It took Clingman and Thoresen seventeen years of working in other restaurants to open Jojo finally. They knew exactly what they wanted and it wasn't glitz, a large operation financed by investors (which they could have attracted in a minute), or a stab at haute cuisine. It was a small place they could decorate and run themselves that would demonstrate why they were drawn to cooking in the first place.

MEZZE . . . .

3407 Lakeshore Avenue
(at Trestle Glen), Oakland
510-663-2500
www.mezze.com
Open Tuesday through Thursday
5:30 to 9 P.M., Friday and
Saturday 5:30 to 10 P.M.,
Sunday 5:30 to 9 P.M.; Brunch on
Saturday 11:30 A.M. to 2:30 P.M.,
Sunday 10 A.M. to 2:30 P.M.
(live music for Sunday brunch)
Moderate
Credit cards: AE, MC, V

Sitting in sophisticated Mezze, which is situated in a funky little shopping area that serves what is known as the Crocker Highlands, I can only surmise that the migration of upwardly mobile, food-and-wine–consuming professionals to areas where housing and rents are still almost affordable has made a restaurant of this kind possible here. Now Crocker Highlanders with disposable income can nibble on Mediterranean-rim tidbits and drink $40 Zinfandels.

The other surprise about Mezze, besides its being so smart, grown-up, and not on College or Piedmont Avenue, is that it doesn't serve meze—North African and Middle Eastern appetizers. In fact, what the menu calls the meze platter is really more of a colorful California medley of marinated olives, roasted peppers, and onion; undercooked French beans; shaved fennel; pickled beets; arugula with a slice of goat cheese; and leek quiche. Fresh, colorful, but certainly not North African.

But *b'stilla*—two crisp phyllo triangles filled with a spicy purée of chicken, ground almonds, and saffron—does evoke the cooking of Morocco, even if Mezze's version is a California riff on the traditional pigeon pie. You can stay Italian with the two daily pizzas that come out of the wood-burning oven, one topped with portobello mushrooms, grilled peppers, and fontina. Or be adventurous with crumbled Moroccan lamb sausage, roasted tomatoes, *kasseri* cheese, and a chiffonade of fresh mint. The best starter has a Northern California pedigree—small pretty lettuces, baked black figs in balsamic vinegar, prosciutto, toasted hazelnuts, and a sharp buttery slice of Cambozola (a mixture of Gorgonzola and Camembert) cheese. These flavors sing together; the textures perform acrobatics on the tongue.

Fish stars in a number of vegetable-rich main courses. Pan-roasted Alaskan halibut tops a pretty mélange of potatoes, roasted tomatoes, and olives scented with marjoram, a combination that doesn't quite suit the delicate flavor and texture of this white-fleshed fish.

Seared rare *ahi* tuna, sliced like a fillet of beef, is draped over a bed of lentils and chanterelles sauced in a veal-based red wine reduction with a drizzle of truffle oil. I particularly enjoyed a large braised lamb shank in a light, cinnamon-scented sauce with apricots, carrots, slightly undercooked chickpeas, and greens.

Abundant choice characterizes the wine list, with wines available by the half and full glass and the bottle. The bar turns out a state-of-the-art martini. The bartender sprays the vermouth onto a chilled glass with an atomizer.

The owners-operators, Solange and Maurice Darwish, are on the floor schmoozing with the customers, supporting the staff, and happily basking in the glory of their popular new restaurant. They live in the neighborhood and opened the restaurant because they wanted to walk over to a place like this themselves. They weren't the only ones. The community has embraced Mezze.

NIZZA LA BELLA . . . .

825 San Pablo Avenue
(near Solano), Albany
510-526-2552
Open Sunday through Thursday
5:30 to 9:30 P.M., Friday and
Saturday until 11 P.M.
Moderate
Credit Cards: MC, V

Bistro Nizza la Bella (Nizza means "Nice" in the local, Italian-influenced patois) not only focuses on the cooking of coastal France along the Mediterranean, but also captures its spirit. The look of the place, down to the graphics on the menu, the shape of the wineglasses, and the color of the walls, transports you to southern France. And frankly, if memory serves, the simple, earthy food at this restaurant tastes better here than there.

The restaurant's sidewalk terrace, curtained in blue mesh during the colder months, catches your eye as you drive along San Pablo Avenue. Inside, you notice first a zinc bar stocked with bottles that reach the ceiling, then the small, closely placed dark wood tables and banquettes and a row of wooden booths. When we arrived for our 8:30 reservation one Friday night, a booking made twenty-four hours in advance as instructed by an answering machine, and confirmed later by telephone, the maitress d' who clearly was the proprietor told us that the dining room was running late. She apologized and gestured to the bar where we drank colorful, delicious cocktails, the fruits of a master bartender. By the time we settled into a dark wood booth, romantically lit by an art deco lamp, we were ready to eat. We could hardly decide what to choose from a traditional brasserie-style menu with a southern French bent. We finally ordered *salade anchoiade*, romaine leaves slathered with a well-balanced Parmigiano-and-anchovy vinaigrette; *limaçons*, snails baked in their shells with anise butter and crisp breadcrumbs; *salada nissarda*, a Niçoise salad with cherry tomatoes, bright-orange-yolked eggs, carrot ribbons, and marinated onions topped with a dryish hunk of house-made tuna confit; and a selection from the *plats du jour* section—a mozzarella ball, bland as mozzarella tends to be, on a bed of arugula, tomatoes, and olives in balsamic vinaigrette. And then the garlic festival began. Fire-roasted mussels were slathered with parsley and garlic and dabbed with pungent, garlicky aioli. A thin Niman Ranch steak, cooked rare, came with terrific french fries with a big spoon of aioli. A half free-range chicken came out of the 800 degrees Fahrenheit wood-burning oven in record time with crisp skin and juicy flesh. My favorite dish was a rich, winey, olivey, tomatoey Provençal beef stew served on noodles. The meat melted into the noodles and the garlic was muted.

The wine list is as pulled together as the cocktail service. The list is stacked with affordable, highly drinkable wines that are chosen to go with the robust food. The waitstaff's familiarity with it points both to personal dedication and good management.

This is not a California restaurant. The food here is not the freewheeling Mediterranean fusion served at seemingly hundreds of restaurants in Northern California—though traditional Niçoise cooking reflects age-old culinary influence with neighboring Italy. Nizza la Bella's food and ambience are so old-fashioned and pure that they seem new and exciting.

O CHAMÉ . . . .

1830 Fourth Street (between Hearst and Virginia), Berkeley
510-841-8783
Open Monday through Saturday 11:30 A.M. to 3 P.M., Monday through Thursday 5:30 to 9 P.M., Friday and Saturday 5:30 to 9:30 P.M.
Moderate
Credit cards: AE, DC, MC, V

David Vardy, the chef-owner of this unique teahouse and restaurant, arrived at his culinary calling by studying tai chi in a monastery in Taiwan with a Taoist master. He traveled to Japan for further study, but became interested in *kaiseki* cooking and the tea ceremony instead. He returned to California with a Tokyo-born wife and opened the Daruma Tea Shop, where he baked tea cakes in such perfect traditional style that teahouses in Japan started importing them. Then he closed Daruma and opened O Chamé, a charming, peaceful tearoom with handcrafted wooden furniture and a menu of noodles, soup, *bento* box lunches, and seasonal Japanese dishes. Many lunches are packaged to go and dispensed from an outdoor kiosk. They disappear very fast.

Indoors, people order surprisingly hearty and tasty Japanese vegetarian stews of wheat gluten and root vegetables like burdock. I'm not kidding; they're really delicious and satisfying. At dinner you can make a meal of all sorts of little dishes served on a striking assortment of Japanese pottery. Start with a smoky miso broth with big cubes of kabocha squash, rings of leek, and shiitakes. Sashimi usually brings two kinds of pristine raw fish, such as halibut and sea urchin roe with *shiso* leaves. If you like your fish cooked, try simmered whitefish dumplings in a clear broth with pale green winter melon, orange squash, and shiitakes, or grilled sea scallops split and filled with a slice of kiwi. One of my favorite dishes is a rich stew of tea-flavored hard-boiled eggs, velvety chicken livers, and diced tomatoes. Cold dishes bring a salad of fine organic greens in a rice-vinegar dressing, and a traditional octopus and cucumber salad. Then, of course, there are many teahouse amenities to be savored after a meal or in the afternoon. Japanese teas are individually brewed in tiny brass pots. I find that the slightly bitter but nutty green teas finish off a Japanese meal like a cup of coffee, though fragrant jasmine tea or a full-bodied Daruma blend served with milk works well, too. Hard, crunchy tea cakes full of peanuts go brilliantly with the teas, though O Chamé's chilled custard studded with pears poached in Zinfandel, or little dumplings made of mashed potatoes topped with plum sauce also are fun. You never know what will turn up on Vardy's menus.

One translation of O Chamé is "precious little girl." At the opening of the restaurant, Vardy's then one-year-old daughter, half Californian, half Japanese, charmed the room with her laughter. Though it was her mother who designed the lovely space, the little girl seemed to be the very incarnation of O Chamé's spirit.

OLIVETO . . . .

5655 College Avenue
(at Shafter), Oakland
510-547-5356
www.oliveto.com
Open Monday through Friday
11:30 A.M. to 2 P.M., Monday
5:30 to 9 P.M., Tuesday and
Wednesday 5:30 to 9:30 P.M.,
Thursday through Saturday
5:30 to 10 P.M., Sunday 5 to 9 P.M.
Expensive
Credit cards: AE, DC, MC, V

Recently, I took on the task of guiding three food product developers from England around the Bay Area. During these research tours, an unconscionable amount of food is sampled, and our last stop after a full day of nonstop tasting was Oliveto. This restaurant, headed by purist Paul Bertolli, sets the standard for Italian cooking anywhere, including Italy. But could we face it?

When we sat down at one of Oliveto's coveted window tables overlooking the street, with a bowl of marinated olives, crusty white Italian bread, sweet butter, and a bowl of kosher salt on a clean canvas of linen, we couldn't help looking forward to what would come next. The smells of roasting herbs and meats, the simple demeanor of the table, the sprawling, busy candlelit room with an epicenter of wild, six-foot-high branches and flowers fanned our flickering hunger. We were at it again, and the odd thing is we ate as if we hadn't had a bite all day.

Oliveto can do that to you. Just reading the menu makes you crazy, because you can't possibly consume all the things you want to try. Somehow, being full allowed us to edit our meal more easily. We passed up all the house-made *salumi*; unfaithfully, I turned my back on a favorite terrine of beef tongue and snubbed my beloved spit-roasted Willis farm pork (the best pork dish in the world). Instead, we demurely dipped spring-sweet baby artichokes into tuna-and-anchovy-infused mayonnaise—an artichoke *tonnato*. We disagreed about the cohesiveness of a bracing chopped salad of cooked, celerylike cardoon with a bitter edge, raw celery heart, chopped egg, and slivered anchovies, but cleaned the plate. (I liked it.)

Of course we ordered Paul Bertolli's pastas. No one can resist them. I was wild about *chitarra nera*, thin strands of pasta tinted jet black with squid ink, briny as the sea, but spicy with hot red pepper and garlic. Thin slices of calamari tossed into the noodles were tender, sweet, intrinsic to the dish. The creation was a triumph of pasta cookery. Just to show that he hadn't abandoned the rustic, Bertolli made tagliatelle out of *farro*, a chewy ancient variety of wheat, and dressed the thin ribbons with a long-cooked hen *ragù* that reminded me of a dish I had eaten in a mountain taverna in Greece. The sauce in Oakland was deep and round and it melded with the grain in the pasta.

We had to try the unusual chicken and lobster sausages, a dialectic of tender and chewy in each bite, slathered with tiny bright green fava beans and silken, barely wilted *mâche*. The dish tasted like May. And we called for all the vegetable side dishes: sweet, juicy braised fennel with a toasted Parmigiano crust; spicy braised beet greens; and Bertolli's signature fresh-milled polenta, thick, toothsome, smelling like popcorn.

We even had room for a shimmering *panna cotta*—cream ever so tenuously suspended in gelatin, surrounded by strawberries. It was the best I've ever tasted.

We drank wines that were new to us: a Sinskey Pinot Noir Rose, a pale pink drink that signifies summer, and a contrasting, lush 1998 Fiddlehead Cellar Pinot Noir from Oregon. (Somehow our wine appetite never flagged.)

The product developers told me that the meal was the highlight of their whole trip and I believed them because I, too, was moved by it. I've been to Oliveto many times, always with anticipation and with preparation by eating lightly all day. Often I go for special events—truffle dinners, tomato festivals, a celebration of the pig—but this time, on a regular night, choosing from the regular menu, the food was so sparkly, unique, artfully prepared, resonant of Bertolli's deep knowledge of and respect for beautiful ingredients that it made four overstuffed food nuts genuinely hungry again.

PICANTE COCINA MEXICANA . . . .

1328 Sixth Street
(at Gilman), Berkeley
510-525-3121
www.picantecocina.citysearch.com
Open Monday through Thursday
11 A.M. to 10 P.M.,
Friday 11 A.M. to 11 P.M.,
Saturday 10 A.M. to 11 P.M.,
Sunday 10 A.M. to 10 P.M.,
Saturday and Sunday brunch
10 A.M. to 3 P.M.
Inexpensive
Credit cards: AE, MC, V

Jim Maser, the manager of Café Fanny, and Alice Waters's brother-in-law, bought this straight-ahead flatlands taqueria eight years ago and continues to improve it. Maser draws on his own experiences in Mexico, where he spent quite a bit of time traveling, eating, and taking classes from Diana Kennedy. When he opened Picante taqueria, he consulted with Rick Bayless, the chef of the peerless Frontera Grill and Topolobambo in Chicago. Picante makes tortillas to order from fresh *masa*; serves whole black beans slowly simmered with *epazote* and other Mexican herbs; and offers delicate little soft tacos laid flat on a plate and piled with beautiful fillings, including house-made chorizo and potatoes with an avocado-tomatillo sauce, *rajas* (roasted pepper strips) topped with *queso fresco*, and moist, long-cooked pork *carnitas* topped with fresh tomato salsa among other things. The house-made tamales are light and tender, filled with zucchini, corn, poblano chiles, and pork braised in ancho-chile sauce. The fresh tortillas and Picante's carefully made fillings give new vitality to the traditional taqueria menu. With lots of tasty vegetarian alternatives, house-baked rolls for Mexican sandwiches, avocado-rich guacamole, fried-to-order chips, and many other carefully rethought components of the basic menu, Picante takes the genre to new, interesting heights. Two long bars that serve lots of margaritas and Mexican beer, two large, gaily painted dining rooms, lots of room for families at booths and large tables, and inexpensive prices for high-quality food make Picante a destination taqueria.

RIVOLI . . . .

1539 Solano Avenue (between
Neilson and Peralta), Berkeley
510-526-2542
www.rivolirestaurant.com
Open Monday through Thursday
5:30 to 9:30 P.M., Friday 5:30 to
10 P.M., Saturday 5 to 10 P.M.,
Sunday 5 to 9 P.M.
Moderate
Credit cards: AE, DC, D, MC, V

Chef-owner Wendy Brucker has polished her gem of a neighborhood restaurant to a high gleam, supported by her partner-husband who keeps the dining room working like a fine Swiss watch. He also hones a strong, interesting wine list that spans California and the Mediterranean to match the style of the food. Reasonable prices and personal involvement have kept the restaurant vital and well attended. The cooking has become more consistent and elegant over the years, but still maintains market-driven freshness. The Rivoli classic, portobello mushroom fritters, are still crisp and juicy, dusted with Parmigiano and served with aioli and arugula salad; and the Bay Area classic of endive and arugula with pears and blue cheese satisfies. Main courses tend to be rich and meaty like red wine–braised lamb shank with an eggplant, tomato, and goat cheese gratin; or rich and not meaty like butternut squash-and-ricotta-filled ravioli liberally sauced with leeks and sage-infused brown butter. Wild steelhead salmon, perfectly grilled, might come with a ragout of potatoes and artichokes plus a lagniappe of velvety carrot custard. Rivoli plates always deliver an extra surprise. Though there are warm chocolate soufflé cakes and warm fresh fruit *galettes* for dessert, I see a lot of hot fudge sundaes with whipped cream and toasted nuts scattered around the small dining room. Bistro-style small tables are closely packed together, but the space is opened up by a windowed back wall that looks out onto a secret garden. For a city full of professors, Rivoli strikes the right balance of intimacy, intelligence, and price.

SIAM CUISINE . . . .

1181 University Avenue (between
San Pablo and Curtis), Berkeley
510-548-3278
www.dreamwater.org
Open Monday through Saturday
11:30 A.M. to 10:30 P.M.,
Sunday 4 P.M. to 10:30 P.M.
Inexpensive
Credit cards: MC, V

My chile-addicted friend, Niloufer Ichaporia King, and I had a splendid meal at Siam Cuisine before a performance at Zellerbach (on the UC Campus) the other night. As we sat down at a window table in the long, dark dining room, we recalled that we actually had been introduced to each other there two decades ago at a party given by the late Barbara Tropp. The food we had then—incendiary, alive, exciting—was the same as the food we had that evening, Thai dishes of such smoldering intensity that by the end of the meal smoke came out of our ears. Recently we began with a warm eggplant salad, slender Asian eggplants and shrimp in a brilliantly hot, sweet-and-sour dressing. We ate the intricately carved half-cucumber garnish between us and went on to attack a medium-hot green shrimp curry redolent of fresh herbs; a crispy, deep-fried whole fish in a sweet-and-hot sauce; and an unconquerable wild boar curry that was so hot even Niloufer cried. Tears streamed down her face as she ate. Usually a pre-performance meal works against alertness during the performance. After the Siam Cuisine meal, we felt invigorated and vowed to return with a group for reexploration of this excellent restaurant's long, intriguing menu.

388 9th Street (between Webster
and Franklin), 2nd floor, Oakland
510-893-9663
www.sushizone.com
Open Monday through Friday
11 A.M. to 2:30 P.M., Monday
through Thursday 5 to 9:30 P.M.,
Friday and Saturday until 10:30 P.M.
Moderate
Credit cards: MC, V

Sushi Zone, a sleek, handsome, modern Japanese restaurant situated in Oakland's Chinatown, delivers an evocatively different kind of Japanese experience. Though the chef, Peter Day, is Japanese (he changed his Japanese name to please his American daughter) and the menu is Japanese—no fusion here except for some of the California-style *maki* or sushi rolls—it's as if the cooking has taken a quarter turn to the West, which is this case, happens to be China.

The menu is eight pages long, like those tomes in Chinese restaurants, and offers different categories of dishes—sushi, of course, *maki*, appetizers from the sushi bar, first courses, salads, noodles, main courses, and sushi dinner combinations. This whole range of Japanese cooking is laid out, open and accessible. You don't have to depend on the whim of the sushi chef or squint at blackboards or decode the menu. English is the lingua franca of the Sushi Zone—the name, you realize, refers to this bit of Japan in the midst of a Chinese neighborhood in the middle of Oakland—and the Japanese culinary experience there is straightforward, filtered through three cultures. Customers get uncommonly generous servings of well-made Japanese food in an international context. Sushi Zone epitomizes the twenty-first-century Pacific Rim restaurant.

As in Chinese restaurants, Sushi Zone's T-shirted waitstaff assumes that you will share. They place the food in the middle of the spacious tables and bring everyone small empty plates.

Start with a juicy seaweed salad, a tangle of dark green seaweed and shredded cucumber dressed with red chile, sesame seeds, and just the right amount of sesame oil so as not to be overpowering. Also, don't miss an appetizer made in the sushi bar called *sake kinutamaki*, delicate rolls of salmon, flying fish roe, avocado, cucumber, burdock root, and pickled ginger wrapped in pickled daikon.

The deep-frying here produces crisp, lacy tempura. I particularly like the appetizer-sized portion of vegetables and shrimp, still generous enough to share. Even more seductive is deep-fried tofu. The fat cubes have a thin, crisp exterior and velvety, creamy interior with a slightly smoky flavor. The chef showers it with threads of scallion and grated radish, a lovely dish.

Sushi and sashimi range from sublime to so-so. Ask for what's fresh and you might get superb buttery albacore tuna or creamy local halibut. The *hamachi* (yellowfin) has been frozen here on my visits, a disappointment when farmed fresh *hamachi* from Japan is now usually available. Of many seaweed-wrapped sushi rolls on a long list, one of the liveliest is 49'er Maki, filled with salmon, flying fish roe, and topped with a tissue-thin slice of lemon that you eat. The rice is firm, sweet, and nutty, the plump grains barely adhering to one another. The sliced rounds are served on a length of ceramic that looks like tree bark. The live lobster sashimi service makes for a grand finale. The soft, sweet tail meat is sliced very thin and mounded on a plate with crunchy flying fish roe. The shell, body, and claws go into a refreshing broth with thick udon noodles, which comes later.

Sushi Zone has become a very popular outpost of Japanese dining in Oakland's Chinatown. Though the cooking of these two cultures really is radically different, many tastes are indeed shared—the love of rice, the appreciation of seafood, and the insistence that it be as close to alive as possible when you eat it. The Chinese barely cook their seafood and the Japanese like eat it raw, but either method does it justice.

UZEN. . . . .

5415 College Avenue (at Hudson), Oakland
510-654-7753
Open Monday through Friday 11:30 A.M. to 2 P.M., Monday through Saturday 5:30 to 9:45 P.M.
Moderate
Credit cards: MC, V

Any sushi bar that serves its sushi on a bright green taro leaf earns my devotion, but Uzen, for all its edgy, arty, minimalist decor, blown-glass sake cups, and hip ceramics, won my heart with its fish. You order by checking off the sushi you want from a printed sheet, writing in any daily specials that catch your fancy. We ate sparkling young yellowtail from Japan, superb, almost moving *mirugai* (giant clam), sweet *unagi* (freshwater eel), slightly watery *uni* (sea urchin roe), buttery bluefin tuna, lightly pickled fresh sardine from Spain; and a spicy tuna roll from the daily special list that I never should have ordered. Both concept and flavor were all wrong. But sticking to the traditional at Uzen with some chef-inspired variations satisfies my Japanese yearnings. Uzen is worth the trip from San Francisco and the wait at the door.

ZAX TAVERN. . . . .

2826 Telegraph Avenue (3 blocks north of Ashby), Berkeley
510-848-9299
Open Tuesday through Thursday 5:30 to 9:30 P.M., Friday and Saturday until 10 P.M.
Moderate
Credit cards: MC, V, AE

Chef-owners Barbara Mulas and Mark Drazek moved their small, hidden San Francisco Zax to tony new digs in the former Mazzini space in Berkeley. The move allowed them to expand the menu and seating as well as offer the amenities of a full bar. The Zax favorites are better than ever: crusty, twice-baked goat cheese soufflés with perfect green salad; the scrumptious warm frisée salad with duck livers, poached egg and bacon; roasted chicken with wilted greens; panko-crusted hake with shoestring potatoes and wonderful lemon-caper aioli; and a man-sized Niman Ranch pork chop. Now Zax patrons can drop in for juicy Niman hamburgers and pressed sandwiches accompanied by a glass of wine or a cocktail. And with a bigger restaurant, Mark Drazek can make more of his beautifully constructed desserts—angel food cake with chocolate-hazelnut ice cream; lemon soufflé tart, warm apple galette.

Everything that comes out of the kitchen radiates brightness and freshness. Though Mulas and Drazek have always been drawn to straightforward, hearty food that belongs in a place that calls itself a tavern, their style of cooking has such refinement and integrity, you feel as it you're tasting these much-prepared dishes anew. If I lived near Zax Tavern, I'd be a regular; since I don't, it has become a bonafide East Bay destination.

CAFFÉ 817 . . . .

817 Washington Street (between
8th and 9th streets), Oakland
510-271-7965
www.cafe817.com
Open Monday through Friday
7:30 A.M. to 4 P.M.,
Saturday 9 A.M. to 3 P.M.
Credit cards: AE, MC, V

In a narrow high-ceilinged storefront that adjoins G.B. Ratto, Oakland's great international foods store (see page 425), Sandro Rossi, a former electrical engineer from northern Italy, and Teresa Sevilla, a Peruvian architect-designer, have created a resonant, art-filled, modern café that serves great coffee and miraculously inexpensive but authentic Italian cafe food. I was originally hooked by a small caffe latte made from Illy espresso beans and served in a short tumbler, my idea

of heaven. The coffee, aromatic and deep in flavor without bitterness, was smoothed with just the right amount of velvety steamed milk. Acme baguettes, *levain*, and focaccia are used for delicious sandwiches: combinations of ham, fontina, and marinated artichokes; or warm grilled prosciutto, mozzarella, and *tapenade*, crisp and buttery, accompanied with a little green salad. The few hot dishes come straight from Rossi's home village and northern Italian soul. You practically can taste the Italian countryside in a Tuscan bean soup thick with cabbage and chard and topped with grated real Parmigiano. A bowl of soft, cheesy polenta is striped with mushroom ragout, sausage, and cherry tomatoes. Only light chianti and vernaccia wines are poured, and they taste terrific with the grilled sandwiches and soups. Medium-sized bottles of cold San Pellegrino come with just the right little glasses. In fact, all the carefully chosen plates, glassware, and cups, and the exquisitely designed room, make the food and drinks taste even better, one more proof that a great café can turn the act of drinking a cup of coffee into a religious experience.

CAFÉ FANNY . . . .

1603 San Pablo Avenue
(at Cedar), Berkeley
510-524-5447
Open Monday through Friday
7 A.M. to 3 P.M., Saturday 8 A.M.
to 4 P.M., Sunday 8 A.M. to 3 P.M.
Credit cards: MC, V

Café Fanny is a charming little stand-up cafe in the tradition of French *tabacs* and Italian espresso bars, but the open-faced sandwiches, pizzas with bright Provençal toppings, house-baked pastries, and oven-fresh Acme breads are a cut above anything else of their kind. You get salads made of the tiniest lettuces topped with baked goat cheese; or a farm-egg salad sandwich moistened with house-made mayonnaise, topped with

Italian sun-dried tomatoes and anchovies. The café au lait comes in bowls. The house-made granola has become so popular it has been packaged for customers to take home. You have to get to the cafe early to snag the lacy buckwheat crepes with fresh fruit conserves. They always run out. The crunchy millet muffins are some of the best I've ever tasted—a recipe I tried to get for this book, but manager-owner Jim Maser (who also started Picante Cocina Mexicana nearby, see page 409) wouldn't let me have it. Even the orange juice is extraordinary, usually mixed with tangerine or blood orange juice and always freshly squeezed. Though there is only a stand-up bar, an indoor bench, and some outdoor tables that are always full during nice weather, the satisfaction you get from a quick, informal meal here lasts all day. Café Fanny's location between two great culinary destinations, the Acme bread bakery (see page 420) and Kermit Lynch wine store (see page 439), make a visit here all the more compelling.

CAFE AT OLIVETO. . . . .

5655 College Avenue
(at Shafter), Oakland
510-547-4382
www.oliveto.com
Open daily 10 A.M. to 7 P.M.
Credit cards: AE, DC, MC, V

One reason this partially outdoor café is a popular spot is that people can get Oliveto-quality food at a cheaper price. In these more casual surroundings, diners can order quick, savory little bites such as a plate of braised fresh shell beans topped with shaved Parmigiano, or bruschetta with roasted yellow peppers in anchovy vinaigrette with black olives. Warm toasts piled with marinated tomatoes look very appealing, as do pretty green salads. Pizzas cooked in the wood-fired pizza oven and focaccia sandwiches provide more substantial sustenance, and of course there's coffee, wine, and Oliveto desserts. At night, a full café dinner menu makes tables scarce. I've often waited at the marble bar in front of a tidy open kitchen framed in stone and then, when a seat opened up there, stayed and ordered dinner. The food comes on handsome gray-green pottery plates. Daytime, people covet the tables by the open French doors.

CAFFE STRADA. . . . .

2300 College Avenue
(at Bancroft Way), Berkeley
510-843-5282
Open daily 6:30 A.M. to midnight
Cash only

In a choice location across the street from Boalt Hall, the architecture building, and the anthropology museum, Caffe Strada rises to the challenge of supplying thousands of students in this part of the University of California campus with first-rate coffee, especially their fortifying *cappuccino doppio*, and surprisingly fine croissants baked on the premises. The croissants are buttery, flaky, and crisp, though I can't recommend any other baked goods here. With more outdoor seating than indoor, even on the coolest days the outdoor tables stay full. The large, constant flow of customers, morning, noon, and night, gives Caffe Strada the vitality of the great urban cafés in Europe.

BARS

BRENNAN'S . . . .

720 University Avenue
(at 4th Street), Berkeley
510-841-0960
Open daily 11 A.M. to 9:30 P.M.;
bar open Sunday through Tuesday
until midnight, Wednesday
and Thursday until 1 A.M.,
Friday and Saturday until 2 A.M.
Credit cards: MC, V

Berkeley's blue-collar horseshoe bar serves good mixed drinks at people's prices. See page 396 for more information.

CESAR . . . .

1515 Shattuck Avenue (between
Cedar and Vine), Berkeley
510-883-0222
Bar open daily noon to midnight;
kitchen open Sunday through
Thursday noon to 3 P.M. and
4 to 11 P.M., Friday and
Saturday until 11:30 P.M.
Credit cards: MC, V

One of the greatest bars in the world in terms of quality of spirits, selection, and mixology. See page 398 for more information.

DOWNTOWN . . . .

2102 Shattuck Avenue
(at Addison), Berkeley
510-649-3810
www.downtownrestaurant.com
Open Tuesday through Friday
11:30 A.M. to 2 P.M., bar opens at
5 P.M.; Tuesday, Wednesday, and
Thursday 5:30 to 9:30 P.M., Friday
and Saturday 5:30 to 11 P.M.;
late-night menu until midnight;
Sunday 5 to 9 p.m., late-night
menu until 10:30 P.M.
Credit cards: AE, MC, V

A big city bar conveniently located near theaters and UC performance venues in Berkeley. See page 401 for more information.

DELICATESSENS/TAKEOUT

BLONDIE'S . . . .

2340 Telegraph Avenue
(near Durant), Berkeley
510-548-1129
Open Monday through Thursday
11 A.M. to 1 A.M., Friday and
Saturday until 2 A.M.,
Sunday until midnight
Cash only

This original Blondie's location must sell more slices of hot, cheesy, saucy, pillowy pizza than any other place in the world. The lines never stop, and the army of pizza makers barely keep up with the demand. A fresh hot slice of this not-too-oily pizza is dirt cheap and fills you up for most of the day. For other location, see page 120.

CHEESE BOARD PIZZERIA . . . .

1512 Shattuck Avenue (between
Cedar and Vine), Berkeley
510-549-3055
Open Monday 11:30 A.M. to 2 P.M.,
Tuesday through Friday 11:30 A.M.
to 2 P.M. and 4:30 P.M. to 7 P.M.,
Saturday noon to 3 P.M. and
4:30 P.M. to 7 P.M.
Cash only

A line stretches out the front door and onto the sidewalk in wait for the first hot pizzas to come out of the oven. The collective bakes them for lunch, takes a break, and then bakes a new batch for dinner starting late in the afternoon. Once you've had a slice of, say, a crisp, thin-crusted pizza topped with mozzarella, sweet corn, thinly shredded zucchini, red and yellow onions, French feta, cilantro, and olive oil, served with a wedge of lime on the side, you'll understand why people congregate. As soon as the pizzas start coming out, the line moves quickly until the pizzas run out. People buy them by the hot slice to eat at a few communal tables in the shop and on the sidewalk, or they buy whole pies to take home. Tumblers of wine and bottles of beer are also available. The collective makes exactly one type of pizza each day, always vegetarian, the lowest common denominator. I'd call to find out when they're making that sweet corn and cilantro pizza again. It was absolutely scrumptious.

DOUG'S BBQ . . . .

3600 San Pablo Avenue
(at 36th Street), Emeryville
510-655-9048
Open Monday through Thursday
11 A.M. to 8:45 P.M., Friday and
Saturday 11 A.M. to 10 P.M.,
Sunday noon to 7 P.M.
Credit cards: MC, V

I like Doug's. I'm not that much of a barbecue fan, but I like Doug's. I love the fresh green beans cooked with ham and sausage; the smoky baked beans that are whole, firm, but creamy; the potato salad in a pleasant, sweet relish–studded mayonnaise with potatoes that still have texture. When it comes to the barbecue, the pork ribs are meaty and tender; the barbecue sauce balances hot, sweet, and sour with precision in three graduated degrees of fieriness. I actually prefer the gigantic beef ribs, moist and meaty, to the pork ribs, but I'm the exception. Doug's does not stick to the usual; they barbecue goat and turkey and deep-fry turkey as well, which gives the meat a bit of an oily aftertaste, although it stays juicier than the smoked. Both turkeys are immersed in sauce. Doug's calls itself a Texas-style barbecue and underscores the point by displaying several pairs of longhorns above the counter. The people working the counter could not be nicer at this thirty-year-old smokehouse, and when I get the urge for barbecue I seriously consider coming all the way here.

MARKET HALL PASTA SHOP. . . . .

5655 College Avenue
(at Shafter), Oakland
510-547-4005
www.rockridge.com
Open Monday through Saturday
9 A.M. to 8 P.M.,
Sunday 10 A.M. to 7 P.M.
Credit cards: MC, V

The busiest spot in the Market Hall by the College Avenue BART station in Rockridge, the Pasta Shop offers a huge variety of prepared and imported foods. Though it made its reputation on excellent fresh egg pasta used by many restaurants in the Bay Area, its ravioli and pasta sauces are a bit of a disappointment and the filled pastas need some editing. I like the idea of being able to buy house-made mayonnaise by the pound, and natural house-made frozen stocks. Olives in bulk from Liguria, Provence, Peru, California, and Morocco, among others; prosciutto, salami; Hobbs's pancetta; and an extensive cheese department with lots of Italian cheeses and French goat cheeses just begin to scratch the surface of the large inventory here. A gigantic refrigerated counter with salads, highly seasoned house-made sausages, lasagna, meat loaf, grilled marinated half chickens, marinated artichokes, and whole roasted vegetables are always packed two deep. Among the dry goods on freestanding shelves are Rustichella d'Abruzzo dried pastas, fine imported extra virgin olive oils and vinegars, as well as more affordable ones, and small tins of my favorite oil-packed anchovies. Service is relatively fast and efficient and your number comes up quickly. If you don't need anything from the deli counter, you can pay without a number at the cheese counter, a humane system.

A huge second branch of The Pasta Shop has opened next to Café Rouge in Berkeley. Colorful, ready-to-go *panini*, freshly made for the lunch rush, are particularly tempting, wrapped in parchment and then cut in half.

THE PASTA SHOP . . . .

1786 4th Street (between
Hearst and Virginia), Berkeley
510-528-1786
www.markethall.com
Open daily 10 A.M. to 6:30 P.M.
Credit cards: MC, V

A branch of the Italian emporium, well stocked with freshly made sandwiches and other foodstuffs. See description above for more information.

PHOENIX PASTAFICIO . . . .

1786 Shattuck Avenue (between
Francisco and Delaware), Berkeley
510-883-0783
Open Monday through
Saturday 7 A.M. to 8 P.M.,
Sunday 7:30 A.M. to 11:30 P.M.;
cafe open 11:30 A.M. to 2:30 P.M.
Cash only

This small shop makes its own extruded pasta; in other words, huge fresh tubes, shells, and wheels as well as spaghetti, linguine, and tagliarini. In addition, it flavors some of them with dried porcini, saffron, chestnuts, or spinach. The pasta has a fantastic texture, chewy yet tender, and cooks pretty fast, making it easy for restaurant kitchens, many of which use Phoenix pastas. The shop also makes sauces, breads, and sweet rolls in house. They have opened a little café in a space next door where you get your pasta not only fresh, but hot.

VIK'S CHAAT CORNER . . . .

726 Allston Way (between
4th and 5th streets), Berkeley
510-644-4412
Open Tuesday through Sunday
11 A.M. to 6 P.M.
Cash only

Every week half the East Bay Indian community stands around this snack counter next door to an Indian market, slurping down saucy, juicy vegetarian snacks, or *chaat*, out of paper cartons. The lucky find an empty folding chair at a card table. Others eat at a wall counter. The rest just down their snacks out of hand, not worrying about dripping on the cement floor. A variety of snacks, each costing a couple of dollars, are listed on a board. Some are based on crisp, deep-fried hollow spheres called *puri*, which are filled with potatoes, chiles, and onions and sauced with yogurt and tamarind chutney as in *batata puri*. Delicious *sev puri* are flat, crisp disks topped with potato, chickpeas, onions, chiles, tamarind, and mint-cilantro chutney. *Dokla*, light, airy, steamed chickpea cakes sprinkled with coconut and fresh cilantro, constitute another snack category; while *pakori chaat* are soft, light balls of chickpea flour that are deep-fried, soaked in water, then squeezed dry and sauced with tamarind chutney and yogurt. A full range of Indian boiled-milk sweets and desserts are freshly prepared and okay, as Niloufer Ichaporia King, my ethnic-food expert, would say. I like the Indian ice cream called *kulfi kluge*, swathed in cream and clear wheat-starch noodles. The warm *gulab jamun*, fried milk balls soaked in scented syrup, are also nice. At Vik's, you get the flavor of what it's like to eat at crowded snack shops in alleys in Varanasi or New Delhi.

YUNG KEE . . . .

888 Webster Street
(at 9th Street), Oakland
510-839-2010
Open daily 9 A.M. to midnight
Cash

This small shop is regarded as the best place in Oakland's Chinatown for Chinese barbecued pork, ducks, and chickens. You can eat them with noodles and soup at Formica tables in the store, or take them home, chopped into neat pieces through the bone and packed in white cartons.

ACME BREAD COMPANY . . . .

1601 San Pablo Avenue
(at Cedar), Berkeley
510-524-1021
Open Monday through Saturday
8 A.M. to 6 P.M.,
Sunday 8:30 A.M. to 3 P.M.
Cash only

When Steve Sullivan started baking bread at home and then at Chez Panisse, the attenuated natural process dictated the rhythm of his life. He became obsessed with bread making, and judging by the huge success of Acme Bakery, which he opened in 1983, a lot of people have become obsessed with buying Acme bread. Having the right loaf every day is important. Like the French, many of us require an Acme sweet baguette daily. But I keep other longer-lasting loaves on hand, too. I knew that Sullivan's loaves, especially a crusty whole-wheat sourdough round called *levain*, were right for me the moment I tasted them. They have tremendous character and substance without being heavy, which can come only from that long and elusive bread-making process he worked on for so many years. I do buy other breads—there are so many good bakeries in the Bay Area now—and enjoy them, but if I don't have a *levain* on my counter I get edgy, as if I don't really have food at home.

You can buy Acme loaves all over the Bay Area, but the loaves you pick up at the bakery next to Café Fanny (see page 413) and Kermit Lynch wines are always the freshest, the most fragrant, the best bread you will find in America. One of the finest qualities of Acme *levain* is that it lasts; never getting moldy even when it stays in a bag for days. You can take this bread camping: I cart loaves of it to Maui and it lasts the whole vacation. I need my *levain* toast in the morning, just like my special coffee.

BREAD WORKSHOP . . . .

1250 Addison Street, No. 109
(at Bonar), Berkeley
510-649-9735
Open Monday through Friday
7:30 A.M. to 1:30 P.M.
Cash only

The Bread Workshop's focaccia buns have provided a landing for some of the best hamburgers in the Bay Area. They're light and flavorful without being oily and make delicious sandwiches. Hundreds of East Bay mothers depend on the Bread Workshop's partially baked pizza dough rounds, which kids top themselves and finish baking. The multigrain bread is substantial and tasty without being tedious. Started by some ex-employees of Acme, the Bread Workshop supplies restaurants and stores and has a pleasant retail bakery-café in a red brick building that backs onto meadowlike Strawberry Creek Park. Outdoor and indoor tables provide spaces where you can drink coffee and eat freshly baked scones.

1504 Shattuck Avenue (between
Cedar and Vine), Berkeley
510-549-3183
Bakery open Monday
7 A.M. to 1 P.M., Tuesday through
Friday 7 A.M. to 6 P.M., and
Saturday 8:30 A.M. to 5 P.M.
Cash only

The warm, crusty breads that hourly come out of the bakery connected to the famous cheese collective are beloved by everyone. See page 437 for more information.

LA FARINE . . . .

6323 College Avenue (between
Alcatraz and Claremont), Oakland
510- 654-0338
www.lafarine.com
Open Monday through Saturday
8 A.M. to 6 P.M.,
Sunday 8 A.M. to 3 P.M.
Credit cards: AE, MC, V

This authentic French bakery, started by Lili Le Coq, has been passed on to two generations of new owners-bakers, but the quality of the buttery French tarts and cakes, croissants, *pain au chocolat*, and sweet rolls remains stellar. If there is one pastry associated with La Farine, it is the morning bun, a rich, cinnamony, sugared roll made with croissant dough that no one can resist. Whenever I drive by this bakery, I have to stop to buy one. Swiss twinkies, flat, palm leaf–shaped sweet rolls, have many fans, but not as many as the sublime morning bun. The breads here are soft and delicate; the egg bread makes superlative French toast; and this is also the place to buy brioche. The tarts topped with fresh fruit actually taste as appealing as they look. La Farine is one of the few great pastry shops left in the Bay Area, as well as one of my favorites. One hopes that the bakers will continue to pass on the secrets of the morning bun to succeeding generations.

KATRINA ROZELLE . . . .

5931 College Avenue
(near Claremont), Oakland
510- 655-3209
www.katrinarozelle.com
Open Tuesday through Saturday
9 A.M. to 6 P.M.,
Sunday 11 A.M. to 5 P.M.
Credit cards: MC, V

A clean, modern little shop next door to a Dreyer's Ice Cream store, Katrina Rozelle shows particular strength in old-fashioned crumbly, buttery American-style cookies. Her shortbread rectangles are indeed simple perfection, to lift the description on the bakery's brochure. Another standout, almond praline cookies, are full of chopped almonds and bits of praline. Their traditional chocolate chip, the Chocolust, is one of the few crisp chocolate cookies around; and the bright-flavored ginger cookies please both adults and children. This shop's reputation for cookies keeps the inventory turning over, which keeps the cookies fresh, the most important quality of any cookie.

SEMIFREDDI'S . . . .

372 Colusa Street, Kensington
510-596-9935
Open Monday through Friday
6:30 A.M. to 6:30 P.M., Saturday
and Sunday 7 A.M. to 5 P.M.
Credit cards: MC, V

A bakery founded on a seeded baguette, Semifreddi's got its inspiration from breads baked at the Cheese Board (see page 437), where Bob Wax taught many generations of bakers how to make them. Semifreddi's baguettes are on the hard side, very crusty with a meaty interior. The most popular are thickly coated with caraway, fennel, poppy seeds, and sesame seeds, infusing each bite with a riot of flavors. I think the seeds take over the bread, making it conflict with other foods, but I'm in the minority here. A handsome wood and glass case displays other breads as well, including a whole-wheat walnut-raisin that has both flavor and unusual moistness. The Odessa rye is dense and moist with a dark crust and tons of caraway seed flavor. On the counter are wrapped slices of tasty fat-reduced lemon pound cake and whole roasted elephant garlic to squeeze onto bread instead of butter—if you're not going to be around other people for twelve hours after you use it. The bakery also serves espresso.

ICE CREAM/CHOCOLATES

SCHARFFEN BERGER CHOCOLATE MAKER . .

914 Heinz Avenue
(at 7th Street), Berkeley
510-981-4050 (To reserve a place
in a daily tour call 510-981-4066)
www.scharffenberger.com
Open Monday through Saturday
10 A.M. to 5 P.M.

The smell of roasting chocolate wafting out onto the sidewalk by the factory practically pulled me into the retail shop, and I was engulfed with the intoxicating, complex smells as I examined bars of bitter, bittersweet, and semisweet chocolate, tins of cocoa powders and cocoa nibs, cookbooks dedicated to chocolate, and cooking implements for baking with chocolate.

By chance I was able to join the 2:30 public tour of the factory, which allowed me to get to the source of that thrilling aroma. If you know what freshly ground coffee smells like, the fragrance of Scharffen Berger roasted cacao beans being pulverized by two granite wheels is even bigger and more tactile. The smell has a physicality. You can feel it in your nose. You can detect layers of fruit, of smokiness, of high-pitched acidity, of tannin, of mocha, of floral perfume.

Sharffen Berger is one of the few small artisan chocolate makers in this country that manufactures chocolate from bean to bar. It buys beans from Sulawesi (an island in Indonesia), Panama, Venezuela, Madagascar, and Ghana from twelve different growers in all. (All cacao plants grow within twenty degrees of the equator.) Climate and soil give each crop a distinctive flavor, plus there are three different varieties of plants. Most are grown on small farms of less than five acres. Scharffen Berger roasts each kind of bean separately, grinds them, and then blends them together to achieve the company's signature flavor, much like a winemaker blends the juice from different vineyards or different grape varieties. For out-of-hand eating or cooking, such nuanced chocolate delivers much pleasure.

CHOCOLATE

On a tour of the Scharffen Berger chocolate factory you learn that the cacao plant is native to the Amazon basin. A cocoa drink (like an *atole*, for those of you who have had them in Oaxaca) was much prized by the Aztecs in Mexico. (Montezuma reputedly drank fifty cups a day.) They ground cacao beans into a drink with cornmeal and chiles—and no sugar. The beans were also used as currency. In 1520, Hernando Cortés brought the first cargo of cacao beans to Spain. By 1600, cacao caught on as a drink, but it was not made into the hard chocolate we love until the late 1800s. Powdered cocoa was first made in the United States by Baker in 1765. Ghirardelli started in San Francisco during the gold rush, followed by Guittard in the 1860s. The technology needed to pulverize the cacao beans into smooth liquor was not invented until the end of the Industrial Revolution. Heavy granite wheels take two hours to turn the roasted beans into a slushy, grainy mass, called the chocolate liquor. Even today it takes thirty hours of "conching" in another machine to mix cane sugar, the cacao liquor, and some added cacao butter to form a smooth, mass that then gets molded into bars. When you eat a fine bittersweet chocolate bar after seeing how it is made, you appreciate its nuances.

If you're a chocolate lover, you should know that bittersweet chocolate is practically a health food. The February 2002 issue of the *Harvard Women's Health Watch* newsletter claims that chocolate, like red wine, is good for you. Cocoa and chocolate contain antioxidants that reduce the risk of heart attack. Nutritional studies published in the *American Journal of Clinical Nutrition* (November 2001) found that a diet supplemented with cocoa powder and dark chocolate slowed the oxidation of bad cholesterol and slightly increased the level of good cholesterol. Even more interesting, volunteers who ate two chocolate bars laced with calcium a day, along with their regular diet, lowered their bad cholesterol by 15 percent! Apparently, the calcium binds with fatty acids in chocolate, making them more difficult for the body to absorb, so you get all the good effects of dark chocolate and none of the bad. If this study is true, I predict that next year we'll be giving calcium-enriched bittersweet chocolate bars to our valentines. In the meantime, I'll still accept my See's.

HOT CHOCOLATE SOUFFLÉS

SERVES 8

This supereasy recipe for do-ahead chocolate soufflés comes from Alice Medrich's charming book, *A Year in Chocolate: Four Seasons of Unforgettable Desserts.*

About 2 tablespoons unsalted butter, softened, to butter the soufflé cups

About 2 tablespoons granulated sugar, to coat the soufflé cups

8 ounces bittersweet or semisweet chocolate, coarsely chopped

1 tablespoon unsalted butter

1 tablespoon all-purpose flour

⅓ cup milk

3 egg yolks

2 teaspoons vanilla extract

4 egg whites

⅛ teaspoon cream of tartar

½ cup granulated sugar

2 or 3 tablespoons powdered sugar, for dusting (optional)

Lightly sweetened whipped cream

1 Preheat the oven to 375° F.

2 Butter the bottom and sides of eight 4-ounce individual soufflé dishes. To coat with sugar, fill one of them with the granulated sugar. Tilt the cup and rotate it over a second cup until the sides are completely coasted with sugar. Pour excess sugar into the second cup and repeat until all the cups are coated with sugar. Discard excess sugar.

3 To make the soufflés, put the chocolate in a medium to large bowl set over (not touching) barely simmering water in a saucepan. Stir occasionally until melted and smooth. Remove from the heat. Or melt in a microwave on medium power (50 percent) for about 3½ minutes. Stir until smooth. Set aside.

4 In a small saucepan over medium heat, melt the butter. Add the flour and cook, stirring constantly, for 1 to 2 minutes. Add the milk gradually, whisking briskly until the mixture forms a smooth sauce. Continue cooking and whisking for 1 to 2 minutes, or until the sauce thickens. Remove from the heat and whisk in the egg yolks and 1 teaspoon of the vanilla. Scrape the sauce over the chocolate and whisk until blended. Set aside.

5 In a clean, dry, large bowl, using and electric mixer, beat the egg whites with the cream of tartar at medium speed until soft peaks form when the beaters are lifted. Gradually sprinkle in the granulated sugar and continue to beat at high speed until the egg whites are stiff but not dry.

6 Fold one-fourth of the whites into the chocolate mixture to lighten it, then fold in the remaining whites. Divide the mixture evenly among the sugared cups, filling them up to three-fourths full. (Soufflés may be prepared to this point, covered, and refrigerated for up to 3 days, before serving.)

7 Place the soufflés on a cookie sheet and bake for 15 to 17 minutes, or until a wooden skewer plunged into the center tests moist but not completely gooey or runny. Soufflés will puff and crack before they are done.

8 Remove the soufflés from the oven and lightly sift the powdered sugar over them, if desired. Serve immediately with the whipped cream.

YOGURT PARK . . . .

2433A Durant Avenue (between
Dana and Telegraph), Berkeley
510-549-0570
Open daily 11 A.M. to midnight
Cash only

Gigantic cups of frozen yogurt topped with fresh fruit
and toasted nuts at the cheapest possible price means
that the line never stops forming at Yogurt Park. When
it still had some fat in it, the Honey Hill Farms yogurt
pumped here used to be as satisfying as ice cream. The
nonfat mania has ruined that, but there's usually a
vanilla low-fat yogurt that doesn't taste like chemicals. After every Zellerbach performance I
attend, I wait in line for a small cup of vanilla frozen yogurt topped with toasted almonds.
The small cup is huge and the fast-moving clerks push about a half cup of nuts into the
top. I have an emotional attachment to this yogurt shop, one of the few remaining, because
I used to eat quarts of frozen yogurt when I was pregnant nineteen years ago. My son is
pretty much made of frozen yogurt.

ETHNIC MARKETS

G. B. RATTO AND COMPANY . . . .

821 Washington Street (between
8th and 9th streets), Oakland
510- 832-6503
Open Monday through Friday
9 A.M. to 6 P.M.,
Saturday 9:30 A.M. to 5 P.M.
Credit cards: MC, V

G. B. Ratto, the East Bay's premier international grocer,
stocks hard-to-find items from all over the world, especially from the Middle East, but also from Brazil, the
Caribbean, Africa, Portugal, France, and Italy. When
you need pâté spice, Ratto's has it, along with hundreds
of other specific cooking needs, ranging from the most
exotic spices in bulk, dried beans, flours, couscous,
cooking oils, bottled syrups and pickles, and canned
fruits and vegetables. In the deli cases are olives and hummus, Italian cured meats, an excellent imported salt cod from Italy, cheeses, yogurts, house-made vinegar in barrels, *harissa*,
phyllo dough—the variety of foods sold here is astounding. G. B. Ratto has long been one
of the best international foods stores in the Bay Area and its reputation still stands. If you
can't find it at Ratto's, it's probably not available in the United States.

MILAN INTERNATIONAL. . . . .

990 University Avenue
(at 9th Street), Berkeley
510-843-9600
Open Tuesday through Sunday
9:30 A.M. to 7 P.M.
Credit cards: AE, DC, MC, V

The smell of spices hits you long before you walk in the
front door of this great Indian grocery with aisles and
aisles of imported Indian foods, the longest bulk spice
section you'll ever see, bulk flours, the best basmati rice
being imported at the moment, and a rainbow of dried
legumes. One whole wall is dedicated to shiny stainless-
steel plates, bowls, tiffin carriers and trays; woklike
Indian cooking vessels; and utensils. Every sort of jarred chutney, pickle, and spice paste;
canned fruit; Darjeeling tea; *papadums* (lentil wafers that make the best snack imaginable,

especially with martinis); and ever so much more tempt you to spend hours here imagining how these things taste. Near the front counter on the floor are cartons of fresh items such as ginger, fresh *kari* leaves, fresh turmeric (which looks like thumb-sized tubers), packaged chapati and nan (Indian breads), and once in a while the most flavorful mangoes you'll ever taste in this country. Whoever buys them has flawless taste in this seductive fruit. You can also pick up Indian videos. If being around all the Indian ingredients makes you hungry, you can get a snack next door at Bombay Cuisine.

NEW SAIGON SUPERMARKET

443 9th Street (between Broadway
and Franklin), Oakland
510-839-4149
Open daily 9 A.M. to 6:30 P.M.
Cash only

The Chinatown block of Ninth Street between Broadway and Franklin is lined with Asian grocery stores, their produce displays spilling out on the sidewalk, and shelves inside stacked to the rafters with products from all over the East. New Saigon is the largest and most densely packed of them all, with gorgeous fresh gourds, squashes, Chinese eggplants, green papayas, mangoes, Asian greens, and seasonal delicacies in eye-catching piles. The large meat department is strong in fresh pork, meaty fresh bacon, piles of dewy ground pork, pristine pork liver and tongue, and every other imaginable part of the animal. French-style baguettes, dishware, tofu in bulk, noodles—all the southern Chinese and Southeast Asian cooking necessities are stocked. This is a destination for pork and Asian produce.

OAKLAND MARKET

401 9th Street
(at Franklin), Oakland
510-835-4919
Open daily 9 A.M. to 6:30 P.M.
Credit cards: AE, MC, V

Roomier and easier to negotiate than New Saigon (above), the Oakland Market is a modern pan-Asian grocery with a large section of Asian kitchenware and dishes. You'll see shelves of inexpensive, clean-smelling Panther Peanut Oil in three-liter tins, excellent for deep-frying of all kinds, and more fragrant Lion and Globe peanut oil in plastic containers, good for salad dressings and cooking. There are refrigerated cases with wonton skins, tofu, and pickled greens. The grocery shelves have items like Japanese seaweed and wasabi, along with Thai, Vietnamese, and Filipino products. The selection of Asian goods is not deep, but it's diverse and comprehensive.

SAM YICK

362 8th Street (between
Webster and Franklin), Oakland
510- 832-0662
Open daily 6 A.M. to 6:30 P.M.
Credit cards: MC, V

People love this resonant old-time Oakland Chinatown grocery store with tons of Chinese pottery, dried black mushrooms for good prices, packed and in bulk, and an extensive collection of Asian pantry items and dry goods, as well as a complement of necessary Western groceries like sugar, mustard, and sea salt.

LION'S HEAD

SERVES 4

This is Cecilia Chiang's recipe for that most soulful of Asian casseroles, so-called because the oversized pork meatballs look like they have a shaggy mane of shredded cabbage. The meat takes on a melting texture, and the juices from the cabbage and the seasoned pork give the gravy haunting depth. Buy a clay pot, easily found in Chinatown and very inexpensive, for this dish, because you'll be making it again and again. Serve the dish with rice.

MEATBALLS

1 pound coarsely ground pork
with fat

1 tablespoon chopped scallion

1 tablespoon peeled and minced
fresh ginger

6 fresh water chestnuts,
peeled and finely diced
(optional, but use them)

2-inch square piece silken tofu,
finely diced (optional)

1 tablespoon Chinese rice wine

1 tablespoon soy sauce

1 tablespoon cornstarch

1 teaspoon sugar

1 generous teaspoon kosher salt

½ teaspoon white pepper

CASSEROLE

½ head napa cabbage,
cut into 1-inch wide strips

4 tablespoons peanut or
vegetable oil

1 cup water

1 cup soaked glass noodles
(bean thread noodles, soaked
in hot water for 10 minutes,
cut with scissors, and
measured into a cup)

1 tablespoon soy sauce

1 teaspoon kosher salt

1 To make the meatballs, combine all the ingredients in a large bowl, mixing well with your hands. Then form the mixture into 4 big meatballs.

2 To assemble the casserole, line a large clay pot with the cabbage strips. You can use any large, heavy, flameproof casserole with a cover.

3 Heat the oil in a large skillet and brown the meatballs. Arrange them on the cabbage in the casserole. Add the water, soy sauce, and kosher salt. Cover the casserole and bring to a boil over high heat. Cook over high heat for 5 minutes. Then add the glass noodles, reduce the heat to a simmer, and cook, covered, for another 15 minutes. Remove from the heat and serve.

EATING IN OAKLAND'S CHINATOWN

Good small Vietnamese restaurants have been popping up in Oakland's Chinatown, and several are of note: **Vi's Vietnamese Cuisine**, 724 Webster Street, Oakland (510-835-8375), is a clean and modern dining room that serves excellent Vietnamese noodle salads in deep bowls with shredded vegetables, pieces of grilled pork or chicken, a crisp, delectable deep-fried imperial roll, and a bowl of clear dressing to pour. I highly recommend any of the salads. **Vien Huong**, 712 Franklin Street, Oakland (510-465-5938), is a popular *pho* restaurant, always packed, that specializes in Vietnamese soup and noodles. The ever-popular **Jade Villa**, 800 Broadway Street, Oakland (510-839-1688), for dim sum has some competition from monumental **Restaurant Peony** in the Pacific Renaissance Plaza, second floor, 388 Ninth Street (510-286-8866). Eight hundred people can sit in three gigantic rooms plus some private rooms. As you can imagine, the selection of dim sum, seafood, and Chinese barbecue is huge, and because of the volume, fresh. The variety seems endless.

THE SPANISH TABLE . . . .

1814 San Pablo Avenue (between Hearst and Delaware), Berkeley
510-548-1383
Open Monday through Saturday
10 A.M. to 6 P.M.,
Sunday 11 A.M to 5 P.M.
Credit cards: MC, V

This Berkeley branch of a Seattle company that imports culinary items from Spain has the Bay Area's biggest collection of paella pans, ranging in diameter from several inches to yards in diameter for that outdoor paella party over an open fire. It also carries fine Spanish olive oils, rice, dried beans, chocolate, some cheeses and hams (but not enough), and instant paella mixes. I shop here for one item that has transformed my kitchen, an artisan sherry vinegar, Toro Albalá Reserva 1980, that has a sweet, nutty, aged sherrylike nose and a gently tart finish. It was recommended by the helpful clerk, who picked it from the many others on the shelf at different prices. But this particular vinegar, sprinkled on tomatoes, on greens, on roasted or grilled vegetables, makes them resonate with new flavor. It adds vibrancy to vinaigrettes and sauces for fish and shellfish. It even enhances fruit. Less sweet than balsamic with a complex nose, elegant aged sherry vinegar brings food alive. For $15 and a trip to West Berkeley to the Spanish Table, you, too, can mysteriously make most things taste better, I promise. It's our secret.

BERKELEY BOWL . . . .

2777 Shattuck Avenue
(near Ashby), Berkeley
510-843-6929
Open Monday through Saturday
9 A.M. to 8 P.M.,
Sunday 10 A.M. to 6 P.M.
Credit cards: AE, D, MC, V

There are two destination produce stores in the Bay Area and Berkeley Bowl is one of them. (Monterey Foods, page 430, across Berkeley, is the other.) Your spirits will be lifted when you walk into this expansive former Safeway and see the amazing variety of produce available under one roof. The organic section alone would fill up most small produce stores, and there is a large representation of Asian produce and tropical fruits.

Seasonal fruits and citrus fill table after table. Wild and cultivated mushrooms, lettuces, cooking greens, peppers, chiles, and always lots of tropicals such as plantains, tomatillos, chayotes, pineapples, coconuts, mangoes, papayas, and galangal all beckon at excellent prices. Also near the produce department are fresh breads, eggs, and dairy, plus a large Asian refrigerated section with noodles and tofu.

At the back of the store is a long glass butcher counter featuring a Japanese fish section with fresh fish fillets marinated in *sake kasu* (the lees from sake fermentation) or miso, both yellowfin and white-fleshed *tombo* tuna, Pacific halibut, seaweed salad, and some shellfish. The meat and poultry counter is strong with Niman Ranch beef, the incomparable naturally raised Niman pork from Iowa, and tasty Petaluma Poultry organic Rosie chickens. You can buy huge tins of anchovies packed in salt and other hard-to-find preserved fish. Shelves of groceries take up the middle of the store with beer and wine; Japanese products; grains, nuts, and spices in bulk; and chips. In essence, the Berkeley Bowl has become a supermarket that sells mostly fresh foods. If you live near the Oakland-Berkeley border, Berkeley Bowl should be your market of choice.

BERKELEY FARMERS' MARKET . . . .

Center Street at Martin Luther
King Jr. Way
Saturday 10 A.M. to 2 P.M.

Derby Street between Milvia and
Martin Luther King Jr. Way
Tuesday 2 P.M. to 7 P.M. in summer

Haste Street at Telegraph Avenue
Sunday 11 A.M. to 3 P.M.
May through November

Cash only

With two great permanent produce markets in town, why shop at the farmers' markets? Because you can get produce that has been picked just hours before you buy it, and you also might find some very local organic crops, grown in such small quantity that they could only be sold by the farmer directly. Produce bought directly from the people who grow it always tastes better, even if you can buy it more cheaply, and a bit older, at Monterey Foods (see page 430). I always make a detour for a farmers' market, if only for the pleasure of strolling down a street lined with fruits and vegetables.

KHANH PHONG. . . . .

429 9th Street (between Broadway
and Franklin), Oakland
Open daily 9 A.M. to 6:30 P.M.
Cash only

This Asian supermarket located between New Saigon
and the Oakland Market (see opposite) has the largest
selection of produce on the block, including many
tropicals such as banana flowers, which look like big,
fat, purple buds, and durian, which are spiky and
smelly. For the thrill of exotic produce, much of which you will have never seen before
unless you've traveled to Southeast Asia, head to Khanh Phong.

MARKET HALL PRODUCE. . . . .

5655 College Avenue
(at Shafter), Oakland
510-601-8208
Open Monday through Friday
9 A.M. to 8 P.M., Saturday and
Sunday until 7 P.M.
Credit cards: MC, V

A part of the Market Hall group of food stalls under
one roof, this large, attractively arranged produce store
offers a useful selection of organic and commercial produce at midrange prices. During a fall visit, fresh, dry,
clean chanterelles at a good price, organic apples, baby
lettuces, and very pretty whole heads of organic oak
leaf, red leaf, red butter leaf, and romaine lettuces
caught my eye. Big bunches of arugula and lots of
tomatoes cried out to be bought. The produce department also carries Straus Family
Creamery organic milk and butter.

MONTEREY FOODS. . . . .

1550 Hopkins Street
(at Monterey), Berkeley
510-526-6042
Open Monday through Friday
9 A.M. to 7 P.M.,
Saturday 8:30 A.M. to 6 P.M.
Cash only

This stupendous produce market sets the standard for
all others in price, variety, and completeness. There
aren't many edible plants grown under the sun that
don't show up on one of Monterey Foods's tables.
Outside in the parking lot is a caged-in area with
mountains of the best buys of the season, organic or
not, but usually of excellent quality at phenomenally
low prices. Every cook I know periodically checks
Monterey Foods to see what's available in the Bay Area and what they should be paying for
it. Both big farmers and small producers have established long-term relationships with the
two generations of the Fujimoto family who run this market. Bill Fujimoto knows everyone
who grows in the northern part of the state and then some. Many farmers come to
Monterey Market first because they might not have to go any farther to sell their harvest.
Monterey makes its profits on volume, so they buy big and keep their markup tiny. When I
started my first eight-table restaurant in Berkeley a million years ago, I shopped at
Monterey Foods every single morning, and to tell you the truth, I've never done better on
price for quality since. The store also has a small grocery department with fresh breads,
pasta, and a dairy section.

9th Street at Broadway, Oakland
Friday 8 A.M. to 2 P.M.
Cash only

Next door to Oakland's Chinatown, the Old Oakland market features lots of fresh Asian produce, fresh non-organic fruits and vegetables, and good prices on everything. Asian apple pears, dates, lots of oranges, and the whole spectrum of Asian greens, gourds, and root vegetables are usually represented. Anchored on one side by G. B. Ratto (see page 425), the great international foods store, and Chinatown on the other, a trip to this part of the Bay Area on Friday could fulfill any number of food-shopping goals. The composition of this market is similar to the Civic Center Farmers' Market in San Francisco (see page 65).

MEAT AND POULTRY

ALAN'S MEATS. . . . .

Housewives Market,
907 Washington Street
(at 9th Street), Oakland
510-893-9479
Open Monday through Saturday
9 A.M. to 6 P.M.
Credit cards: AE, D, MC, V

What beautiful smoked and fresh pork this meat stand has! The piles of salt pork, fresh bacon, smoked bacon, ham hocks, smoked ham ends, and fresh, cured, and smoked ham of all sorts make you want to buy some red beans and get cooking. I bought some huge smoked ham hocks, which Alan's sliced, and I made the most delectable split-pea soup with them. They were meaty with lots of marrow and gave the soup an honest, clean, smoky flavor. When you visit the Housewives Market, plan on picking up some bacon.

ENZO. . . . .

Market Hall, 5655 College Avenue
(at Shafter), Oakland
510-547-5839
Open Monday through Friday
10 A.M. to 8 P.M., Saturday and
Sunday until 7 P.M.
Credit cards: AE, MC, V

This small high-quality butcher shop carries Harris Ranch beef, Petaluma Poultry chickens, house-made pork sausage, Grimaud rabbits, osso buco, and some nice-looking lamb from small animals. Enzo is an Italian butcher, so he cuts and grinds for Italian recipes. He also sells big Hebrew National Kosher hot dogs, which are very delicious. For an extra charge depending on the size of the bird, Enzo will cook ducks and turkeys on the rotisserie for you, so you can pick them up hot and ready to serve.

RED BEANS AND RICE

SERVES 4 TO 6

One of the most satisfying dishes in the world is red beans and rice. I first ate it in New Orleans, and now I prepare it for football playoffs on television. The best recipe comes from *American Cooking: Creole and Acadian*, a volume in the unsurpassed Time-Life Foods of the World series. The recipes in these books are so well researched and written that if you follow them carefully, you will always end up with something tasty. You can find these volumes in used-book stores.

The butchers at Alan's will slice their meaty ham hocks for you, which allows the marrow to enrich the beans. You can buy excellent dried beans at the Bean Bag stall in the Housewives Market near Alan's.

6 cups water, plus more as needed

1 pound dried red beans

4 tablespoons butter or olive oil

1 cup finely chopped scallions

½ cup finely chopped yellow onion

1 teaspoon minced garlic

1 pound smoked ham hocks

1 teaspoon kosher salt

½ teaspoon freshly ground pepper, or more to taste

6 to 8 cups freshly cooked long-grain white rice

1 Bring the 6 cups water to a boil in a large saucepan. Add the beans and boil over high heat for 2 minutes. Turn off the heat and let the beans soak for 1 hour. Drain the beans, reserving the liquid. Add more water as needed to make 4 cups liquid.

2 Heat the butter or oil in a heavy 4- to 5-quart casserole over medium heat. Add the scallions, yellow onion, and garlic and cook, stirring, for about 5 minutes, or until soft. Stir in the beans and their liquid. Add the ham hocks, salt, and pepper. Bring to a boil, then reduce the heat to low and simmer gently, partially covered, for about 3 hours, or until the beans are very soft, periodically checking the pot for liquid and adding up to 1 cup water little by little as necessary.

3 Remove the ham hocks. Cut the meat from the bones and return it to the pot. Taste the beans for salt and pepper and adjust the seasonings as necessary. Put the rice in bowls, cover with the beans, and top with the remaining scallions.

1568 Hopkins Street (between
McGee and California), Berkeley
510-528-6370
Open Monday through Saturday
9:30 A.M. to 6 P.M.
Credit cards: MC, V

Chickens and chicken parts, ducks, turkeys, and other poultry are sold here, including superb Hoffman chickens, poussins, and quail. Of note are the rotisserie chickens, one marinated with Italian herbs, mostly lemon and rosemary, the other in a Japanese teriyaki marinade that is a knockout, particularly moist and flavorful. Magnani also sells meat—Sonoma lamb, Harris Ranch beef, and their own sausages. With Magnani's now selling meat, and Monterey Fish and Monterey Foods all within a block, the little Hopkins corridor has become a complete culinary neighborhood.

T & S MARKET . . . .

323 9th Street (between
Webster and Franklin), Oakland
510- 268-1155
Open daily 8:30 A.M. to 6 P.M.
Cash only

This Chinatown poultry wholesaler also has a retail counter, though most of what they carry is kept in walk-in refrigerators in the warehouse. Just ask for what you need: ducks, chickens, chicken parts, poussins, large squab, and exotics like black-skinned chickens and ostrich (red fleshed like duck). To restore a woman after giving birth, boil up a black-chicken broth with ginseng. The Chinese have been doing it for thousands of years. The results are good. So are the prices here.

TAYLOR'S SAUSAGES . . . .

Housewives Market,
907 Washington Street
(at 9th Street), Oakland
510-832-6448
Open Monday through Saturday
9 A.M. to 6 P.M.
Credit cards: MC, V

In the course of doing research for this book, I've sampled many, many fresh sausages, but the ones I like the best come from this little stand in the Housewives Market. Their New Orleans–style *boudin blanc*, a mildly spicy white sausage with rice, is worth a special trip alone without even considering the perfectly seasoned and textured spicy Cajun chicken sausage, the Louisiana hot sausage, the garlic sausage, the Italian— every sausage these people make has balance; melded together, deep, interesting flavor; and just the right amount of fat to keep the sausages juicy and moist. The prices couldn't be better, the sausages fresher, or the variety more pleasing. No weird ingredients like fruit, curry, or sun-dried tomatoes ever ruin a Taylor's sausage. Through several generations of owners, these have always been classic and great. Whoever runs this stand knows they have a good thing in these recipes.

VER BRUGGE MEATS. . . . .

6321 College Avenue (between
Alcatraz and Claremont), Oakland
510-658-6854
Open Monday through Friday
9 A.M. to 6:30 P.M.,
Saturday 9 A.M. to 6 P.M.,
Sunday 10 A.M. to 6 P.M.
Credit cards: AE, D, MC, V

This successful neighborhood butcher has a long
counter filled with moderately priced fresh meat,
including especially good eastern pork and hams. They
will cut to order and can get you anything you need if
you call ahead.

FISH

ABRAHAM'S SEAFOOD . . . .

Housewives Market,
907 Washington Street
(at 9th Street), Oakland
510-835-4565
Open Monday through Saturday
9 A.M. to 6 P.M.
Credit cards: D, MC, V

Next to Monterey Fish, I like this long, immaculate fish
counter in the Housewives Market the best. There are
fish bargains to be found here, if you fancy catfish,
gaspergoo, buffalo fish, and gar. But some sparkling,
bright-eyed wild Louisiana red snappers might be available, and if they are, buy one. They are some of the
tastiest fish you can find. Abraham's will clean it, scale
it, and take out the gills, then you can roast it in salt

(see recipe, page 44) or barbecue it whole. Its flesh is so juicy and flavorful, it doesn't
require a bit of seasoning. If you like your seafood deep-fried, this is the place to find the
fattier fish that lend themselves to this kind of cooking. There is also rex sole in season,
rockfish and lingcod fillets, and shrimp of all sizes and grades. The people behind the
counter know their fish and will be happy to discuss cooking methods with you. They are
exceptionally nice considering how busy they are.

BERKELEY BOWL FISH MARKET . . . .

2777 Shattuck Avenue
(near Ashby), Berkeley
510-843-6929
Open Monday through Saturday
9 A.M. to 8 P.M.,
Sunday 10 A.M. to 6 P.M.
Credit cards: AE, D, MC, V

Pristine Japanese-style fillets as well as a wide range of
other fish and shellfish are available at the long butcher
counter. See page 429 for more information.

MONTEREY FISH . . . .

1582 Hopkins Street
(at Monterey), Berkeley
510-525-5600
Open Tuesday through Saturday
10 A.M. to 6 P.M.
Credit cards: MC, V

This is Paul Johnson and Tom Worthington's retail fish store, and it is the best one in the Bay Area. You can't find a fish purveyor with higher standards or more integrity. Anything you buy from Monterey Fish will smell like the sea and stay fresh for several days at least—a tall order when it comes to seafood. The secret behind Monterey's quality is their buying. They seek out sources, cultivate them, and stick with them. If they can't get something in perfect condition, they don't carry it. A mitigating factor is that Monterey sells to a small number of picky restaurants from their wholesale location on the wharf in San Francisco, so they move what they have quickly and always have a fairly large variety of what they deem best at the moment. Monterey Fish is a source for fresh squid, carefully culled live lobsters and crabs in clean tanks, fresh shrimp, outstanding scallops and blue crab from a long-held source in Rhode Island, first-rate small shucked oysters from Washington State, and oysters in the shell from California on up to British Columbia.

Quality and freshness mean everything in seafood, because you don't even want to go near it if it isn't pristine. If you shop at Monterey Fish you'll start cooking more and more fish at home and discover that it is the best convenience food you can buy. You don't have to do a thing to a fillet of king salmon, a slice of red-fleshed Hawaiian tuna, a slab of San Diego swordfish, or a piece of velvet-textured northern halibut except not overcook it. And though some of this fish is expensive, there's no waste and you don't need a huge portion to satisfy. Fish is a clean, flavorful, elegant source of protein that goes with practically any vegetable and starch, so throwing a meal together with it is a snap. If you love fish, buy it at Monterey, and if you've been afraid to cook with it, come here too. You can't go wrong cooking fish from this market; you can trust them. Johnson and Worthington sell only what they themselves take home to cook and their standards are high.

ROCKRIDGE FISH MARKET . . . .

Market Hall, 5655 College Avenue
(at Shafter), Oakland
510-654-3474
Open Monday through Friday
10 A.M. to 8 P.M., Saturday and
Sunday until 7 P.M.
Credit cards: AE, D, MC, V

The small fish counter in this popular food shopping hall offers fillets of choice fish like mahi-mahi, sword fish, salmon, and tuna, along with fresh shrimp and live crab and lobsters from a tank. Some good-looking calamari salad, seaweed salad, and a few other fish preparations are also sold. The fish is nicely displayed and well cut. There are no bargains; the emphasis is on high-priced, easy-to-cook fish.

THE CHEESE BOARD . . . .

1504 Shattuck Avenue (between
Cedar and Vine), Berkeley
510-549-3183

Bakery open Monday
7 A.M. to 1 P.M., Tuesday through
Friday 7 A.M. to 6 P.M., and
Saturday 8:30 A.M. to 5 P.M.

Cheese shop open Tuesday through
Friday 10 A.M. to 6 P.M., Saturday
10 A.M. to 5 P.M.

Pizzeria open Monday 11:30 A.M. to
2 P.M., Tuesday through Friday
11:30 A.M. to 2 P.M. and
4:30 P.M. to 7 P.M., Saturday noon
to 3 P.M. and 4:30 P.M. to 7 P.M.

Cash only

In its third decade of operation, the Cheese Board not
only stocks the largest collection of cheeses on the West
Coast (or maybe in the United States), but a full-scale
bread bakery and a to-go pizzeria a door away. Once
merely a cheese store, the Cheese Board has become an
important cultural institution. Over the years, this col-
lectively owned shop has created a wide customer base
that regularly makes the pilgrimage to Berkeley to buy
cheese. Cheese Board customers have become sophisticated cheese buyers who will try new things. This
means that the store turns over enormous volume, not
just of common cheeses, but of exotic ones, which in
turn means that all the cheeses stay fresh and in perfect
condition. The Cheese Board has cultivated this kind of
response by requiring every customer to taste every
cheese before they buy it. Every cheese is unwrapped in
a split second and a taste is shaved off and handed over
on waxed paper before you can protest. No one feels
constrained to buy a cheese he or she doesn't like. One
taste follows another until everyone is satisfied—customer and clerk—that the cheese is right. The cheese
sellers taste along with the customers so they intimately know the inventory—which wheel
of Brie is at a certain stage of ripeness, which aged Gouda is the nuttiest. They learn the
characteristics of every new cheese, how to store, cut, order—and how to serve the customers, some of whom could try the patience of a saint. The clerks know which cheese to
pull up for tasting when a customer gives some vague description. They can tell people
what to buy for certain recipes; what to serve the day after tomorrow on a cheese tray; what
to introduce kids to; what they personally love and the customer might like, too. The
Cheese Board system is an amazing way to sell, unlike any other I've encountered. The end
result is that people trust the store and are willing and eager to be turned on to an ever-
expanding repertoire.

The smell of warm breads just out of the oven always wafts around the store, which
only makes you want to buy more cheese. My favorite is a round loaf called Suburban
Bread, which has the most amazing crisp, thin, but chewy crust and a white, sweet, toothsome interior that's charmingly tender—a bread-baking triumph. People also go to the
Cheese Board for fine olives in bulk at excellent prices. The pizza sold in a little shop that
used to house Pig by the Tail (the first charcuterie in America) is sold slice by slice the
minute it comes out of the oven (see page 416). The bakers can barely keep up with the
line. The slices are slapped onto a piece of paper and served on rattan plates. Customers sit
or stand outside the store, eating and talking.

I have one bit of advice when visiting the Cheese Board. Take a playing card–number when you walk in and then look around at the breads and cheeses. Though the clerks are fast and efficient, and there are a lot of them, you never know how long the people in front of you will spend tasting, deciding, discussing. This exchange is the glory of the shop, and it has proven that education, generosity, and communal ownership can achieve the highest and best kind of success.

MARKET HALL PASTA SHOP. . . . .

5655 College Avenue
(at Shafter), Oakland
510-547-4005
www.rockridge.com
Open Monday through Saturday
9 A.M. to 8 P.M.,
Sunday 10 A.M. to 7 P.M.
Credit Cards: MC, V

Clerks offer tastes and recommendations at this well stocked cheese counter. See page 417 for more information.

COFFEE

PEET'S COFFEE & TEA. . . . .

2124 Vine Street
(near Shattuck), Berkeley
510-841-0564
www.peets.com
Open Monday through Saturday
7 A.M. to 7 P.M.,
Sunday until 6 P.M.
Credit cards: AE, D, MC, V

The perpetual crowd in front of the original Peet's never lets up and neither does the line inside the store. Per square inch, this coffee store must sell more beans and more cups of their intensely brewed coffee than any other, and deservedly so. Peet's has become such a social crossroads that a visit to this model for all the multitudinous coffee-store chains in the Bay Area is always an experience. You get a real whiff of old Berkeley milling outside, the maddening, wacky, passionate, political Berkeley that you can walk away from—or join—once you tame your cup of Peet's coffee with half-and-half and sugar. See page 167 for more information.

KERMIT LYNCH WINES . . . .

1605 San Pablo Avenue
(at Cedar), Berkeley
510-524-1524
Open Tuesday through Saturday
11 A.M. to 6 P.M.
Credit cards: MC, V

Just as Berkeley has spawned Chez Panisse, the Cheese Board , Monterey Foods, Monterey Fish, and Acme Bread, it has also nurtured Kermit Lynch, the groundbreaking wine merchant who brought the wines of Bandol from Domaine Tempier to the United States, along with many other wines from previously undiscovered (at least in the United States) wine-growing areas, which have now become icons of sophisticated eating and drinking. If you read Kermit Lynch's book, *Adventures on the Wine Route: A Wine Buyer's Tour of France*, you'll get a first-hand account of what he was looking for: the quality of the land in the wine, the personality of the winemaker, direct purchasing from the people who make the wines (not *négociants*), and artisan, not industrial, wine-making techniques.

In his retail store, a cool red-brick room stacked with cases, you'll be able to buy the beautiful wines he made famous in this country, the Rhônes from Domaine Jean-Louis Chave in Hermitage and Auguste Clape in Cornas, plus many of what Richard Olney in his introduction to Lynch's book describes as inexpensive, clean, refreshing, and undemanding ideal daily aperitif and luncheon wines, such as Jean Berail-Lagardes white Roque Lestière and Yves Laboucaries *vin gris* Domaine de Fontsainte, both from the southwest Corbières apellation. All of Kermit Lynch's wines are imported, with particular strength in Burgundy, Alsace, Provence, and the Rhône, and most recently, a bunch of discoveries from the Loire and the Côte de Roussillon on the southeast coast of France. You won't like all the wines; some are very eccentric. But more often than not I've come around to appreciating them, the way you would a brilliant but slightly obnoxious person. When I first tasted the monumental Chablis from Raveneau, a rich, powerful wine aged in oak, a wine that is usually crisp and tart, I began to realize that every wine, even wines from the most traditional wine-growing areas, are as individual as their winemakers, and it is the winemakers' visions that captures Lynch's interest.

Shopping at the store is low-key and interesting. The friendly and extremely helpful clerks have tasted everything; they've traveled to the vineyards and eaten the foods that go with the wines. They are able to give good advice on food and wine matchups. Like the staff at The Cheese Board (see page 437), they want to turn their customers on to new wines, hear what people think about them, and try to find wines that will please each palate—to be personal wine merchants.

Finally, though some of these wines are found at other stores, since Kermit Lynch is an importer and a wholesaler as well as a retailer, you'll find the most complete collection at the best prices at the store on San Pablo.

ODD LOTS . . . .

1025 San Pablo Avenue
(at Marin), Albany
510-526-0522
Open Tuesday through Friday
11 A.M. to 7 P.M.,
Saturday 10 A.M. to 5 P.M.
Credit cards: MC, V

Morgan Miller, the force behind this modest shop, has been in the wine trade for over a quarter century. He has a great palate and tremendous knowledge, so he is able to pick up off-year vintages from excellent producers at bargain prices and pass them on to his customers. Wines in the store come from all over the world: Australia, Spain, Italy, and small châteaux in Bordeaux. Some 98 percent of the stock is imported. He ferrets out value wherever he finds it. His selections are not about vintage or provenance, only about character, balance, and pleasure for the money.

As he told me, he finds the wines that have fallen through the cracks of the wine market and offers them at small markups, including wines wholesaled by Grape Expectations, who have represented and imported some of the best bottles from Europe over the years.

PAUL MARCUS WINES . . . .

Market Hall, 5655 College Avenue
(at Shafter), Oakland
510-420-1005
www.paulmarcuswines.com
Open Monday through Friday
10 A.M. to 8 P.M., Saturday and
Sunday until 7 P.M.
Credit cards: MC, V

Service is the thing at this small, but very useful wine stall in Market Hall. The selection of wines here is personal and exciting, with a large section of wines well under $8, and a bunch of more expensive ones, particularly from small California producers and Italy. I spied tasty Rhônes from Château de Fonsalette and some swanky but not outrageous ports, Sauternes, and Champagnes. Lots of people walk out with cases. While you won't find the cheapest prices here, what you will find is enlightened selection, a bit of wine education, and a lot of friendly chitchat about what everyone is having for dinner. The vibes are great. Many knowledgeable wine drinkers feel that Paul Marcus is the best wine store in the East Bay.

VINO . . . .

6319 College Avenue (between
Alcatraz and Claremont), Oakland
510-652-6317
Open Monday through Saturday
10 A.M. to 7 P.M.,
Sunday 11 A.M. to 6 P.M.
Credit cards: AE, MC, V

If you're looking for some outstanding buys on imported and California wines, check out Vino, long associated with Mike Temple, a peripatetic wine importer who started Grape Expectations. The buyer at this first of the Vino shops (there are four others scattered around San Francisco and the East Bay) knows how to choose the best bottles from little-known producers around the world, including California. The inventory is half domestic and half imported, but the unifying theme of this eclectic collection is interesting character and good value. As at Odd Lots (above), you can find tasty wines at closeout prices. With so much competition for the wine dollar these days, and such a mindboggling collection of wines from all over the world, a small, expertly run, price-sensitive store like this can be a real boon.

BLACK OAK BOOKS. . . . .

1491 Shattuck Avenue (between
Cedar and Vine), Berkeley
510-486-0698
www.blackoakbooks.com
Open daily 10 A.M. to 10 P.M.
Credit cards: AE, D, MC, V

This independent bookstore has a large section of new and used cookbooks and an active program of visiting authors. Since it's practically next door to Chez Panisse, you can browse the shelves until it's time for your reservation. Its proximity to the destination food stores and restaurants nearby has raised its cookbook consciousness, so you will always be able to find many books by local authors as well as the classics.

CODY'S . . . .

2454 Telegraph Avenue
(at Haste), Berkeley
510-845-7852
www.codybooks.com
Open daily 10 A.M. to 10 P.M.
Credit cards: AE, D, MC, V

1730 4th Street (between
Hearst Avenue and Virginia Street),
Berkeley
510-559-9500
Open daily 10 A.M. to 7 P.M.,
Thursday, Friday, and Saturday
until 8 P.M.

This may be one of the most complete bookstores in the world and certainly one with the best service. If Cody's does not have the book you need on their shelves, they'll track it down for you. The clerks know an astounding amount about what is available on any subject. The cookbook section is one of the most complete and up to date because the Cody's buyer loves and knows cookbooks. As in so many other areas of culinary interest, Berkeley has the stellar resource and Cody's is it.

THE GARDENER . . . .

1836 4th Street (between
Hearst and Virginia), Berkeley
510-548-4545
www.thegardener.com
Open Monday through Saturday
10 A.M. to 6 P.M.,
Sunday 11 A.M. to 6 P.M.
Credit cards: AE, D, MC, V

This enchanting store, constantly re-created by Alta Tingle, has the most unpredictable treasures for the house and garden. They might take the form of certain cookbooks—on rice perhaps; sumptuous, brightly dyed cotton tablecloths from India backed with material, trimmed and hand sewn; market bags; or serving platters in the most arresting shapes and materials. You might find hand-forged iron candleholders or the perfect hand-painted dining room cabinet. There might be an outdoor picnic table and umbrella. The stock is ever changing and every item gives pause. Tingle has an infallible instinct for beautiful, down-to-earth objects that are always useful and well made. Whenever I'm in the neighborhood, having a bite at O Chamé (see page 407), I stroll through the shop to see what I will be buying for the next year, for my friends and myself.

THE SPANISH TABLE . . . .

1814 San Pablo Avenue (between
Hearst and Delaware), Berkeley
510-548-1383
Open Monday through Saturday
10 A.M. to 6 P.M.,
Sunday 11 A.M. to 5 P.M.
Credit cards: MC, V

This store carries paella pans in all sizes. See page xxx
for more information.

SUR LA TABLE . . . .

1806 4th Street (between
Hearst and Virginia), Berkeley
510-849-2252
www.surlatable.com
Open Monday through Saturday
9 A.M. to 7 P.M.
Credit cards: AE, D, MC, V

The Berkeley branch of this serious kitchenware store
throws many a book party for local cookbook writers
and mounts a full schedule of cooking classes. See page
126 for more information.

MARIN COUNTY

SAN FRANCISCO FOOD LOVER'S GUIDE

RESTAURANTS
Frantoio
Insalata's
Lark Creek Inn
Manka's
Rice Table
Roxanne's
Sushi Ran

CAFÉS
Book Passage Cafe
Emporio Rulli

BARS
Guaymas
Sam's

DELICATESSENS/TAKEOUT
Hamburgers

BAKERIES/PASTRIES
Bovine Bakery
Emporio Rulli

ICE CREAM/CHOCOLATES
Lyla's Chocolates
Emporio Rulli

PRODUCE
Tomales Bay Produce
Marin County Farmers' Market

CHEESE
The Cheese Shop
Tomales Bay Foods

COFFEE
Emporio Rulli
Peet's Coffee & Tea

FISH
Hog Island Oyster Company

WINES AND SPIRITS
Marin Wine Cellar
Mill Valley Market

COOKWARE AND BOOKS
Book Passage
Viking Homechef
Williams-Sonoma

FRANTOIO . . . .

152 Shoreline Highway
(adjacent to the Holiday Inn
Express), Mill Valley
415-289-5777
www.frantoio.com
Open Sunday through Thursday
5:30 to 10 P.M.,
Friday and Saturday until 11 P.M.
Moderate
Credit cards: AE, DC, D, MC, V

At Frantoio, you can witness the sexiest culinary rite of passage in the Mediterranean world just across the bay in Mill Valley. Locally harvested green and black olives are transformed into precious extra virgin olive oil by a state-of-the-art olive oil press located behind a window at the back of this bustling restaurant. During the day from late December through February, you can observe the whole process and taste the results.

Growers from all over Northern California bring Manzanillo, Sevillano, Picholine, and Mission olives to be pressed. First, the crates of olives are poured into a machine that sprays them with water and shakes away the leaves. Then the olives are slowly fed into the grinder, two massive granite wheels that crush the fruit and pits into a rough paste, which is evenly spread by hand onto round mats and stacked on a spindle between steel plates. A water-driven hydraulic press gently squeezes out the oil and the water. You can see the liquid sensually dripping off the sides and being channeled into a centrifuge, which sends the pure oil into one bucket and the olive water into another. This is the moment to ask if you can have a taste from the golden stream of oil slowly dripping into a pail.

If the owner of the olives being pressed at the moment gives the nod, you will be able to taste a food that radiates raw energy, that dances on your tongue. Put your nose to the brand new oil and then sip it from a spoon, noisily drawing the oil through your teeth with air the way the experts do. Sensations will hit your mouth, starting with the fruitiness of the olives, then the subtle smell of perhaps almonds or apples, then the buttery, unctuous texture, and finally a hot and peppery jolt.

Compare this just-extracted oil to slightly older oils. Frantoio sets its tables with cruets of its own new-press olive oil (my favorite being their Sevillano). You'll learn first hand that each oil has its own character, which, like wine, is due to geography, soil differences, the age and variety of the trees, the blend of the olives that go into the press, and, of course, the method and cleanliness of the pressing. At Frantoio during the olive harvest, you will get to experience something afforded very few Americans, a taste of traditionally extracted, cold-pressed, locally grown extra virgin olive oil.

The restaurant is as professionally run as the olive oil press, with a crowd-pleasing Italian menu strong on pasta dishes and antipasti, and a first-rate, affordable Italian wine list. Prices are refreshingly moderate given the handsome modern dining room and a European level of service. A wood oven–baked pizza, some Italian bread dipped into olive oil while you wait, an arugula salad, and a glass of Italian wine have been my repast at the bar—especially during white truffle season when Frantoio's Italian chef always seems to get his hands on some of the best. The combination of new olive oil and white truffles on anything is priceless.

INSALATA'S . . . .

120 Sir Francis Drake Boulevard
(between Barber and Ross),
San Anselmo
415-457-7700
www.insalatas.com
Open Monday through Saturday
11:30 A.M. to 2:30 P.M. and
5:30 to 9 P.M., Sunday 11 A.M. to
5 P.M., take-out Monday through
Saturday 11 A.M. to 7:30 P.M.;
Sunday brunch 11 A.M. to 2:30 P.M.
Moderate
Credit cards: MC, V

From the moment Heidi Krahling opened her spacious Mediterranean-inspired restaurant (surrounded by convenient parking) five years ago, with high ceilings, an open kitchen, a take-out counter, an attractive little wine bar, tables on several levels, and an ebullient yellow paint job outside and in, she had to turn away customers. Most new restaurants falter under this kind of pressure, but Krahling and her experienced crew maintained control, bringing depth, integrity, and personality to a type of restaurant that has become boilerplate in the Bay Area.

At Insalata's, you can begin with *fattoush*, a Syrian salad of romaine tossed with feta, olives, and croutons of cracker bread in a lemon-mint vinaigrette, all of which melts together to form a creamy dressing. The different salads on the Mediterranean platter—carrot, beet, rice, asparagus, mussels—sparkle. They taste bright, fresh, alive. I've had too many identical pasta dishes from one restaurant to the next, but Insalata's shell pasta bathed in a garlicky broccoli rabe pesto with white beans and Parmesan had an intriguing edge. It was a wonderful dish. I've eaten my way through buttery Catalan-style short ribs glazed in sherry, orange, and chocolate sauce on a bed of potato–celery root purée; a Tunisian Seven Vegetable *tagine* on couscous with *harissa*; a thick, moist pork chop with winter vegetables; and thin slices of rosy lamb sirloin on soft polenta with grilled vegetables and *salsa verde*. I am particularly fond of her Tunisian and Moroccan dishes, fragrant with earthy spices, lemon, and olive oil, and make complete North African meals by choosing them from each section of the menu. Drink a spectacular, Rhône-like Château Musar from the Bekaa Valley in Lebanon and you'll be transported.

LARK CREEK INN . . . .

234 Magnolia Avenue (between
King and Williams), Larkspur
415-924-7766
www.larkcreek.com
Open Monday through Friday
11:30 A.M. to 2 P.M., Sunday
through Thursday 5:30 to 9 P.M.,
Friday and Saturday 5 to 10 P.M.;
Sunday brunch 10 A.M. to 2 P.M.
Expensive
Credit cards: AE, DC, MC, V, D

Lark Creek Inn used to be the only culinary reason for visiting Marin, as far as I was concerned, and it still ranks as a compelling one. This great American restaurant started by Bradley Ogden twelve years ago always aims high and delivers on all levels without being stuffy or formal, anathema to casual Marinites. In fact, visiting Lark Creek is pure fun. Everything that comes to the table, from the basket of warm house-baked breads and corn sticks to the big homey desserts, appeals to American's deepest appetites. People devour plates of vine-ripened tomatoes in creamy onion dressing; baskets of crisply fried calamari and clams with a peppery garlic mayonnaise; hearty Yankee pot roast with lots of gravy, airy onion dumplings, and an array of roasted root vegetables; deep bowls of tender braised pork shoulder with white beans and kale; juicy spit-roasted chicken with chive-flecked mashed potatoes and ears of white corn; and plate-sized grilled lamb steaks with fresh peas and irresistible scalloped potatoes and turnips. Even something as esoteric as ravioli stuffed with shredded ham hock in a roasted tomato broth has a down-home side to it. For dessert, expect fresh fruit pies with house-made ice creams, fruit compotes with crème fraîche, shortcakes, butterscotch pudding, and spectacular versions of homemade pastries, like a many-layered banana cake with mashed bananas and tons of frosting between the layers.

The cheerful yellow dining rooms, housed in a converted Victorian mansion set among towering redwood trees, are flooded with light from windows and skylights, and the service is both friendly and professional, a rare combination north of the Golden Gate Bridge. One of the nicest sights in the main dining room is the red brick wood-burning oven out of which come aromatic stews, suckling pigs, and roast chickens. Other seating alternatives are an outdoor patio shaded by the gigantic trees, a natural form of air-conditioning necessary in this hot pocket of the bay, and a separate bar-café room where you can order from a bar menu or the regular one when you feel like dropping in on the spur of the moment.

All the details here ring true: the all–West Coast wine list with tons of interesting bottles from small producers (no bargains here, but lots of treats), thick, rustic pottery plates and serving dishes that suit the hearty food, thin, simple wineglasses that help you taste a wine, and lots of staff to make sure that everything runs smoothly. Ogden knows what really counts in a restaurant. He's a Midwestern boy (raised in Upper Michigan) who believes in substance. As a Midwestern girl (suburban Chicago), I am 100 percent on the same wavelength. This is one of the few restaurants that both my mother and I agree on. I love it for its inventiveness and charm within an American context; she loves it for the pot roast.

MANKA'S INVERNESS LODGE. . . . .

Corner of Argyle and Callendar (first left turn west of the village of Inverness, off Sir Francis Drake), Inverness
415-669-1034
www.mankas.com
Open for dinner Thursday to Monday 6 to 9 P.M.,
Tuesday and Wednesday seating between 6 and 7 P.M.
(lodge guests only)
Expensive
Credit cards: AE, MC, V

To some extent, we all get to design our own immediate environments, whether it be a desktop, a small city apartment, or a country estate. But Margaret Grade, who eight years ago bought Manka's, an old Czech hunting lodge with buildings that date from before the turn of the last century, has created a whole universe based on both a place (the Inverness–West Marin ecosystem) and a time (vaguely in the past). She has transformed this historic eleven-room property into a luxe, wildly sensual landscape intimately tied to its natural surroundings.

There's no sign for Manka's. You have to know that it's located up Argyle, the first left turn west of the village of Inverness off Sir Francis Drake. The lodge is barely distinguishable from the other large old wooden houses built in the trees you pass along the way. But you notice a small parking area off the street, then a wooden sign leaning against the side of a building, and then a deck above a flight of stairs. The check-in desk for both restaurant and inn is at the top of these stairs in a dark Arts and Crafts parlor. (Every time I've been in this room, a human-sized yellow dog has been asleep on the bench in front of the fireplace, the best spot.)

A year ago, Grade grilled in the fireplace in the parlor. Now she has built a serious wood-burning fireplace and three-tier oven in her kitchen, which allows her to cook whole animals, a passion of hers. Tonight's $40 prix fixe menu (the Sunday that I arrived) only offers parts of animals, but is typical of the ingredient-driven cooking that excites her. Dinner guests (you needn't stay at the inn to eat here Thursday through Monday nights) sit in a low-ceilinged second floor room surrounded by windows and trees. A towering mass of wild foliage takes up the center of the room surrounded by sparsely set, white linen–covered tables. The plain white tables serve as canvases for the food, and the first stroke was a sesame-coated *levain*, baked in-house as is everything, and butter from neighboring Straus Family Creamery.

I want you to read the menu as it was written, to set the context for this meal:

a handkerchief of wild axis deer
ribbonned with a duet of wild inverness blackberries and balsamic
with watercress from the point

a soup of local mussels
and a dollop of local dairy whipped dream (sic)
laced with coastal sorrel

the lodge response to the waldorf
bolinas butter lettuce, peter's pink pear apples and radishes

a chop of local lamb tenderloin grilled in the fireplace
served with a mash of mr. little's butterballs
and a concoction of bolinas torpedoes, figs and wild invernesses mint

local raspberries, raspberries and chocolate

The first entry turned out to be a plate painted with the thinnest tissue of red deer meat, drizzled with a fruity, sweet-and-sour syrup, accompanied with a pouf of peppery watercress. With it, Grade served a rich, oaky, grapey roussane from Bolinas winemaker Sean Thackrey, made for Manka's from John Alban's central coast grapes. The roundness of the white wine completed the dish.

After this austere course, the tongue was ready for the voluptuous, creamy but tart mussel soup delicately sweetened with a huge mound of herbed whipped cream. Thackrey's 1998 Pleiades, a soft, fruity, berryish red wine, seemingly was made for it.

And then the meal jumped back to cleanliness with the sharp flavors of the Waldorf, a soft lettuce leaf, shaved radishes, pink apples, and walnuts softened by thinned mayonnaise. 1995 Thackrey's Orion, a spicy syrah whispering of eucalyptus and mint, melded with a rare T-bone lamb chop licked by the wood fire, served with creamy mashed potatoes and a braised red onion and fig sauce. Grade's feeling for game (she hunts) allows her to come up with these fulfilling meat and fruit combinations so appropriate to a former hunting lodge and so suggestive of the natural surroundings.

"Local raspberries, raspberries and chocolate" turned out to be a melting, hot chocolate cookie, resting on top of powerful raspberry ice cream in a martini glass scattered with fresh, sweet-tart raspberries—one of the only chocolate-raspberry matchups I've ever liked.

What defined this meal was the surprising originality, the naïvete of each dish, yet the kitchen has absolute control. Though Grade is one of the very few chefs I know who cooks only with ingredients of local provenance—with foods she may not know she'll have until they appear at her kitchen door—I have never tasted an unfinished or an unthought-through invention. She relishes the challenge of her restricted West Marin larder and her cooking has deepened as she figures out new ways to use the same ingredients. With her enormous integrity and unique vision, the seasonal-local culinary crowd considers her a creative genius, yet she's humble. She knows what she doesn't know.

When you stay in one of Manka's rooms or cabins you feel as if you are living in the trees and eating off the land. You sense a connection with the Miwoks, the original inhabitants of this area, and the early San Franciscans who had to ferry across the bay at the Golden Gate to catch the single-gauge railroad that took them to choice Inverness hunting and fishing spots. The current Manka's belongs to that earlier era. Grade has fashioned it with such intensity, such intuition about what heightens a sense of place, that Manka's has become a pilgrimage for believers in the expression of locality.

RICE TABLE . . . .

1617 Fourth Street (at G Street),
San Rafael
415-456-1808
Open Wednesday through Saturday
5:30 to 10 P.M., Sunday 5 to 9 P.M.
Moderate
Credit cards: AE, MC, V

The Rice Table has been one of my favorite restaurants for years. The founding chef, the late Leonie Hool, personally cooked each of the myriad dishes that make up the lush Indonesian rice table with uncommon love and attention. One rarely gets to taste authentic home-cooked ethnic food, but at the Rice Table customers felt as if they had been invited to Ms. Hool's own dining room. The food had the freshness and integrity of family cooking.

When Leonie Hool died, her son and daughter-in-law took over and they run the restaurant with an inherited passion to prepare and serve genuine Indonesian food. In fact, they had worked with Ms. Hool for years, learning her recipes and assisting her in the kitchen. Recent visits have produced the same full-flavored, carefully prepared dishes that always have been the hallmark of this unique place. When a family believes in a tradition, they can carry it on. Ms. Hool's love of her native cuisine continues to be expressed in the cozy rattan-lined restaurant she started.

The menu is short and simple. There are only eleven dishes on it and you get all of them on the Rice Table Special, a bargain at $19.95 for a feast so large that it arrives in waves. The meal starts with three extraordinary *sambals*, or dipping sauces, with shrimp chips. The vitality of the *sambals* tells you right off that everything, including condiments and curries, will be made from scratch. One *sambal* is a creamy warm peanut sauce spiked with chiles and ginger. The second is a medium-hot, vinegary fresh green chile and onion salsa; the third, a searing-hot red chile paste, completes the hotness spectrum. Then, a bowl of soothing celery-scented dal-like split pea soup arrives. The deluge begins with crisp thumb-sized *lumpia*, or spring rolls; fabulous Indonesian coleslaw dressed with tiny threads of orange zest and fresh mint leaves; and a salad of crunchy bean sprouts with chopped peanuts.

Next come the satays: chicken in a complex teriyakilike sauce and pork in a creamy peanut sauce. Then the stir-fries: shrimp with fruity tamarind seeds, an enchanting dish, and whole button mushrooms stir-fried with hot red chiles, a startlingly good dish. Then braises: a delicious beef stew called *semur* that seduces you with the sweet bouquet of cloves, and a mild chicken curry with the subtle richness of fresh coconut milk. When you think the table can't hold any more, a crab and bean sprout pancake, kind of an Indonesian egg foo yong in a perky sweet-and-sour sauce, is wedged in. Condiments—toasted coconut, pickled vegetables, cold deep-fried potato sticks coated in hot red chile paste—can be scattered on the curries, stews, and two kinds of fragrant rice: yellow saffron and nutty white basmati. The strategy is to mound a big pile of both rices in the middle of your plate and arrange little piles of the different foods around it. Finally, fried thin rice noodles, lushly sauced and studded with bits of pork and vegetables, banish any remaining hunger at the end of the meal. The problem is that the noodles are so tasty you could make a meal of them alone.

Dessert brings creamy deep-fried bananas sprinkled with powdered sugar; you order a second—even after all that food. Cinnamon-scented Indonesian coffee helps you rise from the table.

I feel almost giddy when I encounter a restaurant that is able to keep up its purity, energy, and spirit year after year, especially when the original chef's passion has been passed on from one generation to the next. Like all the Rice Table's longtime customers, I have been nourished, delighted, and embraced by the restaurant to such a degree that its success and well-being feel like my own. As with all great restaurants, the Rice Table's best patrons have become part of an extended family.

ROXANNE'S . . . .

320 Magnolia Avenue (at King),
Larkspur
415-924-5004
www.roxraw.com
Open Tuesday through Sunday
5:30 to 10 P.M.
Expensive
Credit cards: AE, DC, MC, V

The very thought of a restaurant that serves only uncooked vegetables makes most people shudder. The human animal is an omnivore; cooks consider the discovery of fire as a culinary breakthrough. And if you've ever suffered through a bland and unsatisfying vegan meal (the cooking at Millennium, page 109, in San Francisco is an exception) or a living foods meal (as I did at Raw in the Sunset, thankfully now closed), you might never want to try one again.

But I had to go to Roxanne's, the living foods restaurant in Larkspur. I've known chef-owner Roxanne Klein since she was twenty-two and began cooking. Fourteen years later, she and her environmentalist husband, Michael Klein, opened Roxanne's in a converted coffeehouse in downtown Larkspur. It took two years to redo the space to reflect their eco-logical principles. All materials are "green," either recycled or certified sustainably harvested. No chemical sealants or dyes were used in construction. The walls are painted with a lime-based natural pigment. Counters are made from sunflowers pressed into glossy, marblelike, composite board. Chairs are upholstered in organic hemp chenille. Most of the electricity is generated by solar panels on the roof.

You don't realize all this when you walk into the modern, low-lit room on Larkspur's main street. But the space immediately feels welcoming, sleek but comfortable, and not too large. Settled at tables covered with soft white linen (unbleached organic cotton), you are first handed a page of herbal potions and drinks, and a worldly wine list put together by master sommelier Larry Stone of Rubicon (see page 112). Next, you are given the menu. Dishes with recognizable names inhabit the appetizer, salad, soup, and entrée sections. Hooks such as "pizza," "sushi," "noodle soup," "curry," and *"tagine"* give the diner some-thing to hang onto for the ride, but of course these words are only evocative, not literal, descriptions of the food. On the living foods diet, nothing can be heated above 118 degrees Fahrenheit so you can't fall back on grains of any kind—no rice, wheat, bread, pizza crust, pasta—or tofu (which is cooked in processing). All dishes are composed only of organic vegetables, fruits, nuts, seaweed, herbs, and spices. No eggs or dairy are allowed.

So when your wild mushroom pizza with baby arugula and herbed cashew cheese arrives you get something that may suggest a pizza, but actually is made of almond flour dried in the low-temperature convection oven for two hours with spring water and zucchini added for moisture with maybe a little flaxseed thrown in. This is topped with a sauce of sun-dried tomatoes; the "cheese" is fabricated with cashews soaked overnight, juiced and ground, gently fermented, and mixed with fresh thyme, oregano, basil, and garlic. A stra-tum of puréed zucchini and basil is applied for lightness, and of course the "pizza" is capped with tiny leaves of arugula and marinated wild mushrooms.

Here's what's astounding. This multilayered dish tastes magnificently complete and delicious. It has the rich, mouth-feel of pizza; the perfume of fresh herbs and dark mush-rooms; the complexity of aged cheese; the fullness and savoriness of cooked food. Whatever you call it, the construct works. Flavors are melded; textures balanced; the aromas open up in your mouth. It looks luscious and the experience of eating it is thrilling.

Every other dish I've tasted has impressed me in the same way—after I get over the expectation born of menu titles such as *"samosa"* or *"udon* noodle soup." But these dishes have their own unique charm. A yellow curry of finely cubed winter vegetables on creamy whipped parsnips boasts a satiny curry sauce in which the spices are as bright and skillfully blended as the best *masalas* in India. A *tagine* of vegetables over saffron-scented "couscous" knocks you over with its pungency, its accuracy, its authenticity. The Middle Eastern platter of falafel, hummus, dolmas, and "flat bread" captures the spirit of these age-old foods, but makes them brighter.

It took Roxanne five and a half years of experimentation to achieve this level of mastery. She figured out how to build flavor with this limited pantry of pure ingredients, adding layer upon layer like a painter, until she got the effect she wanted. Through a combination of self-invented techniques and a spot-on palate honed by eating and studying food all over the world, she has created a twenty-first-century, completely sustain-able cuisine.

The food truly tastes alive, vibrant, a little mysterious. From appetizers through desserts (Roxanne allows herself one breach of the living foods diet with chocolate, which is roasted, but she also offers a carob alternative), she strives to make refined and delicious what she believes is the healthiest diet on the planet. When you've had three or four courses at Roxanne's, you're pleasantly full. You don't want another bite but you don't feel stuffed, sluggish, or sleepy. The next morning you hop out of bed energized.

High-end, refined, ultravegetarian cooking is a wide-open field, and no one comes close to Roxanne Klein's level of artistry. While living-foods diet advocates such as Roxanne and Michael Klein claim that eating raw leads to a longer, more energetic life and a more sustainable world, Roxanne's proves that it can be satisfying and exciting on a sensual level.

SUSHI RAN . . . .

107 Caledonia Street (between Pine and Turney), Sausalito
415-332-3620
www.sushiran.com
Open Monday through Friday 11:45 A.M. to 2:30 P.M., Monday through Saturday 5:30 to 11 P.M., Sunday 5 to 10:30 P.M.; wine and sake bar open Monday through Saturday 5 to 11 P.M., Sunday until 10:30 P.M.
Moderate
Credit cards: AE, DC, MC, V

A Marin County institution, Sushi Ran has been dispensing impeccable sushi for fifteen years in a sprawling wood-and-glass space off a courtyard in downtown Sausalito. Seats are hard to come by at the long sushi bar and tables are best reserved. One night, without a reservation, we stood at a wooden counter by the front door, agreeably passing the time shelling salted green soybeans and drinking complex cold sake from wooden boxes (called *masu*). A couple of seats finally came free at the sushi bar, but only after we devoured some cleanly deep-fried tofu squares in a gingery soy sauce (*agedashi-tofu*) and a huge, tasty fluorescent green seaweed salad redolent of sesame oil and toasted sesame seeds. Seated, we enjoyed nutty, creamy *uni* (sea urchin roe), mild *unagi* (freshwater eel) broiled and glazed, fresh *kanpachi* (young yellowtail), exquisite Japanese mackerel with silvery skin garnished with a microscopic mince of ginger, unexceptional *hamachi* (yellowtail), and chewy *mirugai* (long neck clam). The highlight of the evening was a live scallop, thinly sliced and served as sashimi with its toothsome mantle cut into curly threads. Both presentation and specimen were glorious.

The ample Sushi Ran sake list includes region of origin, gives an English translation of the sake's name, and offers a brief description of its character. Five sakes are imported by the Sake Service Institute, which means that they are transported and stored under refrigeration. I must say that one of these, Ginyushizuku sake from Tochigi, which translates as "nature's dew," lives up to its name.

BOOK PASSAGE CAFE . . . .

51 Tamal Vista Boulevard
(Market Place Shopping Center),
Corte Madera
415-927-0960
Open Monday through Saturday
10 A.M. to 9:30 P.M.,
Sunday 10:30 A.M. to 9 P.M.
Credit cards: AE, DC, D, MC, V

The bookish *barriste* make suprisingly delicious coffee at this bookstore dedicated to travel and of course, food travel. See page 461 for more information.

EMPORIO RULLI . . . .

464 Magnolia Avenue
(between King and Ward), Larkspur
415-924-7478
www.rulli.com
Open Monday through Friday
7 A.M. to 5:30 P.M., Saturday and
Sunday 8 A.M. to 5:30 P.M.
Credit cards: AE, MC, V

This authentic, elegant Italian pastry shop and café is mentioned in many categories because Emporio Rulli does everything—espresso, pastries, candies, biscotti, gelati, *panini*—so brilliantly.

You can begin with a grilled sandwich filled with prosciutto and mozzarella, all toasty from the Italian sandwich press. Or you can have a cold *panino*, filled with Italian tuna. But save room for dessert and coffee at the marble tables, indoors or out, surrounded by hand-painted murals and beautiful dark-wood paneling. Many informed clerks—efficient, helpful, smiling true professionals—work the counter, pulling out goodies from a sparkling glass case full of luscious cream cakes with names like Brasiliana (a chocolate sponge cake brushed with espresso liqueur, filled with whipped cream, and covered with chocolate shavings) and San Francesco (baked meringue filled with fresh fruit and pastry cream, topped with whipped cream and crumbled toasted meringue). The most elegant possible versions of *sacripantina* and St. Honoré cakes, the staples of North Beach, are made here with all-butter puff pastry, the tenderest sponge cake soaked with fine wines and spirits, and freshly made custard. You can buy these dreamy cream cakes by the slice or whole. Above the cakes is a shelf of tiny cookies, fresh and crisp, like miniature *palmiers* (palm leaf–shaped cookies made of puff pastry glazed with sugar), amaretti, hazelnut balls, and meringues dipped in chocolate. You need to taste Emporio Rulli's version of Italian cookies to appreciate how unique they are, crumbly with breadcrumbs or ground nuts, full of interesting flavors, often dense, but meltingly tender. You can choose a little sampler of them to eat with some of the café's superb coffee, among the best I've had here or in Italy. When you decide which cookies you adore, you can have the clerks pack an exquisite box of them to take home or give as a gift with a pound of Emporio Rulli's house-roasted coffee beans. For ice cream lovers, house-made *sorbetti* and gelati, made with natural essences and fresh fruits, are scooped into tiny cones or glass dishes. Or Rulli's satiny hand-dipped chocolates might tempt you. There's such an embarrassment of riches here you don't know which way to turn. The son of a famous Turin pastry maker founded this *pasticceria*, and why he settled in Larkspur, I can't imagine. The place belongs on a chic alley off Union Square. It's a completely first-class operation offering the world of Italian sweets at the highest level of quality. Marin doesn't deserve Rulli. I want Rulli in the city!

BARS

GUAYMAS . . . .

5 Main Street (at Tiburon
Boulevard), Tiburon
415-435-6300
Open Monday through Thursday
11:30 A.M. to 10 P.M., Friday and
Saturday 11:30 A.M. to 11 P.M.,
Sunday 10:30 A.M. to 10 P.M.
Credit cards: AE, DC, D, MC, V

There are far, far worse hours you can spend than those lounging on the sunny deck of Guaymas, right on the water, drinking fresh-lime margaritas and dunking chips into three appealing house-made salsas. This massive, airy restaurant, done in blond wood, red tile, white adobe, and bright yellow furniture, reminds me of dining rooms in Mexican resorts during high season when everyone is on the American plan: three meals included in the price of a room and everyone eating at the same time. The place roars and the kitchen does its best to keep up. Still, the location of this restaurant can't be beat, and Guaymas's long menu offers lots of tasty tidbits that go with drinks. If you bike over from the city, which isn't all that difficult, believe it or not, you can take the ferry back to Fisherman's Wharf. It loads on a dock right next to Guaymas.

SAM'S . . . .

27 Main Street (near Tiburon
Boulevard), Tiburon
415-435-4527
www.samscafe.com
Open Monday through Thursday
11 A.M. to 10 P.M.,
Friday 11 A.M. to 10:30 P.M.,
Saturday 10 A.M. to 10:30 P.M.,
Sunday 9:30 A.M. to 10 P.M.;
bar open nightly until 2 A.M.
Credit cards: AE, DC, D, MC, V

All the old salts dock their boats at Sam's and climb up the ramp onto the huge outdoor deck with a great view for a cold beer and a hamburger. The food is of absolutely no consequence here, but seats on the deck in this protected corner of the bay are much coveted and feel very good after beating into the wind to get there. After a few bloody Marys, neither the trip nor the food seems so bad. Many reluctant sailors like me consider Sam's to be the high point of a day on the bay.

HAMBURGERS . . . .

737 Bridgeway (at Tracy Way),
Sausalito
415-332-9471
Open daily 11 A.M. to 5 P.M.
Cash only

For those of you taking the ferry ride over to Sausalito from San Francisco, the preferred place to grab a bite is at the nameless hamburger joint with a round charcoal grill in the window and the line out the door. I don't know why or how, but these big, juicy, fire-licked burgers taste better than any others. Get some fries and lots of napkins and eat in the aquatic park across the street. These hamburgers rank with the best food you can find in this charming, if touristy little village. You have to take them to go—there are maybe two unpleasant tables squeezed in the back of the room—but the weather in this protected part of the bay is usually mild.

BAKERIES/PASTRIES

BOVINE BAKERY . . . .

11315 State Route 1 (between 3rd
and 4th streets), Point Reyes Station
415-663-9420
Open Monday through Friday
6:30 A.M. to 5 P.M., Saturday and
Sunday 7 A.M. to 5 P.M.
Cash only

Ocean-pounded West Marin has developed into a culinary destination and the village of Point Reyes Station is the epicenter, a magnet for weekend bikers on Harleys, hikers, tourists, and second-home owners from Inverness. Everyone stops by Bovine Bakery on the main drag of the town for a generously filled bear claw, heavy with almond paste and poppy seeds, and arguably the best bread in the Bay Area. Their thick-crusted, light-textured, wonderously delicious loaves come from Brickmaiden Breads, which operates out of what looks like a wooden Point Reyes house a few blocks away. It's where one of the first commercial wood-fired bread ovens was built by a local artisan. The original bakers moved on to open Tartine in San Francisco (see page 201), where they do not use a wood-fired oven. But some bakers stayed in Point Reyes and they are putting out spectacular bread. I can't stop eating it. The crunchy, fire-licked crust, chewy at first, dissolves in your mouth without a hint of bitterness. I particularly love the crust coated with sesame seeds. The fragrant whole-wheat interior is light but substantial at the same time, delivering enormous, vivacious flavor. Brickmaiden bread has so much character, so much charm, that it becomes a complete meal. You don't want the distraction of cheese or cured meats or even butter. You just want to rip pieces off the warm loaf the minute you buy it—and you better get there early before they run out.

EMPORIO RULLI . . . .

464 Magnolia Avenue (between
King and Ward), Larkspur
415-924-7478
www.rulli.com
Open Monday through Friday
7 A.M. to 5:30 P.M., Saturday and
Sunday 8 A.M. to 5:30 P.M.
Credit cards: AE, MC, V

A fantasy of nut-rich Italian cookies and elegant
cakes will sweep you away. See page 453 for more
information.

ICE CREAM/CHOCOLATES

LYLA'S CHOCOLATES. . . . .

417 Miller Avenue (between
Evergreen and Reed), Mill Valley
415-383-8887
www.lylaschocolates.com
Open Monday through Friday
10 A.M. to 6 P.M.,
Saturday 10:30 A.M. to 5 P.M.
Credit cards: AE, MC, V

Lyla's luscious handmade chocolates fall somewhere
between See's and Godiva, and they earn extra marks
for invention. The peanut butter swirls, rich milk
chocolate with creamy peanut butter mixed in, or
peanut butter frogs with centers of sweetened fresh
peanut butter, make Reese's Peanut Butter Cups pale by
comparison. Lyla takes all sorts of American favorites—
rocky road, honeycombs, caramels—and makes them
with top-notch ingredients in small, rich, beautifully
formed pieces, creating a unique line of elegant chocolates with a homey ethos. The store in
Corte Madera sometimes puts two or three specially made tiny samples on the counter that
will get you hooked. This candy shop is worth a special trip for the quality and interesting
variety of its chocolates.

EMPORIO RULLI . . . .

464 Magnolia Avenue (between
King and Ward), Larkspur
415-924-7478
www.rulli.com
Open Monday through Friday
7 A.M. to 5:30 P.M., Saturday and
Sunday 8 A.M. to 5:30 P.M.
Credit cards: AE, MC, V

This multifaceted Italian café and pastry shop makes
many different seasonal flavors of *sorbetti* and gelati
plus its own line of chocolates. See page 453 for more
information.

GOLDEN POINT PRODUCE . . . .

80 Fourth Street (between B Street
and Route 1), Point Reyes Station
415-298 9619
Open Wednesday through
Sunday 10 A.M. to 6 P.M.
Cash only

This little produce stand in the sheet-metal building
that houses Tomales Bay Foods and the Cowgirl
Creamery sells organic fruits and vegetables, much of
them locally grown and some of them wild, foraged
from berry patches and the nearby coastal forests.
Someone with a backyard tree full of tiny plums or a
stand of heirloom apples trees might bring their harvest
to Denice Beaux of Golden Point to sell. I picked up some intensely flavorful tart-sweet
Gala apples there recently with a soft crunch and unusual, almost floral fragrance from a
small basket of them. "That's all I have," Denice told me. If I had known how good they
were, I would have bought them all. I guess I'll have to wait a year and hope she can score
them again.

Though Golden Point Produce shelves can look meager compared to other produce
sellers, what they do have is so special you don't want to pass it up. Take what they have
and be thankful you got a chance to taste it.

MARIN COUNTY FARMERS' MARKET. . . . . .

Marin Civic Center, San Rafael
Thursdays and Sundays 8 A.M. to
1 P.M. year-round
Cash only

This is one of the most vital farmers' markets in the
Bay Area, much frequented by San Francisco cooks
from the north end of the city until the Ferry Plaza
Farmers' Market on the Embarcadero came along.

Drawing many farmers of both organic and non-
organic produce in different price ranges, the large Marin County market is known for its
out-of-season, locally raised, organic hothouse Wilgenburg tomatoes (people wait in line at
the opening of the market to get them), dates, good medium-priced stone fruits in season,
handicraft stalls, and lots of side events for kids. A strawberry farmer not only sells the fruit,
but a refreshing strawberry-cream sorbet made by his wife; an organic vegetable stand also
sells natural wool, gathered from the sheep on the property. Each skein is a different color,
ranging from white to dark gray-brown; one could imagine a magical garment knitted from
them. The Marin market has the luxury of space, so the stalls are spread out, and the variety and quality is large, concentrated mostly on produce with a little cheese, eggs, and some
expensive, highly smoked salmon thrown into the mix. This is one of the few places where
delectable wood-fired Brickmaiden bread (see Bovine Bakery, page 455) is sold. Look for it.

CHEESE

THE CHEESE SHOP . . . .

38 Miller Avenue (at Sunnyside),
Mill Valley
415-383-7272
Open Tuesday through Saturday
10 A.M. to 6 P.M.
Credit cards: D, MC, V

This tiny, hidden-away shop is worth seeking out if you're a cheese lover. Owner Forrest Young has collected an eclectic group, which he keeps in top condition. A cheese expert, he knows how every cheese is made. He understands seasonality, the influence of locale, and the pleasure of eating cheeses when they are ripe and perfect. His attitude might seem prickly at first encounter, defensive somehow, as if he had had too many run-ins with customers who weren't serious about cheese, but once he sees you're a believer, the tastes are offered and the genealogies of the cheese explained. On one visit I came away with a Spanish Mahón, a nutty, buttery, slightly sharp cow's milk cheese made in the Balearic Islands (Minorca), and a wedge of tangy Saint André in perfect condition, both cut to specification. Young's current favorite is a *dolce latte* Gorgonzola from Galbani, which has huge flavor without tasting strong. Unlike regular Gorgonzola made with soured milk, *dolce latte* is brilliant with pears, elegant in ravioli, and delicate on salads. But of course you can taste for yourself before making the decision to buy.

There's no prewrapping here, which keeps the cheese smelling more like cheese and less like plastic and refrigeration. Much information is forthcoming as each cheese is lovingly set on the counter. Wines, baguettes, and crackers fill up every inch of the wood-lined store all the way up to the ceiling. But cheese is the thing here, and Young's personal selections make the store interesting.

TOMALES BAY FOODS

80 Fourth Street (between B Street
and Route 1), Point Reyes Station
415-663-9335
www.cowgirlcreamery.com
Open Wednesday through Sunday
10 A.M. to 6 P.M.
Credit Cards: MC, V

What an amazing collection of cheeses to find in a village in West Marin! British cheese expert Kate Ardle, formerly of Neal's Yard Dairy, the great cheese shop in London, buys an international selection of artisan cheeses for this stand, including the earthy, complex cheeses of famous Bordeaux *affineur* Jean d'Alos; English farmhouse cheeses from Neal's Yard; some beautiful local cheeses made with organic Straus Guernsey cow milk by Sue Conley, who works next door at the Cowgirl Creamery; plus some amazing new American artisan cheeses that have only recently become available. Put together a picnic of fruit from Golden Point produce; some of these beautiful cheeses, which you can taste before you buy; and a loaf of wood-oven Brickmaiden bread (see Bovine Bakery, page 455) and you will be eating one of the best meals in the world. For more on the cheeses sold here, see Artisan Cheese, page 284.

EMPORIO RULLI . . . .

464 Magnolia Avenue (between
King and Ward), Larkspur
415-924-7478
www.rulli.com
Open Monday through Friday
7 A.M. to 5:30 P.M., Saturday and
Sunday 8 A.M. to 5:30 P.M.
Credit cards: AE, MC, V

Emporio Rulli also roasts and blends coffee beans, so
you can make your own coffee at home to eat with
their cookies. See page 453 for more information.

PEET'S COFFEE & TEA. . . . .

88 Throckmorton Avenue (at
Miller), Mill Valley
415-381-822
www.peetscoffee.com
Open Monday through Thursday
6 A.M. to 7 P.M.,
Friday 6 A.M. to 8 P.M., Saturday
6:30 A.M. to 8 P.M.,
Sunday 6:30 A.M. to 7 P.M.
Credit cards: MC, V

A branch of the Bay Area's most impeccable coffee. See
page 167 for more information.

FISH

HOG ISLAND OYSTER CO. . . . .

20215 Route 1, Marshall
415-663-9218
www.hogislandoyster.com
Open Wednesday through
Sunday 9 A.M. to 5 P.M.
Credit cards: MC, V

Nothing, and I mean nothing, tops the pleasure of eating fresh oysters pulled from the pristine waters of
Tomales Bay while you're sitting on the edge of the
inlet where they are grown. The Hog Island Oyster
Company strategically has placed a few weathered
picnic tables on a rise overlooking the beach, the narrow bay, and the green hills of Point Reyes. The vista is
unsurpassed, especially on clear, sparkly days, and raw oysters have never tasted better.

Hog Island produces four different varieties: their famous Hog Island Sweet Water, a
Pacific genus bedded in a part of the bay that is flushed with fresh water from a western
Marin river; an Atlantic Virginicus oyster that does particularly well in Pacific waters in
the summer; the coppery tasting, flat Belon oyster; and the lush, deep-shelled little
Kumomoto, a sweet Pacific oyster. Depending on the season, you may find one, two, or
all of them.

I like to bring my oyster knife and shuck them myself, but the superfast shuckers in the shed will do it for you. It's best to get there early because the oysters do run out, especially on the weekends. Orders for a hundred oysters or more can be made in advance.

WINES AND SPIRITS

MARIN WINE CELLAR . . . .

2138 Fourth Street (1.5 miles west of Highway 101), San Rafael
415-459-3823
www.marinwinecellar.com
Open Tuesday through Friday
9 A.M. to 1 P.M. or by appointment
Credit cards: AE, MC, V

This large, air-conditioned wine warehouse behind a locked iron gate (you have to buzz to get in) is stacked floor to ceiling with cases of wine. A small desk with many phones and a wooden rack with some of the most amazing bottles you'll ever see are the only islands in the sea of cases. At the back are wine lockers rented by private individuals. There must be millions of dollars worth of wine here, and it's traded mostly over the phone like a commodity. Harvey Buchbinder, the rotund, bearded, sandled partner of this operation calls wine collecting a rich man's sport. However, he says, certain classics are better investments than the stock market.

I asked him if he knew the lineage of some of the blockbuster bottles I saw scattered around—where they came from, how they were cellared and shipped. He shrugged, and it made me wonder about the value of something like a 1918 Mouton Rothschild with an exquisite art deco label. If you open it, what do you have? A dead liquid? A taste memory of the wine in whatever condition it happens to be, a ceremony around opening it, a trophy empty bottle? Displayed on the rack the day I was buzzed in were both 1935 and 1945 Lafites, the 1918 Mouton, and a 1955 Mouton with a beautiful Georges Braque label, a 1954 La Tâche, a bunch of magnums of 1989 Petruswell—you get the idea. I asked Harvey who buys these wines. He told me that 98 percent of his business is done over the phone, all over the world. He has many private buyers in France, Switzerland, London, Mexico, and Hong Kong, and most sales involve single bottles—though he sends cases, like one of 1961 Latour, to celebrities like Barbra Streisand in Las Vegas. Harvey confided that he loves Vegas; high rollers like big wines. He buys through auction and from private individuals and keeps a one-hundred-year backlist for birthdays.

When you visit the Marin Wine Cellar, if only to see millions of dollars of wine bottles piled up on top of one another, get a copy of the catalog, a fascinating document. You can price out a birth-year wine dinner, estimate the value of your own cellar, and actually find some affordable bottles from recent vintages. There's all sorts of fun to be had, but you take your chances. To Harvey, every bottle is a crapshoot. You have to decide how much to lay down.

MILL VALLEY MARKET. . . . .

MARIN COUNTY

12 Corte Madera Avenue (at
Throckmorton), Mill Valley
415-388-3222
Open Monday through Saturday
7 A.M. to 7:30 P.M.,
Sunday 9 A.M. to 7 P.M.
Credit cards: MC, V

An adjunct to the popular Mill Valley Market grocery store, this rustic wood-lined, red-tiled, air-conditioned wine cellar is stacked to the rafters with well-chosen California wines, often from such hard-to-find tiny producers as The Terraces and Sky Vineyard, both noteworthy for their Zinfandels, or Abreu Cabernet from Rick Forman. Top-of-the-line imports from Kermit Lynch and Diamond and Italian wines from Estate are all present and accounted for. This is a Marin County outpost for the Bandols of Domaine Tempier. Finally, the shop has a good selection of high-end spirits, including lots of fancy tequilas and scotches.

COOKWARE AND BOOKS

BOOK PASSAGE . . . .

51 Tamal Vista Boulevard
(Market Place Shopping Center),
Corte Madera
415-927-0960
Open Monday through Saturday
10 A.M. to 9:30 P.M.,
Sunday 10:30 A.M. to 9 P.M.
Credit cards: AE, DC, D, MC, V

Anyone who travels should know about this excellent bookstore specializing in travel books and, hence, international restaurant and food guides. If you're going anywhere in the world, you will want to check out the guides, maps, and travel literature on your destination, if only to get an overview. You'll find hard-to-come-by restaurant guides like *Eating Out in Provence and the Côte d'Azur* by Edward Roch, Gaston Wijnen's *Discovering Paris Bistros*, and Faith Willinger's *Eating in Italy*, which includes restaurants, cafés, outdoor markets, wineries, bakeries, kitchenware shops, and picnic spots throughout northern Italy. You can spend hours browsing the huge travel section, concocting trips and adventures you never even knew you wanted to take. When you tire of this, you can have a first-rate Illy espresso or cappuccino and a nice, light, health-foody Marin County bite at the Book Passages Cafe in one corner of the bookstore near the magazine racks. The café gets special credit for using real plates, glasses, and silverware. Finally, Book Passage publishes a yearly catalog and bimonthly newsletter, sixty-four pages long, with all sorts of information on which guides to buy for different parts of the world. If you're an omnivorous, international eater like me, you will find a trip to Book Passage essential before a trip out of town.

VIKING HOMECHEF . . . .

329 Corte Madera Town Center,
Corte Madera
415-927-3191
Open Monday through Thursday
9:30 A.M. to 9 P.M., Friday and
Saturday 9:30 A.M. to 7 P.M.,
Sunday 11 A.M. to 6 P.M.
Credit cards: AE, MC, V

This branch has the advantage of having a large,
airy shopping mall site so that the merchandise can
be readily seen, examined, and plucked from
attractive displays. See page 288 for more information.

WILLIAMS-SONOMA . . . .

1802 Redwood Highway (in
Nordstrom Shopping Center
on east side of Highway 101),
Corte Madera
415-924-2940
www.williams-sonoma.com
Open Monday through Friday
10 A.M. to 9 P.M.,
Saturday 11 A.M. to 7:30 P.M.,
Sunday until 6 P.M.
Credit cards: AE, MC, V

Another branch of the tony kitchen and tableware
chain started in San Francisco by Chuck Williams.
See page 127 for more information.

WINE
COUNTRY

RESTAURANTS
Auberge du Soleil
Bistro Don Giovanni
Bistro Jeanty
Bistro Ralph
Cafe La Haye
Dry Creek Kitchen
Foothill Cafe
French Laundry
Julia's Kitchen
K & L Restaurant
Manzanita
Martini House
Miramonte
Mustards Grill
Napa Valley Wine Train
Pearl
Piatti
Ravenette/Ravenous
Santi
Terra
Tra Vigne
Wappo Bar Bistro
Willow Wood Market

CAFÉS
Flying Goat Cafe

BARS
Catahoula
Greystone Restaurant
Martin's John and Zeke's

DELICATESSENS/TAKEOUT
Cantinetta at Tra Vigne
Dean & Deluca
Jimtown Store
Oakville Grocery

BAKERIES/PASTRIES
Downtown Bakery and Creamery
Sciambra French Bakery

ICE CREAM/CHOCOLATES
Downtown Bakery and Creamery

MARKETS
Sunshine Foods

ETHNIC MARKETS
La Luna Market
Napa Valley Olive Oil
   Manufacturing Company

PRODUCE
Healdsburg Farmers' Market
Middleton Farm
St. Helena Farmers' Market

MEAT AND POULTRY
Big John's Food Center
Keller's Market
Sonoma Saveurs
Sunshine Foods

CHEESE

The Cheese Shop of Healdsburg

Dean & DeLuca

Oakville Grocery

Vella Cheese Co.

WINES AND SPIRITS

All Seasons Cafe and Wine Store

J. V. Warehouse

Russian River Wine Shop

St. Helena Wine Center

St. Helena Wine Merchants

Tip Top

COOKWARE AND BOOKS

Cornucopia

Dean & DeLuca

The Gardener

Josephine European Tableware

Niebaum-Coppola Winery Store

RESTAURANTS

AUBERGE DU SOLEIL . . . .

180 Rutherford Hill Road (off the
Silverado Trail, at the Rutherford
Crossroad), Rutherford
707-963-1211
www.aubergedusoleil.com
Open Monday through Friday
6 to 9:30 P.M., Saturday and
Sunday, 5:30 to 9:30 P.M.
Expensive
Credit cards: AE, DC , D, MC, V

Until relatively recently, the luxurious Auberge du
Soleil, the wine country hotel in an unsurpassable
location off the Silverado Trail, never had a dining
room that lived up to its posh three-star demeanor.
Now it does. Chef Richard Reddington has transformed the dining experience at the Auberge, and it
has become a culinary destination on the level of the
French Laundry.

Reddington's cooking is complex and original,
classic haute cuisine that uses the magical tool of
French technique to reveal the nature and the taste
possibilities of beautiful ingredients. When you eat his food you're not struck by how
clever it is. Rather, you're swept away by the food itself—by its lusciousness, its sensuality,
its surprise.

Here's an example from a meal I had in summer, sitting outdoors at a pale yellow
linen–covered table on a warm Napa Valley night. Sautéed nuggets of veal sweetbreads,
beautifully crisp outside, voluptuously creamy in, were teamed with an equal portion of
whole tender braised radishes, radish-sized baby turnips, pearl onions, and leaves of tart,
wilted sorrel. The chef knitted together this now seemingly inevitable combination of ingredients with a coffee-colored molasses butter. Each bite delighted with the play of textures;
the conjunction of chthonic flavors in innards and roots, the successful transposition of
port, which traditionally accompanies sweetbreads in the French lexicon, to molasses; the
use of sorrel as a brightening agent. The size of the dish was perfect. There was just the
right number of bites—enough to fully appreciate, but not so many as to sate the appetite.
I'm deconstructing this dish now, but while I was eating it I didn't have to. It was immediately scrumptious.

Dish after dish like this came out of the Reddington kitchen that night, one more
delectable than the next. Three different cold preparations of foie gras—a mousse, a *torchon*
encrusted with pistachios, a terrine with spiced cherries—were arranged on a white rectangular plate with warm brioche, each delicately resonant of its fruit or nut accompaniment.
Blood-rare slices of squab breast interwoven with a compote of Santa Rosa plums infused
with ginger and cinnamon and a syrah reduction with the fragrance of tea came with a foie
gras–brioche toast just to clean up any remaining juices.

Yes, we got a foam course—a crisp-skinned fillet of wild sea bass and tiny deep-fried
oysters immersed in a froth of corn studded with red and white corn kernels—but it didn't
taste like a gimmick. You felt as if you were eating an intense seafood chowder, without the
cream but with all the flavor.

Young Reddington, in his thirties, may be the most unsung cooking talent in the Bay
Area. A completely inexperienced Reddington walked into La Folie and asked Roland
Passot if he could just follow him around for one day to see what it was like to be a chef.
Passot agreed and Reddington fell in love with the kitchen. He convinced Passot to take
him on as an apprentice for two months, and his mentor was so impressed with his progress

that he actually hired him. Thus started a ten-year culinary pilgrimage that found him cooking in New York, France (where he cooked in a trio of three-star kitchens, including Arpège in Paris when it ascended from two to three stars), Los Angeles, and back to San Francisco to help open Jardinière.

At this point, what he really wanted was to open his own restaurant: sleek, smallish, very high end with lots of quiet service and restrained, classical French food to pair with classy wines. The grapevine has it that he tried hard to get the Fifth Floor job, but the Kimpton group hired the more experienced Laurent Gras.

All I can say is that the situation at Auberge du Soleil must be working for him because I have never tasted a meal made with more conviction, more passion, more precision, more joy. This was a meal from a happy chef. When I cornered him in the kitchen, ecstatic about the meal I'd just had, Reddington told me that he had been given carte blanche at Auberge and that he'd inherited a staff of forty whom he retrained. The Auberge du Soleil may not be the small swank club he wanted, but he has made it his own.

BISTRO DON GIOVANNI . . . .

4110 St. Helena Highway
(Highway 29, between Oak Knoll
and Salvador), Napa
707-224-3300
www.bistrodongiovanni.com
Open Sunday through Thursday
11:30 A.M. to 10 P.M., Friday and
Saturday 11:30 A.M. to 11 P.M.
Moderate
Credit cards: AE, D, MC, V

In a modern, barnlike space with tall windows that look out to a sea of vines and distant mountains, two expatriates from Piatti (see page 480), Donna and Giovanni Scala, are cooking up a storm. Their winsome Italian fare includes thin-crusted, wood-fired pizzas, fabulous deep-fried matchsticks of zucchini with Parmigiano grated over them, and an antipasto of broccoli rabe sautéed with lots of garlic and Tuscan olive oil and draped with thin slices of fresh mozzarella. The pastas, such as thin, tender ravioli filled with ricotta in a delicate cream sauce flecked with lemon zest; or rustic handmade *pappardelle* in a juicy stew of braised rabbit, sage, and pancetta, are the high point of the menu. Focaccia sandwiches filled with grilled vegetables, slathered with lots of aioli, and served with warm lattice potato chips are dreamy. Summery appetizers of large marinated shrimp grilled in the shell and served with a warm corn salad make for an appealing alfresco lunch on the broad wooden porch that rims the restaurant. Eating lunch outside near the herb garden is one of the pleasures of visiting the Napa Valley.

BISTRO JEANTY . . . .

6510 Washington Street (at
Mulberry Street), Yountville
707-944-0103
www.bistrojeanty.com
Open daily 11:30 A.M.
with a last seating at 10:30 P.M.
Moderate
Credit cards: AE, MC, V

I like everything about Bistro Jeanty: its modest size, traditional but breezy decor, decidedly moderate cost, continuous hours, small, manageable menu, and versatile wine list. (For a version in San Francisco, see Jeanty at Jack's, page 105.) It's a mature, fully realized restaurant from a French chef who had plenty of time to work out what he would do in his own place while heading a more formal kitchen across the highway at Domaine Chandon for eighteen years.

Philippe Jeanty has natural bistro instincts. All the details of his bistro are perfect, starting with his mouthwatering list of appetizers. No one else serves *pieds de cochon* in the Bay Area, and Bistro Jeanty's are so delicious I think about driving up to Yountville just to eat them. How can anyone get that excited over pig's feet? Wait until you taste these cold, jellied, slightly pickled cubes of shredded pork morsels drizzled with mustardy, capery dressing on a bed of baby green beans. Only the French can make them like this and few chefs even bother. A lamb's tongue and potato salad in a creamy dressing comes from the same school of charcuterie: buttery, rich, tender meat served cold. Jeanty's duck rillettes, a ramekin of shredded duck cooked in its own fat, served with toasts and a pile of bracing tiny pickles and onions, is another treat for us fat aficionados.

The real fat celebration comes in the form of silken rabbit terrine, a huge moist slab with a buttery layer of liver pâté in the middle just to gild the lily. (At Jeanty I like my lilies gilded.) The salad of julienned celery root and apple on the side is a refreshing accompaniment. If for some odd reason you prefer a lighter starter, you have nothing to worry about. A pretty little platter of raw, shredded vegetable salads—cucumber, celery root and apple, and carrot—is cleanly dressed with some sweet baby beets. Thick, meaty hunks of smoked trout had an assertively smoky flavor, quite delicious with sliced new potatoes and mustardy dressing. An individual soup tureen, covered with a golden cap of puff pastry, has a lovely cream of fresh tomato soup underneath.

Though the starters tend to be voluptuous, somehow the proportion allows you appetite for the equally substantial and skillfully made main courses. Coq au vin comes in a deep earthenware crock, very handsome, which holds melting chicken in delicious salty, bacony red wine cooking juices—unthickened and unreduced, just the way I like it. Cassoulet is also served in earthenware, a flavor exchange of smoky white beans, fresh fennel sausage, pork, and duck leg. The vibrant house-made sausage is the star of the dish. *Daube de boeuf,* velvety beef simmered in red wine, is served in a deep bowl over mashed potatoes with fresh peas and baby carrots thrown on at the last minute. But so far, my favorite main course of all on the changing menu is *ragoût de lapin*, a bowl of corkscrew pasta, white beans and tiny new potatoes, tender loin of rabbit and nuggets of sweetbreads, all perfumed with white truffle oil. It's ravishing.

As can be expected, the wine list is disproportionately large compared to the menu, a deep and stylish survey of California and French bottles with a whole section of half bottles. The list offers opportunities to taste French and California wines of the same varietal in a similar price range, an interesting exercise. You won't get much advice from the waitstaff and the wines by the glass are unimaginative, but the dining rooms are filled with wine people who presumably know what they're looking for anyway. I am not as tempted by the desserts as I am by the other courses here. I have liked a thick rice pudding that is mostly cream topped with strawberries and purée, and loved a hot crepe Suzette slathered with orange butter served unfolded on an oversized cake plate.

Though not a big, fancy experience, I consider Bistro Jeanty the ideal wine country destination. It feels like it belongs here. Because the bistro stays open all day, you can spend a whole afternoon lingering at the table, an increasingly rare pleasure, and not have to sleepily drive back to the city after dinner. How lucky to have this welcoming orange cottage with shuttered windows and cozy dining rooms, hung with cooking implements and bakers' racks of baguettes, so readily available! Bistro Jeanty is as French as you can get, either here or in France. It reminds me how good French restaurants can be.

109 Plaza Street (between
Healdsburg Avenue and
Matheson), Healdsburg
707-433-1380
Open Monday through Friday
11:30 A.M. to 2:30 P.M.
and nightly 5:30 to 10 P.M.
Moderate
Credit cards: MC, V

Ralph Tingle, the chef-owner of this stunning-looking restaurant, happens to be the son of Alta Tingle, the creative genius behind The Gardener (see pages 441 and 498), who in turn happens to be a very good friend of conceptual artist David Ireland. (Ireland's seminal work was the stripping back of layers of paint and wallpaper in his turn-of-the-century Mission District house, treating the wadded-up peelings as art objects, then fixing the raw interior in varnish, making it look like a resonant, old Italian villa. Then he took the idea a step further by using the stripped-away materials to make utilitarian objects like lamps.) Tingle enlisted Ireland's energy in designing her son's restaurant, and the result of their collaboration is one of the most compelling restaurant spaces in all of Northern California. Ireland's deconstructive inventiveness combined with Alta Tingle's intuitive understanding of materials created a room of surprising simplicity and beauty with completely unexpected forms, like a long, undulating wood-and-metal wine rack behind the counter and an entrance of raw concrete and steel. I like to be in this room at night when everything takes on a romantic Italian villa glow, although it looks nothing like one.

The cooking can be a bit uneven and quirky, but the whole-leaf Caesar is tasty and pretty, the spicy lamb burger, made with local C. K. Lamb and Downtown Bakery (see page 487) buns, is just plain delicious, and Ralph's sautéed chicken livers with onions in intense balsamic reduction has become a Healdsburg classic. Bistro Ralph is a destination, if only to experience the restaurant dining room as a work of art.

CAFE LA HAYE . . . .

140 E. Napa Street (between
1st and 2nd streets), Sonoma
707-935-5994
www.cafelahaye.com
Open Tuesday through Saturday
5:30 to 9 P.M.; Sunday brunch
9:30 A.M. to 2 P.M.
Moderate
Credit cards: MC, V

As far as I'm concerned, there are two reasons to stop in the town of Sonoma—Ig Vella's cheese factory (see page 494) and this small, cheerful restaurant–art gallery a block off the main plaza. Cafe La Haye serves colorful plates of local food that bear the world-beat signature of one of the restaurant's well-traveled chef-owners. His partner runs the dining room with professional attention to detail—perfect espresso, a provocative revolving art collection on the walls, a gem of a local wine list—and small town graciousness.

One summer evening, three of us ate our way through the menu, starting with bracing Hog Island oysters and a fabulous presentation of house-smoked salmon arranged in piles on a black, rectangular plate with crispy potato-carrot pancakes and crème fraîche in the middle. It cools off at night in Sonoma, so a corn chowder swirled with chipotle cream is not out of the question. In late summer I like to order the sweet heirloom tomato salad of slices and wedges in all colors simply seasoned with shaved Manchego (a dry, buttery Spanish cheese), aged *balsamico*, and excellent extra virgin olive oil. Each night the kitchen comes up with a few specials of international parentage. If juicy marinated pork kabobs with Middle Eastern–style marinated red onions, bulgur pilaf, olives, feta, and yogurt and cucumber salad happen to be available, order them. It's a fresh, luscious plate of food. You will always find the signature golden-crusted chicken breast with herbed Laura Chenel goat cheese stuffed under the skin, accompanied with tender chard and buttery mashed potatoes. For dessert have the deeply chocolate but not overly rich *pots-de-crème* and one of those stellar espressos. The tiny open kitchen has room for only two cooks, and the small interesting menu is composed so that it can be executed perfectly. The two-level dining room with big front windows and red-tile floors in a historic Sonoma building only has about a dozen tables, so it's best to reserve ahead if your heart is set on dinner here.

DRY CREEK KITCHEN . . . .

317 Healdsburg Avenue (at Matheson), Healdsburg
707-431-0330
www.drycreekkitchen.com
Open daily noon to 2:30 P.M. and 5 to 10 P.M.
Expensive
Credit cards: AE, MC, V,

The opening of the fancy Healdsburg Hotel from New York restaurateur Charlie Palmer delivered the final blow of gentrification to once sleepy Healdsburg. The new hotel and spa right on the main plaza of town boasts a polished restaurant, the Dry Creek Kitchen, which serves exciting, highly composed wine country dishes to pair with the greatest collection of Sonoma wines I've ever encountered. Chef Mark Purdy, an accomplished Aureole veteran, weaves local ingredients into stunning creations, like a pile of baby arugula and pickled cherries hiding a big, rich dollop of soft duck rillettes, the plate elaborated with a drizzle of port reduction, roasted red onions, and crispy deep-fried ribbons of fennel. All of these foods sang together. Purdy's rethought steak tartare—a hand-cut mince of beef seasoned with tons of shallots and chervil, molded on the plate next to a pool of sticky sweet balsamic syrup and a salad of miniscule french beans split lengthwise—is a cool and wonderful summer bite. Luxury rules at the Dry Creek Kitchen. Sand dabs, succulent little local Pacific flatfish, come boned and slathered with toasted cashews and frilly hen-of-the-woods mushrooms. A thick piece of snowy Alaskan halibut melts into a ragout of buttery corn and baby squashes with blossoms. The wine list forces you to lose your head and drink expensive Russian River pinot noirs—they're aromatic and delicious but very pricey here.

The large vaulted dining room that looks onto the plaza has a bit of a corporate feel, as if it could be anywhere. On warm days and nights the place to sit is outdoors on the sidewalk patio where you still get a sense of the small town place that Healdsburg used to be, and still is midweek.

FOOTHILL CAFE . . . .

2766 Old Sonoma Road
(at Foothill Road in the J&P
Shopping Center), Napa
707-252-6178
Open Wednesday through Sunday
4:30 to 9:30 P.M.
Inexpensive
Credit cards: AE, MC, V

Each year 4.7 million tourists visit the Napa Valley and I'll bet none of them eat at the Foothill Cafe, a beloved local institution that serves big, luscious plates of food. Located in a funky mini–shopping center in a residential neighborhood, the Foothill Cafe may be the valley's best-kept secret. When I was calling around to fact check the tourism statistic, everyone I spoke to admonished me not to write about the Foothill Cafe. "It's our place," they said. "It serves the best food in the valley and we want to get in."

I don't blame them. Chef-owner Jerry Shafer puts out huge plates of smoky meats roasted in his oak-wood oven, colorful salads and soups, crispy deep-fried appetizers, and dreamy homemade desserts. Ever since he left Masa's eleven years ago, where he worked with Julian Serrano—and before that with the legendary Udo Nechutnys at the old Miramonte in St. Helena—this hometown Napa boy has focused on pleasing an appreciative local clientele. He learned from Serrano about the importance of always being present in the kitchen. He's only open five nights a week, a sustainable personal schedule. And he doesn't cook fancy food, French food, or even stylish food, but Napa Valley–California food, which features lots of fresh vegetables and a gently eclectic international pantry of ingredients. There might be some Mexican, Asian, or Italian themes in the dishes, but the overall character of his cooking is California-American.

The decor of the Foothill Cafe's dining room matches the food—warm, colorful, endearingly retro. The golden yellow sponged walls, white linen, flower-and-vegetable print china, wrought-iron wall hangings, framed mirrors, cactus-filled flower box outside the front window, and ceiling fans successfully transform what was formerly a barbecue joint. Customers feel comfortable the moment they walk in. The dining room staff may seem casual and low key, but they know every detail of the menu and the mostly local wine list. Their enthusiasm adds considerably to the pleasure of eating there.

We started with bowls of bright green, creamy spinach soup and a tall pile of oven-roasted mussels with clarified garlic butter as a dipping sauce. Every mussel was perfect. We ate crispy fried rock shrimp like popcorn, swiping them with spicy ancho chile aioli and fork-dueling over the juicy jicama, avocado, mango, and papaya slaw underneath. Hearts of romaine with dabs of mayonnaisey blue cheese dressing and candied walnuts was the major concession to the salad eater in our midst.

And then the monumental main courses arrived. I've never seen my significant other so delighted as when he worked his way through a thick slab of oak-roasted Angus prime rib with potato-Stilton gratin and a bouquet of spring vegetables. The beef was delicately smoky and buttery, like none I've ever tasted. Slow-smoked baby back ribs, tender and very meaty, almost melted into creamy mashed potatoes and the signature cornucopia of vegetables. Even more fabulous were juicy charcoal-grilled loin lamb chops served with classic béarnaise, potato purée, and a garland of crisp-tender artichoke hearts, snow peas, cauliflower, carrots, and green beans. The lighter eater was hard put to share even a bite of his Peking duck breast, grilled to a perfect medium-rare, complemented by a sweet-and-sour dried cherry sauce.

The wine list, like the menu, delivers good value, so it's a joy to choose. The 2000 White Oak Napa Sauvignon Blanc and the 1999 Pagor California Tempranillo, made from a red Spanish grape cultivated in California, were both rewarding at a very affordable price. If you are willing to spend more on a red wine these days, look to pinot noirs from the Russian River. This appellation now rivals Oregon and Carneros for complex, slightly bigger, but still feminine wines with distinctive pinot noir character. A 1998 Russian River Valley pinot noir from Olivet Lane proved to be just that, a lot of wine for the money. After such generous starters and main courses, we ordered desserts just to taste and ended up eating them all, especially a fresh strawberry shortcake with poufs of whipped cream scented with orange liqueur, layers of flaky biscuit, and tons of sweet berries. Heaven.

The Foothill Cafe may not have the cachet of up-valley operations, but I challenge anyone to find a better place for a deeply satisfying dinner in the Napa Valley. With the revitalization of the city of Napa, more of those five million or so tourists will be starting their visit at the southernmost end of the valley. But they'll never find the Foothill Cafe unless some beneficent local tells them. I wonder if the good people of Napa will keep their favorite place a secret.

FRENCH LAUNDRY . . . .

6640 Washington Street
(at Creek), Yountville
707-944-2380
Open nightly 5:30 to 9:30 P.M.;
lunch served Friday, Saturday, and
Sunday 11 A.M. to 1 P.M.
Expensive
Credit cards: AE, CB, MC, V

Thomas Keller, who has received enormous international attention for his lapidary meals of tiny, witty dishes, has turned the Napa Valley town of Yountville into his backyard. It may take months to get a reservation at the French Laundry, but diners can console themselves with a visit to his smart bistro nearby, Bouchon, or buy bread and pastries from his bakery, which should be open by the time you read this.

Many a pilgrimage to the Napa Valley centers around a visit to the French Laundry and rightly so. Keller's poetic style, based on tiny portions of dishes inspired by both local and offbeat ingredients in pristine condition, adds up to an epic experience. The dishes seem to have become even smaller and more numerous on the French Laundry's prix fixe meals, which take about four hours to be served. When you reserve you get a table for the evening, and Keller makes use of every minute of it. He starts sending out food, little bites that precede the five courses you've so carefully chosen. An oversized French tablespoon cradled in a linen napkin becomes the serving vessel for a tiny poached quail egg napped in beurre blanc and fragrant fresh herbs, one ethereal slurp. A martini glass filled with clear tomato water appears with one grilled shrimp hooked onto its side. As you move into the meal you've actually selected, from a menu that offers four or more choices in each category plus a complete five-course vegetarian meal, the serving size hardly gets bigger than a few bites. A cold stew of tiny artichokes, a slice of monkfish in a verbena-scented tomato *coulis*, a round of veal breast layered with root vegetables, a potato-chip sandwich filled with peppery Brie next to a pile of miniature lettuces, and a warm individual chocolate cake that oozed in the middle made up my meal one night. You end up being entertained all evening by a parade of stylish dishes, amazingly unrepetitious when you consider how many ingredients are involved, without feeling stuffed. Keller has mastered the tasting menu by reducing it to edible scale. It's ingeniously put together like a jigsaw puzzle, so that no matter what you order, it adds up to a sweeping, seamless canvas.

The setting is as much a part of the experience as the cooking. When Keller bought the historic Yountville building from its former owners, he decided to keep its name and its identity as a prix fixe, evening-long destination restaurant. Though diners are no longer encouraged to stroll midmeal in the pretty garden, the current experience of eating there still resonates from the first, more countrified French Laundry. The two-story stone building, like a French country house, has tables in two serene dining rooms, upstairs and down, with windows that look out to vines and greenery. At lunch and earlier in the evening before the chill sets in, you can eat outside on a beautifully manicured lawn enclosed by trees and flowers where you can run your bare feet in the grass while you nibble on the elegant morsels.

The windowed kitchen, open to view both from the downstairs dining room and the garden, is an intrinsic part of the restaurant. You don't feel a separation between the kitchen and the dining room here, because Keller so consciously molds your experience. A meal at the French Laundry is as much performance art as a culinary experience. From the wooden clothespin with the French Laundry logo holding your napkin at the beginning, to the check printed on a laundry list at the end, the culinary puns, twists, and thrills never stop. Though the check does add up, you feel that you haven't been taken to the cleaners.

JULIA'S KITCHEN . . . .

500 First Street
(inside Copia), Napa
707-265 5700
www.copia.org
Open Wednesday through Monday
11:30 A.M. to 3 P.M., Thursday
through Sunday 5:30 to 9 P.M.
Moderate
Credit cards: AE, MC, V

While touring Copia (see page 474), I naturally worked up an appetite, so we walked downstairs for lunch at Julia's Kitchen. Good thing we'd reserved several days in advance, because every seat in the relatively small, modern dining room, dominated by a huge open kitchen, was full. The concrete floors and high ceilings were softened by huge window-doors on one side that look out to the olive grove and garden. White tablecloths also dampened noise and added comfort.

The food is unabashedly and surprisingly French. Somehow I expected something more informal, more ingredient driven, more vegetable-y. Portions are small and artfully presented. Flavors are big. Every effort is made to use herbs, vegetables, and fruits from the surrounding gardens, as well as other local ingredients, but in small proportions. Though the cooks have a cornucopia of beautiful foods to choose from, technique and composition set the tone.

A "farmers' market" salad of tiny lettuces, shaved fennel, and radishes came dressed in a mild vinaigrette made from tart grape juice instead of vinegar so it would not conflict with wine. A small slab of seared foie gras was sublimely set off by a purée of dates, a miniscule dice of quince, and a syrupy Madeira reduction. A hot crab consommé didn't work because the natural sweetness of the crab was defeated by a strong broth. A pretty frisée, beet, and warm goat cheese salad shone in a dressing aromatic with fresh walnut oil.

The star main course paired seared scallops with pancetta, yellowfoot chanterelles, creamy potato purée, and a frothy port wine reduction. It wasn't as rich as it sounds and the flavors melted together poetically. I also liked a browned medallion of monkfish in a mild, mustard seed–thickened vinaigrette. For dessert I easily had room for an airy Meyer lemon soufflé cake with a meringue top and tart huckleberry compote.

I liked my glass of fruity, grassy, full-bodied Provenance cabernet from the Napa Valley, which I chose from a long list of wines by the glass. The extensive list is divided by varietal, chardonnay and French white Burgundies in one category; cabernets and meritages bundled together, and so forth. For those who have the resources to do some serious wine exploration, I can think of no finer museum restaurant in the world, and I am sure that the smallish dining room will become a destination restaurant in the Napa Valley, especially given its glamorous location.

COPIA, THE AMERICAN CENTER FOR WINE, FOOD & THE ARTS

Nailing down the concept behind Copia, The American Center for Wine, Food & the Arts in Napa, an institution passionately wrought by Robert and Margrit Biever Mondavi, has not been easy for anyone, including the people who created it. This museum, exhibition hall, botanical garden, theater, restaurant, and teaching facility, which rose like the phoenix from the floodplain of the Napa River in 2001, offers something for everyone who sets foot in the Napa Valley. The Napa Valley draws as many tourists as Disneyland, and Copia plans on attracting a large proportion of them, as well as locals who come for the day and the swelling ranks of those who work in the wine industry.

Winemaker Mondavi long has played a vocal role as a wine advocate, believing that education will convince Americans of the health benefits and sensual pleasures of drinking wine. He wants more and more of us to regard wine as Europeans do, as part of our daily lives. Self-serving for an industry giant? Of course, but he believes in a society that regularly sits down together at the table, cooks meals, celebrates food, and, yes, drinks wine. Most Americans don't seem to have the time.

Copia is a work in progress. What makes this instant institution worth talking about is its scale, its ambitions, and the phenomenal amount of private and corporate money poured into it. Anyone who is anyone in West Coast wine and food wanted to be part of the party and put up substantial sums to ensure a place at the A table.

Copia's white marble and glass Polshek-designed building rises elegantly against a backdrop of green rolling hills. An undulating roofline mirrors the landscape. A long, riverlike fountain runs through expanses of organic exhibition gardens. Mature olive trees shade an eating patio in the front. Patrons enter the building and emerge into a tall atrium with a floor-to-ceiling glass wall that looks out to a sloping green lawn and the Napa River.

On our way in we were intercepted by a docent who handed us a schedule of the day's activities: several orientation tours; a thirty-minute tasting of and lecture on molasses; a sixty-minute garden tour of Copia's three and a half acres of edible landscape; a forty-five-minute art tour; a thirty-minute workshop on wine etiquette; a twenty-dollar, hour-long workshop called "Deconstructing Dessert: Beignets"—to learn how to make and taste them with New Orleans–style chicory coffee. That night at 8 P.M. a multicultural percussion group called the Rhythmix was holding forth.

After listening to a minute of the orientation tour, we realized that we could easily negotiate Copia ourselves. We began upstairs at a small collection of ancient food-related artifacts starring a translucent, breathtakingly thin, alabaster Egyptian feast bowl, dated 4000 B.C. Having established that humankind set a festive table from earliest times, Copia leaps into the present with state-of-the-art interactive exhibits. One had us guessing the origins of common foods—watermelons, potatoes, coffee, pineapples, almonds. Another taught us to read food labels; another chronicled the rise of fast food. One exhibit built around a huge wine bottle demonstrated that wine is an "all-American food." You could enter a booth to videotape a food memory and to listen to those of others. A small movie theater with benches played a loop of food clips exploring our food obsessions. In the Opinion Corner, visitors are asked to fill out response cards to issues such as the politics of hunger, "frankenfood," and the beneficial effects of alcohol.

Clever exhibits track the origins of culinary icons—Wonder Bread, sugar, fast-food packets of ketchup and mustard, toasters—or celebrate the diversity and the inclusiveness of our melting-pot American culture. One in ten Americans is foreign born, we learn, and American cooking incorporates a world of ingredients into its pantry. In the Thanksgiving room, for example, we hear how Americans of Japanese, Latin American, Greek, and Inuit descent stuff their turkeys. If Copia has any cultural clout, the next wave of American diners will be pouring wine in their igloos and at luaus on the beach.

The fine arts galleries take up the rest of the second floor, and the architectural space allotted for them feels empty and lifeless. The opening show of commissioned, food-themed art called Active Ingredients seemed forced, a little too obvious, and not as engaging as the peppy interactive displays. The most successful of the art installations is a series of evocative black-and-white photographs by different photographers curated around the theme of lunch.

But is there any reason to return? Absolutely. The fact is that Copia, with all its far-flung intentions, offers a full day of entertainment loosely unified by the theme of food—production, preparation, consumption, and representation. It's Los Angeles's Museum of Jurassic Technology—a celebration of the weird and wacky; a museum of science and industry; and an art museum all rolled into one. With its sleek restaurant, a well-curated gift shop, and a café that sells artisan foods, Copia embodies the luxurious wine country lifestyle statement. But it doggedly maintains its democratic outreach. In order to serve a potential consumer base of Disneyland proportions, it has created a core of sophisticated theme park–like attractions and self-consciously celebrates culinary cultural diversity. Once everyone—attendees and program directors alike—figures out what works, Copia's mission no doubt will deepen. At its best, Copia could become a think tank for food issues—food and history, food and the economy, food and health, food and science. At its most fun, Copia is a grand monument to the pleasures of food and wine. For more information, consult www.copia.org.

K & L RESTAURANT . . . .

119 South Main Street (just south of Highway 101), Sebastapol
707-823- 6614
Open Tuesday through Saturday
11:30 A.M. to 3 P.M. and 5 P.M. to 10 P.M., Sunday 5 to 9 P.M.
Moderate
Credit cards: MC, V

I personally experienced a strong wave of déjà vu as I ate at K & L Bistro, which is owned by two former chefs at Hayes Street Grill (see page 53), now married and resettled in a Sonoma county town surrounded by small farms. Lucas Martin makes great use of all the beautiful vegetables and fruits, grown practically next door, in straight-ahead, full-flavored dishes. His wife–pantry chef regularly goes to the Marin Farmers' Market for a wider range of ingredients. The other day she brought back fresh Mission figs for a quintessential summer salad of figs, ripe Sharlyn melon, and prosciutto, topped with a pouf of watercress in a mint-scented vinaigrette. Of course I ordered my seasonal favorite, a big plate of local tomatoes with fresh mozzarella, good olive oil, and grilled bread.

Martin has a way with braised meats, and his Atkins Ranch lamb shank served in a bowl with chickpeas, feta, roasted peppers, and wilted greens, all moistened with eloquent natural juices, is worth a drive from the city. A Hereford rib-eye steak perfectly grilled over mesquite and slathered with crisply sautéed button mushrooms is another treat, especially with a big pile of dressed arugula and perfect french fries.

The small red brick room is furnished with banquettes and tables in crisp white linen and butcher paper, with a minibar at the front and the open kitchen at the back. Oil paintings from San Francisco artist Leslie Andelin decorate the walls and also happen to be on sale. Very much a hands-on operation with Martin always there, the kitchen can get backed up, but otherwise the service is rather sophisticated. The waiters really know the wines, reasonably priced imports and an interesting range of local bottles, as well as every dish on the menu. Though a course may come out slowly, your patience will be rewarded by some absolutely delicious, real food.

MANZANITA . . . .

336 Healdsburg Avenue
(at North), Healdsburg
707-433-8111
Open Wednesday through
Sunday 5:30 to 10 P.M.
Moderate
Credit cards: MC, V

When edgy, modern Manzanita opened last year just off the main plaza in Healdsburg, locals thought that it represented the end of their small-town world. Then the massive, upscale Dry Creek Kitchen in the Healdsburg Hotel came along, which made Manzanita feel like the homegrown, personally run operation that it is. Now everyone embraces Manzanita.

This interesting space, with its hard surfaces, high wooden barnlike ceiling, a counter made of stacked manzanita logs, and a centerpiece manzanita-burning brick oven, provides a fitting backdrop for cutting-edge country-style food. This description may sound like an oxymoron, but chef Bruce Frieseke, with consultation from San Francisco's Loretta Keller of Bizou (see page 346), gathers his ingredients from the backyard and prepares them with a sophisticated global sensibility.

To start you get a basket of warm, yeasty house-baked bread. What could be better? A fabulous beet salad with a carpaccio of pickled beets, wedges of Chioggia beets, baby mustard greens, and pickled sweet carrots—a root vegetable fantasia resonating with the aroma of their earthy sister, the white truffle.

A thin, crackery pizza crust, aromatic from the wood-burning oven, is slathered with Santa Rosa plums, prosciutto, and naturally truffly Italian fontina. Crispy battered and deep-fried green beans taste lovely accompanied with an anisey mayonnaise. The kitchen makes tender Yukon Gold potato gnocchi with chanterelles and shavings of pecorino, and one of the best steak preparations ever with rich red-wine sauce, a thick marrowbone, a cloud of deep-fried sweet potato strings, and rosemary-scented white beans. Desserts like a soft, pillowy lemon-blueberry trifle or a dreamy nectarine cobbler warmed in the manzanita-wood oven, topped with vanilla ice cream, are worth saving room for. While the local wine list may not be as extensive as the tome down the street at the Dry Creek Kitchen, it offers offbeat choices such as chilled Scherer rosé that can really hit the spot on a warm night.

Manzanita strikes the right tone. It's exciting in both design and menu, yet casual and easy to enjoy. The small dining room is just what you're looking for in a country restaurant, while the lush, modern cooking would please anyone, anywhere. When it comes down to a Healdsburg destination, Manzanita is my choice.

MARTINI HOUSE . . . .

1245 Spring Street
(at Oak), St. Helena
707-963-2233
www.martinihouse.com
Open daily 11:30 A.M. to 3 P.M.,
afternoon menu in bar 3 to 5 P.M.,
dinner 5:30 to 10 P.M.
Expensive
Credit Cards: AE, DC, D, MC, V

The open kitchen, once a porch in this 1920s Craftsman-style bungalow, looks too small for the wildly popular Martini House, converted into a restaurant by the indefatigable Pat Kuleto. The chef, Todd Humphries, who created his own signature cuisine in the ample quarters of the Greystone Restaurant in the CIA up-valley, and at Campton Place before that, has a tough challenge in getting the Martini House kitchen to execute his complex menu consistently. Inspired by hyperlocal and unusual ingredients, many of them foraged from the wild or grown especially for him, his plates depend on precise technique, juxtaposition, infusion, and sensual high design. Flavors are delicately woven together and every dish takes an unexpected turn. Humphries likes butter-poached lobster; seared, rare foie gras; salads of fruits and bitter greens; thick juicy hunks of pork with rich potatoes and a garden of tender baby vegetables.

Though I've had some disappointing dishes at this new restaurant, I have faith in Humphries's ultimate ability to control the kitchen.

I love his cooking and am certainly looking forward to eating at Martini House on a weeknight in the dead of winter when the crush of tourists and seasonal residents has let up. I'll sneak into the clubby downstairs bar where the locals hang out for a martini or a glass of wine from the extensive list. Afterward I'll claim my reserved seat upstairs, next to a fireplace, in what looks like an Adirondacks hunting lodge decorated by Native American craftsmen. Undoubtedly I will discover new ingredients in Humphries's stunning preparations and bask in the luxury of a romantic Napa Valley bungalow.

MIRAMONTE . . . .

1327 Railroad Avenue
(near Hunt), St. Helena
707-963-1200
Open Sunday through Thursday
11:30 A.M. to 9 P.M., Friday and
Saturday until 10 P.M.
Moderate
Credit Cards: AE, DC, D, MC, V

No one knows how to write a better menu than Cindy Pawlcyn, the brains behind Fog City Diner and Mustard's Grill (see opposite), among many others, and now the new Miramonte in St. Helena. She bought and smartly refurbished the building that once housed Udo Nechutny's Miramonte, Napa Valley's first sophisticated French restaurant. The Pawlcyn Miramonte is more roadhouse than temple of haute cuisine, half bar and half restaurant with a small outdoor eating area in a brick courtyard shaded by an old fig tree. Her chef is Oaxacan Pablo Jacinto and the menu explores the foods of the Americas, Latin and North, filtered through Pawlcyn's iconoclastic, fun-loving culinary voice. She's always been an artist, actually a ceramicist, with an instinct for arousing people's attention and appetites—always on a gut level. When she moved to California three decades ago, she foresaw that the state would become Asian and Latino, and the menus at her restaurants are energized by these diverse pantries. In her hands, all traditional ingredients, whether they be American, Brazilian, Mexican, or Korean, become unique Cindy Pawlcyn dishes, all the more delicious for having been filtered through her sensibility.

At lunch the other day in Miramonte's barroom, we ate our way through a huge artichoke, charred on the grill, the smokiness from the fire adding delectable dimension. Mild red *chiles rellenos* stuffed with braised beef, in a creamy, charred tomato sauce have become a Miramonte signature dish. Another favorite here, Pablo's Pollo Loco, a half chicken flattened and charcoal grilled, served with a big dollop of avocado salsa, a juicy sweet corn stew, and a roasted stuffed green Anaheim chile, has become a destination dish.

Juicy top-shelf margaritas made with fresh lime, and wines from all over the Americas—Argentina, Chile, Mexico, Oregon, and California—go beautifully with the spicy food. House-made fresh fruit sorbets will cool you down after a foray into chile land. For casual lunch or dinner in the valley, you can't do better than Miramonte. It's still a bit undiscovered, which means that you'll be able to inform your friends about it. You'll want to. Miramonte is that kind of place.

MUSTARDS GRILL . . . .

7399 St. Helena Highway
(1 mile north of Yountville
on Highway 29), Napa
707-944-2424
www.mustardsgrill.com
Open Monday through Thursday
11:30 A.M. to 9:30 P.M.,
Friday 11:30 A.M. to 10 P.M.,
Saturday 11 A.M. to 10 P.M.,
Sunday 11 A.M. to 9:30 P.M.
Moderate
Credit cards: AE, DC, D, MC, V

In some ways this first large-scale restaurant to open in the Napa Valley remains its most successful. Mustards is universally loved by local residents and tourists alike for its smoky, tender, spicy baby-back ribs; cornmeal-coated fried green tomatoes; tasty Asian-marinated flank steak; Chinese chicken and noodle salad; and of course, Mustards always-crisp tangle of deep-fried onion threads. The enduring vitality of this place perhaps comes from the fact that this was chef Cindy Pawlcyn's first endeavor and she put all of the dishes she loved on the menu: country dishes transformed by her sprightly offbeat style and sparkle.

Surrounded by a parking lot, the restaurant feels like the quintessential roadhouse with an airy, porchlike dining room and constantly busy bar. The very mention of Mustards in the valley conjures up fun. It's the place that launched the other Real Restaurants (Fog City Diner, et al.) and in some ways will always be the guiding light.

NAPA VALLEY WINE TRAIN . . . .

1275 McKinstry Street
(between 1st Street and Soscol),
Napa
707-253-2111
www.winetrain.com
Departs daily
Expensive
Credit cards: AE, DC, D, MC, V

Disdain may rain down on me from a certain group of zenophobic valley residents for touting the much-opposed wine train, but the slow-rolling, luxuriously appointed dining cars on this resurrected railway line offer lovely views of the valley and pretty decent food during its two-hour journey into the wine country. Winemakers are often in attendance, giving tastes and informal seminars on wine making, while the train staff coddles passengers from the moment they board. Meals begin informally in the wood-paneled club car with tasty appetizers, and continue in the romantic dining car with straightforward preparations of salmon, chicken, or red meat. Remember, the food is not the main motivation for a tour, but a context for taking the train through a unique stretch of countryside. You can use your visiting relatives as an excuse to take the ride.

PEARL . . . .

1339 Pearl Street (between Franklin and Polk), Napa
707-224-9161
www.therestaurantpearl.com
Open Tuesday through Saturday
11:30 A.M. to 2 P.M.,
Tuesday through Thursday
5:30 to 9 P.M., Friday and
Saturday 5:30 to 9:30 P.M.
Inexpensive
Credit cards: MC, V

Owners Nickie and Peter Zeller of the Brown Street Grill moved their operation over to Pearl Street and continue to prepare homey, fresh, inexpensive fare. Sit on the sidewalk patio shaded by an awning for softshell crab BLTs with a pile of crispy roasted new potatoes, or Pearl's signature grilled mozzarella, tomato, and basil sandwich with a deliciously dressed green salad, or their beloved, generous scallion–corn cakes with smoked salmon and lemon-dill sour cream. Pearl knows how to put out food with optimum flavor— the vinaigrettes are bright, the roast chicken and mashed potatoes just what you'd hope for, and the desserts are inspired by ripe, local fruit. This is where Napa residents eat.

PIATTI . . . .

6480 Washington Street
(at Oak Circle), Yountville
707-944-2070
www.paitti.com
Open daily 11:30 A.M. to 10 P.M.
Moderate
Credit cards: AE, MC, V, DC

You can always find a good dish on the exuberant menu of this Italian chain, which started here in Yountville. It inhabits an airy wooden building with two outdoor patios and an open kitchen boasting a wood-fired rotisserie and a pizza oven. The menu concentrates on pizzas and pastas, some interesting appetizers, and chicken and rabbit cooked on the rotisserie. Though the pasta dishes have their ups and downs, look for the little ear-shaped *orecchiette* tossed with cabbage, pancetta, and fontina, and the satiny, house-made ravioli. Not every dish gets the attention it needs, but a clever orderer can eat well. Ask your waiter for suggestions.

RAVENETTE/RAVENOUS. . . . .

117 North Street (for lunch; one
block north of the main square),
Healdsburg
707-431-1770

420 Center Street (for dinner),
Healdsburg
707-431-1302

Open Wednesday through Sunday
11:30 A.M. to 2:30 P.M., Wednesday
through Sunday 5 to 9 P.M.
Inexpensive
Credit Cards: MC, V

For homey, satisfying, buoyant cooking inspired by
seasonal organic ingredients, the locals head to
Ravenette, a small, always-crowded café actually inside
the Raven movie theater. People order from a small
menu of daily specials written on a blackboard.
Everything I've tried here sparkles, from grilled quail to
chile verde over rice, pretty salads to house-made
desserts. All prices are amazingly reasonable, including
those for local wines. If you can't get into Ravenette,
members of the family have opened a full-scale restaurant around the block called Ravenous—actually,
Ravenette used to be called Ravenous—which offers a
larger menu of more elaborate dishes prepared in the
same spirit. Somehow my heart will always be with
the little original place where the cooking seems so
spontaneous and authentic.

SANTI . . . .

21047 Geyserville Avenue (at
Highway 128), Geyserville
707-857-1790
www.tavernasanti.com
Open Tuesday through Saturday
11:30 A.M. to 2 P.M., Tuesday
through Sunday 5:30 to 9 P.M.
Moderate
Credit cards: AE, MC , V

The two chef-owners of this Geyserville roadhouse
produce some amazingly soulful Italian dishes in what
used to be a sleepy wine country town. Who would
expect to find a bowl of deep, rich Roman-style tripe,
falling-off-the-bone oxtails with polenta, winsome
chicken liver *crostini*, or grilled sardines in the middle
of nowhere? Somehow Taverna Santi, with its cool, airy,
tiled dining room, romantically lit at night, and reasonably priced California and Italian wine list, has taken
hold in this out-of-the-way location. Though some less

than perfectly conceived dishes may emerge from the kitchen, there is real conviction
behind the oddball dishes that adventurous Italian eaters love. Your waiter can steer you
right to them and a map can steer you to the Geyserville exit on the freeway. Santi makes
the twenty-minute drive from Healdsburg well worth the journey.

TERRA . . . .

1345 Railroad Avenue (between
Adams and Hunt), St. Helena
707-963-8931
www.terrarestaurant.com
Open Wednesday through Monday
6 to 9 P.M., Friday and Saturday
6 to 10 P.M.
Expensive
Credit cards: CB, DC, MC, V

Terra, a fifteen-year-old restaurant, is located in an historic stone building (the registered Duckworth Foundry
building, built in 1884) trimmed with flower boxes
overgrown with edible herbs and blossoms. To my
mind, it epitomizes a perfect wine country restaurant—
impeccably appointed but still casual, with two uncluttered stone-walled dining rooms, terra-cotta tile floors,
massive rough beams across the ceiling, and low
romantic lighting.

The chef-owners, Hiro Sone and Lissa Doumani, met in the kitchen of Spago in Los Angeles. Hiro grew up on a rice farm three hundred miles north of Tokyo. He developed a passion for cooking as a child, attended a famous French cooking school in Japan, and ended up opening Spago in Tokyo for Wolfgang Puck. His cooking benefits from his flawless technique in French, Italian, and Japanese cooking, which allows his menu to deliver multicultural surprises. He likes to work with underused ingredients like tripe, sweetbreads, fish roe, and eel among others, and he prepares them so well that he has converted many a squeamish diner. His al dente spaghetti with tripe, white beans, and tomatoes has become a favorite for me as well. He also cooks luscious beef fillet and osso buco, and some of the loveliest fish dishes I've ever encountered. His sake-glazed Alaskan black cod in a *shiso*-scented broth afloat with gossamer shrimp dumplings comes to mind. You'll find velvety terrine of foie gras and a fantastic rustic *sopa de ajo*, a garlic soup thickened with toasted bread, a poached egg in the center waiting to be swirled into the peppery red broth. Tiny fried oysters served in their shell, sweetbreads in a ragout of chanterelles, prosciutto, and white truffle oil, and rosy-fleshed roast squab served with pumpkin ravioli with shaved white truffles in season have delighted his diners over the years.

Lissa does the witty desserts (a tiramisu served in a deep pottery bowl, cannoli filled with orange-scented risotto), and also runs the dining room and manages the extensive, politically sensitive wine list. Every local winemaker is represented and they all come in to order their own wine with the delicious food. I really love Terra. I feel close to the vineyards here, in tune with the seasons, and always astonished by something I haven't tasted before on the menu.

TRA VIGNE. . . . .

1050 Charter Oak Avenue (at Highway 29), St. Helena
707-963-4444
Open daily 11:30 A.M. to 10 P.M.
Moderate
Credit cards: D, DC, MC, V

The tree-shaded courtyard and canopied terrace of this little piece of the Italian countryside in the Napa Valley transform the eating experience here. You can't stay grumpy in this marvelous setting, even if the service is sometimes amateurish or the smell of old garlic over takes the olive oil set out to moisten crusty country bread. Although the stunning tiled floors have now been covered with utilitarian carpeting, and the marvelous faux stone walls have been softened with huge Milanese *aperitivo* posters from the 1930s, the lofty, indoor dining room still represents classic 1980s Limn design; minimal but opulent in use of luxurious materials.

The kitchen has always been maddeningly inconsistent, coming up with some real treats from an enticing menu, but disappointments as well. Crunchy, perfectly fried calamari in an Arborio rice flour batter were delicious one day, if you could fish them out of a pool of sweet mustard sauce; but some delicate Hobbs's prosciutto paired with strong pecorino and fresh cherries one early summer day didn't really taste all that good together. At that same summer lunch, a wonderful bowl of tiny, tender spinach-and-ricotta-filled ravioli in a rich, buttery cheese sauce shone, while some overcooked curly strands of pasta suffered in a reduced rabbit and mushroom sauce with soapy-tasting pieces of rabbit. The most recent dinner I had there, one winter evening when the dining room wasn't so frantic, turned out to be the best of all, interesting Italian dishes executed without mistakes. Well-chosen wines by the glass, like a lush California sangiovese, and some of the best restaurant espresso I've tasted only make you wonder why the food sometimes misses the mark. In the ever more crowded St. Helena corridor, Tra Vigne remains a haven for its lyrical setting.

WAPPO BAR BISTRO . . . .

1226B Washington Street (at
Lincoln Avenue), Calistoga
707-942-4712
www.wappobar.com
Open Wednesday through Monday
11:30 A.M. to 2:30 P.M. and
6 to 9:30 P.M.
Moderate
Credit cards: AE, MC, V

The local secret in Calistoga is this small, stylish, home-grown café with a wonderful outdoor seating area in a brick courtyard shaded by trees and overgrown trellises. During lunch one hot day we stayed cool by ordering a leafy version of Greek salad flanked by tomatoes and tossed with sheep milk feta, olives, and pine nuts, and a tasty Asian noodle salad topped with grilled chicken. A Mexican plate brought *masa* cakes topped with black beans, strips of sirloin, *queso fresco*, guacamole, and fresh salsa. For dessert we had lovely pecan shortcake with fresh peaches and cream.

Indoors, the small copper bar offers a long list of beers and generally inexpensive, well-chosen local, Italian, and French wines. Also fun and refreshing are fresh fruit *licuados* (delicious mango and nectarine), mango *lassi*, citrus spritzers, and Javanese iced coffee.

A second dining room in a cottage on the other side of the brick patio has been annexed and handsomely decorated with handmade copper lamps and Provençal print tablecloths. The dinner menu has also expanded, taking diners to even more corners of the culinary world with Middle Eastern *fattoush* salad with heirloom tomatoes, traditional Milanese-style osso bucco with saffron risotto, and Brazilian chocolate torte layered with coconut-almond filling one night. Culinary common sense in the kitchen and integrity about ingredients assure that whatever international creation emerges will be brightly seasoned, well balanced, and tasty. In Calistoga, Wappo is my restaurant of choice.

WILLOW WOOD MARKET . . . .

9020 Graton Road (between
Eddison and Ross streets), Graton
707-823-0233
Open Monday through Thursday
8 A.M. to 9 P.M., Friday and
Saturday 8 A.M. to 9:30 P.M.,
Sunday 9 A.M. to 3 P.M.
Inexpensive
Credit cards: MC, V

I actually thought I discovered Willow Wood when I was driving on the scenic back roads of western Sonoma. I walked into a charming old general store and noticed that people were eating at gaily painted tables amid the shelves of olive oil, local preserves, and breakfast cereals. So I sat right down and ate a luscious, homey, country-style dinner prepared in an open kitchen that looked like a checkout counter. I had a beautiful salad with fresh figs and blue cheese expertly dressed with olive oil and balsamic; an amazingly vibrant slab of swordfish with mashed potatoes, braised greens, and a fennel-caper vinaigrette; and a bowl of creamy polenta with freshly grated Parmigiano and pesto.

Open for breakfast, lunch, and dinner, with lunch and dinner menus pretty much the same, you can always opt for juicy sandwiches that come with a Willow Wood salad, or a bowl of that good polenta with roasted vegetable ragout. When I exclaimed to the surprisingly professional waiter how lucky I was to have discovered Willow Wood, she dryly informed me that it had been open for eight years. Now I'm going to figure out how to find the tiny village of Graton again.

CAFÉS

FLYING GOAT COFFEE ROASTING CAFE . . .

324 Center Street (north of Plaza Street), Healdsburg
707-433-9081
www.flyinggoatcoffee.com
Open Monday through Friday
7 A.M. to 6 P.M., Saturday and Sunday 8 A.M. to 6 P.M.
Cash only

For a first-rate latte or cappuccino, and freshly baked breakfast pastries, head for the Flying Goat, a handsome, airy café right on the main square. The house-roasted coffee has depth of flavor without bitterness. The *barriste* judiciously pour in properly steamed milk to create a proper balance. Newspapers, including the *New York Times*, are scattered around the attentively wiped, generously spaced tables. Ceiling fans keep the air moving. Any town would be happy to have a coffeehouse like the Flying Goat, and the locals show their appreciation by supporting it.

BARS

CATAHOULA . . . .

1457 Lincoln Avenue (in the Mount View Hotel between Fair Way and Washington), Calistoga
707-942-2275
www.catahoularest.com
Open Monday through Thursday
5 to 10 P.M.,
Friday and Saturday until 11 P.M.
Credit cards: D, MC, V

A lively scene happens in Jan Birmbaum's Catahoula saloon on one side of the lobby of the Mount View Hotel almost every evening. (The stylish restaurant dining room is on the other side of the lobby.) Mud bath–relaxed diners order from a menu of small plates: wood-fired oven pizzas, crawfish tamales, fried green tomatoes with shrimp *rémoulade*, duck confit salad, richly topped flat breads, and the signature brick-oven roasted chicken with a divine, crusty, herbed potato cake. The informality here allows for a wide taste of real down-home food that this New Orleans–born chef loves to cook. You can sit at the bar or at counters, quaff artisan beers, or explore local wines by the glass.

2555 Main Street (Highway 29 just
north of St. Helena), St. Helena
707-967-1010
www.ciachef.edu
Open Sunday through Thursday
11:15 A.M. to 9 P.M., Friday and
Saturday until 10 P.M.
Credit cards: AE, DC, MC, V

This glamorous tapas bar and restaurant, with outdoor tables that overlook the Napa Valley, is really part of a highly regarded continuing education facility for food and wine professionals run by the Culinary Institute of America in Hyde Park, New York. The cooking school took over the majestic old stone Christian Brothers Winery and installed state-of-the-art kitchens and a dining room appointed with Christofle silverware, Villeroy & Boch china, and Reidel wineglasses. Yet the feeling, thank goodness, is very much wine country casual.

My favorite way to visit Greystone, and I do practically every time I stay in the valley, is to sit at the tapas bar where I get the best view of the expansive open kitchen. There I sample chilled local rosé wines with dishes of marinated olives, freshly baked breads, and current chef Pilar Sanchez's "temptations," a series of five little bites each presented on its own miniature plate. The lineup might include a tiny square of country pâté dabbed with a curry mayonnaise; a bite of raw marinated tuna wrapped in a *shiso* leaf; a bite of minted melon wrapped in prosciutto; a hot corn fritter with ancho chile sauce; and a thin slice of skewered, grilled pork with red chile–spiked mustard. My long-suffering dining companion (husband) orders a top-shelf margarita and always comments that it's perfectly made with lots of fresh lime. The efficient bartenders guide me to special glasses and couldn't be more welcoming.

MARTIN'S JOHN AND ZEKE'S . . . .

111 Plaza Street (between
Healdsburg Avenue and
Matheson), Healdsburg
707-433-3735
Open daily 10 A.M. to 2 A.M.
Credit cards: AE, MC, V

Oversized sports' televisions, two good pool tables, hot cashews and pistachios, big microwaved hot dogs with all the fixings, an excellent selection of local wines, a good liquor selection featuring high-end tequilas, tasty margaritas, keno, well-made drinks, friendly people on both sides of the bar, and it's clean and well kept. What more can I say?

DELICATESSENS/TAKEOUT

CANTINETTA AT TRA VIGNE . . . .

1050 Charter Oak Avenue (at
Highway 29), St. Helena
707-963-8888
Open daily 11:30 A.M. to 5 P.M.,
wine bar 11 A.M. to 7 P.M.
Credit cards: DC, D, MC, V

One of the most pleasant places to have a bite in the Napa Valley is under a shade tree in the courtyard of Tra Vigne. A glass of wine and a slice of pizza from the Cantinetta, a freestanding adjunct of the restaurant, can hit the spot on a warm Napa Valley afternoon. This delicatessen–wine bar sells prepared food, breads, and wine by the bottle and glass either to have outdoors here at the wrought-iron café tables under the plane trees, or to take home. The handsome breads from Pan-O-Rama bakery based in Petaluma, an in-house operation that supplies all the bread needs of Real Restaurants, can be paired with spicy, dry Calabrese sausage, delicious small oil-cured black olives, cold roast poussin, and a green salad for a first-rate picnic. The long wine bar buzzes with activity as visitors to the Napa Valley taste the most interesting local wines. The Real Restaurants people seem to know instinctively what makes a food operation exciting. In the case of the Cantinetta, they cater to every visitor's desire to eat food that goes with wine outdoors in a beautiful setting, without paying restaurant prices for it. Once again, they've struck gold.

DEAN & DELUCA. . . . .

607 South St. Helena Highway
(at Inglewood), St. Helena
707-967-9980
www.deansdelucca.com
Open daily 9 A.M. to 7 P.M.,
espresso bar 7:30 A.M.
Credit cards: AE, D, MC, V

Anyone who has visited the mother ship in Manhattan knows that Dean & DeLuca is the ultimate upscale food emporium with ridiculously extravagant imports, an extensive cheese department, a sexy prepared food and charcuterie counter, and shelves of baked goods. At the St. Helena branch, all of the above is present, plus a pretty produce section with lots of organic fruits and vegetables from local farms, and a wine shop loaded with local bottles. I have to watch myself in the seductive housewares section or I just might end up with one more egg-poaching doodad. I didn't think that the Napa Valley could possibly support a high-end store with such a wide range of highly perishable items, but I was wrong. Frequented by high-living locals, seasonal residents who entertain, and the flood of tourists that have now made the Napa Valley one of the most popular destinations in the world, Dean & DeLuca thrives. I challenge anyone to walk through the store and not end up buying something—fancy chocolate bars, a piece of rare cheese, a quarter pound of *serrano* ham, some baby lettuces from a nearby garden, a grilled vegetable salad, two crystal wineglasses, or a state-of-the-art corkscrew. If you've read about a brand new product in a food magazine, Dean & DeLuca will have it. Better pick it up because you may not find it again.

JIMTOWN STORE . . . .

6706 State Highway 128
(near the conjunction of Alexander
Valley Road and Highway 128),
Healdsburg
707-433-1212
www.jimtown.com
Open Monday through Friday
7 A.M. to 5 P.M., Saturday and
Sunday 7:30 to 5 P.M.
Credit cards: D, MC, V

You will find sandwiches, breakfast pastries, salads, box lunches, toys, antiques, oilcloth, and dime-store notions in this resonant old wooden building on a beautiful, undertraveled road that links the Sonoma and Napa valleys. The owner of the store, Carrie Brown, and her late husband, John Werner, former Silver Palate veterans from New York, fell in love with the dilapidated piece of real estate as they were driving through the Anderson Valley. They bought it and transformed it into the Jimtown Store, which prides itself on stocking the most eclectic and quirky inventory of merchandise you could ever imagine. Vineyard workers and antique collectors regularly shop at Jimtown for candy, Mexican sodas, tamales, chic-distressed farmhouse cupboards, and terra-cotta planters. Jimtown olive spreads and condiments have become so popular that you can find them packaged and distributed to other stores, or you can make them yourself by buying a copy of *The Jimtown Store Cookbook*. Even if this stretch of 128 weren't so beautiful, a visit to the Jimtown Store is well worth a detour.

OAKVILLE GROCERY . . . .

7856 St. Helena Highway (at
Oakville Crossroad), Oakville
707-944-8802
www.oakvillgrocery.com and
www.oakvillewine.com
Open daily 9 A.M. to 6 P.M.,
espresso bar 7 A.M.
Credit cards: AE, MC, V

Early on, the Oakville Grocery knew that the Napa Valley couldn't live without prosciutto from Parma, six kinds of imported olives, cheeses from all over the world, Italian salami and cured meats, Passini baguettes, and a worldwide selection of mustards, jams, pastas, vinegars, and olive oils. To go with these choice food-stuffs, the Oakville wine buyer (one of the partners is Joe Phelps, from Phelps winery) put together a distinguished group of Napa Valley and imported wines. Add a sprinkling of local and organic produce, particularly fruits, and you have one of the most important food resources in the area. Yes, you could find many of these things at stores and delicatessens in San Francisco—and indeed, up-valley at Dean & DeLuca—but the charming wood-frame building, with plank floors and old-fashioned corner store refrigerators at the Oakville crossroad, gives everything a fresh, appealing context. The store is so well-managed, the food so nicely displayed, the inventory of tempting things so creative, that the Oakville Grocery has become a destination in its own right. When you rent a house in the valley, Oakville becomes a regular stop for essentials—the *New York Times*, coffee beans, Clover dairy products, and fresh baguettes. Once you are there, how can you pass up a piece of super-aged Parmigiano-Reggiano or a pint of that luscious-looking potato salad? Prices are astronomical, but the quality of everything is high. The cheeses are well cared for, the cured meats expertly sliced. Sometimes the produce looks sparse and a little tired, but greengrocer is not Oakville's identity. It supplied high-end foods to the wine country when no one else was doing it. Relatively small yet packed with temptations, I stop here for picnic supplies rather than at bigger stores. I like Oakville's scale.

BAKERIES/PASTRIES

DOWNTOWN BAKERY AND CREAMERY . . . .

308A Center Street (between
Matheson and Plaza), Healdsburg
707-431-2719
www.downtownbakery.net
Open weekdays 6 A.M. to 5:30 P.M.,
Saturday 7 A.M. to 5:30 P.M.,
Sunday 7 A.M. to 4 P.M.
Cash only

Kathleen Stewart continues to turn out the desserts of the late Chez Panisse pastry chef and cookbook writer Lindsey Shere, plus a whole repertory of her own, at this quintessential country bakery, a bakery everyone wishes they had next door. Every morning a seeming army of workers in the open kitchen turns out baskets of warm sticky buns and buttery almond-encrusted sweet rolls, hefty baguettes, and flavorful country breads. The fresh-fruit *galettes* are dreamy: buttery dark-brown crusts folded over fillings of fresh plums, nectarines, and wild blackberries or rhubarb. They come in a variety of sizes; I eat a small one, still warm from the oven, for breakfast on a bench on the street. The fresh fruit tiramisu layered with berries and peaches has become a birthday classic. Dense, crumbly tea cakes are elegantly glazed with white icing and decorated with tiny tea roses. You can't go wrong with any of the beautiful-looking, simply decorated confections in the case. The main problem is deciding which to pick—and that goes for freshly baked cookies and biscotti and a few choice muffins like the sugar-topped doughnut muffin. Several days a week the famous Como bread is baked, a rectangular loaf with the most delectable crumb and yeasty flavor, divine toasted and slathered with the bakery's jam. From the creamery department comes a seasonal selection of intensely flavored fruit sorbets and ice creams, which are scooped from a small ice cream freezer between the bakery cases. An espresso machine is constantly at work. In addition to being a pastry chef, Kathleen is notorious for the six hundred rose bushes in her backyard. She brings in huge bouquets of the most exquisite antique varieties to decorate the bakery.

SCIAMBRA FRENCH BAKERY . . . .

685 South Freeway Drive
(off Imola), Napa
707-252-3072
Open Monday through Saturday
7 A.M. to 5 P.M.,
Sunday until 2 P.M.
Cash only

I don't necessarily recommend that you visit this retail outlet store in Napa, but I highly recommend the bread, first baked by the Passini family in 1909. In 1972, Sciambra bought the operation and the baguettes are still fantastic, chewy, sweet (or sour if you prefer), full of character, and denser than most. I discovered Passini baguettes at the Oakville Grocery, but they're distributed all over the Napa Valley, Sacramento, Palo Alto, and Vallejo. You can call the bakery to find out where the nearest retail outlet might be. When I visit the valley, I look forward to making a picnic around them with some olives, cheese, and a bottle of local red wine. The bread makes the meal.

ICE CREAM/CHOCOLATES

DOWNTOWN BAKERY AND CREAMERY . . . .

308A Center Street (between
Matheson and Plaza), Healdsburg
707-431-2719
www.downtownbakery.net
Open weekdays 6 A.M. to 5:30 P.M.,
Saturday 7 A.M. to 5:30 P.M.,
Sunday 7 A.M. to 4 P.M.
Cash only

This exemplary bakery also makes its own ice creams and sorbets inspired by locally grown wild fruits. You can buy them by the cup, cone, or pint. See page 487 for more information.

SUNSHINE FOODS . . . .

1115 Main Street
(at Spring), St. Helena
707-963-7070
Open daily 7:30 A.M. to 9 P.M.
Credit cards: AE, D, MC, V

Poised between Safeway and Dean & DeLuca, Sunshine has a strong cheese department, an excellent wine section, a big deli counter with imported prosciutto, and aisles of cereal and laundry soap. See page 493 for more information.

ETHNIC MARKETS

LA LUNA MARKET . . . .

1153 Rutherford Road (just east
of Highway 29), Rutherford
707-963-3211
Open Monday through Saturday
8 A.M. to 8 P.M.,
Sunday 8 A.M. to 7 P.M.
Credit cards: AE, D, MC, V

Many essential Mexican culinary and cultural needs are supplied at this general store: tortillas, tomatillos, thinly sliced beef for *carne asada* at the butcher counter, white confirmation dresses, high, black patent leather boots with pointy heels, piñatas, and videos in Spanish. Vineyard workers order their lunches of tacos and burritos in the morning and stop by at noon to pick them up, hot and ready to go. The house-made tamales,

warm from the steamer in their corn husks, filled with spicy pork, taste mighty good with either cold beer or a bottle of soft Napa Valley red wine.

NAPA VALLEY OLIVE OIL
MANUFACTURING COMPANY . . . .

835 Charter Oak Street
(at Alison Street), St. Helena
707-963-4173
Open daily 8 A.M. to 5 P.M.
Cash only

This ancient store hidden away in a residential section of St. Helena actually used to house an olive oil press. The old hydraulic equipment and cement floor with tracks for the hoppers of olives are now almost concealed by piles of excellent Molinari salami, bottles in all sizes of delicious California extra virgin olive oil

at everyday prices, big hunks of imported fontina and Parmigiano, which are cut to order, sacks of dried beans, shelves of canned Italian tuna packed in olive oil (you'll never go back to Chicken of the Sea once you taste it), tins of salt-cured anchovies, and stacks of dried Italian pasta. The Recco olive oil sold here is now pressed in Orland, California, but for my money, it's the most versatile and affordable high-quality olive oil made in the United States. The Italian owners–store clerks think so too, as do thousands of customers who have left their business cards taped to the walls. The olive oil factory, as it's locally called, is well worth searching out in the back streets of St. Helena.

PRODUCE

HEALDSBURG FARMERS' MARKET . . . .

Just west of the main plaza,
Healdsburg
Saturday 9 A.M. to noon,
Tuesday 4 to 6 P.M.
(on some Tuesday evenings
the market is on the plaza)
Cash only

This is one of the sweetest little farmers' markets in
Northern California, rife with beautiful, young, mostly
organic produce from a scattering of nearby farms.
Before the ring of the opening bell, people line up in
front of their chosen booth to grab the few baskets of
fraises des bois or the limited supply of gold raspberries.
Even if you miss the rarities, you'll find lovely things
like Howard's Miracles, a large, juicy yellow-fleshed

plum with a skin that makes it look like a nectarine, or old-fashioned fragrant strawberries,
both from Middleton Farm, which charges an arm and a leg for them, but they are worth
it. At the Greenman stand next door, you can find equally wonderful Blue Lake beans,
exquisite lettuces, dewy watercress, and chard. Everything is very local—nothing much
exotic or trucked in by farmers from outlying areas—but there's a certain charm to this. You
eat what comes ripe and wait for it all year. You know that fragile apricots, vine-ripened
tomatoes, and strawberries can't travel, making them all the more valued. If you're planning
to visit the wine-growing areas around Healdsburg from May through December, try to
take in this farmers' market, even if only to taste, and make a stop at the Downtown Bakery
and Creamery (see page 487) for bread and pastries.

MIDDLETON FARM . . . .

2651 Westside Road (at Felta),
Healdsburg
707-433-4755
Open daily 7:30 A.M. to 4:30 P.M.,
Sunday 3:30 P.M. to 5 P.M.
Cash only

Ring the brass bell behind the weathered barn to get
one of the gardeners to weigh your produce. This
dreamy-looking organic garden and farm, overgrown
with flowers and herbs, is a mecca for the highest-
quality produce from April through October. You
might find sweet red torpedo onions; garlic braids;
asparagus; tomatoes; squashes; root vegetables; peaches;

sugary, fragrant, tiny, strawberries; raspberries; plums; pears; melons; figs; walnuts; and fresh
eggs, all put out on the rough wooden tables in the cool barn. Pay whatever you're charged,
because you won't find better.

ST. HELENA FARMERS' MARKET . . . .

Railroad Avenue at Pine Street,
St. Helena
Friday 7:30 to 11:30 A.M., May
through November
Cash only

This bustling, all-encompassing market not only offers
local produce, but farm eggs, mushrooms, Bellwether
Farms sheep's milk cheeses, and put-up products like
jams and vegetable sauces. At a typical late-June market
you will find the first flavorful Early Girl tomatoes
you've been hungering for all winter, tiny *haricots verts*,

Santa Rosa plums, intensely flavored Blenheim apricots, some very nice lettuces, pickling
cucumbers, blueberries, and fresh herbs. People know each other at this market, and I have
spotted many chefs from Napa Valley restaurants talking up the growers.

UPSIDE-DOWN APRICOT OR PLUM TART

MAKES ONE 12-INCH TART; SERVES 8

I have found small, fragrant Blenheim apricots in the spring, and intensely flavored French sugar (prune) plums at the end of the summer and early fall. This recipe from Anne Haskell, one of my original partners at Hayes Street Grill (see page 53), puts either fruit to brilliant use in a rustic country tart. I am scared to death of pastry, but I followed this recipe exactly and made a wonderful tart. I know you can do it, too.

DOUGH

1 cup (2 sticks) cold butter

2 cups all-purpose flour

½ teaspoon kosher salt

7 tablespoons ice water

1 To make the dough, cut the butter into the flour until it is pea sized. I use my fingers, rubbing the butter into the flour and working quickly, but you can also use a wire pastry cutter. Stir in the water to form a dough. On a lightly floured board, form the dough into a disk. Wrap in plastic and chill for at least 1 hour.

2 Preheat the oven to 425°F.

FILLING

6 tablespoons unsalted butter

⅔ cup sugar

3 pounds firm apricots or prune plums, halved and pitted

3 To make the filling, melt the butter in a 12-inch cast-iron skillet over medium-high heat, and stir in the sugar until it dissolves. Turn off the heat.

4 Starting from the outer edge of the pan, lay the apricots or plums cut-side up around the pan. The fruit should fit snugly, with each circle slightly overlapping. Cut the remaining apricots or plums in quarters and scatter over the halved fruit.

5 Place the pan on the stove over low to medium heat. When the fruit starts to release some juice, raise the heat to medium-high and cook for about 25 minutes. The juices will get syrupy and eventually begin to caramelize.

6 While the apricots are cooking, roll out the tart dough slightly larger than the circumference of your skillet. The dough should be about ⅛ inch thick.

7 When the apricots are ready, remove the pan from the stove and cover with the dough. I just drape it over the pan and cut off the extra. The dough kind of falls down over the fruit by itself. Bake for 35 minutes. The crust will be nicely browned. Allow to rest 5 minutes.

8 Have a large flat plate ready. Place it over the tart. Wearing oven mitts and using both hands, flip the pan over so that the plate is on the bottom. If any fruit sticks to the pan, just use a spatula to place it on the tart.

9 The tart can be eaten warm, or within 3 to 4 hours of baking. (The dough doesn't get soggy.) Serve with sweetened whipped cream or vanilla ice cream.

MEAT AND POULTRY

BIG JOHN'S FOOD CENTER . . . .

1345 Healdsburg Avenue (at Dry
Creek Road), Healdsburg
707-433-7151
Open daily 8 A.M. to 8 P.M.
Credit cards: D, MC, V

The old-fashioned meat counter at this large, independently owned grocery store is manned by butchers who still cut to order. Featured here are treasures like Bruce Campbell's C. K. Lamb, exceptionally sweet, tender, juicy, and full of character without being muttony; excellent Petaluma Poultry chickens; and corn-fed, naturally raised pork.

KELLER'S MARKET . . . .

1320 Main Street (between Hunt
and Adams), St. Helena
707-963-2114
www.kellersmarket.com
Open daily 6 A.M. to 8 P.M.,
butcher shop 6 A.M. to 7 P.M.
Credit cards: AE, MC, V

One of the attractions of this useful grocery store in downtown St. Helena is a small, but complete independently owned butcher counter that makes its own mild and hot Italian sausages, as well as four or five other kinds. Besides the usual cuts of beef, you will find quick-cooking pork tenderloins wrapped in pancetta for the grill, Fulton Valley and Rocky chickens, and Sonoma lamb. The surrounding grocery gets fresh bread deliveries from Passini (see Sciambra Bakery, page 488) and others, and stocks imported pasta, olive oil, and other necessities of life.

SONOMA SAVEURS. . . . .

487 1st Street West
(near West Napa), Sonoma
707-938-1229
www.sonomafoiegras.com
Open Monday through Saturday
10 A.M. to 6 P.M.
Credit cards: AE, MC, V

Junny and Guillermo Gonzales produce the highest quality fresh duck foie gras in California, a product that certainly rivals the fine Hudson Valley foie gras from New York. You can visit their website or call to find out how to order some (their foie gras is always available at Polarica in San Francisco, see page 209), or to make an appointment to visit the farm.

You can buy prepared terrines and other delicacies made with their foie gras and duck at Sonoma Saveurs, a shop, delicatessen, and tasting room on the main plaza in Sonoma. Sonoma Saveurs is a collaboration between the producers of this fine foie gras and a team of French chefs who will be developing products made with it. Chef Laurent Manrique, former Campton Place chef, who grew up in the foie gras region of southwestern France, is a partner in the project.

Raw foie gras is actually simple to prepare. Get a cast-iron frying pan really hot and sear slices of the foie gras for just bit (15 seconds) on each side; any longer and the foie gras will melt like butter. Drape the warm slices on a very lightly dressed salad of haricots verts and baby lettuces in a sherry vinegar–shallot vinaigrette. Foie gras is expensive, but it's one of those ingredients that always seems worth it.

1115 Main Street
(at Spring), St. Helena
707-963-7070
Open daily 7:30 A.M. to 9 P.M.
Credit Cards: AE, D, MC, V

The large, pretty meat counter is a big draw here. Pristine fish, Rosie organic chickens, ducks, quail, poussin, handsome short ribs, and other braising cuts of beef, plus lamb and pork look fresh and well cared for. The butchers will cut, bone, and grind to specification, and they will order special items from their suppliers if you ask. This large independent grocery also has a well-tended and extensive cheese department and a prepared foods department that will slice prosciutto and cured meats to order. If you're setting up household in the Napa Valley, Sunshine is an invaluable resource.

CHEESE

THE CHEESE SHOP OF HEALDSBURG

423 Center Street (between
North and Piper), Healdsburg
707-433-4998
Open Wednesday through Monday
10 A.M. to 6 P.M.,
closed Tuesday
Credit cards: MC, V

This cheese shop run by Susan Walrabenstein, who used to run the cheese department at the Healdsburg branch of the Oakville Grocery (see page 487), provides personal service, many tastes, and much guidance so that you always leave having discovered a brilliant new cheese. The other day Susan touted a sweet, creamy, washed rind semisoft Italian, an aged brescianella, which was so delectable that my family gobbled it up before I even had a bite. Lucky I tasted it at the shop. She carries lots of artisan cheeses from local, national, and international producers, including Britain's Neal's Yard Dairy. All the cheeses stay in perfect condition in her cool, airy shop. She'll help you pull together a cheese plate and you can accessorize it with items from the shop, like wood oven–baked Della Fattoria breads, cheese knives, dried fruits, and nuts. You can also sign up for a cheese class. The Cheese Shop joins the Downtown Bakery (see page 487) and Middleton Farm (see page 490) as a mandatory stop in the ever-expanding Healdsburg food universe.

DEAN & DELUCA . . . .

607 South St. Helena Highway
(at Inglewood), St. Helena
707-967-9980
www.deansdelucca.com
Open Monday through Sunday
9 A.M. to 7 P.M.,
espresso bar 7:30 A.M.
Credit cards: AE, D, MC, V

Like all the other merchandise at this high-end food store, a wide range of cheeses are beautifully displayed and look absolutely mouthwatering. Be sure to taste before you buy. See page 486 for more information.

OAKVILLE GROCERY . . . .

124 Matheson Street (at Center),
Healdsburg
707-433-3200
www.oakvillgrocery.com and
www.oakvillewine.com
Open daily 9 A.M. to 6 P.M.,
espresso bar 7 A.M.
Credit cards: AE, MC, V

The Healdsburg Oakville branch has a particularly strong cheese section, plus the unusual collection of pricey oils, vinegars, and mustards. Patrons order sandwiches and salads to go from the deli counter and sit outside on the patio under umbrellas. See page 487 for more information.

VELLA CHEESE CO. . . . .

315 2nd Street East (between Spain
Street and Blueing Drive), Sonoma
707-938-3232
www.vellacheese.com
Open Monday through Saturday
9 A.M. to 6 P.M.
Credit cards: AE, MC, V

Ig Vella and his staff of thirteen have been making Monterey Jack and Cheddar by hand since 1931 in this small plant with stone aging rooms a few blocks off Sonoma's central plaza. He is famous for his crumbly aged Monterey Jack, which has won every cheese competition in the country. The two- to five-year-old wheels have a nutty, buttery flavor and can be shaved onto salads or pasta with a potato peeler. I eat it by the chunk. His new Mezzoseco, a semihard cheese, is winning awards, too. You can watch Ig and his crew making the cheese Monday through Thursday at 12:30 p.m. and 2:30 p.m. and get a tour of the aging rooms. You can taste cheese at the retail counter every day. A wheel or half wheel of Vella's Golden Bear, the longest-aged dry jack, makes for a lavish gift or souvenir of a trip to Sonoma.

WINE AND SPIRITS

ALL SEASONS CAFE AND WINE STORE . . . .

1400 Lincoln Avenue
(at Washington), Calistoga
707-942-6828
Open Thursday through Monday
11 A.M. to 7 P.M.
Credit cards: MC, V

This wineshop-café has put together a wonderful collection of both European and local wines at decent prices. You can buy French and California wines made with the same varietals to compare, or find tiny bottlings from small vineyards nearby to immerse yourself in Napa Valley wine making. One of the best ways to taste wine is with food, which the café end of the operation prepares with special attention to seasonal produce and artisan ingredients. For a $7.50 corkage, you can pick out any bottle, pay the retail price for it (a big savings over wine list prices even with the corkage), and drink it with a charming country meal of one of the house-made pastas, sprightly salads, or well-prepared fish and meat dishes that go particularly well with wines. The desserts carry on the fresh seasonal commitment with the likes of summer berry pie with house-made vanilla ice cream; or consider the cheese plate, which makes perfect sense when you're eating in a room full of red wine waiting to be opened.

J. V. WAREHOUSE. . . . .

Vallergas Market
426 1st Street (at Juarez), Napa
707-253-2624
www.jvwarehouse.com
Open daily 8 A.M. to 9 P.M.
Credit cards: AE, D, MC, V

Just as its name implies, wine, beer, and liquor are set out on shelves and you help yourself. The warehouse has lots of Napa Valley wines, including some old vintages. If you know what you're looking for, as the winemakers and growers in the valley who shop here do, you can find some terrific bargains. You can walk over here after a visit to Copia.

RUSSIAN RIVER WINE COMPANY . . . .

132 Plaza Street (between
Center and East), Healdsburg
707-433-0490
www.russianriverwineco.com
Open Wednesday through Sunday
11 A.M. to 4 P.M.
Credit cards: MC, V

This little wine shop specializes in hard to find artisan wines produced in very small lots. If you're a Russian River pinot noir fanatic, and are prepared to spend about $60 a bottle, this is the wine shop for you. The enthusiastic clerk on duty will guide you to bottles in the style you prefer, and the shop will let you know when new bottlings arrive. A tasting room is soon to open. Personal service is a specialty.

ST. HELENA WINE CENTER . . . .

1321 Main Street (between
Spring and Adams), St. Helena
707-963-1313
www.shwc.com
Open daily 10 A.M. to 6 P.M.
Credit cards: AE, DC, D, MC, V

Lots of local wines at good prices here, along with a few imports. Helpful and knowledgeable owner Fred Barringer can steer you to the right wines.

ST. HELENA WINE MERCHANTS . . . .

699 St. Helena Highway (Highway
29 at Inglewood), St. Helena
707-963-7888
www.sainthelenawinemerchants.com
Open daily 10 A.M. to 6 P.M.
Credit cards: AE, D, MC, V

Formerly called Ernie's, this wine store has always stocked high-quality Napa Valley bottles. Now, a good selection from other areas in California coupled with wines from all over the world are included, making this a useful resource for Napa Valley winegrowers in search of taste models. The prices are not terribly competitive, but the clerks are competent and enthusiastic. Savvy collectors used to be able to find quirky old vintages of European wines, but, alas, the buyers have caught up with the inventory.

90 Dry Creek Road (at Healdsburg
Avenue), Healdsburg
707-431-0841
Open Sunday through Thursday
9 A.M. to 8 P.M., Friday and
Saturday 9 A.M. to 10 P.M.
Credit cards: AE, MC, V

In an unlikely spot on the edge of Healdsburg, a funky, cool cement-floored wine and liquor store offers a surprisingly diverse selection of spirits and wines—a selection that includes all the major growing areas of California and a commendable selection of wines from wine-growing regions all over the world.

Some examples: the beautiful local Russian River Lynmar pinot noirs, fine pinots from Oregon, like Adelsheim; an array of Ridge Vineyard wines; representative bottles of one of my favorite Bordeaux, Château La Lagune from the Haute Medoc, not to mention a good selection of others. Though more of a liquor store than a wineshop, Tip Top's buyers know that descriptive signage can sell wine.

COOKWARE AND BOOKS

CORNUCOPIA . . . .

Copia: The American Center for
Wine, Food & the Arts
500 First Street, Napa
707-265-5800 or 888-51-COPIA
www.copia.org

Summer hours: Monday,
Wednesday, and Sunday
10 A.M. to 5 P.M., Thursday
through Saturday until 7 P.M.

Winter hours: Thursday through
Monday 10 A.M. to 5 P.M.

Credit cards: AE, D, MC, V

The gift shop is filled with books, kitchen gadgets, tableware, and anything else imaginable related to the production and joyous consumption of food and wine.

DEAN & DELUCA . . . .

607 South St. Helena Highway
(at Inglewood), St. Helena
707-967 9980
www.deansdelucca.com
Open Monday through Sunday
9 A.M. to 7 P.M.,
espresso bar 7:30 A.M.
Credit cards: AE, D, MC, V

This capacious food emporium has room for a large, densely stocked cookware and tableware department full of gadgets you never thought you needed until they somehow ended up in your shopping basket. See page 486 for more information.

THE GARDENER . . . .

516 Dry Creek Road (just west of
Highway 101 exit), Healdsburg
707-431-1063
Open Thursday through Monday
10 A.M. to 4 P.M.
Credit cards: AE, MC, V

The wine country outpost of Alta Tingle's brilliantly
curated "garden store" in Berkeley (see page 441), displaying Laguiole knives, maroon-and-gold tablecloths,
bags, furniture, sun hats, ceramics, and much more
outdoor furniture and garden ornaments than the
Berkeley store.

JOSEPHINE EUROPEAN TABLEWARE . . . . . .

1407 Lincoln Avenue
(at Washington), Calistoga
707-942 8683
www.josiesdishes.com
Open Monday, Wednesday,
Thursday, and Friday 10:30 A.M.
to 5 P.M., Saturday 10 A.M. to 5 P.M.,
Sunday 11 A.M. to 4 P.M.
Credit cards: AE, MC, V

Stepping off Calistoga's main street into this long,
narrow shop of hand-painted Italian dishware transports you to Deruta, the pottery capital of northern
Italy. Rustic, elaborately painted plates, bowls, and cups
call out for pasta, caffe latte and fruit. Simpler French
pieces will set a more restrained table. I myself have a
whole set of hand-painted Italian dishware that I
ordered in Deruta. It took eight months for it to be
delivered, but has given me years of pleasure. Everyday
food looks bright and appetizing on these plates deco-
rated with rich, colorful, historical patterns encircling the rim and sometimes covering the
whole plate or bowl. The only other place that has as large a collection as Josephine is
Biordi (see page xxx) in San Francisco.

NIEBAUM-COPPOLA WINERY STORE . . . . . .

1991 St. Helena Highway (at
Rutherford crossroad), Rutherford
1-800-782-4266
www.niebaumcoppola.com
Open daily 10 A.M. to 5 P.M.
Credit cards: AE, DC, D, MC, V

The extensive shop and tasting room in the historic
stone Niebaum-Coppola winery showcases Francis Ford
Coppola's lifestyle collection. The Martha Stewart of all
things Italian, he has called on his crew of movie set
designers to build a fantasy store stocked with glassware, dishes, cookbooks, napkins, wine paraphernalia,
and his line of bottled pasta sauces and dried pasta. I
can't walk through it without inadvertently finding something, like a large, deep, yellow
ceramic bowl with a fluted rim and thin green edge. It was ridiculously expensive, but I had
to have it. It is one of the most beautiful bowls I've ever seen and I use it all the time. The
Coppola lifestyle bowl has paid for itself in the thrill I get every time I put something in it.
Whoever buys for the Coppola collection knows what excites food maniacs like me. I figure
that all the money I've saved by drinking Coppola *rosso*, the soft, fruity, very affordable red,
with my pasta, has made up for my extravagances in pottery buying.

INDEXES

INDEXES

Alphabetical

Restaurants

Cuisine

Price

Food Service at Counter or Bar

Food Service after 10 P.M.

Breakfast or Weekend Brunch

Outdoor Seating

Child Friendly

Banquet Room

Of Historic Interest

Bakeries/Pastries

Bars

Cafés

Cheese

Coffee

Cookware and Books

Delicatessens/Takeout

Ethnic Markets

Fish

Ice Cream/Chocolates

Markets

Meat and Poultry

Produce

Wine and Spirits

Recipes

Sidebars

ALPHABETICAL

A Clean Well-Lighted Place for Books, 66

Abraham's Seafood, 434

Absinthe Brasserie and Bar, 50

Acme Bread Company, 420

Acme Chophouse, 344

Acquerello, 292

Ajanta, 394

Al-Masri, 316

Alan's Meats, 431

Alemany Farmers' Market, 204

Alfred's Steak House, 94

All Seasons Cafe and Wine Store, 494

Allstar Donuts, 331

Alma, 174

Amphora Wine Merchant, 65

Amrie Antionette, 271

Andalu, 175

Andronico's, 381

Angkor Borei, 176

Anjou, 94

Antica Trattoria, 293

Antonelli's Meat, Fish, and Poultry, 281

Anzu Sushi Bar, 95

Aqua, 95

Arabi, 83

Arizmendi Bakery, 379

Arlequin, 60

Armani Cafe, 116

Artisan Cheese, 284

A. Sabella & La Torre, 80

Asia SF, 358

Auberge du Soleil, 466

B 44, 96

Bacar, 345

Bagelry, The, 305

Balboa Cafe, 161

Balompie Cafe, 176

Bay Bread, 274

BayWolf, 394

Beach Chalet, 377

Bean There, 136

Beanery, The, 381

Berkeley Bowl, 429

Berkeley Bowl Fish Market, 434

Berkeley Farmers' Market, 429

Betelnut, 150

Big John's Food Center, 492

Biordi Art Imports, 258

Bi-Rite Market, 202

Bistro Aix, 150

Bistro Don Giovanni, 467

Bistro Jeanty, 467

Bistro Ralph, 469

Bix, 97, 119

Bizou, 346

Black Oak Books, 441

Bliss Bar, 220

Blondie's, 120, 416

Bob's Donuts, 305

Bombay Bazaar, 203

Bombay Ice Creamery, 201

Book's, Inc., 285

Book Passage, 461

Book Passage Cafe, 453

Boudin Sourdough Bakery and Café, 80, 84

Boulange de Cole Valley, 137, 140

Boulangerie de Polk, 306

Boulevard, 70

Bovine Bakery, 455

Bow Hon, 24

Brain Wash, 356

Bread Workshop, 420

Breads of India & Gourmet Curries, 395

Brennan's, 396, 415

Brother-in-Law's Bar-be-que, 138

Bryan's Quality Meats, 273, 281, 282, 284

Burger Joint, 132, 177

Burgermeister, 132

Burma's House, 98

Bus Stop, 161

Butler & The Chef, The, 366

Butler & The Chef Cafe, The, 356

butterfly, 177

Caffé 817, 413

Café at Chez Panisse, 396

Cafe at Oliveto, 414

Café Claude, 117

Café de la Presse, 117

Cafe Fanny, 413

Cafe Flore, 220

Café Jacqueline, 234

Cafe Kati, 262

Cafe La Haye, 469

Cafe Marimba, 151

Cafe Merenda, 163

Cafe Niebaum-Coppola, 117

Cafe Prague, 118

Cafe Rouge, 397

Caffe Centro, 357

Caffè Greco, 244

Caffè Roma Coffee Roasting Company, 244, 357

Caffè Strada, 414

Caffè Trieste, 244

Caffé Trinity, 60

California Hornblower, 79

California Sunshine, 363

California Wine Merchant, 168

Cal-Mart, 276

Cantinetta at Tra Vigne, 485

Canvas Cafe/Gallery, 377

Casa Lucas, 203, 205

Casa Orinda, 398

Castro Village Wine Company, 229

Catahoula, 484

Cesar, 398, 415

Cha Cha Cha, 132

Chapeau!, 317

Charanga, 176

Chaz, 152

Cheese Board, The, 421, 437

Cheese Board Pizzeria, 416

Cheese Shop, The, 458

Cheese Shop of Healdsburg, The, 493

Chenery Park, 214

Chez Maman, 347

Chez Nous, 263

Chez Panisse, 399

Chez Papa, 347

chez spencer, 348

Chung Hing Produce Co., 38

Chong Imports, 45

Chow, 214

Cinch Saloon, 302

Citizen Cake, 50, 63

Citron, 399

City Discount, 312

Civic Center Farmers' Market, 65

Clean Well-Lighted Place for Books, A, 66

Clement Produce, 336

Clementine, 318

Cliff's Hardware, 230

Club Deluxe, 137

Cody's, 441

Coffee, Tea and Spice, 141

Coit Liquors, 257

Columbus Cutlery, 258

Cookin', 146

Cooper's, 228

Copia, 474

Cordon Bleu, 293

Cornucopia, 497

Cosmopolitan Café, 82

Cost Plus Imports, 90

Country Cheese, 145

Cozmo's Corner Grill, 161

Crate&Barrel, 125

Daimo, 400

Dalva, 194

Danilo, 253

Dean & DeLuca, 486, 493, 497

Delanghe Patisserie, 274

DeLessio, 61

Delfina, 179

Desiree, 163

Destino, 52

Dianda's Italian-American Pastries, 200

Dol Ho, 24

Dolores Park Cafe, 193

Doña Tere's Cart, 195

Doña Tomas, 401

Double Rainbow, 379

Doug's Bar-B-Q, 416

Downtown, 401, 415

Downtown Bakery and Creamery, 487, 488

Dragon House, 318

Drewes Brothers Meat, 227

Dry Creek Kitchen, 470

E'Angelo, 154

East Coast West Delicatessen, 294, 304

Eastern Bakery, 34

Economy Restaurant Supply, 366

El Balazito, 180

El Perol, 180

El Tonayense Taco Trucks, 195

Elisabeth Daniel, 100

Ella's, 263

Emporio Rulli, 453, 456, 459

Encantada Gallery of Fine Arts, 210

Enrico's Sidewalk Cafe, 245

Enzo, 431

Eos, 133

Estella's Fresh Sandwiches, 139

European Food, 328

Farley's, 357

Farallon, 100

Fattoush, 215

Ferry Plaza Farmers' Market, 85

Fifth Floor, 101

Fina Estampa, 181

Firefly, 216

Fleur de Lys, 102

Florio, 264

Fly Trap Restaurant, 349

Flying Goat Cafe, 484

Fog City Diner, The, 70

Fog City News, 123

Fonda Solana, 402

Foothill Cafe, 471

Foreign Cinema, 182

Forrest Jones, 286

4th Avenue and Geary
Farmers Market, 336

42 Degrees, 359

Frantoio, 445

Freddie's, 248

Fredericksen's Hardware, 170

French Laundry, 472

Fringale, 350

Fruit Basket, 337

Fruit City, 38

G Bar, 272

G.B. Ratto and Company, 425

Gardner, The, 441, 498

Gary Danko, 71

Gastronom, 329

Gelato Classico, 141, 255, 332

Gin Joint

Ginn Wall, 45

Gino and Carlo's, 245

Globe, 103

Golden Boy, 249

Golden Gate Bakery, 34

Golden Point Produce, 457

Golden Turtle, 294

Gourmet Delight, 33

Graffeo, 254

Grand Cafe, 104

Grasshopper, 403

Great Eastern Restaurant, 25

Green Apple Books, 339

Greens, 154

Greens to Go, 164

Greystone Restaurant, 485

Guang Zhou King & King Sausage, 40

Guaymas, 454

Guerra's, 385

Haig's Delicacies, 329

Hama-ko, 134

Hamburgers, 455

Hana, 370

Harbor Village, 72

Harris' Restaurant, 295, 303

Harry Denton's Starlight Room, 119

Harvest Ranch Market, 226

Hawthorne Lane, 351, 359

Hayes and Vine Wine Bar, 66

Hayes Street Grill, 53

Healdsburg Farmers' Market, 490

Helmand, 234
Hing Lung, 25
Hog Island Oyster Co., 459
Home, 216
House, 370
House of Bagels, 331
House of Nanking, 26
House of Prime Rib, 295
House, The, 235
Il Pollaio, 236
Imperial Tea Court, 31
Incanto, 218
In-N-Out Burger, 83
Insalata's, 446
Iroha, 271
Irving Housewares & Gifts, 388
Isa, 155
Isobune, 271
J. V. Warehouse, 496
Jackson Fillmore, 265
Jade Villa, 428
Jardinière, 55
Java Beach Cafe, 377
Jeanty at Jack's, 105
Jimtown Store, 486
Joe's Ice Cream, 334
Jojo, 404
Joseph Schmidt, 223
Josephine European Tableware, 498
Juban Yakiniku House, 265
Jug Shop, The, 311
Juicey Lucy's Organic Juice and
    Food Bar, 249
Julia, 266
Julia's Kitchen, 473
Just Desserts, 165
Just Won Ton, 371
K & L Restaurant, 476
K & L Wines, 365
Kabuto, 319
Khanh Phong, 430
Kamei Household Wares, 339
Kamei Restaurant Supply, 339
Katia, A Russian Tea Room, 320

Katrina Rozelle, 421
Kay Cheung, 27
Keller's Market, 492
Kelly's Mission Rock, 359
Kermit Lynch Wines, 439
Kezar Bar & Restaurant, 137
King of Thai Noodles, 320
Kinokuniya Bookstore, 286
Kiss, 267
Kokkari, 106
Kyo-Ya at the Sheraton Palace
    Hotel, 352
L'Osteria Del Forno, 237
La Corneta Taqueria, 183, 218
La Farine, 421
La Felce, 236
La Folie, 296
La Gallinita, 208
La Loma Produce, 199, 205
La Luna Market, 489
La Nouvelle Pâtisserie, 165
La Palma Mexicatessen, 197, 199
La Raccolta, 256
La Taqueria, 184
Lam Hoa Thuan , 371
Lark Creek Inn, 446
Last Supper Club. The, 183
Laurel Court Bar, 303
Lazlo, 194
Le Central, 107
Le Petit Robert, 297
Lee's Sandwiches, 121
Lehr's German Specialties, 230
Leonard's 2001, 311
Liberty Cafe
Lichee Garden, 27
Lien Hing Supermarket, 36, 38, 40
Lien Hing Supermarket No. 2, 40
Lien Hing Supermarket No. 3, 335
Liguria, 253
Li-Po, 33
Little City, 257
Limon, 185
London Wine Bar, 124

Lorca, 186

Los Jarritos, 186

Lucca, 164

Lucca Ravioli Company, 197

Lucky Pork Store, The, 208

Luen Sing Fish Market, 43

Lulu, 353

Luna Park, 187

Lyla's Chocolates, 456

Macy's, 125

Magnanis Poultry, 433

Make-Out Room, 195

Maki, 268

Man Sung, 41

Manka's Inverness Lodge, 447

Manzanita, 477

Marin County Farmers' Market, 457

Marina Super, 167

Marin Wine Cellar, 460

Mario's Bohemian Cigar Store, 244

Market Hall Pasta Shop, 417, 438

Market Hall Produce, 430

Martini House, 478

Martin's John and Zeke's, 485

Maruwa Foods Company, 279

Maruya Sushi, 273

Masa's, 107

Mashiko Folkcraft, 286

Matrix/Fillmore, 162

Mayflower, 321

May's Coffee Shop, 271

MC², 108

Mecca, 222

Mee Mee Bakery, 35

Meetinghouse, 268

Merenda, 156

Mezze, 405

Middleton Farm, 490

Mifune, 269

MikeyTom, 226

Milan International, 425

Millennium, 109

Mill Valley Market, 461

Ming Kee Game Birds, 42

Miramonte, 478

Miss Millie's, 219

Mission Market Fish and Poultry, 209

Mission Market Meat, 208

Mitchell's Ice Cream, 202

Mo's Grill, 237

Molinari Delicatessan, 252

Momi Toby's Revolution Café, 60

Monterey Fish, 436

Monterey Foods, 430

Moose's, 239

Morrow's Nut House, 123

Moscow and Tbilisi Bakery, 332

Mr. Liquor, 387

Mustards Grill, 479

Naan 'N' Curry, 110

Napa Valley Olive Oil Manufacturing Co., 489

Napa Valley Wine Train, 479

Nature Stop, The, 256

New Chiu Fong Company, 64, 65

New Hai Ky, 372

New Korea House, 269

New May Wah Supermarket, 335

New On Sang, 42, 337

New Saigon Supermarket, 426

New Sang Sang, 42

New World Foods, 330

Nick's, 80

Niebaum-Coppola Winery Store, 498

Nizza La Bella, 406

Nob Hill Grille, 298

Noc Noc, 138

Noe Valley Bakery, 222

North Beach Pizza, 252

O Chamé, 407

Oakland Market, 426

Oakville Grocery, 487, 494

Odd Lots, 440

Old Krakow, 372

Old Oakland Farmers' Market, 431

Oliveto, 408

Oliviers & Co., 279

One Market Restaurant, 73
Oriental Pearl, 28
Original Joe's, 110
Original U.S. Restaurant, 239
Ozumo, 75
Palatino, 188
Palio d'Asti, 111
Palio Paninoteca, 121, 378
Panaderia La Mexicana, 200
Pancho Villa Taqueria, 188
Pane e Vino, 156
Papa Toby's Cafe, 194
Parc Hong Kong, 322
Park Chow, 373
Pasha, 303
Pasta Shop, The, 417
Pat O'Shea's Mad Hatter, 328
Paul Marcus Wines, 440
Pearl, 480
Pearl City, 29
Peet's Coffee & Tea, 166, 167, 276,
    307, 381, 438, 459
Perry's, 162
Pesce, 298
Pho Hoa Hiep II, 373
Phoenix Pastaficio, 418
Piatti, 480
Picante Cocina Mexicana, 409
Piccadilly Fish and Chips, 304
Pier 23 Café, 83
Piperade, 76
Pizzetta 211, 323
PlumpJack Cafe, 156
PlumpJack Wines, 168, 229
Polarica, 209
Polly Ann Ice Cream, 380
Postrio, 112
Q, 324
R & G Lounge, 29
Rainbow Grocery, 361, 363
Ramp, The, 360
Ravenette/Ravenous, 481
Real Food Company, 142, 226, 307,
    310

Red Room, 119
Redwood Room, 120
Restaurant Peony, 428
Rice Table, 449
Ristorante Bacco, 219
Ristorante Marcello, 373
Ritz-Carlton Dining Room, 299
Riverside Seafood Restaurant, 374
Rivoli, 410
RNM Restaurant, 134
Rockridge Fish Market, 436
Rosamunde Sausage Grill, 139
Rose Pistola, 240
Rose's Cafe, 159
Roxanne's, 450
Rubicon, 112
Russian River Wine Company, 496
Saigon Sandwich Café, 61
Saloon, The, 245
Sam and Henry's Cool Beans, 327
Sam Yick, 426
Sam's, 454
Sam's Grill, 113
Samirami's Imports, 204
San Francisco Art Institute Cafe, 241
San Francisco Spirit, 79
San Miguel, 189
San Tung, 375
Sanko Cooking Supply, 287
Sanraku Four Seasons, 114
Santi, 481
Sapporo-Ya, 271
Savoy Tivoli, 247
Say Cheese, 146
Scharffen Berger Chocolate Maker,
    422, 423
Schubert's, 332
Sciambra French Bakery, 488
Seafood Center, 338
Seakor Polish Delicatessen, 331
Sear's Fine Foods, 114
See's Candies, 84, 124, 306, 334, 380
Semifreddi's, 422
Shalimar, 115

Shanghai 1930, 77

Shanghai Restaurant, 375

Siam Cuisine, 410

Slanted Door, 78, 189

Soko Hardware Co., 287

Soma Caffe, 358

Sonoma Saveurs, 492

South Beach Café, 82

South Park Cafe, 354

Spanish Table, The, 428, 442

Spec's, 247

Specialty's Cafe and Bakery, 122

Spoon, 300

St. Helena Farmers' Market, 490

St. Helena Wine Center, 496

St. Helena Wine Merchants, 496

Stella, 254

Straits Cafe, 324

Sue Fisher-King, 287

Sun Fat Seafood Company, 210

Sunrise Deli & Cafe, 378

Sunset Super, 383, 387

Sunshine Foods, 489, 493

Super Mira, 280

Super Tokio Japanese Market, 335

Suppenküche, 55

Sur La Table, 126, 442

Sushi Ran, 452

Sushi Zone, 411

Swan Oyster Depot, 300, 310

Sweet Stop, 275

Sweet World, 35

Swenson's, 306

T & S Market, 433

Tadich Grill, 115

Tai Chi, 301

Tai Yick Trading Company, 46

Taiwan, 325

Takara, 271

Tan Tan, 272

Tango Gelato, 275

Taqueria el Balazo, 135

Tartine Bakery, 201

Taylor's Sausages, 433

Teatro ZinZanni, 81

Tekka, 326

Terra, 481

Thep Phanom, 136

Ti Couz Crêperie, 190

Timo's, 190

Tip Top, 497

Tomales Bay Foods, 458

Tommaso's, 242

Ton Kiang, 327

Tony Nik's, 247

Top of the Mark, 304

Toronado, 138

Tortas Los Picudos, 198

Tosca, 247

Tower Market, 224

Tra Vigne, 482

Trader Joe's, 361

21st Amendment, 354

22nd and Irving Market, 383, 385

23rd and Mission Produce, 205

24th Avenue Cheese Shop, 228

Twilight Café and Deli, 140

Umbria, 355

Universal Cafe, 355

Uoki Market, 280, 284

Uzen, 412

Val 16 Market, 204

Valencia Whole Foods Market, 200

Vella Cheese Co., 494

Venticello, 301

Ver Brugge Meats, 434

Vesuvio, 248

Via Vai Trattoria, 159

Vicolo Pizzeria, 56

Victoria Pastry Co., 254

Vien Hong, 428

Vietnam II, 57

Viglizzo's Meat, 227

Viking Homechef, 288, 462

Vik's Chaat Corner, 418

Village Market, 337

Vino, 440

Vi's Vietnamese Cuisine, 428

Vivande Porte Via, 270, 274

Walzwerk, 191

Wappo Bar Bistro, 483

Warming Hut Cafe and Bookstore, The, 160

Washington Square Bar & Grill, 242

Watergate, 192

Whole Foods Market, 309, 310, 311

William Cross Wine Merchants, 312

Williams-Sonoma, 90, 126, 170, 388, 462

Willow Wood Market, 483

Win's, 376

Wine House Limited, 365

Wine Impression, 285

Wo Chong, 40

Woodward's Garden, 192

Wycen Foods, 338

XOX Truffles, 255

XYZ, 360

Y Ben House Restaurant, 31

Yank Sing, 81

Yee's Restaurant, 34

Yogurt Park, 425

Yukol Palace, 160

Yum Yum, 387

Yumma's, 378

Yummy Yummy, 376

Yung Kee, 418

Zarzuela, 302

Zax Tavern, 412

Zero Degrees, 118, 124

Zuni Café, 57

RESTAURANTS

Acme Chophouse, 344

Acquerello, 292

Ajanta, 394

Al-Masri, 316

Alfred's Steak House, 94

Alma, 174

Andalu, 175

Angkor Borei, 176

Anjou, 94

Antica Trattoria, 293

Anzu Sushi Bar, 95

Aqua, 95

Auberge du Soleil, 466

B 44, 96

Bacar, 345

Balompie Cafe, 161

BayWolf, 394

Betelnut, 150

Bistro Aix, 150

Bistro Don Giovanni, 467

Bistro Jeanty, 467

Bistro Ralph, 469

Bix, 97, 119

Bizou, 346

Boulevard, 70

Bow Hon, 24

Breads of India & Gourmet Curries, 395

Brennan's, 396, 415

Burger Joint, 132, 177

Burgermeister, 132

Burma's House, 98

butterfly, 177

Café at Chez Panisse, 396

Café Jacqueline, 234

Cafe Kati, 262

Cafe La Haye, 469

Cafe Marimba, 151

Cafe Rouge, 397

Caffe Centro, 357

Casa Orinda, 398

Cesar, 398, 415

Cha Cha Cha, 132

Chapeau!, 317

Charanga, 176

Chaz, 152

Chenery Park, 214

Chez Maman, 347

Chez Nous, 263

Chez Panisse, 399

Chez Papa, 347

chez spencer, 348

Chow, 214

Citizen Cake, 50, 63

Citron, 399

Clementine, 318

Cordon Bleu, 293

Daimo, 400

Delfina, 179

Destino, 52

Dol Ho, 24

Doña Tomas, 401

Downtown, 401, 415

Dragon House, 318

Dry Creek Kitchen, 470

E'Angelo, 154

East Coast West Delicatessen, 294, 304

El Balazito, 180

El Perol, 180

Elisabeth Daniel, 100

Ella's, 263

Eos, 133

Farallon, 100

Fattoush, 215

Fifth Floor, 101

Fina Estampa, 181

Firefly, 216

Fleur de Lys, 102

Florio, 264

Fly Trap Restaurant, 349

Fog City Diner, The, 70

Fonda Solana, 402

Foothill Cafe, 471

Foreign Cinema, 182

Frantoio, 445

French Laundry, 472

Fringale, 350

Gary Danko, 71

Globe, 103
Golden Turtle, 294
Grand Cafe, 104
Grasshopper, 403
Great Eastern Restaurant, 25
Greens, 154
Hama-ko, 134
Hana, 370
Harbor Village, 72
Harris' Restaurant, 295, 303
Hawthorne Lane, 351, 359
Hayes Street Grill, 53
Helmand, 234
Hing Lung, 25
Home, 216
House, The, 235
House of Nanking, 26
House of Prime Rib, 295
Il Pollaio, 236
Incanto, 218
Insalata's, 446
Iroha, 271
Isa, 155
Isobune, 271
Jackson Fillmore, 265
Jardinière, 55
Jeanty at Jack's, 105
Jojo, 404
Juban Yakiniku House, 265
Julia, 266
Julia's Kitchen, 473
Just Won Ton, 371
K & L Restaurant, 476
Kabuto, 319
Katia, A Russian Tea Room, 320
Kay Cheung, 27
King of Thai Noodles, 320
Kiss, 267
Kokkari, 106
Kyo-Ya at the Sheraton Palace Hotel, 352
La Corneta Taqueria, 183, 218
La Felce, 236
La Folie, 296
La Taqueria, 184

Lam Hoa Thuan , 371
Lark Creek Inn, 446
Last Supper Club, The, 183
Le Central, 107
Le Petit Robert, 297
Liberty Cafe, 184
Lichee Garden, 27
Lorca, 186
Los Jarritos, 186
L'Osteria Del Forno, 237
Lulu, 353
Luna Park, 187
Maki, 268
Manka's Inverness Lodge, 447
Manzanita, 447
Martini House, 478
Masa's, 107
Mayflower, 321
MC², 108
Meetinghouse, 268
Merenda, 156
Mezze, 405
Mifune, 269
Millennium, 109
Miramonte, 478
Miss Millie's, 219
Mo's Grill, 237
Moose's, 239
Mustards Grill, 479
Naan 'N' Curry, 110
Napa Valley Wine Train, 479
New Hai Ky, 372
New Korea House, 269
Nizza La Bella, 406
Nob Hill Grille, 298
O Chamé, 407
Old Krakow, 372
Oliveto, 408
One Market Restaurant, 73
Oriental Pearl, 28
Original Joe's, 110
Original U.S. Restaurant, 239
Ozumo, 75
Palatino, 188

Palio d'Asti, 111
Pancho Villa Taqueria, 188
Pane e Vino, 156
Parc Hong Kong, 322
Park Chow, 373
Pearl, 480
Pearl City, 29
Pesce, 298
Pho Hoa Hiep II, 373
Piatti, 480
Picante Cocina Mexicana, 409
Piperade, 76
Pizzetta 211, 323
PlumpJack Cafe, 156
Postrio, 112
Q, 324
R & G Lounge, 29
Ravenette/Ravenous, 481
Rice Table, 449
Ristorante Bacco, 219
Ristorante Marcello, 373
Ritz-Carlton Dining Room, 299
Riverside Seafood Restaurant, 374
Rivoli, 410
RNM Restaurant, 134
Rose Pistola, 240
Rose's Cafe, 159
Roxanne's, 450
Rubicon, 112
Sam's Grill, 113
San Francisco Art Institute Cafe, 241
Samirami's Imports, 204
San Miguel, 189
San Tung, 375
Sanraku Four Seasons, 114
Santi, 481
Sapporo-Ya, 271
Sear's Fine Foods, 114
Shalimar, 115
Shanghai 1930, 77
Shanghai Restaurant, 375
Siam Cuisine, 410
Slanted Door, 78, 189
South Park Cafe, 354

Spoon, 300
Straits Cafe, 254
Suppenküche, 55
Sushi Ran, 452
Sushi Zone, 411
Swan Oyster Depot, 300, 310
Tadich Grill, 115
Tai Chi, 301
Takara, 271
Taiwan, 325
Taqueria el Balazo, 135
Teatro ZinZanni, 81
Tekka, 326
Terra, 481
Thep Phanom, 136
Ti Couz Crêperie, 190
Timo's, 190
Tommaso's, 242
Ton Kiang, 327
Tra Vigne, 482
21st Amendment, 354
Umbria, 355
Universal Cafe, 355
Uzen, 412
Venticello, 301
Via Vai Trattoria, 159
Vicolo Pizzeria, 56
Vietnam II, 57
Vivande Porte Via, 270, 274
Walzwerk, 191
Wappo Bar Bistro, 483
Watergate, 192
Willow Wood Market, 483
Win's, 376
Woodward's Garden, 192
Y Ben House Restaurant, 31
Yank Sing, 81
Yukol Palace, 160
Yummy Yummy, 376
Zarzuela, 302
Zax Tavern, 412
Zuni Café, 412

AFGANI
Helmand, 234

AMERICAN
Bix, 97, 119
Brennan's, 396, 415
Casa Orinda, 398
Chenery Park, 214
Chow, 214
Ella's, 263
Fly Trap Restaurant, 349
Fog City Diner, The, 70
Foothill Cafe, 471
Home, 216
Lark Creek Inn, 446
Liberty Cafe, 184
Luna Park, 187
Meetinghouse, 268
Miss Millie's, 219
Mustards Grill, 479
Nob Hill Grille, 298
Pearl, 480
Q, 324
San Francisco Art Institute Cafe, 241
Sear's Fine Foods, 114
Spoon, 300
21st Amendment, 354
Willow Wood Market, 483
Woodward's Garden, 192

ASIAN
Betelnut, 150
butterfly, 177

ASIAN FUSION
Eos, 133
House, 370
House, The, 235

ASIAN/SMALL PLATES
Grasshopper, 403

BASQUE
Piperade, 76

BURMESE
Burma's House, 98

CALIFORNIA
Bacar, 345
BayWolf, 394
Bistro Ralph, 469
Boulevard, 70
Café at Chez Panisse, 396
Cafe Kati, 262
Cafe La Haye, 469
Cafe Rouge, 397
Chez Panisse, 399
Citizen Cake, 50, 63
Downtown, 401, 415
Dry Creek Kitchen, 470
Firefly, 216
Gary Danko, 71
Globe, 103
Hawthorne Lane, 351, 359
Julia, 266
K & L Restaurant, 476
Lulu, 353
Manka's Inverness Lodge, 447
Manzanita, 447
Martini House, 478
Moose's, 239
Napa Valley Wine Train, 479
One Market Restaurant, 73
Park Chow, 373
PlumpJack Cafe, 156
Postrio, 112
Ravenette/Ravenous, 481
Rubicon, 112
Terra, 481
Universal Cafe, 355
Wappo Bar Bistro, 483
Zuni Café, 57

CALIFORNIA/MEDITERRANEAN
Mezze, 405
Rivoli, 410
Zax Tavern, 412

CALIFORNIA/SMALL PLATES
RNM Restaurant, 134

CAMBODIAN
Angkor Borei, 176

CARIBBEAN
Cha Cha Cha, 132

CHICKEN
Il Pollaio, 236

CHINESE
Bow Hon, 24
Daimo, 400
Dol Ho, 24
Dragon House, 318
Great Eastern Restaurant, 25
Harbor Village, 72
Hing Lung, 25
House of Nanking, 26
Jade Villa, 428
Just Won Ton, 371
Kay Cheung, 27
Lichee Garden, 27
Mayflower, 321
New Hai Ky, 372
Oriental Pearl, 28
Parc Hong Kong, 322
Pearl City, 29
R & G Lounge, 29
Restaurant Peony, 428
Riverside Seafood Restaurant, 374
San Tung , 375
Shanghai 1930, 77
Shanghai Restaurant, 375
Tai Chi, 301
Taiwan, 325
Ton Kiang, 327
Win's, 376
Y Ben House Restaurant, 31
Yank Sing, 81

CRÊPES
Chez Maman, 347
Ti Couz Crêperie, 190

FISH AND SHELLFISH
Aqua, 95
Farallon, 100
Hayes Street Grill, 53
Sam's Grill, 113
Pesce, 298
Swan Oyster Depot, 300, 310
Tadich Grill, 115

FRENCH
Auberge du Soleil, 466
Anjou, 94
Bistro Aix, 150
Bistro Jeanty, 467
Bizou, 346
Café Jacqueline, 234
Chapeau!, 317
Chaz, 152
Chez Papa, 347
chez spemcer, 348
Clementine, 381
Elisabeth Daniel, 100
Fifth Floor, 101
Fleur de Lys, 102
Florio, 264
French Laundry, 472
Fringale, 350
Grand Cafe, 104
Isa, 155
Jardinière, 55
Jeanty at Jack's, 105
Jojo, 404
Julia's Kitchen, 473
La Folie, 296
Le Central, 107
Le Petit Robert, 297
Masa's, 107
Merenda, 156

FRENCH, continued
Nizza La Bella, 206
Ritz-Carlton Dining Room, 299
South Park Cafe, 354
Watergate, 192

FUSION/SMALL PLATES
MC², 108

GERMAN
Suppenküche, 55
Walzwerk, 191

GREEK
Kokkari, 106

GUATEMALAN
San Miguel, 189

HAMBURGERS
Burger Joint, 132, 177
Burgermeister, 132
Mo's Grill, 237

INDIAN
Ajanta, 394
Breads of India & Gourmet Curries, 395
Naan 'N' Curry, 110
Shalimar, 115

INDONESIAN
Rice Table, 449

ITALIAN
Acquerello, 292
Antica Trattoria, 293
Bistro Don Giovanni, 467
Delfina, 179
E'Angelo, 154
Frantoio, 445
Incanto, 218
Jackson Fillmore, 265
L'Osteria Del Forno, 237
La Felce, 236
Last Supper Club, The, 183
Oliveto, 408
Original Joe's, 110
Original U.S. Restaurant, 239
Palatino, 188
Palio d'Asti, 111
Pane e Vino, 156
Piatti, 480

Ristorante Bacco, 219
Ristorante Marcello, 373
Rose Pistola, 240
Rose's Cafe, 159
Santi, 481
Tra Vigne, 482
Umbria, 355
Venticello, 301
Via Vai Trattoria, 301
Vivande Porte Via, 270, 274

JAPANESE
Hana, 370
Iroha, 271
Juban Yakiniku House, 265
Kiss, 267
Maki, 268
May's Coffee Shop, 271
Mifune, 269
O Chamé, 407
Sanraku Four Seasons, 114
Takara, 271
Tekka, 326

JAPANESE/SUSHI
Anzu Sushi Bar, 95
Hama-ko, 134
Isobune, 271
Kabuto, 319
Kyo-Ya at the Sheraton Palace Hotel, 352
Ozumo, 75
Sushi Ran, 452
Sushi Zone, 411
Uzen, 412

JEWISH DELICATESSEN
East Coast West Delicatessen, 294, 304

KOREAN
New Korea House, 269
LATIN AMERICAN
Alma, 174
Charanga, 176
Destino, 52
Fonda Solana, 402
Miramonte, 478

MEDITERRANEAN
Absinthe Brasserie and Bar, 50
Chez Nous, 263
Citron, 399
Foreign Cinema, 182
Insalata's, 446
Last Supper Club, The, 183
Teatro ZinZanni, 81

MEXICAN
Doña Tomás, 401
El Balazito, 180
El Perol, 180
La Corneta Taqueria, 183, 218
La Taqueria, 184
Los Jarritos, 186
Pancho Villa Taqueria, 188
Picante Cocina Mexicana, 409
Taqueria el Balazo, 135

MIDDLE EASTERN
Al-Masri, 316
Fattoush, 215

PERUVIAN
Fina Estampa, 181

PIZZA
Pizzetta 211, 323
Tommaso's, 242
Vicolo Pizzeria, 56

POLISH
Old Krakow, 372

PRIME RIB
House of Prime Rib, 295

RUSSIAN
Katia, A Russian Tea Room, 320

SALVADORAN
Balompie Café, 176

SINGAPOREAN
Straits Cafe, 324

SPANISH
B 44, 96
Café Marimba, 151
Zarzuela, 302

SPANISH/TAPAS
Cesar, 398, 415
Lorca, 186
Timo's, 190

STEAK HOUSE
Acme Chophouse, 344
Alfred's Steak House, 94
Harris' Restaurant, 295, 303

TAPAS/FUSION
Andalu, 175

THAI
King of Thai Noodles, 320
Siam Cuisine, 410
Thep Phanom, 136
Yukol Palace, 160

VEGETARIAN
Greens, 154
Greens to Go, 164
Millennium, 109
Roxanne's, 450

VIETNAMESE
Cordon Bleu, 293
Golden Turtle, 294
Lam Hoa Thuan, 371
Pho Hoa Hiep II, 373
Slanted Door, 78, 189
Vien Huong, 428
Vietnam II, 57
Vi's Vietnamese Cuisime, 428
Yummy Yummy, 376

PRICE

INEXPENSIVE

Ajanta, 394

Andalu, 175

Angkor Borei, 176

Balompie Cafe, 176

Bow Hon, 24

Breads of India & Gourmet Curries, 395

Brennan's, 396, 415

Burger Joint, 132, 177

Burgermeister, 132

Burma's House, 98

Cafe Marimba, 151

Cesar, 398, 415

Cha Cha Cha, 132

Charanga, 176

Chez Maman, 347

Chez Papa, 347

Chow, 214

Cordon Bleu, 293

Daimo, 400

Dol Ho, 24

Dragon House, 318

East Coast West Delicatessen, 294, 304

El Balazito, 180

El Perol, 180

Ella's, 263

Fina Estampa, 181

Fonda Solana, 402

Foothill Cafe, 471

Golden Turtle, 294

Grasshopper, 403

Hana, 370

Helmand, 234

Hing Lung, 25

Home, 216

House of Nanking, 26

Il Pollaio, 236

Just Won Ton, 371

Katia, A Russian Tea Room, 320

Kay Cheung, 27

King of Thai Noodles, 320

La Corneta Taqueria, 183, 218

La Felce, 236

La Taqueria, 184

Lam Hoa Thuan, 371

Lichee Garden, 27

Los Jarritos, 186

L'Osteria Del Forno, 237

Luna Park, 187

Mifune, 269

Miss Millie's, 219

Mo's Grill, 237

Naan 'N' Curry, 110

New Hai Ky, 372

New Korea House, 269

Nob Hill Grille, 298

Old Krakow, 372

Original Joe's, 110

Original U.S. Restaurant, 239

Palatino, 188

Pancho Villa Taqueria, 188

Park Chow, 373

Pearl, 480

Pearl City, 29

Pho Hoa Hiep II, 373

Picante Cocina Mexicana, 409

Pizzetta 211, 323

Q, 324

Ravenette/Ravenous, 481

Riverside Seafood Restaurant, 374

Rose's Cafe, 159

San Francisco Art Institute Cafe, 241

San Miguel, 189

San Tung, 375

Sear's Fine Foods, 114

Shalimar, 115

Shanghai Restaurant, 375

Siam Cuisine, 410

Tai Chi, 301

Taiwan, 325

Taqueria el Balazo, 135

Thep Phanom, 136

Ti Couz Crêperie, 190

Tommaso's, 242

Ton Kiang, 321

Via Vai Trattoria, 159

Vicolo Pizzeria, 56

Vietnam II, 57

Walzwerk, 191
Willow Wood Market, 483
Win's, 376
Y Ben House Restaurant, 31
Yukol Palace, 160
Yummy Yummy, 376

INEXPENSIVE-MODERATE
Citizen Cake, 50, 63
Doña Tomás, 401
Kabuto, 319
Umbria, 355

MODERATE
Absinthe Brasserie and Bar, 50
Al-Masri, 316
Alma, 174
Anjou, 94
Antica Trattoria, 293
Anzu Sushi Bar, 95
B 44, 96
BayWolf, 394
Betelnut, 150
Bistro Aix, 150
Bistro Don Giovanni, 467
Bistro Jeanty, 467
Bistro Ralph, 467
Bix, 97, 119
Bizou, 346
butterfly, 177
Café at Chez Panisse, 396
Café Jacqueline, 234
Cafe Kati, 262
Cafe La Haye, 469
Cafe Rouge, 397
Casa Orinda, 398
Chapeau!, 317
Chaz, 152
Chenery Park, 214
Chez Nous, 263
Citron, 399
Clementine, 318
Delfina, 179
Destino, 52
Downtown, 401, 415

E'Angelo, 154
Eos, 133
Fattoush, 215
Firefly, 216
Florio, 264
Fly Trap Restaurant, 349
Fog City Diner, The, 70
Foreign Cinema, 182
Frantoio, 445
Fringale, 350
Globe, 103
Grand Cafe, 104
Great Eastern Restaurant, 25
Greens, 154
Greens to Go, 164
Hama-ko, 134
Harbor Village, 72
Hayes Street Grill, 53
House, 370
House of Prime Rib, 295
House, The, 235
Incanto, 218
Insalata's, 446
Isa, 155
Jackson Fillmore, 265
Jeanty at Jack's, 105
Jojo, 404
Juban Yakiniku House, 265
Julia, 266
Julia's Kitchen, 473
K & L Restaurant, 476
Kiss, 267
Le Central, 107
Le Petit Robert, 297
Liberty Cafe, 184
Lulu, 353
Maki, 268
Manzanita, 477
Mayflower, 321
MC², 108
Meetinghouse, 268
Merenda, 156
Mezze, 405
Millennium, 109
Miramonte, 478

Moose's, 239
Mustards Grill, 479
Nizza La Bella, 406
O Chamé, 407
Oliveto, 408
Oriental Pearl, 28
Palio d'Asti, 111
Pane e Vino, 156
Parc Hong Kong, 322
Piatti, 480
Piperade, 76
R & G Lounge, 29
Rice Table, 449
Ristorante Bacco, 219
Ristorante Marcello, 373
Rivoli, 410
RNM Restaurant, 134
Rose Pistola, 240
Sam's Grill, 113
Sanraku Four Seasons, 114
Santi, 481
Slanted Door, 78, 189
South Park Cafe, 354
Spoon, 300
Straits Cafe, 324
Suppenküche, 55
Sushi Ran, 452
Sushi Zone, 411
Swan Oyster Depot, 300, 310
Tadich Grill, 115
Tekka, 326
Timo's, 190
Tra Vigne, 482
21st Amendment, 354
Universal Cafe, 355
Uzen, 412
Venticello, 301
Vivande Porte Via, 270, 274
Wappo Bar Bistro, 483
Watergate, 192
Woodward's Garden, 192
Yank Sing, 81
Zarzuela, 302
Zuni Café, 57

MODERATE-EXPENSIVE

Acme Chophouse, 344
Bacar, 345
Kyo-Ya at the Sheraton Palace Hotel, 352
Shanghai 1930, 77

EXPENSIVE

Acquerello, 292
Alfred's Steak House, 94
Aqua, 95
Auberge du Soleil, 466
Boulevard, 70
Chez Panisse, 399
chez spencer, 398
Dry Creek Kitchen, 470
Elisabeth Daniel, 100
Farallon, 100
Fifth Floor, 101
Fleur de Lys, 102
French Laundry, 472
Gary Danko, 71
Harris' Restaurant, 295, 303
Hawthorne Lane, 351, 359
Jardinière, 55
Kokkari, 106
La Folie, 296
Lark Creek Inn, 446
Manka's Inverness Lodge, 447
Martini House, 478
Masa's, 107
Napa Valley Wine Train, 479
One Market Restaurant, 73
Ozumo, 75
PlumpJack Cafe, 156
Postrio, 112
Ritz-Carlton Dining Room, 299
Roxanne's, 450
Rubicon, 112
Teatro ZinZanni, 81
Terra, 481

FOOD SERVICE AT COUNTER OR BAR

Absinthe Brasserie and Bar, 50

Acme Chophouse, 344

Al-Masri, 316

Alfred's Steak House, 94

Alma, 174

Andalu, 175

Anjou, 94

Anzu Sushi Bar, 95

Aqua, 95

Auberge du Soleil, 466

B 44, 96

Bacar, 345

Balompie Cafe, 176

Betelnut, 150

Bistro Aix, 150

Bistro Don Giovanni, 467

Bistro Jeanty, 467

Bistro Ralph, 469

Bix, 97, 119

Bizou, 346

Boulevard, 70

Brennan's, 396, 415

butterfly, 177

Cafe Marimba, 151

Cafe Rouge, 397

Casa Orinda, 398

Cesar, 398, 415

Cha Cha Cha, 132

Charanga, 176

Chaz, 152

Chenery Park, 214

Chez Maman, 347

Chez Nous, 263

Chez Papa, 347

Chow, 214

Citizen Cake, 50, 63

Citron, 399

Clementine, 318

Cordon Bleu, 293

Delfina, 179

Destino, 52

Doña Tomás, 401

Downtown, 401, 415

Dry Creek Kitchen, 470

Ella's, 263

Eos, 133

Farallon, 100

Fifth Floor, 101

Firefly, 216

Fleur de Lys, 102

Fly Trap Restaurant, 349

Fog City Diner, The, 70

Fonda Solana, 402

Foreign Cinema, 182

Frantoio, 445

Fringale, 350

Gary Danko, 71

Globe, 103

Grand Cafe, 104

Grasshopper, 403

Hama-ko, 134

Hana, 370

Harris' Restaurant, 295, 303

Hawthorne Lane, 351, 359

Hayes Street Grill, 53

Home, 216

House, 370

House of Nanking, 26

House of Prime Rib, 295

Incanto, 218

Insalata's, 446

Isa, 155

Jackson Fillmore, 265

Jardinière, 55

Jeanty at Jack's, 105

Juban Yakiniku House, 265

Julia, 266

Julia's Kitchen, 473

K & L Restaurant, 476

Kabuto, 319

King of Thai Noodles, 320

Kiss, 267

Kokkari, 106

Kyo-Ya at the Sheraton Palace Hotel, 352

La Felce, 236

La Folie, 296

Lark Creek Inn, 446

Le Central, 107

Le Petit Robert, 297

Los Jarritos, 186

Lulu, 353

Luna Park, 187

Maki, 268

Manzanita, 477

Martini House, 478

Masa's, 107

MC², 108

Meetinghouse, 268

Merenda, 156

Mezze, 405

Millennium, 109

Miramonte, 476

Mo's Grill, 237

Moose's, 239

Mustards Grill, 479

Napa Valley Wine Train, 479

Nizza La Bella, 406

Nob Hill Grille, 298

O Chamé, 407

Oliveto, 408

One Market Restaurant, 73

Original Joe's, 110

Ozumo, 75

Palio d'Asti, 111

Parc Hong Kong, 322

Park Chow, 373

Pearl, 488

Piatti, 480

Picante Cocina Mexicana, 409

Piperade, 76

Postrio, 112

Q, 324

R & G Lounge, 29

Ristorante Marcello, 373

Ritz-Carlton Dining Room, 299

RNM Restaurant, 134

Rose Pistola, 240

Rubicon, 112

Sam's Grill, 113

Santi, 481

Sear's Fine Foods, 114

Shanghai 1930, 77

Siam Cuisine, 410

Slanted Door, 78, 189

South Park Cafe, 354

Spoon, 300

Straits Cafe, 324

Suppenküche, 55

Sushi Ran, 452

Sushi Zone, 411

Swan Oyster Depot, 300, 310

Tadich Grill, 115

Tai Chi, 301

Tekka, 326

Ti Couz Crêperie, 190

Timo's, 190

Tra Vigne, 482

21st Amendment, 354

Umbria, 355

Universal Cafe, 355

Uzen, 412

Venticello, 301

Vivande Porte Via, 270, 274

Wappo Bar Bistro, 483

Woodward's Garden, 192

Yank Sing, 81

Zuni Café, 57

FOOD SERVICE AFTER 10 P.M.

Absinthe Brasserie and Bar, 50

Acquerello, 292

Al-Masri, 316

Alma, 174

Andalu, 175

Antica Trattoria, 293

Aqua, 95

Auberge du Soleil, 466

B 44, 96

Bacar, 345

Balompie Cafe, 176

Betelnut, 150

Bistro Don Giovanni, 467

Bistro Jeanty, 467

Bix, 97, 119

Bizou, 346

Boulevard, 70

Bow Hon, 24

Brennan's, 396, 415

Burger Joint, 132, 177
butterfly, 177
Café at Chez Panisse, 396
Café Jacqueline, 234
Cafe Rouge, 397
Cesar, 398, 415
Cha Cha Cha, 132
Chapeau!, 317
Charanga, 176
Chez Maman, 347
Chez Nous, 263
Chez Papa, 347
Chow, 214
Daimo, 400
Delfina, 179
Destino, 52
Downtown, 401, 415
E'Angelo, 154
Elisabeth Daniel, 100
Eos, 133
Farallon, 100
Fifth Floor, 101
Fleur de Lys, 102
Florio, 264
Fog City Diner, The, 70
Fonda Solana, 402
Foreign Cinema, 182
Frantoio, 445
Fringale, 350
Globe, 103
Golden Turtle, 294
Grand Cafe, 104
Grasshopper, 403
Great Eastern Restaurant, 25
Helmand, 234
Hing Lung, 25
Home, 216
House, 370
House, The, 235
Isa, 155
Jackson Fillmore, 265
Jardinière, 55
Jeanty at Jack's, 105
Jojo, 404
Kabuto, 319

King of Thai Noodles, 320
Kokkari, 106
La Folie, 296
Le Central, 107
Le Petit Robert, 297
Luna Park, 187
Mayflower, 321
Mezze, 405
Moose's, 239
Naan 'N' Curry, 110
New Korea House, 269
Nizza La Bella, 406
Original Joe's, 110
Ozumo, 75
Pancho Villa Taqueria, 188
Park Chow, 373
Picante Cocina Mexicana, 409
Piperade, 76
Postrio, 112
Q, 324
Ristorante Bacco, 219
Ristorante Marcello, 373
RNM Restaurant, 134
Rose Pistola, 240
Rose's Cafe, 159
Rubicon, 112
Shalimar, 115
Shanghai 1930, 77
Slanted Door, 78, 189
Spoon, 300
Straits Cafe, 324
Sushi Ran, 452
Sushi Zone, 411
Tai Chi, 301
Taiwan, 325
Taqueria el Balazo, 135
Tekka, 326
Thep Phanom, 136
Ti Couz Crêperie, 190
Timo's, 190
Tommaso's, 242
Ton Kiang, 327
21st Amendment, 354
Umbria, 355
Universal Cafe, 355

Vicolo Pizzeria, 56
Vietnam II, 57
Walzwerk, 191
Watergate, 192
Yukol Palace, 160
Zarzuela, 302
Zuni Café, 57

**BREAKFAST OR
WEEKEND BRUNCH**
Absinthe Brasserie and Bar, 50
Auberge du Soleil, 466
Balompie Cafe, 176
Citizen Cake, 50, 63
Dol Ho, 24
East Coast West Delicatessen, 294, 304
El Perol, 180
Ella's, 263
Grand Cafe, 104
Hing Lung, 25
Insalata's, 446
Lark Creek Inn, 445
Liberty Cafe, 184
Lichee Garden, 27
Los Jarritos, 186
Lulu, 353
Meetinghouse, 268
Mezze, 405
Miss Millie's, 219
Moose's, 239
Nob Hill Grille, 298
Pearl City, 29
Picante Cocina Taqueria, 409
Postrio, 112
Q, 324
Rose's Cafe, 159
San Francisco Art Institute Cafe, 241
Sear's Fine Foods, 114
Suppenküche, 55
Universal Cafe, 355
Vietnam II, 57
Y Ben House Restaurant, 31
Zuni Cafe, 57

OUTDOOR SEATING
Absinthe Brasserie and Bar, 50
Acme Chophouse, 344
Auberge du Soleil, 466
B 44, 96
BayWolf, 394
Betelnut, 150
Bistro Aix, 150
Bistro Don Giovanni, 467
Bistro Jeanty, 467
Bistro Ralph, 469
Burgermeister, 132
California Hornblower, 79
Cafe Rouge, 397
Citron, 399
Dry Creek Kitchen, 470
Fog City Diner, The, 70
Foreign Cinema, 182
French Laundry, 472
Globe, 103
Jackson Fillmore, 265
La Taqueria, 184
Lark Creek Inn, 446
Le Petit Robert, 297
Martini House, 478
Miramonte, 478
Park Chow, 373
Pearl, 480
Piatti, 480
Rose Pistola, 240
Rose's Cafe, 159
San Francisco Art Institute Cafe, 241
San Francisco Spirit, 79
Tra Vigne, 482
Universal Cafe, 355
Wappo Bar Bistro, 483
Zuni Café, 57

CHILD FRIENDLY
Ajanta, 394
Balompie Cafe, 176
Bow Hon, 24
Brennan's, 396, 415
Burger Joint, 132, 177

Burgermeister, 132

Café at Chez Panisse, 396

Casa Orinda, 398

Charanga, 176

Chow, 214

Citizen Cake, 50, 63

Cordon Bleu, 293

E'Angelo, 154

East Coast West Delicatessen, 294, 304

El Balazito, 180

Ella's, 263

Fattoush, 215

Fonda Solana, 402

Grand Cafe, 104

Grasshopper, 403

Home, 216

House of Prime Rib, 295

Il Pollaio, 236

Just Won Ton, 371

K & L Restaurant, 476

La Corneta Taqueria, 183, 218

La Felce, 236

La Taqueria, 184

Liberty Cafe, 184

Lichee Garden, 27

Los Jarritos, 186

Luna Park, 187

Mayflower, 321

Mifune, 269

Miramonte, 478

Miss Millie's, 219

Mo's Grill, 237

Nob Hill Grille, 298

Original Joe's, 100

Original U.S. Restaurant, 239

Pancho Villa Taqueria, 188

Parc Hong Kong, 322

Park Chow, 373

Pearl, 480

Pearl City, 29

Picante Cocina Mexicana, 409

Q, 324

Riverside Seafood Restaurant, 374

Rose's Cafe, 159

San Francisco Art Institute Cafe, 241

San Miguel, 189

San Tung, 375

Sear's Fine Foods, 114

Taqueria el Balazo, 135

Ti Couz Crêperie, 190

Tommaso's, 242

Ton Kiang, 327

Vicolo Pizzeria, 56

Vietnam II, 57

Willow Wood Market, 483

Win's, 376

Y Ben House Restaurant, 31

Yank Sing, 81

BANQUET ROOM

Absinthe Brasserie and Bar, 50

Aqua, 95

Boulevard, 70

Dry Creek Kitchen, 470

Farallon, 100

Fly Trap Restaurant, 349

Grand Cafe, 104

Greens, 164

Harbor Village, 72

Harris' Restaurant, 295, 303

Hawthorne Lane, 351 359

Incanto, 218

Kokkari, 106

Kyo-Ya at the Sheraton Palace Hotel, 352

Maki, 268

Masa's, 107

Moose's, 239

Napa Valley Wine Train, 479

Oliveto, 408

One Market Restaurant, 73

Oriental Pearl, 28

Parc Hong Kong, 322

PlumpJack Cafe, 156

R & G Lounge, 29

Ritz-Carlton Dining Room, 299

Shanghai 1930, 77

Yank Sing, 81

OF HISTORIC INTEREST

Boulevard, 70
Casa Orinda, 398
Chez Panisse, 399
Fly Trap Restaurant, 349
French Laundry, 472
Grand Cafe, 104
Harris' Restaurant, 295, 303
Jeanty at Jack's, 105
Maki, 268
Napa Valley Wine Train, 479
Original Joe's, 110
Sam's Grill, 113
Sear's Fine Foods, 114
Swan Oyster Depot, 300, 310
Tadich Grill, 115
Terra, 481
Tommaso's, 242

BAKERIES/PASTRIES

Acme Bread Company, 420
Allstar Donuts, 331
Arizmendi Bakery, 379
Bagelry, The, 305
Bay Bread, 274
Bob's Donuts, 305
Boudin Sourdough Bakery and Café, 453
Boulange de Cole Valley, 137, 140
Boulangerie de Polk, 306
Bread Workshop, 420
Cheese Board, 421, 437
Citizen Cake, 50, 63
Danilo, 353
Delanghe Pâtisserie, 274
Dianda's Italian-American Pastries, 200
Downtown Bakery and Creamery, 487, 488
Eastern Bakery, 34
Golden Gate Bakery, 34
House of Bagels, 331
Just Desserts, 165
Katrina Rozelle, 421
La Farine, 421
La Nouvelle Pâtisserie, 165
Liguria, 253
Mee Mee Bakery, 35

Moscow and Tbilisi Bakery, 332
Noe Valley Bakery, 222
Panaderia La Mexicana, 200
Schubert's, 332
Sciambra French Bakery, 488
Semifreddi's, 422
Stella, 254
Sweet Stop, 275
Tartine Bakery, 201
Victoria Pastry Co., 254

BARS

Asia SF, 358
Bacar, 345
Balboa Cafe, 161
Beach Chalet, 377
Bix, 97, 119
Bliss Bar, 220
Brennan's, 396, 415
Bus Stop, 161
Catahoula, 484
Cesar, 398, 415
Cinch Saloon, 302
Club Deluxe, 37
Cosmopolitan Café, 82
Cozmo's Corner Grill, 161
Dalva, 194
Downtown, 401, 415
Enrico's Sidewalk Cafe, 245
42 Degrees, 359
G Bar, 272
Gino and Carlos, 245
Greystone Restaurant, 485
Harris' Restaurant, 295, 303
Harry Denton's Starlight Room, 119
Hawthorne Lane, 351, 359
Kelly's Mission Rock, 359
Kezar Bar & Restaurant, 137
Laurel Court Bar at the Fairmont, 303
Lazlo, 194
Li-Po, 33
Make-Out Room, 195
Martin's John and Zeke's, 485
Matrix/Fillmore, 162
Mecca, 222

Noc Noc, 138

Pasha, 303

Pat O'Shea's Mad Hatter, 328

Perry's, 162

Pier 23 Cafe, 83

Ramp, The, 360

Red Room, 119

Redwood Room, 120

Saloon, The, 245

Savoy Tivoli, 247

Spec's, 247

Tony Nik's, 247

Top of the Mark, 304

Toronado, 138

Tosca, 247

21st Amendment, 354

Vesuvio, 248

XYZ, 360

CAFÉS

Arlequin, 60

Armani Cafe, 116

Bean There, 136

Boulange de Cole Valley, 137, 140

Brain Wash, 356

Butler & The Chef Cafe, The, 356

Caffé 817, 413

Cafe at Oliveto, 414

Café Claude, 117

Café de la Presse, 117

Cafe Fanny, 413

Cafe Flore, 220

Cafe Niebaum-Coppola, 117

Cafe Prague, 118

Caffè Centro, 357

Caffè Greco, 224

Caffè Roma Coffee Roasting Company, 244, 357

Caffè Strada, 414

Caffè Trieste, 244

Caffé Trinity, 60

Canvas Cafe/Gallery, 377

DeLessio, 61

Dolores Park Cafe, 193

Farley's, 357

Flying Goat Cafe, 484

Imperial Tea Court, 31

Java Beach Cafe, 377

Mario's Bohemian Cigar Store, 244

Momi Toby's Revolution Café, 60

Palio Paninoteca, 121, 378

Papa Toby's Cafe, 194

Sam and Henry's Cool Beans, 327

Soma Caffè, 358

South Beach Café, 82

Specialty's Cafe and Bakery, 82

Tan Tan, 272

Warming Hut Cafe and Bookstore, The, 160

Zero Degrees, 118, 124

CHEESE

Artisan Cheese, 284

Cheese Board, The, 421, 437

Cheese Shop of Healdsburg, The, 493

Cooper's, 228

Country Cheese, 145

Dean & DeLuca, 486, 493, 497

Leonard's 2001, 311

Market Hall Pasta Shop, 417, 438

Oakville Grocery, 487, 494

Say Cheese, 146

24th Avenue Cheese Shop, 228

Vella Cheese Co., 494

Whole Foods Market, 309, 310, 311

COFFEE

Beanery, The, 381

Coffee, Tea and Spice, 141

Graffeo, 254

Peet's Coffee and Tea, 166, 167, 276, 307, 381, 438, 459

COOKWARE AND BOOKS

Clean Well-Lighted Place for Books, A, 66

Biordi Art Imports, 258

Black Oak Books, 441

Book's, Inc., 285

Butler & The Chef, The, 366

Chong Imports, 45

City Discount, 312
Cliff's Hardware, 230
Cody's, 441
Columbus Cutlery, 258
Cookin', 146
Cornucopia, 497
Cost Plus Imports, 90
Crate&Barrel, 125
Dean & DeLuca, 486, 493, 497
Economy Restaurant Supply, 366
Encantada Gallery of Fine Arts, 210
Forrest Jones, 286
Fredericksen's Hardware, 170
Gardner, The, 441, 498
Ginn Wall, 45
Green Apple Books, 339
Irving Housewares & Gifts, 388
Josephine European Tableware, 498
Kamei Household Wares, 339
Kamei Restaurant Supply, 339
Kinokuniya Bookstore, 286
Lehr's German Specialties, 230
Macy's, 125
Mashiko Folkcraft, 286
Niebaum-Coppola Winery Store, 498
Sanko Cooking Supply, 287
Soko Hardware Co., 287
Spanish Table, The, 428, 442
Sue Fisher-King, 287
Sur La Table, 126, 442
Tai Yick Trading Company, 46
Viking Homechef, 288, 462
Williams-Sonoma, 90, 126, 170, 388, 462

DELICATESSENS/TAKEOUT
Arabi, 83
Blondie's, 120, 416
Brother-in-Law's Bar-be-que, 138
Bryan's Quality Meats, 273, 281, 282, 284
Cafe Merenda, 163
Cantinetta at Tra Vigne, 485
Cheeseboard Pizzeria, 416
Dean & DeLuca, 486, 493, 497
DeLessio, 61

Desiree, 163
Dona Tere's Cart, 195
Doug's Bar-B-Q, 416
East Coast West Delicatessen, 294, 304
El Tonayense Taco Trucks, 195
Estella's Fresh Sandwiches, 129
European Food, 328
Freddie's, 248
Gastronom, 329
Golden Boy, 249
Gourmet Delight, 33
Green's to Go, 164
Haig's Delicacies, 329
In-N-Out Burger, 83
Jimtown Store, 486
Juicey Lucy's Organic Juice Bar, 249
La Palma Mexicatessen, 197, 199
Lee's Sandwiches, 121
Lucca, 186
Lucca Ravioli Company, 197
Market Hall Pasta Shop, 417, 438
Maruya Sushi, 273
Molinari Delicatessen, 252
New World Foods, 330
North Beach Pizza, 252
Oakville Grocery, 487, 494
Pasta Shop (see Market Hall Pasta Shop),
    417, 438
Palio Paninoteca, 121, 378
Phoenix Pastaficio, 418
Piccadilly Fish and Chips, 304
Rosamunde Sausage Grill, 139
Saigon Sandwich Café, 61
Seakor Polish Delicatessen, 331
Specialty's Cafe and Bakery, 122
Sunrise Deli & Cafe, 378
Tortas Los Picudos, 198
Valencia Whole Foods Market, 200
Vik's Chaat Corner, 418
Vivande Porta Via, 270, 274
Yee's Restaurant, 34
Yumma's, 378
Yung Kee, 418

ETHNIC MARKETS

G.B. Ratto and Company, 425

La Luna Market, 489

Lien Hing Supermarket, 36, 38, 40

Maruwa Foods Company, 279

Milan International, 425

Napa Valley Olive Oil Manufacturing Co, 489

New Chiu Fong Company, 64, 65

New Saigon Supermarket, 426

Oakland Market, 426

Oliviers & Co., 279

Sam Yick, 426

Spanish Table, The, 428, 442

Super Mira, 280

Uoki Market, 280, 284

FISH

Abraham's Seafood, 434

Antonelli's Meat, Fish, and Poultry, 281

Berkeley Bowl Fish Market, 434

Bryan's Quality Meats, 273, 281, 282, 284

California Sunshine, 363

Luen Sing Fish Market, 43

Mission Market Fish and Poultry, 209

Monterey Fish, 436

New Sang Sang, 42

Rockridge Fish Market, 436

Seafood Center, 338

Sun Fat Seafood Company, 210

Sunset Super, 383, 387

Swan Oyster Depot, 300, 310

Uoki Market, 280, 284

Yum Yum, 387

ICE CREAM/CHOCOLATES

Arlequin, 60

Bombay Ice Creamery, 201

Citizen Cake, 50, 63

Double Rainbow, 379

Downtown Bakery and Creamery, 487, 488

Fog City News, 123

Gelato Classico, 141, 255, 332

Joe's Ice Cream, 334

Joseph Schmidt, 223

Mitchell's Ice Cream, 202

Morrow's Nut House, 123

Polly Ann Ice Cream, 380

Scharffen Berger Chocolate Maker, 422, 423

See's Candies 84, 124, 306, 334, 380

Sweet World, 35

Swenson's, 306

Tango Gelateria, 275

XOX Truffles, 255

Yogurt Park, 425

Zero Degrees, 118, 124

MARKETS

Andronico's, 381

Big John's Food Center, 492

Bi-Rite Market, 202

Bombay Bazaar, 203

Cal-Mart, 276

Casa Lucas, 203, 205

La Palma Mexicatessen, 197, 199

La Raccolta, 256

Lien Hing Supermarket No. 3, 335

Marina Super, 167

Nature Stop, The, 256

New May Wah Supermarket, 335

Rainbow Grocery, 361, 363

Real Food Company, 142, 226, 307, 310

Samirami's Imports, 204

Sunset Super, 383, 387

Sunshine Foods, 489, 493

Super Tokio Japanese Market, 335

Tower Market, 224

Trader Joe's, 361

22nd and Irving Market, 383, 385

Val 16 Market, 204

Whole Foods Market, 309, 310, 311

MEAT AND POULTRY

Alan's Meats, 431

Antonelli's Meat, Fish, and Poultry, 281

Big John's Food Center, 492

Bryan's Quality Meats, 273, 281, 282

Drewes Brothers Meat, 227

Enzo, 431

Guang Zhou King & King Sausage, 40

Guerra's, 385

Keller's Market, 492

La Gallinita, 208

Lien Hing Supermarket, 36, 38, 40

Little City, 257

Lucky Pork Store, The, 208

Magnanis Poultry, 433

Man Sung, 41

Ming Kee Game Birds, 42

Mission Market Meat Department, 209

New On Sang, 42, 337

Polarica, 209

Real Food Company, 142, 226, 307, 310

Sonoma Saveurs, 492

Sunshine Foods, 489, 493

T & S Market, 433

Taylor's Sausages, 433

Ver Brugge Meats, 434

Viglizzo's Meat, 227

Whole Foods Market, 309, 310, 311

Wycen Foods, 338

PRODUCE

Alemany Farmers' Market, 204

Berkeley Bowl, 429

Berkeley Farmers' Market, 429

Casa Lucas, 203, 205

Civic Center Farmers' Market, 65

Clement Produce, 336

4th Avenue and Geary
    Farmers Market, 336

Fruit Basket, 38

Harvest Ranch Market, 226

Khanh Phong, 430

La Loma Produce, 199, 205

Market Hall Produce, 430

MikeyTom, 226

Monterey Foods, 436

New Chiu Fong Company, 64, 65

Old Oakland Farmers' Market, 431

Real Food Company, 142, 226, 307, 310

22nd and Irving Market, 383, 385

23rd and Mission Produce, 205

Val 16 Market, 204

Village Market, 337

Whole Foods Market, 309, 310, 311

WINE AND SPIRITS

All Seasons Cafe and Wine Store, 494

Amphora Wine Merchant, 65

California Wine Merchant, 168

Castro Village Wine Company, 229

Coit Liquors, 257

Hayes and Vine Wine Bar, 66

Jug Shop, The, 311

J. V. Warehouse, 496

K & L Wines, 365

Kermit Lynch Wines, 439

London Wine Bar, 124

Mr. Liquor, 387

Odd Lots, 440

Paul Marcus Wines, 440

PlumpJack Wines, 168, 229

Russian River Wine Company, 496

St. Helena Wine Center, 496

St. Helena Wine Merchants, 496

Tip Top, 497

Vino, 440

William Cross Wine Merchants, 312

Wine House Limited, 365

Wine Impression, 285

RECIPES

Avocado Quesadillas, 206

Best Macaroni and Cheese, 145

Buttermilk Bread, 308

Cherry Clafoutis, 278

Chocolate Sauce, 275

Chicken with Yogurt and Mustard, 87

Crab, Endive, and Radicchio Slaw, 54

Fresh Egg Pasta, 86

Fresh Peas with Shallots, 142

Hot Chocolate Soufflés, 424

Insalata Rustica L'Osteria, 238

Lamb's Tongue Salad, 283

Lion's Head, 427

Luscious Chile-Oil Tofu, 41

Milk Chocolate Pecan Clusters, 362

Mussels with Black Beans and Flowering
Garlic Chives, 384

Niloufer's Turkey Kabobs, 382

Orecchiette with Cauliflower and
Pecorino, 309

Pasta with Fava Beans, Potatoes,
and Basil, 169

Patricia Wells's Choucroute Garni, 224

Pickled Salmon, 330

Pork and Chile Wedding Stew, 207

Pot Stickers, 39

Raised Waffles, 128

Red Beans and Rice, 432

Red-Braised Whole Pork Shoulder, 340

Red Lentil Soup with Lime, 364

Roasted Asparagus with Shaved
Dry Jack, 89

Salt-Roasted Whole Fish, 44

Savory Meatballs with Spaghetti, 250

Spaghettini with Percorino and
Black Pepper, 51

Upside-Down Apricot or Plum Tart, 491

Watermelon and Pineapple-Ginger
Aguas Frecas, 153

SIDEBARS

A Coffee Tasting, 166

A Small Japantown Detour, 288

A Strategy for Visiting
Fisherman's Wharf, 80

Chocolate, 423

Copia: The American Center for
Wine, Food, and the Arts , 474

Eating in Oakland's Chinatown, 428

Fresh Peas, 143

Laurie MacKenzie's Walking Tours
of the Mission, 210

Shopping in Chinatown, 37

Specialty Restaurants in Japantown
that do a Good Job on a Single
Type of Dish, 271

Taking Advantage of the Bay:
Where to Eat with the Best View, 79

Tamales in the Mission with a
Mural Detour, 199

SUBSCRIBE!

UNTERMAN ON FOOD

Keep your *San Francisco Food Lover's Guide* up to the minute!
Subscribe to *Unterman on Food,* a newsletter dedicated to
contemporary eating in and around San Francisco, written by
restaurant critic and food writer Patricia Unterman. Each issue
includes reviews of new restaurants and old favorites, plus
recipes and articles on what to look for in markets and culinary
travel. *Unterman on Food* is published six times a year.

"Lively, comprehensive, indispensable for people who love
good food."
—Alice Waters

"I trust Unterman's palate. She loves the authentic."
—Paula Wolfert

To subscribe, send a check for $30, payable to
Patricia Unterman, c/o Hayes Street Grill,
320 Hayes Street, San Francisco, CA 94102.

www.unterman-on-food.com
info@unterman-on-food.com